Tourism Informatics:
Visual Travel Recommender Systems, Social Communities, and User Interface Design

Nalin Sharda
Victoria University, Australia

Information Science REFERENCE

INFORMATION SCIENCE REFERENCE
Hershey · New York

Director of Editorial Content: Kristin Klinger
Senior Managing Editor: Jamie Snavely
Assistant Managing Editor: Michael Brehm
Publishing Assistant: Sean Woznicki
Typesetter: Michael Brehm, Kurt Smith
Cover Design: Lisa Tosheff
Printed at: Yurchak Printing Inc.

Published in the United States of America by
Information Science Reference (an imprint of IGI Global)
701 E. Chocolate Avenue
Hershey PA 17033
Tel: 717-533-8845
Fax: 717-533-8661
E-mail: cust@igi-global.com
Web site: http://www.igi-global.com/reference

Library of Congress Cataloging-in-Publication Data

Tourism informatics : visual travel recommender systems, social communities, and user interface design / Nalin Sharda, Editor.
p. cm.
Includes bibliographical references and index.
Summary: "This book presents innovative research being conducted into Travel Recommender Systems, travel related on-line communities, and their user interface design"--Provided by publisher.
ISBN 978-1-60566-818-5 (hardcover) -- ISBN 978-1-60566-819-2 (ebook) 1. Tourism--Computer network resources. 2. Internet. 3. Online social networks. I. Sharda, Nalin, 1952-
G156.5.I5.T68 2010
910.285'5678--dc22

2009031089

British Cataloguing in Publication Data
A Cataloguing in Publication record for this book is available from the British Library.

Editorial Advisory Board

List of Reviewers

Table of Contents

Foreword xv

Preface xvi

Acknowledgment xviii

Section 1
Travel Recommender Systems for E-Tourism

Chapter 1
Building Visual Travel Recommender Systems and Tourism Communities for Effective User Experience 1
Nalin Sharda, Victoria University, Australia

Chapter 2
Semantic User Model Inferences for Travel Recommender Systems 22
Yanwu Yang, Chinese Academy of Sciences, China

Chapter 3
Developing Knowledge-Based Travel Advisor Systems: A Case Study 38
Dietmar Jannach, Technische Universität Dortmund, Germany
Markus Zanker, University Klagenfurt, Austria
Markus Jessenitschnig, University Klagenfurt, Austria

Chapter 4
Multiagent Truth Maintenance Applied to a Tourism Recommender System 54
Fabiana Lorenzi, Universidade Federal do Rio Grande do Sul (UFRGS), Brasil and Universidade Luterana do Brasil (ULBRA), Brasil
Ana Bazzan, Universidade Federal do Rio Grande do Sul (UFRGS), Brasil
Mara Abel, Universidade Federal do Rio Grande do Sul (UFRGS), Brasil

Chapter 5
Exploiting a Map-Based Interface in Conversational Recommender Systems for Mobile Travelers 73
Francesco Ricci, Free University of Bolzano, Italy
Quang Nhat Nguyen, Hanoi University of Technology, Vietnam
Olga Averjanova, Image Data Systems Ltd, UK

Section 2
Social Communities in E-Tourism

Chapter 6
A Study of Web 2.0 Tourism Sites: A Usability and Web Features Perspective 95
Carmine Sellitto, Victoria University, Australia
Stephen Burgess, Victoria University, Australia
Carmen Cox, Southern Cross University, Australia
Jeremy Buultjens, Southern Cross University, Australia

Chapter 7
Facebook, Friends and Photos: A Snapshot into Social Networking for Generating Travel Ideas 115
Leanne White, Victoria University, Australia

Chapter 8
Virtual Travel Community: Bridging Travellers and Locals 130
Jin Young Chung, Texas A&M University, USA
Dimitrios Buhalis, Bournemouth University, UK

Chapter 9
Progressive Tourism: Integrating Social, Transportation, and Data Networks 145
Edward Pultar, University of California, Santa Barbara, USA
Martin Raubal, University of California, Santa Barbara, USA

Section 3
User Interface Aspects of E-Tourism

Chapter 10
Model-Based User Interface Generation for Mobile Tourism Applications and Services 161
M. O. Adigun, University of Zululand, South Africa
A. O. Ipadeola, University of Zululand, South Africa
O. O. Olugbara, University of Zululand, South Africa

Chapter 11
Visiting Tourist Landmarks in Virtual Reality Systems by Real-Walking.. 180
F. Steinicke, Westfälische Wilhelms-Universität Münster, Germany
G. Bruder, Westfälische Wilhelms-Universität Münster, Germany
J. Jerald, University of North Carolina at Chapel Hill, USA
H. Frenz, Westfälische Wilhelms-Universität Münster, Germany
M. Lappe, Westfälische Wilhelms-Universität Münster, Germany

Chapter 12
Developing Web3D Tools for Promoting the European Heritage.. 194
Francesco Bellotti, University of Genoa, Italy
Riccardo Berta, University of Genoa, Italy
Alessandro De Gloria, University of Genoa, Italy
Ludovica Primavera, University of Genoa, Italy

Chapter 13
Itchy Feet: A 3D E-Tourism Environment.. 209
Ingo Seidel, Matrixware Information Services GmbH, Austria
Markus Gärtner, Matrixware Information Services GmbH, Austria
Michael Pöttler, Vienna University of Technology, Austria
Helmut Berger, Matrixware Information Services GmbH, Austria
Michael Dittenbach, Matrixware Information Services GmbH, Austria
Dieter Merkl, Vienna University of Technology, Austria

Chapter 14
The Use of Photographs on Consumer Generated Content Websites:
Practical Implications for Destination Image Analysis... 243
Doris Schmallegger, James Cook University, Australia
Dean Carson, Charles Darwin University, Australia
Damien Jacobsen, Charles Darwin University, Australia

Section 4
Selected Further Reading

Chapter 15
Developing Visual Tourism Recommender Systems... 262
Mohan Ponnada, Victoria University, Australia
Roopa Jakkilinki, Victoria University, Australia
Nalin Sharda, Victoria University, Australia

Detailed Table of Contents

Travel recommender systems and virtual tourism communities are now playing an important role in providing better tourism experience to many travellers. These technologies have become possible due the recent advancements in information and communication technology (ICT) systems and their application to tourism. Chapter I presents an overview of the three main topics covered in this book: visual travel recommender systems, social communities and user interface design. It shows how visual travel recommender systems and tourism communities can be advanced along with user experience.

Building a model of the user is important for developing effective recommender systems that can match the travel recommendations closely to the user's requirements. Many users do not feel comfortable answering too many personal questions; therefore the use of inference logic to build a semantic model is a promising approach. Chapter II presents a semantic user model for advancing travel recommender systems (TRS). This model uses description logic to represent user's knowledge and information, in conjunction with domain-dependent rules to derive user interests.

Travel recommender systems often require extensive knowledge about catalogued items and the customer requirements. Being interactive Web applications, their development can be costly and time-consuming. However, building these from off-the-shelf components can reduce cost and development time. Chapter III covers a recommender system called "VIBE virtual spa advisor". This system is based on an off-the-shelf knowledge-based and domain-independent framework called ADVISOR SUITE.

A multiagent approach can be used with distributed knowledge to develop a travel recommender system (TRS). In this approach, agents cooperate with each other to make the recommendations. Each agent uses a truth maintenance system component to access information during the recommendation process. Chapter IV presents a multiagent recommender system developed to deal with distributed expert knowledge. In this system agents work as cooperating experts that exchange information to generate the best possible recommendations.

Travel and tourism websites can provide copious amounts of travel related information. Much of this information can be accessed over mobile devices, including mobile phones and personal digital assistants (PDAs). However, this large volume of information can become too much for the limited screen size of these mobile devices. Therefore, we need to develop better techniques for information visualisation on mobile devices. Chapter V presents a recommendation methodology that integrates a conversational approach for preference acquisition with map visualization for mobile travellers, along with a usability study for the same.

Section 2
Social Communities in E-Tourism

Chapter 6
A Study of Web 2.0 Tourism Sites: A Usability and Web Features Perspective 95
Carmine Sellitto, Victoria University, Australia
Stephen Burgess, Victoria University, Australia
Carmen Cox, Southern Cross University, Australia
Jeremy Buultjens, Southern Cross University, Australia

In recent years many Web 2.0 sites have immerged for promoting tourism. These Web 2.0 travel sites use multimedia information including text, video, still images, animation and sound. More importantly, these sites allow users to contribute, update or alter existing content. Chapter VI investigates Web 2.0 tourism sites vis-à-vis their usability and the novel types of content available on these. It explores how embedding an application within a website influences design complexity and modifies the user experience.

Chapter 7
Facebook, Friends and Photos: A Snapshot into Social Networking for Generating Travel Ideas 115
Leanne White, Victoria University, Australia

The social networking site Facebook was launched in 2004, and by now it has over 100 million users who are posting around 500 million photographs per month. Facebook has now become a platform for sharing holiday snapshots and travel ideas as well. Chapter VII explores social aspects of tourism informatics by using travel photographs posted on Facebook. It examines the semiotics of visual images and written messages based on tourism experience of ten individuals.

Chapter 8
Virtual Travel Community: Bridging Travellers and Locals 130
Jin Young Chung, Texas A&M University, USA
Dimitrios Buhalis, Bournemouth University, UK

Virtual travel communities (VTCs) are now emerging by combining social networking and the advanced capabilities of the Web 2.0 technologies. These VTCs can be used in a novel way for connecting travellers with the locals in the destination region. Chapter VIII examines the state of virtual travel community (VTC) research from this new perspective. Current VTC research has focused mainly on consumer behavior from the travellers' viewpoint. This research examines how the VTCs can be used for connecting travellers to the locals at the destination.

Chapter 9
Progressive Tourism: Integrating Social, Transportation, and Data Networks 145
Edward Pultar, University of California, Santa Barbara, USA
Martin Raubal, University of California, Santa Barbara, USA

Many social networking websites have been created to provide information about free lodging with local residents at the destination. However, the geographical spread of people also influences their travel choices; and specific groups of people using these networks are influenced by factors such as transport and cultural issues. Chapter IX examines tourism behavior using Internet-based websites that provide free lodging with local residents. It investigates factors that influence the development of a general model describing traveller behavior within a cost-free lodging social network.

Section 3
User Interface Aspects of E-Tourism

Chapter 10
Model-Based User Interface Generation for Mobile Tourism Applications and Services 161
M. O. Adigun, University of Zululand, South Africa
A. O. Ipadeola, University of Zululand, South Africa
O. O. Olugbara, University of Zululand, South Africa

As tourism information becomes available on mobile devices, there is a need to create user-centric interfaces that can provide the tourist with self-customized interfaces for efficient access to mobile applications and services. Polymorphic logical description (PLD) model offers an interface description methodology to address the diverse needs of users in a mobile computing environment. Chapter X presents a model-based approach for automatic generation of user-centric interfaces for mobile tourists leading to efficient access to mobile applications and services. It presents the polymorphic logical description (PLD) model for interface description to address the diverse needs of the different mobile users.

Chapter 11
Visiting Tourist Landmarks in Virtual Reality Systems by Real-Walking.. 180
F. Steinicke, Westfälische Wilhelms-Universität Münster, Germany
G. Bruder, Westfälische Wilhelms-Universität Münster, Germany
J. Jerald, University of North Carolina at Chapel Hill, USA
H. Frenz, Westfälische Wilhelms-Universität Münster, Germany
M. Lappe, Westfälische Wilhelms-Universität Münster, Germany

Virtual environments (VEs) have become popular for 3D city visualization applications. Older 2D visualization systems did not provide natural interfaces for navigation within complex 3D scenes. More recent virtual reality (VR) systems make use of tracking technologies and stereoscopic projections to create 3D synthetic worlds that allow the users to explore virtual worlds in an intuitive manner. For example, in a virtual 3D city environment, users can visit landmarks virtually. Chapter XI presents a VE for redirected walking that allows users to walk through large-scale immersive virtual environments (IVEs), such as a virtual city. It explores two main questions: firstly, how well does redirected walking work, and secondly, the degree to which the users can be manipulated?

Chapter 12
Developing Web3D Tools for Promoting the European Heritage.. 194
Francesco Bellotti, University of Genoa, Italy
Riccardo Berta, University of Genoa, Italy
Alessandro De Gloria, University of Genoa, Italy
Ludovica Primavera, University of Genoa, Italy

Virtual reality (VR) environments are now being made available online as well. These environments provide novel opportunities for cultural tourism. The Travel in Europe (TiE) project aims to build virtual environments in which the user can explore faithfully represented European cultural sites from within these information-rich artifacts. Chapter XII looks at online virtual reality environments in the context of the Travel in Europe (TiE) project. It explores tools for building enriched virtual environments where the player can explore reconstructed virtual places creating an information-rich and contextualized experience.

Chapter 13
Itchy Feet: A 3D E-Tourism Environment.. 209
Ingo Seidel, Matrixware Information Services GmbH, Austria
Markus Gärtner, Matrixware Information Services GmbH, Austria
Michael Pöttler, Vienna University of Technology, Austria
Helmut Berger, Matrixware Information Services GmbH, Austria
Michael Dittenbach, Matrixware Information Services GmbH, Austria
Dieter Merkl, Vienna University of Technology, Austria

E-Tourism environments are being developed that emphasize a community-driven approach to create a society of travelers. These environments enable them to exchange travel experiences, recommend destinations, or exchange interesting snippets of information. In these environments interactions take place in a game-like 3D virtual world where each tourist is an avatar. Chapter XIII presents such an e-tourism environment that uses a community-driven approach to encourage the development of a society of travelers, to be able to exchange travel experiences, recommend tourism destinations or just catch on some interesting gossip.

Chapter 14
The Use of Photographs on Consumer Generated Content Websites:
Practical Implications for Destination Image Analysis.. 243
Doris Schmallegger, James Cook University, Australia
Dean Carson, Charles Darwin University, Australia
Damien Jacobsen, Charles Darwin University, Australia

Word-of-mouth has become an important source of information for tourists when making decisions about their destinations. Social networking sites using Web 2.0 applications that use consumer generated photographs are now being used for spreading this virtual word-of-mouth. Chapter IX shows how photographs make a substantial contribution to virtual word-of-mouth exchange using Web 2.0 applications. It presents a destination image analysis framework that allows a comparison of images posted by marketing organisations and consumers.

Section 4
Selected Further Reading

Tourism recommender systems (TRS) have become popular in recent years; however, most lack visual means of presenting the recommendations. This paper presents ways of developing visual travel recommender systems (V-TRS). The two popular travel recommender systems being used today are the TripMatcher and Me-Print. Tour recommendation using image-based planning using SCORM (TRIPS) is a system that aims to make the presentation more visual. It uses SCORM and CORDRA standards. SCORM (sharable content object reference model) is a standard that collates content from various websites, and CORDRA (content object repository discovery and registration/resolution architecture) aims to locate and reference SCORM repositories throughout the Internet. The information collected is stored in the form of an XML file. This XML file can be visualised by either converting it into a Flash movie or into a SMIL (synchronized multimedia integration language) presentation. A case study demonstrating the operation of current travel recommender systems is also presented. Further research in this area should aim to improve user interaction and provide more control functions within a V-TRS to make tour-planning simple, fun and more interactive.

This chapter provides an overview of tourism ontology and how it can be used for developing e-tourism applications. The Semantic Web is the next generation Web; it uses background knowledge captured as an ontology and stored in machine-processable and interpretable form. Ontologies form the core of the Semantic Web and can be used to develop intelligent applications. However, generating applications based on ontology still remains a challenging task. This chapter presents a framework that provides a systematic process for developing intelligent e-tourism applications by using a tourism ontology.

Foreword

Whilst the substantial contribution that tourism makes to many economies is now well known, there is less recognition of the fact that the tourism industry has been the catalyst for many of the advances in information technology since the 1980s. The early advances related largely to booking and reservation systems particularly through the activities of airlines, travel agencies and hotels. In more recent times, advances in informatics have influenced, if not determined, not only how tourists access information pertinent to their needs, but also how they engage with and record the tourist experience. Research in this field has advanced at a rapid rate. In Australia's national Cooperative Research Centre in Sustainable Tourism (STCRC), which is probably the largest tourism research organisation in the world, one of the major research programs related specifically to tourism informatics as this was seen by industry partners to be the area of tourism that had most potential for competitive advantage. Dr. Nalin Sharda was one of the STCRC's key researchers in this field who applied his expertise in informatics to tourism. It is pleasing to see that Dr Sharda has continued his interest in this field with the production of this text on tourism informatics.

In this text, Dr. Sharda has brought together a range of well credentialed academics with expertise in informatics to provide a comprehensive coverage of advances that have been made in tourism informatics as well as indications of future research and development opportunities in this fast moving field. This text, which has been written in a most accessible form, will be a valuable asset for developers and researchers as well as those with simply an interest in this exciting field.

Professor Leo Jago
Director,
Centre for Tourism and Services Research
Victoria University

Dr. ***Leo Jago*** *is a Professor in Tourism and Director of the Centre for Tourism and Services Research at Victoria University. He was formerly the Deputy CEO and Director of Research for the national Sustainable Tourism Cooperative Research Centre. Leo has researched and published in a range of fields including event evaluation, small enterprise management and volunteers. He is a Director for a range of public and private organizations and on the Editorial Board of six journals.*

Preface

Tourism informatics has come a long way since the development of computerised airlines booking systems in the 1960s. Information and communication technology (ICT) systems have penetrated almost all aspects of modern tourism. The focus of this book is on two important aspects, namely: travel recommender systems (TRS) and social communities. A third aspect, user interface design, is important for all ICT systems. The aim of this book is to cover these three important aspects in one volume, and bring out the latest research being conducted in these three areas, as well as their interrelationship.

The first chapter presents an overview of the three main topics covered in this book: visual travel recommender systems (VTRS), social communities and user interface design. The author shows how visual travel recommender systems and tourism communities can be advanced along with user experience.

The remaining four chapters in **section 1** focus on the latest research on travel recommender systems (TRS). The second chapter presents a semantic user model for advancing travel recommender systems (TRS). This model uses description logic to represent user's knowledge and information, in conjunction with domain-dependent rules to derive user interests. This model is then connected to a Web application scenario for providing personalized information to assist a traveller in an urban space. The third chapter covers a recommender system called "VIBE virtual spa advisor". This system is based on an off-the-shelf knowledge-based and domain-independent framework called ADVISOR SUITE. This suite allows rapid development of advisory applications and therefore reduces development costs. This chapter also reports the authors' practical experiences, and opportunities for future research in the domain. Chapter four presents a multiagent recommender system developed to deal with distributed expert knowledge. In this system agents work as cooperating experts that exchange information to generate the best possible recommendations. To validate the system, the author carried out simulations in which agents collaborate to recommend travel packages, enhancing the efficacy of the system. In the fifth chapter, the authors present a recommendation methodology that uses a conversational approach for preference acquisition, in conjunction with map visualization for mobile travellers. Their usability study demonstrates that integrating map-based visualization and critiquing-based interaction improves the system's recommendation effectiveness, thereby enhancing user satisfaction.

The four chapters in **section 2** look at social communities for e-tourism, and present research into their usability as well as their effectiveness in bridging the tyranny of distance. The emergence of Web 2.0 has dramatically changed the look and feel of websites and applications available on these. Chapter six investigates Web 2.0 tourism sites vis-à-vis their usability and the novel types of content available on these. It explores how embedding an application within a website influences design complexity and modifies the user experience. The seventh chapter explores social aspects of tourism informatics by using travel photographs posted on Facebook. It examines the semiotics of visual images and written messages based on tourism experience of ten individuals. The author explores how photographs reinforce the travel experience of those who took these photos, and how it can influence the travel decisions of those who view them. Chapter eight examines the state of virtual travel community (VTC) research from a new perspective. Current VTC research has focused mainly on consumer behavior from the travellers' viewpoint. This research examines how the VTCs can be used for connecting travellers to the locals at the destination. The authors present empirical evidence from a substantial virtual community, namely: CouchSurfing.com. Their research demonstrates that there is ample opportunity to build relationships between potential travellers and locals by using VTCs. In chapter nine the authors examine tourism behavior using Internet-based websites that provide free lodging with local residents. This research investigates factors that influence the development of a general model describing traveler behavior within a cost-free lodging network. The authors present an information representation and visualization methodology that is based on time-geographic dimensions.

The five chapters in **section 3** focus on user interface aspects of e-tourism systems. The first chapter in this section, chapter ten, presents a model-based approach for automatic generation of user-centric interfaces for mobile tourists leading to efficient access to mobile applications and services. The authors present a polymorphic logical description (PLD) model for interface description to address the diverse needs of mobile users. A toolkit developed by the authors, based on the PLD model, and its evaluation results are also provided. Chapter eleven presents a virtual environment (VE) for redirected walking that allows users to walk through large-scale immersive virtual environments (IVEs), such as a virtual city. The authors explore two main questions: firstly, how well does redirected walking work, and secondly, the degree to which the users can be manipulated? Chapter twelve looks at online virtual reality (VR) environments in the context of the Travel in Europe (TiE) project. This project is developing tools to build enriched virtual environments where the player can explore reconstructed virtual places creating an information-rich and contextualized experience. Authors' tests indicate that enriched 3D environments can support contextualized promotion of artifacts, products and services. In chapter thirteen the authors present an e-tourism environment that uses a community-driven approach to create a society of travelers, in which they can exchange travel experiences, recommend tourism destinations or just catch some interesting gossip. It also includes facilities for business transactions; including booking a trip or seeking assistance from a travel agent within an integrated, game-like 3D virtual world, in which each tourist is represented by as an avatar. The final chapter shows how photographs make a substantial contribution to virtual word-of-mouth exchange using Web 2.0 applications. The authors articulate the need for tools that can help in interpreting destination based photographs; and discuss a destination image analysis framework that allows a comparison of images posted by marketing bodies and consumers.

The additional **section 4** includes reproductions of two chapters by the editor from a previous IGI Global book titled *Information and Communication Technologies in Support of the Tourism Industry.* The first reproduced chapter is titled *Developing Visual Tourism Recommender Systems*. This chapter expounds the original motivation for including visualization aspects in travel recommender systems, and became the motivation for producing the current book. The second reproduced chapter is titled *A Framework for Ontology-Based Tourism Applications*. This chapter presents a framework for developing intelligent e-tourism applications with the help of a tourism ontology.

This book will be useful for researchers and practitioners who wish to explore some innovative research being conducted into travel recommender systems, travel related on-line communities, and their user interface design. It can also be used as a reference for senior undergraduate and postgraduate studies in tourism informatics. I hope that you benefit from it, and are inspired to create more innovative solutions for e-tourism.

Nalin Sharda
Victoria University, Australia

Acknowledgment

Editing this book has been an exciting project, which began many years before it was conceived. My foray into Tourism Informatics was launched by the research funding granted over a number of years by the Sustainable Tourism – Collaborative Research Centre (ST-CRC), Australia. I am thankful to ST-CRC for giving me the funding to create new research opportunities. I am particularly indebted to Prof. Leo Jago, the research director of ST-CRC during this period for his support and guidance. I am also thankful to my research partners, namely: Prof. Michael McGarth, Dr. Leisa Armstrong, Dr. Mladen Georgievski, Ms. Roopa Jakkilinki, Mr. Jayden Kimber, Mr. Imran Ahmad, and Mr. Mohan Ponnada.

Book publishing is a challenging business, however, very important for disseminating new knowledge. IGI Global has taken on this task with great enthusiasm. I am thankful to all IGI Global staff for their support and guidance throughout this project. Thank you Jan Travers, Lindsay Johnston, Heather Probst, Tyler Heath, Neely Zanussi, Elizabeth Ardner, and those working in the background. I am also thankful to all the members of the Editorial Advisory Board for supporting the book concept, and helping me in disseminating its call for chapters. Thank you Prof. Borko Furht, Prof. Michael McGrath, Prof. Leo Jago, Prof. Margaret Deery, Prof. John Zeleznikow, Dr. Suzanne Bergin, Dr. Klemens Waldhör, Dr. Jamie Murphy, Prof. Dean Carson, and Mr. Paul Baron.

All authors of this book have been great partners in producing well written chapters while meeting tight deadlines. Most of the authors have also supported the editorial process; a big round of applause for you all. Dr. Klemens Waldhör, Prof. Antony Sofo, and Dr. Subhash Sharma have participated in the editorial process as additional reviewers; thank you all for sparing your valuable time and meeting tight deadlines.

Most families are affected by book writing or editing projects, mine was an exception. Nonetheless, I am thankful to my lovely wife Prof. Hema Sharda, my beautiful daughter Pallavi Sharda, and my fantastic son Ankur Sharda, for being away from home most of the time on their respective business ventures, giving me all the time in the world to work on this project. However, and more importantly, flying back whenever I missed them too much.

Finally, I would like to thank my parents, Shri Gian Chand Sharda and Dr. Krishna Sharda for their inspiration and love, which has always guided me towards the pursuit of knowledge.

Nalin Sharda
Victoria University, Australia

Section 1
Travel Recommender Systems for E-Tourism

Chapter 1
Building Visual Travel Recommender Systems and Tourism Communities for Effective User Experience

Nalin Sharda
Victoria University, Australia

ABSTRACT

Modern information and communication technology (ICT) systems can help us in building travel recommender systems and virtual tourism communities. Tourism ICT systems have come a long way from the early airline ticket booking systems. Travel recommender systems have emerged in recent years, facilitating the task of destination selection as well activities at the destination. A move from purely text-based recommender systems to visual recommender systems is being proposed, which can be facilitated by the use of the Web 2.0 technologies to create virtual travel communities. Delivering a good user experience is important to make these technologies widely accepted and used. This chapter presents an overview of the historical perspective of tourism ICT systems and their current state of development vis-à-vis travel recommender systems and tourism communities. User experience is an important aspect of any ICT system. How to define user experience and measure it through usability testing is also presented.

INTRODUCTION

Tourism related applications are some of the oldest and the most prolific users of information and communication technology (ICT). Various terms such as eTourism, Tourism Informatics, and Tourism ICT are used to describe such systems, and we use these terms interchangeably in this chapter. The goal of all such systems is to enhance the tourism experience, before, during, and after the tour. This chapter presents an overview of modern eTourism systems with a focus on Travel Recommender Systems, Tourism Communities, and their relationship to user interface design.

Tourism is fundamentally a social activity. In planning a tour, people take suggestions about the destination from friends and colleagues; interact with agents to plan and book the travel itinerary and accommodation; partake in the travel and destination activities with family and friends; meet new people

DOI: 10.4018/978-1-60566-818-5.ch001

and develop friendships–at times everlasting ones; share the travel experience with many other people. All these interactions and communications lead to the creation of a myriad of travel communities. In the past, these communities were developed when face-to-face contact occurred. With the advent of the social networking systems on the Internet, such communities are proliferating in the virtual world as well.

Tourism Informatics began with the introduction of the first air ticket booking system introduced in 1950s by the American Airlines; since then the tourism domain has adopted and utilized advancements in ICT systems soon after these have been developed. Now booking tickets and hotels on the Internet is common. However, many more Internet-based facilities have become available within the eTourism gambit; all of these aim to make tour planning a more enjoyable experience.

The concept of recommender systems has been adopted widely by almost all business areas where a consumer needs to make an informed choice. Websites selling books, recommend more books based on the user's current choice and the related books chosen by previous consumers who also bought the same book. Google has built a billion dollar business in recommending advertisements based on the topic a user is searching for. Travel recommender systems apply this concept in helping travelers to choose their destination, accommodation, and activities at the destination. Tourism is a very sensual experience, involving all senses. However, most recommender systems present their recommendations as textual information, thereby underselling the destination and its sensual aspects. Visual travel recommender systems are being developed to overcome this limitation. Some of the proposed systems can capture information from a variety of websites and link these together into a continuous visualization like a video clip (Ponnada, Jakkilinki, & Sharda, 2007).

Good user interface design is of paramount importance, because an ineffective user interface can turn a good idea into a failed product. The ICT world has realized lately that the user experience must be given as much attentions, if not more, as the technical details of any ICT system. While there are many more aspects of user experience with any ICT system, the user interface is the 'face' of the system, and this 'face' is often taken by the users as the 'soul' of the system. To ensure that the user interface is effective and easy to use, usability studies should be carried out using well established usability testing methods (Neilson, 1993).

This chapter explores the evolution of Tourism ICT systems, with a focus on travel recommender systems, virtual travel communities and their user interface design.

Chapter Aim and Objectives

The main aim of this chapter is to build a holistic view of tourism ICT systems and their role in advancing tourism communities.

Some of the specific objectives of this chapter include:

- To understand fundamentals of Tourism ICT systems
- To build a big-picture view of Travel Recommender Systems (TRS)
- To appreciate how tourism ICT systems can help in creating travel communities.
- To understand the importance of good User Interface (UI) design and techniques for enhancing user experience.

Chapter Layout

Section-1 introduced the motivations, aims and objects for this chapter. Section-2 presents history and fundamentals of tourism informatics. Section-3 presents an overview of travel recommender systems. Section-4 explores the concept of travel communities. Section-5 discusses the concept of user experience and how it may be used to advance tourism ICT systems with future research. Conclusions are given in section-6.

TOURISM INFORMATICS

Information and Communication Technologies (ICT) systems have always been adopted by the tourism industry with great enthusiasm. According to Houghton (2007), "In OECD countries, the adoption of e-commerce and online service delivery in tourism has been rapid, and the tourism sector is among the leaders in online marketing and sales" (p. 2). While the tourism sector began its foray into the use of computers with airline booking systems, by now it has adopted most of the technological innovations in ICT for enhancing the whole of tourism experience: from tour planning to execution, as well as from partaking to ruminating. In this section we briefly explore the evolution of Tourism ICT systems from early Computer Reservation Systems (CRS) to the modern web-based Travel Recommender Systems (TRS).

History of Tourism Informatics

Marten (2007) articulates how the airlines industry advanced rapidly in the post-World War II era with innovations in the technologies for building aircrafts and their support systems, such as Radar and other navigation systems. This boom led to an exponential growth in air travel, leading to the need for more efficient booking systems. The development of the first-generation reservation systems such as SABER (Semi-Automated Business Environment Research) was inspired by the need to replace relatively slow and expensive processes such as telex, telephone, and postage, being used for booking airline tickets at that point in time.

Along with other technological innovations, World War II also triggered the development of computer technology. The use of data communication links for transmitting digital information over long distances also became possible around the same time. This convergence of computer and communication technologies made it possible for the airlines industry to develop reservation systems that minimized manual intervention. However, such reservation systems still required a well trained operator (e.g. a travel agent) to be able to use the same.

Much research was carried out during the 1970s, 80s and the 90s into all aspects of computer technology, such as database systems, wired and wireless communication, and artificial intelligence. These technologies became useful for advancing tourism ICT systems as well. While many improvements were made in the airline reservations systems over these decades, a quantum boost to tourism ICT systems came with the proliferation of the World Wide Web (web) in the 1990s. By mid to late 1990s, increasing number of households were connecting to the Internet for using new and exiting services becoming available on the web. Furthermore, information representation transformed from being purely text to multimedia information, including audio and video content, which could be transmitted over the Internet with relative ease (Sharda, 1999). The confluence of these information and communication technologies made the scene ripe for enhancing the Tourism Informatics systems into online services available freely on the web.

Current State of Tourism Informatics

Tourism is a complex industry and each of its aspects can benefit from the use of latest ICT systems (Houghton, 2007). It includes a wide range of activities including travel, accommodation, dinning and recreation. The service providers for these activities are also diverse, from Small to Medium Enterprises (SMEs) to large corporations. Furthermore, a well connected tourism infrastructure requires participation of public as well as private sector enterprises. While market economy is considered the hallmark of a vibrant tourism sector in any country, the need for having sustainable tourism requires some government support. Finding a balanced regulatory environment becomes essential for ensuring a competitive but healthy tourism sector in any country (Forsyth, 1997). ICT systems have been developed to support almost all aspects of tourism. Tourism sector often uses ICT services as the glue that links different tourism sector players, and the disparate ICT systems used by them. However, at times, this linking is hampered due to the lack of common terminology and standards; this drawback can be tackled by developing a common ontology (Jakkilinki & Sharda, 2007).

Tourism Business Models

Tourism systems involve both business-to-business (B2B) and business-to-consumer (B2C) interactions. The early ICT systems catered mainly for B2B transactions; however, the current web-based systems can cater for both types of interactions. The factors that make tourism services amenable for online delivery include the following (Houghton, 2007):

Standardization: Tourism transcends national boundaries by its very nature. To ensure interoperability of global systems, it is important to standardize information formats, operational procedure, and communication codes. The Internet and the web provide underlying standard codes and communication protocols to make this possible; however, further standardization is required for specific tourism ICT systems.

Task complexity: Most tourism related tasks are complex, requiring cooperation of various systems and organizations. ICT systems make it possible to hide some of this complexity from the user, and provide a more manageable experience. Most Tourism ICT systems, such as Visual Travel Recommender Systems are complex, however, the aim is to have the technology manage this complexity, while the user interacts through a simple user interface (Venkataiah, Sharda, & Ponnada, 2008).

Knowledge coding: Knowledge can be tacit or codified. Often, knowledge that can be codified is easier to include in online systems, while tacit knowledge needs to be derived through human interaction. Some newer recommender systems aim to move closer to accessing tacit information, such as the Adaptive Recommender System proposed by Mahmood, Ricci, Venturini & Höpken (2008).

Problem nature: So called 'tame' problems are easy to solve, and are straightforward vis-à-vis their implementation when done with the help of ICT systems. On the other hand, the so called 'wicked' problems are difficult to describe and can only be solved by working out a series of intermediate solutions, which lead to a better understanding of the problem. The problem of creating better tourism communities is such a 'wicked' problem; therefore it needs much more research before we can find the ultimate solution.

Delivery context: At a high-level context, any problem needs cooperation amongst many co-workers, making it difficult to create an ICT-based solution for it. While low-level, or context-specific problems have clear solutions, independent of other factors, therefore these can be solved by ICT systems more readily.

In developing Tourism ICT systems the above listed factors must be considered carefully, to ensure that these new Tourism ICT systems are accepted by the user community.

Tourism Services

The wide range of tourism services that make up the entire tourism sector can be grouped into the following categories (Houghton, 2007):

1. Transport services,
2. Intermediation services,
3. Recreation and amusement services,
4. Accommodation and food services.

Most of the early tourism ICT services were business to consumer (B2C) services, and were therefore less amenable to the development of a community; however, many current internet-based services provide consumer to consumer (C2C) interactions; therefore, these are more amenable to the development of a community.

Impact of Innovations in Tourism ICT Systems

Technologies advance due to innovations that often make only an incremental change in the system, or in its application processes, but with a dramatic effect on the outcomes vis-à-vis factors such as: ease of use, market share and profit. However, an innovation can be a sustaining innovation or a disruptive innovation.

A sustaining innovation does not result in the closure of established companies but improves the performance of existing products for some parameters that are of value to the customers. The original airlines booking systems –such as SABER– were, therefore, sustaining innovations. A disruptive innovation often produces a less expensive product –at times of inferior quality; however, it erodes the current product's market share, and can lead to some companies going broke. Many of the newer Tourism ICT systems have had disruptive effect on the earlier tourism services supply chains; for example, because of the internet-based booking systems, "disintermediation of agencies is being exacerbated by the cutting of commissions by airlines and, increasingly, hotel chains" (Houghton, 2007, p. 13).

While some of the tourism ICT systems have been disruptive innovations, others systems, such as Travel Recommender Systems, are sustaining innovations; consequently, these will add value to the tourism supply chain, and the proposed Visual Travel Recommenders Systems will enhance these even further (Ponnada, Jakkilinki & Sharda, 2007). Similarly, the social networking systems will add value to the travel industry as a whole by building better travel communities (Chung & Buhalis, 2008).

Impact of Advancements in Tourism Informatics

Just as in the past the tourism industry has adopted innovations in ICT systems, it can be expected that future technological innovations will keep penetrating the tourism supply chain; consequently, new and innovative eTourism systems will be created incessantly. As mobile computing penetrates almost all facets of our lives, many tourism services are being morphed into mobile tourism services; for example, airlines are now using the short message service (SMS) for sending flight information to their customers. Location Based Services (LBS) are providing a plethora of travel related information on mobile phones, including route, location of restaurants and latest shows (Lee & Mills, 2007).

TRAVEL RECOMMENDER SYSTEMS

Travel Recommender System (TRS) technology has been developing for about a decade now. A TRS accepts inputs form a prospective traveler, and provides some recommendations, for possible tours that match the users input information (Berka & Plößnig, 2004). A simple TRS undertakes a dialog with the user, asking various questions and then provides one or more recommendations for travel itineraries that match the user's preferences (Ricci, 2002). A basic TRS provides recommendations as textual information, so that the user has to browse many information resources such as travel brochures or web pages related to the suggested destinations and activities, so as to mentally visualize the complete trip (Venkataiah, Sharda, & Ponnada, 2008). With recent advancements in multimedia technologies it is possible to build a system that allows one to enter information such as chosen destination, transport, and

Figure 1. A classification of recommender systems and content type

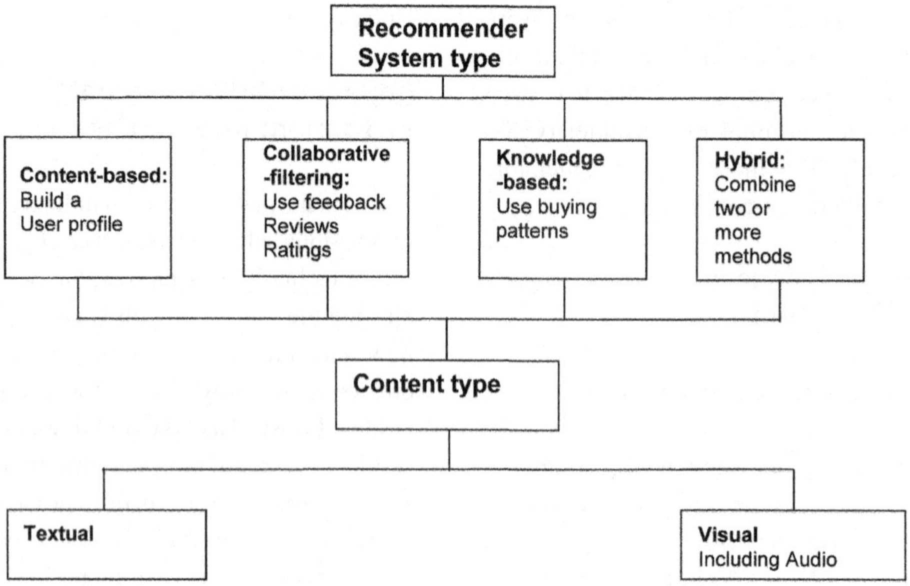

accommodation; and then see all this information as a continuous video presentation, leading to the development of a Visual Travel Recommender System (VTRS) (Ponnada & Sharda, 2007).

Recommender System Types

Recommender systems are essentially e-commerce applications (Mahmood, Ricci, Venturini, & Höpken, 2008). Their function is to assist the user in selecting the most suitable product, within the range of product types being searched for, by having an interactive session with the user on the Web (Adomavicius & Tuzhilin, 2005).

All recommender systems require that the system understands the user's requirements, and "These systems acquire the user needs and wants, either explicitly (by asking) or implicitly (by mining the users' online activity logs)" (Mahmood, Ricci, Venturini, & Höpken, 2008). Most recommender systems employ a user interaction methodology that is specified at the design stage. Mahmood et al. (2008) show how an adaptive recommender system can be developed, "which uses Reinforcement Learning techniques in order to autonomously learn an adaptive interaction strategy".

A variety of recommendation methodologies have been developed to suit different applications, and the ICT systems used for their deployment. While the general concepts used in recommender systems have some commonality, these can be divided into four broad classes (Stabb et al., 2002). A brief description of each is given in the following sections, and an overview of their classification is presented in Figure 1.

Content-Based Recommender System

A content-based recommender system begins by understating the users' needs and preferences, as well as constraints, if any. This information is combined with a log of the user's previous interactions (if any) to build a user profile. Then the recommender system matches the user profile with the information about various products already stored in its database. Often a user is asked to rate exiting items vis-à-vis their suitability, to develop a clear understanding of the user's needs and preferences.

However, this method for generating recommendations suffers from the following limitations (Balabanovi & Shoham, 1997). A new user is required to rate a number of items for the content-based recommender system to build an understanding of the user's needs and preferences. Furthermore, the recommendation depends upon the item features entered in the database in text form. Multimedia features, e.g. graphics, audio and video cannot be included in the selection process. Such recommender systems suggest items that have best match of features; and do not give the user the opportunity to check the suitability of the item being recommended.

Collaborative-Filtering Recommender System

In collaborative-filtering methodology, user feedback, reviews and rating given by previous users are used as the basis for recommending the items (Hill, Stead, Rosenstein, & Furnas, 1995). However, in this methodology providing recommendations can be problematic for new items entered in the system's database. The solution lies in developing hybrid recommender system that combine collaborative, content-based, and demographic filtering to overcome this problem (Pazzani & Billsus,1999).

Knowledge-Based Recommendation Systems

These systems apply the knowledge about the user's current choice and their relation to the other similar products. Such a system does not require detailed knowledge about an item. However, it requires some knowledge of the user's buying patterns, which can be obtained by posing a series of questions.

Hybrid Recommender Systems

Hybrid recommender systems combine two or more techniques to overcome the limitations of the individual methods. Collaborative-filtering is commonly combined with some other techniques, these can include: artificial neural networks (Pazzani & Billsus, 1997) and Bayesian classifiers (Mooney, Bennett, & Roy, 1998).

As recommender systems are becoming an integral part of most e-commerce systems, the mode of recommendation presentation is also changing from purely textual information to multimedia information.

Textual Travel Recommender Systems

With the proliferation of tourism Websites since the mid 1990s, users have been able to plan and preview their holiday locations online. Around the same time, travel recommender systems (TRSs) were developed to recommend holiday locations and activities to match the user needs and preferences. Two popular recommender systems are TripMatcher™ system (Delgado, 2001) used by Ski-Europe, and VacationCoach Me-Print™ system used by Travelocity (Ponnada et al., 2007).

TripleHop's Trip Matcher™

TripleHop's Trip Matcher™ aims to simulate a face-to-face counselling session with a travel agent, similar to the ones conducted by persons wanting to go on a holiday. Just as a travel agent analyses the needs and the preferences of a customer and recommend the most suitable destination to visit, the recommendation software is designed to understand the user's requirements and constraints, and then match these with the locations and activities entered in the system catalogue, or database. This system has been used by the Ski-Europe.com website.

The TripleHop system uses a sophisticated approach to reduce the need for extensive user input. This is done by guessing some of the attributes, especially if the user does not explicitly enter these. Then it combines statistics gathered from past user interactions, and predictions are computed by taking weighted averages of importance assigned by similar users to these missing attributes (Ricci, 2000). Furthermore, the software remembers user preferences by recording navigation patterns as the user browses the Website. Thus, it uses contextual filtering and attribute-based collaborative filtering.

VacationCoach Me-Print™

The Me-Print™ system applies three techniques to generate personalised travel recommendations: intelligent profiling, expert knowledge, and robust advice engineering (Ponnada et al., 2007). Me-Print™ builds user profiles and categorizes them. This user profile includes lifestyle and leisure preferences relative to other options; e.g. a user may have higher preference for golf, as compared to tennis or swimming. Such preferences are used to recommend the most appropriate destination, e.g. one with good golfing facilities. At times a recommender system has to work with under, or over specification. This can be handled by either applying "constraint relaxation" if the user has over-specified, or "tightening", if the user preferences have been under specified. This type of system uses case-based reasoning to provide the most appropriate recommendations (Ricci, 2002).

Services offered by a Textual TRS

The main service offered by a textual TRS is the ability to select holiday destination and activities without leaving a computer workstation. These systems aim to reduce the time taken to make the selection, as compared to the time it would take to visit various Websites, gather information, match it with personal preference and then select the most suitable destination. Such a TRS has the ability to formulate queries for the databases of available services; if a user is not experienced enough to answer all the questions, then it presents examples of the various services for the user to choose from. Thus, a good TRS should allow users to explore different options available, apart from providing a selection of recommendations (Ricci, 2002).

While most textual recommender systems provide some visual information, the recommender systems discussed in the following section use visual information much more directly for the recommendation and destination selection process.

Visual Travel Recommender Systems

With a textual TRS the system provides recommendations for the most suitable destination and services, nonetheless, the user still has to browse through many web pages to build a holistic mental picture of the complete trip. The aim of a Visual Travel Recommender System (VTRS) is to overcome this limitation. A VTRS uses audio visual information to present the choices as well as the recommendations.

Two important aspects of any VTRS are: visual input and visual output (Ponnada et al., 2007). The first aspect –visual input– focuses on presenting destination information as visual content to help the user in making the destination selection; and the second aspect –visual output– relates to presenting the selected tour as an audio visual presentation of the entire trip by combining content from existing websites.

Visual Input Systems

Most textual TRSs focus on destination selection and do not deliver a complete itinerary. The traveller then has to brows the Internet and look for different attractions at the suggested destination. As the Internet has become popular for booking almost all aspects of travel, Websites now provide a lot of visual information to help the travellers in their decision-making process. Kimber, Georgievski,

& Sharda (2006) proposed the Tourism Recommendation using Image-based Planning (TRIP) systems to incorporate visualisation of destination information into recommender systems.

The motivation for the development of the TRIP systems stems from the difficulty in finding the required details about a trip: generally one has to brows through a large number of Websites to gather the required information and sort out the relevant details. The TRIP system aims to overcome this drawback by presenting customised details visually.

Another system for visual input based recommendation has been proposed by Keen and Rawlings (as cited in Sharda, Jakkilinki, Georgievski & Ponnada, 2008). This system facilitates the decision making process by using a visual scrapbook. In this system, information is provided on a wide range of tourism products as images and videos. As the user browses through this information, the system tracks the browsing pattern, and constructs a statistical profile, with the assumption that: the more time a user spends on viewing a particular item, the more the user is interested in that type of activity. This is therefore used for building the user profile. This profile is stored in an electronic scrapbook (e-scrapbook) for that particular user and is used in making future recommendations.

Therefore, the e-scrapbook becomes a personalised storage in which the items of interest for a specific user are placed. Typical information stored in the e-scrapbook could be product information, e.g., cost of accommodation at various hotels. The user could also include personal information such as travel schedule, accommodation booking, and recreational activities. The user can also delete or update items in the e-scrapbook. Thus the e-scrapbook can become not only input for the recommender system, but also a storage mechanism for the individual user. This system lets users post their e-scrapbooks, and also permits them to import partial or entire e-scrapbooks produced by other users. In this method, a user is able to narrow down choices until satisfied, all along having a graphical overview of the trip (Sharda, Jakkilinki, Georgievski, & Ponnada, 2008).

Visual Output Systems

The aim of a Visual Travel Recommender System (VTRS) is to present the entire trip as sequence of images, in a form that makes it easy to visualise the complete trip. To categorise two ways in which images can be used for visualisation, Venkataiah, Sharda and Ponnada (2008) define the concepts of Discrete and Continuous Visualisation.

Discrete Visualization occurs when the user has to view many individual images to visualize the trip. The general process begins with the user entering a query in a search oriented interface. Generic search engines such as Google can be used, or destination specific portals may be accessed directly. The search process lists a series of 'hits' that link to individual web pages. Then these web pages need to be browsed one-by-one by the user to build a complete mental picture of the entire trip. While a lot of information can be gathered in a Discrete Visualization system, it is rather disjointed, and the user has to spend much effort in accessing and using the required information (Venkataiah et al., 2008).

Continuous Visualization retrieves and combines information dynamically, and displays it almost like a video clip. To tailor this information for various user devices, such as a Notebook computer or a Mobile phone, this information content can be 'repurposed'. 'Content repurposing' is a techniques that modifies the available content's parameters, such as resolution and frame rate, to fit the display device, and to match the available communication bandwidth.

Sharda et al. (2008) show how discrete content taken from various exiting websites can be combined into a continuous visualization, either as a Flash movie or as a presentation based on the Synchronized Multimedia Integration Language (SMIL). One of the advantages of the SMIL standard is that it is possible to play-out the presentation for different lengths and in different formats depending upon the user requirements.

Alfaro et al. (2004) present the idea of using cinematic techniques to create effective visualizations. They propose the use of the Rhetoric Structure Theory (RST) (Taboada & Mann, 2006) to create a framework for the multimedia presentation. While some research has been conducted into the production of effective visual output systems, much more work is required before is becomes possible to produce a continuous visualization of a proposed trip, tailored to the user devices and other requirements, such as the time available to view the presentation. However, the advent of the Web 2.0 technologies is expected to further support the implementation of this idea.

Web 2.0 Systems

The concept of Web 2.0 emerged to enhance and rescue the original World Wide Web (Web 1.0) from the ashes of the dot-com crash that took place in the early part of the new millennium (O'Reilly, 2005). The Web 2.0 model transformed the way information is presented on the Web, and exponentially enhanced the level of user interactivity provided by web sites. One of the most important aspects of the Web 2.0 concept is that users are not just passive consumers of information, but also active content creators. The content on a Web 2.0 based website is therefore highly audio visual, with much faster response time than that on the earlier versions available on the Web 1.0 systems (Lin, 2007).

The Web 2.0 concept has been developed to create a variety of web system. The most widely used Web 2.0 systems include: blogs (web-logs), wikis, podcasts and social networks. These are briefly describe in the following, with some relevant tourism examples (Kolbitsch & Maurer, 2006):

- **Blog:** Web logs (Blogs) are websites that allow user to publish their own content as they would in a personal journal. However, on a Blog they can add images and connect these with hyperlinks to other entries on their Blog or to items on other web pages. Many Blogging web sites are available where the user can setup the Blog with relative ease. The Blog site is managed by the professional organization owning the same; the users just provide content using predefined methodology. A sequence of Blogs on a given topic is listed chronologically, where the newest posting is most often listed first. Many travel and tourism-related websites (such as http://www.itourism.com/) now provide the opportunity to create tourism related blogs.
- **Wiki:** Wikis are also websites, but with aim of creating collective knowledge. These websites allow most users to add content, as well as edit or supplement existing content. Wikipedia is the most well known such web site, and it contains over two million articles in English (http://en.wikipedia.org). Wiki systems create a web environment that enhances collaboration between contributors to provide reliable information in any domain. In the travel domain, Wikitravel (http://wikitravel.org) is a wiki that aims to provide a reliable worldwide travel guide.
- **Podcast:** A podcast allows digital recording and distribution of audio and video files from a website. The Lonely Planet website (http://www.lonelyplanet.com/travelstories/podcast) offers many podcasts that describe tourism locations, activities and their special features.
- **Social Network:** These websites aim to develop web communities or social networks using web technologies. Their strength is in providing the ability to build relationships with people from around the globe.

Prime examples of such sites include Facebook (http://www.facebook.com), MySpace (http://www.myspace.com), and LinkedIn (http://www.linkedin.com). Each social networking site has a particular focus, for example Facebook and MySpace target younger people who what to build new friendships, whereas LinkedIn aims to connect like minded professionals. Driftr (http://www.driftr.com) is a travel community building website. On the Drifter site one can keep track of ones travels, post photos, write reviews and blogs to share with family and friends. Additionally, one can get information on destinations before planning a trip.

VIRTUAL TRAVEL COMMUNITIES

The concept of communities is as old a humanity, and even predates civilization when early humans lived in groups, or communities; even some animals live in communities. The Oxford dictionary defines the various types of communities as (http://www.askoxford.com):

1. a group of people living together in one place.
2. the people of an area or country considered collectively; society.
3. a group of people with a common religion, race, or profession: the scientific community.
4. the holding of certain attitudes and interests in common.
5. a group of interdependent plants or animals growing or living together or occupying a specified habitat.

These definitions apply to the 'real' communities, in which real people, animals or plants interact. However, recently many new types of communities have been created with the help of the Internet technologies, such as Communities of Practice (CoP) (Nickols, 2003), Virtual / Web Communities (Cantoni, L., Tardini, S., 2006), and Travel Communities (Chung & Buhalis, 2008). While the concept of community has a well understood meaning, it needs some formal foundations, before we can analyse existing communities or synthesis newer communities that operate effectively.

Essential Aspects of Communities

Nisbet (1970, p. 47) called the concept of a community "The most fundamental and far-reaching of sociology's unit-idea", that renders legitimacy to a wide variety of associations, including "state, church, trade unions, revolutionary movements, professions, and cooperative(s)". These are all 'real' communities, where the members physically meet each other at one point in time or another.

Cantoni, and Tardini (2006, p. 157) suggest two essential aspects to be able to identifying that a community exits, namely:

1. A set of people have something in common.
2. A group of people interact with each other physically or electronically.

Canter and Siegel (1994) were early users of the Usenet in 1993 and used it extensively for spamming their law services. They were vehemently criticized for doing so; however, in their book *How to Make a Fortune on the Information Superhighway* they stated, "It is important to understand that the Cyberspace community is not a community at all" (as cited in Werry, & Mowbray 2001, p. 4). This assertion highlighted the fact that there were no well established norms for operating in the Cyberspace at that point in time, and therefore it could not qualify as a community according to Canter and Siegel (1994). However, as web / virtual communities matured it became essential to develop norms for interacting with the other members of the virtual community.

Web / Virtual / Online Communities

In recent times Internet technologies have provided an unprecedented variety of means for communicating with each other by electronic means, including, email, blogs, wikis, and social networking sites. Consequently, these communication technologies provide the opportunity of creating virtual communities (Cantoni, L., Tardini, S., 2006), as opposed to real communities. These are also called web communities or online communities. While giving a precise definition of a virtual community is difficult, Cantoni and Tardini (2006, p. 159) provide a provisional definition as: "a group of people to whom interactions and communications via computer play an important role in creating and managing significant social relations".

The main facets that validate a group as a virtual community include the following:

1. Sharing online (electronic) communications environment to connect the group members.
2. Developing and maintaining interpersonal relationships by using the online communications environment.
3. Creating a sense of belonging to the group by using the online communications environment.
4. Having a group structure, that facilitates interaction.
5. Identifying a set of shared norms, values and interests.

However, the three most essential aspects of a community are belonging, identity, and interest (Cantoni, L., Tardini, S., 2006).

Belonging

Belonging is the feeling that a community member gets when he / she is a part of the community. However, this awareness may not be pronounced if the strength of the connection is 'weak'; for example a resident of a country may not have strong sense of belonging to that country, and thus may not feel a part of that community. On the other hand, members of religious group are likely to have a 'strong' sense of belonging to their community.

Virtual communities often have weak ties or connections if the electronic communication is not frequent enough. The lack of face-to-face contact can also lead to a weak connection. For example, when we start communicating with the members of a special interest group via email and web postings, the sense of belonging is weak to begin with. However, if we meet the members of the group at a conference, thereafter the sense of belonging becomes stronger.

Identity

The identity of a community member is used to identify the person. In a real community the identity is often the person's real name or a pet name. Even if a pet name is used by most people for someone, the identity of that person is rarely in doubt. However, in virtual communities the identity is just an identifier to address a member; it may have nothing to do with the real identity of the individual. At times people take on a virtual identity or 'avatar' that identifies with who the person would like to be, and not who they are; for example, the skinniest person can call himself or herself Hercules.

Interest

The topic of interest often delineates the boundary of a virtual community, because virtual communities are not bound by other factors such as geographical location. This topic of interest can be made as wide or as narrow as possible. Having a narrow topic of interest can lead to a lack of healthy debate that often takes place in real communities. In this sense web-based travel communities can be rather narrow focused. A group, or community, based on a topic of interest develops its norms of behavior; these norms often evolve informally with time, and then are turned into a formal set of guidelines for interaction as the need arises–often as community membership grows.

Online Travel Communities

Tourism has always been at the forefront of using the latest ICT systems for advancing business opportunities and the tourist's experience. As the technology for establishing and running virtual communities matured over the last decade many virtual travel communities have also been setup. According to Chung and Buhalis (2008), "Online communities have been increasingly recognized as important information sources for consumers and as effective marketing channel for marketers".

One of the basic needs that these virtual travel communities fulfill is: to search for authentic travel experience by others, to be able to make informed decisions and travel plans. Much of this interaction is based on the creation of User Generated Content (UGC) on blogs, wikis and other social networking sites. However, not all users participate equally in the creation and consumption of the UGC. Based on the level of participation Wang and Fesenmaier have classified these users into the following four classes (as cited in Cantoni, Tardini, Inversini, & Marchiori, 2009, p. 16).

1. Tourists: Mostly brows content, do not have strong ties with other members, and rarely contribute
2. Minglers: Maintain good social ties and contribute occasionally
3. Devotees: Maintain strong social ties and contribute often
4. Insiders: Maintain extensive social ties and contribute regularly

Initially the social networking sites were setup to cater for providing essential information that would help in decision making. However Vogt and Fesenmaier argue that with time, these functional needs have expanded to included higher level needs such as: hedonic, innovation, aesthetic, and sign needs (as cited in Chung, & Buhalis, 2008, p. 72).

1. Hedonic needs relate to the desire for enjoying the experience.
2. Aesthetic needs relate to the desire for having appealing audio visual experience.
3. Innovation needs relate to the desire to develop new ways of enhancing the experience.
4. Sign needs relate to the desire to assert status, and earn recognition form peers.

Consequently, the importance of online travel communities is increasing in promoting travel and tourism. However, in parallel, it is becoming more important and challenging to create good user interfaces. A bad user interface can turn a good system difficult to use, and discourage prospective users for coming back to it. A good user interface is particularly important for fulfilling hedonic, aesthetic and innovation needs. How to generate good user experience is discussed in the next section.

USER INTERFACE DESIGN

This section explores how new eTourism systems should approach User Interface (UI) design issues to make the best use of the newer Web 2.0 technologies for creating effective tourism communities. User-centered design of UI has been considered essential for some time now. Zappen, Harrison, and Watson (2008, p. 19) predicate that, "User-centered approaches to system development recognize that users are helpful and even essential contributors to the design process". This approach has led to the development of UI design methodology in which usability testing become a part of the UI design cycle; where "Usability testing involves measuring the quality of user experience in deploying a particular application, such as: software applications, websites, electronic devices, mobile phones etc." (Georgievski, & Sharda, 2006. p. 224).

User Interface Design Paradigms

From the software designer viewpoint a system must deliver the intended functionality, whereas the user also looks for a good experience while using the system. This dichotomy is articulated by Nielsen (2000) by distinguishing between two approaches to UI design (as cited in Zappen, Harrison, & Watson, 2008, p. 19):

1. Task-oriented paradigm
2. Experience-oriented paradigm

Nielsen seems to prefer the task-oriented approach to UI design, when he states, "There are essentially two basic approaches to design: the artistic ideal of expressing yourself and the engineering ideal of solving a problem for a customer. This book is firmly on the side of engineering. While I acknowledge that there is a need for art, fun, and a general good time on the Web, I believe that the main goal of most web projects should be to make it easy for customers to perform useful tasks" (p. 11).

However, experience production is becoming more important in the current hedonic society. In particular, tourism is an experience industry, and the users of this industry's web systems (i.e. tourists) are more likely to be experience oriented. Therefore, it will be more useful to design eTourism websites and systems using the experience-oriented paradigm.

User Experience Models

Experience is a nebulous concept and difficult to define, and therefore, before we can use it effectively for system design, it needs to be placed on a firm theoretical ground. Theory of experience generation is still work in progress, and the following sections present some of the theoretical models that can be used for further research.

User Experience Production Models

Many attempts have been made at defining the concept of experience. However, associating buzz words such as extraordinary experience, memorable experience, total experience, powerful experience etc. do not help in pinning down this concept (Gelter, 2006, p. 32). The 'Lapland Centre of Expertise for the Experience Industry' defines experience as "a multisensory, memorable, positive and comprehensive emotional experience that can lead to personal change of a subject person" (Gelter, 2006, p. 32). A fuller explanation of this definition is provided by the experience production models given in figures 2 & 3.

The user experience significance model shown in Figure 2 depicts that experience is a continuous phenomenon (Gelter, 2006, p. 34). It flows like an unbroken stream of experience that persists in our conscious mind, as well as in our unconscious (or sub-conscious) mind when we sleep. So called peak experiences are of significant strength and have the potential to make a lasting difference to the individual. Every-day experiences just coast along, while the sub-conscious experiences, especially during sleep lie below the conscious mind; however, even these can have significant effect depending upon their significance.

Furthermore, we can divide experience into internal (thought) experiences and external (physical) experience; and these are of course linked. Figure 3 presents the user experience type model giving a classification of different experiences of various strengths on both internal and external planes (Gelter, 2006, p. 36).

While the experience significance mode (Figure 2) and the experience type model (figure

Figure 2. The user experience significance model

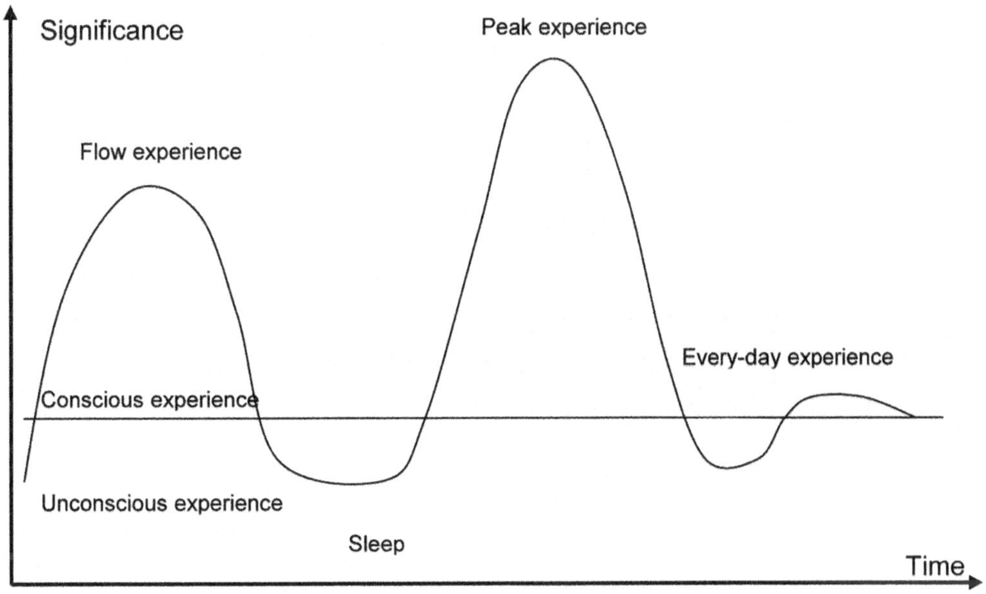

Figure 3. The user experience type model

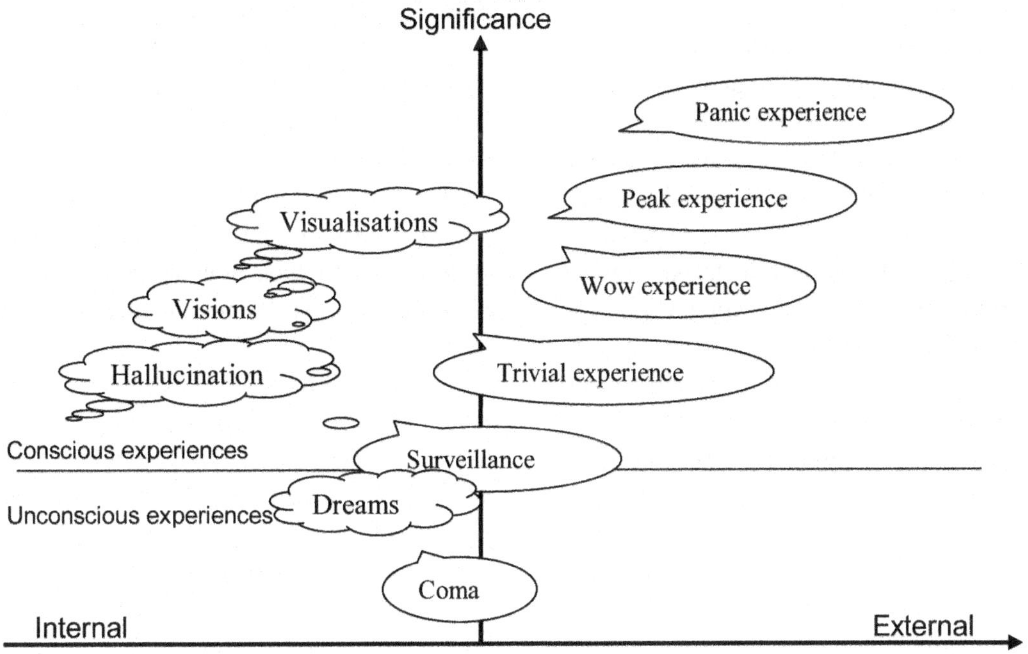

Figure 4. The user experience research (UXeR) model

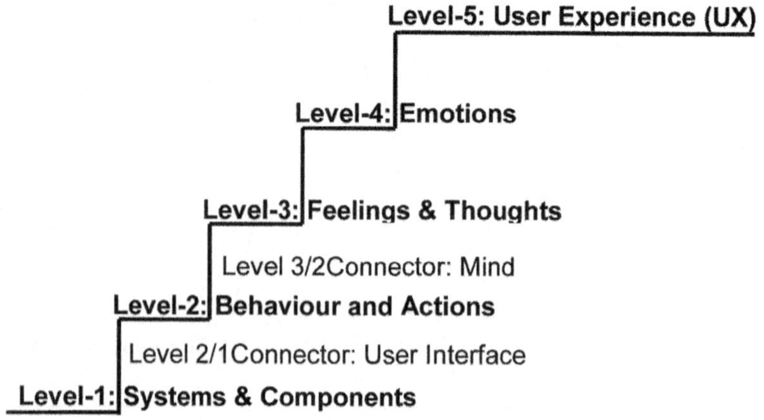

3) clarify some aspects of user experience, these do not show how to relate the user experience to the process for designing UIs. The User Experience Research model presented in the next section show how to make this link.

User Experience Research (UExR) Model

As stated earlier, Neilson (2000) has indicated preference for task-oriented UI design, while current hedonic society is moving towards experience-oriented design. In reality tasks are connected to the user experience (UX). We need a model that connects user actions to the user experience. The User Experience Research (UExR) model presented in figure 4 make this connection over five levels (Sharda, 2008).

We need to appreciate that "User experience (UX) is a gestalt, i.e. a 'holistic outcome' of the inputs received by the human senses and what is already stored in the memory. However, as yet, we do not have standard formal models to measure UX" (Sharda, 2008). According to Hassenzahl and Tractinsky (2006), UX is a strange phenomenon; often criticized for being "vague, elusive, and ephemeral". According to them UX is a multidimensional phenomenon that is: "Experiential: dynamic, complex, unique, situated, and temporally bounded. Beyond the instrumental: holistic, aesthetic, and hedonic. Emotional: subjective, positive, with antecedents, and consequences"

While, the concept of being able to measure UX is still a contentious issue (Ben-Bassat, Meyer, & Tractinsky, 2006), we need to find some formal techniques for doing this, to be able to place UX on a firm scientific ground.

Given that UX is a difficult concept to define, we connect it with more tangible concepts taken from cognitive and behavioral sciences as shown in the five layer User Experience Research (UExR) model presented in Figure 4. In this model we place UX (which is the most ephemeral concept) at level-5; and then connect it with the most physical concept (systems and their components) placed at level-1.

From cognitive science literature we can confirm that the emotions play a central role in any user experience (Mutlu, 2004), therefore, emotions are placed at level-4, just below the experience layer. Feelings and thoughts are responsible for producing emotional responses, therefore these are placed at level-3; here feelings relate to emotional feelings such as happy or sad, and not physical feeling such as hot or cold (Sharda, 2008).

Thoughts occur in the brain and are at times accompanied by verbal and/or visual responses in the mind. Furthermore, thoughts create feelings, for example positive thoughts create positive feeling such as happiness, and negative thoughts create native feelings making one feel sad, angry, jealous etc. These feelings exist in the mind, and connect thoughts to behavior.

Mind is also a nebulous concept, and there are many arguments about where it resides in the human self. However, cognitive science literature views mind as the total information flow taking place in the body. Therefore, mind can be seen as the sum of information stored in the brain, and all the information flowing through the body, including the conscious as well as the sub-conscious mind (Murphy, 1988).

As the mind links thoughts with behavior and actions these are placed at level-2 in the UXeR model. Behaviors are patterns of actions. Thus physical entities are placed at level-1, which comprise the system including all of its components such as user interface entities and hardware devices used to perform actions and tasks.

Thus, the UXeR model provides a step-by-step link that can bridge the gap between task-oriented and experience oriented UI design paradigms. However, more formal relations need to be developed to provide a systematic process for creating effective user interfaces that meet the user's task performing needs while providing a peak experience.

However, the UXeR model is still under development and cannot yield a measure of user experience from the user interface design. Therefore, Usability testing needs to be used for measuring the user experience for any user interface.

Usability Testing

Usability testing is based on the measurement of the quality of user experience when using a specific system or application, such as: software applications, websites, electronic devices, or even mobile phones (Georgievski, & Sharda, 2006). The International Standards Organization (ISO) defines usability as the "effectiveness, efficiency and satisfaction with which a set of users can achieve a specified set of tasks in a particular environment." (as cited in Georgievski, & Sharda, 2006, p 224).

An example of usability testing has been provided by Venkataiah, Sharda and Ponnada (2008) in a research project which demonstrated the greater effectiveness of Continuous Visualization as compared to Discrete Visualization of tourism information.

This usability study focused on specific usability goals and evaluated how well these goals were satisfied in visualization of tourism information. The main usability goals investigated in this usability study were:

1. Navigation: how well is the user able to navigate through the user interface?
2. Collecting information: how well is the user able to gather information from the application?
3. User interface satisfaction: how satisfied is the user with the interface when using the application?

Participants were required to carry out specific task-based scenarios. In each task, participants were presented with a set of objectives that had to be satisfied while carrying out the specified tasks. Participants were then asked to give feedback on their interaction with the Continuous and Discrete Visualization systems in relation to usability goals.

In addition, participants were required to complete the following questionnaires:

1. <u>Pre-experiment questionnaire:</u> To obtain the technical background and details of the participants, e.g.: name, age, gender, if professional: occupation/industry, if student: level and field of study, computer skills, Internet usage, travel experience, use of internet to gather information for your travel,

2. Scenario-questionnaires: These were completed by the participants after each task to capture the users' feedback on their experience regarding each activity. A few sample questions are listed here with the answer choices.
    - Rate how easy or difficult was to find the icon of the continuous visualization system application
    - Rate how easy or difficult was to create a user account
3. Post-experiment questionnaire: These were used to get the users' feedback. Some sample questions are listed here:
    - Rate how easy or difficult was to enter and alter data over the user Interface on the continuous visualization system application
    - Rate how easy or difficult was it to navigate from one page to other page of the user interface
    - Rate how fast or slow was the application to retrieve the data
    - Was the movie (data) related with your query?
    - Rate how informative was the movie (data)

A short interview was also conducted to share the user's experience and any other suggestions regarding the procedures used in the usability study. This research demonstrated that users have a better experience when presented with tourism information as a Continuous Visualization rather than Discrete Visualization. The knowledge gained form this research project will help in developing more advanced Visual Travel Recommender Systems in the future.

Future Research Directions

Future research in this area should focus on the technical as well user experience aspects. Technical aspects should explore how to create more reliable recommender systems, which provide users a trustworthy virtual experience of the proposed tour, to be able to make informed travel plans. Development of virtual social communities is a recent phenomena; it requires more thorough research to understand the factors that will support long-term viability of such communities, especially in the tourism domain. The user experience aspects should focus on enhancing the hedonic aspects of the user interface, to provide a more enjoyable user experience. However, in any system task oriented and hedonic aspects are equally important, and neither should be developed at the expense of the other.

CONCLUSION

Tourism has been a major user of Information and Communication Technology (ICT) systems. Some of the main tourism ICT systems developed in the recent years include Visual Travel Recommender Systems (VTRS) and virtual communities. With the advent of Web 2.0 technologies we can create highly interactive TRS and virtual travel communities. When developing Tourism ICT systems, factors such as Standardization, Task complexity, Knowledge coding and Problem nature must be considered carefully. Some of the tourism ICT systems have been disruptive innovations, while others systems, such as Travel Recommender Systems, are sustaining innovations adding value to the tourism supply chain. Visual Travel Recommenders System is one such sustaining innovation that will further enhance tourism. Web 2.0 systems such as Blogs, Wikis, Podcasts and Social Networks provide new ways to create virtual travel communities. To be able to provide a good user experience with any tourism ICT system, we need to conduct a usability study of the system, thereby keep the user in the design loop.

REFERENCES

Adomavicius, G., & Tuzhilin, A. (2005). Towards the next generation of recommender systems: A survey of the state-of-the-art and possible extensions. *IEEE Transactions on Knowledge and Data Engineering, 17*(6), 734–749. doi:10.1109/TKDE.2005.99

Alfaro, I., Nardon, M., Pianesi, F., Stock, O., & Zancanaro, M. (2004). Using cinematic techniques on mobile devices for cultural tourism. *Journal of Information Technology & Tourism, 7*(2), 61–71. doi:10.3727/1098305054517309

Balabanovi, M., & Shoham, Y. (1997). Content-based, collaborative recommendation. *ACM communication, 40*(3), 66-72.

Ben-Bassat, T., Meyer, J., & Tractinsky, N. (2006). Economic and subjective measures of the perceived value of aesthetics and usability. *ACM Transactions on Computer-Human Interaction, 13*(2), 210–234. doi:10.1145/1165734.1165737

Berka, T., & Plößnig, M. (2004). Designing recommender systems for tourism. In *Proceedings of The Eleventh International Conference on Information Technology in Travel & Tourism, ENTER 2004,* Cairo, Egypt.

Canter, L., & Siegel, M. (1994). *How to make a fortune on the information superhighway*. New York: Harper Collins.

Cantoni, L., & Tardini, S. (2006). *Internet*. New York: Routledge.

Cantoni, L., Tardini, S., Inversini, A., & Marchiori, E. (2009). From paradigmatic to syntagmatic communities: a socio-semiotic approach to the evolution pattern of online travel communities. In W. Hopken, U. Gretzel, & R. Law (Eds.), *Information and Communication Technologies in Tourism 2009 - Proceedings of the International Conference*, Amsterdam, The Netherlands (pp. 13-24). Wien, Austria: Springer.

Chung, J. Y., & Buhalis, D. (2008). Web 2.0: A study of online travel community. In *Proceedings of ENTER 2008: International Conference on Information and Communication Technologies in Tourism*, Innsbruck, Austria (pp. 70-81).

Delgado, J. (2001). Who's who in recommender systems. In *Proceedings of the ACM SIGIR Workshop on Recommender Systems*, New Orleans, LA.

Forsyth, T. (1997). Environmental responsibility and business regulation: The case of sustainable tourism. *The Geographical Journal*, 163.

Gelter, H. (2006). Towards an understanding of experience production. In M. Kylänen (Ed.), *Digital media & games* (pp. 28-51). Rovaniemi, Finland: University of Lapland Press.

Georgievski, M., & Sharda, N. (2006). Re-engineering the usability testing process for live multimedia systems. [EIMJ]. *Journal of Enterprise Information Management, 19*(2), 223–233. doi:10.1108/17410390610645094

Hassenzahl, M., & Tractinsky, N. (2006). User experience - a research agenda. *Behaviour & Information Technology, 25*, 91–97. doi:10.1080/01449290500330331

Hill, W., Stead, L., Rosenstein, M., & Furnas, G. (1995). Recommending and evaluating choices in a virtual community of use. In *Proceedings of the CHI-95 Conference*, Denver, USA.

Houghton, J. W. (2007). Online delivery of tourism services: Development, issues, and challenges. In W. Pease, M. Rowe, & M. Cooper (Eds.), *Information and communication technologies in support of the tourism industry* (pp. 1-25). Hershey, PA: IGI Publishing.

Jakkilinki, R., & Sharda, N. (2007). A framework for ontology-based tourism applications. In W. Pease, M. Rowe, & M. Cooper (Eds.), *Information and communication technologies in support of the tourism industry* (pp. 26-49). Hershey, PA: IGI Publishing.

Kimber, J., Georgievski, M., & Sharda, N. (2006). *Developing a visualisation tool for tour planning*. Paper presented at the IFITT Global Travel & Tourism Technology and eBusiness Conference, Lausanne, Switzerland.

Kolbitsch, J., & Maurer, H. (2006). The transformation of the Web: How emerging communities shape the information we consume. *Journal of Universal Computer Science, 12*(2), 187–213.

Lee, J. K., & Mills, J. E. (2007). Exploring tourist satisfaction with mobile technology. In *Proceedings of ENTER 2007: 14th annual conference of IFITT, the International Federation for IT & Travel and Tourism*, Ljubljana, Slovenia (pp. 141-152).

Lin, K.-J. (2007). Building Web 2.0. *Computer, 40*(5), 101–102. doi:10.1109/MC.2007.159

Mahmood, T., Ricci, F., Venturini, A., & Höpken, W. (2008). Adaptive recommender systems for travel planning. In *Proceedings of ENTER 2008: International Conference on Information and Communication Technologies in Tourism*, Innsbruck, Austria (pp. 1-11).

Marten, P. S. (2007). The transformation of the distribution process in the airlines industry empowered by information and communication technologies. In W. Pease, M. Rowe, & M. Cooper (Eds.), *Information and communication technologies in support of the tourism industry* (pp. 76-113). Hershey, PA: IGI Publishing.

Mooney, R., Bennett, P., & Roy, L. (1998). *Book recommending using text categorization with extracted information.* Paper presented at the AAAI Workshop on Recommender Systems, Madison, WI.

Murphy, J. (1988). *The power of your subconscious mind.* London: Simon & Schuster.

Mutlu, B. D. (2004). *The chaotic nature of human experience: Insights on the subject matter of design towards establishing a science of design.* Unpublished master's thesis, Carnegie Mellon University, USA.

Nickols, F. (2003). *Communities of practice: An overview*, Retrieved January 2009, from http://home.att.net/~discon/KM/CoPOverview.pdf

Nielsen, J. (1993). *Usability engineering.* Boston, MA: Academic Press.

Nielsen, J. (2000). *Designing Web usability: The practice of simplicity.* Indianapolis, IN: New Riders Publishing.

Nisbet, R. A. (1970). *The sociological tradition.* London: Heinemann Educational.

O'Reilly, T. (2005). *What Is Web 2.0: Design patterns and business models for the next generation of software.* Retrieved March 2009, from http://www.oreillynet.com/pub/a/oreilly/tim/news/2005/09/30/what-is-web-20.html

Pazzani, J. M., & Billsus, D. (1997). Learning and revising user profiles: The identification of interesting Web sites. *Machine Learning, 27*(3), 313–331. doi:10.1023/A:1007369909943

Ponnada, M., Jakkilinki, R., & Sharda, N. (2007). Developing Visual Tourism Recommender Systems, in *Information and Communication Technologies in Support of the Tourism Industry, Pease, W., Rowe, M. & Cooper, M. (Eds.), IGI Global, 162-179.*

Ponnada, M., & Sharda, N. (2007). A high level model for developing intelligent visual travel recommender systems. In *Proceedings of ENTER 2007: 14th annual conference of IFITT, the International Federation for IT & Travel and Tourism,* Ljubljana, Slovenia (pp. 33-42).

Ricci, F. (2002). Travel recommender systems. *IEEE Intelligent Systems*, 55–57.

Sharda, N. (1999). *Multimedia information networking*. Upper Saddle River, NJ: Prentice Hall.

Sharda, N. (2008). *Creating ambient multimedia experience on-demand.* In *Proceedings of the Semantic Ambient Media Experience Workshop (SAME 2008) in conjunction with ACM Multimedia 2008,* Vancouver, BC, Canada (pp. 41-48).

Sharda, N., Jakkilinki, R., Georgievski, M., & Ponnada, M. (2008). *Intelligent visual travel recommender systems model for e-tourism websites*. Queensland, Australia: CRC.

Stabb, S., Werther, H., Ricci, F., Zipf, A., Gretzel, U., & Fesenmaier, D. R. (2002). Intelligent systems for tourism. *IEEE Intelligent Systems*, *17*(6), 53–66. doi:10.1109/MIS.2002.1134362

Taboada, M., & Mann, W. C. (2006). Applications of rhetorical structure theory. *Discourse Studies*, *8*(4), 567–588. doi:10.1177/1461445606064836

Usability Net. (2003). *International standards for HCI and usability*. Retrieved July 2004, from http://www.usabilitynet.org/tools/r_international.htm

Venkataiah, S., Sharda, N., & Ponnada, M. (2008). A comparative study of continuous and discrete visualisation of tourism information. In *Proceedings of ENTER 2008: International Conference on Information and Communication Technologies in Tourism,* Innsbruck, Austria (pp. 12-23).

Werry, C., & Mowbray, M. (2001). *Online communities: Commerce, community action and the virtual university*. Upper Saddle River, NJ: Prentice Hall.

Zappen, J. P., Harrison, T. M., & Watson, D. (2008). A new paradigm for designing e-government: Web 2.0 and experience design. In *Proceedings of the 2008 international conference on Digital government research, Digital Government Society of North America* (pp. 17-26).

Chapter 2
Semantic User Model Inferences for Travel Recommender Systems

Yanwu Yang
Chinese Academy of Sciences, China

ABSTRACT

This chapter proposes a semantic user model based on a description logic language to represent user's knowledge and information, and a set of domain-dependent rules specific to the tourism domain in terms of spatial criteria (i.e., distance) and cognition to infer useful user features such as interests and preferences as important inputs for travel recommender systems (TRS). We also identify a spatial Web application scenario in the tourism domain, which is intended to provide personalized information about a variety of spatial entities in order to assist the user in traveling in an urban space.

INTRODUCTION

Personalization offers many opportunities to improve the way web information is delivered to the users with different culture and backgrounds. Among personalization tools developed so far, recommender systems and Web personalization are successful examples of solutions recently introduced to improve Web documents searching, and information filtering such as products recommendation in E-Commerce (Shahabi & Chen, 2003).

Electronic tourism is one of the leading industries of E-business. In the travel and tourism domain many systems have been implemented to support personalized services. A wide range of heterogeneous information is available, and the complexity of product descriptions in the field of tourism is growing (Werthner & Klein, 1999). Travel Recommender Systems (TRS) are viewed as one of the important application domains, in order to assist the user in traveling, e.g., in an urban space. They are intuitive and valuable extensions to, and meanwhile a common means for tourism information systems based on observations in the real world (Berka & Plößnig, 2004).

In most user modeling and preference elicitation applications, there are many cases where no sufficient information and assumptions about the user

DOI: 10.4018/978-1-60566-818-5.ch002

are available to support user preference elicitation and personalization strategies. Usually, the user may either distrust a personalization system or be reluctant to be simulated and tracked by a user modeling component due to some privacy issues. In case of being required to fill a registration form, the user may do it so quickly that some inevitably incomplete user profiles and inconsistency of user's information occur. On the other hand, concerning user modeling in the tourism domain, there is still to explore semantic user model and inference rules for travel recommender systems, especially with consideration of spatial criteria. Amongst many techniques currently developed, the semantic web provides one of the most promising solutions for describing and inferring user models, deriving inference rules for approximating user preferences. Semantic user models play a kernel role for recommender and web personalization systems. In a knowledge-based system, a semantic user model serves as an important input for personalizing human-computer interactions and interfaces. Particularly, travel recommender systems have direction relationships with the spatial dimension. That is, the spatial criteria, relationships and cognition have big infulences on the perceptions and interactions between and the user and information systems. However, to the best of our knowledge, there is few (if any) research to explore the effects of the spatial dimension on the representation of user model and the generation of recommender services.

This chapter introduces a semantic user model and inference rules based on a description logic language to represent and manipulate user information relevant to Travel Recommender Systems, with particular attention to the spatial domain. Description logics are effective to describe user's information and knowledge at the semantic level, besides, they can efficiently handle inconsistency checking and incompletion issues, e.g., infer missing user information items. The logic-based modelling framework acts as a support for user classification and semantic web personalization, to favour the generation of additional information services to the users. The semantic user model can be used to represent a user's knowledge and information (i.e. demographics), and with a set of domain-dependent rules specific to the tourism domain in terms of spatial criteria (i.e. distance) and cognition to infer useful user features such as interests and preferences. The user features serve as important inputs for Travel Recommender Systems to generate and deliver semantically rich, personalized information services to users. The objective of this research is to enhance the representation, reasoning and inference of user's information and knowledge, such as interests and preferences, with semantic techniques and taking spatial cognition and criteria into account. The user-modelling approach is illustrated in the context of a tourism case study.

The remainder of this chapter is organized as follows. The second section, "User modelling and preference elicitation," presents a semantic user model and inference rules for travel recommender systems. The section "DL user model inferences: an illustrative case" gives an illustrative case in the e-tourism domain. In the fourth section we discuss some implementation issues, and conclude this chapter in the last section.

USER MODELLING AND PREFERENCE ELICITATION

In order to acquire accurate, relevant user information, personalization techniques take the construction of user model and preference elicitation as a prerequisite for information retrieval and filtering. User modelling and preference elicitation is a key factor in personalization systems (Kobsa, 2000; Fink & Kobsa 2000) in that it acts as main inputs (about user information) to personalization components. User profiles are approximated for the evaluation of system reliability and retrieval effectiveness (Yao, 1995), optimisation of search engines (Joachims, 2002), refinement of search results (Sugiyama et al., 2004) and smart back navigation (Milic-Frayling et al., 2004). Smart back navigation takes into account user profiles to provide the user intelligent "back" navigation to retrospect to his/her historical Web pages.

Eliciting user's preferences is a non-deterministic process that involves many intuitive and non well-defined criteria that are difficult to model. Identifying user's preferences over a given domain knowledge requires either observing user's choice behaviours or directly interacting with the user with pre-defined questions. A key issue in eliciting user's preferences is the problem of creating a valid approximation of the user's intentions with a few information inputs. The measurement process for modelling user's preferences consists in the transformation of user's intentions towards a classifier or regression model that rank different alternatives. Several knowledge-based algorithms have been developed for eliciting user's preferences from pairwise-based comparisons to value functions. An early example is the pairwise algorithm comparison applied on the basis of ratio-scale measurements that evaluate alternative performances (Saaty, 1980). Artificial neural networks approximate people preferences under certainty or uncertainty conditions using several attributes as an input and a mapping towards an evaluation function (Shavlik & Towell, 1989; Haddawy et al., 2003). Fuzzy majority is a soft computing concept that provides an ordered weighted aggregation where a consensus is obtained by identifying the majority of user's preferences (Kacprzyk, 1986; Chiclana et al., 1998). Preference elicitation is already used in E-Commerce evaluation of client profiles and habits (Riecken, 2000; Schafer et al., 1999), flight selection using value functions (Linden et al., 1997), apartment finding using a combination of value function and user's feedbacks (Shearin & Lieberman, 2001).

However, elicitation of user preferences on the Web is a non-straightforward task as the amount of information available on the user profile, and the extent to which the system might interact with a given user is limited. In spite of the heterogeneity of the user communities that interact with Web applications, there is a lack of a-priori knowledge on the user profiles, cultural and knowledge backgrounds. Meanwhile it's a non-straightforward task to derive user's information needs during system running time. User preference elicitation techniques should consider minimal user input at the beginning stage, and collect as much user information as possible through user's behaviours. This implies to explore and develop unsupervised mechanisms that facilitate manipulation and analysis of information on the Web, that is, to approximate user preferences and intentions in order to guide and constrain information retrieval processes. Last but not the least, a preference elicitation process should also be flexible in order to favour interactions between the user initial intentions, and the preference elicited by the system.

SEMANTIC USER MODEL INFERENCES

A Semantic User Model Based on Description Logics

Logic-based approaches, especially description logics, are dominant for the design and management of ontologies and knowledge bases, due to their strength of specifying primitive and defined concepts, and strong reasoning abilities (Calvanese et al., 1998). Semantic user modelling and Web personalization on the semantic Web require techniques under the open-world assumption. In other words, what is not stated is currently unknown, opposite to the closed world assumption which holds that any statement that is not known to be true is false. One of the distinguishing features of description logics with conventional modelling languages is the non-finiteness of the domain and the open-world semantics. Description logics turn into relevant candidates for ontology languages due to their availability of a well-defined semantics and powerful reasoning tools (Baader et al., 2003). Research achievements and insights from the description logics research community have a strong influence on the design of Web ontology languages such as RDF (RDF Core Working Group, 2004) and OWL (Web Ontology Working Group, 2004), particularly on the formation of semantics, the choices of language constructors, and the integration of data types and data values (Horrocks et al., 2003). Therefore a user model represented with description logics can be transformed with Web ontology languages to support personalized semantic Web services.

From a logical perspective, description logics become a member of the family of knowledge representation formalisms once they are equipped with a proper syntax and semantics, model and proof theory. Consequently, connections between description logics and other areas of logics particularly modal logics have received considerable research attention. As first observed by (Schild, 1991), the description logics ALC can be viewed as a syntactic variant of multi-modal K. However, concrete domain constructor and n-ary relations that are the two main factors in our UMKB case, have no counterpart in modal logic, and there does not exist a translation from description logics with concrete domain extension. ALC(D) related concepts into formulas of the two-variable fragment of first order and modal logics or of the guarded fragment (Lutz, 2003).

Description logics are effective to describe user's information and knowledge at the semantic level. Besides, they can efficiently handle inconsistency and incompletion issues, particularly to infer missing user information. Recently, several research proposals tried to apply description logics to represent and reason about user assumptions in user modeling systems. Description logic is proposed as a representation language for profile information to address matchmaking of demands and supplies of personal profiles in the business of recruitment cases (Calì et al., 2004). (Sinner et al., 2004) used description logics as a semantic language to describe services and user profiles, and determine whether a given profile is semantically compatible to particular services. Cali and his colleagues presented a richer set of description logic formalisms that encode various kinds of user information. Particularly, the former takes advantage of description logics with a concrete domain extension in order to manage "concrete" data in user profiles, e.g. the level of interest in a certain field (e.g. football). Semantic user profile representations are tailored for matchmaking operations and dating services, instead of user model construction and personalization services. However, there is still to explore to utilize description logics to represent and reason user models in concrete applications, especially in spatially-related applications (such as e-tourism) that need a diversity of more complex representation structures and reasoning modules beyond the SHIQ. This chapter makes some preliminary efforts in this directions, namely to extend the description logics with concrete domains and n-ary relations to represent and reason user models. To the best of our knowledge, this might be one of few (if any) works on the adaption of description logics to concrete applications, i.e. travel recommender systems.

In a related work (Yang, 2006), we proposed a semantic user model based on stereotype approaches, with a particular attention to the tourism domain, which is expressed with an extended concept language SHIQ(DR), with concrete domains and n-ary relations. The framework applies hierarchical user stereotypes identified according to several user features relevant to a specific application, e.g., the tourism domain. We combine two distinct types of user information to design a user model, that is, explicit, static user information from registration or interview processes, and implicit, dynamic user information derived from user's behaviors while interacting with the application system. Both explicit and implicit user features are used to identify a stereotype to which a given user belongs. While implicit user information is also used to dynamically update user stereotypes. The framework employs a description logics language SHIQ(DR) to construct and reason an ontology-based UMKB.

The concept language SHIQ is supported by modern description logic system such as FACT and RACER, which extends ALC with several expressive constructors: transitive roles, role hierarchies, inverse roles, and qualifying number restrictions. SHIQ(DR) is an extension of SHIQ to encode concrete domains and n-ary relations, these being motivated by the requirement for modeling and reasoning about an ontology-based UMKB. Concrete datatypes and n-ary relations are particularly useful.

The reasoning capabilities of description logics express inference rules for a user model. The user model can derive profiles for a given user who accesses to and interacts with the application system starting from her/his static (e.g. demographic data) and dynamic information (e.g. behaviors). A user profile contains the corresponding user's personal information, interests and preferences to assist searching, navigation in an information space.

- **Concrete domain** such as number and string are used to represent user information contained in a stereotype (e.g. age, gender). A concrete domain D consists of a set dom(D) (the domain of D) and a set pred(D) (the predicate names of D). Each predicate name P is associated with an arity n and an n-ary predicate over this set. For example, using the set of non-negative integer as concrete domain, we can describe a woman who is at least 20 years old as the concept:

$$\text{Human} \sqcap \text{hasGender.Female} \sqcap \text{hasAge.} \geq 20$$

  Here ≥ 20 stand for the set of the nonnegative integer greater or equal to 20, $\geq$ the binary predicate.
- **N-ary relations** can describe roles that link an individual to more than just one individual or value.

The tourism user community can be ordered in a hierarchy according to these user features, in which the contents of super stereotypes are inherited by the subordinate stereotypes (Figure 1). For example, a tourist is described as a non-inhabitant without temporal address in the residence center of the destination city.

$$\text{DResidence\_center} \equiv \text{Residence} \sqcap \text{locateIn. Destination}$$

$$\text{Tourist} \equiv \text{Non\_inhabitant} \sqcap \forall \text{ hasTAddress.} \neg \text{DResidence\_center}$$

Figure 1. Hierarchical representation of stereotype

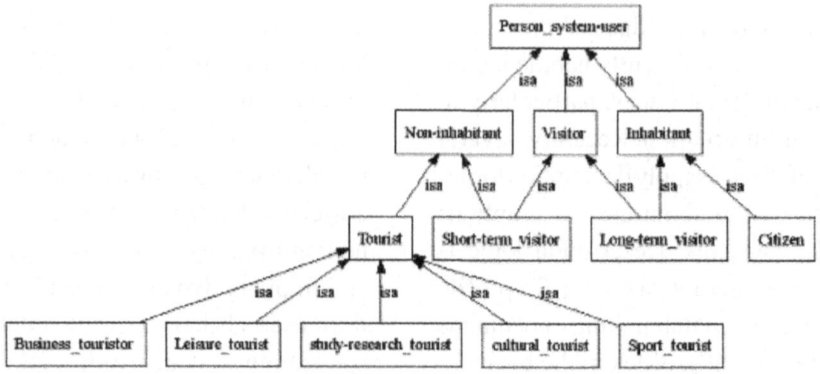

Implicit User Information Extraction

This chapter emphasizes on inference rules to derive user features highly relevant to the tourism domain: familiarity with an urban space, physical and cognitive capability, and interests and preferences. On the application side these are used to build utility functions of the tourism services to a given user.

Familiarity with an Urban Space

Familiarity is one of determinant features that can significantly affect the interactions between the user and a given physical space. For instance, a given urban space to a user with little knowledge of it and another, who is familiar with it, is quite different. High familiarity to an urban space may facilitate the user's decision-making, way-finding, travel routine and time, and *vice versa*. In this user model, we identify and infer the user's familiarity with two factors: role (e.g. tourist) and the access times (i.e., how many times a user accessed to a given urban space, physically or virtually like throug the web). User's role may imply what type of activities a user takes in an urban space and user's familiarity. Each user group in a stereotype hierarchy refers to a specific role for users classified in it. We distinguish four roles: citizen, long-term_visitor, short-term_visitor and tourist, following the descending level of familiarity. Meanwhile, the access times can be used to decide user's familiarity degrees as: high, middle, and low. This tourism user model describes a person with low familiarity to a given urban space as

PersonLF ≡ Person ∩ [$1]hasFamilarity.($2: City $3:Low) ∪ [$1]hasAccessTimes.($2: City $3: ≤ 1) ∪ Tourist (you use different styles for code)

Physical and Cognitive Capability

In comparison to many other kinds of electronic commerce, a tourism application is immaterial and difficult to model. Thereby the range of user's cognitive capabilities is of highest importance: high demands for cognitive capability. Exceeding user's capabilities may give rise to service exclusion and difficulties for her/him to get the right information and make the right decisions. Tourism services are spatially related, and should act as assistants for the user to physically interact with a given spatial environment. Accordingly, spatial proximity measures are an indispensable factor to tailor information to a specific user's personal and contextual situation (Worboys, 2001; Yang & Claramunt, 2004). User's physical capability is in turn one of important factors that should be taken into account in spatial proximity and similarity measures (Yang, 2006).

According to Piaget's theoretical framework genetic epistemology, there are four cognitive structures (i.e., development stages): sensorimotor, preoperations, concrete operations, and formal operations (Piaget & Inhelder, 1969). In previous stages children cannot reason abstractly or test hypotheses systematically. They begin to reason abstractly in the fourth stage (12-15 years). Statistical surveys on physical and cognitive capability show that physical and cognitive function decrease with age among people aged over 50, and the trends of cognitive and physical decline are in prevalence over the age of 75 (Steel et al., 2004). They also find that cognitive capabilities are likely to be related to measures of physical functions, particularly the ability to perform instrumental activities of daily living. For instance, using a map to figure out how to act in an unknown environment, requires both physical and cognitive capabilities. Therefore, user's physical and cognitive capability with age can be considered as a determinant factor. Physical and cognitive capabilities are classified as three degrees: low (less than 12 years, over 75 years), middle (from

12 to 18 years, from 50 to 75 years), high (from 18 to 50 years). Moreover, users with a variety of physical impairment conditions such as athetoid, ataxic, require more efforts and attentions for tourism service personalization. There are very important performance and acceptance differences between them and healthy user, when they interact either with computers or with physical environments. These differences in the interaction cycles should be qualified at the level of user model design (Keates et al., 2002), since disabled users may demand additional services especially while delivering personalized services to a user group, e.g. a family (Ardissono et al., 2001). A disabled user's physical state is often at the low level. Then we describe a person who has low physical capabilities using the concept:

PersonLP $\equiv$ Person $\cap$ hasAge. ≤ 12 $\cup$ hasAge. >75 $\cup$ hasPhyDisable.true

User's Interests and Preferences

User's interests and preferences can be implicitly identified either from user's personal information, or from user's behaviors, as the way that an adept guide does in the tourist domain. First of all, we can infer user's interests and preferences from her/his personal information, e.g., hobbies. Profession and hobby, to some degree, can be employed to infer user's interests and preferences. A person who likes football may have strong interests in sportive issues. A professor in history may prefer to visit historic sites and museums.

Activity $\subseteq$ Thing $\cap$ occurIn.Spatial_entity

relateTo= $\neg$ occurIn

$\exists$ HasHobby(Activity) $\Rightarrow$ $\exists$ hasInterest($2:Place $\cap$ relateTo.Activity $3:High)

Secondly, user's interests and preferences evolve over time. This implies to explore user's dynamic interactions with an information space. It also reflects the observation that a given user shows some interests to a type of spatial entities if she/he performs some actions on an entity that falls into this type, either physically or on the Web. The possible actions include visit, pass by, browse, search for further information, include in travel routine, etc. These actions lead to different degrees of user's interests and preferences according to a type of spatial entities. For example, visit, search for further information, select and include in travel routine reflect high interests and preferences. The family of tourist stereotype classifies the user according to her/his interests and preferences in the topics of the tourism domain. For instance, a person with high interests and preferences over the domain *Culture* can be described using the concept:

//Interests and preferences

hasActivity. Place $\Rightarrow$ hasInterest$|_{\$2}$. Place

hasVisit $\subseteq$ has Activity

hasSearchFurther $\subseteq$ has Activity

hasBookmark $\subseteq$ has Activity

hasBrowse $\subseteq$ has Activity

hasSelect $\subseteq$ has Activity

hasPassby $\subseteq$ hasActivity

$\exists$ hasActivity. (Business_center $\cup$ Administrative_center) $\Rightarrow$ $\exists$ hasInterest$|_{\$2}$.Business

$\exists$ hasActivity. (Gymnasium $\cup$ Beach) $\Rightarrow$ $\exists$ hasInterest$|_{\$2}$.Sport

$\exists$ hasActivity. (Historic_site $\cup$ Culture_area $\cup$ Museum $\cup$ Church) $\Rightarrow \exists$ hasInterest$|_{\$2}$.Culture

$\exists$ hasActivity. (Research_center) $\Rightarrow \exists$ hasInterest$|_{\$2}$.StudyResearch

$\exists$ hasActivity. (Garden $\cup$ Theater $\cup$ Cinema) $\Rightarrow$ $\exists$ hasInterest$|_{\$2}$.Leisure

$\exists$ hasVisit $\Rightarrow \exists$ hasInterest$|_{\$3}$.High

$\exists$ hasSearchFurther $\Rightarrow \exists$ hasInterest$|_{\$3}$.High

$\exists$ hasBookmark $\Rightarrow \exists$ hasInterest$|_{\$3}$.High

$\exists$ hasBrowse $\Rightarrow \exists$ hasInterest$|_{\$3}$.Middle

$\exists$ hasSelect $\Rightarrow \exists$ hasInterest$|_{\$3}$.Middle

$\exists$ hasPassby $\Rightarrow \exists$ hasInterest$|_{\$3}$.Low

Thirdly, it's reasonable and natural to recommend particular places in a given urban space, e.g., the Eiffel tower in Paris, especially if the user has visited them. Sometimes these places might act as one of the main impetus to the interactions between the user and a city. These inference rules can be given as:

Spe_place $\subseteq$ Place

$\exists$ visit.City $\Rightarrow \exists$ hasInterest.(\$2:Spe_place $\cap$ locateIn.City \$3:High)

DL USER MODEL INFERENCES: AN ILLUSTRATIVE CASE

In description logics, basic inferences operating on concept description and a terminological axiom include subsumptions and satisfiability.

- Subsumption checks whether a concept description is more general than another, which is employed to organize the concepts in a taxonomy according to their generality.
- Satisfiability concerns if a concept description is satisfiable with respect to a terminological axiom.

Concerning a knowledge base with the TBox (assertions on concepts) and the ABox (assertions on individuals), and the inference mechanisms for reasoning on both the TBox and the Abox include are consistency and instance checking.

- Consistency is to check if an ABox is consistent with respect to a TBox, e.g. there is an interpretation that is a common model of the two.
- Instance checking verifies if an individual in an ABox is an instance of a concept description with respect to a TBox.

In order to achieve an efficient implementation, it's necessary to consider more complex inferences that can be reduced to multiple invocations of the more basic inference problems mentioned above: retrieval and realization.

- Retrieval is, given an Abox A, a TBox and a concept C, to find all individuals a such as that $A|=_T C(a)$.
- Realization is, given an Abox A, a TBox, and an individual a, to find the most specific concept C from the set such that $A|=_T C(a)$.

All the relevant inference problems can be reduced to the consistency problem for ABox, provided that the DLs at hand allow for conjunction and negation. The Tableau Algorithms have turned out to effectively handle this issue, and to obtain sound and complete satisfiability algorithms for a great variety of DLs (Baader & Sattler, 2001).

Subsumption and concept satisfiability inferences are used to check if there exist some inconsistencies in the terminological axioms of the user modeling knowledge base, and to add a new user concept to a stereotype hierarchy. As an example we consider a person who visits a given urban space, e.g. Christian visits Beijing for the first time (Table 1). Besides her registration information, we get the fact that she also visited the Great Wall after arrival.

Consistency inference will be used to check if Christian's description is consistent with the terminological axioms, and instance checking to identify her to the right stereotypes. The Great Wall is figured out to be a historic site (realization). The user with similar features can be sorted out through retrieval inference. The logic-based user modeling system encodes and analyzes Christian's personal and behavioral information, then infers some implicit information about her, e.g. familiarity, physical and cognitive capability, and interests and preferences.

These inference results show that various user features about Christian, and who is identified as a culture tourist, studyresearch tourist (Table 2). The contents of the Culture_tourist and StudyResearch_tourist stereotypes with respect to user's interests and preferences are used to predict some information about her through a conjunction operator (Table 3). The multi-dimensional user information is merged through a disjunction operator to form a complete user profile (Carmagnola et al., 2005). The application system employs this information to tailor information services delivered to her in order to facilitate her travel in Beijing.

IMPLEMENTATION ISSUES

User Profiles Retrieval and Matching

In a user model knowledge base, each user is attached with a static profile and a dynamic profile.

Table 1. Christian's personal information

Name: Christian
hasCode: BJ0001
Gender: Female
Age: 30~40
Address: Roma
Nationality: French
Temporary address: Beijing Hotel
Family visit: No
Profession: Professor
haHobby: Gardening...
hasAccessTimes: the first time
hasVisit: GreatWall
...

Table 2. User profile for Christian

// Assertions
//Basic user information
hasCode(Christian, BJ0001)
hasGender(Christian, Female)
hasAge(Christian, $\geq 30 \cap \leq 40$)
hasPAddress(Christian, Roma)
hasTAddress(Christian, BeijingHotel)
hasNationality(Christian, French)
hasProfession(Christian, Professor)
hasHobby(Christian, Gardening)
hasAccessTimes(Christian, Beijing, ≤ 1)
hasVisit(Christian, GreatWall)
...
//Destination information
Destination(Beijing)
Spe_place(GreatWall)
Spe_place(ForbiddenCity)
...
//Derived user information
hasFamilarity($1:Christian, $2:Beijing, $3:Low),
hasCogCapability(Christian, High)
hasPhyCapability(Christian, High)
FTourist(Christian)
Culture_tourist(Christian)
StudyResearch_tourist(Christian)

Table 3 Partial description of the combination of Culture_tourist and StudyResearch_tourist stereotypes

Culture_tourist ∪ StudyResearch_tourist ⊆ Tourist ∩
∩ [$1] $ hasInterest.($2:Business_center $3:Low)
∩ [$1] $ hasInterest.($2:Culture $3:High)
∩ [$1] $ hasInterest.($2:Leisure $3:Middle)
∩ [$1] $ hasInterest.($2:Sport $3:Middle)
∩ [$1] $ hasInterest.($2:Research_center $3:High)
∩ [$1] $ hasInterest.($2:Transportation $3:Middle)
∩ [$1] $ hasInterest.($2:Administrative_center $3:Low)

The former from user's registration and relevant reference operations, the latter is from user's current actions and usage logs. The two profiles can also be viewed as the static and dynamic part of a user profile, as they are interwoven through some domain-dependent rules. When a new user begins to interact with the application system, according to her/his static information (if available), she/he is initially classified to a user group. With further interacting actions, the user might move from one group to another. A general user profile can be generated from a stereotype group, which can be populated with detailed information during interactions between the user and the application system.

Case-based reasoning technique solves a new problem by retrieving the olds that are likely to have similar solutions (Hammond, 1989; Riesbeck & Schank, 1989; Kolodner 1993). User profiles are derived either from a web query, an original example entity of interest, or from an explicit user model (Towle & Quinn, 2000). To a specific user, intuitively we can first search for the most similar user profile, whose corresponding personalization solution can be used as a basis for the generation of personalization services. Then a series of tweaking actions are executed to alter characteristics of the original example solution to make it more closely match the problem situation according to either explicit or implicit user relevance feedbacks. The process is repeated until the system reaches a satisfiable solution. In our user model knowledge base, user profiles are organized based on a domain-dependent stereotype, then user profile retrieval means to fetch user profiles relevant to a user group. The most common approach used to compute a degree of similarity between two vectors in Web information retrieval is the standard cosine similarity. Accordingly, and in order to deal with spatial semantics in user profiles, we applied the adjusted cosine similarity introduced by (Sarwar et al., 2001) to determine the semantic similarity between two user profiles. The semantic function $Sem(x_i, x_j)$ is given as

$$Sem(x_i, x_j) = \frac{\sum_{h=1}^{m} (x_i^h - \overline{x^h}) \times (x_j^h - \overline{x^h})}{\sqrt{\sum_{h=1}^{m} (x_i^h - \overline{x^h})^2 \times \sum_{h=1}^{m} (x_j^h - \overline{x^h})^2}}$$

The domain of the semantic function is given by the unit interval [0, 1]. A semantic parameter x_i^h (x_j^h) reflects a demographical (or inferred) feature of a user profile x_i (x_j). These features are valuded by fuzzy quantifiers bounded by the unit interval $[0,1]$. $\overline{x^h}$ is the average value of a specific feature of the user profiles. The value domain of $Sem(x_i, x_j)$ is given by the interval [-1, 1].

System Architecture

The user modeling module interacts with the application systems using inter-process communications, e.g., "*tell*" and "*ask*" operations (Figure 4). A semantic user model can be considered as a formal representation of a given user background information, interests and preferences. Web application systems unobtrusively observe and record user's behaviors, then send such information to the user modeling component that allows the inference of domain-dependent user features. The application system then performs a matching between the user's query and her/his profile to provide services tailored to the user.

There are two different approaches relevant to the implementation of our semantic user model to support semantic spatial web personalization applications, e.g., e-tourism personalization. The first approach is that, it seems natural to build a user modeling system based a DL reasoner to manipulate logic-based user model. The DL reasoner can be used to check consistency of user profiles, and infer relevant user features while being required by a personalization component. The second approach is to implement it on the

Figure 2. Personalization system

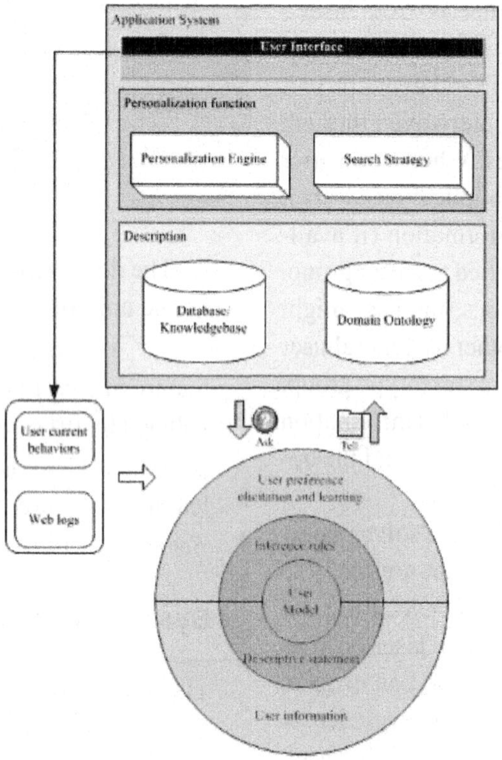

platform of an ontology editor integrated with a rule engine. The first approach may produce light-weight user modeling component that fit mobile devices however is hard to maintain and update. The latter provide a visual environment for developers to edit and maintain ontologies, which also provide a set of flexible interfaces to DL reasoners and rule engines. Semantic user modelling component can be used to support value-added web services because of its functions for representation and reasoning about a variety of assumptions about the user.

We developed a prototype of semantic user model (Figure 3) in the environment of Protégé (Noy et al., 2000), in which the abstract reference rules can be implemented in the integrated Semantic Web Rule Language (SWRL) editor (Horrocks et al., 2004) and Java Expert System Shell (JESS) (Friedman-Hill, 1995). Protégé is a frame-based tool that offers classes, slots, facets, instances, and slot values as building blocks for ontology editing and knowledge representation and acquisition. Protégé is available as an open source software with a well-documented plugin architecture, which allows a third party to easily create a variety of extensions. The Protégé OWL Plugin provide abilities for loading, edit and save OWL and RDF ontologies and individuals to build knowledge bases. The ontologies and knowledge bases built in Protégé can be exported as OWL files to provide semantically enriched information across several application systems in a distributed environment or on the Web. As well as providing a set of APIs to explore and edit OWL ontologies, Protégé OWL plugin is also equipped with a set of reasoning APIs, which can be used to access to an external DIG compliant reasoner to enable a variety of inference rules. The SWRL editor is an extension of the Protégé OWL plugin that permits the interactive editing of SWRL rules. SWRL is proposed based on a combination of the OWL DL and OWL Lite sublanguages of the OWL Web Ontology Language with the Unary/Binary Datalog RuleML sublanguages of the Rule Markup Language. It enables Horn-like rules to extend OWL ontologies and knowledge bases. Moreover, the SWRL editor uses a subsystem called the SWRL factory that supports a rule engine plugin mechanism that permit API-level interoperation with existing rule engines (O'Connor et al., 2005). Jess is a popular rule engine for reasoning about knowledge bases in the form of declarative rules. We choose Jess due to the fact that it can works seamlessly with Protégé OWL APIs in Java. OWL concepts and individuals, and SWRL rules can be represented with Jess programs.

Preliminary Application on Spatial Personalization in the Tourism Domain

Without loss of generality, we consider an application scenario in which an urban space represented on the Web. In a given city, there are diverse sightseeing places, distributed in space and that contain some semantic contents. Additionally, reference locations that are easy to find and where people can act from to visit the spatial entities are available. In our case, spatial entities of interest are modelled as places that might present an interest to a user who wants to visit the city of Kyoto, reference locations as hotels where the user will be able to act from in the city. We assume no prior – if any – little knowledge of the Web GIS environment presented by the Web interface, neither experiential nor survey knowledge1. Given a Web GIS environment of interest (i.e. the historical city of Kyoto in the prototype developed so far), the user is expected to plan a trip or to find valuable information in the city, and where she/he would like to find out some spatial entities of interest, and a reference location from which she/he will be able to act in the spatial environment.

The Web personalization system developed so far encodes two main levels of information inputs: places and hotels. Several sight-seeing places of diverse interests in the city of Kyoto have been pre-selected to give a large range of preference opportunities to the user. These places are referenced by image schemata and encoded

Figure 3. Implementation architecture of DL-based user model

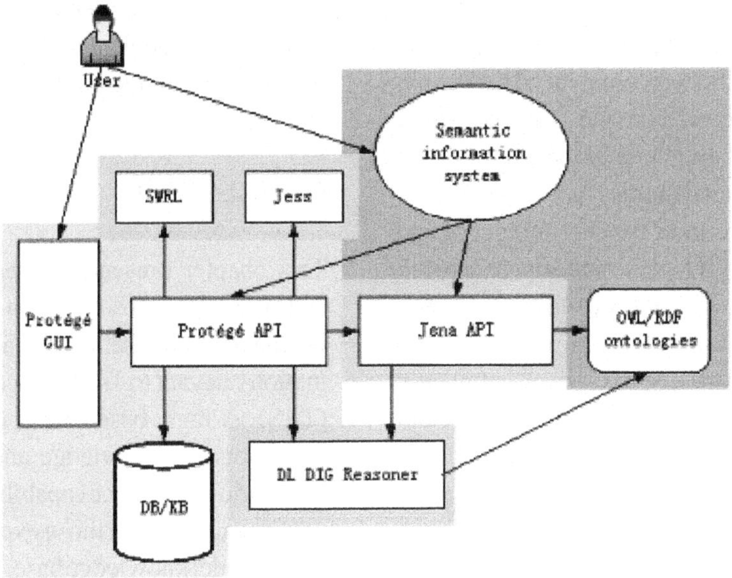

using fuzzy quantifiers according to predefined semantic classes (e.g. urban, temple, garden and museum) and geo-referenced. Hotels are represented by a list of hotels also offered for user's selection.

The spatial web personalization system supports personalized search strategies, a hybrid personalization engine, and a spatially enriched user interface. From user preference elicitation and personalization mechanisms, the personalized search strategies and the hybrid personalization engine are based on different principles. The former are based on static inferences, the latter, on dynamic inferences as the personalization engine takes into account user's current navigations. The former allows for active interactions, while the latter performs in a passive mode. Integration of these personalized search strategies and the personalization engine gives flexible mechanisms for supporting interactions between the user and spatial web applications. Personalization services also supports a Web-based interface enriched with image schemata and affordance concepts that facilitate interactions between the user and the spatial Web, and user preference elicitation process. The whole personalized search strategy is implemented as an iterative process, namely an initial and a series of successive refinement steps based on the BNAM mechanism, taking into account user's interests and preferences as described previously, to search for the best reference location and top-n spatial entities recommended to the user. The direct result from initial personalized search process recalls the best reference location and a set of top-n ranked spatial entities, whose names are displayed at the interface. We also introduced and implemented a hybrid personalization approach and reinforcement process that facilitate user's navigations and interactions with spatial entities embedded in web pages. Markov chains implicitly monitors and records user's trails on the Web, and derives navigational patterns and knowledge in order to predict user's interactions on the web. A reinforcement process complements the approach by adapting the interactions between the user and the web, that is, a sequence of iterative negative/positive rewards evaluated on the basis of user's relevance feedbacks to personalized presentations.

Research Opportunities

We believe that user's multi-dimensional characteristics are intimately and semantically interrelated. This paper makes some preliminary efforts on the elicitation of implicit assumptions from user characteristics explicitly provided by the user in registration procedure. There are still some inference rules among user's characteristics that remain unexplored. For instance, some useful information is concealed in culture- or region-specific user features. This will be covered in future work. The future work is intended to further explore semantic user model for the generation of semantically enriched user profiles, and inference rules for the elicitation of implicit user features from explicit user information. It also deserves further investigation about effects of space and time on personalization, user model and preference elicitation. This concerns how to identify and qualify preference aspects relevant to the spatial and temporal dimensions, construct and populate user model with them, and extract the knowledge with some inference mechanisms. Furthermore, we also plan to implement and evaluate our semantic user model and inference rule in concrete travel recommender system applications.

CONCLUSION

This chapter presented a semantic user model and inference rules based on a description logic language to represent and manipulate user information relevant to Travel Recommender Systems (TRS). A logic-based semantic user model describes user's knowledge and information, and with various inference capabilities to elicit implicit user's features from those explicit descriptions in a user model knowledge base. Domain-dependent user features inferred act as the main inputs for travel recommender systems to generate and deliver personalized information services.

ACKNOWLEDGMENT

We are thankful to the reviewer for the detailed comments and recommendations. This work was supported by the Hi-tech Research and Development Program of China (863) (2008AA01Z121).

REFERENCE

Ardissono, L., Goy, A., Petrone, G., Segnan, M., & Torasso, P. (2001). Tailoring the recommendation of tourist information to heterogeneous user groups. In *Proceedings of the Hypermedia: Openness, Structural Awareness, and Adaptivity, Int. Workshops OHS-7, SC-3 and AH-3* (LNCS 2266, pp. 280-295). Berlin, Germany: Springer Verlag.

Baader, F., Calvanese, D., McGuinness, D., Nardi, D., & Patel-Schneider, P. (2003). *The description logic handbook: Theory, implementation and applications*. Cambridge, UK: Cambridge University Press.

Baader, F., & Sattler, U. (2001). An overview of tableau algorithms for description logics. *Studia Logica, 69*, 5–40. doi:10.1023/A:1013882326814

Berka, T., & Plößnig, M. (2004). Designing recommender systems for tourism. In *Proceedings of ENTER 2004, Kairo.*

Calì, A., Calvanese, D., Colucci, S., Di Noia, T., & Donini, F. M. (2004). A logic-based approach for matching user profiles. In M. Gh. Negoita, R. J. Howlett, & L. C. Jain (Eds.), *Proceedings of the Knowledge-Based Intelligent Information and Engineering Systems, 8th International Conference, KES 2004*, Wellington, New Zealand (pp. 187-195).

Calvanese, D., De Giacomo, G., & Lenzerini, M. (1998). On the decidability of query containment under constraints. In *Proceedings of the 17th ACM SIGACT SIGMOD SIGART Symposium on Principles of Database Systems (PODS'98)* (pp. 149-158).

Carmagnola, F., Cena, F., Gena, C., & Torre, I. (2005). A multidimensional approach for the semantic representation of taxonomies and rules in adaptive hypermedia systems. In *Proceedings of the PerSWeb'05 workshop (UM 2005).*

Chiclana, F., Herrera, F., & Herrera-Viedma, E. (1998). Integrating three representation models in multipurpose decision making based on preference relations. *Fuzzy Sets and Systems, 97*, 33–48. doi:10.1016/S0165-0114(96)00339-9

Fink, J., & Kobsa, A. (2000). A review and analysis of commercial user modeling servers for personalization on the World Wide Web. *User Modeling and User-Adapted Interaction, 10*(3-4), 209–249. doi:10.1023/A:1026597308943

Friedman-Hill, E. (1995). *Jess: The rule engine for the Java platform*. Retrieved from http://herzberg.ca.sandia.gov/jess/

Haddawy, P., Ha, V., Restificar, A., Geisler, B., & Miyamoto, J. (2003). Preference elicitation via theory refinement. *Journal of Machine Learning Research, 4*, 317–337. doi:10.1162/153244304773633843

Hammond, K. (1989). *Case-based planning: Viewing planning as a memory task*. San Diego, CA: Academic Press.

Horrocks, I., Patel-Schneider, P. F., Boley, H., Tabet, S., Grosof, B., & Dean, M. (2004). *SWRL: A Semantic Web rule language combining OWL and RuleML* (W3C Member Submission, 21 May 2004). Retrieved from http://www.w3.org/Submission/2004/SUBM-SWRL-20040521/

Horrocks, I., Patel-Schneider, P. F., & van Harmelen, F. (2003). From SHIQ and RDF to OWL: The making of a Web ontology language. *Journal of Web Semantics*, *1*(1), 7–26. doi:10.1016/j.websem.2003.07.001

Joachims, T. (2002). Optimizing search engines using clickthrough data. In *Proceedings of the 8th ACM SIGKDD International Conference on Knowledge Discovery and Data Mining (KDD-02)* (pp. 133-142). New York: ACM Press.

Kacprzyk, J. (1986). Group decision making with a fuzzy linguistic majority. *Fuzzy Sets and Systems*, *18*, 105–118. doi:10.1016/0165-0114(86)90014-X

Keates, S., Laddon, P., Clarkson, P. J., & Robinson, P. (2002). User models and user physical capability. [UMUAI]. *Journal of User Modeling and User-Adapted Interaction*, *12*, 139–169. doi:10.1023/A:1015047002796

Kobsa, A. (2000). *User modeling as a key factor in system personalization*. Retrieved September 16, 2005, from http://www.zurich.ibm.com/~mrs/chi2000/contributions/kobsa.html

Kolodner, J. (1993). *Case-based reasoning*. San Mateo, CA: Morgan Kaufmann.

Linden, G., Hanks, S., & Lesh, N. (1997). Interactive assessment of user preference models: The automated travel assistant. In *Proceedings of User Modeling*.

Lutz, C. (2003). Description logics with concrete domains - a survey. In P.Balbiani, N.-Y. Suzuki, F. Wolter, and M. Zakharyaschev (Eds.), *Advances in modal logics* (Vol. 4). London: King's College Publications.

Milic-Frayling, N., Jones, R., Rodden, K., Smyth, G., Blackwell, A., & Sommerer, R. (2004). Smartback: Supporting users in back navigation. In *Proceedings of the 13th conference on World Wide Web*, New York, USA.

Noy, N. F., Fergerson, R. W., & Musen, M. A. (2000). The knowledge model of Protege-2000: Combining interoperability and flexibility. In *Proceedings of the 2nd International Conference on Knowledge Engineering and Knowledge Management (EKAW'2000),* Juan-les-Pins, France.

O'Connor, M. J., Knublauch, H., Tu, S. W., & Musen, M. A. (2005). Writing rules for the Semantic Web using SWRL and Jess. In *Proceedings of the 8th International Protege Conference, Protege with Rules Workshop*, Madrid, Spain.

Piaget, J., & Inhelder, B. (1969). *The psychology of the child*. New York: Basic Books.

RDF Core Working Group W3C Semantic Web Activity, W3C. (2004). *Resource description framework (RDF)* (W3C Recommendation, 10 February 2004). Retrieved from http://www.w3.org/TR/rdf-primer/

Riecken, D. (2000). Introduction: Personalized views of personalization. *Communications of the ACM*, *43*(8), 27–28.

Riesbeck, C. K., & Schank, R. C. (1989). *Inside case-based reasoning*. Hillsdale, NJ: Lawrence Erlbaum.

Saaty, T. L. (1980). *The analytic hierarchy process*. New York: McGraw-Hill.

Sarwar, B., Karypis, G., Konstan, J., & Riedl, J. (2001). Item-based collaborative filtering recommendation algorithms. In *Proceedings of the 10th International WWW Conference*, Hong Kong.

Schafer, J. B., Konstan, J., & Riedl, J. (1999). Recommender systems in e-commerce. In *Proceedings of the ACM Conference on Electronic Commerce* (pp. 158-166).

Schild, K. (1991). A correspondence theory for terminological logics: Preliminary report. In *Proceedings of IJCAI-91, 12th International Joint Conference on Artificial Intelligence,* Sydney, Australia (pp. 466-471).

Shahabi, C., & Chen, Y. (2003). Web information personalization: Challenges and approaches. In *Proceedings of the 3nd International Workshop on Databases in Networked Information Systems (DNIS 2003),* Aizu-Wakamatsu, Japan (pp. 5-15).

Shavlik, J., & Towell, G. (1989). An approach to combining explanation-based and neural learning algorithms. *Connection Science, 1*(3), 233–255. doi:10.1080/09540098908915640

Shearin, S., & Lieberman, H. (2001). Intelligent profiling by example. In *Proceedings of the International Conference on Intelligent User Interfaces (IUI 2001),* Santa Fe, NM (pp. 145-152).

Sinner, A., Kleemann, T., & von Hessling, A. (2004). Semantic user profiles and their applications in a mobile environment. In *Proceedings of the Artificial Intelligence in Mobile Systems 2004 (AIMS 2004).*

Steel, N., Huppert, F. A., McWilliams, B., & Melzer, D. (2004). *Physical and cognitive function.* Retrieved from http://www.ifs.org.uk/elsa/report03/ch7.pdf

Sugiyama, K., Hatano, K., & Yoshikawa, M. (2004). Adaptive Web search based on user profile constructed without any effort from users. In *Proceedings of the WWW 2004*, New York, USA (pp. 675-684).

Towle, B., & Quinn, C. (2000). *Knowledge-based recommender systems using explicit user models* (Tech. Rep. WS-00-04, 74-77). Paper presented at the AAAI workshop.

Web Ontology Working Group W3C Semantic Web Activity, W3C. (2004). *OWL Web ontology language* (W3C Recommendation, 10 February 2004). Retrieved from http://www.w3.org/2001/sw/WebOnt/

Werthner, H., & Klein, S. (1999). *Information technology and tourism - a challenging relationship*. Berlin, Germany: Springer.

Worboys, M. F. (2001). Nearness relations in environmental space. *International Journal of Geographical Information Science, 15*(7), 633–651. doi:10.1080/13658810110061162

Yang, Y. (2006). *Towards spatial Web personalization.* Unpublished doctoral dissertation, Naval Academy Research Institute, France.

Yang, Y., & Claramunt, C. (2004). A flexible competitive neural network for eliciting user's preferences in Web urban spaces. In P. Fisher (Ed.), *Developments in spatial data handling* (pp. 41-57). Berlin, Germany: Springer-Verlag.

Yao, Y. (1995). Measuring retrieval effectiveness based on user preference of documents. *Journal of the American Society for Information Science American Society for Information Science, 46*(2), 133–145. doi:10.1002/(SICI)1097-4571(199503)46:2<133::AID-ASI6>3.0.CO;2-Z

ENDNOTE

1 Experiential knowledge is derived from direct navigation experience while survey knowledge reflects geographical properties of the environment (Thorndyke & Hayes-Roth, 1982).

Chapter 3
Developing Knowledge-Based Travel Advisor Systems:
A Case Study

Dietmar Jannach
Technische Universität Dortmund, Germany

Markus Zanker
University Klagenfurt, Austria

Markus Jessenitschnig
University Klagenfurt, Austria

ABSTRACT

In the domain of travel and tourism, recommender systems have proven to be valuable tools for supporting potential customers during the decision making process. In contrast to other domains, however, travel recommendation systems must not only include extensive knowledge about catalogued items but also require interactive elicitation of customer requirements. As a consequence, such systems often become highly-interactive and personalized Web applications, whose development can be costly and time-consuming. The authors see these factors as major obstacles to the widespread adoption of this type of recommender system in particular with respect to small and medium-sized companies and e-tourism platforms. The "VIBE virtual spa advisor" presented in this chapter is an example of a recommender system offering such high level interaction. It has been built with the help of ADVISOR SUITE, an off-the-shelf knowledge-based and domain-independent framework for the rapid development of advisory applications. The chapter discusses how development costs can be reduced by using a framework that supports graphical domain modeling, domain-independent recommendation algorithms and semi-automated generation of production quality web applications. The authors also report on practical experiences and give an outlook on future work and opportunities in the domain of travel recommendation.

DOI: 10.4018/978-1-60566-818-5.ch003

INTRODUCTION

The travel and tourism sector is not only a leading industry with substantial growth rates, but is also a sector in which the web already forms the primary source of information. Today, people searching for travel destinations or planning a trip typically consult a web-based information system first. Furthermore, recent studies (such as those conducted by the European Travel Commission) show that the share of customers that actually book their travel arrangements online is constantly growing, which in turn means that sales opportunities can be easily missed if appropriate electronic online services are not provided on travel agency web sites or e-tourism platforms. Consequently, the online market in the travel and tourism domain has become highly competitive, supporting a vast number of information and booking platforms. However this has also resulted in the fact that online service providers are finding it increasingly harder to attract (new) customers to their sites, and more importantly, to turn these potential customers into buyers; see (Werthner & Ricci, 2004) for a detailed discussion on the role of e-commerce for tourism industry.

In this context, Recommender Systems can be seen as a promising opportunity to add value to online services that can help to differentiate a platform from its competition. Such systems have already been successfully deployed in various domains and have proven to be valuable tools for coping with information overload and for guiding online customers through the decision-making and purchase process.

Although there has been extensive research into recommender systems over the last decade especially concerning community-based approaches – see, e.g., (Adomavicius & Tuzhilin, 2005) for an overview – the tourism domain shows some specific particularities. First, most travel recommender applications are content or knowledge based (Burke, 2000) i.e., the system possesses deep knowledge of the catalogued items; and can determine that the alternatives are simply not viable.

For example, community-based approaches require a minimal size of the user community, which is hard for small- and medium sized e-tourism platforms to achieve. In addition, without a detailed buying history for each customer, customers with similar preferences and tastes cannot be identified by collaborative approaches.

However, following a content-based approach also means that the customer's travel preferences have to be elicited interactively using a complex elicitation, as it must support a heterogeneous user community including first-time visitors, occasional users, as well as experienced travelers who have very concrete and detailed requirements. Consequently, the user interface for such a system should be conversational, adaptive and personalized in order to be suitable for all these different user groups, see (Bridge, 2000), (Carenini, Smith & Poole, 2003) and (Thompson et al., 2004). Finally, there are also special requirements with respect to the generation of proposals, i.e. the recommendation algorithms.

The most prominent content-based systems utilize Case-Based Reasoning, see e.g., (McSherry, 2005; Ricci & Del Messier, 2004; Ricci & Werthner, 2002), as well as Critiquing (Reilly et al., 2005) techniques. Utility functions for ranking or constraint-based filtering are also commonly used (Burke, 2000), either alone or in combination with other recommendation techniques. Furthermore, with respect to proposal generation algorithms, there are other specific problems to be solved in the travel and tourism domain such as the consistent "bundling" of several items, cf. (Ricci, 2002), which shall be discussed in a later section.

Compared with self-adapting collaborative systems, the well-known drawback of all these knowledge-intensive approaches is that the required domain expertise, such as similarity functions, has to be formalized in an initial modeling and formalization phase, and has to be maintained and updated on a regular basis.

Overall, we conclude that the development of a value-adding recommendation service in the travel and tourism domain is far more challenging than in well-known 'quality-and-taste' application areas such as books or movies.

This chapter discusses the cost-effective development of an advanced, conversational recommender application for the tourism domain using the knowledge-based Advisor Suite system (Felfernig et al., 2007). The system presented here follows a comprehensive and interactive approach to recommendation ("advisory") and comprises a graphical environment supporting the elicitation of the different pieces of knowledge, pre-implemented recommendation algorithms, as well as a mechanism for the automated generation of web applications from customizable templates. Here, the term "advisory" is used to indicate that the task of a virtual advisor built with the system is not limited to retrieving a suitable set of products for a given set of customer requirements, it shall for instance also be able to elicit the real customer requirements in a personalized way, be capable of explaining the proposal, finding alternatives, explaining differences and similarities between products, or provide additional help and guidance to match the user's needs.

The chapter is organized as follows. After discussing previous work, we will give an overview of an end user's view of the "Vibe virtual advisor", an application developed and deployed for an Austrian spa resort, which was built with the Advisor Suite development environment. Subsequently, we will sketch the system's general architecture and the design rationale behind selected components. After a discussion of experience gained from several projects, the chapter gives an outlook on future work.

PREVIOUS WORK

Although tourism is an enormous industry sector and despite the fact that the Web is already one of the most important search mediums, interactive and personalized recommender systems can rarely be found on commercial e-tourism sites. Today's booking platforms and tourism information portals are instead typically comprised of the following features:

1. Static search forms for information filtering
2. Availability checks and online booking
3. Popularity-based recommendations or paid promotions
4. Discussion forums
5. Additional information such as maps and further links, e.g. to the country or city homepage.

With respect to the search functionality, today's e-tourism platforms – and most of the academic systems – are limited to pre-trip destination or package selection. Comprehensive itinerary planning or dynamic packaging and bundling of different tourism services is typically not available on commercial websites; see also the final section for a discussion of future research directions.

Although no detailed study about the reasons for this lack of integrated planning tools or full tourist life-cycle support is available, we suppose that the major causes are:

1. Such advanced systems are *knowledge intensive* and require significantly increased ramp up costs.
2. The problem of data integration and harmonization is not yet solved, and no broadly-accepted standards exist – especially in the context of bundling of services. In particular, interoperability between tourism IT systems is an area of active research.

A recent example is the EU-funded "Harmonise" project (Fodor & Werthner, 2005), which aims to provide ontology-based mediation and loose coupling between the different information systems. The ADVISOR SUITE presented in this paper does not cover this latter aspect of data integration; nonetheless, it supports XML-based importation of catalog items, and therefore addresses factors of knowledge acquisition and maintenance through appropriate editing tools and automated user interface generation.

On the research side, several prototype systems – some of which have also been successfully deployed for at least a limited period of time – have been developed over recent years. The Intelligent Travel Recommender (ITR) system described in (Ricci & Del Messier, 2004; Ricci et al., 2002) and (Mizardeh & Ricci, 2007) is one example of such a system that encompasses different techniques and algorithms in one travel advisory framework that supports single-item recommendation as well as larger queries for whole travel itineraries.

In the "single item search" scenario, the user initially enters personal preferences and requirements using a Web interface: e.g. the desired region, the type of accommodation, and preferred activities. These selections are used by the system to filter out suitable items from the catalogue.

The user can make individual selections for different aspects of the trip such as accommodation, locations, activities or events and add interesting items to his/her *travel bag*. If the search for suitable items leads to no results or if there are too many matching items, an *Interactive Query Management* module is used to overcome these undesirable situations. If no item matches, the system evaluates whether slightly "relaxed" queries lead to a non-empty result set. Relaxed queries allow some user constraints to be ignored, and in case of numeric attributes their ranges to be extended.

If, on the other hand, there are too many matching items, the system may ask the user to add an additional constraint based on the expected information gain. Once the set of items has been reduced to a manageable size, a Case Based Reasoning (CBR) technique may be used to rank these items. Here, a collaborative aspect comes into play, as the CBR technique selects and ranks items according to their appearance in previous searches.

The ITR framework and the two prototype systems built on top of it have several elements in common with the ADVISOR SUITE system, which form the base of the travel advisor presented in this chapter. In both cases, the user is explicitly asked for preferences, allowing a set of suitable items to be retrieved in a query-like fashion.

Both systems support query relaxation and interactive and cooperative query answering (Jannach, 2006). Query tightening and re-writing for numerical attributes is however not supported in ADVISOR SUITE. Collaborative item ranking is also not part of the standard functionality of ADVISOR SUITE. However, the system supports the more general concept of utility-based ranking, effectively allowing the incorporation of past recommendation sessions.

Personalized preference elicitation, where every user is not asked the same set of questions, as well as automated user interface generation, is missing in ITR. While the provisioning of a general reasoning framework like the ITR is helpful for reducing the costs of building travel recommenders, a more flexible interaction style is more effective for many applications, in particular when guiding inexperienced users or persuading an indecisive customer.

As an example of a different approach to building a travel recommender system we consider the system described by Wallace et al (2004). Their work is inspired by the problem that standard collaborative filtering techniques do not work when the history of user interactions is too sparse. The basic idea of the proposed approach is to analyze the complete usage history of the system, i.e. the complete transaction log, and to identify typical patterns appearing in "travel plans", such as sets of services that were for instance often bought together.

Pattern analysis is conducted using hierarchical clustering; the results are fed into a neural network to provide online recommendations and constantly retrained the system based on new user inputs. An evaluation based on artificially created data sets has demonstrated the general applicability of the approach.

When compared with the ADVISOR SUITE system, the main advantage of the approach described in (Wallace et al., 2004) lies in its self-adapting and learning nature, i.e., no initial knowledge acquisition or periodic maintenance activities are required. Furthermore, the mining-based method does not even need to have detailed knowledge about the features of the items at its disposal.

The only information that is typically required beside the item ID is the availability of the service to avoid the recommendation of items which are currently not available. In the knowledge-based ADVISOR SUITE system, knowledge acquisition and behaviour modelling is a costly task. Once the knowledge base has been setup, however, requests for changes in the recommendation rules occur infrequently – according to our experience.

What remains unclear with the usage mining approach by Wallace et al. (2004), is how large the user community has to be for the system to be effective and how well the system overcomes typical ramp-up problems of learning-based approaches.

In the following section, we briefly describe the end user's view of the system before presenting a summary of the underlying technology of the ADVISOR SUITE system.

VIBE: THE VIRTUAL SPA ADVISOR

The VIBE virtual advisor is hosted on the web portal of the Warmbad-Villach resort, one of Austria's most renowned spas, offering a variety of different tourism products that range from four and five-star hotel accommodation to a variety of recreational and sporting facilities, as well as health and beauty therapy (Jannach et al., 2007). As a part of the resort's web portal, the goal of the virtual advisor VIBE (named after the ancient goddess of springs) is to welcome online visitors and provide them with a single point of contact for multi-lingual guidance and preference elicitation.

Figure 1 and Figure 2 show how the end user sees the virtual advisor application. ADVISOR SUITE applications such as VIBE follow a system-guided, conversational interaction style based on personalized fill-out forms that incrementally elicit the customer's requirements.

The system constantly monitors and evaluates the input of the current user and adapts the dialog in several dimensions. Depending on the previous and current input, the system's dialog model and the personalization rules in the underlying knowledge base, the application decides which variants of which questions to ask next (thus catering for both experts and first time users), whether additional situation-dependent information or help should be displayed, and so forth. The usage of a personal "avatar" as shown in Figure 1 is optional in ADVISOR SUITE applications. Commonly, however, such life-like, animated avatars are used to make advisory applications more persuasive by the means of "personification" (Zanker et al., 2006).

When the system decides that enough input has been provided or the customer wants to receive a recommendation based on the inputs so far, VIBE enters the proposal generation phase and comes up with a personalized recommendation.

Figure 2 depicts the main result page, which displays the details of the best-matching product in the center of the screen. The selection of suitable items in ADVISOR SUITE is based on two mechanisms. Firstly, filtering rules and an additional "relaxation" algorithm (Jannach, 2006) are used to retrieve catalogue items that match as many of the customer's constraints as possible.

Secondly, the remaining products are ordered according to a multi-attribute-utility (MAUT) technique that takes the customer's preferences into account. Since the determination of products is based on explicit recommendation rules, the

Figure 1. Virtual advisor screenshot (www.warmbad.com)

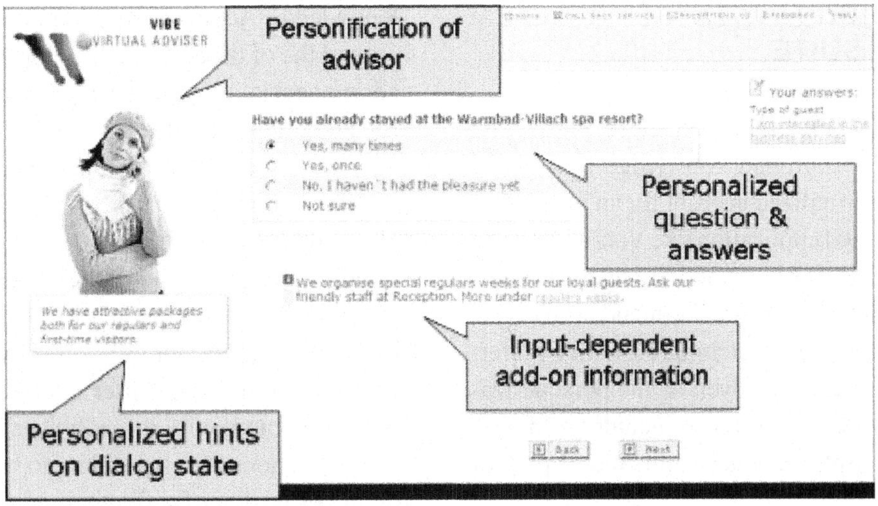

Figure 2. VIBE's personalized recommendation

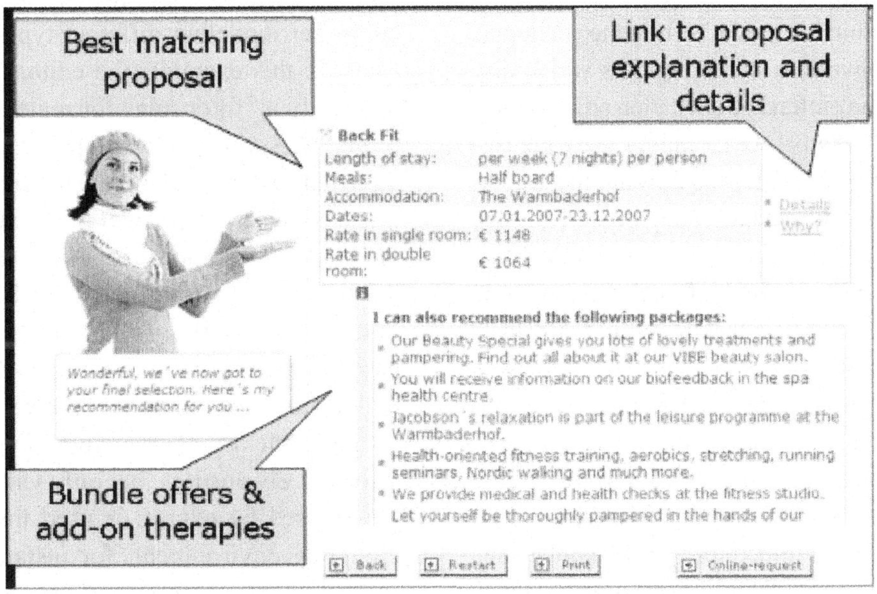

system is also capable of explaining the reasons for the proposal.

Thus, when the user clicks on the "explanations" link, the system generates a human-readable list of arguments which is internally composed by retrieving pre-defined text fragments for each applied rule from the knowledge base. Finally, the system also generates a personalized list of possible add-on services that the customer may choose together with the proposed vacation package. The contents of this list depend both on the user's input (e.g. whether he/she was interested in beauty treatments or not) and the main spa or accommodation packages proposed. Again, the rules for constructing the list of possible add-on packages are contained in the underlying knowledge base.

RAPID APPLICATION DEVELOPMENT WITH ADVISOR SUITE

As is evident in the discussion above, significant amounts of background knowledge have to be elicited and formalized in order for an interactive and personalized application like VIBE to function effectively. This background knowledge is comprised of both the core recommendation logic, such as the rules for matching customer preferences with products, as well as the personalization logic, which for instance includes a 'dialog model' or the rules that determine the display of personalized hints.

Many of today's content-based approaches to product recommendation focus only on the former, i.e. on methods and techniques for retrieving and ranking suitable products from the catalogue. However, conversational approaches which also personalize the preference elicitation process itself (and not only the proposal) cannot view the two pieces of knowledge independently due to the interdependencies between them (Jannach & Kreutler, 2005). If, for instance, the "product model" that describes the characteristics of catalogue items is to be extended with a new feature, we not only have to consider how this new feature should be taken into account for the retrieval and ranking process but also about appropriate methods for acquiring the customer's preference with respect to the new feature, as well as how and when the system should ask for it. Furthermore, such maintenance problems also affect the graphical user interface. Once we decide to introduce a new question (or a new answering option) into the preference elicitation dialog, the HTML-based user interface has to be changed accordingly.

The ADVISOR SUITE framework, on which VIBE is based, is an off-the-shelf, integrated development environment for the rapid development and deployment of conversational recommender systems (Felfernig et al., 2007) and is designed to address the above-mentioned challenges as follows.

As illustrated in Figure 3, the Integrated Knowledge Acquisition Component lies at the core of the of the ADVISOR SUITE framework. This component is comprised of a set of graphical tools for modeling the different pieces of knowledge which are used by the domain expert and a supporting knowledge engineer. During the design phase of the framework, a strong focus was laid on improving the usability of the system for domain experts who are in general not IT experts. Usability in this context not only refers to providing a comfortable graphical user interface but also to reducing complexity through user-oriented conceptualizations of the problem to be designed or by the provision of different, manageable views of the problem. Examples of this approach are given in Figure 4 and Figure 5.

Figure 4 depicts the ADVISOR SUITE expression editor for modeling different types of business rules. In this example, the editor is being used to specify a "filter rule" for matching customer preferences with product properties. Although the modeled filter constraints are internally compiled into a conjunctive query of the catalogue and exploited by a relaxation procedure (Jannach, 2006), the domain expert can express his/her knowledge in terms of IF-THEN-style business rules, which based on our experience are more comprehensible to domain experts than declarative constraints.

The context-sensitive expression editor which also actively ensures that only valid statements are entered by expert, is used throughout the modeling environment, for instance to model conditions for state transitions in the "dialog model" depicted in Figure 5. In this "dialog model" view, the domain expert describes the possible paths that the user may follow in the preference elicitation process and describes how the previously defined questions should be displayed.

Although the model is internally transformed into a predicate-augmented state automaton, the domain experts can express this knowledge in terms of dialog pages and questions (instead of

Figure 3. Recommendation process overview (Jannach & Kreutler, 2007)

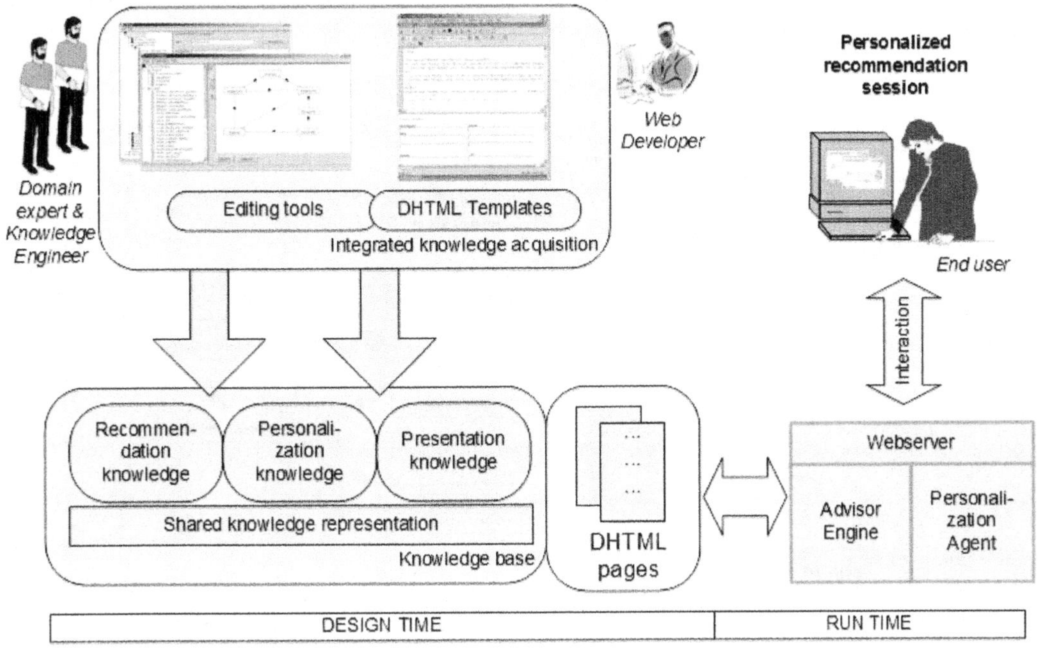

Figure 4. Expression editor

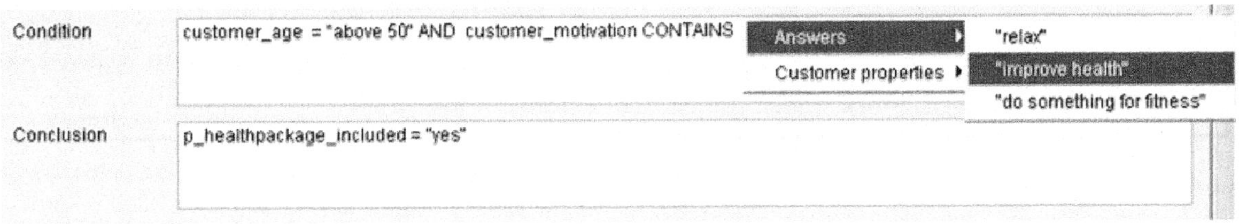

states, state variables and transition predicates). The integrated modeling environment stores all the information contained in the models in a shared knowledge base, which is evaluated at run-time by the advisor engine hosted on a web server, as shown in Figure 3.

In summary, a significant reduction of development costs is achieved through the application of a "model-driven" approach in which the domain expert (instead of the IT-expert) directly formalizes his/her knowledge with the help of a *domain-specific modeling language*. Domain specific languages typically trade expressiveness for ease of use and thus lead to reduced software construction and maintenance costs, see e.g., (Mernik et al., 2005).

As mentioned above, the development of the graphical user interface (GUI), i.e. the implementation of the dynamic HTML pages that make up the user dialog, is another critical step in the construction of interactive advisory applications. ADVISOR SUITE follows an approach based on page templates which are subsequently utilized to automatically generate dynamic web pages, as outlined

Figure 5. Dialogue modeling view

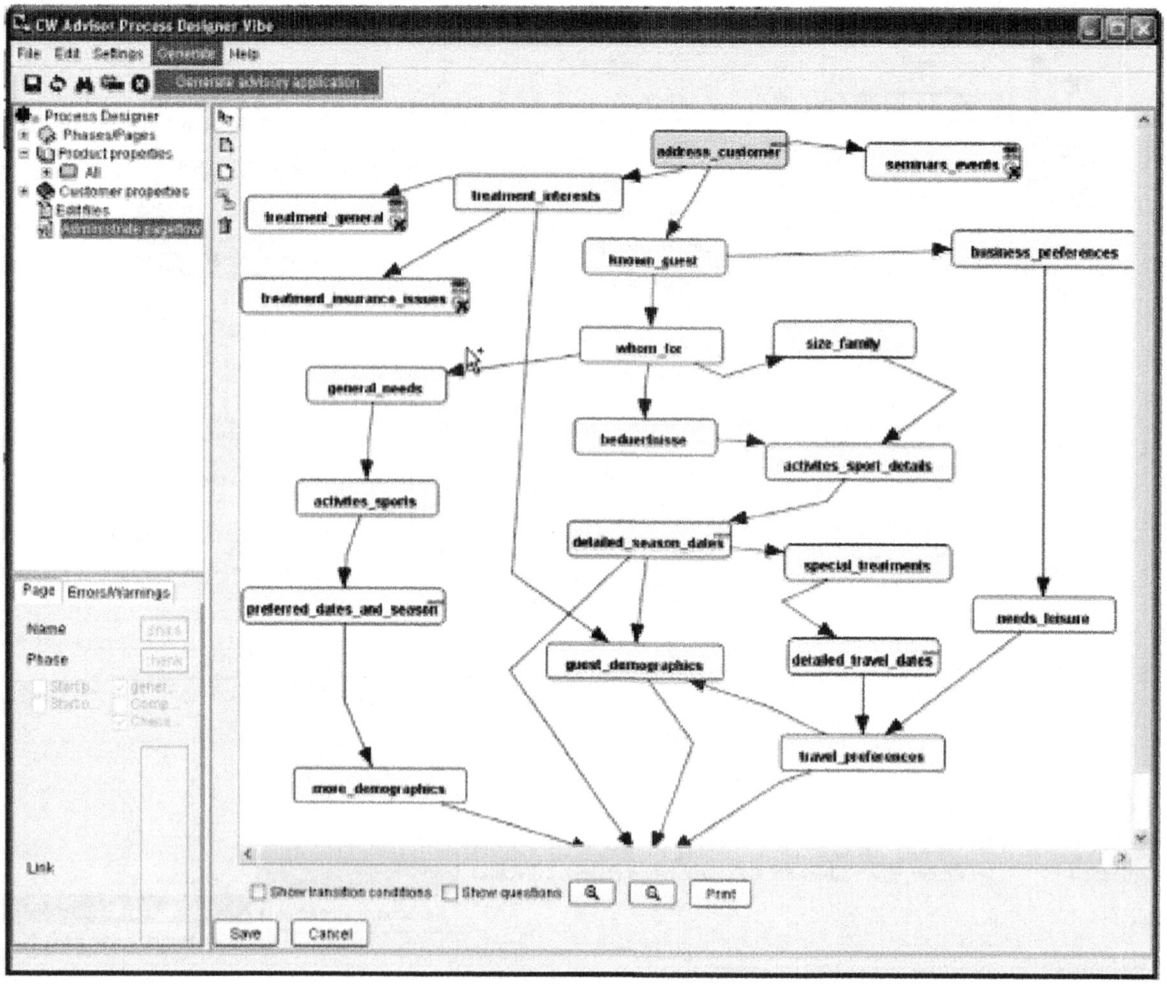

in Figure 3. The main idea behind this mechanism, which is described in more detail in (Jannach & Kreutler, 2007), is to provide small page fragments (e.g., question display, navigation area, progress information and so forth) which are edited by a web developer. Within these templates, we use Java Server Pages Custom Tags that can be used like ordinary HTML tags within the templates but implement the complex logic required for evaluating the personalization rules. Thus, after the recommendation dialog has been modeled and the page templates are prepared, a GUI generation module automatically assembles the source code for the final dialog pages from the page fragments.

At run-time, the "advisor engine" running on a web server (see right-hand side of Figure 3) first pre-loads all relevant information from the knowledge base into its internal cache since most pieces of information, such as the items in the catalog or the general rules, can be shared between parallel advisory sessions. The generic "personalization agent" handles the interaction with the individual clients and uses the advisor engine's pre-implemented recommendation algorithms to determine the proposal for the current client as shown in Figure 2.

Overall, the integrated nature of the framework supports a consistent model-based software development approach. Thus, it provides the cost-reducing benefits of "round-trip-engineering" such as the full automation of programming tasks through code-generation or warranting the quality of the produced code (Selic, 2003).

EXPERIENCES & RESULTS

In this section, we first report on the experience obtained from our model-driven approach to developing interactive virtual advisors. These findings are based on a variety of applications that have been developed in different domains and are supported by anecdotal evidence. Next, we discuss the findings of a preliminary evaluation of the usage of the VIBE virtual spa advisor over a period of four months.

Questions concerning the general acceptance and usefulness of recommender systems are not the focus of this paper. Nonetheless, the results of the evaluation demonstrate that knowledge-based advisory systems – which, with systems such as the ADVISOR SUITE, are relatively inexpensive to build and are not dependent on a large user community – can be a valuable decision aid for customers, and serve as a means to measurably influence the behavior of online customers.

Our general findings are based on more than two dozen different conversational recommender applications that have been developed and commercially deployed using the basis of the ADVISOR SUITE framework. Beside the e-tourism application presented in this chapter, advisory systems have been implemented for various other domains such as consumer electronics and home entertainment, financial services, as well as for "quality-and-taste" goods such as fine wines or cigars (Zanker et al., 2006). The following findings informally summarize the experience gained while working with end users to create the initial knowledge base for the VIBE virtual spa advisor, see also (Jannach et al., 2007).

Development process and knowledge base complexity: In general, the broad spectrum of application domains where the ADVISOR SUITE framework has been applied provides two observations:

1. The overall system design and algorithm implementations are domain-independent and sufficiently general.
2. This framework has proven to be flexible and extensible enough such that domain-specific extensions and characteristics can be easily taken into account.

From the perspective of the time and effort required to develop and maintain a virtual advisor, the benefits of using the presented off-the-shelf system as opposed to creating a new solution from scratch have even surpassed our expectations.

Furthermore, in most cases the initial sketch of the knowledge base including product data, questions, basic recommendation rules and a first dialog model can be drafted in a full-day workshop, assuming wholehearted participation form the stakeholders.

In this first project phase, the ability to quickly generate functional prototype applications proved to be advantageous. This feature helped us on the one hand to establish a common understanding of the projected project outcomes in the early project phases; on the other hand, it also increased the stakeholders' involvement as they see their suggestions and ideas immediately taken into account. In addition, we noticed that the number of core recommendation rules in most domains (including the tourism domain) remains manageable, e.g. a few dozen. The overall costs are mainly determined by the amount of additional information to be provided by the system, the fine-tuning of the different personalization rules, as well as the time required for setting up the layout or integrating external data sources.

For VIBE application, the complexity of the knowledge base can be summarized as follows.

About thirty questions were modeled, out of which only a personalized subset is posed to each user to have a succinct dialog. About the same number of rules and hints were designed, which – together with a custom relaxation rule for searching for suitable arrival and departure dates – were sufficient to generate personalized recommendations.

One particularity of the domain however lies in the limited number of available "products": In the consumer electronics domain, for instance, sometimes hundreds of different products are available, whereas in this domain typically only a small number of products or packages are available.

These problems were addressed with the help of two mechanisms. First, we relied on "query relaxation" as described by Jannach (2006). Query relaxation in this context instructs the system to automatically retrieve a set of items that fulfils as many of the requirements as possible in situations where no single catalog item fulfils all the requirements of the user. In addition, we enhanced the recommender system with the option to propose "bundles" consisting of a basic package plus a personalized set of add-on activities and side-offers.

The design of ADVISOR SUITE's user-oriented conceptualizations and graphical modeling tools is driven by the idea that the domain experts themselves should formalize the system's expert knowledge. However, in most projects the help of a knowledge engineer is required, at least in the early phases or to design more complex business rules. After the initial phase, however, many of the domain experts became capable of modifying and updating the system's knowledge base by themselves (Felfernig et al., 2007) – especially when supported by a comprehensive test and debugging environment. Although these experiences are encouraging, further improvements in the direction of usability are suggested as future work.

Preliminary evaluation of interaction logs: In the following, we will report on initial findings from an evaluation of the usage of the web portal of the Warmbad-Villach resort and the virtual advisor VIBE over a period of 4 months during the second half of 2006 (Zanker et al., 2008). Due to the lack of an integrated user tracking environment we based our work on the raw logs of the web server and the logging facility of the advisor component for reconstructing the actual user behavior. We identified more than 40,000 (actual 40516 online visits) distinct user sessions out of which approximately 2% could be unambiguously associated with an advisory session with our conversational recommender system. Approximately the same share of sessions could not be related to web log entries due to unresolved DNS-names of accessing hosts or the use of proxy servers.

At first we researched if the relative use of the virtual travel advisor varied depending on contextual parameters of the user sessions such as duration, access time or language preference.

Table 1 splits user sessions into different classes according to their duration. Not surprisingly, longer lasting sessions (longer than 5 minutes) use the virtual advisor significantly more often than short online visits. We applied Pearson's chi square test to evaluate the statistical independence of variables. It proves that the hypothesis of statistical independence between the use of advisor and the sessions' durations can be dismissed with a probability of error below 0.1% (i.e. $\chi2(4) = 360.67$; $p < 0.001$). See Backhaus et al. (2003) for reference on the computation of the statistical test. However, when users access the web portal on weekends we could only observe a slightly higher relative frequency for accesses to VIBE ($\chi2(1) = 3.848$; $p < 0.05$; see Table 2). From a cultural point of view, most online visits are from German speaking countries and Italy. It is quite interesting to observe that Italians are more likely to use such an innovative interactive tool than German speaking people ($\chi2(3) = 208.11$; $p < 0.001$; see Table 3). Further experiments are however required to determine whether an actual cultural difference in Internet use exists between these two language groups.

In a further step we wanted to evaluate the hypothesis that users who interact with a recommender system are more likely to request information about the availability of accommodation. From Table 4 we can see that a significantly larger share of those online visits that employed the virtual advisor also triggered a request for availability information than of those users that did not use the advisor. Thus, we can observe that the usage of the conversational recommender system positively correlates with accommodation requests ($\chi 2(1) = 62.87$; $p < 0.001$).

Overall, these results indicate that interested web site users are willing to use the additional feature of an interactive advisor; furthermore, such systems also measurably influence the behavior of the users, e.g. by promoting interest in the offerings.

FUTURE RESEARCH DIRECTIONS

This section presents an overview of research directions in the area of knowledge-based travel recommender systems, relates our current work to these dimensions, and proposes future extensions to our system (Jannach et al., 2007).

1. **Intelligent bundling:** The current implementation of VIBE only recommends pre-bundled packages consisting of hotel accommodation, beauty and health treatments and so forth. In addition to each package, VIBE also proposes a suitable set of individual add-on services (Figure 2), whose selection is based on rather simple business rules. However, current trends suggest that in the future the demand for individualized tourism arrangements will increase even further. Thus, we are currently exploring mechanisms that allow individual combinations to be "configured" and validated (Zanker et al., 2007). We plan to employ a constraint-based configuration approach (Mailharro, 1998),

Table 1. Use of advisor with respect to duration of online visits

	Advisor used	Advisor not used
Session duration	in %	in %
Up to 5 min.	0.98	99.02
5 to 15 min.	3.64	96.36
15 to 30 min.	4.00	96.00
30 to 60 min.	4.56	95.44
Over 60 min.	2.70	97.30

Table 2. Use of advisor with respect to access times

	Advisor used	Advisor not used
Access at weekend	in %	in %
Yes	2.07	97.93
No	1.77	98.23

Table 3. Use of advisor with respect to language preferences

	Advisor used	Advisor not used
Language preferences	in %	in %
German	1.42	98.58
Italian	3.14	96.86
English	0.46	99.54
Unknown	0.91	99.09

Table 4. Probability of booking request with respect to the use of VIBE

	Advisor used	Advisor not used
Availability Request	in %	in %
Yes	8.91	3.49
No	91.09	96.51
Total	100	100

to support more complex dependencies and bundling rules. However, the main challenge lies once again in the area of modeling, i.e. how can we find simple conceptualizations and tools such that a domain expert can set up and maintain possibly complex bundling rules.

2. **Group recommendation:** Often recommendations need to be accepted by a group of people rather than by a single person, particularly in the tourism domain. The question of how a recommender system should be designed in order to support such a group decision process is largely open. Initial experiments in the domain of movie recommendation on a test-bed for the development of a group recommendation system. Also, the Collaborative Advisory Travel System described by McCarthy et al., (2006) address the problem of information visualization and the mutual awareness of the preferences of other users. How such techniques can be embedded into the ADVISOR SUITE system and what other mechanisms are suitable for making effective group decisions remain the subject of future research.
3. **Mobile recommendation applications:** VIBE is a pre-trip information and decision support tool. However, travel advisory and recommendation could also be a source of added value for the customer during and even after his or her journey: The etPlanner project (Höpken et al., 2006), which is partially based on the ADVISOR SUITE technology, comprehensively examines the electronic services required for supporting users from the pre-trip until the post-trip phase. Context-aware information and recommendation services provide adaptive and personalized user interfaces. Furthermore, an information-push service actively communicates with tourists during their stay. A typical problem in this context is the acquisition and revision of the user preferences on small mobile devices, as addressed by Ricci and Nguyen (2007), who propose a critique-based approach and interaction style.
4. **Advanced data analysis:** The ADVISOR SUITE system includes a built-in logging component which can be configured to record the full history of interactions of each individual user, as that ADVISOR SUITE's interaction logs are much more detailed and structured than standard web server logs. These logs provide an easy method of obtaining important information about the customer as well as his/her preferences. One can, for instance, determine whether typical customer profiles exist or whether certain combinations of services are requested by customers despite not being part of a package. This additional knowledge could be used to offer new services. The second type of information contained in the logs is related to the advisory service itself and pertains to the effectiveness of the application. Typical questions in this context include whether the virtual advisor is a) accepted and used by customers and b) whether the system is actually capable of influencing buyer behavior, which is of particular importance for determining the business value of providing such an add-on service. Although ADVISOR SUITE in its current state already includes a "statistics" module, which documents the distribution of user answers to specific questions or the ratio of successfully completed user sessions, further engineering and research are still required, and are a part of our ongoing work. On the engineering side, we are currently aiming to integrate a data mining component for detecting correlations hidden in user preferences. On the research side, we are interested in new metrics that allow us on the one hand to measure changes in actual sales when using such a system, and on the other hand on finding basic concepts and guiding principles that are capable of

allowing recommender systems to become an even more persuasive technology (Zanker et al., 2006).

5. **Self-adaptation and learning:** An obvious shortcoming of the described system compared with other approaches to recommendation lies in the static nature of the system's behavior. While, for instance, in systems based on collaborative filtering or case-based reasoning recommendations continuously improve over time, our system currently exhibits no learning behavior. In the context of our system, such an improvement would have to be based on advanced techniques for log data analysis. Current extensions hope to accommodate such learning behavior by taking community ratings into account when generating proposals. The question of how such hybrid systems can be fine-tuned (e.g., balancing the weight of community ratings vs. expert opinions) remains the subject of further research.
6. **Persuasiveness:** Recommender systems, especially those that interactively converse with their users, must not only be seen as neutral search tools, but instead must actually "persuade" their human counterparts to click on offerings or even to buy items they might otherwise have overlooked. Gretzel and Fesenmaier (2007) conducted an empirical study that investigated some of the factors of the preference elicitation process that influence the perception of received recommendations and concluded that recommender systems can influence consumers in a systematic and predictable manner. Zanker et al. (2006), present a conceptual scheme for classifying the driving factors behind persuasive recommendation applications. A long-term study of actual sales figures from an online store for fine Cuban cigars gave us further evidence that the introduction of the conversational recommender system can change the buying habits of users. Sales of items that were frequently recommended by the system significantly increased after deployment of the conversational recommender.

CONCLUSION

The development of an interactive travel recommendation service can often be challenging and prove too costly, especially for small and medium-sized e-tourism platforms or service providers. In particular, such highly-interactive applications require significant knowledge acquisition and maintenance efforts. Standard self-adapting recommendation systems based on collaborative filtering adapt their behavior automatically based on user feedback, are only applicable to websites with a broad user-community.

The Advisor Suite presented in this chapter represents an approach to providing an off-the-shelf software framework for rapid and cost-effective development of online pre-trip travel advisory services. The novel features of this system include the model-driven development approach and the support for the automated generation of web applications. With the help of an example of a commercially-deployed travel advisory application for an Austrian spa resort, we have shown how the development process is supported by the tool and how the typical knowledge-acquisition bottleneck of knowledge-based approaches can be overcome by using an adequate modeling environment and user-oriented conceptualizations.

REFERENCES

Adomavicius, G., & Tuzhilin, A. (2005). Toward the next generation of recommender systems: A survey of the state-of-the-art and possible extensions. *IEEE Transactions on Knowledge and Data Engineering*, *17*, 734–749. doi:10.1109/TKDE.2005.99

Backhaus, K., Erichson, B., Plinke, W., & Weiber, W. (2003). *Multivariate analysemethoden* (10th ed.). Berlin, Germany: Springer.

Bridge, D. (2002). Towards conversational recommender systems: A dialogue grammar approach. In *Proceedings of the Workshop in Mixed-Initiative Case-Based Reasoning, at the 6th European Conference in Case-Based Reasoning*, Aberdeen, Scotland (pp. 9-22).

Burke, R. (2000). Knowledge-based recommender systems. In *Encyclopedia of library & information systems* (Vol. 69, pp. 180-200). Boca Raton, FL: CRC Press.

Carenini, G., Smith, J., & Poole, D. (2003). Towards more conversational and collaborative recommender systems. In *Proceedings of the 8th International Conference on Intelligent User Interfaces,* Miami, FL (pp. 12-18). New York: ACM Press.

Felfernig, A., Friedrich, G., Jannach, D., & Zanker, M. (2007). An integrated environment for the development of knowledge-based recommender applications. *International Journal of Electronic Commerce, 11*, 11–34. doi:10.2753/JEC1086-4415110201

Fodor, O., & Werthner, H. (2005). Harmonise: A step toward an interoperable e-tourism marketplace. *International Journal of Electronic Commerce*, *9*(2), 11–39.

Gretzel, U., & Fesenmaier, D. (2007). Persuasion in recommender systems. *International Journal of Electronic Commerce, 11*, 81–100. doi:10.2753/JEC1086-4415110204

Höpken, W., Fuchs, M., Zanker, M., Beer, T., Eybl, A., & Flores, S. (2006). etPlanner: An IT framework for comprehensive and integrative travel guidance. In [Berlin, Germany: Springer.]. *Proceedings of the Information and Communication Technologies in Tourism, ENTER, 2006*, 125–133. doi:10.1007/3-211-32710-X_20

Jameson, A., Baldes, S., & Kleinbauer, T. (2004). Two methods for enhancing mutual awareness in a group recommender system. In *Proceedings of the Working Conference on Advanced Visual interfaces*, Gallipoli, Italy (pp. 447-449). New York: ACM.

Jannach, D. (2006). Finding preferred query relaxations in content-based recommenders. In *Proceedings of the IEEE Intelligent Systems Conference IS'2006*, Westminster, UK (pp. 355-360).

Jannach, D., & Kreutler, G. (2005). Personalized user preference elicitation for e-services. In *Proceedings of the IEEE International conference on e-Technology, e-Commerce and e-Service*, Hong Kong (pp. 304-611).

Jannach, D., & Kreutler, G. (2007). Rapid development of knowledge-based conversational recommender applications with advisor suite. *Journal of Web Engineering*, *6*(2), 165–192.

Jannach, D., Zanker, M., Jessenitschnig, M., & Seidler, O. (2007). Developing a conversational travel advisor with ADVISOR SUITE. In A. J. Frew (Ed.), *Information and communication technologies in tourism* (pp. 43-52). Berlin, Germany: Springer.

Mailharro, D. (1998). A classification and constraint-based framework for configuration. *AI in Engineering . Design and Manucturing, 12*, 383–397.

McCarthy, K., Salamó, M., Coyle, L., McGinty, L., Smyth, B., & Nixon, P. (2006). Group recommender systems: A critiquing based approach. In *Proceedings of the 11th international Conference on intelligent User interfaces*, Sydney, Australia (pp. 267-269). New York: ACM.

McSherry, D. (2005). Retrieval failure and recovery in recommender systems. *Artificial Intelligence Review, 24*, 319–338. doi:10.1007/s10462-005-9000-z

Mernik, M., Heering, J., & Sloane, A. M. (2005). When and how to develop domain-specific languages. *ACM Computing Surveys, 37*(4), 316–344. doi:10.1145/1118890.1118892

Mirzadeh, N., & Ricci, F. (2007). Cooperative query rewriting for decision making support and recommender systems. *Applied Artificial Intelligence, 21*, 1–38. doi:10.1080/08839510701527515

O'Connor, M., Cosley, D., Konstan, J. A., & Riedl, J. (2001). PolyLens: A recommender system for groups of users. In W. Prinz, M. Jarke, Y. Rogers, K. Schmidt, and V. Wulf (Eds.), *Proceedings of the Seventh Conference on European Conference on Computer Supported Cooperative Work* (pp. 199-218). Norwell, MA: Kluwer Academic Publishers.

Reilly, J., McCarthy, K., McGinty, L., & Smyth, B. (2005). Incremental critiquing. *Knowledge-Based Systems, 18*, 143–151. doi:10.1016/j.knosys.2004.10.005

Ricci, F. (2002). Travel recommender systems. *IEEE Intelligent Systems*, 55–57.

Ricci, F., Arslan, B., Mirzadeh, N., & Venturini, A. (2002). ITR: A case-based travel advisory system. In S. Craw & A. D. Preece (Eds.), *Proceedings of the 6th European Conference on Advances in Case-Based Reasoning* (LNCS 2416, pp. 613-627). London: Springer.

Ricci, F., & DelMissier, F. (2004). Supporting travel decision making through personalized recommendation. In B. C.-M. Karat & J. Karat (Eds.), *Designing personalized user experiences for ecommerce* (pp. 231-251). Amsterdam: Kluwer Academic Publisher.

Ricci, F., & Nguyen, Q. N. (2007). Acquiring and revising preferences in a critique-based mobile recommender system. *IEEE Intelligent Systems, 22*(3), 22–29. doi:10.1109/MIS.2007.43

Ricci, F., & Werthner, H. (2002). Case-based querying for travel planning recommendation. *Information Technology and Tourism, 4*, 215–226.

Selic, B. (2003). The pragmatics of model-driven development. *IEEE Software, 20*(5), 19–25. doi:10.1109/MS.2003.1231146

Thompson, C. A., Göker, M. H., & Langley, P. (2004). A personalized system for conversational recommendations. *Journal of Artificial Intelligence Research, 21*, 393–428.

Wallace, M., Maglogiannis, I., Karpouzis, K., Kormentzas, G., & Kollias, S. (2004). Intelligent one-stop-shop travel recommendations: Using an adaptive neural network and clustering of history. *Information Technology & Tourism, 6*(3), 181–193. doi:10.3727/1098305031436971

Werthner, H., & Ricci, F. (2004). E-Commerce and Tourism. *Communications of the ACM, 47*, 101–105. doi:10.1145/1035134.1035141

Zanker, M., Aschinger, M., & Jessenitschnig, M. (2007). Development of a collaborative and constraint-based Web configuration system for personalized bundling of products and services. In B. Benatallah et al. (Eds.), *Proceedings of the 8th International Conference on Web Information Systems Engineering*, Nancy, France (pp. 273-284). Berlin, Germany: Springer.

Zanker, M., Bricman, M., Gordea, S., Jannach, D., & Jessenitschnig, M. (2006). Persuasive online-selling in quality & taste domains. In Proceedings of the *International Conference on Electronic Commerce and Web technologies - EC-WEB*, Krakow, Poland (pp. 51-60). Berlin, Germany: Springer.

Zanker, M., Fuchs, M., Höpken, W., Tuta, M., & Müller, N. (2008). Evaluating recommender systems in tourism - a case study from Austria. In P. O'Connor et al. (Eds.), *Proceedings of the Information and Communication Technologies in Tourism (ENTER 2008)* (pp. 24-34). Berlin, Germany: Springer.

Chapter 4
Multiagent Truth Maintenance Applied to a Tourism Recommender System

Fabiana Lorenzi
Universidade Federal do Rio Grande do Sul (UFRGS), Brasil Universidade Luterana do Brasil (ULBRA), Brasil

Ana L. C. Bazzan
Universidade Federal do Rio Grande do Sul (UFRGS), Brasil

Mara Abel
Universidade Federal do Rio Grande do Sul (UFRGS), Brasil

ABSTRACT

This chapter presents a multiagent recommender system applied to the tourism domain. The multiagent approach is able to deal with distributed expert knowledge to support travel agents in recommending tourism packages. Agents work as experts cooperating and communicating with each other, exchanging information to make the best recommendation possible considering the travelers' preferences. Each agent has a truth maintenance system component that helps the agents to assume information during the recommendation process as well as to keep the integrity of their knowledge bases. The authors have validated the system via simulations where agents collaborate to recommend travel packages to the user and specialize in some of the tasks available. The experiments show that specialization is useful for the efficacy of the system.

INTRODUCTION

The Internet is a rich source of information where users search for contents about products and services related to their interests and preferences. However, this has generated some problems. In fact, the overload of information may divert the users and ultimately make it very hard to locate the desired information (Maes, 1994). Moreover, the relevant data required is usually distributed over several repositories.

In the tourism domain a variety of services can be recommended such as restaurants, places to visit, better opportunities of accommodation,

DOI: 10.4018/978-1-60566-818-5.ch004

or travel packages. Recommender systems have the objective of helping customers in selecting services more suitable to their needs. They have the ability of aggregating information in order to match the recommendations with the information users are looking for.

However, it may be possible that a single source does not have all the information needed to make the full recommendation process. The available data may be fragmented, overspecialized or over generalized, or even irrelevant to the recommendation at hand. There are several data sources and services distributed in the Internet, which, are not always available, or are ambiguous or wrong.

A travel package recommendation is typically supported by several service providers for transportation, accommodations and attractions. Besides, specific knowledge is required to assemble all the components (Ricci, 2002). Usually this information cannot be found in a single repository. The tourism market is distributed, and several service providers and intermediaries manage and store service information and users data in their repositories. Also, the domain can change quickly, requiring the information to be frequently updated. To recommend a travel package, a travel agent must construct a model containing all the elements (information) required for generating this recommendation. This model can be implicitly defined in the travel agent's mind, or explicitly documented in a formal plan stored at the travel agency. These elements would include resources (information, products or services), customers and their requirements, factors influencing the recommendation (such as the season), and strategies for finding the best options for the user.

To cope with these problems – distributed source of information and frequent updating – we propose the application and integration of two technologies: distributed recommender systems and multiagent technologies. We claim that a multiagent recommender system can be applied for retrieving, filtering and using the information that is relevant to the recommendation task, and deals better with dynamic changes that occur in the data sources, as compared with more traditional non-distributed recommender systems (Montaner et al., 2003).

The main goal of a multiagent recommender system is therefore to facilitate the cooperation among the agents. Each agent works as an expert, helping to compose the final recommendation. This work presents a distributed and knowledge-based recommender system implemented in a multiagent environment. The recommendation process (travel package) is based on the collaboration of multiple agents exchanging information stored in their local knowledge bases. A recommendation request is decomposed into sub-tasks handled by different agents, each one maintaining its own knowledge base and participating in the composition of the final recommendation.

The proposed model supports agent specialization where agents become experts in specific tasks. This agent specialization mimics what happens in the real world, where it is common for the travel agents to specialize in a particular kind of service (travel packages, interchanges, conferences, etc.) to provide better recommendation to the customers. Another feature presented in the proposed model is the ability to access and maintain the integrity of the exchanged information among agents. Agents employ a truth maintenance component that helps to revise the shared data among agents to guarantee the integrity of the agents' knowledge bases.

This chapter is organized as follow: section 2 presents the background of recommender systems and truth maintenance systems and discusses related works on multiagent recommender systems. Section 3 describes the multiagent recommender approach and section 4 presents the experiments we conducted. Section 5 presents some ideas for future work and finally section 6 summarizes the contributions of this chapter.

BACKGROUND

This section introduces the fundamental concepts underpinning the technologies applied in our research, and used later in this chapter.

Recommender Systems

The three main techniques that can be used in recommender systems are: collaborative filtering, content-based filtering and knowledge-based systems.

Collaborative filtering is one of the most popular techniques and it aggregates customer' preferences, expressed as product ratings, to recommend new products (Resnick et al., 1994). There are two kinds of collaborative filtering techniques: item-item and user-user. Item-item based techniques identify correlations between products to define new items to be recommended to the users; recommended items are often similar to the items already associated with the user, possibly based on previous usage. User-user based techniques evaluate the similarity between different users to find users with similar tastes or needs; in this case, items that will be recommended to a test user, are already associated with similar users' previous usage.

In the content-based filtering approach, the preferences of a specific user are exploited to build new recommendations. Only data related to the current user are exploited in building a recommendation. It requires a description of user's interests that matches the item in the catalog to generate a recommendation.

Collaborative and content-based filtering can deliver poor recommendations if not trained with an adequate number of examples (product ratings or pattern of user preferences). This limitation motivates the development of the knowledge-based approach. A knowledge-based system learns about user preferences over time and automatically suggests products that fit the user model. This technique tries to better utilize preexisting knowledge, derived from the application domain, to build a more accurate prediction model, which is based on a limited number of user preferences, used as training instances to train the recommender system (Burke, 2000).

Knowledge-based recommender approaches, such as case-based reasoning (Smyth, 2007; Lorenzi & Ricci, 2005), can be combined with collaborative or content-based filtering to provide better recommendations. Knowledge about customers and the application domain is used to reason about the products that fit the user's preferences. The most important advantage of the combined approach is that it does not depend (exclusively) upon customer's rates, hence avoiding the mentioned difficulty in bootstrapping the system. The knowledge that improves the recommendation can be expressed as a detailed user model; a model of the selection process or a description of the items that will be suggested.

Multiagent Applications in Tourism Domain

Autonomous agents are being used in a large number of Internet applications due to their ability to decide what tasks must be performed to achieve their goals. This is true especially for those systems that help the user in the decision-making process in the tourism domain (AlNazer & Helmy, 2007; Wu et al., 2006; Buffett et al., 2004).

In e-commerce applications, agents work on behalf of users, trying to help these users during the decision-making process. However, some limitations remain, i.e.:

1. Depending on the complexity of the problem, the agent may need deep knowledge about the domain to answer the user requests;
2. Complex tasks normally are based on the evaluation of heterogeneous data;
3. Agents responsible for gathering information are not able to get updated information;

4. A single agent may not have complete knowledge needed to solve a problem. When the task is complex and the agent does not have enough knowledge, it needs to ask other agents to perform its task.

SmartClients System

Torrens et al. (2002) presented the *SmartClients* system. This system exploits the possibilities of representing spaces of solutions as constraint satisfaction problems to help the user to plan a flight route. The user has to inform some preferences such as city of departure, destination and the dates of the travel. Knowing these preferences in hand, the system builds a network capable of exploiting the possible routes. Some disadvantages can be found in this approach, such as:

1. The system collects information from the server only once, to avoid several accesses. However, this feature limits the search space because it is not possible to modify the user preferences, and thus, refine the query; and
2. The variables of the domains are predetermined by the system and it is not possible to explore solutions that are not in that search space. To overcome this problem, the search space should be dynamic.

Heracles II System

Heracles II is another example of a system developed in the travel planning domain (Ambite et al., 2005). Its framework of planning and information gathering determines how to reach the destination (flights, taxi, bus, etc) and how to choose a hotel option. The system models each piece of information as a variable in a constraint network. The system partitions the network hierarchically corresponding to the task structure of the application domain. The application designer groups variables and constraints related to a distinct task into a package. Each package is called a *template*. These *templates* are presented to the user following the hierarchy defined by the system. For instance, the system shows how the user can arrive in the chosen city, and later, how to arrive in some hotel.

The user can interact with the system at any point during the planning process, changing the values of variables throughout the network. It means that the user can guide the process to find a better plan. However, the system does not deal with expert knowledge or with previous user's experiences. In each new query, the planning process starts from scratch. The authors do not mention if the system receives any evaluation from the user, such as satisfaction with the system operation.

MAPWEB System

The MAPWEB is another example of a system that plans travels according to the user's preferences (Camacho et al. 2002). It integrates planning agents and Web information retrieval agents. MAPWEB is a multiagent framework applied to a travel planning assistant domain, where users need plans for travelling to several places. Each plan determines which steps the user should take, and which information sources should be accessed.

Different agents were developed: *UserAgent* is responsible for the communication between the user and the system. This agent receives the user request, and it is also responsible for presenting the final result; *PlannerAgent* is responsible for planning the travel; the *Webbot is* responsible for searching information into the Internet; the *CoachAgent* acts like a coach to the entire group of agents, controlling them and allocating tasks to them.

This system presents important features: agents store the planning performed and use the knowledge (past cases) to get new plans; there is a communication among agents that allows an agent to help another one to complete the task.

Table 1. Comparison of multiagent systems applied to e-commerce

System	Information gathering	Criticizing	Learning	Specialization
MAPWEB	Yes	No	Yes	No
Heracles II	Yes	Yes	No	No
Smartclients	Yes	No	No	No

However, there is a further agent that controls the possible communication and indicates the agent that needs to help another agent. The system is distributed, but the control and management of the tasks are centralized in the *CoachAgent*. However, agents may work with information that is not up-to-date.

Comparing the Three Systems

Table 1 shows a comparison of the three multiagent recommender systems described in this section, by indicating the main features presented in each one.

As shown in table 1, all three systems have an information-gathering component. It means that the information is collected automatically, ready for use when needed. In a dynamic domain, this feature may introduce errors because the information can be incorrect, or not updated. Regarding the critique component, only the *Heracles II* system allows the user to criticize the result. Only the MAPWEB system has a learning component, where plans are stored as cases. We can see also that none of the systems allows agent specialization.

Multiagent Recommender Systems

Multiagent systems can be applied to retrieve, filter and use information relevant for recommendations as they are able to deal with distributed information sources with several advantages over other approaches. These are: 1) the information sources may be inherently distributed so that it would be wasteful to replicate agent information gathering and problem-solving capabilities for each user and each application; 2) agents can interact flexibly in new configurations on demand; and 3) the system performance can degrade gracefully when some agents are out of service temporarily.

In classical recommender systems one single intelligent system provides the recommendation function, whereas in a multiagent recommender system a collection of interacting agents manages the recommendation generation process, trying to improve the recommendation quality obtained by each single agent. The agents cooperate and negotiate to satisfy the users, interacting among themselves to complement their partial solutions or even solve conflicts that may arise.

Fab System

Fab is a pioneer multiagent recommender system. It recommends web pages to the user through the combination of collaborative filtering and content-based techniques (Balabanovic & Sholam, 1997). The goal is to explore the advantages presented in each recommendation technique, minimizing the disadvantages of each one. The system uses content-based filtering to create user's profiles. With these profiles, it is possible to identify similar users, and then the system applies the collaborative filtering to get the items it recommends to the user. There are three main components in this system: collection agents (that find pages for a specific topic), selection agents (that find pages for a specific user) and the central router.

The recommendation process is performed as follows: the *collection* agents find pages for a specific topic, the *selection* agents select the pages that will be recommended to the user and send these pages to the *central router*. The *central router* forwards them to those users whose profiles match, given some threshold. Each user receives pages matching their profile from the *collection* agents. Every agent maintains a profile, based on words contained in web pages that have been rated. A *collection* agent's profile represents its current topic and a *selection* agent's profile represents a single user's interests.

Once the user receives the recommendation, this is evaluated by the user who assigns ratings on a 7-point scale. These ratings are used to update the user personal *selection* agent's profile, and also to adapt the *collection* agent's profile. This hybrid implementation confers FAB some advantages, such as:

- By using collaborative recommendations, experiences of other users are included in the recommendation process;
- By using content-based recommendations, the system to able to deal with items that have not yet been rated by any user;
- It is possible to recommend suitable items to the user even when there is no similar users' experience stored in the system.

Multiagent System for Planning Meetings

Another example of a multiagent recommender system is presented by (Macho et al., 2000). This system arranges meetings for several participants taking into account various constraints, and personal agendas. Every participant has an agenda, which is accessible by an agent through the Internet.

In this system, three different agents were proposed: the *personal assistant* agent is the interface between the user and the MAS; the *flight travel* agent is connected to a database of flights and it has access to flight schedules and availability; and the *accommodation hotel* agent is responsible for finding accommodation in the cities connected with the meeting venue. All the information implied in the recommendation process and the problem modeling is formalized using constraint satisfaction techniques.

A disadvantage of this approach is that the problem is not solved dynamically, because to solve it the recommender system has to collect information from different information gathering agents. Moreover, this approach does not learn from previous experiences. Considering that the system knows user's preferences, it should take into account this information to arrange next meetings for that user.

Truth Maintenance Systems

Truth Maintenance Systems (TMS) are based on algorithms that help to maintain the knowledge base integrity (Doyle, 1979). The first TMS presented was the JTMS (Justification Truth Maintenance System) that has two components: a problem solver that draws inferences (beliefs) and an annotated knowledge base, which records these inferences (called justifications).

JTMS consists of several nodes that have a label associated to them: *in* (believed) or *out* (not believed). The TMS believes in a node if it has an argument for it. Associated with a node there is a list of justifications that explain the labels of the node. These justifications can be used to provide an explanation to the user.

Assumption-based Truth Maintenance System (ATMS) (deKleer, 1986) is an extension of the basic TMS concept. The ATMS is based on the manipulation of assumption sets and also on every data being labeled with a set of assumptions. Results are computed by the ATMS from the justifications supplied by a problem solver. In this approach, the belief label can be a set of assumptions instead of just labels of the type *in* or *out*. The assumption sets, called environment, can be manipulated more conveniently than the data sets. Different contexts can be formed by

Table 2. Comparison of truth maintenance systems

System	Number of agents	Possible Labels	Assumptions
JTMS	1	In/Out	No
ATMS	1	In/Out	Yes
DATMS	2 or more	In/Out	Yes
DTMS	2 or more	Internal/External/Out	No

consistent environments and all nodes derived from it. A label is consistent if all of its environments are consistent.

A distributed ATMS was introduced by (Mason & Johnson, 1989). The Distributed Assumption Based Truth Maintenance System (DATMS) was developed to guarantee the consistency of assumptions of each agent. The TMS is applied to a multiagent system where agents make decisions based on their evidences and information. Agents can share information in order to help the consolidation of their decisions, but the labels of the information in any of the agents is not changed.

Distributed Truth Maintenance System (DTMS) is the distributed form of TMS (Huhns & Bridgeland, 1991). This algorithm aims to seek local consistency for each agent and global consistency for the data shared by the agents. Given a network of several agents, they interact by exchanging data. Each agent has two kinds of data: *shared* and *private*. A private data becomes shared data when the agent exchanges it with another agent. The concern of this approach is maintaining the consistency of the shared data, because it affects the problem-solving ability of another agent.

Table 2 presents a comparison of the existing truth maintenance systems. The first important feature is the number of agents involved in the maintenance process. JTMS and ATMS are mono-agent systems. It means that the system cares about the consistency of the agent's own knowledge base. DATMS allows two or more agents to interact with each other; however it is considered mono-agent system because agents do not consider the other agent's opinion to make a decision. DTMS is considered multiagent as it deals with two or more agents that interact and can share information and effectively use it

With respect to the labels, DTMS is the only one that works with a three valued labels: *internal*, *external* and *out*; this is necessary because it allows agents to share information. JTMS, ATMS and DATMS work with a two values status: *in* and *out*.

An open challenge for multiagent systems is to maintain the logical consistency between collaborative agents operating asynchronously to solve a problem. Multiagent systems can solve problems by assigning different aspects of the problem to different agents. Each agent may have a different perspective of the problem; consequently, the definition of consistency may be different from agent to agent. However, multiagent systems require solutions that have the highest possible level of consistency. For this reason, TMS has become an important approach to deal with the consistency issue.

THE MULTIAGENT RECOMMENDER APPROACH

Planning a travel itinerary is a complex task even for an expert travel agent. The travel agent needs to know many details about the destination chosen by the passenger and many features of the whole trip such as the attractions, hotels, flights timetable and costs. In many cases, this knowledge is distributed among different travel agents, and they must communicate and exchange information to come up with the final recommendation.

This work presents a multiagent recommender approach where agents can cooperate to get a recommendation. These agents are able to exchange information when necessary. To accomplish this goal, two important features are included in this approach: 1) Agents are able to access and maintain the integrity of the exchanged information; and 2) Agents perform their tasks in an asynchronous way. When some agent depends on information from another agent, it must be able to start the process by making some assumptions, even when the information is not available. To implement these features, we propose the utilization of a TMS component. It is used to revise the shared data, while keeping the integrity of the agents' knowledge bases.

In summary, the proposed approach deals with the following issues:

- Information sources can be distributed in different places;
- The domain is dynamic and knowledge can change over time and this has to be considered during the recommendation process;
- A recommendation can be built from different tasks that can be performed in an asynchronous way;
- Expert knowledge is necessary to perform the tasks, and it can be distributed among different experts.

The architecture proposed in this work was designed to deal with the tourism domain, which is dynamic and requires specific knowledge to compose a recommendation. Furthermore, we propose an innovative method for keeping the integrity of the agent knowledge bases involved in the recommendation process. The TMS also allows agents to assume initial information, when it lacks a piece of this information to assemble a recommendation.

We created a multiagent recommender system where a community of agents shares a common goal (the travel package recommendation) as well as individual goals (the travel components that each one must identify). A community C of agents consists of n agents, i.e. C = a_1, $a_{2,}$ ..., $a_{n,}$ where each agent a_i has the following features:

- **Cooperation**: Agents cooperate to achieve their goal with high efficiency;
- **Knowledge**: An agent has its own knowledge base. All tasks solved by the agent are stored in its knowledge base as cases;
- **Specialization**: A human travel agent becomes an expert in a specific type of task over time in a travel agency; this specialization increases agent's confidence and improves the quality of the service. For this reason, the proposed approach replicates this behavior by allowing software agents to specialize in one task;
- **Truth maintenance system component**: agents have a truth maintenance system component that deals with inconsistencies in their knowledge bases. This component is responsible for keeping the knowledge bases consistent;
- **Assumptions**: an agent is capable of assuming missing or lacking information during the recommendation process.

The Recommendation Process

Figure 1 shows the recommendation process, which starts when the user asks for a recommendation. The user inputs relevant preferences, such as accommodation type, departure date or number of passengers. From these user's preferences the system creates a list of tasks to be solved and communicated to the agents.

Each agent chooses a task and all of them must cooperate to assemble a recommendation and present it to the user. Each agent can perform one task in the recommendation cycle. When an agent

Figure 1. Agents working in a cycle of recommendation

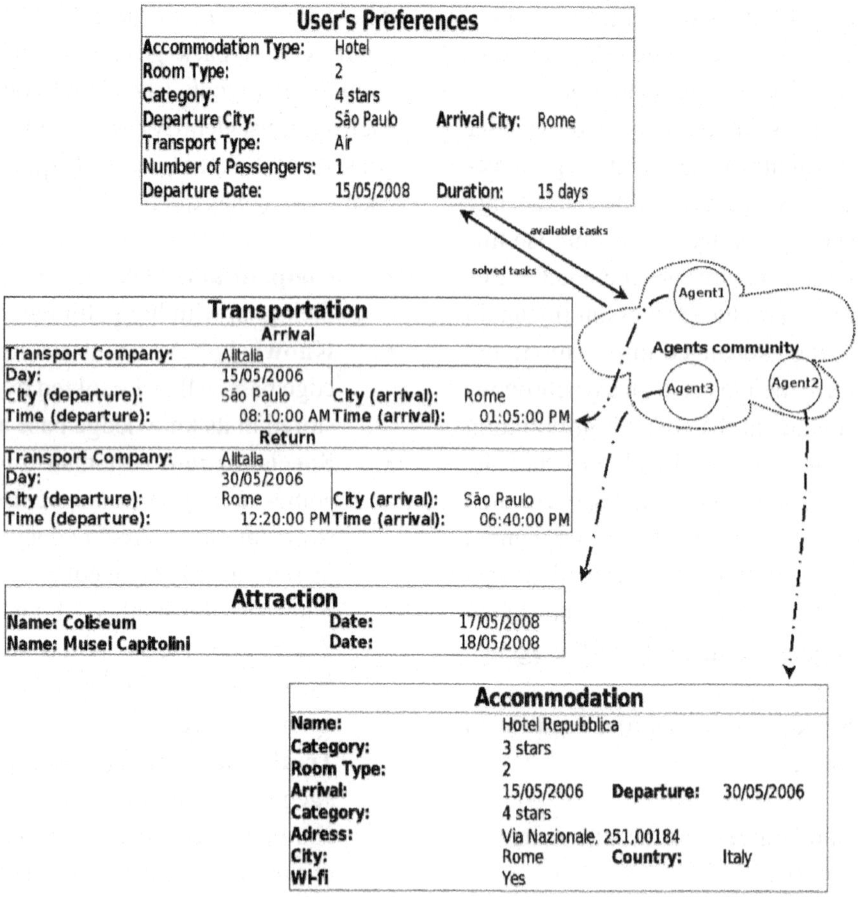

chooses a task, the status of the task is changed to "not available". It means that two different agents cannot perform the same task at the same time. As shown in figure 1, there are three agents working in the recommendation process. *Agent1* is working in the **transportation** task, *Agent2* is working in the **accommodation** task, and the **attraction** task is with *Agent3*.

As we can see in figure 2, in order to perform a task the agent searches for the information in its knowledge base. If the agent does not find the information needed, it starts a communication with agents in the community to exchange information.

Agents can obtain new information during the recommendation process as well. If some inconsistency is found in the knowledge base (or some conflict of knowledge appears among agents), the TMS component is run to maintenance the integrity of the knowledge bases.

Agent Specialization

The specialization of the agents enables them to deal with the task more efficiently, since it was not necessary to look for information to answer the requisites of the task. With the use of the system, the agents become *experts* in some kind of task. Figure 2 shows the agent architecture and the data flow required for a single agent to perform a single task (a piece of the recommendation).

To choose the task according to its specialty,

Figure 2. Flow diagram of tasks performed in the agent architecture

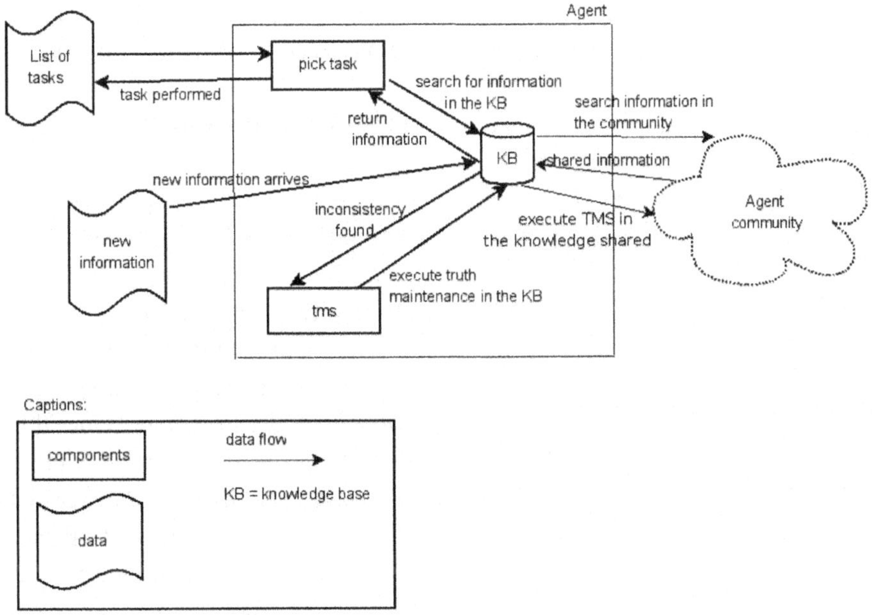

the agent calculates a *confidence index* (confind) for each type of task that it is able to perform. These confidence indexes represent the level of expertise an agent has acquired from the time it was executing each type of task.

Each task solved by an agent receives an evaluation from the user; with a rate ranging from 0 to 7, where 0 is the worst and 7 is the best rating. The task evaluation is then used in the agent confidence index computation so that the agent increases its confidence when it provides a better solution to the task.

We are looking for two features when applying user evaluations to calculate the confidence index: quality and uniformity. The quality aims to provide the best recommendation, and thereby obtain a high user evaluation. The uniformity aims to obtain homogeneity in user evaluations, where lower variability in evaluations implies more reliable results. Thus, high quality and uniformity would imply that a set of evaluations has a high average value for evaluation, and low standard deviation. Equation 1 shows how the confidence index of each type of task t is calculated.

$$confind(t) = \frac{\sum_{i=0} F_i(t)}{\sum_{k \in K} \sum_{i=0} F_i(k)} \times \phi(t) \quad (1)$$

Where: t is the type of task;

$F_i(t)$ is the number of tasks of type t performed by the agent;

K is the set of all types of tasks;

$F_i(k)$ is the number of tasks of all types performed by the agent;

$\Phi(t)$ is the evaluation of the user to that type of task t, defined by equation 2.

$$\phi(t) = \begin{cases} \alpha\left(\dfrac{\mu(t)}{\Sigma_{j \in K}\mu(j)}\right) & if\,\Sigma_{l \in K}\sigma(l) = 0 \\ \alpha\left(\dfrac{\mu(t)}{\Sigma_{j \in K}\mu(j)}\right) + (1-\alpha)\left(\dfrac{\dfrac{1}{\sigma(t)}}{\Sigma_{l \in K}\dfrac{1}{\sigma(l)}}\right) & otherwise \end{cases} \quad (2)$$

where:

$\mu(t)$ is the average of the evaluations of type of task *t* performed by the agent;

σ (t) is the standard deviation of the evaluations of type of task *t* performed by the agent;

α is the coefficient to determine the relevance of μ and σ over the confidence index.

To get the normalized evaluation average value of the type of task *t*, the value is divided by the number of different types of tasks. The standard deviation value is calculated in the same way. The coefficient α determines the relevance of the average and the standard deviation over the confidence indexes. For instance, if we set this coefficient to 0.5, the average and the standard deviation will have the same importance in the calculation of each of the confidence indexes. This value should be set during the experiments.

Thus, the confidence index must be proportional to the average and inversely proportional to the standard deviation, which means that we will get best results with a high average evaluation and a low standard deviation. Equation 2 expresses the influence that the evaluations of the tasks have over the confidence indexes.

The agent updates the confidence index every time it must choose a task to perform. Based on the index, it checks which type of task among those available would be the best to be performed. This behavior helps the agent to become an expert in a task type. Also, if the agent has enough information about a task type in its knowledge base, it can provide a faster recommendation for that kind of service. Moreover, it yields, in the long run, high quality recommendations because the agent becomes an expert in that type of recommendations.

This agent specialization mimics what happens in the real world, where it is common for human travel agents to specialize in a particular kind of service (accommodation, transportation, interchanges, conferences, etc) in order to provide better recommendations to the customers.

The Recommendation Algorithm

Using the confidence indexes, the agent chooses the task that fits its specialty best. As shown in algorithm 1, agents perform different procedures to find the information.

In the procedure **PickTask** the agent chooses a task to perform (β), as already explained in *section Agent Specialization*. Once the agent chooses a task, it starts to search for the information to solve the task. In the first step, when executing the procedure **SearchLocalKB**, the agent searches for the information in its own knowledge base. The knowledge is stored as cases in the agent's knowledge base. Each task performed becomes a case solved, increasing the knowledge base according to the number of performed tasks.

The selection of the information to solve the task by the agent is done according to the similarity of the attributes of the pieces of the task to be solved with those of the previous solved tasks in the agent's knowledge base. For example, comparing the type of accommodation or transport in

Algorithm 1. Multiagent recommendation

```
{ C is the agents community; }
   { T is the set of tasks to be solved; }
   { β is the task to be solved}
{ an is the agent}
Function Recommendation (an, β,T)
     repeat
               β = PickTask (an, T)
               T = T - β
               S = SearchLocalKB (β)
               if (S = Ø)then
                         for each an  in C
                           S = CommunitySearch (ay, β)
                           if S = Ø then
                               T = T U β
                           end if
                         end for
               end if
     until (T = Ø)
Return S
```

user's preference, or class of attraction (museum, art galleries), who those previously stored in the agent knowledge base. To do this comparison, we apply a simple nearest neighbor algorithm (Watson, 1997) where the similarity function of each attribute just compares if the value of the attribute is equal or not.

The goal is to recommend the most similar information. The new task is considered the "new problem" and it is compared with all cases stored in the agent's knowledge base. If no similar case is found in the knowledge base (no cases has reached the threshold set), then the agent has to search for the information in the community (other agents). In the procedure *CommunitySearch* the agent starts the communication with other agents, asking for the information needed.

Truth Maintenance System Component

In our multiagent recommender system, agents work in a cooperative way to assemble a recommendation to the user. Each agent is responsible for a piece of the recommendation (called task). When the agent does not have the information necessary to complete the task in its knowledge base, it communicates with agents in the community to get the information. It means that agents can exchange information during the recommendation process.

However, conflicts may arise when agents share knowledge, such as:

- Some information can be shared among different agents with different status;
- An agent can assume some information and realize later that the assumption is not correct.

The truth maintenance system (TMS) component is used to keep integrity among agents' knowledge bases. Figure 3 shows communication among agents that share information during the recommendation process. *Agent3* is looking for attractions in Rome and *Agent7* answers its request, informing that it has information about "Musei Vaticani" in Rome. From this moment on, *Agent7* and *Agent3* are sharing this information. When some conflict arises, the TMS component is triggered and it executes the maintenance, considering the conflicting information and maintaining the integrity of the knowledge bases.

Algorithm 2 shows the truth maintenance steps necessary to keep the integrity of the agents'

Figure 3. Agents exchanging information

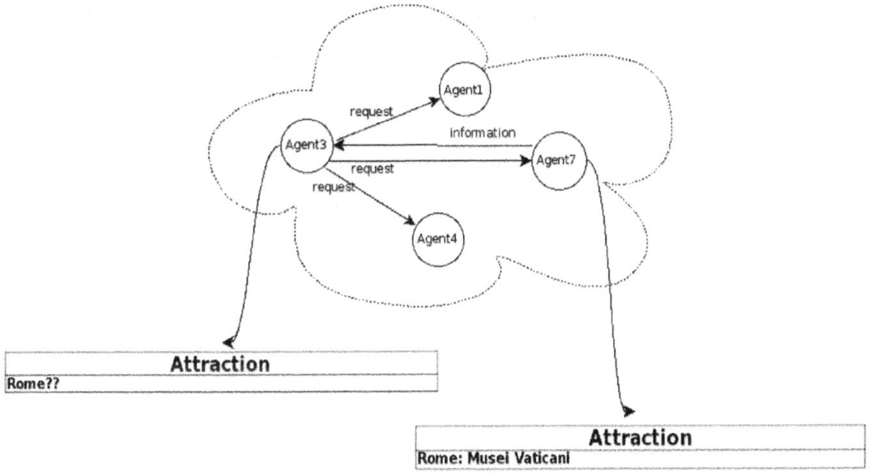

Algorithm 2. Truth maintenance

```
{C is the community of agents}
 {γ is the conflicting information}
 {a_n is the agent}
 {A is the set of agents that share information γ}
 Procedure Truth maintenance (an, γ, C)
 repeat
   {Search for agents who share the information γ}
   A = Search_Agents (a_n, γ)
   {Find the agent with the initial information and classify the set of agents from it}
   A = Classify (A)
   for each a in A do
     {Label the knowledge status in each agent (a)}
     Label (a, status)
   end for
 until (A = ∅)
```

knowledge bases. It is necessary to review the knowledge label in each agent that is sharing it. The TMS finds the agent that has the original information, and starting with this agent changes the label in each agent according to the new information received. The goal is to achieve the same status of the knowledge in every agent who is sharing it. It is important to mention that we will think about the possibility of agents having different points of view; however this issue is not covered in this first approach.

When the system detects inconsistent information, the first step is to search for all agents that share this information. For example, if an agent has information about *Hotel Libertel* in Paris and another one has the information that *Hotel Libertel* is out of service, the system detects an inconsistency (γ).

The procedure **Search_Agents** is responsible for finding all agents that share this information. Then, with this set of agents, the procedure **Classify** is executed to identify the agent source, i.e., the agent that shared the information for the first time. This is necessary because consistency requires that the information γ reaches the same status in all agents that share it. Once we have the ordered set of agents, the procedure **Label** starts, changing the label of the information γ to the new status.

Assumptions

This approach has the ability of manipulating assumption sets. Using assumptions is a desirable feature in a tourism multiagent recommender system, since the use of agents can work in an asynchronous way. For instance, the agent responsible for the accommodation needs information about the flight (day and time of arrival) to choose the better hotel for the user.

Two different situations that happen in the real travel scenario need to be mapped into the recommender system: 1) when the travel agent needs to wait for information from another agent (this causes a delay in the process); and 2) when the travel agents has to guess the information about the user during the recommendation process (lack of preferences of the user, for instance).

The assumptions used by the agent during the recommendation process can be reviewed when the user evaluates the result, i.e., in the iterate step of the recommender system. This feature will be developed in the next step of this work.

EXPERIMENTS

A set of experiments was developed in order to validate the proposed multiagent recommender approach. Two different kinds of simulations were run to analyze agents' behavior. In the first simulation, we verified if specialization really improves the quality of the recommendations. In the second simulation, we checked the scalability of the agents, i.e., the performance of the agents when the number of agents is increased in the system.

We simulated different user queries and 45 of them were used to create 120 new tasks (the list of tasks was created from these new queries). These 120 tasks were representing 3 types of tasks: transportation, accommodation and attractions. A step of knowledge acquisition was done to include some cases into the knowledge bases of the agents and to evaluate each task performed by the agents.

To provide the initial state to start the experiments, some initial sets were necessary, such as:

- At instant 0, it was considered that each agent has performed one task for each type (accommodation, transportation and attraction);
- These 3 tasks were evaluated with 5 (a neutral rate) to each agent;
- The coefficient α was set with 0.5 that is the optimal value according to our tests. It allows getting the average and the standard deviation with the same importance in the calculation of the confidence indexes;
- There is no standard deviation in the beginning, which means that the standard deviation is not considered in the first time the agent calculates the confidence indexes.

With these initial settings, the confidence indexes of each agent have the same initial value and therefore the first task will be chosen randomly.

Simulation 1: Specialization

In this simulation we focus in the agent's behavior. The scenario was created with 3 agents, 3 types of tasks (transportation, accommodation and attraction) and 120 new tasks.

Two different situations were considered to validate the results: 1) the confidence indexes of the agents were considered for choosing the tasks (specialized agents); 2) the agents did not consider the indexes to choose their tasks (non-specialized agents), i.e., in this simulation, agents did not become experts during the process and the choice of tasks were done randomly. Thus, we could compare the results got from specialized agents with the results got from agents that were not specialized.

First, agents had to perform the tasks considering their confidence indexes. Figure 4 shows *agent1* behavior through the 45 cycles of recommendation (we considered that one user query is equal to 1 cycle of recommendation).

We can see that *agent1* starts of becoming expert in the type of task **attraction** and increases its confidence index in this type. However, near cycle 20, where the tasks of **attraction** end, it has to perform another type of tasks, and the respective confidence index starts to decrease. This happens because the agent performs other types of tasks. The confidence index of **accommodation** starts to increase from this point.

Figure 5 shows *agent1*'s behavior in a non-specialized simulation. Here, the agent chose the tasks to perform in a random way. It means that the agent did not consider the confidence index to choose the task. Thus, it does not become expert during the process. We calculated the confidence indexes just to compare with the indexes obtained in the specialized simulation. We can note that, in the beginning, the values are instable but from cycle 3, the confidence indexes keep linear until the end of the process.

We can conclude from this simulation that specialized agents have better results while they

Figure 4. Agent1 – specialized

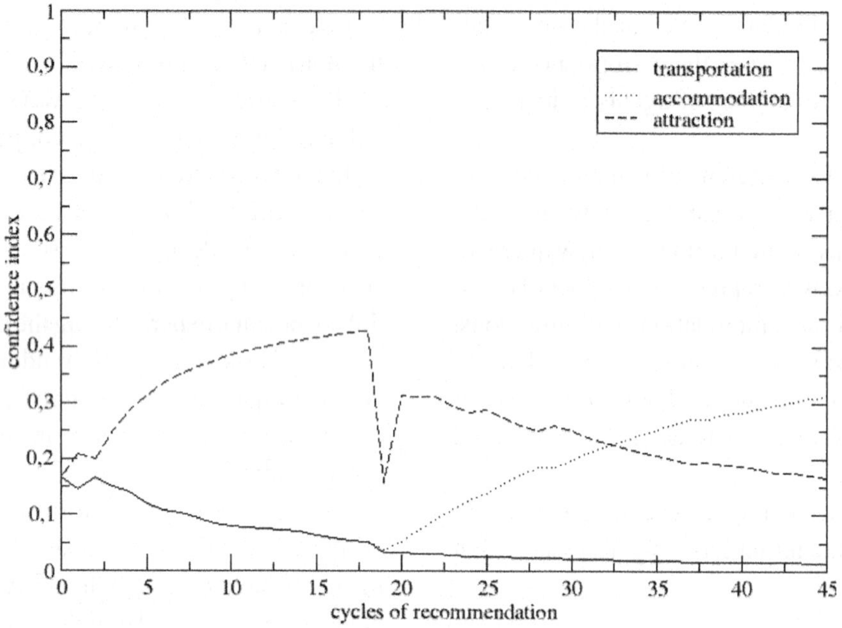

Figure 5. Agent1 – non-specialized

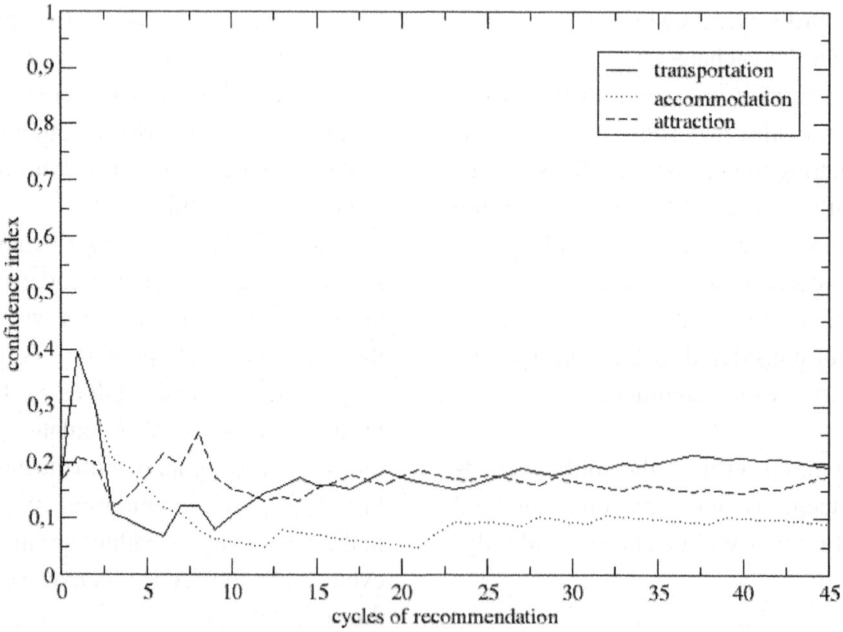

find tasks of the type they are becoming experts. When the agent has to perform another type of tasks, it decreases its performance since it has to start to learn about that type of task.

Simulation 2: Performance of the Agents

In the second simulation, the goal was to validate the performance of the agents, comparing results of specialized and non-specialized agents. We wanted to verify the agents' behavior if we increase the number of agents. The idea is to use different number of available agents and analyze the performance of the system, verifying if the quality of the recommendations increase according to the number of agents available to perform the recommendations.

We run simulations with 3 different numbers of agents: 3, 10 and 15 agents. In all these simulations, we considered specialized and non-specialized agents to compare the results of the agents in both situations.

To verify the quality of the recommendations, we calculated the average of the evaluations received in each task performed by the agent. A travel agent analysed this step to evaluate the real recommendations done by the agents. In figures 6, 7 and 8, the Y-axis represents the average evaluation value, calculated in each cycle of recommendation. The X-axis represents the number of tasks performed in the experiment.

In the first simulation we used 3 agents to perform the 120 tasks. Figure 6 shows that the results from specialized agents (the average of evaluations was almost 7) were better than the results from non-specialized agents (average 4).

Analyzing figure 7 we can see the average evaluation value resulting from the simulation with 10 agents working. Specialized agents have got better results than non-specialized agents. They reached 4.5 of average value and the result

Figure 6. Average of evaluations with 3 agents

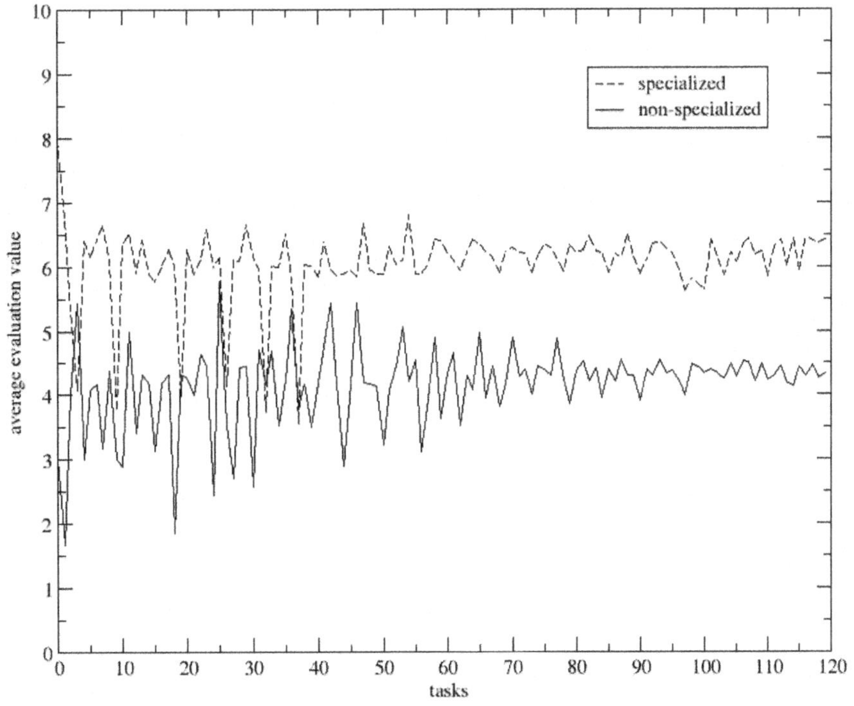

Figure 7. Average of evaluations with 10 agents

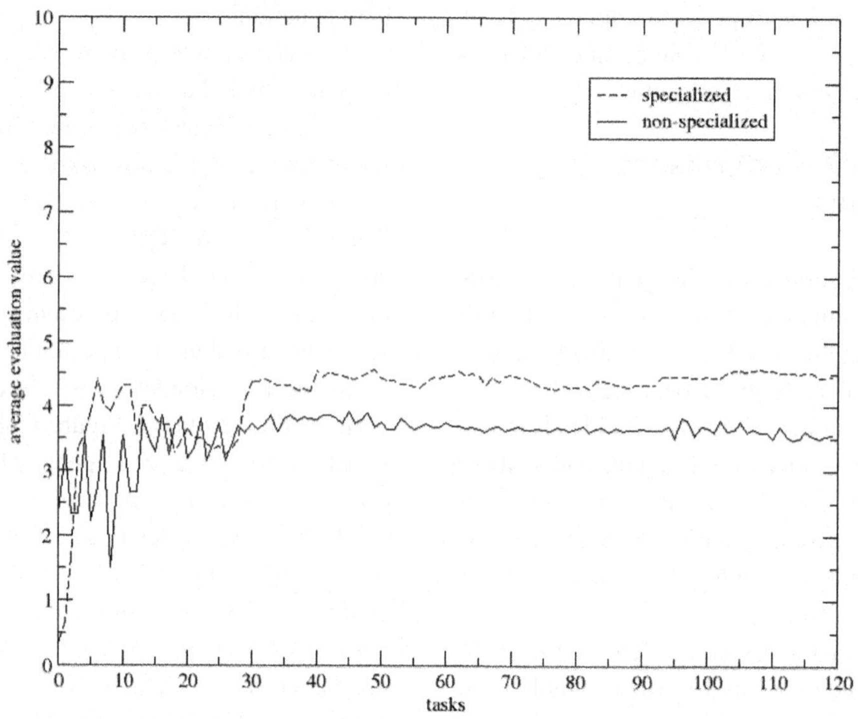

Figure 8. Average of evaluations with 15 agents

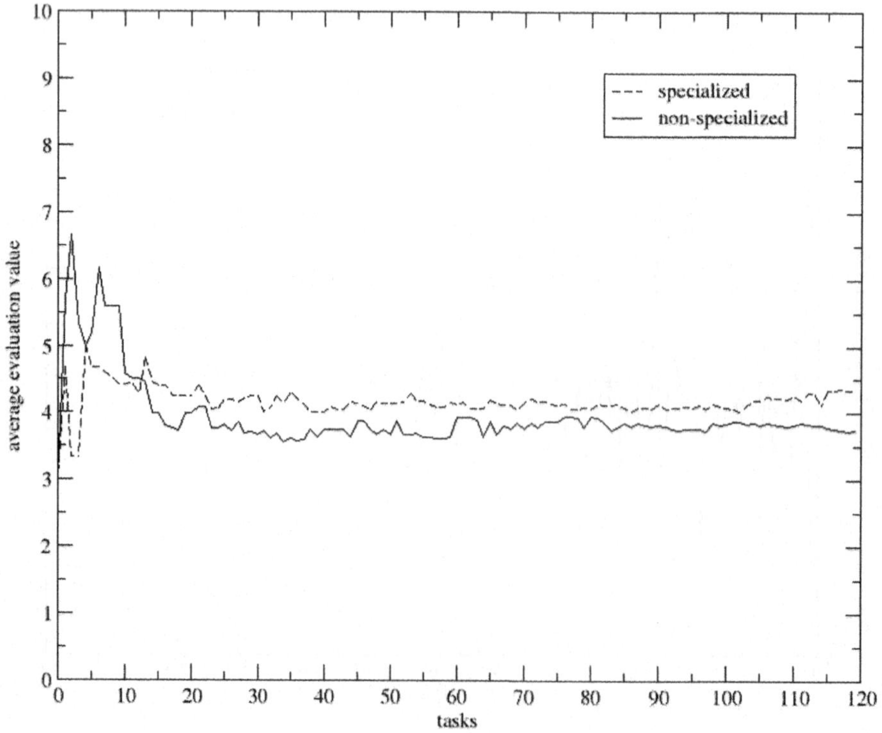

was stable starting from task 30. Considering that we had 10 agents and 120 tasks to be performed, the results of specialized agents have shown the advantages of specialization.

The second simulation has increased the number of agents and has kept the same number of tasks. As expected, the average evaluation value is lower for the specialized agents than in the previous scenario (with 3 agents).

Figure 8 shows the average evaluation value when we used 15 agents working to solve the tasks. Despite the specialized agents started with unstable values, the evaluation average became stable soon and kept the same performance until all the tasks were completed. The average evaluation value was a little bit higher than 4, while the average evaluation value got from non-specialized agents was lower than 4.

We can conclude that the system is scalable; however the variety of tasks is an important factor to determine how many agents should work to perform the available tasks.

OPPORTUNITIES FOR FUTURE WORK

As future work, we intent to deliver more attention to the step where the user evaluates the recommendation received. We aim to create a learning mechanism inside the system where agents would be able to review their assumptions according to the user's evaluation to get better recommendation and learning with this process. Furthermore, new tests will be run to verify the results with different agents performing the same task.

CONCLUSION

This chapter has presented a multiagent recommender approach applied to the tourism domain to deal with dynamic and distributed knowledge necessary to compose a travel package recommendation. Agents work in a cooperative way to recommend travel packages to the user. A recommendation is divided in tasks and each agent is responsible to perform some tasks.

Agents become experts in a specific type of task over time. Decomposing the problem and distributing it to several different agents, which become more and more specialized, can yield better recommendations than the current algorithms of recommendation that we have studied. This is especially recognized when applied to the tourism area, which is a complex domain that needs specific knowledge distributed over different sources.

Agents have a TMS component that helps to keep the integrity of the knowledge bases, avoiding inconsistencies. This is an important feature to be developed in a multiagent recommender system, because it allows sharing of information among agents, keeping the consistent of the knowledge bases. The validation of the TMS component is being done with a real travel agency, due to the lack of similar systems to compare the results obtained. So far, we have already concluded that the TMS component avoids incorrect recommendations.

A set of experiments were carried out, where we learned that specialized agents deliver better recommendations than non-specialized agents. We have tested also the scalability, where we saw that the number of agents should be increased according to the number of types of tasks.

REFERENCES

Al-Nazer, A., & Helmy, T. (2007). A Web searching guide: Internet search engines and autonomous interface agents collaboration. In *Proceedings of the wi-iatw*, Los Alamitos, CA, USA (pp. 424-428).

Ambite, J. L., Knoblock, C. A., Muslea, M., & Minton, S. (2005). conditional constraint networks for interleaved planning and information gathering. *IEEE Intelligent Systems, 20*(2), 25–33. doi:10.1109/MIS.2005.24

Balabanovic, M., & Shoham, Y. (1997). Fab: Content-based, collaborative recommendation. *Communications of the ACM, 40*(3), 66–72. doi:10.1145/245108.245124

Buffett, S., Keping, J., Liu, S., Spencer, B., & Wang, F. (2004). Negotiating exchanges of P3P-labeled information for compensation. *Computational Intelligence, 20*(4), 663–677. doi:10.1111/j.0824-7935.2004.00259.x

Burke, R. (2000). Knowledge-based recommender systems. In J. E. Daily, A. Kent, & H. Lancour (Eds.), *Encyclopedia of library and information science*. New York: Marcel Dekker.

Camacho, D., Molina, J. M., Borrajo, D., & Aler, R. (2002). MAPWEB: Cooperation between planning agents and Web agents. *Information & Security, 8*(2), 209–238.

deKleer, J. (1986). An assumption-based tms, extending the ATMS, and problem solving with the ATMS. *Artificial Intelligence, 28*(2), 127–224. doi:10.1016/0004-3702(86)90080-9

Doyle, J. (1979). A truth maintenance system. *Artificial Intelligence, 12*(3), 231–272. doi:10.1016/0004-3702(79)90008-0

Huhns, M. N., & Bridgeland, D. M. (1991). Multiagent truth maintenance. *IEEE Transactions on Systems, Man, and Cybernetics, 21*(6), 1437–1445. doi:10.1109/21.135687

Lorenzi, F., & Ricci, F. (2005). Case-based recommender systems: A unifying view. In *Intelligent techniques for Web personalization* (pp. 89-113). Berlin, Germany: Springer.

Macho, S., Torrens, M., & Faltings, B. (2000). A multi-agent recommender system for planning meetings. In *Proceedings of the Workshop On Agent-Based Recommender Systems (WARS'2000).*

Maes, P. (1994). Agents that reduce work and information overload. *Communications of the ACM, 37*(7), 30–40. doi:10.1145/176789.176792

Mason, C., & Johnson, R. R. (1989). DATMS: A framework for distributed assumption based reasoning. *Distributed Artificial Intelligence, 2*, 293–317.

Montaner, M., Lopez, B., & de la Rosa, J. L. (2003). A taxonomy of recommender agents on the Internet. *Artificial Intelligence Review, 19*(4), 285–330. doi:10.1023/A:1022850703159

Resnick, P., Iacovou, N., Suchak, M., Bergstrom, P., & Riedl, J. (1994). GroupLens: An open architecture for collaborative filtering of netnews. In *Proceedings of the ACM Conference On Computer-Supported Cooperative Work* (pp. 175-186).

Ricci, F. (2002). Travel recommender systems. *IEEE Intelligent Systems, 17*(6), 55–57.

Smyth, B. (2007). Case-based recommendation. In *The adaptive Web* (pp. 342-376). Berlin, Germany: Springer.

Torrens, M., Faltings, B., & Pu, P. (2002). SmartClient: Constraint satisfaction as a paradigm for scaleable intelligent information systems. *Constraints: An International Journal, 7*(1), 49–69. doi:10.1023/A:1017940426216

Watson, I. (1997). *Applying case-based reasoning: Techniques for enterprise systems*. San Francisco: Morgan Kaufmann.

Wu, S., Ghenniwa, H., Zhang, Y., & Shen, W. (2006). Personal assistant agents for collaborative design environments. [f]. *Computers in Industry, 57*(8), 732–739. doi:10.1016/j.compind.2006.04.010

Chapter 5
Exploiting a Map-Based Interface in Conversational Recommender Systems for Mobile Travelers

Francesco Ricci
Free University of Bolzano, Italy

Quang Nhat Nguyen
Hanoi University of Technology, Vietnam

Olga Averjanova
Image Data Systems Ltd, UK

ABSTRACT

Nowadays travel and tourism Web sites store and offer a large volume of travel related information and services. Furthermore, this huge amount of information can be easily accessed using mobile devices, such as a phone with mobile Internet connection capability. However, this information can easily overwhelm a user because of the large number of information items to be shown and the limited screen size in the mobile device. Recommender systems (RSs) are often used in conjunction with Web tools to effectively help users in accessing this overwhelming amount of information. These recommender systems can support the user in making a decision even when specific knowledge necessary to autonomously evaluate the offerings is not available. Recommender systems cope with the information overload problem by providing a user with personalized recommendations (i.e., a well chosen selection of the items contained in the repository), adapting this selection to the user's needs and preferences in a particular usage context. In this chapter, the authors present a recommendation approach integrating a conversational preference acquisition technology based on "critiquing" with map visualization technologies to build a new map-based conversational mobile RS that can effectively and intuitively support travelers in finding their desired products and services. The results of the authors' real-user study show that integrating map-based visualization and critiquing-based interaction in mobile RSs improves the system's recommendation effectiveness, and increases the user satisfaction.

DOI: 10.4018/978-1-60566-818-5.ch005

INTRODUCTION

The users of travel and tourism web sites often find it difficult in choosing their desired travel products and services due to an overwhelming number of options to consider, and the lack of the system's help in making product selection decisions. The problem becomes even harder for users of the mobile Internet, who browse travel sites and their product repositories using a mobile device. This additional difficulty is due to the intrinsic obstacles of the mobile usage environment, i.e., mobile devices have small screens and the data transfer rates of wireless networks are typically lower than those of wired ones.

Recommender Systems RSs are decision support tools aimed at addressing the information overload problem, providing product and service recommendations personalized to the user's needs and preferences at a particular request context (Resnick & Varian, 1997; Adomavicius & Tuzhilin, 2005). However, existing recommendation technologies have not been developed specifically for mobile users; and this chapter shows that recommendation techniques developed for the wired web must be adapted to the mobile environment in order to better exploit the available information, and provide software tools usable on mobile devices.

The evolution of mobile devices (e.g., PDAs and mobile phones), wireless communication technologies (e.g., wireless LAN and UMTS), and position detection techniques (e.g., RFID beacon-based and GPS), have created favorable conditions for the development and commercialization of a large number of location-based mobile services (Mohapatra & Suma, 2005; Steinfield, 2004), i.e., information services accessible by mobile devices through the mobile network, and utilizing the geographical position of the mobile device. As a consequence, many location-based mobile services have been introduced in the recent years, including emergency services, information services, navigation support services, etc.

For example, mobile travelers can access local tourist information services providing information about nearby points of interests (Pospischil et al., 2002), such as pubs and restaurants (Dunlop et al., 2004), or get routing guidance from their position to a target location (Pospischil et al., 2002). In many of these systems, maps and map-based interfaces are used to visualize points of interests (e.g., restaurants, museums, or hotels), their spatial relations, and various kinds of information related to these points (e.g., menus, opening hours, or in-room services).

However, map-based interfaces do not solve all the information access problems. In fact, a major problem in map-based visualization is the need to keep the display readable and free from irrelevant information. This is particularly true in the mobile usage environment. Because of the limitations of mobile devices, especially small screens and limited computing power, displaying on an electronic map a large number of objects and their related information is computationally expensive and usually not effective. Hence, systems providing mobile travel services should employ filtering mechanisms to reduce the amount of data (information objects) that is displayed on an electronic map.

Though the specific benefits of map-based interfaces and recommendation technologies have been demonstrated in a number of previous research projects, the integration of these two technologies and their empirical evaluation, in terms of usability and effectiveness, in mobile travel support systems have not been studied yet. In this chapter, we present an approach for integrating recommendation technologies and electronic map visualization technologies to build a map-supported travel RS that can effectively and intuitively provide personalized recommendations on mobile devices.

Our recommendation methodology integrates long-term and session-specific user preferences, uses a composite query representation, employs a case-based model of the recommendation problem and its solution, furthermore, it exploits a critique-based conversational approach (Ricci & Nguyen, 2007). The integration of long-term and session-specific user preferences enables the exploitation of multiple knowledge sources of user's data. The long-term user preferences are derived (inferred) from past recommendation sessions, and on the other hand, the session-specific user preferences are collected through the user's explicit input including the critiques made in the current session.

The composite query representation consists of a logical query and a favorite pattern. This allows using both strict logical constraints and weak similarity-based conditions. The logical query component helps the system to precisely focus on the most relevant subsets of the product space, whereas the favorite pattern component enables the system to correctly sort the relevant products, ranking higher the products that are most suitable for their needs and wants.

In our approach, a travel product recommendation session is modeled as a case, and the Case-Based Reasoning (CBR) problem solving strategy is used (Aamodt & Plaza, 1994). CBR is based on learning from previous experiences, and case-based RSs exploit (reuse) the knowledge contained in a set of past recommendation cases. In our recommendation methodology, CBR is used for building a personalized user-query augmenting (by specializing) the original query derived from the conditions explicitly entered by the user. This personalized query is adapted in such a way that, taking into account the knowledge contained in the case base, the set of recommended products better match the user's preferences, even if these preferences are not expressed in the original query entered by the user.

Furthermore, our recommendation approach is based on the interactive elicitation of the user's preferences through critiques. The user, instead of being required to formulate a precise search query at the beginning of the interaction, is involved in a dialogue where the system's product suggestions interleave with the user's critiques to the recommended products. A user's critique is a comment (judgment) on a displayed product, which points out an unsatisfied preference (e.g., "I would like a cheaper restaurant") or confirms the importance of a product feature for the user ("I'd like to have dinner in a restaurant with a garden terrace"). This critique-based user preferences elicitation procedure results in the system building a better understanding the user's needs and preferences, and hence, in constantly improving the recommendations.

Our recommendation methodology has been firstly implemented in MobyRek (Ricci & Nguyen, 2007), a mobile RS that supports travelers in finding their desired travel products (restaurants). The results of some previous empirical evaluations of MobyRek, consisting of a live-user test (Ricci & Nguyen, 2007) and a number of simulations (Nguyen & Ricci, 2007; 2008a), showed that our critique-based recommendation methodology is effective in supporting mobile travelers in product selection decisions. However, MobyRek employs a text-based interface for recommendation visualization and system-user interaction, where the recommendations are presented to the user in a ranked list, as in a standard search engines like Google. We conjectured that this visualization and interaction approach may not be optimal for mobile devices and for mobile recommendation problems. We believed that this type of "standard" interface used for web applications can, in fact, cause some difficulties and inconveniences for mobile users in their interactions with the system.

Hence, in this chapter, we analyze the usability limitations of MobyRek, which we believe are typically found in all list-styled RSs, and we illustrate how this analysis leads to the design of an extended and improved version of the system called MapMobyRek. MapMobyRek implements the same core recommendation techniques used in MobyRek, i.e., the computation of the recommended items and their ranking are done exactly as in MobyRek. However, MapMobyRek uses maps as the main user interface for information display and access; furthermore, it provides new decision-support functions based on the map. The design of the map-based interface of MapMobyRek focused on the ability to offer the following user functions:

- to enter the search query by specifying preferences for item features,
- to see the system's recommendations on the map,
- to recognize immediately the differences between good and weak recommendations,
- to compare two selected recommendations,
- to input critiques to the recommended items,
- to see on the map how the expressed critique influences the system's recommendations, and
- to select the best item(s).

MobyRek and MapMobyRek are then compared, through a real-user test, with respect to functionality, efficiency, and convenience. The objective measures taken during the test and the subjective evaluations of the real-users show that the map-based interface is more effective than the list-based one. We also find that the integration of a map-based interface in a RS results in increased user satisfaction.

The remainder of this chapter is organized as follows. In the next section, we survey some related work. Then, we present our recommendation methodology, we discuss the limitations of MobyRek's user interface, and we present MapMobyRek – the improved system. Next, we state our research hypotheses, describe the test procedure, and present and discuss the test results. Finally, we give our conclusions and indicate some avenues for future research. We note that this chapter extends (Averjanova et al., 2008) that more briefly describes MapMobyRek and its validation.

RELATED WORK

There have been several research works focusing on map-based mobile services (Meng et al., 2008), map-based mobile travel guides (Baus et al., 2005), recommender systems (Adomavicius & Tuzhilin, 2005; Burke, 2007), and travel RSs (Ricci, 2002; Fesenmaier et al., 2006). In this section, we first discuss traditional recommendation techniques, and then we focus on related works that aim to integrate mobile computing, map visualization and recommendation technologies in providing personalized travel products and services to tourists.

Recommendation Techniques

Many recommendation methods have been introduced in the RSs literature. Nevertheless, they are often classified into four well-known categories: collaborative, content-based, knowledge-based, and hybrid (Adomavicius & Tuzhilin, 2005; Burke, 2007).

Collaborative RSs generate recommendations using the information of the ratings given by users on items. In the collaborative recommendation approach, the system recommends to a given user those items that have been highly rated by the other users who have similar taste (i.e., similar ratings for co-rated items). The collaborative recommendation approach is inspired by the daily habit of people, i.e., when finding information or choosing between options, people often consult friends who have similar likes and tastes.

Content-based RSs generate recommendations for a given user exploiting feature-based descriptions of items and the ratings that the user has given on some items. In the content-based recommendation approach, a user is modeled by a profile that represents the user's needs and preferences with respect to item's features; and the system recommends to the user those items whose features (highly) match the user's profile.

The *knowledge-based* recommendation approach uses specific domain knowledge to reason on the relationship (i.e., suitability/appropriateness) between a user's needs and preferences and a particular item. In knowledge-based RSs, the system acquires the user's requirements on items (e.g., the user's query), and then consults the knowledge base to determine the best fitting items.

Each of the three recommendation approaches (i.e., collaborative, content-based, and knowledge-based) has its own limitations and disadvantages (Adomavicius & Tuzhilin, 2005; Burke, 2007). Therefore, some RSs take a *hybrid* recommendation approach that combines two (or more) recommendation techniques in order to take full advantages of each individual technique, or to overcome some of their disadvantages (Burke, 2007). With respect to this categorization of recommendation methods, our recommendation approach can be considered a knowledge-based approach.

Many RSs, such as those based on collaborative filtering, follow the *single-shot* recommendation strategy, i.e., for a given user's request the system computes and shows to the user the recommendation list, and the session ends. If the user is not satisfied she could enter a new query, if possible, but this process is up to the user and the system does not provide any support through this sequence of requests.

Conversely, in *conversational* RSs a recommendation session does not terminate immediately after the first set of recommendations are shown to the user, but it evolves in a dialogue where the system tries to elicit step-by-step the user's needs and preferences to produce better recommendations (Bridge et al., 2005). In our approach, the system-user conversation is supported through critiquing, where the system's recommendations are interleaved with the user's critiques to the recommended items (Burke, 2002; McGinty & Smyth, 2006).

Mobile Recommender Systems

The systems and techniques described above have been mostly applied in the Web usage context, without any special concern with the context of the user, i.e., in particular, if she is on the go and accesses the information service using a mobile device. In the rest of this section we will review some personalized travel and tourism support systems that have been specifically designed for the mobile usage context.

CityGuide (Dunlop et al., 2004) is designed for PalmOS devices and helps tourists in finding attractions (such as restaurants) around a city. This recommender system uses the constraint-based filtering approach to control which attractions are shown on the map. In particular, the user, through the system's map interface, is asked to specify constraints on attraction type, restaurant cuisine and price. The system retrieves from the database only those attractions that satisfy the user's indicated constraints, and then ranks these retrieved attractions according to their match to the preferences stored in the user's profile. The system builds and updates the user's profile, which maintains her long-term preferences, by mining and interpreting the user's actions (such as writing a restaurant review, reading a review, viewing a restaurant's details, etc.) and collecting the user's ratings to the restaurants. Though the system ranks the recommended attractions and shows them on the map, it does not visualize how close each recommended attraction is to the user's preferences (i.e., the recommendation level).

Burigat et al. (2005) illustrate a system running on PDA devices that supports tourists in searching for travel products (i.e., hotels or restaurants) in a geographic area that best satisfy their needs and preferences. The system builds the user-query used to search in the services repository by asking the user to indicate her constraints on the service attributes, e.g. the facilities offered by the hotel or the restaurant. However, the system does not employ the constraint-filtering approach or a multi-attribute utility function. Instead, the system constructs the recommendation list by ranking the services according to their satisfaction score. A service's satisfaction score is measured by the number of constraints (indicated in the user's query) that are satisfied by the service. Hence, each recommended service is visualized by an icon superimposed on the map of the geographic area, augmented by a "filled-in" vertical bar representing how much the service satisfies the user's query. We observe that this system does not reuse the knowledge derived from past user interactions to provide better recommendations.

Dynamic Tour Guide (*DTG*) (ten Hagen et al., 2005) is a mobile tour guide system that helps travelers in discovering a destination. Given a user's request, the system computes a personalized tour in the city by asking the user her interests and the time she would like to spend for the visit. In *DTG* a tour is composed of a set of points of interest (i.e., restaurants, attractions and events). The system then presents the recommended tour on the map and provides some audio guide information. This audio visual presentation lets the user to visualize the tour itinerary. The system computes and presents just one tour per user request, instead of providing a list of recommended tours. *DTG* also utilizes the content-based approach for building the recommendations (Burke, 2007), just as the previous one.

The *George Square* system (Brown et al., 2005) runs on handheld tablet PCs. It is designed for supporting visitors to explore a city as well as share their visit experiences. As the user moves in the city and visits the attractions, her positions and activities are automatically recorded (logged) by the system. The user's activities include the attractions she encounters, the web pages (i.e., weblogs created by previous visitors) she browses, and the photographs she takes. To build the recommendation list, the system makes use of patterns of co-occurrence of positions and activities, and employs the collaborative filtering recommendation technology (Adomavicius & Tuzhilin, 2005). In particular, the system uses the user's recent activities (i.e., in the last few minutes) to define the user's current context, then finds in the previous visitors' log data those periods of time with similar contexts, and finally includes in the recommendation list the activities done in those periods of time by these visitors. In addition, when showing the recommended items (i.e., attractions, web pages, photographs) on the map, the system displays the positions of nearby visitors and supports their leisure collaboration. For instance, the system let the user to collaboratively producing pictures of the attractions, or to have (voice-over-IP) discussions on co-interested attractions and objects.

Mobile Piste Map (Dunlop et al., 2007) is designed to support mobile users in selecting ski routes, i.e., individual or combined runs appropriate to their level of ability, preferences, and current mood and track conditions. The system first asks the user to indicate her ski-run preferences, for instance the route difficulty level, and then uses the indicated preferences to compute a list of recommended routes. The system presents on the map the recommended routes and their suitability for the user.

Park et al. (2007) presents a restaurant RS for mobile users. The system computes personalized recommendations using a Bayesian Network (Pourret et al., 2008) that models the probabilistic influences of the input parameters, i.e., the user's personal and contextual information, in relation to the restaurant attributes. This approach represents a restaurant by three discrete-valued attributes: class (e.g., Korean or Italian restaurant), price (e.g., low or medium), and mood (e.g., romantic or tidy). The Bayesian Network is defined by an expert, and is trained using a training dataset. To begin with, each user is required to provide personal information (e.g., age, gender, income, preferred restaurant class, etc.). The user's contextual information is automatically collected (detected) by the system, including season (e.g., spring), time in day (e.g., breakfast), position, weather (e.g., sunny), and temperature (e.g., warm). When a user requests for a restaurant recommendation, the system computes the recommendation score for all the restaurants in the database. A restaurant's recommendation score is a weighted sum of the conditional probabilities of the restaurant's attribute values, where these conditional probabilities are derived (inferred) from the learned Bayesian network. The system presents on the map a small set of the restaurants, i.e., those achieving the highest recommendation scores.

Research Goals

The main goal of our research work is similar to that addressed by the papers presented in the previous section, i.e., to provide personalized suggestions for travel products and services to mobile travelers, and to use th e map as primary tool for visualizing these suggestions. However, our approach differs in the following aspects.

- In our approach, the recommendation process begins with the user specifying explicit preferences, however, this user input is optional in our system, i.e., the user can obtain some recommendations even without explicitly providing any initial input. The main rationale for this design solution is that the user's preferences can be also acquired during the product search interaction phase, using the critiquing function (discussed in details in the next section) and exploiting the knowledge derived from the previous recommendations. We note that in all the referenced approaches either it is mandatory for the user to input initial preferences (Dunlop et al., 2004; Burigat et al., 2005; ten Hagen et al., 2005; Dunlop et al., 2007) or the user is not even given the option to specify initial preferences (Brown et al., 2005; Park et al., 2007). In this respect, our approach is more flexible, since it give the option to the user to specify preferences if she wants.
- In most of the systems described earlier, the user is not supported in providing feedback to the system's recommendations; or if supported, as in *CityGuide* (Dunlop et al., 2004), such a feedback is exploited only in future recommendation sessions, but not immediately for personalizing the current one. In our approach, various types of feedback are supported, i.e., critiquing the recommended items and rating the selected product(s). Moreover, critiquing is used immediately to refine the current user query.
- Our approach allows the users to indicate their preferences at different levels, in particular as a wish or a must satisfy criteria, and it utilizes these preferences in computing the system's recommendation(s). None of the earlier mentioned approaches support such a real-time use of user's preferences and critiques.
- Furthermore, none of the systems described earlier support the users in comparing two recommended items. In fact, given the system's recommended items, a user may first focus her interest on a few items, and then she may compare pairs of items by browsing their characteristics (see Figure 5, presented later on). Hence, our approach supports an item-to-item comparison, highlighting the differences between the two compared items, and hence provides additional support to users in selecting the best item.
- In our approach, case-based reasoning and user-interaction mining methodologies are used to exploit the knowledge contained in the past recommendation cases for learning how to rank the recommendations. Of the systems discussed earlier, only *CityGuide* (Dunlop et al., 2004) and *George Square* (Brown et al., 2005) learn from past recommendation interactions; whereas, *CityGuide* exploits the users' ratings and implicit feedback, and *George Square* exploits the users' past activities.

RECOMMENDATION METHODOLOGY

In this section we summarize our proposed methodology for travel product recommendation in a mobile context, providing details about the product representation and the user preferences model. Moreover, we illustrate how the user can critique a product recommendation and how this action is interpreted and exploited by the system. A more detailed description of the recommendation methodology is provided by Ricci & Nguyen (2007).

We observe that both MobyRek -- the system using text-based display of recommended items, and MapMobyRek -- the system using a map-based interface, identify the recommendation set, i.e., the restaurants to suggest to the user, in the same way. The two systems differ only in the way they present the results to the user, i.e., in their user interface.

Product Representation and User Preferences Model

In our recommendation technology, a travel product is represented as a feature values vector $x = (x_1, x_2, \ldots, x_n)$, where a feature value x_i may be numeric, nominal, or a set of nominal values. For instance, the restaurant x= ("Dolomiti", 1713, {pizza}, 10, {air-conditioned, smoking-room}, {Saturday, Sunday}, {credit-card}) has: name x_1="Dolomiti", distance from the user's position x_2=1713 meters, type x_3={pizza}, average cost x_4=10 Euros, characteristics x_5={air-conditioned, smoking-room}, opening days x_6={Saturday, Sunday}, and payment method x_7={credit-card}.

Any recommender system, for generating personalized recommendations, requires a representation of the user's preferences. Preferences vary from user to user, and even the same user in different situations (contexts) may have different preferences. In our approach, the user preferences model, which is encoded in a product search query, includes both contextual preferences (such as the space-time constraints) and preferences on product features. Contextual preferences characterize a user's current context of request, whereas product preferences express a user's taste and like. In the restaurant recommendation problem, for example, space-time constraints guarantee that the recommended restaurants are open on the day of the request and not too far from the user's position. Preferences on product features may state that the user, for instance, is interested in cheap restaurants, or prefers to go for pizza.

The user preferences model incorporates both long-term and session-specific user preferences (Nguyen & Ricci, 2008a; Ricci & Nguyen, 2007). Long-term (stable) user preferences, such as a preference for non-smoking room, are inferred from the user's recent interaction sessions with the system, and remain true throughout these sessions. In contrast, session-specific user preferences, such as a wish to eat pizza, are transient and specific to a session. Acquiring session-specific preferences helps the system to effectively capture the transient needs of the user, whereas exploiting long-term preferences allows the system to rely on more stable preferences, or default choices, and also avoids interrupting the user or requiring her effort in specifying preferences when these are not needed.

Session-specific and long-term preferences must be combined and used in the most appropriate way. In our approach, the system acquires session-specific user preferences in two ways: by user's initial specifications and by user's critiques. The user's initial preferences explicitly specified at the beginning of the recommendation session help orient the system's initial search. Meanwhile, the user's critiques to the recommended products help the system refine its understanding of the user's needs and preferences. As noted earlier the initial preference specification is optional in our system.

In a recommendation session, the user query has the function of encoding the user's preferences (both session-specific and long-term), and is used by the system to compute the recommendation list (more on this subject will be provided later). In our model, the user-query q consists of three components, $q = (q_l, p, w)$.

- The *logical query* (q_l) models the conditions that must be satisfied by the recommended products. The logical query is a conjunction of constraints: $q_l = (c_1 \wedge c_2 \wedge \ldots \wedge c_m)$, where c_j is a constraint on j-th feature. A constraint deals with only one feature, and a feature appears in only one constraint.
- The *favorite pattern* (p) models the conditions that the recommended products should match as much as possible. The wish conditions allow the system to make trade-offs. The favorite pattern is represented in the same vector space of the product representation: $p = (p_1, p_2, \ldots, p_n)$, where x_i and p_i belong to the same feature type, $\forall \forall i=1..n$.
- The *feature importance weights vector* (w) models how much each feature is important for the user with respect to the others: $w = (w_1, w_2, \ldots, w_n)$, where w_i ($\in [0,1]$) is the importance weight of i-th feature. The system refers to the feature importance weights when it needs to rank the products or make trade-offs or to find relaxation solutions for over-constrained logical queries.

For instance, the query $q = (q_l = (x_2 \leq 2000) \wedge (x_6 \supseteq \{\text{Saturday, Sunday}\}), p = (?, ?, \{\text{pizza}\}, ?, ?, ?, ?), w = (0, 0.4, 0.2, 0, 0, 0.4, 0))$ models a user interested only in those restaurants within 2 km from her position, open on Saturday and Sunday, and preferring pizza restaurants to the others. The user considers the distance and the opening day as the most important features and then the restaurant type, and she is indifferent to the other features.

Recommendation Process

In our approach, the overall model of a recommendation session is logically divided into three phases: 1) initialization, 2) interaction and adaptation, and 3) retaining, as shown in Figure 1. Given a user's request for a product recommendation, the system builds the initial representation of the user's query. Then, the system finds the products most suitable to the initial query, and recommends them to the user. Given these recommendations the user can browse and evaluate them. Then the user may critique the recommended products, e.g., "This product is too expensive for me". This user's evaluation helps the system to adapt (update) the current understanding of the user's needs and preferences encoded in the user-query representation. These two steps, i.e., the system's recommendation and the user's critiquing, iterate until when the user is satisfied with one of the recommended products or when she terminates the session with no product selection. At the end of the session, the system records the current recommendation session for future exploitations.

Hence, a recommendation session starts when a user asks for a product suggestion (Figure 2a) and ends when the user selects a product or when she quits the system. A recommendation session evolves in cycles. In a recommendation cycle, MobyRek shows a ranked list of recommended products (Figure 2b) that the user can browse and criticize (Figure 2c), and the cycle ends when a new recommendation list is requested and shown.

At the beginning of the recommendation session, MobyRek and MapMobyRek offer the user three options for search initialization (Figure 2a).

- "*No, use my profile*". To let the system automatically construct the initial search query.
- "*Let me specify*". To let the user explicitly specify some initial preferences.
- "*Similar to*". To let the user specify a known product, which the user has consumed

Figure 1. The recommendation process

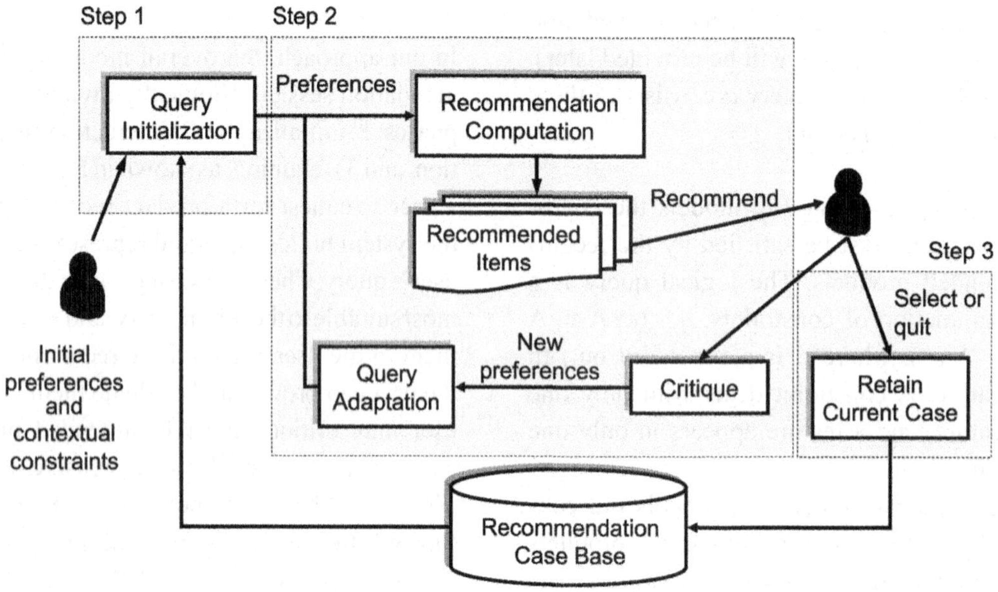

previously, as the starting point of the system's search.

Once the user selects an initialization option, the system builds the initial query (q^0) exploiting multiple knowledge sources of users-related data, including a) the current user's space-time information, b) the current user's previous products' selections, c) the past selections of other users of the system, and d) the current user's initial preferences, explicitly specified at the beginning of the interaction with the system. Basically, the initial logical query (q_l^0) is built based on the user's space-time constraints and initial preferences stated as a must-have option. The initial favorite pattern (p^0) is built by integrating the user's long-term preferences pattern, the characteristics of the product that was selected in a past case that is most similar to the current case, and the initial preferences of the current user stated as a wish-have conditions. The initial feature weights vector (w^0) is built by exploiting data collected in previous user's interactions with the system. The details of the query representation initialization are discussed in (Nguyen & Ricci, 2004; Ricci & Nguyen, 2007).

The initial query (q^0) is then used by the system to compute the first recommendation list. In the computation of the recommendation list, the system first filters out those products that do not satisfy the logical query (q_l), and then ranks the remaining products according to their similarity to the (p, w), i.e., the favorite pattern and the feature weights vector, respectively. The ranking is done so that the more similar to (p, w) a product is the higher that product appears in the ranked list of MobyRek. A product's similarity score is computed as described in Equation (1). It is 1, i.e., the maximum value for similarity, minus the generalized weighted Euclidean distance, $d(x,p,w)$, between the product x and the favorite pattern p, using the weights in the vector w:

$$sim(x,p,w) = 1 - d(x,p,w) = 1 - \frac{\sum_{i=1}^{n} w_i d(x_i, p_i)}{\sum_{i=1}^{n} w_i} \tag{1}$$

where $d(x_i, p_i)$ is the distance (dissimilarity) between product x and the favorite pattern p with

Figure 2. MobyRek user interface

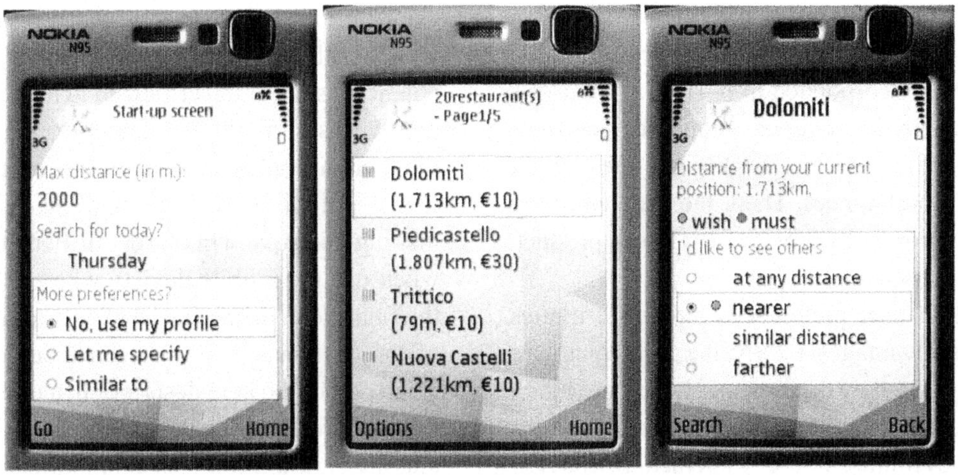

(a) (b) (c)

respect to feature f_i, and w_i is the importance weight of feature f_i.

In the computation of the recommendation list, if no products in the catalogue satisfy the logical query (q_l), then the system attempts to discard the minimum number of constraints for making the query satisfiable, i.e., such that the new relaxed query returns a non-empty set of items. In this procedure, which is a kind of constraint relaxation, a constraint involving a less important feature is eliminated before another involving a more important one. The relaxed constraints are then converted to wish conditions and incorporated in the favorite pattern *p*.

When MobyRek shows the recommendation list to the user (Figure 2b), for each recommended product the system also displays the product's basic information (i.e., name, average cost, and distance) together with an icon (on the left of the restaurant's name) that provides a hint about how close the product matches the user's preferences. Looking at the recommendation list, the user could quickly understand the "appropriateness" of the recommended product. Moreover, to inform the user of the number of available options matching her preferences, the system displays this number on top of the screen . In MobyRek the recommendation list is divided into "pages" so that the number of products displayed on one page fits the mobile device's screen size.

Given the recommendation list shown to the user (Figure 2b), if she is satisfied with a recommended product, the user can select and save it for future reference, and the session ends successfully. However, if the user is somewhat interested in, but not completely satisfied with, a recommended product, then she can criticize that product to express her additional preferences on the unsatisfactory feature values (Figure 2c) or to indicate that some product feature is more important for her (e.g., "I like to have lunch in an air-conditioned room"). When making a critique, the user is supported by the GUI to express the strength of the preference implied in that critique, i.e., as a must or a wish condition. This helps the system to correctly exploit the user's critique, i.e., whether to focus on a certain part of the product repository (by using the must conditions) or to refine the products' ranking (by using the wish conditions). In particular, a critique stated as a must is incorporated in q_p, whereas a critique stated as a wish is incorporated in p. Hence, the user's critiques help the system to adapt the query representation, i.e., refining its previous guess about the user's preferences. Then, the adapted query representation is used by the system to produce a new recommendation list.

Eliciting user preferences through critiques has some advantages. Firstly, the preferences are explicitly stated by the user, and hence, are much more reliable than those implicitly collected, for instance, by mining the user's interaction behavior. Secondly, the user effort to make a critique is low, as compared to other methods using interviews or early ratings. In practice, a critique to a recommended product is done simply by a few button clicks (Figure 2c). Finally, compared to the explicit request to specify preferences, the request to criticize a real product is more convincing, because in the latter approach the system first provides some immediate benefit to the user showing some recommendations and motivating the user to further reveal her preferences, and only after that it requires the user to provide additional input (critique). All these considerations convinced us to conjecture that critiquing could be a viable and preferred approach to collect user preferences in a mobile application.

We note that our critiquing approach is different in several aspects from others that were developed primarily for web applications. For instance, in the notable approaches used by Burke(2002); and McGinty & Smyth (2006) the criticized item defines the new user-query, i.e., at the next interaction the items closer in similarity to the criticized item are retrieved, and the user's critique on a specific feature is used as a constraint to reduce the number of items retrieved. Conversely in our approach the query is modified incorporating the user critique and the selected item is just used to elicit the user preference encoded in a critique. The rationale of our choice, which departs from these more common approaches, is based on the peculiar characteristics of the mobile usage environment. In fact, in these approaches, by transferring all the characteristics of the criticized item into the user query, it is implicitly assumed, or required, that the user has looked at many of the recommended items, and all of the features of an item, before making a critique. This is very difficult to achieve when using a mobile device, where, because of the small screen, one can have only a partial view of the critiqued item, and can focus only on a small part of the item description, namely just the critiqued feature. Finally, in our approach, when making a critique, the user is supported to indicate the preference strength (i.e., wish or must) of the critique; and this functionality is not provided by other critique-based RSs.

When a recommendation session finishes, it is retained as a case in the system's case base for future references (Aamodt & Plaza, 1994). In this way, the past recommendation sessions can be exploited by the system in making new recommendations for the future users as described by Nguyen & Ricci (2008b).

VISUALIZATION AND INTERACTION ISSUES IN MOBYREK'S USER INTERFACE

The proposed recommendation methodology has been implemented in MobyRek, a restaurant RS for mobile travelers. A live-user evaluation of MobyRek showed that it can effectively support mobile users in finding their desired travel products (Ricci & Nguyen, 2007).

However, that live-user evaluation, and some further analysis pointed out the following limitations of the MobyRek's user interface.

- *User perception of the influence of a critique on the new recommendation list.* After making a critique, it might be difficult for the user to get an immediate feedback of 1) how the expressed critique has influenced (changed) the ranking of the recommended items, or 2) the inclusion of new recommendations, or 3) the elimination of items that were previously recommended. To determine which items lose/gain higher/ lower recommendation score, and consequently their rank, in MobyRek the user must remember the previous recommendation list (i.e., that produced in the previous cycle). This is clearly quite difficult, and the result is that users feel unsure about the changes produced by their input and the system looses transparency.

- *Clear perception of the restaurant's distance from the user's position.* When a user is on the go, it is very important to illustrate how far the recommended venues are from the user's current position. In MobyRek, it is difficult for the user to get an immediate understanding of the position of the recommended restaurants. In fact, the user, in order to evaluate this aspect, must scroll down the recommendation list and compare the recommended items' distances to her position, as it is displayed close to the name of the restaurant (Figure 2b).
- *Inconvenience and difficulties in accessing an item's description.* In MobyRek, a user may find it inconvenient to access an item appearing in a long recommendation list. For instance, if a user is interested in a recommended item and, after browsing other recommendations, decides to come back to see that item, she must remember its position in the list, or its name.
- *Items comparison.* Given a list of recommended items, a user may be uncertain of the choice between two or more items. In such a situation, a system function providing item-to-item comparison could help the user in identifying the most appropriate items. This useful function, however, is not supported by MobyRek.

To overcome these limitations and increase the usability of MobyRek, we developed an extended system called MapMobyRek that provides the following new features.

- *Map-based visualization of the recommendations.* In MapMobyRek, the recommended items are shown as objects placed on a map (Figures 3a, 4a). The map interface supports typical electronic map features, such as zooming in/out or panning up/down/left/right. On the map, a user can easily perceive the recommended items' relative distance from the user's position, and can easily access any of the recommended items.
- *Color-encoded representation of the item's recommendation level.* Instead of showing in a ranked list the recommended items, as in MobyRek, MapMobyRek uses a range of colors to show the predicted degree of suitability of the recommended items. The colors range is red-orange-yellow-green, where the best recommendations are shown in green and the worst in red. In other words, the ranked list produced by the recommendation algorithm is divided into four parts, where the highest ranking items are encoded in green, those ranked lower are encoded in yellow, and so on. Smiley icons, shown on the top of the mobile screen, help the user understand the meaning of these colors (Figures 3a, 4a). We believe that these visual clues of the recommendation score are easier to grasp, and provides better support for filtering items; the user can easily focus on the green-colored (and yellow-colored) items if she wants to rely on the filtering provided by the recommendation algorithm.
- *Visualization of the influence of a critique on the next recommendations.* As discussed in the previous section, in our recommendation methodology a critique

stated as a must condition changes the recommendation list, i.e., some new items may be recommended whereas some previously recommended items may be removed. On the contrary, a critique stated as a wish condition only changes the ranking of the recommended items. In MapMobyRek, the influence of the user critique is visualized immediately and intuitively on the map.

In fact, after the user has made a wish critique, MapMobyRek gradually changes the colors of the icons on the map (from red to green, or from green to red) and draws an arrow (upward or downward) on each recommended item to show the change (increase or decrease) of its recommendation level (Figure 3b). Moreover, the system displays a progress bar showing the progress of display update (above the wish critique).

After the user has expressed a must critique, some previously recommended items may not satisfy the new condition, and hence these should be removed from the map. MapMobyRek shows this by using an animation that gradually reduces the size of the icons of the removed items until they disappear. Similarly, MapMobyRek attracts the attention of the

Figure 3. MapMobyRek user interface

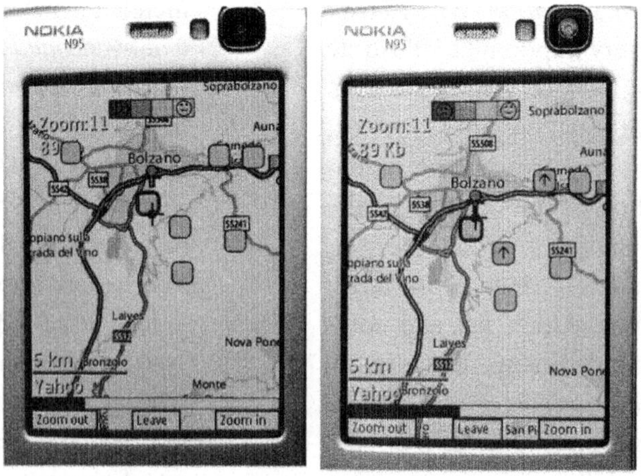

(a) (b)

Figure 4. MapMobyRek user interface

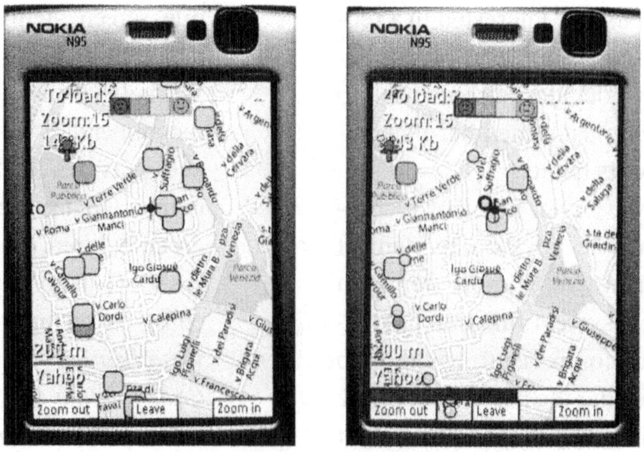

(a) (b)

Figure 5. Items comparison functionality

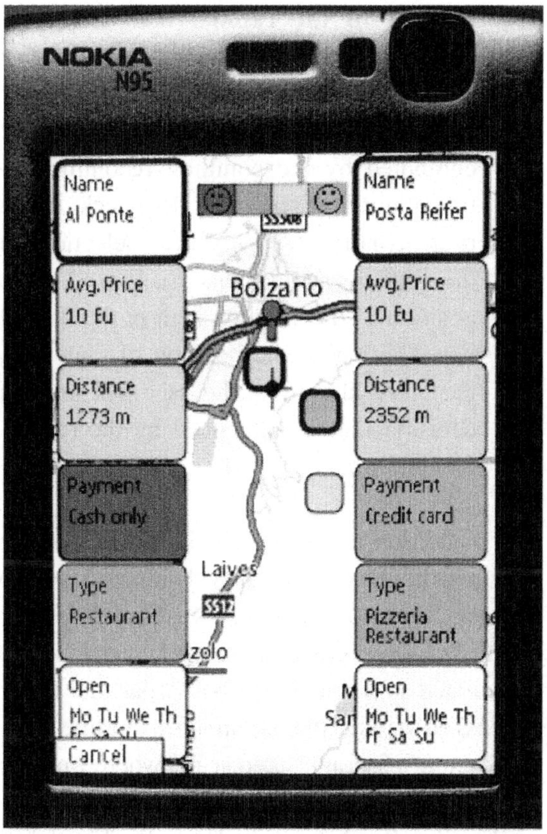

user on the new recommended items by gradually increasing their icon size up to the final standard dimension. When updating the display upon a must critique, the system displays a progress bar showing the progress of the display update.

- *Items comparison functionality*. During the interaction with MapMobyRek a user can compare two interesting items. After she has selected the two items, their characteristics are displayed side-by-side on the screen; so their advantages and disadvantages can be easily compared ( ).

As described earlier, MobyRek and MapMobyRek implement the same recommendation methodology and ranking algorithm; however, they utilize different user interfaces. This is important because any measured difference in the users' evaluation must be tracked back to the changes in the graphical user interface (i.e., list-based vs. map-based).

To implement map visualization in MapMobyRek we used J2meMap (a freeware library for Java MIDP applications, available on http://j2memap.landspurg.net/) that allows the management and display of map-related content. For displaying graphical objects as an overlay on the map, we exploited the J2ME SVG (Scalable Vector Graphics) library for drawing various geometrical shapes and text objects.

EMPIRICAL EVALUATION

In this section, we present the live-user evaluation of MapMobyRek that we conducted in February, 2008. This test was aimed at comparing MobyRek and MapMobyRek with respect to the recommendation effectiveness and the system usability. We first state the research hypotheses and the test procedure, and then we present and discuss the test results.

The Research Hypotheses and the Test Procedure

Based on the features incorporated in MapMobyRek we hypothesize that MapMobyRek, as compared to MobyRek, provides the following benefits:

- increased system usability and user satisfaction,
- reduced interaction length, i.e., the number of recommendation cycles produced by user critiques,
- reduced the time to complete the user task, i.e., finding a suitable product in a particular context of usage, and
- MapMobyRek users tend to rely more

on the recommendation score computed by the system and choose the items with higher score, i.e., with a green color.These are the top ranked items as computed by the recommendation algorithm ((Ricci & Nguyen, 2007).

To validate our research hypotheses we ran a user study, which involved twenty testers, using a mobile phone (Nokia N95) with both MobyRek and MapMobyRek installed. 18 testers were male and 2 female; most of them were aged below 30 with only 3 testers above that age. In this experiment each tester was asked to use both systems, MobyRek and MapMobyRek, and to express her subjective opinions. Each tester used both systems, one after the other, to find her desired restaurant and add it to her travel notes. The travel notes are a container for the selected travel products, services, and information that the user can easily access and consult. The order in which the two systems were used was assigned randomly to compensate any learning effect. In fact, it could be easily guessed that the users will perform the task better with the latter system, as they will get more familiar with the product domain and the task itself.

In the comparative evaluation of the two systems, we collected some objective and subjective measures. The objective measures consisted of:

- **Average interaction length**. This is the average number of recommendation cycles, where a cycle is defined by the application of a critique. This is an important metric to consider, since if the two systems give the same user satisfaction, one must prefer the system that enables to complete the task quicker.
- **Average time required to complete the task**. This is the elapsed time of the user-system interaction. The motivation for considering this metric is similar to that mentioned above for the interaction length metric.
- **Average position of the selected restaurant in the ranked list**. The color encoding the recommendation score of a recommended restaurant is computed by considering its position in the ranked list computed by the common recommendation algorithm. In order to check if the user actually based her item selection on the system's suggestions, we looked at the position of the selected item in the ranked list. The higher the position of that item, the more likely that the user will make a decision that is influenced by the recommender system.

In addition to these objective measures, we obtained the subjective user evaluations of the two systems. The tester, after she has used each system, was asked to complete a usability questionnaire articulated in Table 1). In particular, the tester was asked to judge the statements in the questionnaire using a 5-point Likert scale, where 1 means "strongly disagree" and 5 "strongly agree".

Finally, after the users had tested both systems, they were asked to complete a final questionnaire

Table 1. The usability questionnaire

Statement	Description
S1	It was simple to use this system.
S2	It was easy to find the information I needed.
S3	The information (such as on-screen messages, and other documentation) provided by this system was clear.
S4	It was easy to learn to use this system.
S5	The information is effective in helping me complete the task and scenario.
S6	The interface of this system is pleasant.
S7	I found it easy to understand what the best recommended items are.
S8	I found it useful to criticize a restaurant and get new offers.
S9	This system has all the functions and capabilities I expected.
S10	Overall, I am satisfied with this system.

Table 2. The final preference questionnaire.

Question	Description
Q1	What system do you find more informative?
Q2	What system has the better interface?
Q3	What system do you find more useful?
Q4	What system do you prefer?

to express their preference between MobyRek and MapMobyRek based on the questions listed in Table 2. We observe that a similar test approach has been used in the experiment discussed by Reilly et al. (2007). This questionnaire asks the user to compare the two systems along the following dimensions: informativeness (Q1), user interface (Q2), usefulness (Q3), and overall preference (Q4).

The Test Results

In addition to the quoted measure we logged all the testers' actions when interacting with both systems. By mining the log file, which recorded the testers' recommendation sessions data, we found that for both systems, the majority of the testers could find their desired restaurant within 2-3 recommendation cycles. Furthermore, the average interaction length, i.e., the average number of recommendation cycles in each recommendation session, for MapMobyRek was 17% shorter than that for MobyRek (Figure 6), which proves our hypothesis that MapMobyRek improves (reduces) the interaction time.

Regarding the average time needed to accomplish the task, the user interaction with MapMobyRek was 1.43 minutes longer than with MobyRek (Figure 7). This result contradicts our hypothesis that users can accomplish the task faster with MapMobyRek than with MobyRek. However, we observed that with MapMobyRek the time required to download the maps on the phone caused significant delays. Hence, as the previous result on the interaction length illustrates, this increased task completion time was not due to additional interactions, or cognitive load on the user; therefore, it could be reduced by a better implementation of the map management functionality. In fact, in the future we plan to use caching techniques to avoid repeated downloading of the same map data.

The average position of the selected item in the final recommendation list is an indication of the goodness of the ranking algorithm. In other words, if the user on average selects higher ranking items, i.e., those mapped to the green color, then either the user agrees with the recommendation, or she is influenced by the system and follows its suggestion. The average position of the selected restaurant was high, 2.65 for MobyRek and 2.3 for MapMobyRek (Figure 8). This is quite surprising, given the fact that MapMobyRek does not show precisely the items' positions in the recommendation list, and just uses a rough scale (4 levels corresponding to the four colors). We explain this by conjecturing that MapMobyRek users

Figure 6. Comparison on the average interaction length in recommendation cycles

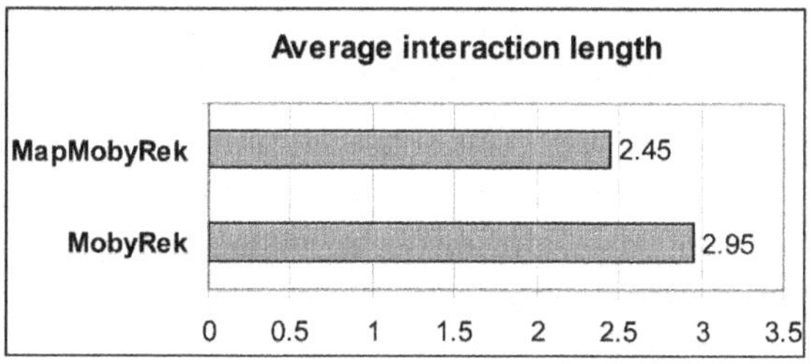

Figure 7. Comparison on the average time to complete the task in minutes and seconds (m:ss)

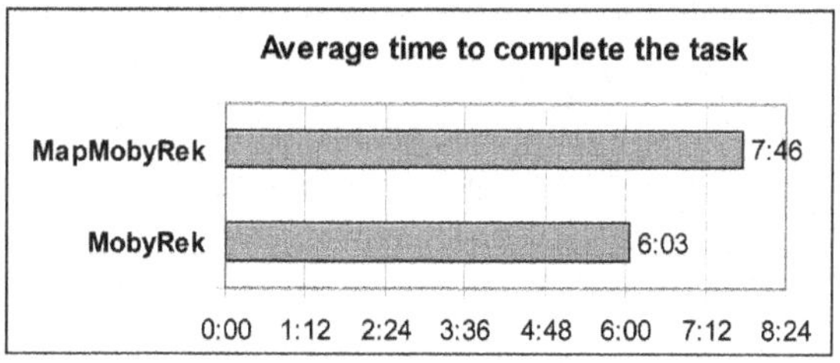

were strongly influenced by the color encoding and that MapMobyRek users selected the "green" restaurants on the maps more often than MobyRek users selected the top restaurants in the ranked lists. This result is quite interesting and suggests that the user interface for a mobile application should be different from those used, and even validated for the corresponding web-based information service.

Figure 9 shows a comparison of the testers' average rating for the statements contained in the usability questionnaire. As shown in Figure 9, both systems received a positive evaluation. However, overall MapMobyRek received higher evaluations than MobyRek on all the inspected dimensions. We performed a two-tailed, paired t-test, of statistical significance on each statement's result. We found that the significant differences between the two systems relate to the statements S2, S3, S6, S7, S9, and S10. This implies that MapMobyRek provides an easier information search tool, it has a clearer information display and a more pleasant interface, it is more transparent for the users, it has a richer set of system functionalities, and it is generally preferred by the users. Nonetheless, with respect to some statements, such as S1 and S8, there is no significant difference between the two systems. For instance, the result for statement S8 ("it is useful to criticize a restaurant and get new offers") shows that the map-based interface does not change the user evaluation on this aspect. This is a reasonable conclusion and provides a counter check, since the same critiquing functionality (and the same user interface for critiquing) is implemented in both systems.

In the final questionnaire we asked each tester to vote for the preferred system. The comparative results show that almost all the testers stated that the map-based system is better than the list-based one in terms of usefulness, interface and informativeness (Figure 10). Hence, overall we can conclude that MapMobyRek represents a step ahead for mobile RSs, and its main characteristic, i.e., of being based on a map-based display, should be used as the basis for future developments.

Figure 8. Comparison on the average position of the selected restaurant

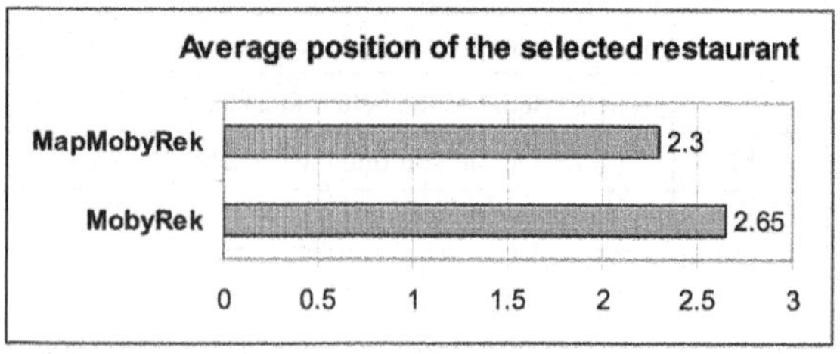

Figure 9. Comparison on the statements in the usability questionnaire

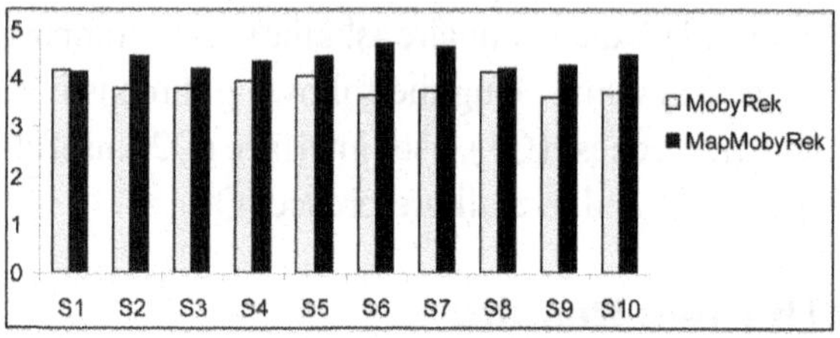

Figure 10. Comparison on the questions in the final preference questionnaire

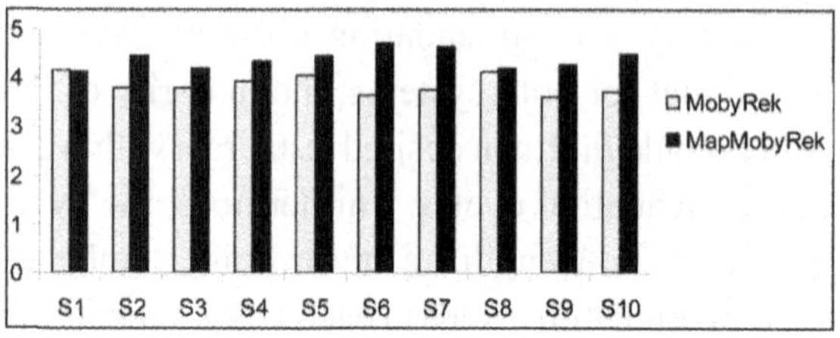

FUTURE WORK

Notwithstanding the success of this research, there are several open issues that can be further investigated for applying the proposed solutions to other systems and in other application contexts. Firstly, we did not investigate how different mappings of rank values to colors could influence the user decision. It would be interesting to analyze to what extent we can push the extension of "green" items (i.e., strongly recommended), and how an overabundance of "green" items can influence the user decision. This touches a fundamental issue of RSs, i.e., whether this technology really offers to the user a tool for making better decisions or the effects of recommendations must be considered as manipulations of the user preference, i.e., the recommender system just persuades the user that the recommended items are suitable for her (Gretzel & Fesenmaier, 2005).

The second aspect that requires a better analysis relates to the fact that in MapMobyRek the user cannot review the recommendation lists produced in previous cycles. In fact, it could be helpful if the system records the recommendation states and supports the user (with an "undo" or "review" button) to view a previous recommendation state.

The third aspect relates to the system's user interface. MapMobyRek, by presenting the recommended items on the map, is very useful in helping users perceive the geographical relations between the items. Notwithstanding that MapMobyRek supports users to understand the items' recommendation level using a color encoding, it cannot visualize fine-grained differences of the match of the items to the user's preferences. For example, in Figures 3a and 4a the user cannot know how well the yellow-colored items match with her preferences. Moreover, the ranked-list style has been often used in RSs, and it is still liked by some users. Hence, it would be beneficial for the users if a RS can support both types of interface (i.e., map- and ranked list-based) and provides a menu function for users to switch between these two types of interface during their interaction with the system.

Finally, an important topic for further investigations is how to integrate recommendations for different product types (e.g., restaurant, hotel, activities, etc.) so that the system can suggest them as a single travel package. This would be very important for a real commercial implementation of the system, and would open the road to dynamic packaging of mobile commerce.

CONCLUSION

In this chapter we have presented an approach for integrating recommendation and electronic map technologies to build a map-based mobile recommender system that can effectively and intuitively provide personalized travel suggestions to mobile users. Our system cope with the information overload problem, e.g., which is produced by the large number of restaurants available in a city, by providing a user with personalized restaurant recommendations, i.e., a well chosen selection of restaurants. The information about the restaurants is contained in a Web repository, and the system recommendations are adapted to the user's needs and preferences in the particular mobile usage context. Our recommendation approach integrates a conversational preference acquisition technology based on "critiquing" with map visualization technologies to build a new map-based conversational mobile RS that can effectively and intuitively support travelers in finding their desired products and services.

Our real-user study showed that the map-based interface is more effective than the traditional list-based interface that was typically used in RSs so far. We also found that the integration of a map-based interface in an RS increases user satisfaction, with the only additional cost of a slightly longer recommendation session.

This work provides a clear example of the fact that mobile recommender systems deserve specific methods and technologies. They cannot be simply engineered with techniques that have been proved to be successful in the wired Web applications. The user mobility, the device mobility and the wireless networking technology have a profound impact on the user task and on the system usage and they all deserve special and careful attention in order to develop effective solutions for the user information needs.

REFERENCES

Aamodt, A., & Plaza, E. (1994). Case-based reasoning: Foundational issues, methodological variations, and system approaches. *AI Communications*, *7*(1), 39–59.

Adomavicius, G., & Tuzhilin, A. (2005). Toward the next generation of recommender systems: A survey of the state-of-the-art and possible extensions. *IEEE Transactions on Knowledge and Data Engineering*, *17*(6), 734–749. doi:10.1109/TKDE.2005.99

Averjanova, O., Ricci, F., & Nguyen, Q. N. (2008). Map-based interaction with a conversational mobile recommender system. In *Proceedings of the 2nd International Conference on Mobile Ubiquitous Computing, Systems, Services and Technologies*.

Baus, J., Cheverst, K., & Kray, C. (2005). A survey of map-based mobile guides. In L. Meng, A. Zipf, & T. Reichenbacher (Eds.), *Map-based mobile services: Theories, methods and implementations* (pp. 193-209). Berlin, Germany: Springer.

Bridge, D., Göker, M., McGinty, L., & Smyth, B. (2005). Case-based recommender systems. *The Knowledge Engineering Review*, *20*(3), 315–320. doi:10.1017/S0269888906000567

Brown, B., Chalmers, M., Bell, M., Hall, M., MacColl, I., & Rudman, P. (2005). Sharing the square: Collaborative leisure in the city streets. In *Proceedings of the 9th European Conference on Computer Supported Cooperative Work* (pp. 427-447).

Burigat, S., Chittaro, L., & De Marco, L. (2005). Bringing dynamic queries to mobile devices: A visual preference-based search tool for tourist decision support. In *Proceedings of the 10th IFIP TC13 International Conference on Human-Computer Interaction* (*INTERACT 2005*) (pp. 213-226).

Burke, R. (2002). Interactive critiquing for catalog navigation in e-commerce. *Artificial Intelligence Review*, *18*(3-4), 245–267. doi:10.1023/A:1020701617138

Burke, R. (2007). Hybrid Web recommender systems. In P. Brusilovsky, A. Kobsa, & W. Nejdl (Eds.), *The adaptive Web: Methods and strategies of Web personalization* (pp. 377-408). Heidelberg, Germany: Springer.

Dunlop, M. D., Elsey, B., & Montgomery Masters, M. (2007). Dynamic visualisation of ski data: A context aware mobile piste map. In *Proceedings of the 9th International Conference on Human Computer Interaction with Mobile Devices and Services* (*Mobile HCI 2007*) (pp. 211-214).

Dunlop, M. D., Morrison, A., McCallum, S., Ptaskinski, P., Risbey, C., & Stewart, F. (2004). Focussed Palmtop information access combining Starfield displays with profile-based recommendations. In *Proceedings of Workshop on Mobile and Ubiquitous Information Access* (pp. 79-89).

Fesenmaier, D. R., Werthner, H., & Wöber, K. (Eds.). (2006). *Destination recommendation systems: Behavioral foundations and applications*. London: CAB International.

Gretzel, U., & Fesenmaier, D. (2005). Persuasiveness of preference elicitation processes in destination recommendation systems. In *Proceedings of the 12th International Conference on Information and Communication Technologies in Travel and Tourism* (*ENTER 2005*) (pp. 194-204).

McGinty, L., & Smyth, B. (2006). Adaptive selection: An analysis of critiquing and preference-based feedback in conversational recommender systems. *International Journal of Electronic Commerce*, *11*(2), 35–57. doi:10.2753/JEC1086-4415110202

Meng, L., Zipf, A., & Winter, S. (2008). *Map-based mobile services: Design, interaction and usability*. Berlin, Germany: Springer.

Mohapatra, D., & Suma, S. B. (2005). Survey of location based wireless services. In *Proceedings of the 2005 IEEE International Conference on Personal Wireless Communications* (pp. 358-362).

Nguyen, Q. N., & Ricci, F. (2004). User preferences initialization and integration in critique-based mobile recommender systems. *Proceedings of the 5th International Workshop on Artificial Intelligence in Mobile Systems*, 71-78.

Nguyen, Q. N., & Ricci, F. (2007). Replaying live-user interactions in the off-line evaluation of critique-based mobile recommendations. In *Proceedings of the 2007 ACM Conference on Recommender Systems* (pp. 81-88).

Nguyen, Q. N., & Ricci, F. (2008a). Long-term and session-specific user preferences in a mobile recommender system. In *Proceedings of the 2008 International Conference on Intelligent User Interfaces* (pp. 381-384).

Nguyen, Q. N., & Ricci, F. (2008b). Conversational case-based recommendations exploiting a structured case model. In *Proceedings of the 9th European Conference on Case-Based Reasoning*.

Park, M. H., Hong, J. H., & Cho, S. B. (2007). Location-based recommendation system using Bayesian user's preference model in mobile devices. In *Proceedings of the 4th International Conference on Ubiquitous Intelligence and Computing* (pp. 1130-1139).

Pospischil, G., Umlauft, M., & Michlmayr, E. (2002). Designing LoL@, a mobile tourist guide for UMTS. In *Proceedings of the 4th International Conference on Human Computer Interaction with Mobile Devices and Services* (*Mobile HCI 2002*) (pp. 140-154).

Pourret, O., Naïm, P., & Marcot, B. (2008). *Bayesian networks: A practical guide to applications*. New York: Wiley.

Reilly, J., Zhang, J., McGinty, L., Pu, P., & Smyth, B. (2007). Evaluating compound critiquing recommenders: A real-user study. In *Proceedings of the 2007 ACM Conference on Electronic Commerce* (pp. 114-123).

Resnick, P., & Varian, H. R. (1997). Recommender systems. *Communications of the ACM, 40*(3), 56–58. doi:10.1145/245108.245121

Ricci, F. (2002). Travel recommender systems. *IEEE Intelligent Systems, 17*(6), 55–57.

Ricci, F., & Nguyen, Q. N. (2007). Acquiring and revising preferences in a critique-based mobile recommender system. *IEEE Intelligent Systems, 22*(3), 22–29. doi:10.1109/MIS.2007.43

Steinfield, C. (2004). The development of location based services in mobile commerce. In B. Preissl, H. Bouwman, & C. Steinfield (Eds.), *E-Life after the dot com bust* (pp. 177-197). New York: Springer.

ten Hagen, K., Kramer, R., Hermkes, M., Schumann, B., & Mueller, P. (2005). Semantic matching and heuristic search for a dynamic tour guide. In *Proceedings of the 12th International Conference on Information and Communication Technologies in Travel and Tourism* (*ENTER 2005*) (pp. 149-159).f

Section 2
Social Communities in E-Tourism

Chapter 6
A Study of Web 2.0 Tourism Sites:
A Usability and Web Features Perspective

Carmine Sellitto
Victoria University, Australia

Stephen Burgess
Victoria University, Australia

Carmen Cox
Bond University, Australia

Jeremy Buultjens
Southern Cross University, Australia

ABSTRACT

The term Web 2.0 was coined around 2004 and was used to describe more interactive types of websites developed after the dot-com crash. An important characteristic of Web 2.0 sites is premised on being able to incorporate various technologies and applications within the site to enhance functionality. This enhanced functionality is primarily associated with such sites being able to publish and display diverse content— content that is user-contributed, or where the site might draw information synergistically from a third party. This increased functionality potentially affects two traditional areas of website implementation. Firstly, the embedding of applications within a website tends to increase design complexity that can contribute to a detrimental user experience when browsing— in turn, affecting website usability. Secondly, Web 2.0 sites in allowing users to publish, display and list diverse views, opinions, pictures, sounds, and so forth, will impact content and design features that are not encountered on traditional websites. Consequently, this chapter investigates a set of Web 2.0 tourism sites for their usability as well as reporting an overview of website content encountered. In examining these issues the paper provides a background primer on the advent of Web 2.0 sites, novel aspects of their design, including the potential for incorporating user content. Tourism sites are the focus of this chapter— both commercial and non-commercial Web 2.0 sites being of interest.

DOI: 10.4018/978-1-60566-818-5.ch006

INTRODUCTION

Tourism is an information-based and information-intensive industry (Werthner & Ricci, 2004)—with tourism promotion and documentation being well suited to the Internet environment. Indeed, travellers using websites plan and purchase their travel is arguably now the norm, whereby the Internet "has become one of the most successful channels used by consumers to research travel options, compare prices and make reservations" (Collins, Buhalis & Peters, 2003, p. 484). This type of information seeking behaviour tends to result in a higher involvement of customers in the planning process (Buhalis, 1999) of which the Internet becomes an integral part.

In recent times many Web 2.0 sites have been implemented within the tourism sphere. These Web 2.0 travel sites involve the use of a diverse range of presentation formats—text, video, images and sound—with some formats having functionality that allows a website user to contribute, update or alter existing content.

The information that is posted on Web 2.0 sites is known as user-generated-content (UGC)— a feature that delineates such sites from the older, more traditional websites that have been referred to as Web 1.0 (O'Reilly, 2005). Arguably, the opportunity available to individuals to post content on such sites is an important value-adding feature.

The emergence of Web 2.0 sites in the tourism domain allow the visitor to potentially access a greater variety of information from a myriad of sources about all aspects of travel. With respect to travel and tourism content, these UGC sites have also been referred to as Travel 2.0 sites (Merritt, 2006)— a term that reflects industry-specific activities and one that can be applied to the broad information content that is associated with the latest tourism websites.

Indeed, Web 2.0 can be viewed as a general term, and a noted trend is to refer to these newer forms of websites with a domain-focussed terminology— a terminology that attempts to define a more specific application sphere. Hence, different authors have used terms such as Library 2.0 (Bolan, Canada, & Cullin, 2007), Mobile-web 2.0 (Yamakami, 2007), Enterprise 2.0 (Knight, 2007) and Semantic Web 2.0 (Greaves, 2007) when referring to a specific industry area or domain.

An important aspect of Web 2.0 sites is premised on their ability to embed applications within the site to enhance functionality— functionality that allows users to contribute content, or to draw synergistically from third-party content. With respect to past website design and usability, the embedding of applications within a website tends to add a degree of complexity that can result in a sub-optimal user experience when browsing (Nielsen, 2007). Given the high degree of application functionality that Web 2.0 sites incorporate, they may not address or embrace aspects of the traditional user interface design— website interfaces that were developed and refined in the Web 1.0 era and have been generally based on good design practice.

This chapter explores and investigates a set of Web 2.0 oriented tourism websites and their usability based on Nielsen's approach for usability evaluation. Moreover, given that Web 2.0 sites are deemed to allow new and potentially different forms of online presence, the study also presents an overview of some of the identified website components associated with these tourism sites.

The structure of the chapter is as follows. Firstly, a background section describes the advent of the Web 2.0 phenomena with respect to website features, design elements and typical content that might be encountered on such sites. The next section of the chapter deals with how tourism entities have come to use various Web 2.0 related features— features that includes blogs (web-logs), wikis, podcasts and social networks. A small section on website usability and design follows, before another component of the chapter describes how the study was undertaken (methodology). The last section of the chapter discusses the results of the study, the implications of findings,

Table 1. Web 1.0 and 2.0 comparison (adapted from O'Reilly (2005)

Web 1.0	Web 2.0
DoubleClick	Google AdSense
mp3.com	Napster
Britannica Online	Wikipedia
Personal Websites	Blogging
Domain Name Speculation	Search engine optimization
Page Views	Cost per click
Screen Scraping	Web services
Publishing	Participation
Content Management Systems	Wikis
Directories (taxonomy)	Tagging ("folksonomy")
Stickiness	Syndication

before documenting the salient conclusions of the research. The chapter includes the important areas identified for future research.

BACKGROUND

The term Web 2.0 was coined around 2004 when O'Reilly and MediaLive International commenced using the moniker to describe the new types of websites that manage to survive the dot-com crash (O'Reilly, 2005). These websites tended to be associated with mature applications that allowed increased user-functionality. As a consequence of this increased website functionality, visitors to a site have an opportunity to contribute an array of UGC through different media types— be they text, video, sound or a hybrid of these forms.

Any application that allows a user to create and update website content can be viewed as being part of the Web 2.0 phenomenon (Lin, 2007). Indeed, the names of many Web 2.0 associated features have now entered the everyday lexicon and include web-blogs (blogs), wikis, syndication (RSS), mashups and many others— features that have an ever increasing influence over transforming the web environment (Gillmor, 2008).

The concept of Web 2.0 is well established and one that reflects the popularity of interactive information content in contrast to websites that provided static information sources (Newitz, 2008). Moreover, some of the popular Web 2.0 sites such as Facebook® and MySpace® are well known through their overt media coverage.

Just as Web 2.0 can be a reference to new types of websites that have appeared post dot-com bust, the old types or traditionally implemented websites are referred to as Web 1.0 sites. O' Reilly (2005), initially characterised the different aspects of Web 1.0 and 2.0 sites— this comparison can be based on functionality, underlying website development principles, or even the names of companies associated with the site's conception. Table 1 provides a comparison of some of the Web 1.0 and Web 2.0 characteristics.

Lin (2007) further suggests that although Web 2.0 features and applications are important, the technology can be viewed as being secondary, with such websites needing to be simple and provide an interface that is usable by even the less technically savvy. Knight (2007) also identifies and compares different aspects of Web 1.0 and Web 2.0 sites suggesting that the difference is one of higher functionality amongst the newer generation of Web 2.0 sites. Knight also highlights the important marketing value that a social website might provide in that it is a powerful means to disseminate opinions— either complimenting or condemning a product or service. Moreover, the advent of Web 2.0 sites can be used to test new product ideas and provide important feedback that potentially shortens development times for new products or services.

Web 2.0 Sites and Their Design

Lin (2007) advocates that Web 2.0 sites should be systems that are simple to use, scalable and sensible— highlighting that not all web-users are technologically apt and that input design is important. Some of the most desirable features can be described as follows:

- Simplicity associated with Web 2.0 design should be reflected in an interface that provides even the unsophisticated user an opportunity to publish content. The provision of a simple and user-friendly interface precludes discrimination on the basis of technological expertise of some users and can be seen as addressing equal opportunity.
- Scalability of Web 2.0 systems needs to accommodate the web's global presence and provide for universal and geographically disparate user access. Arguably, scalable Web 2.0 design may be assisted through the implementation of accepted and broadly known protocols— allowing access to the broadest audience.
- Sensible Web 2.0 design should also accommodate a range of input, however, it should be balanced so that these are considered sensible by most users.

Lin further relates to several technologies that can contribute to making Web 2.0 interfaces intuitive— amongst them being Ajax, JavaScript, cascading style sheets and extensible HTML. Many of these have also been used in the Web 1.0 era (Knight, 2007)— although not to the extent that is prevalent today.

With respect to website implementation, O'Reilly (2005) identifies a set of Web 2.0 design features that appear to reflect the functional value of Web 2.0 sites and the applications that they embrace. These design characteristics include:

- **The Long Tail:** an observation that reflects that the great majority of smaller websites that form the cornerstone of web's content are an important source for Web 2.0 implementers.
- **Data is the Next Intel Inside:** a design pattern that recognises that Web 2.0 applications should be data-driven and that the greater uniqueness of that data the higher its value.
- **Users Add Value:** embraces the notion that use-generated content is the most important feature of the Web 2.0 phenomenon.
- **Network Effects by Default:** recognises that the contribution of each individual user will only be incremental in improving the data or information value of the site. However, the collective aggregation of all input provides enhanced value for all subsequent users.
- **Some Rights Reserved:** applications should be designed for high flexibility that embraces re-use and re-configuration with minimal restrictions.
- **The Perpetual Beta:** update applications incrementally for maximum user value and to enhance user experience.
- **Cooperate, Don't Control:** Data interaction and integration are a feature of Web 2.0 applications and premised on providing a user service— services that embrace syndication and data re-use.
- **Software Above the Level of a Single Device:** recognise the diverse nature of current and future devices that can be used to deliver Web 2.0 sites— the mobile networked environment is pervasive and becoming the norm.

An examination of these design patterns highlights their potential for use in the development of the different aspects of Web 2.0 functionality that tends to be a defining characteristic of these sites. Arguably, these functional design features do not address or embrace aspects of the traditional user interface design— website interfaces that were developed and refined in the Web 1.0 era and have been generally accepted as being good design practice.

Given the existence of many more Web 1.0 than Web 2.0 sites, it is unlikely that the user preferences for interacting with a user-friendly website interface will have radically altered. Clearly an important consideration when it comes to these newer Web 2.0 sites is the usefulness of their information content and the usability of their interfaces.

The Tourism Industry: Website Content and Emerging Web 2.0 Sites

The adoption of the Internet by the tourism industry has been widely reported. For example, A.M. Morrison, Taylor, A.J. Morrison & A.D. Morrison (1999) investigated Internet adoption by small Scottish hotels reporting that many websites tended to be electronic brochure in nature.

Lituchy and Rail (2000) examined how accommodation providers such as bed and breakfasts (B&Bs) used the Internet and concluded that their websites delivered benefits that included lower marketing costs, immediate customer communication and broader customer reach when compared to traditional media.

Procaccino and Miller (2000) investigated the technical capabilities of US and French-based hotel, museum, restaurant and airline websites associated with marketing, including sales and customer support functionality. The authors concluded that websites of US-based tourism enterprises were technically more proficient when it came to business functionality than comparable French websites.

Lexhagen (2005) reported a customer's perspective of the value-added services provided by the websites of tour operators and travel agencies. As such these website services were perceived to be important by customers, including features that embraced product price comparison before purchase, location maps, email contact, booking forms and search facilities.

Sellitto (2005) identified the website features associated with wine-tourism, concluding that many wineries used their website to promote themselves as tourism entities, rather than for direct wine sales. The winery website features tended to include specific information about tourism activities ancillary to the winery, such as restaurants, accommodation, tours and regional attractions.

Sellitto and Burgess (2007) researched website planning processes amongst small to medium size tourism enterprises (SMTEs) identifying that functional implement ation practices were important when it came to website adoption. Burgess, Sellitto and Karanasios (2009) further document a small business perspective to website adoption and give salient examples of web presence by different tourism enterprises— examples that included bed and breakfast establishments, tour operators, museums and galleries. The authors also report on the use of the Internet amongst small tourism enterprises in Malaysia and Ecuador.

Nusair, Yoon and Parsa (2008) propose that travel website quality is related to improved customer satisfaction. The authors suggest that website visual and emotional appeal, information content and response time are some of the important website quality dimensions that need to be considered to enhance customer satisfaction.

Clearly, much of the previous scholarly literature relating to the perceived value of tourism websites reports from a traditional Web 1.0 viewpoint or approach— Web 2.0 descriptions being nascent. Indeed, the tourism and travel industry appears to have had a varied response to the emergence of Web 2.0 sites and the UGC published on these.

Whilst the general tourist seems to be embracing the concept, constituent elements associated with the travel industry are still somewhat unsure of how to respond to the Web 2.0 phenomenon (Kelly, 2007). Notwithstanding this ambivalence, there appears to be growing interest in facilitating the integration of user-derived information as a component of online tourism sites. This is understandable given the important role that the Internet plays in the information search stage of the traveller's itinerary planning process (Collins et al., 2003) .

Elliott (2008) suggests that tourism Web 2.0 sites incorporate features that include cutting edge technology, interesting website design and creative applications— all features that can potentially entice a critical mass of travellers to use these sites. As previously indicated, Web 2.0 has also been referred to as Travel 2.0 (Merritt, 2006)— whereby such Travel 2.0 sites allow readers to interact in the virtual environment to contribute reviews and images that provide a forum for people to gain insights about aspects of tourism (Breslow-Sardone, 2006).

The delineating elements and features of Web 2.0 sites relate to some of their application-centric user functions. In the tourism sphere, the more commonly encountered Web 2.0 features that appear to have gained acceptance include blogs (web-logs), wikis, podcasts and social networks. It is useful to briefly describe them with some relevant tourism examples (Kolbitsch & Maurer, 2006; Reactive, 2007):

- **Blogs:** These websites allow people to publish their own journal-style text, images and hyperlinks to other entries. Generally the newest posting is listed first with subsequent information threads being listed in reverse chronological order. Examples of travel and tourism-related blogs can be experienced on websites associated with Starwood, Eurostar and STA Travel Australia.
- **Wikis:** These websites allow users to readily contribute new content, edit and/or alter existing content to suit individual preferences. The wiki environment is particularly conducive to collaboration between contributors and can strengthen the underlying information that is published. Examples of wikis include the Wikitravel website that embodies a freely created and reliable worldwide travel guide. World66 is another example of how the wiki feature can be used, allowing users to read and edit travel information.
- **Podcasts:** Podcasting is an activity that allows the recording and/or distribution of audio using the website as the primary access point. In terms of travel and tourism, these podcasts allow a website to facilitate an audible experience for the potential tourist about a place, environment or destination. Indeed, the online travel guidebooks, such as Lonely Planet, provide excellent examples of how podcasts can be used with respect to tourism.
- **Social Networks:** These websites promote and encourage relationship development in the virtual environment by those visiting social websites. Some of the leading social networking sites included MySpace® and YouTube®— sites that allowed friends, peers and like-minded individuals to communicate, chat and share information on topics of interest. An emerging aspect of social networks within the tourism sphere is that they enable travellers to contribute and share information that is unbiased and free of marketing so as to inform others. This has a commensurate value of building website loyalty resulting in repeat traveller visits. An example of a travel social website is Driftr®, where individuals are able to share their travel/tourism information amongst the online Driftr® community— potentially allowing members to use this information for their travel plans.

Clearly there is a diverse range of websites emerging that contain UGC related to travel and tourism. These range from generic social networking sites such as MySpace.com which contain travel sections through to individual blogs that have been created by avid travellers to showcase a set of destination reviews to a global audience. As previously indicated, many of these Web 2.0 features tend to be reliant on functional applications being embedded in the website. The technical aspect of the application will be seamless to the user, however, the website's usability and content may deviate from commonly expected features associated with the traditional user interface design.

The next section introduces website usability and design issues as a prelude to reporting on a study that examined a series of tourism Web 2.0 sites for these issues.

Usability and Website Design Features

Formal definitions of website usability have been proposed including one associated with the International Standards Organisation (ISO) that conceptualises usability as a means of providing effectiveness, efficiency and satisfaction with the aim of achieving these goals in a specific environment (Alva, Martínez, Cueva, Sagástegui, & López, 2003). Government agencies advocate good practices when it comes to website usability in an endeavour to improve the general design and navigation features of websites.

Indeed, the US government advocates a step-by-step usability approach to achieving website design that enhances usability and proposes a set of 209 guidelines that addresses several areas—planning, analysis, design, user testing and further website refinement (US-GSA, 2006). The MIT Usability Group (MUG) has proposed website usability guidelines that assist with aspects of navigation, site functionality, accessibility and information content (MIT, 2008).

One of the well documented and easiest approaches to understanding and examining usability has been proposed by usability expert Jakob Nielsen (Nielsen, 2000; Nielsen & Tahir, 2002; Nielsen & Loranger, 2006). Much of Nielsen's works tend to be based on behavioural research and observational studies of the website user and his work appears to have gained widespread acceptance amongst the web development community. Nielsen's (2000) approach tends to be premised on the notion that website usability is associated with features that allow websites to be easy to learn and remember, are reliable and efficient to use, and impart user satisfaction. Thereby improved visitor experience is achieved if it provides the website visitor an effective, efficient and satisfying experience with any aspect of the site. These tenets also embrace some of the fundamental aims of the ISO in their guidelines on usability.

Nielsen and Tahir (2002) have proposed a series of homepage design features that could be used to enhance the usability of the organisational website. The authors highlighted the importance of the home page as a virtual showcase for people when they visit a website. Indeed, an appropriately designed and usable website allows prospective customers and users to gain an initial positive impression of the organisation, as well as being able to effectively access published information. Some 40 recommended design elements were grouped by the authors in order of importance based on a 1, 2 or 3 star rating— with the 3 star design elements being deemed as essential when it came to website design.

The essential design features were associated with website searching, data collection and privacy, avoiding the use of deleterious and non-functional features, and an acceptable web page download time. Arguably, many of these essential design features have, or are becoming, design conventions, and should be incorporated by all website implementation projects— not just on the home page, but throughout the site.

With respect to Web 2.0 sites, it can be assumed that these types of websites will also need to conform to the designated essential usability design recommendations. Hence, the selection of Nielsen and colleague's (Nielsen, 2000; Nielsen & Tahir, 2002; Nielsen & Loranger, 2006) essential website design features can potentially be used to evaluate usability elements of Web 2.0 defined sites. These essential website elements address a myriad of usability design features such as inclusion of a company logo and search feature; appropriate down load time; providing organisation details and a privacy declaration and the use/non-use of frames (see Appendix for detailed list and classification).

The next section details the research design and approach to evaluating a set of travel and tourism Web 2.0 sites with respect to Nielsen's work associated with essential usability features, as well as identifying important website content.

METHODOLOGY: AN APPROACH TO EXAMINING WEB 2.0 USABILITY AND CONTENT

In previous sections it was argued that design features associated with Web 2.0 sites potentially deviate from the traditional user interface design, i.e. guidelines developed and refined in the Web 1.0 era, and generally accepted as good design practice. Hence, one of the questions directing this research is— how the newer types of Web 2.0 sites perform with respect to traditionally usability criteria?

Understanding that Web 2.0 sites allow users to publish, display and list diverse views, opinions, pictures, sounds, etc, the research seeks to explore and categorize content published on Web 2.0 tourism sites. Hence, the second question guiding the research relates to— what type of content is associated with Web 2.0 tourism websites?

In examining the research questions a set of Web 2.0 tourism websites were examined for their adherence to traditional website usability, as well as the content elements that might be associated with these types of sites. The procedures associated with the analysis of Web 2.0 tourism sites included the following:

- Select an appropriate set of Web 2.0 tourism and travel sites,
- Evaluate the sites with respect to a set of usability criteria, and
- Report on content associated with these Web 2.0 sites

The website analysis and investigation was conducted by an experienced research assistant in August-September 2007 based on a previously reported approach (McMillan, 2000). The use of the same research assistant, who had experience in this type of website analysis ensured consistency and reproducibility in the evaluation process.

Selection of an Appropriate Set of Web 2.0 Tourism and Travel Sites

The researchers worked closely with Tourism New South Wales (one of the largest State tourism organisations in Australia) who had an active interest in the research and was instrumental in proposing a set of Web 2.0 sites as appropriate to use in the study.

These websites embraced some of the features proposed by O'Reilly (2005), as listed in Table 1, reflecting different functionality and/or underlying website principles that are typically associated with Web 2.0. Indeed, the sites represent a broad selection of websites with different degrees of Web 2.0 functionality.

Arguably, sites such as Expedia and Travelocity that might have been considered as non-Web 2.0 sites by some people, where also included in the study as they captured customer reviews and content— a notable Web 2.0 feature. Given this website selection process, the authors acknowledge that the study may not be fully representative of some of the multi-functional Web 2.0 tourism sites—this is considered a limitation of this study, therefore the results should be interpreted bearing this in mind.

The researchers also classify these sites as commercial and non-commercial sites to reflect the two main types of tourism information sources commonly encountered in the online environment. The commercial Web 2.0 sites were further classified into sites that allowed visitors to apply a star (*) rating (the academic version of a 5 scale Likert rating) to the content that was posted. This rating system has been previous used by Cox, Burgess, Sellitto and Buultjens (2008), who found this to be an appropriate manner to classify Web 2.0 tourism sites. Table 2 lists the Web 2.0 sites evaluated in this study under three groupings: a) Commercial Sites-5-Star Ratings, b) Commercial Sites– No Ratings, and c) Non Commercial Sites.

Evaluating the Sites with Respect to a Set of Usability Criteria

The usability features used in this study are those proposed in Nielsen's related work (Nielsen, 2000; Nielsen & Tahir, 2002; Nielsen & Loranger, 2006) and are summarised in Table 3. A description of each feature and a set of affirmative response question(s) used to test for each specific design feature is detailed in the Appendix. It would be assumed that the new and emerging Web 2.0 sites would be expected to embody these usability features given their high reliance on engaging users to gather appropriate content that is subsequently published on the site.

Reporting Content Associated with Web 2.0 Tourism Sites

Given that there are few studies of Web 2.0 sites in the travel and tourism sector that have categorized content, the authors draw from their many years of research and teaching experience in the web design, management and e-business area to propose a simple, but workable set of content areas to examine Web 2.0 tourism sites. Indeed, although Web 2.0 sites can be considered a new form of online presentation, there is still a requirement for these sites to reflect features that allow website visitors to be well informed about potential services or products. Hence, features such as online bookings, diversity of booking offers, marketing, searching for business information and trip planning are reported. Furthermore, the notion of community or building social networks is a functional component of Web 2.0 sites that tends to delineate them from the traditionally implemented website. Moreover, the provision for capturing UGC, particularly in the form of blogs is also included in the examination of the content of such sites.

DISCUSSION AND FINDINGS: WEB 2.0 USABILITY AND CONTENT

As previously indicated, the websites were individually examined and grouped into either *commercial* or *non-commercial* types. If the website was operated by a business entity then it was classified as *commercial*. Indeed, many of the businesses identified with commercial Web 2.0 sites were notable names such as Yahoo Travel, Trip Advisor and Lonely Planet.

In other instances it appeared that the website was the primary purpose for setting up the related company (for example, *Trav Buddy* was operated by Travbuddy LLC and *Schmap* was operated by Schmap, Inc.). The non-commercial websites tended to be associated with individuals or groups that supported their operation. From the 31 websites evaluated— 23 (74.2%) websites were deemed to be commercial, whilst 7 (22.6%) websites were of a non-commercial type. One of the noted features of travel-related websites is that they allow users to rate various aspects or information content published on the site.

Table 2. Web 2.0 sites evaluated in the study

Type of Site	Website Name and Address (URL)
a) Commercial Sites - 5-Star Ratings	Trip Advisor (www.tripadvisor.com)
	Epic Trip (www.epictrip.com)
	IgoUgo (www.igougo.com)
	Lonely Planet's Bluelist (www.lonelyplanet.com/bluelist)
	Orbitz (www.orbitzinsider.com)
	Mapsack (www.mapsack)
	Virtual Tourist (www.virtualtourist.com)
	Trip Up (www.tripup.com)
	Travelocity (www.travelocity.com)
	Expedia (www.expedia.com/destinations)
	Yahoo Travel (travel.yahoo.com)
	TravBuddy (www.travbuddy.com)
	STA Travel Blogs (www.statraveljournals.com)
b) Commercial Sites - No Ratings	Flickr Travel (www.flickr.com/travel)
	Gusto (www.gusto.com)
	Travelistic (www.travelistic.com)
	The Lobby (www.thelobby.com)
	Kayak (www.kayak.com)
	Visit Victoria (www.visitvictoria.com)
	Lonely Planet TV (www.lonelyplanet.tv)
	Schmap (www.schmap.com)
	Trip Hub (www.triphub.com)
	Del.icio.us (www.del.icio.us)
c) Non Commercial Sites	This Place I Know (www.thisplaceiknow.com)
	Wikitravel (www.wikitravel.com)
	Travel Blog (www.travelblog.com)
	Travel Rants (www.travelrants.com)
	Trips Log (www.tripslog.com)
	You Tube Travel (www.youtube.com/travel)
	V Carious (www.vcarious.com)
	World 66 (www.world66.com)

This type of rating system generally involves allocating a score of between one to five to travel information associated with accommodation and/or tourism destinations. Some of these scoring systems were found to be controlled by the website, whilst on some sites users had the freedom to score a particular feature or rate information content. Amongst the websites evaluated, some two out of every five sites embraced this user-generated rating feature, with the majority having no user-generated ratings at all.

The thirty-one websites evaluated were examined for their particular tourism focus and application area. Table 4 summarises the website

Table 3. Usability design criteria used to evaluate Web 2.0 tourisms sites

Usability Features	
1. No splash page	6. Privacy Policy
2. No frames	7. Body text - adjusts for screen size
3. Logo present	8. Unvisited links - blue
4. The About Us Page	9. Visited links - non-blue
5. The search feature	10. Download time

(Adopted from Nielsen (2000), Nielsen and Tahir (2002) and Nielsen and Loranger (2006) with modifications by authors).

focus area as well as the star rating it addressed. Some 77% of websites examined were solely devoted to tourism, whilst the rest of the sites incorporated features or aspects in addition to the tourism theme.

Usability of Web 2.0 Tourism Sites

The concept of usability embodies the notion that websites need to have characteristics that make them learnable, easy to remember, reliable and efficient to use, and impart audience satisfaction. The adoption of website usability values can be easily achieved with noted benefits found to be associated with an improved visitor experience.

One of the motivations for this research was to investigate how the newer types of Web 2.0 sites perform with respect to traditional usability. Traditional usability website features have been developed and refined in the Web 1.0 era and have been generally accepted as being good practice design. The ten usability features derived from Nielsen's work (Nielsen, 2000; Nielsen & Tahir, 2002; Nielsen & Loranger, 2006) were used to evaluate the tourism websites in this study. These usability design features addressed areas associated with website searching, data collection and privacy, navigation, functionality and acceptable web page download time. Table 5 summarises the results obtained after evaluating the tourism website against this set of ten usability features.

The general adherence and implementation of usability features in this set of Web 2.0 sites is encouraging. The website splash page as a visual design feature, which is purely used for embellishing the look of the site, was not encountered. Frames were only found in one non-commercial website, whilst all websites used some business logo or representative emblem in the appropriate or recommend position on website pages. Indeed, the logo on the majority of websites was a means of returning to the home page as a hypertext link.

Websites need to always have an 'About the company' component. This usability design feature tends to address a trust element that is associated with online publishing and should be used by all organisations regardless of size, affiliation or commercial type. The results of the study found that not all tourism websites include this feature suggesting that this may be an area for design improvement. Three out of ten 'Commercial no-rating' websites did not address this design feature.

The search feature is a fundamental website design element that users appreciate and expect to find on websites. Design convention suggests that

Table 4. Website tourism focus, type and available rating system

Website Content	Overall	Website Category		
		Commercial (5-star-rating)	Commercial (No-rating)	Non-Commercial
Tourism	77%	0%	100%	0%
Tourism & Other	17%	48%	30%	22%
General that included tourism	7%	40%	20%	40%

Table 5. Web 2.0 usability evaluation of tourism sites

Usability feature	Proportion of websites meeting evaluation criteria		
	Commercial-5-star	Commercial-no-rating	Non-commercial
1. No splash page	100%	100%	100%
2. No frames	100%	100%	86%
3. Logo present	100%	100%	100%
Logo - top left	100%	100%	100%
Logo - link to home	92%	90%	86%
4. About Us Page included	77%	90%	86%
5. Search feature on home page	85%	70%	86%
Search feature - search box	77%	70%	86%
Search box - upper section	77%	70%	71%
Search box - labelled as 'Search'	77%	60%	86%
Search box - allows > 25 chars	77%	70%	86%
Search box - white text entry area	77%	70%	86%
6. Privacy Policy	77%	60%	43%
7. Body text - adjusts for screen size	23%	10%	29%
8. Unvisited links - blue	8%	0%	0%
9. Visited links - non-blue	8%	0%	0%
10. Download— T1 <10seconds	62%	70%	57%
Download— 56k <10seconds	0%	0%	0%

for best effect and usability it should be located on the home page. The study results indicate that around eight out of ten 'commercial-5-star' rating and 'non-commercial' websites performed well in this area. However there were still a number of tourism websites that did not adhere to this convention.

When organisations collect data via their website it has become an expected design feature to include a privacy policy. This policy should be easily identifiable and accessible. A high proportion (77%) of 'commercial-5-star' rating websites had this feature. Disappointingly, four out of ten 'commercial–no-rating' and more than half of non-commercial tourism websites did not provide an easily accessible privacy policy— suggesting that this is a significant issue requiring design attention. Indeed, given that one of the fundamental tenets of Web 2.0 sites is to gather user content, it seems almost remiss that a clear, unambiguous declaration of how user content is used, or can be potentially used, is absent on many of the sites examined.

The evaluation of tourism websites for features associated with visual display and navigation identified that many did not conform to expected usability conventions. The use of specific body text sizing that does not adapt to a user's browser is problematical—with displays staying the same regardless of window size. Good website design uses relative sizing of text in the coding of the website allowing each page layout to be easily adapted for different screen sizes and browser windows. Only a small proportion of websites addressed this usability feature.

With respect to website navigation, the standard convention is to use blue links for unvisited web pages and a less saturated non-blue for unvisited links. Only one site used this navigation convention, with all other sites using a variant navigation protocol.

Individual web page download time should be less than 10 seconds. Even with the advent of broadband that has led to website designers increasing the number of images and graphics in pages, this 10 second rule should hold. The results of the study indicate that the evaluated Web 2.0 tourism sites are not viable for people with a 56k dialup connection. Notably, some 40% of the Web 2.0 websites could not be downloaded with a high-powered broadband (T1) connection within the ten-second limit.

Content Associated with Web 2.0 Tourism Sites

The second question explored in this research related to the type of information content given on the Web 2.0 tourism websites. Although Web 2.0 tourism sites can be considered to embrace a new form of online presentation, there is still a requirement for these sites to provide appropriate content for website visitors to be informed about the use of their services or products.

Furthermore, website features may also reflect marketing activities that may be an extension of those undertaken by the business with other forms of traditional media. Features such as online bookings, diversity of booking offers, marketing, searching for business information and trip planning are included. Community or social networking features are also a functional component of Web 2.0 sites, thus traveller blogs and reviews can be examined to investigate the content features of such sites.

Search Options

The websites were examined for several types of search conventions that were classified as of the following:

- **User Generated Tags:** This is where users of the website have the opportunity to create tags that reflect different types of UGC. Any search results with various keywords will match up to these user-originating tags.
- **Controlled Tags:** Content is categorised and determined by the website operator. Search results tend not to reflect any previous users' views or opinions, but the website operators governing rules and values.
- **Location Map:** This is where interactive geographical maps are provided allowing the user to access particular information associated with a tourism destination.
- **Hierarchy:** Refers to a traditional search hierarchy available on the website? Users can select from a number of topics on the home page and 'drill-down' to the destination or website service they wish to investigate.

Table 6 provides details of the types of search options available on the websites investigated.

Most of the websites had one or more different search option available— the most popular being user-generated keyword tags. This type of search was popular on non-commercial websites (86%)—

Table 6. Search options by website category

Search Option	Overall	Commercial - 5-star	Commercial - No-rating	Non-commercial
Keyword: User generated tags	73%	69%	70%	86%
Location map	40%	62%	10%	43%
Hierarchy	30%	38%	30%	14%
Keyword: Controlled tag	27%	31%	40%	0%
Other	7%	8%	0%	14%

indeed, no non-commercial website operator used a keyword search associated with controlled tags. Similarly, 'commercial-5-star' rating websites were also much more likely to have location maps and hierarchy search options.

Sponsored Advertising and Links

The Web 2.0 sites were investigated for the types of marketing features reflected by sponsored advertisements and links. Table 7 summarizes the marketing features across the commercial and no-commercial websites evaluated.

Seven out of ten of the websites had sponsored advertisements and just over half had sponsored links— consequently such features were not only prominent, but potentially provided the sites with important revenue. The '5 star' rating websites were quite overt in providing sponsored advertisements and links. Notably, websites that were classified as *non-commercial* websites had more sponsored advertising features than the *commercial* websites that did not offer '5 star' ratings.

Online Booking Options

Table 8 shows the different online (real time) booking options provided on the Web 2.0 sites. The most prevalent type of online booking was associated with airline flights, accommodation and rental car booking engines—potentially reflecting consumer expectations that such a feature is a mandatory function of such sites. A number of 'other' options not specifically listed emerged during the analysis. These included the options to book package deals and travel insurance plans via the website. Notably, only one non-commercial website offered any type of online booking option (accommodation) when compared to commercial sites. Furthermore, some of the 'commercial-5-star' rating websites provided a greater number of online booking options than the other commercial websites.

Table 7. Website sponsored advertising and links

Commercial Features	Overall	Commercial-5-star	Commercial no-rating	Non-commercial
Sponsored Advertisements	70%	92%	50%	57%
Sponsored Links	57%	69%	40%	57%
Other	13%	15%	10%	14%

Table 8. Online booking options

Online Booking Option	Overall	Commercial-5-star	Commercial (no-rating)	Non-Commercial
Flights	43%	69%	40%	0%
Accommodation	40%	62%	30%	14%
Rental Cars	30%	54%	70%	0%
Other	33%	62%	20%	0%
Rail	10%	23%	0%	0%
Attractions (tickets)	7%	15%	0%	0%
Ferry	7%	15%	0%	0%
Ship	3%	0%	10%	0%
Side Trips	3%	8%	0%	0%

Planning, Mapping and Other Tourism Support Features

The Web 2.0 tourism sites were investigated for both mapping and planning features that potentially assist prospective travellers in exploring different vacation scenarios. Only the 'commercial-5-star' rating websites had a trip planner facility. Two 'commercial no-rating' sites and one non-commercial website had a street directory feature. The Microsoft® Virtual Earth or Google® Maps were the respective application engines used to support this feature. Interestingly, more than seven out of ten non-commercial sites had some type of ancillary-support feature that included:

- An optional version of the site available for mobile (cellular) phone display.
- Real-time picture feeds of particular destinations.
- Information feeds of the sites most frequently updated content done through RSS (Really Simple Syndication).
- Travel journals.

Only one website was available in multiple languages— possibly highlighting an English-speaking bias of the selected sites. Although the original intention of evaluating the websites was to only identify features such as trip planners and street directories, these ancillary-support features tend to be an important and obvious customer support feature. Table 9 summarizes the mapping, planning and ancillary features across the different types of sites.

Traveler Blogs and Reviews

Website features that embrace the notion of community and social networks are a functional component of Web 2.0 site that delineates them from traditionally implemented websites. The websites were examined for features that encouraged users to establish online communities. Half of the websites examined allowed users to set up a group of friends or contacts. These features were slightly more prevalent on non-commercial websites. A non-commercial site (Trips Log) allowed users to set up their own blog and Travelocity (a 'commercial-5-star' rating website) allowed users to become members of the site to receive newsletters and updates that related to fare increases and changes. Overall, 14 of the 30 websites had content associated with blogs that were derived from user's publishing their comments in the online environment.

User comments published on these sites were found to be of two distinct types— blogs that allowed a form of interactive-response with previous postings and clearly identifiable reviews of different aspects of travel and tourism issues. Indeed, over half of the non-commercial websites allowed for general comments or blog activity by website visitors, however, not one of these non-commercial sites allowed users to enter their own reviews— reviews that may have captured traveller experiences associated with accommodation or a visit to a tourism area.

Indeed, a higher proportion of the commercial-5-star websites allowed general blog comments than their commercial no-rating counterparts. The published content associated with blogs and

Table 9. Mapping and other tourism support features

Feature	Overall	Commercial - 5 star	Commercial - no rating	Non-commercial
Trip Planner	13%	31%	0%	0%
Street Directory	13%	8%	20%	14%
Other	27%	23%	0%	71%

reviews had a different emphasis. Blog content was found to have a relatively high focus on documenting user activity and experiences associated with a destination, whilst review comments focussed primarily on accommodation. It was found that many of the comments associated with destinations tended to have a value-added nature— whereby, it is assumed that the writer had visited the area and was able to draw from their experiences. Table 10 summarises the different tourism and travel categories identified with comments and the relative occurrence between blogs and reviews (Collectively 1240 comments were examined across the set of websites using a random selection of comments from each site to achieve this).

A further evaluation of comments identified that some 84% of all comments were associated with expressing an opinion on aspects of travel. A high degree of comments (60%) were found to be associated with informing or updating other travellers. Notably, very few comments (0.5%) revealed that people had altered plans as a result of viewing the website's blog comments.

FUTURE TRENDS AND RESEARCH

There is an expectation that tourism and travel sites will embrace many of the Web 2.0 features providing the traveller with enhance functionality and appropriate content. The concept of Web 2.0 has arguably ushered in a new paradigm in the travel industry with respect to the way that content is captured and published. Indeed, already the literature alludes to the next generation of travel websites that have a higher degree of functionality and tend to be referred to by a numerical increment— such as Web or Travel 3.0 sites. Indeed, tourism and travel related organisations that have online presence should explore the various options available through Web 2.0 features— allowing them to further engage their constituent audience.

With respect to the research reported in this article— several extensions and investigations to the research can be identified. The sampled Web 2.0 sites were classified into commercial 5-star, commercial no-rating, non-commercial categories based on previous work by Cox et al., (2008). The use of other classification system to reflect other forms of business perspectives, such as, business mission, specific audience, or even grouping of sites based on functionality— can be different avenues of investigation in future research.

A further examination and analysis of blog and review comments can potentially allow those comments to be categorised in different travel genres while identifying their business value. The linking of comments to different genres can provide an organisation with a better understanding of individual travel groups— which has intrinsic marketing applicability.

With respect to Web 2.0 design and usability, further evaluation of these features could incorporate laboratory investigations such as eye-tracking

Table 10. Categorising blog and review comments

Comment Category	Blogs	Reviews
Destinations	46%	13%
Attractions	17%	20%
General	11%	-
Accommodation	5%	53%
Transport	4%	4%
Other (mainly non-travel related comments)	18%	10%

and perception studies. Such an approach although resource-intense, can be used to explore the finer aspects of Web 2.0 design and usability for different user groups. For example, young people and older travellers— important age groups to the global travel industry— tend to operate with different cognitive and visual perceptions when accessing online information. Arguably, these groups of travellers would behaviour differently from a usability perspective in the Web 2.0 environment. Hence, research that allowed specific improvements to Web 2.0 design elements would enhance the information search and planning features for these groups. Future researchers might also choose to specifically evaluate the user-participation aspects of Web 2.0— for example blogs, wikis and mashups— to see if there are any usability issues associated with these aspects.

CONCLUSION

The term Web 2.0 was coined around 2004 and was used to describe the new types of websites that had survived the dot-com crash. An important characteristic of Web 2.0 sites is how they incorporate various technologies and applications that enhance the site's functionality. Given this increased functionality, the traditional manner associated with website implementation can be affected— a site's usability, as well as content design features, can be potentially impacted. This article explored and investigated a set of Web 2.0 tourism sites for their usability as well as reporting an overview of some of the website content.

Web 2.0 tourism sites performed well when evaluated against many of the chosen website usability criteria. However, relatively poor usability associated with the provision of a company's privacy policy and web page download times was noted and should be of concern. Arguably, when organisations collect data via their website it has become an expected design feature to include a privacy policy. A relatively high number of both commercial and non-commercial tourism websites did not provide an easily accessible privacy policy— suggesting that this is a significant issue requiring design attention. Indeed, given that one of the fundamental tenets of Web 2.0 sites is to gather user content, it seems almost remiss that a clear, unambiguous declaration of how user content is used, or can be potentially used, is absent on many of the sites examined. Individual web page down load time should be less than 10 seconds. Even with the advent of broadband that has led to website designers increasing the number of images and media types on each page, this 10 second rule should hold. The results of the study indicate that the evaluated Web 2.0 tourism sites are not viable for people with a 56k dialup connection and notably, some 40% of the Web 2.0 websites could not be downloaded with a high-powered broadband (T1) connection within the ten second limit.

In terms of the identified content associated with Web 2.0 tourism sites a number of differences between commercial and non-commercial sites were noted. Proportionally, more commercial websites had sponsored advertisements than non-commercial websites. The commercial websites had multiple search features— the non-commercial websites more likely to support user-generated tags, whilst commercial websites more likely to provide their own controlled tags. Commercial Web 2.0 travel sites provide a greater number of online booking features than their non-commercial counterparts. Non-commercial websites seemed more willing to provide and/or experiment with mobile-phone versions of their site, online cameras and RSS feeds. Blog and review comments were an important feature Web 2.0 sites and an evaluation of comments identified that some 84% of all comments were associated with expressing an opinion on some aspect of travel. When posted, a high degree of comments (60%) were found to be associated with informing or updating other travellers. Notably, very few comments (0.5%) revealed that people had altered plans as a result of viewing the website's blog comments.

ACKNOWLEDGMENT

This research was supported by a grant from the Sustainable Tourism Cooperative Research Centre, Australia.

REFERENCES

Alva, M. E. O., Martínez, A. B., Cueva, J. M., Sagástegui, H. T. C., & López, B. P. (2003). Comparison of methods and existing tools for the measurement of usability in the Web. In *Web engineering* (LNCS 2722, pp. 386-389). Berlin, Germany: Springer.

Bolan, K., Canada, M., & Cullin, R. (2007). Web, library, and teen services 2.0. *Young Adult Library Services*, *5*(2), 40–43.

Breslow-Sardone, S. (2006). *Travel 2.0*. Retrieved May 12, 2008, from http://web.archive.org/web/20060811192611/http://honeymoons.about.com/od/smarttravel/qt/travel2pointoh.htm

Buhalis, D. (1999). Information technology for small and medium sized tourism enterprises: Adaptation and benefits. *Information Technology & Tourism*, *2*(2), 79–95.

Burgess, S., Sellitto, C., & Karanasios, S. (2009). *Effective Web Presence Solutions for Small Businesses: Strategies for Successful Implementation,* Hershey, PA: IGI Global

Collins, C., Buhalis, D., & Peters, M. (2003). Enhancing SMTEs' business performance through the Internet and e-learning platforms. *Education and Training*, *45*(8/9), 483–494. doi:10.1108/00400910310508874

Cox, C., Burgess, S., Sellitto, C., & Buultjens, J. (2008). *The influence of user-generated content on tourist travel behaviour*. Lismore, NSW: Australian Regional Tourism Research Centre.

Elliott, C. (2008). Next up: Travel 2.0. *National Geographic Traveler*, *25*(2), 14–18.

Gillmor, D. (2008). Bloggers and mash. *New Scientist*, *197*(2649), 44–47. doi:10.1016/S0262-4079(08)60675-2

Greaves, M. (2007). Semantic Web 2.0. *IEEE Intelligent Systems*, *22*(2), 94–96. doi:10.1109/MIS.2007.40

Kelly, M. (2007). *Heard about user generated content? It's the new word of mouth (Travel trends: Incorporating travel trends and novacancy)*. Retrieved April 18, 2008, from http://web.archive.org/web/20070313203812/http://www.travel-trends.biz/ttn17-user-generated-content

Knight, M. (2007). Web 2.0. *Communications Engineer*, *5*(1), 30–35. doi:10.1049/ce:20070104

Kolbitsch, J., & Maurer, H. (2006). The transformation of the Web: How emerging communities shape the information we consume. *Journal of Universal Computer Science*, *12*(2), 187–213.

Lexhagen, M. (2005). The importance of value-added services to support the customer search and purchase process on travel websites. *Journal of Information Technology and Tourism*, *7*(2), 119–135. doi:10.3727/1098305054517336

Lin, K.-J. (2007). Building Web 2.0. *Computer*, *40*(5), 101–102. doi:10.1109/MC.2007.159

Lituchy, T. R., & Rail, A. (2000). Bed and breakfast, small inns, and the Internet: The impact of technology on the globalization of small businesses. *Journal of International Marketing*, *8*(2), 86–97. doi:10.1509/jimk.8.2.86.19625

McMillan, S. J. (2000). The microscope and the moving target: The challenge of applying content analysis to the World Wide Web. *Journalism & Mass Communication Quarterly*, *77*(1), 80–98.

Merritt, J. (2006). Web 2.0 becomes travel standard. *Business Travel News*, *23*(20), 28–30.

MIT. (2008). *Usability guidelines (Massachusetts Institute of Technology)*. Retrieved April 17, 2008, from http://web.mit.edu/is/usability/usability-guidelines.html

Morrison, A. M., Taylor, S., Morrison, A. J., & Morrison, A. D. (1999). Marketing small hotels on the World Wide Web. *Information Technology & Tourism*, *2*(1-4), 97–113.

Newitz, A. (2008). Web 3.0: What will the next era of Web culture bring? *New Scientist*, *197*(2649), 42–43. doi:10.1016/S0262-4079(08)60674-0

Nielsen, J. (2000). *Designing Web usability: The practice of simplicity*. New York: New Riders Publishing.

Nielsen, J. (2007). *Web 2.0 can be dangerous*. Retrieved April 21, 2008, from http://www.useit.com/alertbox/web-2.html

Nielsen, J., & Loranger, H. (2006). *Prioritorizing Web usability*. Berkeley, CA: New Riders Publishing.

Nielsen, J., & Tahir, M. (2002). *Homepage usability*. Salem, VA: New Riders Publishing.

Nusair, K. K., Yoon, H.-J., & Parsa, H. G. (2008). Effect of Utilitarian and hedonic motivations on consumer satisfaction with travel websites. *Information Technology & Tourism*, *10*(1), 75–89. doi:10.3727/109830508785058977

O'Reilly, T. (2005). *What is Web 2.0: Design patterns and business models for the next generation of software*. Retrieved January 1, 2009, from http://www.oreillynet.com/pub/a/oreilly/tim/news/2005/09/30/what-is-web-20.html

Procaccino, D. J., & Miller, R. F. (2000). Tourism on the World Wide Web: A comparison of Web sites of United States- and French-based businesses. *Information Technology & Tourism*, *1-4*(1), 173–183.

Reactive. (2007). *Web 2.0 for the tourism & travel industry*. Melbourne, Australia: Reactive.

Sellitto, C. (2005). A study of emerging tourism features associated with Australian winery websites. *Journal of Information Technology and Tourism*, *7*(3/4), 157–170. doi:10.3727/1098305057742972 83

Sellitto, C., & Burgess, S. (2007). Planning and implementing the websites of Australian SMTEs. *Journal of Information Technology and Tourism*, *9*(2), 115–131. doi:10.3727/109830507781367366

US-GSA. (2006). *Research-based Web design & usability guidelines*. Washington, DC: U.S. Department of Health and Human Services (HHS) and the U.S. General Services Administration (GSA).

Werthner, H., & Ricci, F. (2004). Tourism and development II: E-commerce and tourism. *Communications of the ACM*, *47*(12), 101–105. doi:10.1145/1035134.1035141

Yamakami, T. (2007). MobileWeb 2.0: Lessons from Web 2.0 and past mobile Internet development. In *Proceedings of the International Conference on Multimedia and Ubiquitous Engineering (MUE '07)*, Korean Bible University, Seoul, Korea. Washington, DC: IEEE Computer Society.

APPENDIX

Criteria used for testing the usability features of Web 2.0 sites

Usability Feature	Description	Evaluation criteria
1. No splash page	The website splash page as a visual design feature that is purely used for embellishing the look of the site and should not be used in website design.	Splash pages are NOT used? (Y/N)
2. No frames	Frames are a poor design feature, that can impart poor website functionality and should not be used.	Frames are NOT used? (Y/N)
3. Logo present	All websites need to use a business logo or emblem in the appropriate position on each website page.	Do pages have a logo? (Y/N) Is the logo located in the top left hand corner of pages? (Y/N) Is the logo a linked to the homepage? (Y/N)
4. The About Us Page	This design feature tends to address a trust element that is associated with online publishing. Appropriate for all organisations regardless of size, affiliation or commercial type.	Is there an 'About us' page? (Y/N)
5. The search feature	The search feature is a fundamental website design element that all users appreciate and expect to find on large websites.	Is there a search facility located on the home page? (Y/N) Is the search facility in the form of a box? (Y/N) Is the search box on the upper part of the home page? (Y/N) Labelled as 'Search' (Y/N)? Allows for 25-30 characters? (Y/N)
6. Privacy Policy	When organisations collect data via their website it has become an expected design convention to include a privacy policy. This policy should be easily identifiable and accessible.	Is there a privacy policy? (Y/N)
7. Body text - adjusts for screen size	Good website design is to use relative sizing of text in the construction of the website allowing each page layout to be easily adapted for different screen sizes and browser windows.	Does the website use relative body text sizing? (Y/N)
8. Unvisited links - blue 9. Visited links - non-blue	With respect to website navigation, the standard convention is to use blue (unvisited) and non-blue links (visited).	Are the website's unvisited links blue? (Y/N) Are visited links a non-blue colour? (Y/N)
10. Download	Individual web page down load time should be less than 10 seconds.	Report download** times for modem (56k) and T1 (256k) connections. Are they under 10 seconds? (Y/N)

Chapter 7
Facebook, Friends and Photos: A Snapshot into Social Networking for Generating Travel Ideas

Leanne White
Victoria University, Australia

ABSTRACT

This chapter undertakes a 'snapshot' or glimpse into social aspects of tourism informatics with specific reference to the travel photographs posted on the social networking site 'Facebook'. This analysis will focus on the travel images (photographs) generated by 10 individuals (five male and five female) from the Facebook community. It must be emphasised that the study is deliberately narrow in its focus and does not attempt to make generalisations about how photos are used by other Facebook users. The aim of the study is to begin a dialogue about the use of travel photos on this popular social networking site. Examined in this chapter are a selection of visual images and written messages surrounding the tourism encounters of the particular Facebook members between September 2007 and September 2008. As Urry (1995) has argued, "the consumption of tourist services is important yet by no means easy to understand and explain" (p. 139). Tourism is experienced in a highly visual manner and there is a need for further research in this area. This chapter explores how the photographs taken, displayed and recorded on Facebook reinforce the travel experience for the tourist; and furthermore, how these images might influence the travel decisions of those who view the photos. Wider implications resulting from this type of research for the future development for tourism informatics (e-tourism) is also explored.

INTRODUCTION

The popular site Facebook was launched in February 2004 as an online version of the hard-copy face-books which college students in the United States are given at orientation to help in getting to know their fellow students (Dulworth, 2008, p. 135). Facebook boasts more than 100 million users (Moses, 2008) uploading around 500 million photos per month (Nash, 2008). In a relatively short time Facebook has become a critical form of social media. The exponential growth of the Facebook community

DOI: 10.4018/978-1-60566-818-5.ch007

is so profound that when this book is published, it is quite possible that the number of Facebook users worldwide may have exceeded 500 million. A recent book on Social Networking sites discusses Facebook as "a site specifically for students" with around eight million members (Engdahl, 2007, p. 183) – information that was clearly inaccurate by the time the book was published.

Nine of the 10 Facebook users chosen for investigation in this study have more than 100 'friends', and all have more than two photo albums displayed on their site. A highly focused analysis of one aspect of the Facebook phenomenon was undertaken with a small sample (10 participants) by examining the travel photographs circulated in the 'electronic space' of Facebook at a particular time. The photographs examined in this chapter were taken in a range of countries including: the United States, Canada, Mexico, Italy, Greece, France, Germany, Spain, the Netherlands, the Czech Republic, Scotland, Ireland, China, Malaysia, Hong Kong, Japan, and the Solomon Islands.

The chapter will undertake an analysis of the photographs by applying aspects of content analysis and (to a lesser extent) semiotics – key quantitative and qualitative research methodologies. Combining different research methodologies is particularly pertinent to this chapter as content analysis can be used to substantiate semiotics. Semiotics (how signs generate meaning) might be considered by some to be a subjective form of analysis as it requires a rather personal view to begin the decoding process. However, the quantitative analysis – which is designed to be undertaken in much the same way by any researcher – works to further validate the results derived from the qualitative analysis. Both qualitative and quantitative research methodologies have particular strengths and using both methods reinforces the final research outcome.

Textual analysis, in particular semiotics and content analysis (studying what is actually evident in one or many photographs), are useful methodologies for deconstructing mediated representations of travel images. A combination of primary and secondary research, semiotic analysis and content analysis will be undertaken to analyse the way in which particular travel images generated in this social networking medium were created, replicated and relayed to other Facebook users across the world.

Having introduced the chapter, some background information will be provided. The background material examines the popular social networking phenomenon known as Facebook, the role travel photos play in this online environment, and the role these images might play in the travel plans of those who view the photos. The research methodologies are then explained in further detail. The quantitative methodology of content analysis and the qualitative methodology of semiotics can be combined to strengthen the data analysis undertaken in this chapter. The 'Issues and Analysis' Problems' section begins with discussing the two main types of travel photograph that Facebook members post in their photo albums. The close analysis of the five females and five males from the Facebook online community is then undertaken. This longer section of the chapter begins with a table summarising the data. The examination of the 10 Facebook members is then briefly summarised with significant similarities, differences and possible trends highlighted. Finally, the 'Summary Analysis…' section draws out the key qualitative and quantitative implications arising from the data, while the 'Conclusion' summarises the key points from the study and identifies further research that might be undertaken in this area.

BACKGROUND

By April 2008 Facebook overtook News Corporation's MySpace as the world's most popular social networking site (ComScore, 2008). Social networking sites such as Facebook, MySpace, Hi5, Friendster, Xanga, Bebo and Orkut allow people to create profiles and share information and files including: photos, videos and messages with online friends. While English is the commonly used language on Facebook, other languages now used to communicate on the site include: Chinese, French, German, Italian, Japanese, Russian and Spanish. Indeed, there are currently 23 languages to choose from when one sets up his/her Facebook account. As McIntyre argues, technology is "helping media audiences swim in more ponds outside the mainstream – blogs, social networks, podcasting, vodcasting, video-sharing sites and the like" (McIntyre, 2008).

Facebook has a repository of 6.6 billion photos – more than any other photo web site. The straightforward interface of Facebook is one of the key reasons for its growing popularity – currently "the fourth most-trafficked site in the world" (Nash, 2008) and valued at $15 billion (Hodgkinson, 2008). Aaron Sorkin, creator of the television drama *The West Wing* and a number of films including *A Few Good Men* is writing a screenplay about the origins of Facebook. The film will be an adaptation of Ben Mezrich's book, *Face Off* which examines the contested and controversial origins of Facebook (Moses, 2008). The site was established by Mark Zuckerberg in 2004 as an online yearbook for students at Harvard University. Needless to say, growth of the site over a period of just four years has been nothing less than phenomenal.

The issue of Facebook and the nature of 'friendship' is one of significant social, cultural and even legal interest. In January 2008, a British judge presiding over a case of Internet stalking ruled that befriending someone on Facebook was a fairly innocuous act and didn't necessarily make them a friend in the true sense of the word (Emerson, 2008). Facebook user Garry Dean claimed that his Facebook friends were really "people I have come into contact with in my life", while Geoff Dick agreed that friends on Facebook were more like 'acquaintances' – "and the more there were, the less friendly the profile owner" was likely to be with them (Emerson, 2008). The true nature of friendship in this site was put to the test by writer Hal Niedzviecki who decided to invite his 700 Facebook friends to a party at a local hotel. While he was expecting up to 75 people (based on replies to the invitation), only one person eventually joined him (Niedzviecki, 2008, p. 3).

Like any technology, Facebook is simply a tool that can be equally used for good or evil. Hodgkinson argues that "Far from connecting us, Facebook actually isolates us at our workstations", it "appeals to a kind of vanity and self-importance in us" and it "encourages a disturbing competitiveness around friendship" where "quality counts for nothing and quantity is king" (Hodgkinson, 2008). When Melbourne backpacker Britt Lapthorne was reported missing in Croatia in September 2008, her family and distraught friends posted numerous items on her Facebook 'wall', and media outlets used many of Lapthorne's Facebook photos in their reports (Costa, Dobbin and Klisanin, 2008). In the case of Britt Lapthorne, the Facebook community united around the missing student and posted messages on her site (which has since been taken down). Some of the Facebook groups that were established after her death included: R.I.P. Britt Lapthorne (4,417 members); We will find justice for Britt Lapthorne and her family (1,911 members); Our love and thoughts go out to Britt Lapthorne's family (771 members); Britt Lapthorne Foundation (747 members); and at least five other groups with fewer members.

Recent studies in tourism have considered the role of tourist attractions in assisting with the creation of an identity. Pretes (2003) notes that tourists receive messages sent to them by the creators of the sites they visit, and these sites of significance, presented as aspects of a national heritage, help to shape a common identity, or 'imagined community' among a diverse population. Rojek (1997) argues that "most tourists feel they have not fully absorbed a sight until they stand before it, see it, and take a photograph to record the moment" (p. 58). If tourism sites can help create a common identity or imagined community, can images of these destinations on the websites of family and friends represent aspects of a culture and help to develop a better understanding of a destination or even a possible desire to travel to that place?

Morgan, Pritchard and Pride (2004) argue that travel for the purpose of leisure is "a highly involving experience, extensively planned, excitedly anticipated and fondly remembered" (p. 4). The photographs that capture the highlights of the travel occasion constitute a vital element of both remembering the event and sharing the experience with others. Urry (1990) argues that visual images generated by travellers provide a strong basis for potential tourists to select places to visit. He argues that when tourists gaze they effectively become semioticians "reading the landscape for signifiers of certain pre-established notions or signs derived from various discourses of travel and tourism" (Urry, 1990, p. 12). Sheldon (1997) argues that the Internet in particular facilitates tourism. Photographs that are posted on websites become part of the visual culture that makes up our world. Rather than these memories being encased in photo albums and stored on bookshelves collecting dust, photos shared on the Internet have a vast potential audience. Pitchford (2008) further argues that tourism promotional materials "speak to tourists in a language that creates a set of expectations about a destination" (p. 98). Friends' Facebook travel photos constitute another form of promotional material and have thus become a part of the overall marketing mix.

METHODOLOGY

Content analysis is a research methodology that is concerned with the frequency of content contained in a particular data set. Berelson (1952) defined content analysis as "a research technique for the objective, systematic and quantitative description" of communications (p. 15). Content analysis is used in this chapter as it is a useful tool for examining content that might assist in interpreting the 'bigger picture'. Content analysis is effectively a counting strategy and is put forward as an objective method for counting content. It is a useful research tool for identifying and describing trends. Content analysis is primarily concerned with studying what is actually evident on the page or the screen.

An essential feature of content analysis is the use of categories. Quantitative content analysis of this kind does not concern itself with questions of quality or interpretation but can easily place data into categories and thus detect systematic patterns and structures. At its most basic level, "content analysis simply entails inspection of the data for recurrent instances of some kind" (Wilkinson, 2004, p. 184). It is concerned with "the denotative order of signification" (Fiske, 1990, p. 136).

Content analysis has been employed by researchers for nearly a century but became a popular form of analysis in the 1950s and is used in a variety of academic disciplines including media studies, tourism, literature, history and marketing. Gerbner used content analysis to illustrate particular patterns that existed across a range of media products. He examined how cultural values (such as violence) are transmitted through an entire message system and not just one particular television program (Fiske, 1990, p. 143). In quantitative content analysis, the researcher "uses objective and systematic counting and recording procedures to produce a numeric description" of what is contained in the text (Neuman, 2006, p. 323). Content is discovered through a more systematic analysis of the text – such as a photograph or an album of photographs – as opposed to a 'normal' reading of the text.

Semiotics is the study of signs, codes and culture, and a methodology for reading 'soft' data such as representations of travel adventures. Semiotics will be occasionally integrated into this chapter as it is a useful tool for examining the sometimes multi-layered images of the encounters and experiences that took place at a destination (albeit as relayed via the photographer through the lens of a camera). Semiotics is the study of how signs operate in society or "the study of the social production of meaning" generated from sign systems (O'Sullivan, Hartley, Saunders, Montgomery and Fiske, 1994, p. 281).

Meaning in this context is the dynamic interaction between the 'reader' and the message. In any semiotic analysis, the reader is an active participant in the process, not simply a passive viewer. Visual images often leave a space within the text for the viewer to occupy and thus engage in the signifying process. The active processes at work in the text, combined with the act of decoding the image by the viewer, create meaning (Williamson, 1978, p. 41). Meaning is influenced by the reader's socio-cultural experiences, and the reader plays a central role in any semiotic analysis. Assorted representations of travel and tourism imagery (as presented in the photo albums of five male and five female Facebook users) can be discovered through an examination of the symbols and images presented to friends on this popular social networking site.

Semiotics is a particularly useful methodology for deconstructing our daily experiences and attempts to capture those experiences more permanently – with tools such as cameras. As Culler argues, "All over the world the unsung armies of semioticians, the tourists, are fanning out in search of the signs of Frenchness, typical Italian behaviour, exemplary Oriental scenes, typical American thruways, traditional English pubs" (Culler, 1981, p. 127). Equally, the search for preferred accounts of travel experiences can be discovered through a close examination of the photographs people choose to share in their Facebook albums.

According to Leiss, Kline and Jhally, the real strength of semiotics is "its capacity to dissect and examine closely a cultural code and its sensitivity to the nuances and oblique references in cultural systems" (Leiss, Kline and Jhally, 1990, p. 214). Leiss and his co-authors developed a research methodology for advertisements which combined the strengths of qualitative semiotics and quantitative content analysis. Their combined research formula is sensitive to the multi-layered levels of meaning in visual texts but at the same time provides for the systematic rigours of quantitative analysis.

Leiss, Kline and Jhally (1990) also incorporate the notion of a cultural frame into their research. They argue that "a cultural frame is the predominant set of images, values, and forms of communication in a particular period that arises out of the interplay between marketing and advertising strategies, the mass media, and popular culture" (p. 62). This notion is important with regard to the primary object of examination in this chapter – the 'cultural frame' of a selection of travel photos on Facebook.

Barthes developed the related concept of 'anchorage', where the caption under a photograph provides crucial information for understanding the intended meaning. In the case of captions, the words "fix the floating chain of signifieds" (O'Sullivan et al., 1994, p. 13) and thus effectively anchor the preferred reading of a text by serving to eliminate other possible readings.

While semiotics is a valuable methodology for undertaking a close analysis of a particular text (such as a particular shot in a television program, an advertisement or a photograph), content analysis is able to perform analysis over a larger sample and thus detect similarities, differences and possible trends. When semiotics meets content analysis, we can interpret key features of a text and also measure the frequency of the specific phenomenon under investigation. These combined research tools (qualitative and quantitative) will be applied to the data examined in this chapter as they provide a rich base from which to undertake a close and thorough analysis of the travel images posted on Facebook.

Figure 1. An example of a 'Type one' photograph. Close shot of human subject/s sometimes with landscape or landmark

ISSUES AND ANALYSIS

In examining the types of photographs that were displayed in the albums, two main types of photograph were identified.

- A 'Type one' photograph includes human subjects such as the individual, family, friends, other tourists, or a combination of these. The human subject/s might be photographed with a close shot or a long shot. These images sometimes might include a landmark or landscape in the background (Figures 1 and 2).
- A 'Type two' photograph is what might be referred to as traditional 'tourist photograph' – visual representations of landscape, landmarks or other images such as streetscapes revealing aspects of the destination (Figures 3 and 4). These images do not include human subjects at all.

The following analysis focuses on the travel photographs generated by 10 individuals (five male and five female) from the Facebook community. The Facebook members that comprise this snapshot sample are people that I know and have befriended. The selection was made by selecting from my friends (approximately 250 when the selection was made) those who had posted the most travel albums on their site. For the purposes of protecting the identity of the individuals, the females are identified (from youngest to oldest) as F1, F2, F3, F4 and F5, while the males – M1, M2, M3, M4 and M5 – are also re-named in order of age. For a summary of the 10 individuals examined, refer Table 1 below. The snapshot begins with a discussion of the females, then moves on to examining the males.

Figure 2. Another example of a 'Type one' photograph. Long shot of human subject/s sometimes with landscape or landmark

Figure 3. An example of a 'Type two' photograph. Image of landscape with no human subject

Figure 4. Another example of a 'Type two' photograph. Image of landmark with no human subject

THE FIVE FEMALE FACEBOOK MEMBERS

Female 1 (F1)

F1 is 23 years of age, has 187 friends and has posted 10 photo albums on her Facebook site. Of the 10 photo albums, five are of destinations she has visited and were posted on Facebook in late 2007. The countries visited were: Italy, Greece, Spain, Germany and the United States, and these albums contain a total of 73 photographs. The album of photographs taken in Italy contains 21 photographs. Greece exhibits 17 photographs, while Spain and Germany contain 16 and 11 images respectively. The single destination in the Unites States displayed on the site is Las Vegas which contains 8 photos.

The majority of photographs in F1's albums are of people and in most cases, of herself often with other females. Of the 73 photographs in the five albums, 56 images or 77% fall into this category. The remaining images presented are what might be referred to as traditional 'tourist' photographs – visual representations of landscape, landmarks or other images such as streetscapes revealing aspects of the destination (type two photos). The food and drink consumed at the various locations are also displayed in F1's travel albums. Such images included pasta consumed in Italy, glasses of Amaretto in Greece, and Paella and Churros in Spain.

Six of the 73 photographs in the albums attracted comments from four of F1's Facebook friends. All of the photographs which attracted comments included human subjects as opposed to images of landmark or landscape devoid of human subjects. The comments were generally of a positive nature. One friend commented that they had sat on the very same beach chair at the same beach – Black Beach in Santorini. The photograph portrays F1 lying on a deck chair while eating a bagel with one hand. F1 is positioned in the centre of the photo and at the base of it. She

Table 1. Summary of the 10 Facebook Members.

Facebook member	Age	Number of friends	Number of travel albums	Number of photos	Photos with human subjects	Photos of landscape/ landmark and surrounds	Number of comments on photos
F1	23	187	5	73	56	17	6
F2	28	141	5	143	110	33	18
F3	30	159	5	107	47	60	2
F4	33	145	4	177	23	154	2
F5	53	30	2	41	14	27	4
M1	22	562	1	47	34	13	2
M2	27	310	4	214	188	26	14
M3	29	206	2	89	49	50	0
M4	32	193	10	204	0	204	2
M5	40	186	4	56	37	19	14

is dressed in bathers, shorts, sunglasses and a hat. The beach scene includes 10 large umbrellas carefully positioned around F1, while the water and other tourists can be seen on one side of the image. The further information that has been added to this photo (by virtue of her friend's comment) provides further meaning to the visual image. The underlying message is that the world is such a small place that two individual tourists can experience much the same location in similar ways at separate times and places.

F2

F2 is 28 years of age, has 141 friends and has posted nine photo albums on her Facebook site. Of the nine albums, five are of destinations she has visited since September 2007. The countries visited were: Italy, France, the Netherlands, Mexico and The Solomon Islands. These five albums contain a total of 143 photographs. The album on Italy presents 40 photographs, France displays 39, while the Netherlands, Mexico and The Solomon Islands displays 11, 22 and 31 photos respectively.

Similarly to F1, the majority of photographs in F2's albums are of people and in most cases, of herself – often with friends and family. Of the 143 photographs in the five albums, 110 images or 76% fall into this category – a surprisingly similar figure to F1's 77%. Type two photographs in the five albums totalled 33 photos. F2's travel albums displayed objects such as food, drink and bicycles as two of the albums presented photographs taken while on cycling tours while in Europe.

Eighteen of the 143 photographs in the albums attracted comments from many of F2's friends. The photograph that received the most comments (four posts) was of the subject and her sisters in a car in Mexico. The comments made by the sisters generally centred around how good/bad each other looked in the particular photograph.

F3

F3 is 30 years of age, has 159 friends and has posted 17 photo albums on her Facebook site. Of the 17 albums, five are of destinations she has visited since September 2007. The countries visited were: Italy, France, Scotland, Ireland and the United States. All albums are given the name of the city or region visited (rather than the country) – in this case Tuscany, Paris, Edinburgh, Dublin and New York. The five travel albums house a total of

107 photographs. The album on Italy presents 26 photographs, France displays 36, while Scotland, Ireland and the United States present 30, 4 and 11 photos respectively.

Unlike F1 and F2, the photographs taken by F3 include more type two photos. Of the 107 photographs in the five albums, 60 images or 56% are travel photos of scenery such as landmarks or landscape including the Eiffel Tower, Edinburgh Castle and the Statue of Liberty. The remaining 47 photographs in the five albums display human subjects. Thus, 44% of the images show the subject alone, with friends or include images of locals or tourists as part of the photograph.

F3 appears to have tried to capture the essence of the city she has visited and also humorously indulges in the anticipated cliché of the location such as drinking Guinness in Ireland, mimicking the pose of sculptures in Italy, or looking up in awe at the Eiffel Tower when in Paris. Despite the generally good quality of the images taken and the deliberate humour injected into some of the imagery, only one of the 107 photographs in the albums attracted comments from F3's friends. It may be that F3's friends are not particularly interested in her photos or do not feel particularly motivated to comment on them. The photograph which attracted comments shows F3 standing in front of a New York skyline. She is positioned in the bottom right-hand corner of the photograph with the backdrop of the skyline to the left. The image is framed in such a way that the blue sky takes up the top half of the photo, while F3 and the skyline take up the bottom half. Of the two comments posted about this photo, one friend remarked on the attractiveness of the backdrop while the other made mention of a suspected Unidentified Flying Object (UFO) – actually an airship or blimp – in the background.

F4

F4 is 33 years of age, has 145 friends and has posted eight photo albums on her Facebook site. Of the eight albums, four are of destinations she has visited since September 2007. The countries visited were: Italy (spread over three albums) and the Czech Republic. The four travel albums house a total of 177 photographs. F4 puts more photos in her albums than the other Facebook users examined and two of these albums hold the maximum number of photos able to be stored in an album – 60. The albums on Italy present 135 photographs, while the Czech Republic album displays 42 images.

Similarly to F3, the photographs taken by F4 mainly represent landscape, landmarks and other images of the destination as opposed to including human subjects. Of the 177 photographs in the four albums, a staggering 154 images or 87% are type two. The remaining 23 photographs (13%) in the four albums display human subjects. Almost all of these subjects are of fellow travellers who happened to find themselves in the photograph because they were simply at the same destination at the same time as opposed to friends or relatives known to F4. As only three of the 177 photographs display F4, one gains the impression that she is a lone traveller. It can also be seen that in two of these photographs (the Trevi Fountain in Rome and eating a gelato at an outdoor café), F4 took a self-portrait. One can only hazard a guess but she may have felt that travel photographs without herself in them might not properly contextualise her album, or that her friends and family might not believe she had actually taken the trip.

Again like F3, despite the excellent quality of the images, only two of the 177 photographs in the albums attracted comments from F4's friends. It may also be the case that younger people are more likely to comment on their friends photos, or even that the nature of these photos (often with human subjects) are such that they generate an increased likelihood that a comment will follow. The two photographs that received comments from two friends were of Cinque Terre in Italy. Both friends remarked on the stunning nature of the landscape and the photographs were composed particularly well. One image was of a five boats on a marina at sunset; while the other showed the coastline and sea of Cinque Terre in equal proportions to the left and right of the striking image.

F5

The final female Facebook member selected was F5. She is 53 years of age, has 30 friends and has posted four photo albums on her Facebook site. Of the four albums, two are of destinations that F5 has visited since September 2007. The country visited was the Unites States (with albums covering Colorado, and a visit to the Grand Canyon). The two travel albums house a total of 41 photographs.

In a similar fashion to F3 and F4, the photographs taken by F5 mainly represent landscape, landmarks and other images of the destination as opposed to a focus on human subjects. Of the 41 photographs in the two albums, 27 images or 66% are type two photos. The remaining 14 photographs or 34% in the two albums display human subjects. Seven of the 41 photographs (17%) reveal F5.

Four of the 41 photographs in the albums attracted comments from F5's friends. Three of the photographs that received comments were of the Grand Canyon (F5 labelled that album 'Third Wonder of the World'). Her friends remarked on the incredible nature of the scenery.

THE FIVE MALE FACEBOOK MEMBERS

Male 1 (M1)

M1 is first of the five male Facebook members selected and is 22 years of age. He has a larger than usual amount of friends (562) and has posted two photo albums on his Facebook site. Of the two photo albums, one is of a destination he visited in late 2007 - Egypt. This album contains 47 photographs. As one might expect from a 22 year-old, the majority of photographs in M1's albums are of himself and other friends and relatives. Of the 47 photographs in the album (which was given the title 'Trip to Egypt'), 34 images or 72% are type one photos. The remaining 13 images in the album (28%) are representations of landscape, landmarks or other photos revealing aspects of the destination with no human subjects displayed.

Two of the 47 photographs in the album attracted comments from two of M1's Facebook friends. Both photographs commented upon were of M1 in front of Egypt's major tourist attraction – the pyramids. In one of the photos M1 was photographed sitting on a horse – an image which one of M1's friends apparently found hilarious. The image is perfectly framed and displays M1 on a horse before three pyramids of descending size from the foreground to the background. In the distance other tourists on horses can be seen. When I asked M1 about the comment made by his friend in relation to this photo, he explained that the friend's expectation was that camel rides were more appropriate for a desert tourism experience.

M2

M2 is 27 years of age, has 310 friends and has posted 14 photo albums on his Facebook site. Of the 14 albums, four are dedicated to a destination he visited in late 2007 – the United States. The four albums contain a total of 214 photographs. Similarly to M1, the vast majority of photographs in M2's four USA albums are of himself, family and friends. Of the 214 photographs, 188 images or 88% fall into this category. Traditional 'tourist' scenes in the four albums such as images of landscape totalled 26 photos (representing just 12%).

Fourteen of the 214 photographs in the four albums attracted comments from three of M2's family and friends. The comments generally revolved around how enjoyable the trip was or how M2 and his wife looked in particular photographs. While comments such as these may appear somewhat flippant, the all-important affirmations provide crucial anchorage as they reinforce the concept that the experience shared on the holiday was a pleasurable one.

M3

M3 is 29 years of age, has 206 friends and has posted 17 photo albums on his Facebook site. Of the 17 albums, two are of destinations M3 has visited since September 2007. The countries visited were Malaysia and China. The two travel photo albums house a total of 89 photographs. The album on Malaysia presents 29 photographs, while the album on China contains 60 photos.

Unlike M1 and M2, the photographs taken by M3 include more than half of landscape, landmarks and other images of the destination without the inclusion of human subjects. Of the 89 photographs in the two albums, 50 images or 56% are type two photos including the Petronas Towers in Kuala Lumpur, the Great Wall of China and the 2008 Beijing Olympic Games stadium colloquially referred to as 'The Birds' Nest'. The remaining 49 photographs in the five albums display human subjects. Thus, 44% of the images show the subject alone or with friends or include images of locals or tourists as part of the photograph. The percentage breakdown of these two categories of photographs is identical to F3 who is just one year older than M3.

Also like F3, M3 tries to capture the essence of the city he has visited and also humorously indulges in the experience. For instance, M3's album on China is given the somewhat postmodern name 'China - Where is the Sky?' (alluding to the air pollution) and in a number of the photos he appears to be looking for the apparently absent sky. Despite the good quality of the photographs and the interesting subject matter, not one of the 89 photographs in the two albums attracted a comment.

M4

M4 is 32 years of age, has 193 friends and has posted 17 photo albums on his Facebook site. Of the 17 albums, 10 are of a destination he has visited since September 2007 – Japan. The 10 albums on Japan house a total of 204 photographs.

Surprisingly, all 204 photographs taken by M4 are of landscape, landmarks and other images of the destination (with many internal locations photographed). Despite the excellent quality and composition of the images, only one of the 204 photographs in the 10 albums attracted comments from M4's friends. The photograph that received comments from two friends was of a seagull swooping down to eat a potato chip while in mid flight. One friend commented, "Nice picture! I hope I can put it in my painting someday", while another said, "You feed the seagull using your left hand, while taking this picture with your right hand? Stunning!" The reply to this second comment from M4 was simply but humorously, "Oh, that's not my hand..." (with a smiley face emoticon). The comments focus on how the image was constructed and both M4 and the friends share in a dialogue about the creation of his craft.

M5

Finally, M5 is 40 years of age, has 186 friends and has posted four photo albums on his Facebook site. All four albums are of destinations he has visited since September 2007. The countries visited were: Canada, France, Italy and Hong Kong. The four travel albums house a total of 56 photographs. The majority of photographs in M5's albums are of himself and other family members. Of the 56 photographs in the albums, 37 images or 66% include people. The remaining 19 images in the album (34%) are type two photos.

Fourteen of the 56 photographs attracted comments from 10 of M5's friends. The photograph that received the most comments was of a hamburger and a bowl of hot chips smothered in tomato sauce. The photo caption by M5 was, "Typical morning after the night before French Canadian breakfast". In this comment M5 is both making a statement about the partying that took place the night before, while expanding upon the culturally appropriate way to recover the next morning. The message provides a glimpse into the travel experience undertaken by M5 and also provides something of a culinary lesson for those not familiar with a 'typical' French Canadian breakfast.

SUMMARY ANALYSIS OF THE 10 FACEBOOK MEMBERS

Having examined the 10 Facebook members, some concluding comments on the analysis are also warranted. While it is obviously extremely difficult to gauge how influential the travel photos of one are on the travel plans of another, it would appear that F2, M2 and M5 (with 18, 14 and 14 comments respectively) certainly generated interest from friends as a result of the photos posted.

Members F1 to F5 ranged from 23 to 53 years of age, with the average age being 33 years. M1 to M5 ranged from 22 to 40 years, with an average age of 30 years. Thus, the male sample was slightly younger than the females examined. Along with being slightly younger, the males also had significantly more friends. The total number of friends for M1 to M5 was 1457, with an average of 291 friends each. For F1 to F5 the total number of friends was 662, thus averaging 132 friends each.

Surprisingly, both sample sets displayed 21 albums amongst the group, with an average of 4.2 albums per person. It should be pointed out however that the data for the males was significantly influenced by the large number of travel albums (10) that M4 displayed on his Facebook site. The average number of travel photographs in these albums was also relatively similar across the two sample sets. While the females displayed a total of 541 photos (averaging 108 each), the males displayed a total of 610 photos – a slightly higher average of 122 each. Amongst the group of five males the data was more varied as M2 and M4 had a total of 214 and 204 travel photos respectively.

Both sample groups also took more photos collectively of type two photographs (images of landscape, landmark and surrounds) as opposed to type one photos. Collectively, the females displayed 291 type two photos, while the males displayed 312. The females displayed 250 type one images (with human subjects), while the males collectively presented 308 of this type of photo. As explained in the above analysis dealing with each Facebook member, F2 displayed 110 type one photos and only 33 type two photos. Her photos also attracted the most number of comments from friends. The male Facebook member who attracted the most comments on photos was M2, and like F2, the majority of his photos (188) displayed human subjects. While this sample size is far too small to draw any substantial conclusions, it would appear that type one images with human subjects (often known to the viewer of the photograph) are more likely to attract a comment from a friend as opposed to images devoid of human subjects. Humans ultimately need to communicate with other humans, and social networking sites such as Facebook trade on this basic human need.

OPPORTUNITIES FOR FUTURE RESEARCH

The significance and potential motivator of this form of promotion cannot be overlooked when it comes to visual Travel Recommender Systems (TRS) or Destination Recommendation Systems (DRS) – a topic which although commands a "high level of interest" from both the academic and commercial sectors remains "rather young" (Stock, Werthner and Zancanaro, 2006, p. 297).

This study seeks to examine just one of the ways in which some travel photographs might be analysed and further extend the body of literature in this area. This chapter also aims to commence a dialogue about the types of images people choose to post on the Internet, and how these images may begin to possibly influence others. How these visual images work to reinforce the memory of the travel experience for the photographer might be explored in further studies. Future studies in Tourism Informatics and the visual culture of Tourism might examine the images generated in the world of Facebook or other social networks on a much larger and more in-depth scale. This study seeks to open the door to that further research by shedding some light on possible forms of analysis.

CONCLUSION

This chapter reflected on social aspects of Tourism Informatics with specific reference to the travel photographs posted on Facebook of 10 people over a one year period. The analysis provided a microscopic glimpse into the types of travel photographs that individuals post and how these images might be received and perceived by other Facebook users.

F2 and M2 (with 18 and 14 comments on their photos respectively) generated the most interest from friends as a result of the photos posted. F2 (who is 28 years of age) had 143 photographs in her five albums. A staggering 76% of these photos included human subjects. It is not surprisingly then that F2's photos also generated more comments than the others in the sample set. Of M2's 214 photographs, 188 images (an even more staggering 88%) included human subjects. M2 is 27 years of age. Comments such as these provide crucial anchorage as they reinforce the concept that the experience shared on the holiday was a pleasurable one, and thus are more likely to influence the viewer of the photograph. This small study also found that younger people generally take more photographs with human subjects while older people take a higher percentage of photos of scenery and landscape.

As outlined, this sample is clearly not representative of all (or possibly even some) Facebook users. However, it seems clear that the images and words projected may have played a role in the way a particular destination is perceived by others. New impressions of a destination may have been gained by those who viewed the photographs. These perceptions will obviously vary depending on whether or not the viewer of the photograph has also travelled to that destination.

Images communicated via social media play a part in the overall promotional package that can work to either reinforce or revise the travel experiences of the viewer. In the highly democratised world of the Internet, one person's travel snapshots can very easily become part of another person's travel plans. As 500 million photos are uploaded to this most popular social networking site each month, the significance of one's Facebook travel photos as a form of TRS should not be underestimated.

REFERENCES

Berelson, B. (1952). *Content analysis in communication research.* New York: Free Press.

Comscore. (2008). *Social networking explodes worldwide as sites increase their focus on cultural relevance.* Retrieved August 12, 2008, from http://www.comscore.com/press/release.asp?press=2396

Costa, G., Dobbin, M., & Klisanin, R. (2008). *Facebook hunt for missing Melbourne woman.* Retrieved September 25, 2008, from http://www.theage.com.au/national/facebook-hunt-for-missing-melbourne-woman-20080925-4nux.html

Culler, J. (1981). Semiotics of tourism. *American Journal of Semiotics, 1*, 127–140.

Dulworth, M. (2008). *The connect effect: Building strong personal, professional, and virtual networks.* San Francisco: Berrett-Koehler Publishers.

Emerson, D. (2008). *Facebook friends not real friends: Judge.* Retrieved March 27, 2008, from http://www.smh.com.au/news/technology/facebook-friends-not-real-judge/2008/03/27/1206207279597.html

Engdahl, S. (Ed.). (2007). *Online social networking.* Farmington Hills, MI: Greenhaven Press.

Fiske, J. (1990). *Introduction to communication studies* (2nd ed.). London: Routledge.

Hodgkinson, T. (2008). *With friends like these...* Retrieved January 14, 2008, from http://www.guardian.co.uk/technology/2008/jan/14/facebook

Leiss, W., Kline, S., & Jhally, S. (1990). *Social communication in advertising: Persons, products and images of well-being* (2nd ed.). Ontario, Canada: Nelson Canada.

McIntyre, P. (2008). *Using social media for commercial gain.* Retrieved December 4, 2008, from http://www.theage.com.au/news/technology/biztech/using-social-media-for-commercial-gain/2008/12/04/1228257189521.html

Morgan, N., Pritchard, A., & Pride, R. (2004). *Destination branding: Creating the unique destination proposition.* Oxford, UK: Elsevier.

Moses, A. (2008). *Coming soon... Facebook: The movie.* Retrieved September 1, 2008, from http://www.theage.com.au/news/web/coming-soon--facebook-the-movie/2008/09/01/1220121111266.html

Nash, K. (2008). *A peek inside Facebook.* Retrieved August 31, 2008, from http://www.pcworld.com/businesscenter/article/150489/a_peek_inside_facebook.html

Neuman, W. L. (2006). *Social research methods: Qualitative and quantitative approaches* (6th ed.). Boston: Allyn and Bacon.

Niedzviecki, H. (2008, November 1). With 700 friends like these, who needs...? [Insight section]. *Age*, 3.

O'Sullivan, T., Hartley, J., Saunders, D., Montgomery, M., & Fiske, J. (1994). *Key concepts in communication and cultural studies* (2nd ed.). London: Routledge.

Pitchford, S. (2008). *Identity tourism: Imaging and imagining the nation.* Bingley, UK: Emerald Group Publishing.

Pretes, M. (2003). Tourism and nationalism. *Annals of Tourism Research, 30*(1), 125–142. doi:10.1016/S0160-7383(02)00035-X

Rojek, C. (1997). Indexing, dragging, and social construction. In C. Rojek & J. Urry (Eds.), *Touring cultures: Transformations of travel and theory* (pp. 52-74). London: Routledge.

Sheldon, P. (1997). *Tourism information technology.* Wallingford, CT: CAB International.

Stock, O., Werthner, H., & Zancanaro, M. (2006). Futuring travel destination recommendation systems. In D. R. Fesenmaier, H. Werthner, & K. W. Wober (Eds.), *Destination recommendation systems: Behavioural foundations and applications* (pp. 297-314). Oxfordshire, UK: CAB International.

Urry, J. (1990). *The tourist gaze: Leisure and travel in contemporary societies.* London: Sage Publications.

Urry, J. (1995). *Consuming places.* London: Routledge.

Wilkinson, S. (2004). Focus group research. In D. Silverman (Ed.), *Qualitative research: Theory, method and practice* (2nd ed.) (pp. 177-199). London: Sage Publications.

Williamson, J. (1978). *Decoding advertisements: Ideology and meaning in advertising.* London: Marion Boyars.f

Chapter 8
Virtual Travel Community: Bridging Travellers and Locals

Jin Young Chung
Texas A&M University, USA

Dimitrios Buhalis
Bournemouth University, UK

ABSTRACT

With the rapid development of Web 2.0 influence in tourism, this chapter aims to examine the current state of virtual travel community (VTC) studies, and to offer an additional perspective of VTC, beyond the conventional research trends. The notion of virtual community includes a group of people who tend to build relationships with one another via computer-mediated communication, regardless of geographical distances (Rheingold, 1991). However, current VTC knowledge has primarily focused on consumer behaviour from the travellers' side (e.g., information search, decision-making process, sharing experience with other travellers), and little attempt has been made to examine the use of VTC for connecting travellers in the generating region to the locals in the destination region. Emerging information communication technologies (ICTs) and the use of technology in tourism e-tourism- make it much easier to communicate between people in both regions. This chapter brings empirical evidence from one virtual community – CouchSurfing.com – and demonstrates that the opportunity to build relationships between potential travellers and locals has increased dramatically through innovative technology services. Further research is recommended through the use of alternative methodologies, such as netnography or social network analysis. This chapter provides both policy and managerial implications by exploring how technology and VTC can support the bridging the gap between locals and prospective visitors.

E-TOURISM DEVELOPMENTS AND WEB 2.0

Information Communication Technologies (ICTs) have been transforming tourism globally. ICTs have been revolutionising the world of Tourism (Buhalis, 2003). This is already evident in a wide range of examples and cases around the world (Egger & Buhalis, 2008). ICTs empower consumers to identify, customise, and purchase tourism products, and support the globalisation of

DOI: 10.4018/978-1-60566-818-5.ch008

the industry by providing tools for developing, managing and distributing offerings worldwide. Increasingly, ICTs play a critical role for the competitiveness of tourism organisations and destinations (Buhalis, 2003). ICTs are a key determinant of organisational competitiveness, and a wide range of technological developments propel the evolution observed. In addition, ICTs enable travellers to access reliable and accurate information as well as to undertake reservations in a fraction of time, cost and inconvenience required by conventional methods.

Buhalis and Law (2008) demonstrated that developments in ICTs have undoubtedly changed business practices and strategies as well as industry structures. If the past 20 years have seen an emphasis on technology per se, then since the Year 2000 we have been witnessing the truly transformational effect of the communications technologies. This has given scope for the development of a wide range of new tools and services that facilitate global interaction between players around the world. Increasingly, ICTs play a critical role for the competitiveness of tourism organisations and destinations as well as for the entire industry as a whole. Developments in search engines, carrying capacity and speed of networks have influenced the number of travellers around the world that use technologies for planning and experiencing their travels. ICTs have also radically changed the efficiency and effectiveness of tourism organisations, the way that businesses are conducted in the marketplace, as well as how consumers interact with organisations. The ICT-driven business processes re-engineering observed in the industry gradually generates a new paradigm shift. This alters the structure of the entire industry and develops a whole range of opportunities and threats for all stakeholders. Not only ICTs empower consumers to identify, customise and purchase tourism products but they also support the globalisation of the industry by providing effective tools for suppliers to develop, manage and distribute their offerings worldwide.

Since 2007, Web 2.0 has been developed to represent the wide range of peer-to-peer interactions between individuals online. The emergence of Web 2.0 or Travel 2.0 brings together the concept of social networking/virtual communities and applies it to the tourism industry. The integration of information processing, multimedia and communications created the 'World Wide Web' (WWW) to enable the near instant distribution of media-rich documents and to revolutionise the interactivity between computer users and servers. Perhaps one of the most interesting current developments is the development of Web 2.0, a phrase coined by O'Reilly (2005) that refers to a second generation of web-based services based on citizens/consumer generated content—such as social networking sites, blogs, wikis, communication tools, and folksonomies—that emphasize online collaboration and sharing among users. A Web 2.0 website may feature a number of the following techniques including: Rich Internet application techniques, optionally Ajax-based; Cascading Style Sheets (CSS); Semantically valid XHTML markup and the use of Microformats; Syndication and aggregation of data in Really Simple Syndication (RSS/Atom; Clean and meaningful URLs; Extensive use of folksonomies (in the form of tags or tagclouds, for example); Use of wiki software; Weblog publishing; Mashups and REST or XML Webservice APIs. Increasingly, the Internet is becoming a platform of data/views/knowledge creation and sharing which harness the network to get better information to all users (See Table 1)(O'Reilly, 2005).

Based on the mainstream of online community research in social science disciplines, online community research is increasingly influential in tourism informatics literature as one of the emerging agendas. The terms online community, virtual community, or online virtual community have been interchangeably used. Virtual travel communities (VTCs) have become popular as credible information sources since they provide potential tourists with up to date, personalised,

Table 1. O'Reilly formulates the sense of Web 2.0 by example

Web 1.0		Web 2.0
DoubleClick	→	Google AdSense
Ofoto	→	Flickr
Akamai	→	BitTorrent
mp3.com	→	Napster
Britannica Online	→	Wikipedia
personal websites	→	Blogging
evite	→	upcoming.org and EVDB
domain name speculation	→	search engine optimization
page views	→	cost per click
screen scraping	→	web services
publishing	→	Participation
multimap	→	Google Earth with content layers
content management systems	→	Wikis
directories (taxonomy)	→	tagging ("folksonom")
stickiness	→	Syndication

Source: Based on O'Reilly, 2005

user-generated content (UGC), including trustworthy reviews and recommendations (Buhalis & Law, 2008). Despite VTCs' large potential impact on the tourism industry, Preece (2000) stated that research on the topic is still at an infancy stage when comparing to other geographical and physical communities.

In a virtual travel community, functioning like social networking sites, users are able to find plenty of information from like-minded users from around the world, beyond their actual friendship circle of family members. They can also build relationships with other users or become involved in the community, regardless of geographical restrictions. They participate in communities for a wide range of purposes which may include fun, companionship, demonstration of expertise, enjoyment, and amusement as an end in itself (Chung & Buhalis, in press). A range of functional, social, psychological, and hedonic benefits have been identified as the main motivators leading online users to participate in VTCs (Wang, Yu, & Fesenmaier, 2002). For example, TripAdvisor (www.tripadvisor.com) is amongst the most successful social networking/virtual community in tourism that facilitates the reviewing of all hotels around the world and brings together individuals in discussion forums. The system provides users with independent travel reviews and comments written from TripAdvisor members and experts, and offers a powerful platform for interaction between peers (Wang & Fesenmaier, 2004). User satisfaction is a major factor for evaluating a travel organization. By analyzing VTCs' content, travel organizations can understand their customers' satisfactions and behaviour, and undertake corrective actions to improve their offering. They can also increase brand awareness and strengthen brand association through the assistance of VTCs.

However, despite the various benefits of VTCs that have been explored, the need for a better understanding of the social aspects of VTC has been recently recognised and undertaken as a research issue. To date, the interactions between users (mainly potential travellers or hedonic surfers) have been investigated. Most researchers have focused on VTCs only from a consumer behaviour perspective, and they have been trying to explain how consumers search/obtain information, maintain connections with other consumers, and eventually make travel decisions. However, little attempt has been made to research the use of VTCs for connecting travellers in generating regions with local communities in destination regions (Leiper, 1990). The extended networks encompassing locals in the destinations and the travellers have been neglected hitherto. Thus, in this chapter, this newly recognised social aspect of VTCs is analysed through a case study using one of the fast-growing VTCs, namely the CouchSurfing.com. This chapter consists of four major parts: introduction, literature review, a case study, and discussion and conclusion. The chapter begins with brief description of a tourism system and literature review on cross-cultural understanding studies. Then, it focuses on major VTC studies conducted over the recent years, and then explores the case study. Finally, it provides further research directions, followed by discussion of the results of a case study.

A DEFINITION OF VIRTUAL COMMUNITY

Although many researchers have defined virtual communities and have attempted to understand their features, the most frequently quoted definition is given by Rheingold (1991): "Virtual communities are cultural aggregations that emerge when enough people bump into each other often enough in cyberspace. A virtual community is a group of people who may or may not meet one another face to face, and who exchange words and ideas through the mediation of computer bulletin boards and networks." (pp. 57-58). Further, Rheingold (1991) extends the scope of an online community to involve individuals' daily activities: chatting, discussing, exchanging knowledge, sharing emotional support, finding friends, playing games, and even falling in love. Preece (2000) also proposes four basic components for organising an online community including people, purpose, policy, and computer system. In other words, a virtual community is defined as a virtual place in which people with a shared purpose interact on the basis of the policies established, by using computer systems (Preece, 2000). From a multidisciplinary perspective, the following core attributes of VTCs can be identified (Whittaker, Issacs, & O'Day, 1997).

- Shared goals, interests, needs, or activities that motivate individuals to belong to the community
- Being engaged in repeated, active participation, and often, intense interaction, emotional ties, and shared activities that occur among participants
- Access to shared resources, and policies that determine the access to those resources
- Reciprocity of information, support, and services among members
- A shared context of social conventions, language, and protocols

In brief, a virtual community is perceived as a cyberspace system in which people with shared goals and needs are engaged regardless of where people are located.

Virtual communities are becoming incredibly influential in tourism as consumers increasingly trust their peers, rather than marketing messages. A Virtual Travel Community (VTC) makes it easier for people to obtain information, maintain connections, develop relationships, and eventually make travel-related decisions (Stepchenkova, Mills, & Jiang, 2007). Vogt and Fesenmaier (1998) stated that participation and attitude are the primary dimensions of consumer behaviour in the virtual communities. Since many travellers like to share their travel experiences and recommendations with others, VTCs have become one of their

Figure 1. The Tourism Industry and the Tourism Systems

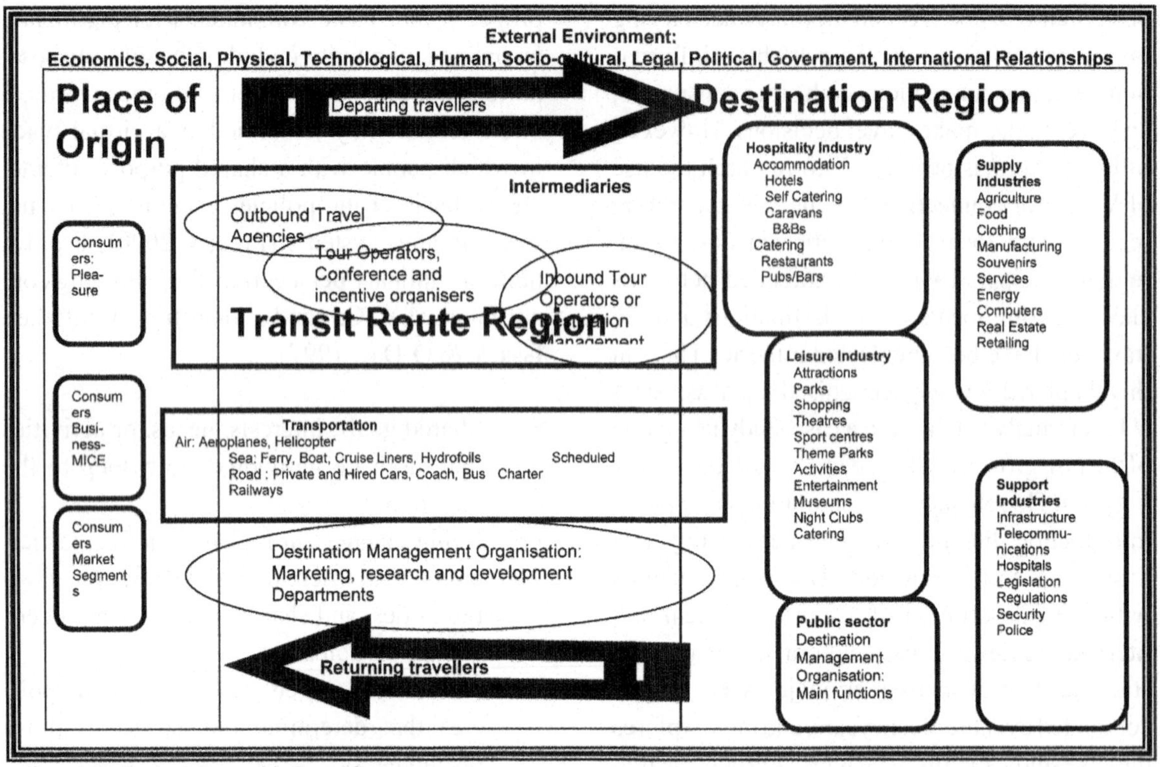

Figure 1. The Tourism Industry and the Tourism Systems
Source: Adapted from Leiper, 1990 and Cooper and Buhalis, 1998

favourite areas to post their travel dairy (Vogt & Fesenmaier, 1998). Additionally, online travellers are enthusiastic to meet other travellers who have similar attitudes, interests and way of life (Wang, et al., 2002). As such, better understanding VTC users' behaviour and motivation can assist tourism practitioners and policy makers to establish, operate, and maintain VTCs in a more efficient way. This, in turn, facilitates consumer centric marketing or relationship marketing (Niininen, Buhalis, & March, 2007). VTCs, however, may be at risk of losing members if their members are not satisfied with the content, design, security policies, and repercussions for non-compliance with community rules (Allison, Currall, Moss, & Stuart, 2005; Wang, et al., 2002).

THE TOURISM SYSTEM

The tourism phenomenon can be observed as a traveller makes a move toward a destination and returns back to the place of origin. Some areas generate travellers, and some areas host them, and vice verse. The transit route connects the traveller in the generating region to the destination region, and travellers are located only in this route. As demonstrated in Figure 1, Buhalis (2003) adopted Leiper's (1990) tourism system and Cooper and Buhalis' (1998) model to include five key elements: a traveller generating region; a destination region; a transit region including Intermediaries, Transportation, and Technology

The tourism system model has been a theoretical framework in many tourism studies over the last two decades (Buhalis, 2002; Cooper & Buhalis,

1998). However, to date, many studies regarding tourist behaviour have examined the individual or group behaviour between prospective travellers, but failed to connect travellers to the locals in destinations. Even the research on Virtual Travel Communities, which operate on the cyberspace, and therefore are free of physical or geographical limitations, have only been examined mainly from a consumer behaviour perspective.

INTERACTION BETWEEN LOCALS AND TRAVELLERS

The interaction between locals and travellers has been widely researched in the tourism literature. Research has particularly, focused on resident's attitudes toward tourists or tourism development. However, several other studies (e.g. Fisher & Price, 1991; Gomez-Jacinto, Martin-Garcia, & Bertiche-Haud'Huyze, 1999) have attempted to investigate attitude changes caused by the interaction between hosts and travellers in terms of cross-cultural understanding (Nyaupane, Teye, & Paris, 2008). While research on residents' attitudes toward travellers includes both intra-cultural and inter-cultural relationships, most studies on cross-cultural understanding emphasize intercultural interactions.

Fisher and Price (1991) argued that some factors such as motivation, satisfaction, and the degree of intercultural interaction need to be considered as predictors of positive attitude changes. Following the Fisher and Price model, Gomez et al. (1999) proposed a structural model depicting the influence of tourists' intercultural experience on changes of attitude toward each other. In their longitudinal study, they added other predictors to Fisher and Price' initial model: previous stereotype of destination people, the amount of tourist activities, and service quality. Most importantly, they found that overall holiday satisfaction has a mediating role of relationship between all predictors and attitude changes. Thyne, Lawson, and Todd (2006) examined the impact of cultural differences between tourists and hosts on local communities by a conjoint analysis. Their empirical study revealed that locals prefer visitors with similar cultural background, and more specifically, residents in New Zealand were more likely to greet with U.S. tourists than other cultures including Japan, Australia, and Germany. Interestingly, Australian tourists were relatively not welcomed to New Zealand residents despite of cultural similarity. Thyne et al. (2006) attributed the discrepancy of this finding to temporal tension between two countries due to a sports rivalry.

Additionally, some other studies found that independent travellers including backpackers and students on study abroad programs are more likely to select exotic cultures, and as a result, to have prior attitude changed. The fact that individual tourists are more easily influenced by intercultural factors compared to organised tour groups is understandable since they are more flexible to experience cultural attributes at a destination, whereas organised groups have to only follow the pre-planned itinerary. It is apparent that a fixed travel schedule limits their opportunities to freely interact with local communities.

VIRTUAL TRAVEL COMMUNITY RESEARCH

The aforementioned definitions and principles have influenced the VTC research. However, although many researchers in tourism have investigated the nature of VTCs, most of their research interests have focused on the consumer side of the tourism system (Table 2).

Research has primarily concentrated on potential travellers' behaviour from a consumer behaviour perspective (e.g. information search behaviour, interaction with information online, electronic word-of-mouth). Nevertheless, the inevitable relationship that develops between travellers and local people has been rarely dealt with as a topic of VTC research.

Table 2. Major VTC studies conducted over the recent years

Authors	Major argument(s)	Focal members in VTC	Main interest(s)
Armstrong and Hagel (1996)	An online travel community meets four different consumers' values: transaction, interest, fantasy, and relationship.	Prospective travellers	Information search behaviour Decision-making
Wang, Yu, and Fesenmaier (2002)	VTC is composed of three core elements such as place, symbol, and virtual; and four peripheral elements including people, policy, purpose, and computer systems.	Prospective and experienced travellers	Information search Network
Wang and Fesenmaier (2004)	Functional, social, psychological, and hedonic benefits perceived by online travel community members, social and hedonic benefits have a major impact on their level of participation in community activities.	Prospective and experienced travellers	Information search behaviour Motivation
Kim, Lee, and Hiemstra (2004)	Three aspects of VTCs have influenced the members' loyalty; and consumer loyalty is strongly associated with purchasing behaviour.	Online community members who are interested in travel	Consumer loyalty Buying behaviour
Niininen, March, and Buhalis (2006)	A number of tourists are connected through virtual communities, and they share their own experiences, exchange valuable information regarding tourism destinations and service.	Experienced travellers	Information search behaviour Information source (e.g. electronic Word-of-Mouth (eWOM))

Armstrong and Hagel (1996) postulated that an online travel community provides four different values to its own members: transaction, interest, fantasy, and relationship. For example, community of transaction may refer to the purchase of airline tickets and making hotel reservations; while the community of interest offers the opportunity to share information and experience with other travellers and residents at the destination. In addition, community of fantasy is associated with hedonic features, such as a game or an event, whilst community of relationship allows community members to find their travel companions for a trip (Armstrong & Hagel, 1996). It is inevitable that multiple benefits may motivate users to participate in communities and this is also reflected in the value that is generated.

Wang, Yu, and Fesenmaier (2002) pointed out that although online communities have been a central element of the Internet, less attention has been paid to the notion of online virtual community in tourism. Thus, in order to define a virtual community, they proposed three core elements, namely: place, symbol, and virtual. Place indicates a certain kind of space where individuals can develop or maintain social relationships. This may not necessarily be a physical space. Symbol refers to meanings or an identity which a virtual community provides to its users (Wang, et al., 2002). If a symbol for the community is absent or lacking, the online community may not be attractive to any online user. Being virtual is literally a salient characteristic which defines the difference between physical and online communities.

In addition, it is suggested that there are peripheral components of a virtual community, including a group of people with specific purposes, policies, and computer systems. Wang et al. (2002) further argued that a virtual community fulfils three sorts of needs from an online user perspective:

1. Functional needs (transaction, information, entertainment, and convenience),
2. Psychological needs (identification, involvement, belonging, and relatedness), and

3. Social needs (relationship, interactivity, trust, and escape).

Moreover, Wang and Fesenmaier (2004) attempted to empirically test Wang et al. (2002) propositions of benefits offered by virtual communities. As a result, they concluded that the main benefits of a virtual community are functional, social, psychological, and hedonic; where social and hedonic benefits have a major impact on the community members' level of participation in its activities (Wang & Fesenmaier, 2004). This empirical research regarding relationships between benefits and member participation is based on a consumer behaviour perspective (e.g. information search and information source).

Kim, Lee, and Hiemstra (2004) also conducted empirical research about the effects of an online community on customer loyalty and purchasing behaviour. They argued that four factors associated with a sense of belonging to a VTC include: membership, influence and relatedness, integration and fulfilment of need, and shared emotional connection. Excluding shared emotional connection, it was found that three senses are significantly related to online community users' loyalty, in particular in engendering a higher degree of loyalty; i.e. a consumer is more likely to buy products or service within a VTC (Kim, Lee, & Hiemstra, 2004).

Recently, Niininen, March, and Buhalis (2006) argued that numerous tourists from around the world are connected via virtual communities, and a variety of experience-based information on tourism places and service are exchanged in these communities. Accordingly, from a tourism marketing perspective, VTCs are becoming an important channel for spreading word-of-mouth to other travellers (Niininen, March, & Buhalis, 2006). Hence, they assert that VTCs provide the opportunity for meeting individuals across the world and making friendships, as it can be demonstrated on the case study on VirtualTourist.com, one of the largest VTCs.

As previously discussed, most current research has dealt with core attributes of VTC such as goals, needs, members' participation, shared resources and information, and computer systems. However, despite many researchers' efforts to explore VTCs over the last decade, they have only focused on potential travellers; locals are of less interest with reference to 'people'. Although developing communication between travellers and locals can be a unique and promising role of VTC, this feature has not been given adequate attention, thus far as VTC has been most widely examined as one of the information sources (e.g. eWOM) in terms of information exchange among consumers.

CASE STUDY: COUCHSURFING.COM

The aim of this study is to explore alternative applications of VTCs, and how these can play new roles as well as what additional benefits can be derived from these. To address these issues, an extensive case study was carried out based on the CouchSurfing.com website (www.couchsurfing.com). This travel-related online community is one of the social networking sites connecting travellers to local communities they will visit (boyd & Ellison, 2007). Information Communication Technology (ICT) including Web 2.0 technologies makes it much easier to communicate among travellers and also between travellers and locals at the destination. Specifically, empirical evidence based on a virtual community (CouchSurfing.com) demonstrates that the opportunity to develop relationships between potential travellers and locals has gradually increased. By definition, CouchSurfing.com encourages communications between prospective travellers and potential hosts at destinations. This case study also provides theoretical and practical implications of such interactions.

Overview

CouchSurfing.com has over 700,000 registered members all over the world (in almost 232 countries). With approximately 754,000 friendships created (CouchSurfing, 2008), it is one of the fast-growing VTCs. The original purpose of this online virtual community was to connect potential travellers to locals who are willing to provide them with free accommodation in their own homes. The statistics report of CouchSurfing.com shows that about 76% of CouchSurfers have experienced hosting or couch surfing some other members. Surfing refers to staying at the other member's place, and hosting indicates the provision of one's own place for accommodation. In particular, almost 99.8% of all hosting or surfing experiences are positive (CouchSurfing, 2008). The main features offered by CouchSurfing.com include:

- Searching a member who is willing to provide you with free accommodation
- Making friendships with other CouchSurfers for consistent relationships
- Organizing off-line gathering or finding collated information for places you plan to visit
- Discussing your own area of interests
- Engaging in chat with other members
- Becoming an ambassador representing your country, city, or the World
- Making a donation to the CouchSurfing community

Beyond the initial purpose, many members also use this website for communicating their personal interests and collecting information on destinations which they plan to visit. In addition, numerous offline meetings and gatherings around destinations have been organized on the website, and face-to-face relationships are expected to enhance online social networks.

VTC Member Profiles

CouchSurfing.com provides various real-time statistics including general website statistics, demographic profiles of online members, and member relationships statistics. Demographic profiles are derived from self-reported personal information only if a member agrees with the disclosure policy. In this study, only parameters related to the present research were collected, and analyzed to identify characteristics of members of CouchSurfing.com. Accordingly, as of 31st, August, 2008, profiles of online members (called CouchSurfers) are as given in Table 3.

Table 3 show that over one half (51.4%) of members are male, and on average they are 27 years old. 'Several people' (6.4%) refers to couples or friends who were registered using a single user account. In addition, while the majority of CouchSurfers at a country level are located in the United States (24.1%), at the region-level Europe has the highest number (49.8%). Many CouchSurfers speak multiple languages, and English (83.7%) is the most spoken language, followed by French (32.7%) and then Spanish (29.6%). In terms of willingness to provide accommodations, 50.9 percent of CouchSurfers have a positive attitude towards hosting visitors. The social-demographic profiles of all members demonstrate that online members in CouchSurfing.com come from diverse regions spread all over the world despite the fact that English is the most spoken language among its members. Note that the dominance of English as the main language of communication is not because a majority of the community members are located at English-speaking countries, but because the majority of websites use English as the language for communication.

Table 3. CouchSurfers profiles

Item		%
Top 3 countries where CouchSurfers are located	United States Germany France	24.1 9.0 8.9
Top 3 cities where CouchSurfers are located	Paris, France London, U.K. Montreal, Canada	1.9 1.6 1.4
Top 3 world regions where CouchSurfers are located	Europe North America Central Asia	49.8 30.9 4.7
Most spoken languages (top 3)	English French Spanish	83.7 32.7 29.6
Willingness to give couches for surfing	Yes Maybe Just coffee or a drink No Definitely! Travelling at the moment	32.4 18.5 16.5 8.8 4.1 19.7
CouchSurfers by age groups	18 to 24 25 to 29 30 to 34 35 to 39 40 to 49 50 to 59 60 to 69 70 to 79 80 to 89	45.7 27.8 11.6 5.8 4.6 2.1 0.6 0.1 0.0
CouchSurfer genders	Male Female Several people Unknown	51.4 40.4 6.4 1.8

Bridging Travellers and Locals

Data Collection

In order to examine to what extent potential travellers and locals are connected, patterns of friendship in online networks were analyzed. In this case study, 100 dyadic friendships (including 100 actors and 100 corresponding friends) were collected from CouchSurfing.com. From November 5 to December 5, 2007, the profiles of subjects (actors and friends) were drawn from the front page of the CouchSurfing.com website where the registered users are randomly displayed. The front page of CouchSurfing.com is composed of search link directing currently available couches, some statistics showing real-time community using history, random CouchSurfers lists, and other quick links including latest news, FAQ, and CouchSurfing introduction.

Randomly selected sample profiles such as gender, age, ethnicity, location, cultural background, language, and number of friends were recorded. These individual records and their attributes are open to the public, as per the privacy guidelines published on the website. In addition, one friend of each actor was chosen to analyse their dyadic relationship. Each CouchSurfer's personal webpage shows a 'Friends' list. 'Friends' are registered using the feature of 'friendship', based on a mutual

Table 4. The profiles of sample (n=100)

Item		
Gender	Male Female	59% 41%
Age	Mean	27.7
Couched	Yes No	53% 47%
Location	33 countries	
Number of friends	Mean Median	27.7 13.0

agreement between two online actors. Although two actors need to mutually agree to make a friendship with each other, the degree of friendship is not necessarily the same. Even if one designates her friend as "Best Friend", he may register her as "Just Friend". For this study, the ith friend in the ith actor's 'Friends' list was therefore selected because friend lists were displayed not at random. For example, for the 8th sample actor, the 8th friend in the 'Friends' list was chosen.

Additional friendship-related information such as the degree of friendship from 1 (Haven't met yet) to 7 (best friend), when and how to meet each other, and whether they have met in person before were obtained by examining both comments and profiles of the actor and the friend. The vast majority of CouchSurfing members make profiles accessible to the public, but when someone who have refused to make them visible were encountered, the following actor or friend were alternatively selected.

Data Analysis

Frequency analysis and the Binomial test were used to obtain research findings. Binomial test is a kind of non-parametric statistical technique for dealing with binomial data when a measurement procedure classifies individual cases into exactly two distinct categories. In this chapter, dyadic friendship with actors and their friends were analyzed with regard to degree of friendships, the experience of face-to-face interaction, and pre-existing relations. The profiles of the sample (Table 4) are consistent with descriptions of profiles of whole populations in CouchSurfing.com: male (59%) vs. female (41%); average age = 27.7.

Also, the majority of CouchSurfers (53%) have been couched (hosting or surfing) before, and the geographical locations of samples vary across 33 countries. The location refers to the place where the actor was currently staying. For example, if a White American who grew up in U.S.A. temporarily lived at Hong Kong when data was collected, his or her location belonged to Asia, instead of North America. However, this is not without limitations because the geographical location information was entirely based on self-reported data from each actor's profile. In addition, the average number of each actor's friends was 27.7, and the median was 13.0.

To get more concrete findings, the binomial test was conducted (Table 5). The binomial test is generally used to identify two categories as A and B, and distinguish the probability (or proportion) associated with each category (p and q, respectively) (Gravetter & Wallnau, 2003). For instance, a coin toss leads to either heads (A) or tails (B), with probabilities p = .50 and q =.50. To conduct the binomial test, two assumptions are required. First, the sample must consist of independent observations. Each case should not be dependent on any other case of observation. Second, the values for each probability (pn and qn, respectively) must be greater than or equal to 10 (Gravetter & Wallnau, 2003). The two assumptions were met in this study. The binomial test was therefore appropriate for this study because the data-set was non-parametric based on the structural similarities.

The null hypothesis was formulated as follows: H0: p = p(identical) = p(not identical) = .50. Depending on whether locations of two actors and friends are identical or not, '1' indicating that

Table 5. Binomial test results

Variable	Category	N	Observed Prop.	Test Prop.	Asymp. Sig. (2-tailed)
Locations	identical	32	.32	.50	.000
	Not identical	68	.68		

both subjects are from the same geographical locations, or '0' indicating that they are from distinct locations was given. The unit of geographical location is a country, and one of the authors made a scientific judgment on their identicalness.

As a result, it revealed that geographical location similarity between actors and their friends significantly tends not to be matched (Prop. = .68, $p < .001$), indicating that the null hypothesis has been rejected. This demonstrates that the difference in location or cultural background of two subjects would be a main predictor of online friendship in VTC.

Based on the fact that sixty six percent of the sample makes friendships after being couched, it is therefore argued that the majority of individuals tend to make relationships with others from different regions for couching. It is revealed therefore that there are lots of ties between travellers and locals who live at the destinations where travellers have visited or want to visit in the future. Assuming that many online users in CouchSurfing.com are potential travellers to search for free accommodations, undoubtedly they would be more likely to contact people who live at a destination. Nonetheless, the findings presented here need to be further investigated because this study did not empirically measure an actor's intrinsic motivation to make a friendship with the other actor.

FUTURE RESEARCH DIRECTIONS

This chapter can provide theoretical implications. As discussed earlier, the results of previous research on cross-cultural understanding, are somewhat mixed: some are consistent with those of the case study in this chapter, and some are not (Gomez-Jacinto, et al., 1999). While some studies showed that hosts or residents prefer travellers with similar cultural background (Thyne, Lawson, & Todd, 2006), some demonstrated that tourists who visited even similar cultural destinations experienced negative attitude changes (Nyaupane, et al., 2008). The mixed findings of previous studies about travellers' or hosts' cultural preferences therefore make it more necessary to investigate the relationship between travellers and locals.

For instance, Thyne et al. (2006) argued that hosts in a destination are more likely to welcome travellers with similar cultural background. Yet, there may be somewhat difference in understanding the word of 'host' in their study. They applied the term of 'host' instead of 'resident', assuming that both terms are used interchangeably. In this chapter, locals (or hosts) indicate those who are willing to be acceptance of travellers, not merely individuals who live at that place. Therefore, it is not surprising for this case study to yield the different results from Thyne et al.'s study because it is understandable that people who are willing to see, meet, or host tourists are more tolerant of visitors with exotic and distinctive cultural background.

Therefore, this study's findings which demonstrate that people tend to make a friend with different cultural background online can be supportive evidence for one side of the debates regarding the role of tourism in cross-cultural understanding. However, to make the findings generalizable, this case study regarding the alternative role of virtual travel communities should be expanded to large-scale empirical research. Specifically, the pattern of online friendship in addition to virtual travel communities can be examined in terms of cultural similarity, and also a survey to online community members will be able to complement the shortcoming of the content analysis-based case study. An email or mail survey will allow researchers to measure the motivation of making friendships online, and enable them to examine why people prefer similar or different cultures when travelling or hosting tourists.

From a methodological perspective, a further study about bridging two sides (travellers in generating region and locals in destination region) is recommended using alternative methodology such as Social Network Analysis (SNA) or netnography. Social Networks refer to structures composed of actors (nodes) and their relationships (links) with a society (Scott, 2000; Wasserman & Faust, 1994). Accordingly, social networks theory is defined as a body of knowledge used to identify entities embedded in a social context, and measure their relations, roles, and ties within networks (Cook & Whitmeyer, 1992; Granovetter, 1985; Monge & Contractor, 2003). The most distinguishing characteristic of SNA is to pay attention to relational data in social structures rather than attribute data. Hence, it is very meaningful to analyse relations between actors in a network. In SNA, several key measurements have been employed to assess various properties at different level of analysis and explain a whole social structure (Wellman, 1983). Specifically, at the individual level, degree, centrality, closeness, and betwenness represent the roles and positions of actors in the network (Monge & Contractor, 2003). On the other hand, some measures such as density, centralization, and size are used to describe entire networks. Thus, the principles of SNA give insights to analyse patterns of relations between travellers and locals, and SNA would be recommended as an additional research method to study online communities.

Netnography is also suggested to understand the nature of online communities. Netnography is a term of combining 'Net' and 'ethnography', and is literally an ethnographic methodology being adapted to study online communities (Kozinets, 2002). Kozinets (2002) argues that compared to ethnography, netnography is less time-consuming and elaborate. This method gives marketing researchers a chance to observe consumer behaviour occurring in an online community. More specifically, he suggests that four different types of online community be appropriate to conduct netnography: electronic bulletin boards (e.g. newsgroup, use-group); independent web-pages; e-mail mailing lists called listservs; multi-user dungeons and chat rooms. Hence, netnography can be a useful and flexible method when studying online communities.

CONCLUSION

This chapter examined the current state of Virtual Travel Community (VTC) studies, and offered an additional social aspect of knowledge about VTC to current research trend. A case study in this chapter also provides theoretical and practical implications. Specifically, the findings of this study assist to understand how a virtual space contributes to improving relationships between individuals from each other, and accordingly how online users extend their social networks throughout the VTC. It is thus expected that this chapter can give insights to understand how pervasive virtual ties between travellers and locals increase cultural understanding all over the world. Furthermore, the findings provide an alternative approach to the social value of VTC, and practical implications of designing and marketing VTC.

Finally, additional methodologies including Social Network Analysis (SNA) or netnography are expected to complement the shortcoming of the case study in this chapter, and provide alternative perspectives to understand the interaction between locals and travellers. The importance of online or mail survey to Virtual Travel Community members were also emphasized since a questionnaire enables researchers to measure diverse psychological constructs such as intrinsic motivation and satisfaction with appropriate scales.

REFERENCES

Allison, A., Currall, J., Moss, M., & Stuart, S. (2005). Digital identity matters. *Journal of the American Society for Information Science and Technology, 56*(4), 364–372. doi:10.1002/asi.20112

Armstrong, A., & Hagel, J. (1996). The real value of on-line communities. Harvard Business Review, (May-June). boyd, d. m., & Ellison, N. B. (2007). Social network sites: Definition, history, and scholarship. *Journal of Computer-Mediated Communication, 13*(1).

Buhalis, D. (2002). The future e-tourism intermediaries. *Tourism Management, 23*, 207–220. doi:10.1016/S0261-5177(01)00085-1

Buhalis, D. (2003). E-tourism: Information technologies for strategic tourism management. New York: Financial Times Prentice Hall.

Buhalis, D., & Law, R. (2008). Progress in information technology and tourism management: 20 years on and 10 years after the Internet - the state of e-tourism research. *Tourism Management, 29*, 609–623. doi:10.1016/j.tourman.2008.01.005

Chung, J. Y., & Buhalis, D. (in press). Information needs in online social networks. *Journal of Information Technology and Tourism.*

Cook, K. S., & Whitmeyer, J. M. (1992). Two approaches to social structure: Exchange theory and network analysis. *Annual Review of Sociology, 18*, 109–127. doi:10.1146/annurev.so.18.080192.000545

Cooper, C., & Buhalis, D. (1998). The future of tourism. In C. R. Cooper (Ed.), Tourism: Principles and practices. London: Addison Wesley Longman.

CouchSurfing. (2008). CouchSurfing statistics. Retrieved August 8, 2008, from http://www.couchsurfing.com/

Egger, R., & Buhalis, D. (2008). E-tourism case studies: Management & marketing issues in eTourism. Oxford, UK: Butterworth Heinemann Oxford.

Fisher, R. J., & Price, L. L. (1991). International pleasure travel motivation and post vacation cultural attitude change. *Journal of Leisure Research, 23*, 193–208.

Gomez-Jacinto, L., & Martin-Garcia, J., & Bertiche-Haud'Huyze, C. (1999). A model of tourism experience and attitude change. *Annals of Tourism Research, 26*(4), 1024–1027. doi:10.1016/S0160-7383(99)00063-8

Granovetter, M. (1985). Economic action and social structure: The Problem of embeddedness. *American Journal of Sociology, 91*, 481–493. doi:10.1086/228311

Gravetter, F. J., & Wallnau, L. B. (2003). Statistics for the behavioral sciences (6th ed.). Belmont, CA: Wadsworth/Thomson Learning.

Kim, W. G., Lee, C., & Hiemstra, S. J. (2004). Effects of an online virtual community on customer loyalty and travel product purchases. *Tourism Management, 25*, 343–355. doi:10.1016/S0261-5177(03)00142-0

Kozinets, R. V. (2002). The field behind the screen: Using netnography for marketing research in online communities. *JMR, Journal of Marketing Research, 39*, 61–72. doi:10.1509/jmkr.39.1.61.18935

Leiper, N. (1990). Tourism systems: An interdisciplinary perspective. New Zealand: Massey University.

Monge, P. R., & Contractor, N. S. (2003). Theories of communication networks. New York: Oxford University Press.

Niininen, O., Buhalis, D., & March, R. (2007). Customer empowerment in tourism through consumer centric marketing (CCM). *Qualitative Market Research, 10*(3), 265–282. doi:10.1108/13522750710754308

Niininen, O., March, R., & Buhalis, D. (2006). Consumer centric tourism marketing. In D. Buhalis & C. Costa (Eds.), Tourism management dynamics: Trends, management and tools (pp. xxiii, 279). London: Buttterworth Heinemann.

Nyaupane, G. P., Teye, V., & Paris, C. (2008). Innocents abroad: Attitude change toward hosts. *Annals of Tourism Research, 35*(3), 650–667. doi:10.1016/j.annals.2008.03.002

O'Reilly, T. (2005). What is Web 2.0: Design patterns and business models for the next generation of software. Retrieved February 20, 2009, from http://www.oreillynet.com/pub/a/oreilly/tim/news/2005/09/30/what-is-web-20.html

Preece, J. (2000). Online communities: Designing usability, supporting sociability. New York: John Wiley.

Rheingold, H. (1991). Virtual reality. New York: Summit Books.

Scott, J. (2000). Social network analysis: A handbook (2nd ed.). Thousands Oaks, CA: Sage Publications.

Stepchenkova, S., Mills, J. E., & Jiang, H. (2007). Virtual travel communities: Self-reported experiences and satisfaction. In M. Sigala, L. Mich, & J. Murphy (Eds.), Information and communication technologies in tourism 2007 (pp. 163-174). New York: Springer-Verlag Wien.

Thyne, M. A., Lawson, R., & Todd, S. (2006). The use of conjoint analysis to assess the impact of the cross-cultural exchange between hosts and guests. *Tourism Management, 27*, 201–213. doi:10.1016/j.tourman.2004.09.003

Vogt, C. A., & Fesenmaier, D. R. (1998). Expanding the functional information search model. *Annals of Tourism Research, 25*(3), 551–578. doi:10.1016/S0160-7383(98)00010-3

Wang, Y., & Fesenmaier, D. R. (2004). Towards understanding members' general participation in and active contribution to an online travel community. *Tourism Management, 25*(6), 709–722. doi:10.1016/j.tourman.2003.09.011

Wang, Y., Yu, Q., & Fesenmaier, D. R. (2002). Defining the virtual tourist community: Implications for tourism marketing. *Tourism Management, 23*(4), 407–417. doi:10.1016/S0261-5177(01)00093-0

Wasserman, S., & Faust, K. (1994). Social network analysis: Methods and applications. New York: Cambridge University Press.

Wellman, B. (1983). Network analysis: Some basic principles. *Sociological Theory, 1*, 155–200. doi:10.2307/202050

Whittaker, S., Issacs, E., & O'Day, V. (1997). Widening the Net. Workshop report on the theory and practice of physical and network communities. [ff]. *SIGCHI Bulletin, 29*(3), 27–30. doi:10.1145/264853.264867

Chapter 9
Progressive Tourism:
Integrating Social, Transportation, and Data Networks

Edward Pultar
University of California, Santa Barbara, USA

Martin Raubal
University of California, Santa Barbara, USA

ABSTRACT

This research examines tourism behavior using Internet-based websites that provide free lodging with local residents. Increases in computing power and accessibility have led to novel e-tourism techniques and the users of such systems utilize an amalgamation of social networks, transportation networks, and data communication networks. The chapter focuses on how the geographical spread of people in a modern, digital social network (CouchSurfing) influences the travel choices of each individual in the network. Activities performed in coordination with this type of system can vary greatly in travel mode, accessibility, mobility, and time, among other factors. This research studies factors that influence a general model describing traveler behavior using a cost-free lodging network. The authors present an information representation and visualization methodology utilizing time-geographic dimensions.

INTRODUCTION

In recent years the flourishing of technology has brought many conveniences, connections, and frustrations for people across the world. Specific to this research, the digital age provides novel ways for humans to discover geography. Means of mobility have greatly increased over the decades, and we are able to travel farther and faster than ever before; however, travel has also become less necessary in some circumstances through the integration of virtual communication and meetings. Physical presence is still required in many instances, but are we seeing an increase or decrease in *time-space compression* (Harvey, 1989)? Part of our interest in time-space compression is the effect that modern technology has on a human's use of time and capabilities for travel.

Modern, internet-based social networks allow individuals to connect unlike ever before with large, geographically spread, culturally diverse, and yet, maintainable structures. While travel behavior with Information Communication Technologies (ICT),

DOI: 10.4018/978-1-60566-818-5.ch009

global transportation, and social networks (Larsen, Urry, & Axhausen, 2006) are currently popular research subjects, a geographer's perspective on the interconnectedness of these topics sheds new light as to how all of these impact *spatial behavior*. In addition, specific groups of people utilizing those networks need to be studied to understand how virtual data networks and contemporary social networks link with transportation and cultural exchange. This chapter aims to gain a better understanding of this challenge, and show how to conduct research in this area.

In this chapter the concept of a *synergy of social, transportation, and data networks* is divided into the following sub-questions:

- How does the geographical spread of people in an internet-based social network influence the travel choices of individuals in the network?
- What behavior do these travelers exhibit, when utilizing a novel amalgamation of social, transportation, and data communication networks?
- How can these network levels be visualized efficiently to be utilized as a decision support tool for travelers and cutting-edge e-tourism systems?

All of these questions require individual in-depth research programs; nevertheless, for developing a more holistic understanding of this topic, all three questions should be integrated. In order to tackle this work of geographic complexity we begin at the conceptual level that first investigates each of the critical elements individually, and then analyzes its potential contribution to the system as a whole. Next, a data model will be created to test, explain, and represent different elements of the complete information. This model will be valuable for any researcher studying single or multi-level network architectures; and, on a broader scale, any individual experiencing geography first-hand, through tourism and travel.

Traveling can be a thrilling and stimulating experience; however, it can also be costly and emotionally draining. Presence in a new environment provokes questions, and demands answers to physical and geographical issues. This research focuses on the existence of hospitality and hosting combined with travel. When visiting a new place individuals are more likely to take on distant and exotic travels if there exists a connection with a local host. This can be beneficial for both the host and the visitor, as this can lead to exchange of culture and food, leading to the development of companionship. Traveling for business as well as for leisure can fit into this category, and relate to these principles. Trips made in this fashion have been common for many years through family, friends, friends of friends, and beyond. However, expanding upon these concepts and using newly developed technological resources brings about a more recent form of travel, yet to be studied in detail.

In order to embark upon this research a sound, existing collection of diverse individuals is needed to demonstrate the power of the network amalgamation. This launches the effort to understand and characterize the unique spatio-temporal behavior of these travelers. In this research we utilize an existing online network as a case study. The CouchSurfing (CS, http://www.couchsurfing.com) project is a free, online social network of people from all over the world, and willing to share time and their homes with travelers. Users provide each other with a space to sleep such as a couch, floor space, or an extra bedroom. Members may also offer guidance with tours or simply meet.

A key element that holds all of these people together in one system is the use of a *digital social network*. Each member creates a profile containing *volunteered geographic information* (VGI) such as their current city of residence, previous travels, and future travel plans. A profile can also contain personal descriptions, hosting capabilities, languages spoken, and photographs. This social network is increasingly important as the links created between nodes can be used to gather a level of safety for travelers as well as a global map with the geographic locations and places of connected friends. Members began signing up for the CS project in 2004 with hundreds joining per month. By 2005 thousands were joining each month and steady growth has continued over the years right up to 2009, by when over ten thousand people were joining during peak months.

Users of CS now cover a vast portion of the globe with members on each continent. It is a contemporary, emerging form of connection. The world is quickly opening its doors more than some may suspect due to current world news, hence the issues related to traveler safety are included in the proposed research design. Further expansion of this non-profit traveler system is expected to carry on well into the future; therefore any results discovered in this research afford a utility for prospective future developments.

The second section presents a background with related work in pertinent fields. The third section, "Impacts, Approach, Methodology," describes the specific methodologies utilized in this research and provides a conceptual framework on which this research is based, in addition to time-geographic visualizations. Section four presents potential areas for future research on this topic, while last section wraps the chapter up with conclusions.

BACKGROUND

This research focuses on how the geographical spread of people in an Internet-based social network can influence the travel choices of each individual in the network. This innovative behavior revolves around the concept of *place* (Couclelis, 1992) as the setting is continually changing on a wide variety of scales from city to country to continent. The role of place is unique in this system where people are searching for subjective places that are not merely space or location but highly personalized (Cresswell, 1996). In this sense hosts can also point guests to places that are more than simple coordinates as the recommendations contain a degree of subjectivity. Hence place in this research is defined by all three network levels working together to provide travel opportunities, as well as link physical locations and subjective places. These places have emphases on any combination of a traveler's preferences for language, culture, guidance, and safety among others.

There is a wide variety of ICT tools at a modern traveler's disposal, and these tools play a major role in their travel choices (Janelle, 2004). Technology affords the participation of distributed individuals in the network to take part in the same project as is done with community modeling (Maechling et al., 2005), public-participation GIS (Keßler et al., 2005), or web-based communities (Pultar et al., 2008). Members of the CS system utilize ICT in combination with *multi-modal transportation:* different modes of transportation such as train, plane, bus, or boat. The use of ICT begins with communication through asynchronous email messages while guest and host are on separate continents. An email request can be viewed at a time convenient to the host, and does not interrupt their regular daily activities. Each member can evaluate the other using the online social network with biographies and references from other members. Further person-to-person communication can be carried out until both parties are satisfied. Later, when the members are on the same continent, more messages may be exchanged until both host and guest are in the same country or city. This is due to the fact that a guest may initially travel to a city in a country such as Berlin in Germany but have a trip planned a week later for Hamburg, Germany. While in Berlin the guest can call their future host in Hamburg to confirm and finalize trip details. After all of this, synchronous communication can occur via means such as a telephone to confirm meeting places, times, and personal descriptions. This process can be seen as taking place in a hierarchy of transportation scales starting at the highest level with cross-continent mobility granted

Figure 1. Various transportation modes with different speed and distance capabilities.

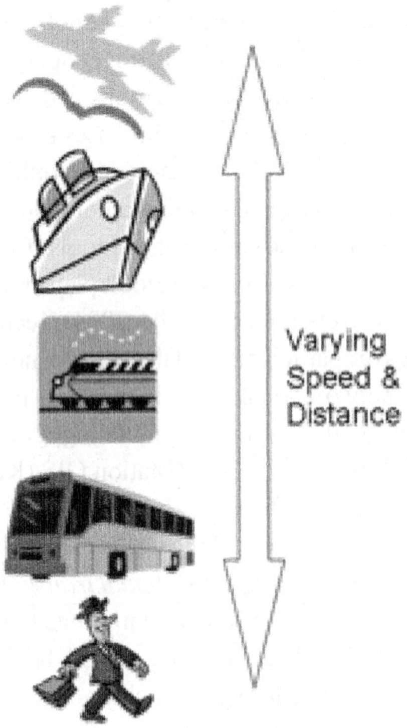

through commercial planes or sea vessels. Below this are forms of travel such as national trains spanning across countries. Another scale lower are local trams and buses in cities until an individual reaches a final destination (Figure 1).

Our study concerning the synergy of multiple networks is built upon earlier research in travel behavior modeling, time geography, and visualization. Work in social activity-travel behavior points towards "the main individuals' driver to perform a trip is mostly with whom they interact rather than where they go." (Carrasco, Miller, & Wellman, 2006, p.1) In other words the social aspects of whom a person interacts with in their travels can be a very important factor in determining where a person goes. However, this can be reversed in the CS system, as this electronic network allows people to select a location first and then decide with whom to interact. "A major part of social activity destinations are at homes of specific persons rather than at places that can be 'chosen' depending on attractors such as costs, environment, and proximity." (Carrasco et al., 2006, p.2) This hints at the lack of choice available in many social activity destinations where in using the CS system places can in a sense be 'chosen' based on factors such as environment and location, in addition to other attributes of potential hosts.

Individual space is space about which an individual can move and perform actions while activity space is the space of potential activities available for a person given their characteristics and attributes. Both individual and activity space are important in the CS system, while place plays a larger role if a traveler has a strong desire to be at a specific place. This alters a guest's preferences and threshold level in choosing a potential host. *Place-based* and *individual-based* decisions (Golledge & Stimson, 1997) play a key role in this process and this work seeks to discover thresholds for people's transportation behavior. For example, a CouchSurfer primarily desiring cultural experiences can adjust her plans mid-trip and travel farther (perhaps at higher cost as well) in order to partake in a more desirable trip (e.g., free surfing lessons at a beach house on an island).

Recent contributions combining social networks with travel have been described by Dugundji, Paez, & Arentze (2008). They state that the contemporary changes in urban transportation show a need for policy integration and that the modern approaches to transportation analysis are pushing the capabilities of the underlying theories. Axhausen & Gärling (1992) have presented related work on conceptual frameworks of travel behavior. Golledge & Stimson (1997) provide a collection of spatial behavior knowledge and models that describe general spatial behavior. These models present a general method for investigating the steps and factors that contribute to travel behavior.

The STARCHILD conceptual framework (Root & Recker, 1983) is an activity-based approach in which individuals are assumed to choose options with optimal utilities. The model characterizes travel behavior elements into pre-travel and travel stages. This classification is used in the conceptual model presented in this chapter, where an individual's pre-travel actions (as well as during, and post-travel actions) include extensive use of ICT in the form of data networks and digital social networks.

The SCHEDULER framework (Gärling, Säisä, Book, & Lindberg, 1986) fits desired activities into a specified time interval. In scheduling, fitting the activities into the timeframe is a key objective of most travelers – apart from others, such as minimizing the travel time or distance. Nonetheless, some travelers may look for the maximum amount of travel for the available time, in order to see as many places as possible, and experience the maximum number of diverse events. Explicit influence of ICT systems on travel behaviors is a modern phenomenon, and is therefore covered in our research.

Another field of research related to this topic is that of *time geography*, i.e. how time and location are related to each other. In general, people and resources are available at a limited number of locations for a limited amount of time. Time geography defines the space-time constraint for being present at a specific location and a specific time (Hägerstrand, 1970). This possibility of being present is determined by one's ability to trade time for space, supported by transportation and communication services.

Space-time paths depict the movement of individuals in space over time. Such paths are available at various spatial and temporal granularities, and can be represented through different dimensions. All space-time paths must lie within space-time prisms (STP). These are geometrical constructs of two intersecting cones (Lenntorp, 1976). Their boundaries limit the possible locations a space-time path can take (Figure 2). The time budget is defined as $\Delta_t = t_2 - t_1$ in which an agent can move away from the origin, limited only by the maximum travel velocity. From a network perspective (Figure 3), such as taken in this research, movement is limited by the network geometry and the maximum travel velocity, which can vary for different edges and times. The geometry of the STP in a network therefore forms an irregular shape. Algorithms for calculating the network time prism (NTP) can be found in (Miller, 1991) and (Raubal, Winter, Teßmann, & Gaisbauer, 2007). A generic procedure involves (1) calculating shortest paths from the travel

Figure 2. Space-time prism as intersecting cones

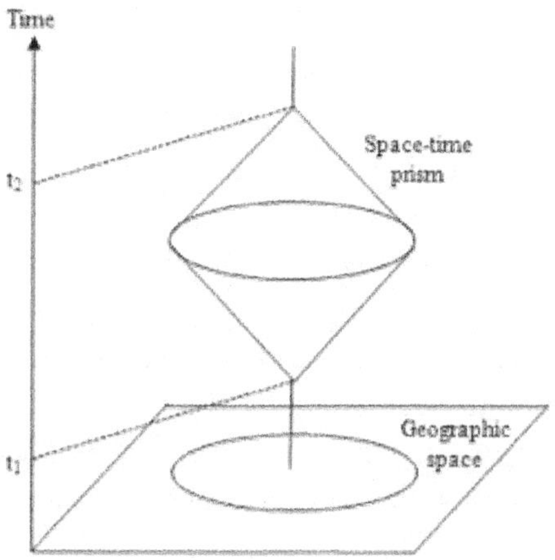

Figure 3. Space-time path from a network perspective

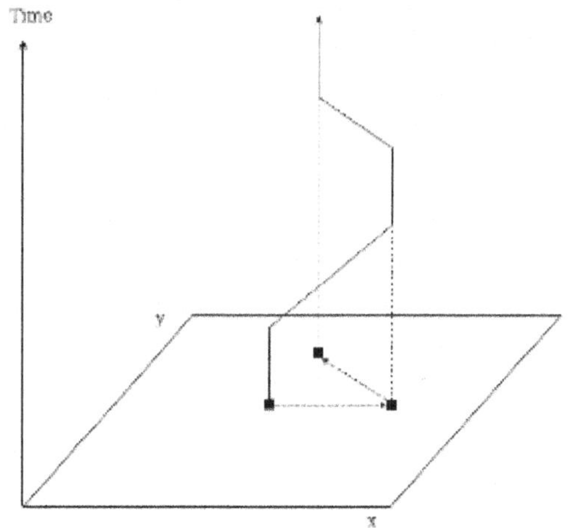

origin up to a cumulative impedance (e.g., travel time) along each path, and (2) testing, for each edge, whether traveling from the origin over the edge and to the destination is possible within the cumulative impedance.

Time geography defines different constraints that limit a person's activities in space and time. Fundamental physical restrictions on abilities and resources are summarized as *capability* constraints. Not having access to a car in order to trade time for space efficiently is one example for this type of constraint. *Coupling* constraints refer to the requirement for a person to be at a specific location at a certain time or for a fixed duration. For example, if two persons want to meet at a physical location, they have to be there at the same time. Certain domains in life are controlled by *authority* constraints, e.g. a person can only shop at a mall when the mall is open, such as between 9am and 8pm.

Time geography has been extended to the area of geographic information systems (GIS) regarding transportation networks to model and measure space-time accessibility (Miller, 1999; Wu & Miller, 2001), and for the analysis and theoretical understanding of disaggregate human spatial behavior (Kwan, 2000). It has also been suggested that it is possible to use time geography in GIS and location-based services (LBS), to achieve more user-centered systems (Miller, 2005b; Raubal, Miller, & Bridwell, 2004). Further applications of time geography include the structuring of dynamic pathfinding environments (Hendricks, Egenhofer, & Hornsby, 2003) and the modeling of *geospatial lifelines*, which represent movement as a time-stamped record of the locations an individual has occupied over a period of time (Hariharan & Hornsby, 2000). Analytical formulations of basic entities and relationships from time geography are presented by Miller (2005a).

Visualization methodologies based on time geography can be utilized to display and analyze the integration of social, data, and transportation networks presented here. Several methods for computing and geographically visualizing human activity patterns based on time geography have been proposed and successfully employed (Kwan, 2004; Ren & Kwan, 2007). Space-time paths allow for depicting both the movement of individual travelers in space over time, and their utilization of the social and communication networks. Yu & Shaw (2008) have presented an adjustment of the STP and utilized a 3D-GIS representation to support visualization and analysis of human activity patterns in physical and virtual spaces. The paths are available at various spatial and temporal granularities, and can be represented through different dimensions. It is important to note that such dynamic spatio-temporal behavior requires attention to the concept of scale with respect to both time and space (Montello, 2001).

IMPACTS, APPROACH, METHODOLOGY

This research makes a contribution to the study of multiple, interrelated network levels in relation to the field of time geography while making use of *volunteered geographic information. Volunteered geographic information* (VGI) is a relatively new area of research targeted towards enabling general audiences to author and submit information about their environment, complementing existing information sources and services with a user volunteered web of places. People should not only be enabled to access spatial information about their current location, but also to author and edit such data, and to interact with systems and friends that are physically separated. This encompasses a seamlessly integrated environment, where the real world is intertwined with the digital, and mobile devices serve as portals and handles to this digital world. The information flow is directed mainly from the user to a growing and distributed set of databases that integrate the volunteered information. The field of VGI has seen tremendous growth in the 21st century (Goodchild, 2007). Previously, information has been volunteered by Internet users across the globe via structures such as Wikipedia. Now those elements are gaining a useful geographical element (Hecht & Raubal, 2008).

CONCEPTUAL MODEL OF TRAVEL BEHAVIOR IN A COST-FREE LODGING NETWORK

Conceptual Model

Figure 4 shows a conceptual model of travel behavior, it highlights the critical elements and factors that affect a user's decisions. This flowchart helps in visualizing each step, in addition to presenting how the whole process fits together. Travel choices are made in a variety of locations and are heavily affected by the synergy of ICT tools, international transportation networks, and web-based social networks. In the absence of any one of these crucial networks the traveler's behavior would be greatly altered. Therefore, this type of travel is quite unique and highly dynamic, and does not lend itself for analysis by traditional travel behavior models. The application of this system is further described in the rest of this section.

Initially a user chooses a place to travel. The individual's choice may be for any purpose including vacation, cultural, and/or business. The concept of scale is important with the initial place decision as users may vary in their desire to visit a specific city, country, or continent. The results and further refinement of their decision behavior will move through various scales (both virtual and physical) before reaching street-level with corporeal presence between guest and host. At this point an initial transportation mode choice may be made or hypothesized by a user but further potential refinement is necessary in this highly dynamic model.

Utilizing any level of initial place and transportation choice the traveler will perform a host search based on their individual criteria. At this step user-based trip preferences are gathered including desired place along with any combination of language, age, verification level, and gender among others. Following criteria specification, possible hosts are generated that match the desired characteristics. This may return no results and require the user to further refine their criteria and search again until at least one host match is found. If one host matches the specified criteria the user can choose that host and move to the next step of checking availability. If more than one host matches the criteria a user may further refine her search to narrow down the results or may choose to contact multiple potential hosts. Also with more than one potential host generated the user has the ability for further evaluation (before contacting via e-mail) by utilizing characteristics of a modern Internet-based social network. These include profile information, number of 'friend'-links, personal references left by other members, and photos. The weights a person applies to each of the criteria vary widely between users. For instance, one traveler may place more weight on staying with a host of a specific gender versus another that may be more concerned with finding a host within a particular age interval.

Once a traveler has chosen to contact a possible host about availability then the asynchronous ICT tool of e-mail is utilized for initial communication. At this step a guest contacts a host that is local to the desired area of travel. Here the highly dynamic nature of this travel behavior is demonstrated as advice may be given that alters a user's transportation mode choice and potentially their place choices at various resolutions. Next, availability is verified and if both parties are satisfied the trip occurs. At this step the model maintains its flexibility as users may check e-mail at an airport and choose different standby flights based upon the current situation potentially leading to

Figure 4. Conceptual model of spatial behavior utilizing three network levels. Green elements are explicit networks utilized in the framework: data, social, and transport networks

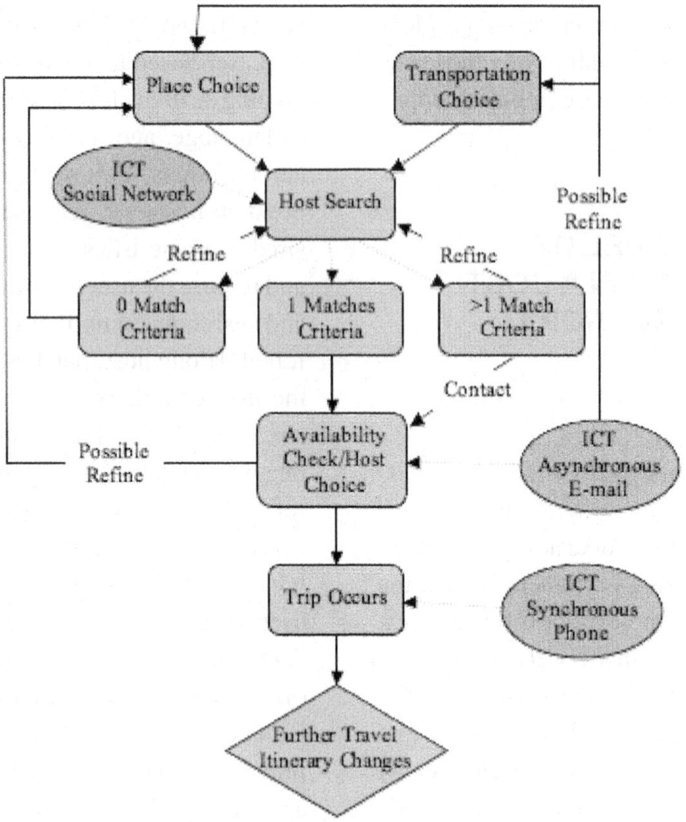

a new place choice or other changes in itinerary. This also relates to the mid-trip itinerary changes described in the next section with sample travel scenarios.

Typically, the travel network infrastructures work as an *enabler* allowing mobility options with planes, trains, and buses. It is important in this system to also consider the potential *barriers* of the transportation network with employee strikes or a natural disaster event. With this system a user can quickly change her place choices and find a new host where there are no transit barriers. Upon arrival at a desired destination travelers may find synchronous ICT technologies such as telephones useful to verify initial meeting locations and acquire personal descriptions. Guest and host meet face-to-face in physical space at this later step making the transition from virtual to corporeal presence. After an individual completes her stay the framework allows for further travel along with itinerary changes. For example, hosts may have strong recommendations of places to see and/or connections with other potential hosts the guest had not originally planned. Here again we see the appropriateness of the highly dynamic and flexible model provided for this travel behavior. The individual may continue travel to any number of places for any time period starting at the top of the framework with a new place and transportation choice. The conceptual framework presented in this section and Figure 4 provides a starting point for how this behavior can be modeled and raises further research questions such as those of traveler safety but especially those of model evaluation. Additional real world accounts such as those given in the next section entitled "Sample Scenarios" may further justify the creation of this new conceptual model. In conclusion, this model serves as a basis for further inputs, datasets, and adjustments into the future.

Sample Scenarios

This section provides travel scenarios using the CouchSurfing system to further demonstrate the necessity for a novel conceptual travel behavior model. Two types of travelers are presented: the first has little to no constraints and the second has many constraints. Different levels of constraints are possible and further apparent as a result of the scenario descriptions, which exemplify the capabilities of this highly dynamic, multi-network system.

Sample North American traveler A desires a trip to Europe to experience different cultures. Using ICT and the dynamic system described here the individual is able to purchase minimal tickets, use a flexible itinerary, and minimize lodging fees. At the start of the trip the individual plans on spending one week in the Netherlands but after three days decides to visit the nearby city of Antwerp in Belgium. A suitable CS host is found the day before who welcomes the arrival, leading to unique food, music, and history knowledge. The traveler discovers discount airline tickets from a previous host and books an inexpensive flight to Brno, Czech Republic. Leading up to the departure of the flight multiple potential hosts have been contacted but final plans are not solidified. Checking e-mail at the airport less than an hour before departure instantaneously reveals solidified plans of what people and places will be visited. Castles, casemates, and college campuses are all part of the tour given by a local but they are only able to host for two days. Traveler A examines a map and notices Vienna, Austria, is nearby. The tourist only has time to record some phone numbers of potential hosts to call once the train arrives in Vienna. The individual calls members of the modern social network and finds a place for the evening and from there is able to call others to stay with for the next nights. The hosts provide museum recommendations, sack lunches, and travel tips for the area increasing the traveler's mobility, efficiency, and overall cultural experience. Traveler A moves north and stops in a small Czech town. She wanders into a local festival and is seen by a friend of a previous host who provides accommodation. After this a member of the network provides accompaniment and knowledge of the buses and trains on an excursion to a national park for a few days. At the end of traveler A's tour a host in Poland gives a knowledgeable tour as the host is training to become a tour guide. After a thorough journey around town the tourist returns home with a multitude of unique experiences in diverse places.

Travel via the CS network can be done for a variety of purposes such as business, leisure, study, culture, and language. The following is an overview travel description of a CS trip for primarily business but provides other purposes as well. Sample South American professor (traveler B) wishes to attend a conference in Barcelona, Spain, where he will give a presentation on a paper he wrote. Since he has never been to this location before, the individual decides to spend some days before and after the conference in Barcelona to gain more experience of the new culture. The traveler discovers a CS host of the same age who has lived over half of his life in Barcelona. The guest and host send each other a series of e-mails to arrive at an initial plan of activities that is convenient for both parties. The host then takes the guest to local museums and eateries not in traveler B's travel guide, but he is pleasantly surprised. After the trip occurs both parties are satisfied with the exchange of culture and experiences and hope to reverse the roles of guest and host in the near future.

TIME-GEOGRAPHIC VISUALIZATION OF TRAVEL BEHAVIOR AND OPTIONS

The research presented here utilizes VGI as a key component for collecting geodata that are visualized as 2-dimensional static spatial maps in a GIS. With the existence and necessity of this multi-network architecture demonstrated, this section focuses on how all of this relates to the field of *time geography*. Table 1 demonstrates sample concepts from time geography and how they relate to this work.

This investigation provides a unique application of user-centered time geography (Raubal et al., 2004) as the travelers have a wide array of journey preferences such as length of stay, gender of host, accessibility to public transport, and host's age among other factors.

Once data has been collected, the information can be further analyzed and visualized via static 2-dimensional individual network maps (Larsen et al., 2006). However, travel is a dynamic activity varying in both space and time, leading to a necessity for more advanced methods of visualization made possible by a recent boom in geospatial technology. For maximum cross-platform utility, a visual portion of these research results is exhibited by means of 3-dimensional space-time maps in a virtual globe environment such as Google Earth (http://earth.google.com/). The extensive information repository of world data currently available in this software makes it an ideal platform to demonstrate and visualize results. This offers the possibility for interactive visualizations of space-time maps with tools affording the ability to control spatial and temporal variables. Of specific importance in this context is the Keyhole Markup Language (KML, http://www.opengeospatial.org/standards/kml), an eXtensible Markup Language (XML) geospatial data file format accepted by the internationally-recognized Open Geospatial Consortium (OGC, http://www.opengeospatial.org/). Using this language environment, the appropriate Features, Placemarks, LineStrings, and other data types are created via scripts based on a given user scenario. This information representation provides a highly flexible and efficient technique for working with modern spatio-temporal data. Once representations have been created, conversion between various geospatial data types can be automated with the Geospatial Data Abstraction Library (GDAL, http://www.gdal.org/). Exploring *time geography* in this novel way supplies useful visualization and analysis tools for geographers and spatiotemporal researchers as a whole.

The visualizations will also be useful for travelers planning a trip. These e-tourism tools will further allow users to see potential paths and therefore their many travel options given their individualized

Table 1. Time geography concepts linked with multi-network travel behavior

Sample Time Geography Concepts	Multi-Network Traveler Examples
Authority constraints	A host provides a guest with information about operating hours of sites in addition to a sequence in which to visit.
Capability constraints	Host shares local and international transportation capabilities as well as the current status.
Coupling constraints	Initial corporeal meeting between guest and host; also synchronicity between a traveler and any mode of transportation.
Fixed vs. flexible activities	Traveler wants to mountain climb meaning the possible locations and schedule are flexible vs. a traveler designating a fixed activity such as visiting the Louvre.
Potential path areas and prisms	These are created using a traveler's desired travel destinations in a specified duration of time along with available modes of transportation.
Space-time stations	Various tourist activities such as a historic church or a host's residence are space-time stations.

constraints of space and time. The results of these tools can also aid further analysis via utilization of spatiotemporal queries available in a dynamic Geographic Information System or GIS (Pultar et al., forthcoming 2009a). A dynamic GIS may also be used to combine layers of networks, such as those of transportation and potential CS hosts, to make travel recommendations (Pultar et al., 2009b). Another key feature of this approach to space-time geography is the wide accessibility to persons of all socio-economic status due to the no-cost software platform of Google Earth. As an experiment of capabilities and proof-of-concept, the sample physical travel scenario described in the previous section is visualized in Figures 5 and 6. In this example each location has a temporal attribute that corresponds with a time slider tool in addition to the visible height variable. Utilizing an intuitive user interface, any traveler will be able to input their preferences, constraints, and capabilities to acquire a 3-dimensional time-geographic representation of their possibilities. For example, the figures also demonstrate a potential solution for a journey involving 6 stops. Given a starting and ending location a traveler recommender system (TRS) (Ricci, 2002) could return this option for travel order based on a user's preferences. The traveler has a space-time prism with height boundaries decided by the traveler's available time. The lowest height represents the beginning of the trip and is bounded above by the ending time of the trip. With respect to the lodging system in this research, different optional sequences may be shown based on host availability. In taking a trip this visualization methodology aids a traveler in making choices and changes in a travel itinerary. These tools exemplify ways of how we see this research contributing to the development of future cutting-edge e-tourism systems (such as a TRS) and also providing high-utility tools for spatio-temporal researchers.

FUTURE TRENDS

In this chapter we have laid a foundation for tourism making extensive use of social, transportation, and data networks. This contemporary form of e-tourism involves cost-free lodging as a novel way to connect travelers and hosts. The behavior makes extensive use of the Internet, which is an important note as the structure of this global system would have to be quite different without the presence of intercontinental data networks. This hints towards further research on the enablers and barriers concerned with this topic. These were mentioned in the context of transportation networks but can also be extended to include the fact that data and access to digital social networks are not ubiquitous worldwide.

On the technical side, the applied methods for visualizing the interaction of the three network levels can be exploited for the design and development of cutting-edge e-tourism systems. Such systems will eventually help to provide higher access to low-income and minority groups to physically experience the geographical world due to lessening the financial burden for traveling by utilizing the type of travel discussed in this chapter.

The approach presented here utilizes qualitative and quantitative techniques in order to collect, evaluate, and visualize the triple network system design. The specific details of going about this task involve VGI. Geographic, anonymous CouchSurfer data can be utilized for spatio-temporal analysis and visualization. City and country of residence, gender, age, and network connections provide an excellent starting point to aid in answering the posed questions. Along the lines of social capital, members of this social network specify a depth level of each connection. This will be valuable in examining the relationship between distance and strength of ties in a social network. Additional discoveries pertaining to network capital could also become evident through the results of a survey.

Figure 5. Space-time path of example traveler scenario in the section "Conceptual Model of Travel Behavior in a Cost-Free Lodging Network".

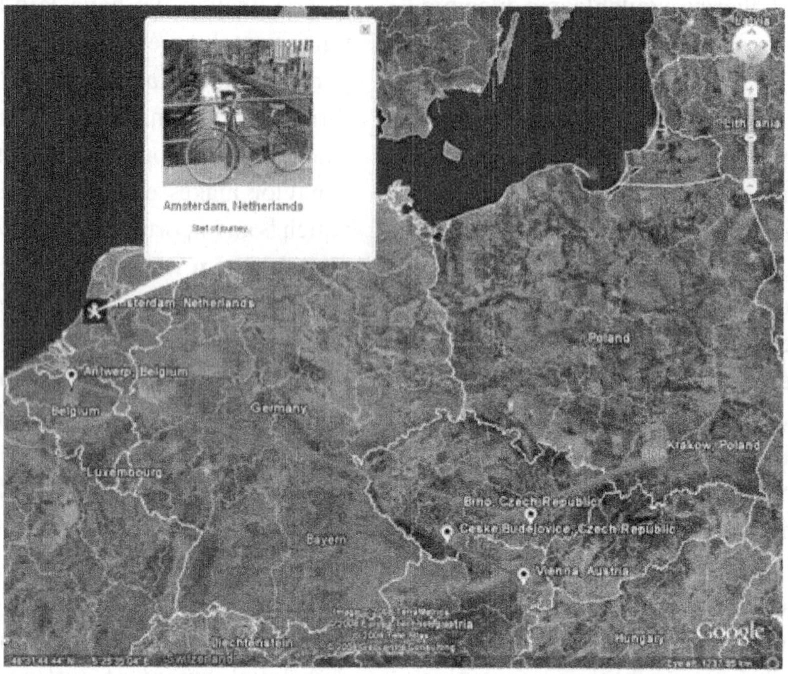

Figure 6. Tilted view of a space-time path showing temporal visualization with height

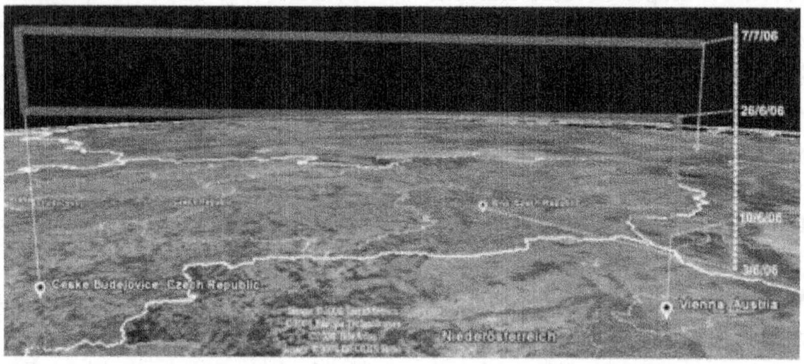

As a preliminary list we foresee VGI and future interview techniques to include, but not be limited to, the following information:

- Age, gender, relationship status, occupation, place of birth, nationality;
- geographical distribution of social network (strong vs. weak ties);
- categories for travel purpose (e.g., business, leisure, language, culture, among others) as called for by (Larsen et al., 2006, p.41).

This list of information provides a starting point for future model evaluation utilizing VGI.

CONCLUSION

A conceptual model for traveler behavior heavily utilizing ICT and multiple networks was presented in the section "Impacts, Approach, Methodology." This forms a prototype but this ongoing research will be aided by further review of travel behavior methods and importantly model validation with real world user data. The next step for this involves survey techniques to learn even more about these hosts and guests from all continents of the world. In-depth survey methods will provide a means to further test this behavioral model in addition to providing input for a tool such as agent-based simulation (Frank et al., 2001). Modeling with agents can be useful for validation and verification as well as guidance for model calibration.

The further development of the time-geographic concepts presented here will provide additional tools for spatio-temporal researchers. With a user able to customize the inputs to the tool using a graphical user interface (GUI) any combination of space and time attributes will be allowed. In the prototype presented here the physical location is taken into account in the geovisualization while the explicit influence of each network needs to be further studied.

In conclusion, these technologies are in a state of constant change and it is important to stay current with the factors mentioned here, all of which play a role in travel informatics. We have presented a unique form of international travel that focuses on personal connections while utilizing multiple network structures. We have begun the groundwork for studying this behavior and will continue to improve upon the designs into the future.

REFERENCES

Axhausen, K., & Gärling, T. (1992). Activity-based approaches to travel analysis - conceptual frameworks, models, and research problems. *Transport Reviews*, *12*(4), 323–341. doi:10.1080/01441649208716826

Carrasco, J., Miller, E., & Wellman, B. (2006). *Spatial and social networks: The case of travel for social activities*. Paper presented at the 11th International Conference on Travel Behaviour Research.

Couclelis, H. (1992). Location, place, region, and space. In R. Abler, M. Marcus, & J. Olson (Eds.), *Geography's inner worlds* (pp. 215-233). New Brunswick, NJ: Rutgers University Press.

Cresswell, T. (1996). *In place/out of place*. Minneapolis, MN: University of Minnesota Press.

Dugundji, E., Paez, A., & Arentze, T. (2008). Social networks, choices, mobility and travel. *Environment and Planning. B, Planning & Design*, *35*(6), 956–980. doi:10.1068/b3506ged

Frank, A., Bittner, S., & Raubal, M. (2001). Spatial and cognitive simulation with multi-agent systems. In D. Montello (Ed.), *Spatial Information Theory - Foundations of Geographic Information Science, Proceedings of COSIT 2001,* Morro Bay, CA, USA (Vol. 2205, pp. 124-139). Berlin, Germany: Springer.

Gärling, T., Säisä, J., Book, A., & Lindberg, E. (1986). The spatiotemporal sequencing of everyday activities in the large-scale environment. *Journal of Environmental Psychology*, *6*, 261–280. doi:10.1016/S0272-4944(86)80001-9

Golledge, R., & Stimson, R. (1997). *Spatial behavior: A geographic perspective*. New York: Guilford Press.

Goodchild, M. (2007). Citizens as sensors: The world of volunteered geography. *GeoJournal*, *69*, 211–221. doi:10.1007/s10708-007-9111-y

Hägerstrand, T. (1970). What about people in regional science? *Papers / Regional Science Association. Regional Science Association. Meeting, 24*, 7–21.

Hariharan, R., & Hornsby, K. (2000). *Modeling intersections of geospatial lifelines.* Paper presented at the First International Conference on Geographic Information Science, GIScience 2000, Savannah, Georgia, USA.

Harvey, D. (1989). *The condition ofpostmodernity.* Oxford, UK: Basil Blackwell.

Hecht, B., & Raubal, M. (2008). GeoSR: Geographically explore semantic relations in world knowledge. In L. Bernard, C. Friis-Christensen, & H. Pundt (Eds.), *The European Information Society - Taking Geoinformation Science One Step Further (Proceedings of the 11th AGILE International Conference on GIScience 2008, Girona, Spain)* (pp. 95-113). Berlin, Germany: Springer.

Hendricks, M., Egenhofer, M., & Hornsby, K. (2003). Structuring a wayfinder's dynamic space-time environment. In W. Kuhn, M. Worboys, & S. Timpf (Eds.), *Proceedings of the Spatial Information Theory - Foundations ofGeographic Information Science, International Conference, COSIT 2003, Kartause Ittingen, Switzerland, September 2003* (Vol. 2825, pp. 75-92). Berlin, Germany: Springer.

Janelle, D. (2004). Impact of information technologies. In S. Hanson & G. Giuliano (Eds.), *The Geography of Urban Transportation* (3rd ed., pp. 86-112). New York: Guilford Press.

Keßler, C., Rinner, C., & Raubal, M. (2005). An argumentation map prototype to support decision-making in spatial planning. In F. Toppen & M. Painho (Eds.), *Proceedings of the AGILE 2005 - 8th Conference on Geographic Information Science* (pp. 135-142). Lisboa, Portugal: Instituto Geografico Portugues (IGP).

Kwan, M.-P. (2000). Analysis of human spatial behavior in a GIS environment: Recent developments and future prospects. *Journal of Geographical Systems, 2*(1), 85–90. doi:10.1007/s101090050034

Kwan, M.-P. (2004). GIS methods in time-geographic research: Geocomputation and geovisualization of human activity patterns. *Geografiska Annaler B, 86*(4), 267–280. doi:10.1111/j.0435-3684.2004.00167.x

Larsen, J., Urry, J., & Axhausen, K. (2006). *Mobilities, networks, geographies.* Aldershot, England: Ashgate.

Lenntorp, B. (1976). Paths in space-time environments: A time-geographic study of the movement possibilities of individuals. *Lund Studies in Geography, Series B*(44).

Maechling, P., Chalupsky, H., Dougherty, M., Deelman, E., Gil, Y., & Gullapalli, S. (2005). Simplifying construction of complex workflows for non-expert users of the Southern California Earthquake Center community modeling environment. *SIGMOD Record, 34*(3), 24–30. doi:10.1145/1084805.1084811

Miller, H. (1991). Modeling accessibility using space-time prism concepts within geographical information systems. *International Journal of Geographical Information Systems, 5*(3), 287–301. doi:10.1080/02693799108927856

Miller, H. (1999). Measuring space-time accessibility benefits within transportation networks: Basic theory and computational methods. *Geographical Analysis, 31*(2), 187–212.

Miller, H. (2005a). A measurement theory for time geography. *Geographical Analysis, 37*(1), 17–45. doi:10.1111/j.1538-4632.2005.00575.x

Miller, H. (2005b). What about people in geographic information science? In P. Fisher & D. Unwin (Eds.), *Re-presenting geographical information systems* (pp. 215-242). New York: John Wiley.

Montello, D. (2001). Scale, in geography. In N. Smelser & P. Baltes (Eds.), *International encyclopedia of the social & behavioral sciences* (pp. 13501-13504). Oxford, UK: Pergamon Press.

Pultar, E., Cova, T. J., Yuan, M., & Goodchild, M. (2009a). EDGIS: A dynamic GIS based on space time points. *International Journal of Geographical Information Science*.

Pultar, E., Raubal, M., Cova, T. J., & Goodchild, M. (2009b). Dynamic GIS case studies: Wildfire evacuation and volunteered geographic information. *Transactions in GIS*, *13*(s1), 85–104. doi:10.1111/j.1467-9671.2009.01157.x

Pultar, E., Raubal, M., & Goodchild, M. (2008) GEDMWA: Geospatial exploratory data mining Web agent. In H Samet, C. Shahabi, & O. Wolfson (Eds.), *Proceedings of the 16th ACM International Symposium on Geographic Information Systems, SIGSPATIAL ACM GIS 2008*, Irvine, CA (pp. 499-502).

Raubal, M., Miller, H., & Bridwell, S. (2004). User-centred time geography for location-based services. *Geografiska Annaler B*, *86*(4), 245–265. doi:10.1111/j.0435-3684.2004.00166.x

Raubal, M., Winter, S., Teßmann, S., & Gaisbauer, C. (2007). Time geography for *ad-hoc* shared-ride trip planning in mobile geosensor networks. *ISPRS Journal of Photogrammetry and Remote Sensing*, *62*(5), 366–381. doi:10.1016/j.isprsjprs.2007.03.005

Ren, F., & Kwan, M.-P. (2007). Geovisualization of Human hybrid activity-travel patterns. *Transactions in GIS*, *11*(5), 721–744. doi:10.1111/j.1467-9671.2007.01069.x

Ricci, F. (2002). Travel recommender systems. *IEEE Intelligent Systems*, (November/December): 55–57.

Root, G., & Recker, W. (1983). Towards a dynamic model of individual activity pattern formulation. In S. Carpenter & P. Jones (Eds.), *Recent advances in travel demand analysis* (pp. 371-382). Aldershot, England: Gower.

Wu, Y.-H., & Miller, H. (2001). Computational tools for measuring space-time accessibility within dynamic flow transportation networks. *Journal of Transportation and Statistics*, *4*(2/3), 1–14.

Section 3
User Interface Aspects of E-Tourism

Chapter 10
Model-Based User Interface Generation for Mobile Tourism Applications and Services

M. O. Adigun
University of Zululand, South Africa

A. O. Ipadeola
University of Zululand, South Africa

O. O. Olugbara
University of Zululand, South Africa

ABSTRACT

The purpose of this chapter is to describe a model-based approach for automatic generation of user-centric interfaces for an individual mobile tourist. The generation of user-centric interfaces can provide a tourist with self-customized interfaces for efficient accessibility to mobile applications and services. The authors' polymorphic logical description (PLD) model is an interface description created at design time to address the diverse needs and preferences of users in a mobile computing environment. A PLD consists of three important modeling elements, namely, polymorphic task modeling (PTM), polymorphic abstract modeling (PAM) and polymorphic concrete modeling (PCM). A toolkit was developed based on the model-based PLD approach to user interface design. The toolkit achieves user-centric and multi-device interface generation with a high degree of dynamism and flexibility. The evaluation results of user satisfaction of the toolkit and usability of the generated interfaces are provided.

INTRODUCTION

The proliferation of mobile computing devices and their continuous injection into the world market at a rapid rate bring about appreciable impacts on e-Commerce applications and services. This proliferation of mobile devices has turned our working environment into multi-device computing environment, providing effective information communication, enhanced business transactions and numerous novel business opportunities. Due to their nomadic nature, the tourists are one of the most potential beneficiaries of mobile applications and services. However, the provision of efficient

DOI: 10.4018/978-1-60566-818-5.ch010

universal accessibility mechanisms to mobile applications and services in a mobile computing environment remains a quandary. Heterogeneity of computing devices, diversity in users' needs and preferences, and changing execution environments are the core challenges to be squarely addressed so as to achieve efficient accessibility to mobile applications and services. Specifically, in the tourism domain, the diversity of users, devices and execution environment is still a palpable challenge.

The objectives of this chapter are to: state the challenges facing universal accessibility to applications and services in a tourism execution environment, present the state-of-the-art knowledge in user interface design, describe a model-based approach called polymorphic logical description for automatic generation of user-centric interfaces for mobile tourism applications and services, and present an evaluation of a model-based toolkit that was implemented based on polymorphic logical description. The toolkit provides a unique opportunity for a tourism application designer, due to its ability to support automatic generation of customized interfaces. The toolkit can be used by a designer of tourist applications and services to provide user-centric interface generation on mobile devices. At design time, the designer provides a polymorphic description of tourism applications and services that are adapted by the toolkit for a particular tourist based on the preference information provided by the tourist.

Section 2 of this chapter gives background information and discusses polymorphic logical description for user-centric interface design. Section 3 presents an architecture for integrating polymorphic logical description into a mobile computing environment. The evaluation and application of an authoring toolkit realized from polymorphic logical description is further presented in section 4. Section 5 describes opportunities for future work in interface generation for mobile tourism applications and services. Conclusions are articulated in Section 6.

BACKGROUND

The dynamic nature of the tourism industry brings about some challenges, which crave for efficient technological solution (Staab, et al., 2002). More importantly, the provisioning of efficient access to Tourism Information Systems (TIS) constitutes to be a big challenge. TIS are software applications that are deployable on the web and accessed over desk-top as well as small hand-held devices, for provisioning of tourism business support services (Daramola, et al., 2008). As mobile devices become more prevalent, universal accessibility to mobile tourism applications and services by tourists becomes of prime significance due to the nomadic nature of tourists. Tourism applications and services must be accessible to tourists who are anonymous or familiar, but differ in race, culture, background, needs, preferences and motivation. Tourists are often faced with unfamiliar territory and languages, as pointed out by Yang, et al. (1999). For tourism applications and services to be universally accessible, they must be able to adapt to the intrinsic characteristics of every tourist, and his or her computing device.

Ongoing advancement in wireless technology and communication devices, such as PDA (Personal Digital Assistant), mobile phones, pagers and WebTV are aiding ubiquitous information accessibility. But, to achieve efficient universal accessibility to mobile applications and services, the diversity in users' preferences must be taken into cognizance. Efficient universal accessibility to mobile applications and services by tourists can only be achieved when the many challenges facing a mobile computing environment are surmounted. We believe that user interface adaptation solutions can play a significant role in adapting tourism applications and services to users' needs, thereby, making TIS more usable. The general challenges of mobile computing environment that can be addressed by user interface adaptation methods are succinctly summarized as device limitations, diversity in users' preferences and heterogeneity of execution environment.

1. **Device Limitations:** The various limitations of mobile computing devices constitute a challenge for efficient access to mobile applications and services. Mobile devices have lower computing power and memory capacity as compared to traditional desktop computers. They have different screen sizes, memory sizes and computing power (Brewster, et al., 1998; Olsen, et al., 1998; Richter, 2005). As a result, it is difficult to conveniently use these devices to access tourism applications and services. Hence, efficacious adaptation mechanisms are required to make tourism applications and services conveniently and efficiently accessible.
2. **Diversity in Users' Preferences:** The diversity in users' preferences constitutes a great challenge for efficient accessibility to mobile applications and services. Mobile tourists for instance, have diversified needs that are defined in terms of their demographics, information seeking strategy and purchasing intent factors (Burns, et al. 2001). In general, different tourists have different preferences, for example, tourists with disabilities require special consideration (Aaron, 2003).
3. **Heterogeneity of Execution Environment:** The heterogeneity of the execution environment and the inherently variable characteristics of the mobile user devices, constitute another challenge for efficient accessibility to mobile applications and services. An environment is a set of objects, persons and stochastic events that are peripheral to the current activity, but may have an impact on the system and/or user's behavior, either now or in the future (David, et al., 2001). A mobile execution environment can experience low network bandwidth with variation in location or increased noise. Low network bandwidth for example, can result into poor quality of service delivery, particularity for high bandwidth traffic, such as video.

The heterogeneity of computing devices and diversity in preferences and requirements of individual users must, therefore, be taken into consideration in order to achieve effective information communication (Constantine, 2000; Graef, et al., 2000). The conventional method of addressing the diversity and limitations of mobile devices is to design device dependent interfaces. This method is considered inefficient, time consuming, error-prone and cost ineffective (Kai, 2005). Consequently, to address these challenges of the mobile tourism environment, user interface adaptation methods can be used to making the mobile environment more efficacious.

Partial interface migration (Bandelloni & Paterno, 2004) is an emerging user interface design solution that can be adopted to solve the challenges of a tourism computing environment. Partial interface migration is the process of breaking a client interface into two main parts, namely, control part for user interaction and visualization part for information presentation. Partial interface migration solutions take advantages offered by the surrounding devices, such as public displays. A partial migration solution assumes that a user is completely immersed in a multi-device environment, and this solution comes with the inherent benefits that the consumer need not own expensive resources to access the services.

However, there are a number of social issues that can limit possible uses of user interface migration solutions in a mobile tourism computing environment. These issues include information security, privacy and confidentiality, and possible spread of diseases through the use of public displays. In tourism computing environment, for instance, security, privacy and confidentiality are important issues that must be taken into consideration when designing partial interface migration solutions. This way, it is possible to protect a tourist who is probably not familiar with the new environment, and is not fully informed of the risks, such as exposing his or her personal information to the public. Consequently, we focus on interface adaptation methods that can address such challenges of the mobile computing environment. The adaptation of an interface to a device, a user or an execution environment is an important step towards realizing efficient universal accessibility to mobile applications and services. Interface adaptation methods can be classified into three major classes, namely, multi-device, multi-environment and multi-target user interfaces (David, et al., 2001).

1. **Multi-Device User Interface Adaptation:** A multi-device or multi-platform user interface is sensitive to multiple classes of platforms, but supports a single class of users and environments (James, 2002; Mori, et al., 2004; Rodrigo, et al., 2006). Multi-device interfaces are limited to devices known at design time and do not automatically support new devices. They do not adapt to user's context, such as user preferences and changes in user execution environment.
2. **Multi-Environment User Interface Adaptation:** A multi-environment user interface supports multiple classes of environments, but it is limited to a single class of devices. Some authors (Anil, et al., 2007) regarded multi-environment interface as context aware user interfaces.
3. **Multi-Target User Interface Adaptation:** A multi-target user interface supports multiple types of devices, users, platforms and environments (Jank, et al., 2005; Banavar, et al., 2004; Bisignano, et al., 2006). A multi-target user interface design is appropriate for adapting mobile tourism applications and services, due to its ability to adapt to diverse devices, users' needs and their execution environments.

Due to the dynamic nature of a tourism computing environment, the need for an automatic user-centric interface generation for efficient access to mobile applications and services becomes highly significant. User-centric interfaces can help a tourist with self-customized interfaces for efficient accessibility to mobile applications and services. Tourists, as unique consumers of mobile applications and services require special consideration during interface generation. It is, therefore, pertinent to involve tourist participation during interface generation. Priority must be given to the preferences and requirements of an individual tourist so as to improve the usability of tourism applications and services. The goal is to provide user-centric interfaces for universal accessibility to mobile tourism applications and services. Specifically, three essential requirements that must be satisfied during an interface generation for efficient universal accessibility to tourism applications and services are: on-demand, user-centric and flexible interface generation. Moreover, user interface adaptation is carried out based on three common approaches, namely, middleware based, mark-up language based, and model-based adaptation approaches (Niklfeld, et al., 2005). These important requirements, adaptation approaches and model-based user interface design approaches are outlined in the following.

1. **On-Demand Interface Generation:** A tourist, who is likely to be a new user in a new execution environment, requires that an interface be generated on request. Such an on-demand interface generation allows for an instant interface delivery for efficient accessibility to mobile applications and services.

2. **User-Centric Interface Generation:** The needs or preferences of a tourist must be addressed through discrete generation of an interface for an individual tourist. The tourist should be actively involved in the selection of every interface component during interface generation so as to achieve interface usability as well as the usability of mobile applications and services.

3. **Flexible Interface Generation:** A tourist should be able to alter his or her interface at any given time by modifying his or her preference information through a proxy application on less constrained devices such as desktop, laptop, and palmtop that can easily be used for submission of user preferences. Hence, through a proxy device, a tourist should be able to specify example preferences and generate specimen interfaces that can be delivered on-request. The proxy application gives a user the flexibility of managing preferences, viewing specimen interface and other preference information supported by the system. Next, we discuss three approaches to user interface adaptation, namely: middleware-based, mark-up language-based, and model-based adaptation approaches.

Middleware-Based User Interface Adaptation

A middleware based adaptation approach translates a single source interface implementation into a device-specific format before the final projection of the interface to the user. The translation is handled by a middleware, which is positioned in the delivery path. Mark-up languages employed for this translation include: IBM's Abstract User Interface Markup Language (AUIML), Universal Interface Mark-up Language (UIML) and Quality of Information Markup Languages (QIML) (Huang, 2001). These markup languages are collectively known as User Interface Description Languages (UIDL). They run simultaneously on different devices, describing user interface in an abstract manner. User interfaces can be adapted to a specific device using a middleware based adaptation approach so as to address the user preference diversity challenge.

Mark-Up Language Based Adaptation

A mark-up based adaptation approach uses an extended mark-up language for interface adaptation. This involves extending existing mark-up languages such as eXtensible Hypertext Markup Language (XHTML) and Cascaded Style Sheet (CSS) with more powerful features, enabling advanced device and modality independence. Braun (2004) extended XForms and XHTML by adding new tags and attributes for spanning diverse user interfaces. Similarly, Grundy, et al. (2002) adapted custom Java Server Pages (JSP) tag libraries for multi-device interface design.

Model-Based User Interface Adaptation

A model-based approach involves the specification of explicit models, ie. preference aware models for the description of the user interface. Model-based approaches allow designers to specify and analyze software applications in a more semantic-oriented level rather than starting to immediately address the implementation details, which can be updated using an appropriate tool (Paterno, 2005a). this user interface model organizes information into three different levels of abstraction, namely, task, abstract and concrete models (Szekely, et al., 1996). The task model provides a description of user tasks. The abstract model comprises of Abstract Interaction Objects (AIO), information elements (e.g. EditObject typifies an abstract interaction object/element for a TextField) and presentation units. A presentation unit is a window perceivable by a user on his/her device at a given time. For instance the current display a MIDlet application is presentation unit). The concrete model specifies the style for rendering the presentation units and their associated information. A concrete user interface is transformed into a final user interface using appropriate implementation language supported by a specific target device. Examples of these implementation languages include: eXtensible HyperText Markup Language (XHTML), Hypertext Mark-up Language (HTML) and Wireless Mark-up language (WML).

Model-Based User Interface Design Approaches

Model-based approaches have wide acceptability and applicability and have been proposed to address the challenges in user interface design. While some works addressed the challenges posed by heterogeneity of mobile devices, others considered the requirements of users during multi-device interface generation. A number of existing model-based approaches for the design of user interfaces to suit device, user, and/or environment can be categorized as: device and user-centric interfaces.

1. **Device Centric User Interface:** A device centric user interface adapts itself to the intrinsic characteristics of a targeted device. The use of multiple logical descriptions based on a model-based approach for achieving device centric interfaces have been proposed, and an authoring environment called TERESA has been realized (Mori, et al., 2004). A hybrid of a model-based approach and design patterns was proposed by James (2002) for device-centric user interface design, and an authoring toolkit called DAMASK was realized. These model-based approaches only catered for design time adaptation of user interfaces for devices whose characteristics or profiles are pre-determined. But, user characteristics and preference information were not considered during interface adaptation.

2. **User-centric User Interface:** A user-centric user interface is usually designed to suit individual user's characteristics. A user characteristic can either be application independent or application dependent. Application independent characteristics include user preferences, capabilities and psycho-motor-skills. Application dependent characteristics include goals and knowledge of the system and the applications. Device-centric user interface design approaches were proposed for addressing the challenges of heterogeneous mobile devices. However, interfaces must be sensitive to user needs, requirements and preferences. Many model-based approaches for device and user-centric interfaces have been proposed (Savidis, et al. 1997; Schlungbaum, et al., 1997; Bisignano, et al. 2006).

Our holistic approach is called Polymorphic Logical Description (PLD) (Ipadeola, et al., 2008a), and is implemented with a model-based toolkit called Custom MADE (CoMADE), which uses Java 2 Micro Edition (J2ME). PLD addresses the challenges of a mobile computing environment by focusing on user participation in interface generation. User participation in automatic interface generation can be helpful for efficient generation of user-centric interfaces. PLD creates alternative interface artifacts based on real-time user preference information and performs automatic artifact selection, user-centric interface generation and packaging for an individual user. This comes with inherent benefits of achieving device and user-centric interface generation for universal accessibility to mobile applications and services.

With CoMADE, an interface designer can create a polymorphic model for an interface at design time, while application developers can simultaneously work on alternative task representations. Additionally, an interface designer can extend a CoMADE generated user interface by applying a new task variant to address one or more users' preferences. A mediator (an intermediary component that uses user preference information for the generation of final user centric interface, created by a designer at design time), together with Sun emulator programs were integrated with CoMADE. This allows for design time testing and evaluation of the generated interface. Furthermore, interface designers can specify example preferences and activate the mediator.

POLYMORPHIC LOGICAL DESCRIPTION FOR INTERFACE GENERATION

PLD is proposed for efficient accessibility to business support services in a tourism application domain. The goal of PLD is to achieve an on-demand as well as user-centric and flexible interface generation for an individual tourist. PLD is an interface description created at design time to address the diverse needs and preferences of users in a mobile computing environment. PLD consists of three important modeling elements, namely, Polymorphic Task Modeling (PTM), Polymorphic Abstract Modeling (PAM) and Polymorphic Concrete Modeling (PCM).

PLD supports direct user participation during interface generation and achieves automatic interface generation for J2ME enabled phones. The J2ME platform provides significant benefits for a mobile tourist, as compared to the conventional browser based environment such as the mobile Web (m-Web) and Wireless Access Protocol (WAP). The benefits offered by the J2ME platform include among others: adequate security system, disconnected access and synchronization, cross-platform compatibility, dynamic delivery of applications and services, enhanced user experience, scalability and performance (Gupta, et al., 2001). Additionally, J2ME enabled phones are readily available in the market (Nasseam, et al., 2003).

Polymorphic Task Modeling

Polymorphic Task Modeling (PTM) is based on hierarchical task decomposition proposed by Savidis, et al. (1997). In this context, we define polymorphism as the representation of an interface artifact in multiple forms. Alternative representations of interface artifacts can be effective for handling the diversity in users' needs and preferences. An interface designer specifies different tasks to be carried out by a user on an interface. Tasks are logical activities that must be performed by a user in order to reach a goal (Paterno, 2005b) and a set of related tasks help to define the requirements for making an interface. First, a polymorphic task model is realized at design time through the analysis of tasks and their associated variants. Next, tasks are represented in a tree structure, showing task hierarchy with each task forming a node. The properties associated with tasks are the task types, operators and relationships between tasks. Besides, there are different types of tasks, which include interaction, user, application and abstraction tasks, as shown in Figure 1, where connector is an operator that connects two or more tasks, T_1, T_2, and T_3 are tasks. A subtask relationship exists between a task its variants, for example V_{11} and V_{12} are subtasks of T_1.

Tasks are given alternative representations, which are called task variants or substitutes so as to cater for diverse users' preferences. For example, a task can be represented in a number of different languages to achieve localized interfaces. An alternative language representation given to a task is an example of a task variation. Additionally, task variants can cater for different device capabilities. For instance, the use of different media contents for the representation of the same task can be employed. Using this approach, different interaction styles and diversities in users' preferences can be addressed by specifying such task variant information during the polymorphic task modeling. User interface designers do not have to design separate interfaces to meet user

Figure 1. Polymorphic task representation

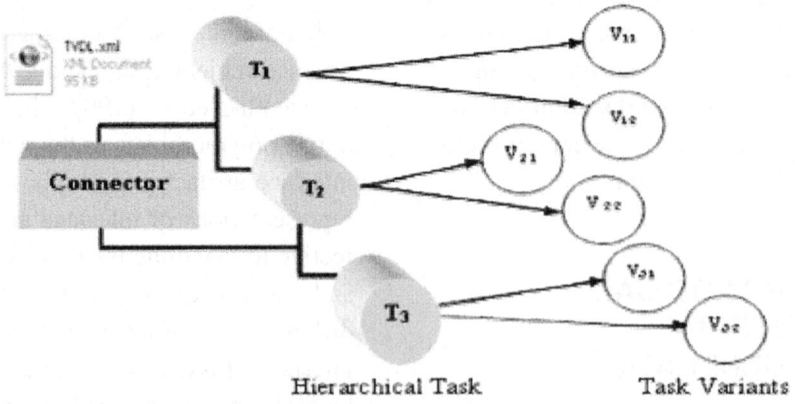

or device specific needs by using task variants. Figure 1 shows a polymorphic task representation, with tasks (T_1, T_2, T_3), task variants (V_{11}, V_{12}, V_{21}, V_{22}, V_{31}, V_{32}) and a connector that shows the relationship between these tasks. For instance, T_1 = "Enter Your Name", T_2 = "Enter Your Password" and T_3 = "LogOn" tasks are required to be performed by a user in order to sign-on to an e-mail account. Any of these tasks can be decomposed into several sub-tasks or given an alternative task representation. The associated task presentations are Shona and Isizulu languages. Hence, the task presentations are V_{11} = Zita Raunoshandisa, V_{12} = Faka Igama Lako, V_{21} = Password Yakho, V_{22} = Faka Inamba Yakho Eyimfihlo, V_{31} = Pinda Mutsamba, and V_{32} = Ngena.

During PTM-based task representation, task variants are given attribute-value pair descriptions. For instance, task variants can have language as an attribute, and English as attribute value. The task variants and attribute-value description considered during the PTM process depend on the preferences of the target user group. This is obtained from an explicit user model (Schlungbaum, 1997) or explicit information provided by tourists. Moreover, the attribute-value description associated with task variants serve as the basis for the selection of a task variant during interface generation. Task and task variant information specified in this phase are generated in hierarchical structure and represented in an XML based language, called Task Variant Description Language (TVDL). The TVDL describes each task variant, its properties, associated task and attribute-value description

Polymorphic Abstract Modeling

Polymorphic Abstract Modeling (PAM) is realized from the transformation of task variants in TVDL (Task Variant Description Language) to AIO (Abstract Interaction Objects). An abstract user interface modeling is a device independent description of an interface. It describes all possible user interface presentations with their associated connections. From TVDL, different presentation task sets are constructed with their associated connections. Every presentation set contains user tasks and the associated variants. Tasks and their associated variants are represented in terms of AIO. The resulting description of a presentation set is represented in a Presentation Set Description Language (PSDL).

Task variants are grouped into different sets, called Presentation Task Set (PTS). A navigation operator or connector is associated with every PTS. A PTS is therefore, a window or a set of task variants perceivable by a user on his or her device at a given time. Figure 2 shows a sample representation of polymorphic abstract presen-

Figure 2. Polymorphic abstract interface representation

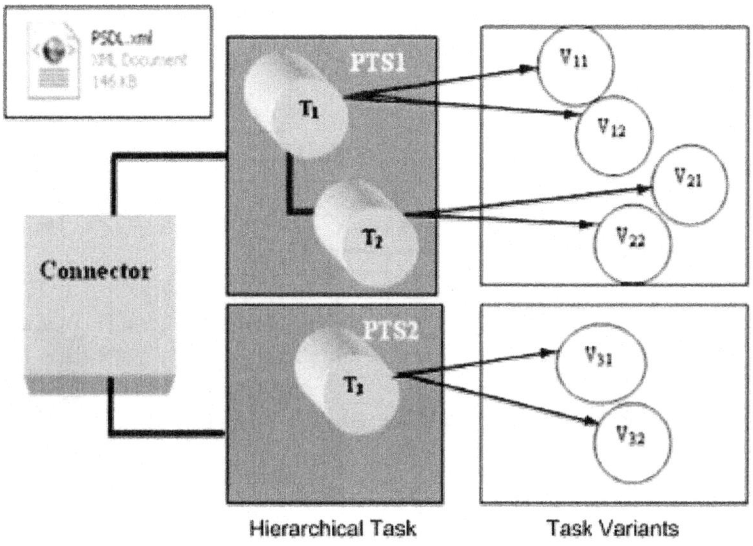

tation. The task variants V_{ij} of a task T_i were represented as AIO.

Polymorphic Concrete Modeling

Polymorphic Concrete Modeling (PCM) facilitates the generation of polymorphic concrete models, also referred to as polymorphic concrete interface. PCM was automated by our CoMADE toolkit (Ipadeola, et al., 2008b) and involves the generation of a device dependent interface description. PCM heavily relies on the information stored in the PSDL (Presentation Set Description Language). Every task variant in PTS stored in PSDL is converted to a Concrete Interaction Object (CIO), represented as variant of Concrete Interaction Object ($_V$CIO). For example, an EditElement object is associated with an implementation method for a TextField interactor and an implementation method for a StringItem is generated for TextOnlyDisplay object.

Figure 3 shows the conversion of Abstract Interaction Objects (AIO) to Concrete Interaction Objects (CIO). A task such as "Select Desired Service QoS (Quality of Service) Metrics" can be represented with a "Select Element" object during the abstract interface description. The concrete description involves a replacement AIO with suitable CIO for a target device. As shown in Figure 3, the AIO is replaced with graphical object such as a Check Box for the mobile phone and voice object for the PDA according to the user preferencesCoMADE generates a supporting implementation method for every $_V$CIO object. The method generated for every $_V$CIO, coupled with its description in the PSDL is persisted in an object database. The concrete descriptions also referred to as Application Dependent implementation Methods (ADM). Specifically, concrete description associated with each task variant was persisted using db4o (an open-source java/.Net object database library). For p sets of task variants in TVDL, there are q sets of AIO in PSDL and consequently, r sets of vCIOs objects in the object database. CoMADE also generates class templates for every user interface. Class templates include, class definition and Application Independent implementation Methods (AIM). These definitions are specified at design time and persisted as objects into db4o database. The designer can modify and update the

Figure 3. Conversion of abstract interaction objects to concrete interaction objects

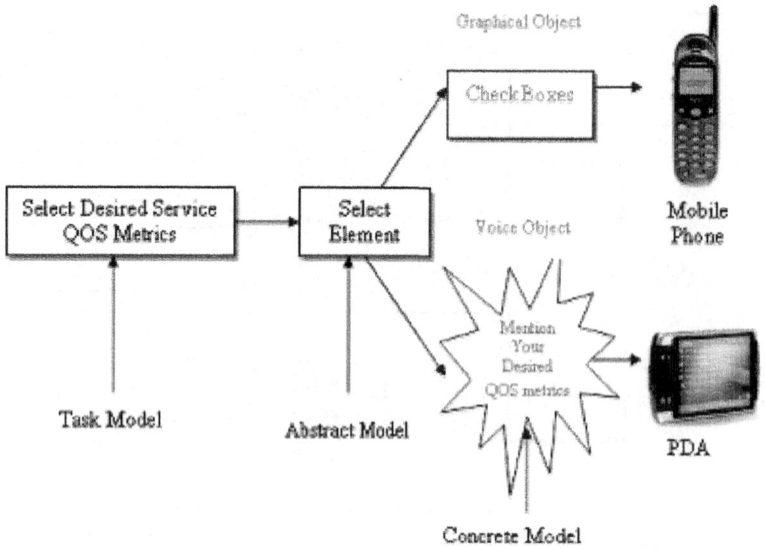

entire interface components generated. Additionally, different designers can update the task variant implementation methods generated by CoMADE with more intriguing functionalities.

The model also supports modularity, whereby different modules created by software experts are associated with different task variants of CIOs. That is, the generated task variant implementation methods and properties can be modified. In CoMADE, a work-board is provided to enable designers or mobile web service developers to import and edit additional files. The output of the concrete interface is an object containing task variants of CIO implementation methods (vCIO) and class template definitions, persisted into the object database. Figure 4 shows the persistence of the concrete description of task variants V_1 and V_2 into an object database.

Figure 4. Polymorphic concrete model persisted into Db4o

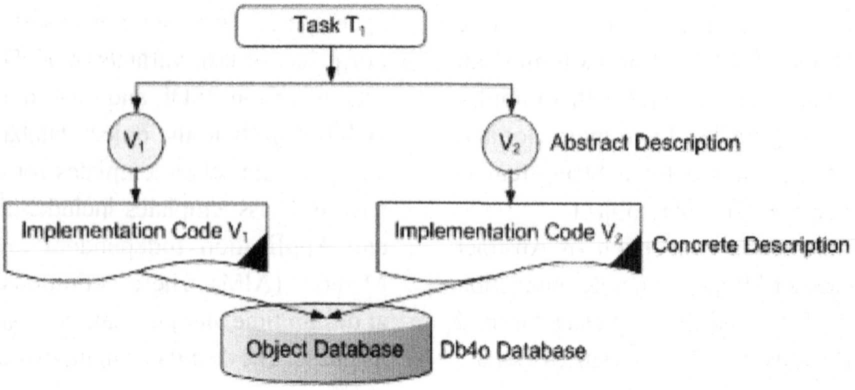

INTEGRATING PLD INTO A MOBILE COMPUTING ENVIRONMENT

Integrating PLD into a mobile computing environment requires that an appropriate mechanism be put in place to retrieve preference information from a user. The preference information forms the basis for the selection of interface artifacts from the PLD model. The interface artifacts are used for interface generation, which is then packaged and delivered to a requesting user. To accomplish the integration of PLD into a mobile computing environment, there are three important integration stages, namely, design time, load time and run time. The design time activities involve the creation of a PTM (polymorphic task model), a PAM (polymorphic abstract model) and a PCM (polymorphic concrete model). The load time activities involve the generation and delivery of an interface to a requesting user. Load time activities are performed during the generation and delivery of a requested interface. The runtime activities include adapting an interface to changes in users' preferences. Runtime activities are those performed during the actual use of a generated interface. An example of runtime activities is response to changes in users' preferences.

Figure 5 shows the architecture for integrating PLD (Polymorphic Logical Description) into a mobile computing environment for direct user participation during interface generation. An interface designer creates task-variant information, which CoMADE converts into a Polymorphic Task Modeling (PTM) and persisted into TVDL. The PTM serves as input to the Polymorphic Abstract Modeling (PAM), which is used as input to generate Polymorphic Concrete Modeling (PCM). The preference of a tourist determines which task variant of a CIO should be selected for a presentation set. For each presentation set, some task variants are selected while some are left disabled. The selected task variants make up a User-centric Presentation Task Set (UPTS). A set of UPTS is compiled, pre-verified and packaged for a requesting user. User request and preference information are conveyed from the user to the mediator for processing. User request and preference information are received through web portal interfaces on proxy devices, user application and Short Message Service (SMS).

Figure 5. Architecture for integrating PLD into a mobile computing environment

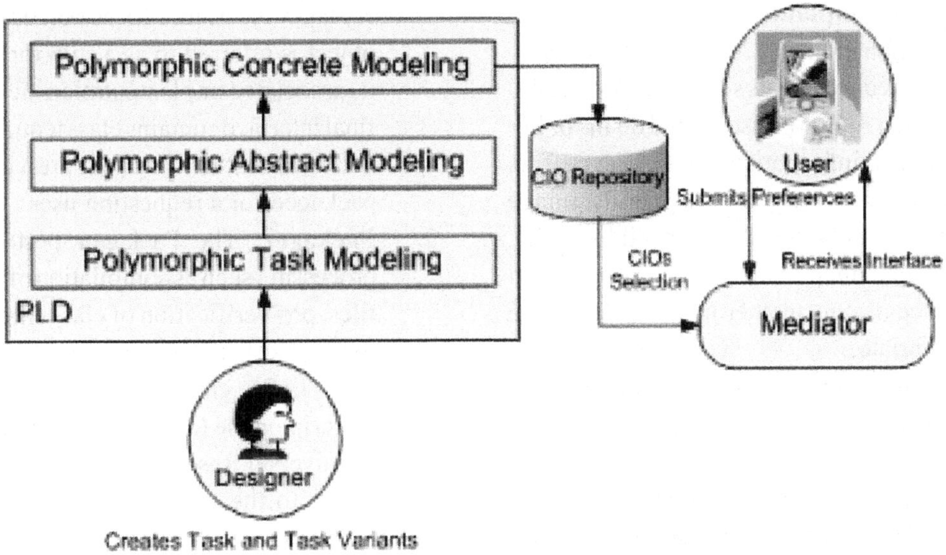

Figure 6. The mediator and supporting components

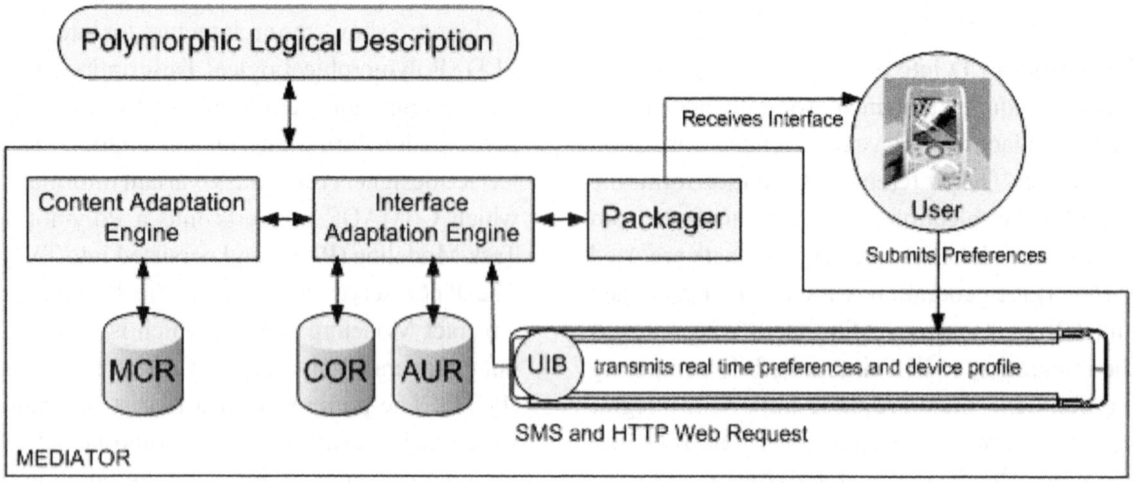

The mediator component plays an important role during the load time and runtime activities. One of the most important functions of the mediator is the selection of interface artifacts for interface generation, packaging and delivery. Figure 6 shows various components of the mediator, which include: Content Adaptation Engine (CAE), Interface Adaptation Engine (IAE), Packager, MCR (Media Content Repository), COR (Concrete Object Repository), Active AUR (User Repository) and UIB (User Information Bus).

1. **Content Adaptation Engine:** The Content Adaptation Engine (CAE performs the selection of media contents such as images, audio and video files for a user based on his or her preference information and device profile. Depending on the device capability, image contents can be transformed. Additionally, audio and video contents can be substituted in place of one another media type, where appropriate.
2. **Interface Adaptation Engine:** The Interface Adaptation Engine (IAE) carries out the generation of the final user interface and is the most significant component of the mediator. It utilizes information from other components during interface generation. A user preference information is received through an explicit proxy, user device or sample preference specified by the designer. The IAE then performs a look-up on the received preference information from the appropriate database object for the requested application interface. When such an object is found, the mediator queries an object database for the selection of task variants (vCIO) having a match with the submitted preference. A task variant is selected for every task object and each selected task variant object is referred to as a stub for retrieving its associated implementation methods. The final interface contains class template, ADM and AIM that is compiled, pre-verified and packaged for a requesting user.
3. **Packager:** The Packager performs final processing such as compilation of all needed files, pre-verification of class files, creation of manifest, packaging into Java Archive File (JAR), creation of Java Application Descriptor file (JAD) and the generation of a Universal Resource Location (URL) that points to the generated user-centric interface. The URL of the generated interface

and the associated preferences are dynamically stored in the AUR (Active User Repository).

4. **Media Content Repository:** The Media Content Repository (MCR)or Interface Resource Directory (IRD) stores various contents for user interface presentation. Media contents such as images, video and audio files are managed by this component. During an interface generation for a requesting user, an appropriate content is selected and adapted by the CAE (Content Adaptation Engine). Adaptation of media contents includes sampling of images and selection of a media content substitute. For example, an audio bite can be selected as a substitute for a video for a low bandwidth connection.
5. **Concrete Object Repository:** Concrete objects or CIOs are stored in the Concrete Object Repository (COR). That is, every task variant, with a concrete description (vCIO) is stored in the COR, which comprises of presentation task sets of vCIO objects. The description associated with every vCIO is also stored in the COR. The COR is queried for the selection of suitable vCIO to service a request for an interface generation. User preferences are used as query parameters during the selection process. User information or requests are received through an information bus.
6. **Active User Repository:** The Active User Repository (AUR) keeps record of all user requests and their corresponding responses in terms of the local addresses of the generated interfaces. For every request received by the mediator, AUR is queried to find any match with existing requests. When a match is found, an already generated interface is retrieved and delivered to a requesting user.
7. **User Information Bus:** The User Information Bus (UIB) conveys request and preference information from the user to the mediator for processing. User request and preference information are received through web portal interfaces, user application and SMS. All requests received by the UIB are logged in the AUR.

EMPIRICAL EVALUATION OF COMADE

A live-user experimental evaluation that we conducted using CoMADE is presented in this section. The purpose of our experimental study was to determine the usability of CoMADE as a toolkit for automatic generation of user-centric interfaces. The usability test was performed for evaluating the system effectiveness and user satisfaction with the toolkit. To evaluate the toolkit we hypothesize that the toolkit:

1. Increases effectiveness in automatic generation of user-centric interfaces
2. Enhances user satisfaction of the generated interface.

To validate the research hypotheses, we conducted a user study involving 30 testers grouped into Expert, Intermediate and Novice categories vis-à-vis their familiarity with technology: 10 experts, 10 intermediates and 10 novices. The testers were students of the university where the study was carried out. The expert users were mainly postgraduate students of computer science who had at least 6 years of programming experience and knowledge of user interface design. The intermediate users were honors students of computer science with at least 4 years programming experience in software development, and the novice users were first and second year students of computer science with at least 6 months programming experience in Java language. In the experiment, the testers were first presented a video demonstration of CoMADE to show how it works. Later each tester was asked to use the system to design an interface for supporting Business news, Sport news, Weather information, Stock quote and Local news services for mobile users. The user preferences to cater for in the user interface include service type, user language (English and IsiZulu) and choice of media content.

The testers developed polymorphic task models, with different task variants to achieve alternative interface presentations for users. A description was associated with each task variant definition during polymorphic task modeling. The toolkit was evaluated based on its ability to effectively generate user interfaces according to specified preferences. We measured the effectiveness of the toolkit for user-centric interface generation as well as the user satisfaction of the generated interface. In this evaluation, we provided subjective measures to capture the opinions of the testers. The questionnaire comprised statements about the system effectiveness, and user satisfaction of the generated user interface. The testers were asked to judge the statements using a 5-point Likert scale, where 1 mean strongly disagree and 5 implies strongly agree. Table 1 shows the effectiveness questionnaire used for the evaluation of the toolkit.

Similarly, the user satisfaction of the generated user interface test was conducted based on subjective measures. Table 3 shows the user satisfaction questionnaire used for the evaluation of the user interface generated by the toolkit.

Test Results

Figure 7 shows the results of some sample user interfaces generated with varying preference information. In particular, Figure 7(a) is an interface generated in English to aid accessibility to the five mobile services. Figure 7(b) is an interface generated IsiZulu for the five mobile services. Figure 7(c) is an interface generated in English and provides accessibility to Business, Weather and Local news. The interfaces were generated according to users' specified preferences. The results show that different request and preference information resulted into efficient automatic generation of different user interfaces.

Table 1. System effectiveness questionnaire

Statement	Description
e_1	I found the toolkit effective in the creation of polymorphic logical description
e_2	The interface adapts to changing new preferences
e_3	The user interface generated met the preferences I specified
e_4	Overall, the toolkit is effective in generating final user-centric interface

Table 2. User satisfaction questionnaire

Statement	Description
s_1	I found the interface of the toolkit simple to use
s_2	I found interaction with the toolkit fascinating
s_3	I found the interface generated by the toolkit usable
s_4	Overall, I am satisfied using the toolkit

Table 3. Result of CoMADE Empirical Evaluation

		Expert	Intermediate	Novice
System effectiveness	Mean	4.08	4.20	4.53
	Stdev	0.16	0.24	0.14
User satisfaction	Mean	4.50	4.10	4.30
	Stdev	0.54	0.24	0.17

Figure 8 presents a comparison of the testers' mean ratings to the statements contained in the effectiveness questionnaire. Interestingly, the novice testers gave the highest positive evaluations for all the system effectiveness questions, followed by the intermediate testers and then the expert testers.

Figure 9 shows a comparison of the testers' mean ratings to the statements contained in the user

Figure 7. User-centric interfaces generated by CoMADE

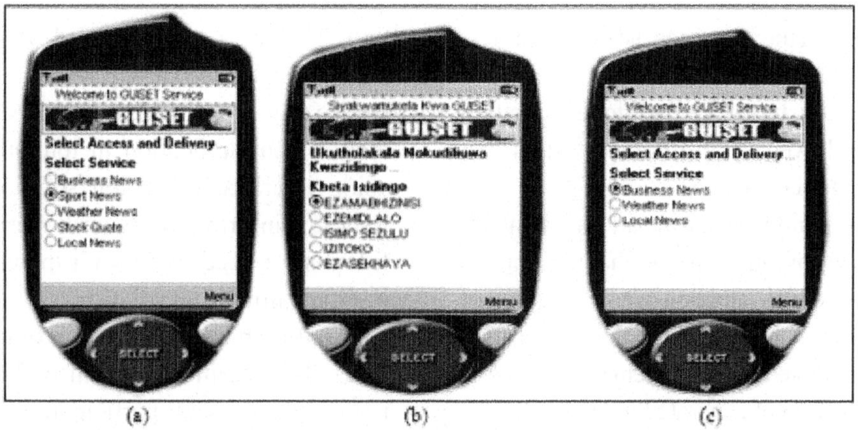

Figure 8. Comparison on the tester evaluation of the effectiveness questionnaire

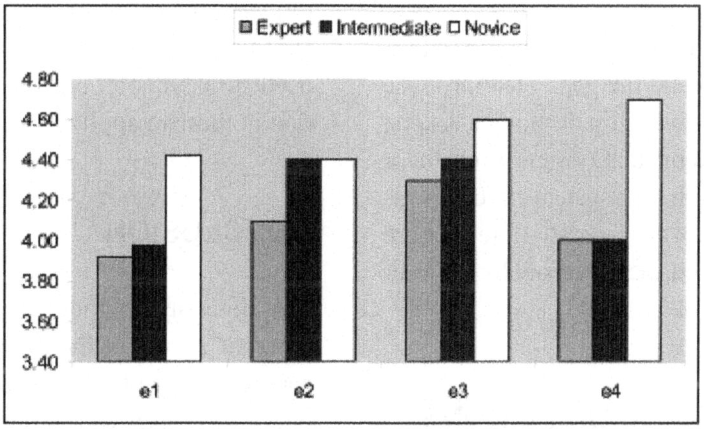

Figure 9. Comparison on the tester evaluation of the user satisfaction questionnaire

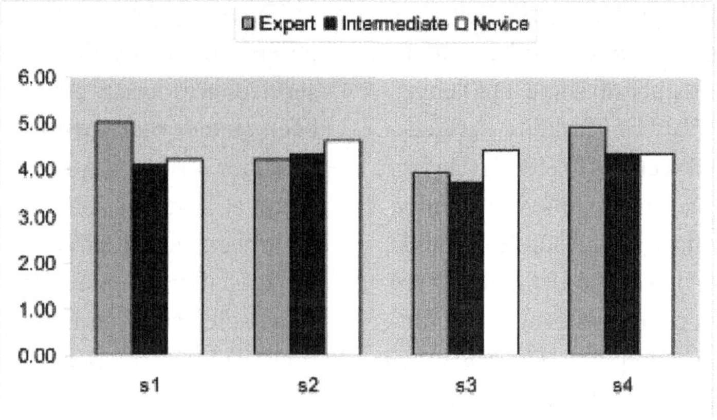

satisfaction questionnaire. The mean evaluation ratings for all classes of testers were higher for the user satisfaction of the generated user interface test as compared to those for the system effectiveness test. The expert testers gave the highest positive evaluation, followed by the novice testers and then the intermediate testers.

Finally, we computed the mean and standard deviation (stdev) of ratings for all the questions to determine the overall evaluation of each category of testers. Table 3 list of the mean and standard deviation of the ratings obtained for the system effectiveness, and user satisfaction of generated interfaces.

We found that overall, the novice testers considered the toolkit most effective, followed by the intermediate testers, and then came the expert testers. These results are different for the user satisfaction of the generated user interface test. The expert testers found the generated interface most satisfactory, followed by the novice testers, and then came the intermediate testers. From these results we can conclude both system effectiveness and user satisfaction of the generated interface are significantly increased, therefore, our hypotheses are upheld.

FUTURE RESEARCH DIRECTIONS

Many current research efforts in tourism application focus on recommender systems design to provide efficient access to information services. Considering the dynamic nature of the tourism industry, which brings about some challenges of efficient accessibility to information services, many future research directions related to tourism applications and services are possible. We mention here two important directions, namely; flexible user interface migration solutions for federated devices to enable task continuity as well as uninterrupted information communication. The other possible research direction is automatic generation of user centric vocal interface for efficient accessibility to tourism application and services.

First, interface migration aims to combine a number of devices for information communication. That is, a constrained device (e.g. mobile phone) can be used along with a less constrained device (e.g. desktop) to establish effective information communication in tourism applications using interface migration solutions. However, issues of information security, privacy and confidentiality need to be well managed in partial interface migration solutions.

Another possible way to provide an efficient accessibility to information in tourism applications is to involve users' participation in the process of interface generation, which is the goal of user centric interfaces. Possible solution methods for the automatic generation of user centric vocal interfaces for tourism applications and services need to be further investigated. This would definitely be useful to achieve efficient accessibility to information in tourism applications and services.

CONCLUSION

The diversity in tourists' preferences and the dynamic nature of the tourism computing environment demands that an efficient mechanism be provided for user-centric interface generation. The usability of interfaces can be efficiently realized in a tourism computing environment, when interfaces can automatically adapt to changing tourists' preferences. The major challenges facing efficient universal accessibility to mobile applications and services in a tourism computing environment have been stated. State-of-the-art knowledge in user interface design and a model-based approach for automatic generation of user-centric interfaces have been presented. A CoMADE authoring toolkit was implemented based on a model-based approach, called, Polymorphic Logical Description (PLD). A PLD consists of three important modeling elements, namely, Polymorphic Task Modeling (PTM), Polymorphic Abstract Modeling (PAM) and Polymorphic Concrete Modeling

(PCM). During PTM-based task representation, task variants are given attribute-value pair descriptions capture diverse user preferences. PAM is realized from the transformation of task variants in TVDL (Task Variant Description Language) to AIO (Abstract Interaction Objects) to achieve device independent description of an interface. PCM facilitates the generation of polymorphic concrete models to generate device specific interface for a particular user. A toolkit was developed based on the model-based PLD approach to user interface design. Evaluation results show that CoMADE has the ability to automatically generate user interface according to specified user preference information, and CoMADE is an effective toolkit for automatically generating user-centric interfaces.

REFERENCES

Aaron, M. (2003). Universal, ubiquitous, user-interface design for the disabled and elderly. *Interaction, 10*(2), 23–27. doi:10.1145/637848.637858

Anil, S., Juan, Q., Sergiu, M. D., Sushil, J. L., & Monica, N. N. (2007). Sycophant: An API for research in context-aware user interfaces. (pp. 83-83). In *Proceedings of the 2nd International Conference on Software Engineering Advances (ICSEA). Cap Esterel.*

Banavar, G., Bergman, L., Cardone, R., Chevalier, V., Gaeremynck, Y., & Giraud, F. (2004). An authoring technology for multi-device Web applications. *IEEE Pervasive Computing / IEEE Computer Society [and] IEEE Communications Society, 3*(3), 83–93. doi:10.1109/MPRV.2004.1321033

Bandelloni, R., & Paterno, F. (2004). Flexible user interface migration. In *Proceedings of the 9th international conference on Intelligent user interfaces* (pp. 148-155).

Bisignano, M., Di-Modica, G., & Tomarchio, O. (2006). An intent-oriented approach for multi-device user interface design. In *Proceedings of the 20th International Conference on Advanced Information Networking and Application* (Vol. 2, pp. 186-194).

Braun, E., Hart, A., & Muhlhauser, M. (2004). Authoring for multi-device interfaces. In *Adjunct Proceedings of the 8th ERCIM Workshop* (pp. 186-194.).

Brewster, S., Leplatre, G., & Crease, M. (1998). Using non-speech sounds in mobile computing devices. In *Proceedings of the First Workshop on Human Computer Interaction of Mobile Devices,* Glasgow, Scotland (pp. 224-259).

Burns, J., & Gregory, R. M. (2001). A framework for effective user interface design for Web-based electronic commerce applications. *International Journal of an Emerging Transdiscipline, 4,* 67–75.

Constantine, S. (2000). *User interfaces for all: Concepts, methods and tools*. Mahwah, NJ: Lawrence Erlbaum Associates, Inc.

Daramola, J. O., Adigun, M. O., & Olugbara, O. O. (2008). A product line architecture for evolving intelligent component services in tourism information systems. In P. O. Connor, W. Hopkin, & U. Gretze (Eds.), *Information and communication technologies in tourism* (pp. 118-145). Berlin, Germany: Springer.

David, T., Joelle, C., & Gaelle, C. (2001). A unifying reference framework for the development of plastic user interfaces. In *Proceedings of the 2001 Engineering of Human—Computer Interaction Conference (EHCI'2001)* (pp. 173-192).

Graef, G., & Gaedke, M. (2000). Construction of adaptive Web-applications from reusable components. In *Proceedings of the 1st International Conference on Electronic Commerce and Web Technologies*(EC-Web) (pp. 1-12).

Grundy, J. C., & Jin, W. (2002). Experiences developing a thin-client, multi-device travel planning application. In *Proceedings of 2002 New Zealand Conference on Computer-Human Interaction*, Hamilton, New Zealand.

Gupta, A., & Srivastava, M. (2001). *Integrated java technology for end-to-end m-commerce*. Retrieved June 4, 2008, from http://developers.sun.com/mobility/midp/articles/mcommerce/

Huang, C. M., & Chao, Y. C. (2001). Universal WWW access for heterogeneous client devices. In *Proceedings of the 27th Euromicro Conference* (pp. 315-322).

Ipadeola, A. O., Olugbara, O. O., Adigun, M. O., & Xulu, S. S. (2008b). A system for dynamically generating user centric interfaces for mobile applications and services. In I. Y. Song, et al. (Eds.), *Proceedings of the ER Workshops 2008* (LNCS 5232, pp. 175-184). Berlin, Germany: Springer-Verlag.

Ipadeola, A. O., Olugbara, O. O., Xulu, S. S., & Adigun, M. O. (2008a). Polymorphic logical description for automatic generation of user centric, multi-device interfaces. In *Proceedings of the third International Conference on Pervasive Computing,* Alexandria, Egypt.

James, L. (2002). Damask a tool for early-stage design and prototyping of cross-device user interfaces. In *Proceedings of the Conference Supplement of UIST 2003: ACM Symposium on User Interface Software and Technology* (pp. 13-16).

Jank, M., & Pospischil, G. (2005). Device independent mobile multimodal user interfaces with the MONA multimodal presentation server. In *Proceedings of the Eurescom Summit* (pp. 89-93).

Kai, R. (2005). A transformational approach to multi-device interface. In *Proceedings of the human Factor in computer System*, Portand OR, USA (pp. 1126-1127).

Mori, G., Paterno, F., & Santoro, C. (2004). Design and development of multi-device user interface through multiple logical descriptions. In *Proceedings on Software Engineering* (pp. 507-520).

Nasseam, E. (2003). *A Web services strategy for mobile phones*. Retrieved June 4, 2008, from http://webservices.xml.com/pub/a/ws/2003/08/19/mobile.html

Niklfeld, G., Anegg, H., Gassner, A., Jank, M., Pospischil, G., Pucher, M., et al. (2005). Device independent mobile multimodal user interfaces with the MONA multimodal presentation server. In *Proceedings of the Eurescom Summit. W3C Workshop on Multi-Modal Interaction.*

Olsen, D., Jefferies, S., Nielsen, T., Moyes, W., & Fredrickson, P. (2000). Cross-modal interaction using XWeb. In *Proceedings of the 13th Annual Symposium on User Interface Software and Technology,* CA, USA (pp. 191-2000).

Paterno, F. (2005a). Model-based tools for pervasive usability. *Interacting with Computers, 17*(3), 219–315. doi:10.1016/j.intcom.2004.06.017

Paterno, F. (2005b). Multimodality and multi-device interfaces. In *Proceedings of the W3C Workshop on Multimodal Interaction.*

Richter, K. (2005). A transformation strategy for multi-device menus and toolbars. In *Proceedings of the CHI '05 Extended Abstracts on Human Factors in Computing Systems* (pp.1741-17).

Rodrigo, O. (2006). Mobile access to Web systems using a multi-device interface design. In *Proceedings of 2006 World congress in Computer Science, Computer Engineering and Applied Computing* (pp. 332-334).

Savidis, A., Alex, P., Demosthenes, A., & Constantine, S. (1997). Designing user-adapted interfaces: The unified design method for transformable interactions. In *Proceedings of the Symposium on Designing Interactive Systems* (pp. 323-334).

Schlungbaum, E. (1997). Individual user interfaces and model based user interface software tools. In *Proceedings of International Conference on Intelligent User Interfaces*.

Staab, S., Werther, H., Ricci, F., Zipf, A., Gretzel, U., & Fesenmaier, D. R. (2002). Intelligent systems for tourism. *IEEE Intelligent Systems*, *17*(6), 53–66. doi:10.1109/MIS.2002.1134362

Szekely, P. (1996). Retrospective and challenges for model-based interface development. In *Proceedings of the 2nd International Workshop on Computer-Aided Design of User Interfaces*, A Presses Universitaires de Namur, Namur (pp. 21-44).

Yang, J., Yang, W., Denecke, M., & Waibel, A. (1999). Smart sight: A tourist assistant system. In *Proceedings of the. 3rd Int. Symposium. Wearabale computers*, San Francisco, CA (pp. 73-78).f

Chapter 11
Visiting Tourist Landmarks in Virtual Reality Systems by Real-Walking

F. Steinicke
Westfälische Wilhelms-Universität Münster, Germany

G. Bruder
Westfälische Wilhelms-Universität Münster, Germany

J. Jerald
University of North Carolina at Chapel Hill, USA

H. Frenz
Westfälische Wilhelms-Universität Münster, Germany

M. Lappe
Westfälische Wilhelms-Universität Münster, Germany

ABSTRACT

In recent years virtual environments (VEs) have become more and more popular and widespread due to the requirements of numerous application areas in particular in the 3D city visualization domain. Virtual reality (VR) systems, which make use of tracking technologies and stereoscopic projections of three-dimensional synthetic worlds, support better exploration of complex datasets. However, due to the limited interaction space usually provided by the range of the tracking sensors, users can explore only a portion of the virtual environment (VE). Redirected walking allows users to walk through large-scale immersive virtual environments (IVEs) such as virtual city models, while physically remaining in a reasonably small workspace by intentionally injecting scene motion into the IVE. With redirected walking users are guided on physical paths that may differ from the paths they perceive in the virtual world. The authors have conducted experiments in order to quantify how much humans can unknowingly be redirected. In this chapter they present the results of this study and the implications for virtual locomotion user interfaces that allow users to view arbitrary real world locations, before the users actually travel there in a natural environment.

DOI: 10.4018/978-1-60566-818-5.ch011

In recent years virtual environments (VEs) have become more and more popular and widespread due to the requirements of numerous application areas in particular in the 3D city visualization domain. Two-dimensional desktop systems are often limited in cases where natural interfaces are desired, for example, when navigating within complex 3D scenes. In such cases virtual reality (VR) systems, which make use of tracking technologies and stereoscopic projections of three-dimensional synthetic worlds, support better exploration of complex datasets.

These VR systems allow user to explore virtual worlds in an intuitive and immersive manner. In virtual 3D city environments people can visit, for instance, tourist landmarks virtually.

However, due to the limited interaction space usually provided by the range of the tracking sensors, users can explore only a portion of the virtual environment (VE). Redirected walking allows users to walk through large-scale immersive virtual environments (IVEs) such as virtual city models, while physically remaining in a reasonably small workspace by intentionally injecting scene motion into the IVE. With redirected walking users are guided on physical paths that may differ from the paths they perceive in the virtual world.

In this context two questions arise: First, how does redirected walking work and second, up to which degree can users be manipulated?

In order to quantify how much humans can unknowingly be redirected, we have performed constant stimuli experiments. In our study, 18 subjects tested in four different experiments: Study E1 explored the difference of user response between virtual and physical rotation; study E2 investigated the difference between virtual and physical translation, and study E3 investigated of the same for walking direction. In experiment E1 subjects performed rotations to which different gains have been applied, and then had to choose whether or not the visually perceived rotation was greater than the physical rotation. In experiment E2 subjects chose if they thought that the physical walk was longer than the visually perceived scaled travel distance. In experiment E3 subjects walked along a path in the IVE, which was physically bent to the left or to the right, and they estimate the direction of the curvature.

In this chapter we present the results of this study and the implications for virtual locomotion user interfaces that allow users to view arbitrary real world locations, before the users actually travel there in a natural environment.

Most of the presented results can be found in the works of Steinicke et al.

INTRODUCTION

Walking is the most basic and intuitive way of moving within the real world.

Navigating through large-scale immersive virtual environments (IVEs) can be used in interesting ways in the e-Tourism domain. Landmarks, historical areas, hotels etc. can be viewed in an IVE before going there physically.

Many domains are inherently three-dimensional and advanced visual simulations often provide a good sense of locomotion, but exclusive visual stimuli cannot address the vestibular-proprioceptive system -- which provide us the ability to know where we are in space and time.

Real walking through IVEs is often not possible (Whitton et al. 2005). However, an obvious approach is to transfer the user's tracked head movements to changes of the virtual camera in the virtual world by means of a one-to-one mapping, i.e., a one meter movement in the real world is mapped to a one meter movement in the virtual one. This technique has the drawback that the users' movements are restricted by a limited range of the tracking sensors and a rather small workspace in the real world. Therefore, concepts for virtual locomotion methods are needed that enable walking over large distances in the virtual world while remaining within a relatively small space in the real world. Various prototypes of interface devices have been developed to prevent a displacement in the real world such that users remain almost at the same position in the physical world even while they walk. These devices include torus-shaped omni-directional treadmills, motion foot pads, robot tiles and motion carpets (Bouguila & Sato, 2002; Iwata, Yano, Fukushima, & Noma, 2006).

Although these hardware systems represent enormous technological achievements, they are still very expensive and will not be generally accessible in the foreseeable future. Hence there is a tremendous demand for more accessible approaches. As a solution to this challenge, traveling by exploiting walk-like gestures has been proposed in many different variants, giving the user the impression of walking. For example, the walking-in-place approach exploits walk-like gestures to travel through an IVE, while the user remains physically at nearly the same position (Feasel et al. 2008).

However, real walking has been shown to be a more presence-enhancing locomotion technique than other navigation methods.

Cognition and perception research suggests that cost-efficient as well as natural alternatives exist. It is known from perceptive psychology that vision often dominates proprioceptive and vestibular sensation when they disagree. When, in perceptual experiments, human participants can use only vision to judge their motion through a virtual scene they can successfully estimate their momentary direction of self-motion but are much less proficient in perceiving their paths of travel (Lappe, Bremmer, & van den Berg, 1999). Therefore, since users tend to unwittingly compensate for small inconsistencies during walking, it is possible to guide them along paths in the real world that differ from the path perceived in the virtual world. This *Redirected walking* enables users to explore a virtual world that is considerably larger than the tracked working space (Razzaque, 2005) (see Figure 1).

In this chapter we present a series of experiments in which we have quantified how much humans can be redirected without observing inconsistencies between real and virtual motions. The remainder of this chapter is structured as follows.

The second section, "Previous Work," summarizes previous work related to locomotion and perception in virtual reality (VR) environments. In the section "Generalized Redirected Walking" we present a taxonomy of redirected walking techniques as used in the experiments that are described in the experiments section. The fifth section, "Visiting Tourist Landmarks," explains how the described concepts can be used to visit tourist landmarks. The final section discusses opportunities for future research and presents our conclusions.

PREVIOUS WORK

Currently locomotion and perception in IVEs are the focus of many research groups analyzing perception in both the real world and the virtual worlds.

For example, researchers have found that distances in virtual worlds are underestimated in comparison to those in the real world (Interrante, Anderson, & Ries, 2006), visual speed during walking is underestimated, and in VEs the total distance one has traveled is also underestimated. Furthermore, users can experience difficulties in orienting themselves in the virtual worlds.

From an egocentric perspective, the real world appears stationary as we move around or rotate our head and eyes. Both visual and extraretinal cues that come from other parts of the mind or body help us to perceive the world as stable.

Extraretinal cues come from the vestibular system, proprioception, our cognitive model of the world, or from an efference copy of the motor commands that move the respective body parts.

Figure 1. Redirected walking scenario for a user walking in the real environment

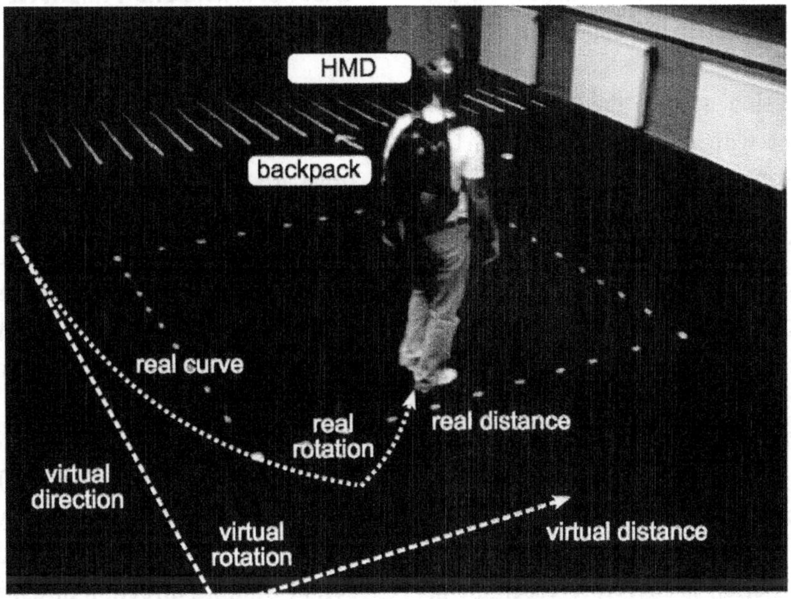

The vestibular system contributes to our sense of spatial orientation and balance; it is the sensory system that provides the dominant input about equilibrioception and movement. Proprioception is the sense of the relative position of neighbouring parts of the body. Efference copy is an internal copy of a motor innervation. When a motor command is sent through the nervous system this copy is used to predict the expected sensation that will occur.

When one or more of these cues conflicts with other cues, as is often the case for IVEs (e.g., due to tracking errors or latency) the virtual world may appear to be spatially unstable. Experiments demonstrate that the user tolerates a certain amount of inconsistency between visual and proprioceptive sensation (Steinicke et al., 2008; Jerald, Peck, Steinicke, & Whitton, 2008; Peck, Whitton, & Fuchs, 2008).

In this context redirected walking provides a promising solution to the problem of limited tracking space and the challenge of providing users with the ability to explore an IVE by walking. With this approach the user is redirected via manipulations applied to the displayed scene, causing users to unknowingly compensate scene motion by repositioning and/or reorienting themselves.

Different approaches to redirect a user in an IVE have been proposed.

An obvious approach is to scale translational movements, for example, to cover a virtual distance that is larger than the distance walked in the physical space. Interrante et al. suggest applying the scaling exclusively to the main walking direction in order to prevent unintended lateral shifts (Interrante, Ries, & Anderson, 2007).

With most reorientation techniques, the virtual world is imperceptibly rotated around the center of a stationary user until he/she is oriented in such a way that no physical obstacles are in front of him/her (Peck et al. 2008).

Then, the user can continue to walk in the desired virtual direction.

Alternatively, reorientation can also be applied while the user walks (Steinicke et al., 2008; Razzaque, 2005).

For instance, if the user wants to walk straight ahead for a long distance in the virtual world, small rotations of the camera redirect him/her to walk unconsciously on an arc in the opposite direction in the real world.

When redirecting a user, the visual sensation is consistent with motion in the IVE, but proprioceptive sensation reflects motion in the physical world.

However, if the induced manipulations are small enough, the user has the impression of being able to walk in the virtual world in any direction without restrictions.

Redirection techniques have been applied particularly in robotics for controlling a remote robot by walking.

For such scenarios much effort has been directed towards preventing collisions, -sophisticated path prediction is therefore essential in order to avoid a collision with physical obstacles. These techniques guide users on physical paths for which lengths as well as turning angles of the visually perceived paths are maintained, but the user observes the discrepancy between the two worlds.

Until now not much research has been undertaken in order to identify thresholds, which indicate the tolerable amount of deviation between vision and proprioception while the user is moving.

Our preliminary studies (Steinicke et al. 2008) have shown that in general redirected walking works as long as the subjects are not focused on detecting the manipulation. In these experiments user had to remark afterwards, if they noticed a manipulation or not. However, quantitative analysis has not been undertaken yet.

In summary, substantial efforts have been made to allow a user to walk through a large-scale VE while physically remaining in a much smaller laboratory space. But this challenge has not yet been addressed adequately.

GENERALIZED REDIRECTED WALKING

Redirected walking can be implemented using gains, which define how tracked real world motions are mapped to the VE.

These gains are specified with respect to a coordinate system. For example, they can be defined by uniform scaling factors that are applied to the virtual world registered with the tracking coordinate system such that all motions are scaled likewise.

Steinicke et al. (2008) have introduced the *human locomotion triple* (HLT) (s,u,w) concept, represented by three normalized vectors, i.e., strafe vector s, up vector u and direction of walk w. The actual walking direction or using proprioceptive cues such as the orientation of the limbs or the view direction can determine the user's direction of walk. In our experiments we define w as the actual walking direction tracked and filtered by the tracking system.

The strafe vector, a.k.a. *right vector*, is orthogonal to the direction of walk and parallel to the walk plane.

Whereas the direction of walk and the strafe vector are orthogonal to each other, the up vector u is not constrained to the cross product of s and w.

Hence, if a user walks up a slope the direction of walk is defined according to the walk plane's orientation, whereas the up vector is not orthogonal to this tilted plane. When walking on slopes humans tend to lean forward, so the up vector is defined in opposite direction to the gravitational force. As long as the direction of walk holds $w!=(0,1,0)$, the HLT composes a coordinate system. In the following sections we describe how gains can be applied to such a locomotion triple. We define u by the up vector of the tracked head orientation.

Assume that the tracking system detects a change in the user's real world position defined by the vector $T_{real}=P_{cur}-P_{pre}$, where P_{cur} is the current position and P_{Pre} is the previous position, T_{real} is mapped one-to-one to the virtual camera with respect to the registration between virtual scene and tracking coordinates system.

A translation gain g_T is defined for each component of the HLT by the quotient of the mapped virtual world translation $T_{virtual}$ and the tracked real world translation T_{real}. A vector consisting of three angles, for pitch, yaw and roll, can specify real world head rotations. The tracked orientation change is then applied to the virtual camera. Rotation gains are defined for each component (pitch/yaw/roll) of the rotation and are applied to the axes of the locomotion triple. A rotation gain g_R is defined by the quotient of the considered component of a virtual world rotation and the real world rotation. The product of the gain and the amount of the real world rotation rotates when a rotation gain g_R is applied to a real world rotation the virtual camera. This means that if $g_R=1$ the virtual scene remains stable considering the head's orientation change.

Instead of multiplying gains with translations or rotations, offsets can be added to the real world movements. Thereby, camera manipulations are enforced if only one kind of motion is tracked, for example, user turns the head, but stands still, or the user moves straight without head rotations. If the injected manipulations are reasonably small, the user will unknowingly compensate for these offsets resulting in curvilinear walk. The gains can be applied in order to inject rotations, while users virtually walk straight, or gains can be applied when users only rotate their heads. The curvature gain g_C denotes the resulting bend of a real path. For example, when the user moves straight ahead, a curvature gain that causes reasonably small iterative camera rotations to one side enforces the user to walk along a curve in the opposite direction in order to stay on a straight path in the virtual world. The curve is determined by a circular arc with radius r, and $g_C=1/r$.

EXPERIMENTS

In this section we present five experiments in which we have quantified how humans can unknowingly be redirected by changing the gain between tracked physical movements and virtual camera motions.

Experimental Design

Since the main objective of our experiments is to allow users to walk freely in 3D city environments, the visual stimulus consisted of virtual scenes of the city of Münster in Germany (see Figure 2). Before each trial a random place and a horizontal gaze direction were chosen. The only restriction

Figure 2. Example scene as used for the experiments

for this starting scene was that no vertical objects were within *10 m* of the starting position in order to prevent collisions in the VE.

We performed all experiments in a *10 x 10 m* darkened laboratory room.

The subjects wore an HMD (3DVisor Z800, 800x600@60 Hz, 40° diagonal field of view (FoV)) for the stimulus presentation. On top of the HMD an infrared LED was fixed for tracking. We tracked the position of this LED within the room with an active optical tracking system (Precise Position Tracking of World Viz), which provides sub-millimeter precision and sub-centimeter accuracy. The update rate was *60Hz* providing real-time positional data of the active markers. For three degrees of freedom (DoF) orientation tracking we used an InertiaCube 2 (InterSense) with an update rate of *180 Hz*. The InertiaCube was also fixed on top of the HMD.

In the experiments we used an Intel computer (host) with dual-core processors, 4 GB of main memory and an *n*Vidia GeForce 8800 system for control and data logging purposes.

Participants were equipped with an HMD backpack consisting of a laptop PC with a GeForce 7700 Go graphics card (see Figure 1).

The scene was rendered using OpenGL and our own software with a frame rate of 60 frames per second.

During the experiment the room was fully darkened in order to reduce the user's perception of the real world. The subjects received instructions on slides presented on the HMD. A Nintendo Wii remote controller served as input device. All computers, including the laptop on the back of the user, were equipped with wireless LAN adapters. The total weight of the backpack was about 8 kg, which is quite heavy. However, no wires disturb the sense of complete immersion, and no assistant needs to walk beside the user to keep an eye on the wires.

In a wired system, any sensations derived from the wires would give subjects a cue to the physical orientation, an issue we had to avoid in our experiments. In order to focus subjects on the tasks no communication between observer and subject was performed during the experiment. All instructions were displayed in the VE, and subjects responded via the WII device. Acoustic feedback was used for generating ambient city noise in the experiment, to emulate the orientation achieved by means of auditory feedback received in the real world.

Participant in this experiment comprised 15 males and 3 females in the age 24-35. Subjects came from backgrounds ranging from students to professionals with expertise in computer science, mathematics, psychology, geoinformatics, and physics. All had normal or corrected to normal vision; 4 wore glasses or contact lenses. 3 had no game experience, 10 had some, and 4 had a lot of game experience. Three of the authors also served as subjects; all other subjects were naive to the experimental conditions. Eight of them had experience with walking in VR environments using an HMD setup. Subjects were allowed to take breaks at any time. Some subjects obtained class credit for their participation. The total time per subject -- including pre-questionnaire, instructions, training, experiment, breaks, and debriefing -- was 3 hours.

For all experiments we used the method of constant stimuli in a *yes/no judgment* task. In the method of constant stimuli, the applied gains are not related from one trial to the next, but presented randomly, and are uniformly distributed. The subject chose between one of two possible responses, e.g. ``Was the physical movement greater than virtual movement: yes or no"; responds like ``I can't tell." were not allowed. In this version, when the subject cannot detect the signal, he/she must guess, and will be correct on average in 50% of the trials.

The gain at which the subject responds ``greater" in 50% of the trials is taken as the *point of subjective equality* (PSE), at which the subject perceives the physical and the virtual movement as identical. As the gain decreases or increases from this value, the ability of the subject to detect the difference between physical and virtual movement increases.

We define the *detection threshold* (DTs) for gains larger than the PSE to be the value of the gain at which the subject has 75% probability of choosing the ``greater" response correctly, and the detection threshold for gains smaller than the PSE to be the value of the gain at which the subject chooses the ``yes, greater" response in only 25% of trials (since the correct response ``no" was then chosen in 75% of the trails).

Experiment 1 (E1): Discrimination between Virtual and Physical Rotation

In this experiment we investigated subject's ability to discriminate whether a physical rotation was greater than the simulated virtual rotation. Therefore, we instructed the subjects to rotate on a physical spot and we mapped this rotation to a corresponding virtual rotation to which different gains had been applied.

Figure 3 shows the mean detection rates together with the standard error over all subjects for the tested gains. The *x*-axis shows the applied rotational gain, the *y*-axis shows the probability for estimating a physical rotation greater than the mapped virtual rotation. We found no difference in results whether we simulated the rotation to the left or to the right, and therefore pooled the two conditions.

Using the sigmoid function we determined a bias for the point of subjective equality resulting in a PSE=0.8403. For individual subjects, we found the PSE varied between 0.54 and 1.24 (2 subjects had PSE greater than 1.0, the rest had it less than 1.0). Detection thresholds were at gains of 0.59 for greater responses and at 1.1 for not greater responses, suggesting that gain differences within this range cannot be reliably estimated, i.e., subjects have serious problems to discriminate between a 90 degrees virtual and real rotations ranging from 81 degrees and 152 degrees. Within this threshold interval, subjects can only guess whether they have been manipulated or not. Hence, subjects can be turned physically about 68% more or 10% less than the perceived virtual rotation.

Experiment 2 (E2): Discrimination between Virtual and Physical Translational Movement

In this experiment we analyzed the subjects' ability to discriminate between virtual and physical translational movements. The virtual movement was a forward movement mapped to physical walking.

In the IVE subjects always had to walk a distance of 5 m. The walking direction was indicated by a green dot in front of the subjects (see Figure 2).

The physical distance the subjects had to walk varied between 3 m and 7 m.

The task was to judge whether the physical walking distance was larger than the virtual travel distance or not.

Figure 4 plots the mean probability for a subject's estimation that the physical distance was larger than the virtual perceived one, as the average over all subjects. The error bars show the standard deviation in the errors.

This data fitted the same sigmoid function as for experiments E1a and E1b. The data sets of two subjects were removed from overall results subjected to further analyses.

One of these subjects always indicated that the physical walking distance is larger than the virtual distance. The second subject either mixed up the answer buttons or misunderstood the task.

The PSE for the pooled data of the remaining 14 subjects is 0.9972. This means the subjects are very accurate in estimating the walking distance in the physical to be the same as in the virtual world.

Figure 3. Pooled results of the discrimination between virtual and physical rotational movement. The x-axis shows the applied translation gain, the y-axis shows the probability that subjects estimate the physical rotation greater than the mapped virtual motion

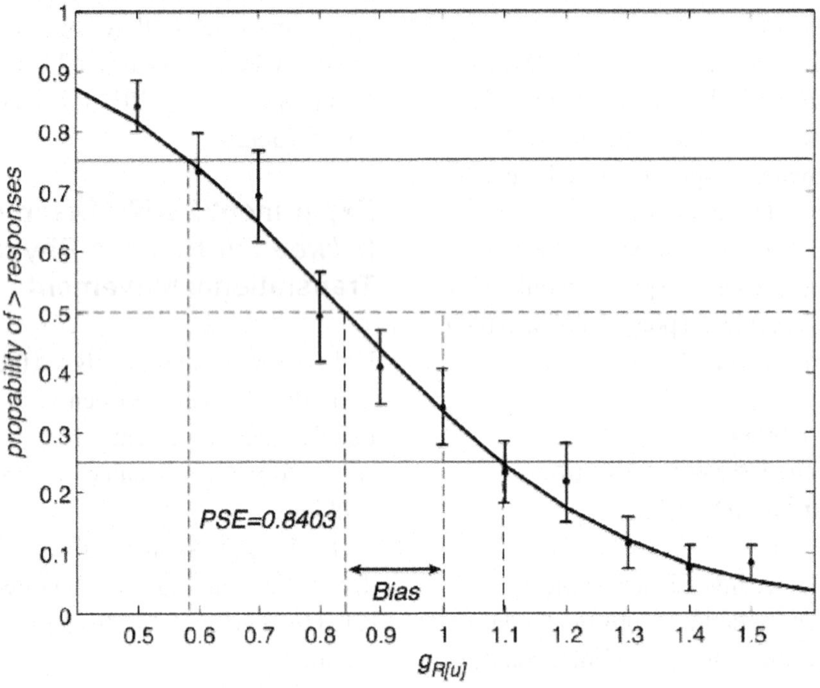

The calculated PSE for individual subjects varied between 0.78 and 1.19 (based on 7 subjects with PSE above or equal to 0.9972, the rest with PSE less than 0.9972). According to Figure 4, DTs for estimation of translational movements are given for gains at 0.78 for greater responses and at 1.22 for not greater responses. These results indicate that human beings can differentiate between virtual and real translational movements accurately when actually walking a distance in a familiar environment such as realistic 3D city model.

Since subjects knew the VE from the real world, it is possible that subjects were able to exploit distance cues such as the height of trees, street sizes etc.

Experiment 3 (E3): Discrimination of Direction of Walk

In this experiment we analyze sensitivity to curvature gains, which enforce the user to walk on a curve in order to stay on a straight path. To support users to virtually walk on a straight path we introduced a 1 m wide pavement in the virtual world.

At the subject's eye level we added a green dot in the scene, which turned red when the subjects had walked 5 m towards it.

While the subjects walked along the pavement, we rotated the scene to either side with a velocity linked to the subject's real movement velocity.

The scene rotated by approximately 0, 5, 10, 20 and 30 degrees after 5 m walking distance. The rotation started immediately when they began to walk. After the subjects walked a distance of 5 m

Figure 4. Pooled results of the discrimination between virtual and physical translational movement. The x-axis shows the applied translation gain, the y-axis shows the probability that subjects estimate the physical translational movement greater than the mapped virtual motion

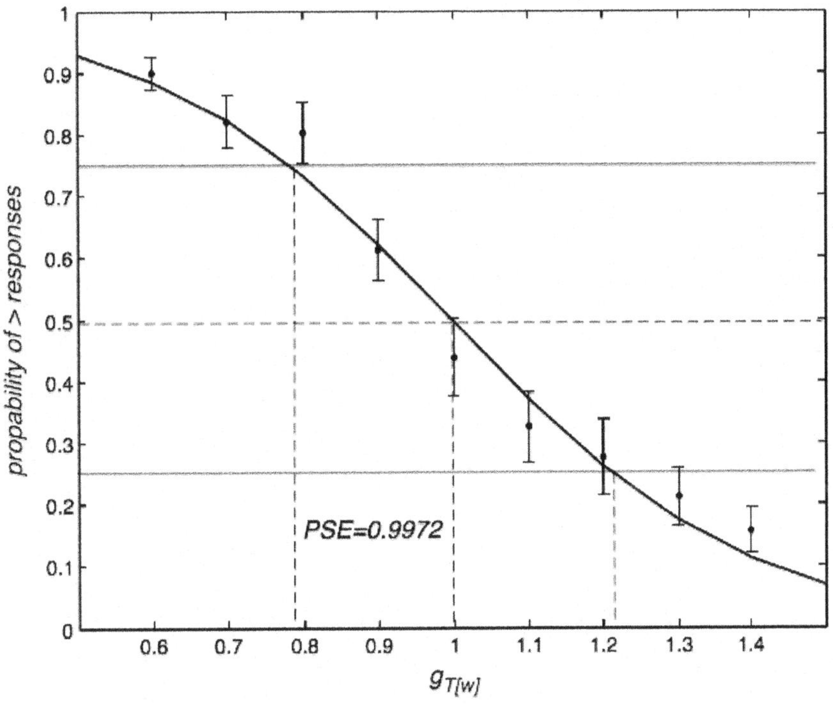

in the virtual world, the screen turned white and the written instruction appeared. The subject's task was to decide whether the physical path was curved to the left or not, by pressing a button on the WII controller. To guide the subjects back to the starting position we used two markers on an otherwise white screen.

Figure 5 plots the mean probability for a subject's estimation that the physical path was curved to the left against the curvature (square symbols).

The variance is the standard error. The DTs is the stimulus intensity at which subjects correctly detect the stimulus 75% of the time. The PSE for the pooled data is -1.74.

The results show that subjects can be reoriented by 18 degrees to the left or 17 degrees to the right after 5 m of walking, which corresponds to walking along a circular arc with a radius of approximately 16 meters. We applied the curvature gain during the entire walk during this experiment. Subjects reported that they had difficulty estimating the direction of the bending particularly during the first few steps. For instance, after two gaits, they left the pavement and had to reorient themselves to the target and continue the walk. Consequently, they tended to walk along a triangle rather than walking on an arc.

Therefore, we introduced a 2 m travel distance without scene manipulation before the curvature gain was applied. The results for this method are plotted in Figure 5 (circle symbols). The error bars are the standard errors. Same comment as above.

Furthermore, we found no significant difference whether we performed a camera rotation to the left or to the right. The PSE for the pooled data is still -1.37.

Figure 5. Pooled results of the discrimination between virtual and physical curvature movement. The x-axis shows the applied curvature gain, the y-axis shows the probability that subjects estimate the physical curve was turned left, or not

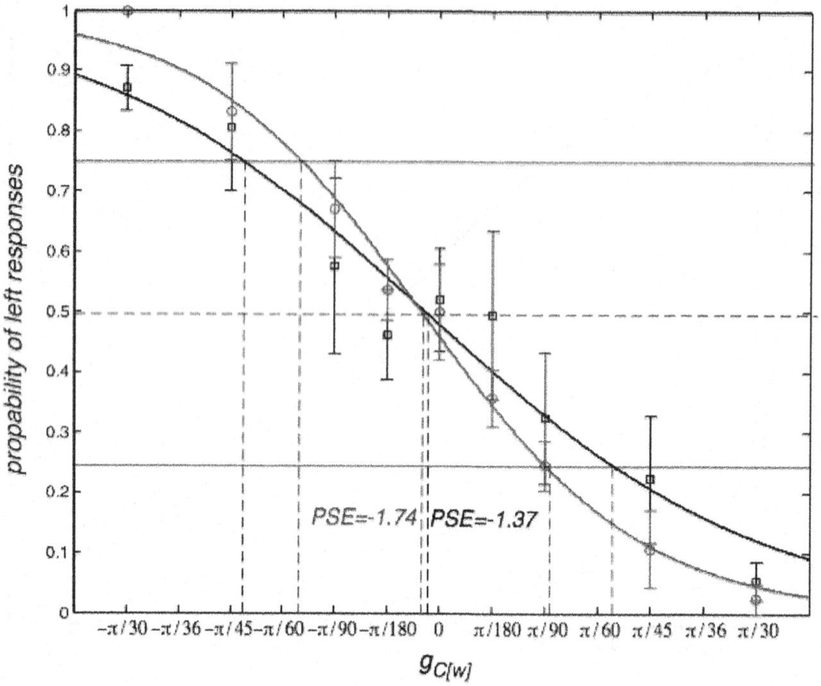

In this experiment the detection thresholds shifted to gains -∏/69.23 for left and -∏/85.71 for right curvatures respectively. Until this DT, subjects cannot estimate reliably if they walk straight or on a curve. Subjects become significantly more sensitive to bending compared to the previous condition in which no pavement was used. With the condition with a 1m pavement subjects can be reoriented by 13 degrees to the left or 10 degrees to the right after 5 m walking without noticing the discrepancy between real and virtual motion.

This corresponds to walking along a circular arc with a radius of approximately 24 meters. When redirected walking is applied guiding users on a circular arc is a typical situation where users first walk a certain distance before the path is curved.

VISITING TOURIST LANDMARKS

In our experiments, we analyzed the users' sensitivity to redirected walking manipulations. We introduced a taxonomy of redirection techniques and tested the corresponding gains in a practical useful range for their perceptibility. The results of the conducted experiments show that users can be turned physically about 68% more or 10% less than the perceived virtual rotation without noticing the difference. Our results agree with previous findings (Jerald et al. 2008) that users are more sensitive to scene motion if the scene moves against head rotation than if the scene moves with head rotation.

Walked distances can be up- and down-scaled by 22%. Hence, when users want to walk 5m through the virtual environment, this distance can be mapped to a physical distance between 3.9m and 6.1m.

When applying curvature gains users can be redirected such that they unknowingly walk along a circular arc when the radius is greater or equal to 24 meters.

Certainly, redirected walking is a subjective matter, but the results have potential to serve as thresholds for the development of future locomotion interfaces.

In another experiment, we applied these guidelines to a walk in the virtual city scene shown in Figure 6. Four users (3 of them had not participated in the previous study) were told to walk within this environment. An essential objective was to keep the user in the tracking area and to prevent collisions with physical objects that were not in the immediate vicinity of the user in the virtual world. When the user potentially left the tracking area, while virtually being located in the center of the room, we determined the angle of intersection between the user's path and the boundary of the tracking area. Corresponding camera modifications were performed to redirect the user on a circle segment with respect to the guidelines such that the user was guided away from the wall back into the interior of the room. Less than 25% of all redirected walks were perceived as manipulated when these guidelines were followed.

The proposed redirect walking techniques allow user to explore virtual worlds in an intuitive and immersive manner. With redirected walking users can walk through large-scale immersive virtual environments such as virtual city models, while physically remaining in a reasonably small workspace by intentionally injecting scene motion into the IVE. In such environments people can visit, for instance, tourist landmarks virtually. In our experiments we have shown that a reasonably small workspace is sufficient to allow users to explore arbitrary virtual environment by real walking.

Users can visit a tourist landmark in the virtual world before they actually visit the landmark in the real world. For example, excursions can be planned and walked in the virtual world, or they can be modified in order to find a desired path. Such a scenario enables users to get an overview about certain features of a virtual city model even before they are at the corresponding locations in real world.

Figure 6. Visiting a 3D tourist landmark in a virtual city model

CONCLUSIONS AND OPPORTUNITIES FOR FUTURE RESEARCH

We have addressed the challenge of unlimited walking through the virtual world in a restricted physical setup. Therefore, we have performed a study from which we derived detection thresholds, which have essential implications for the design of future locomotion user interfaces based on redirected walking.

We have integrated the results of our experiments in a virtual locomotion interface. With this locomotion user interface user are able to explore virtual environments. We use the setup in our virtual city model that allows users to travel through a virtual city via different tourist landmarks.

In the future we will consider other redirection techniques that have not been analyzed in the scope of this paper. Moreover, further conditions have to be taken into account and tested for their influence on redirected walking, for example, distances of scene objects, level of detail, contrast, etc.

Informal tests have motivated that manipulations can be intensified in some cases, e.g., when less objects are close to the camera, which could provide further motions cues while the user walks.

In addition it will be interesting to examine in how far real walking to through a virtual city model affects space perception and cognition in comparison to exploring a city model in the real world or using a standard desktop computer. Therefore, certain experiments have to be performed which analyze how space and topology etc. is perceived using the proposed setup.

These experiments will have great impact on perception research and will help to understand how we perceive the virtual as well as the real environment.

REFERENCES

Bouguila, L., & Sato, M. (2002). Virtual locomotion system for large scale virtual environments. In *Proceedings of Virtual Reality* (pp. 291–292). Washington, DC: IEEE.

Interrante, E. V., Ries, B., & Anderson, L. (2007). Seven league boots: A new metaphor for augmented locomotion through moderately large scale immersive virtual environments. In *Proceedings of the Symposium on 3D User Interfaces* (pp. 167–170). Washington, DC: IEEE.

Interrante, V., Anderson, L., & Ries, B. (2006). Distance perception in immersive virtual environments, revisited. In *Proceedings of Virtual Reality* (pp. 3–10). Washington, DC: IEEE.

Iwata, H., Yano, H., Fukushima, H., & Noma, H. (2005). CirculaFloor. *IEEE Computer Graphics and Applications*, *25*(1), 64–67. doi:10.1109/MCG.2005.5

Jerald, J., Peck, T., Steinicke, F., & Whitton, M. (2008). Sensitivity to scene motion for phases of head yaws. In *Proceedings of the Applied Perception in Graphics and Visualization* (pp. 155–162). New York: ACM.

Kohli, L., Burns, E., Miller, D., & Fuchs, H. (2005). Combining passive haptics with redirected walking. In []. New York: ACM.]. *Proceedings of the Conference on Augmented Tele-Existence*, *157*, 253–254. doi:10.1145/1152399.1152451

Lappe, M., Bemmer, F., & van den Berg, A. V. (1999). Perception of self-motion from visual flow. *Trends in Cognitive Sciences*, *3*(9), 329–336. doi:10.1016/S1364-6613(99)01364-9

Peck, T., Whitton, M., & Fuchs, H. (2008). Evaluation of reorientation techniques for walking in large virtual environments. In *Proceedings of Virtual Reality* (pp. 121–128). Washington, DC: IEEE.

Razzaque, S. (2005). *Redirected walking*. Unpublished doctoral dissertation, University of North Carolina, Chapel Hill.

Steinicke, F., Bruder, G., Jerald, J., Frenz, H., & Lappe, M. (2008). Analyses of human sensitivity to redirected walking. In *ACM Proceedings on Virtual Reality and Software Technology* (pp. 149-156). New York: ACM.

Steinicke, F., Bruder, G., Kohli, L., Jerald, J., & Hinrichs, K. (2008). Taxonomy and implementation of redirection techniques for ubiquitous passive haptic feedback. In *Cyberworlds*. Washington, DC: IEEE Press.

Steinicke, F., Bruder, G., Ropinski, T., & Hinrichs, K. (2008). Moving towards generally applicable redirected walking. In *Proceedings of the Virtual Reality International Conference (VRIC)* (pp. 15-24). Washington, DC: IEEE Press.

Whitton, M., Cohn, J., Feasel, P., Zommons, S., Razzaque, S., Poulton, B., & Brooks, F. (2005). Comparing VE locomotion interfaces. In *Proceedings of Virtual Reality* (pp. 123–130). Washington, DC: IEEE.f

Chapter 12
Developing Web3D Tools for Promoting the European Heritage

Francesco Bellotti
University of Genoa, Italy

Riccardo Berta
University of Genoa, Italy

Alessandro De Gloria
University of Genoa, Italy

Ludovica Primavera
University of Genoa, Italy

ABSTRACT

Virtual reality environments are ever more going online. This trend, opened by videogames, will open new important opportunities to enhance cultural tourism, given the possibility of creating compelling virtual adventures set in the context of artistic and natural beauties. The authors are exploring these challenges in the context of the Travel in Europe (TiE) project, and developing tools to build enriched virtual environments where the player could explore faithfully reconstructed places and live there information-rich, contextualized experiences. The TiE architecture is based on a state-of-the-art commercial game engine, with massive multiplayer online games (MMOG) facilities that support access to multiple concurrent users, plus ad-hoc designed modules. The 3D model is completely geo-referenced. In each covered area, a few points-of-interest (POIs) are implemented. These buildings are rigorously reconstructed at a high level of detail. The textures for the rest of the palaces are built dynamically by the TiE system using a statistical template-based algorithm that exploits local characterizations of common architectonic elements. The TiE virtual world is enriched by geo-localized, contextualized MicroGames (mGs). mGs are simple, short games that focus the player's attention on a particular item that is found during exploration of the 3D world. mGs are typically taken from well known simple game models, such as Puzzle, MemoryGame, and FindTheWrongDetails. The main concept that underpins mGs is that, they should be intuitive and easy to play, so that the player can focus on the contents rather than on learning

DOI: 10.4018/978-1-60566-818-5.ch012

how to play. Preliminary informal tests have suggested that the approach is valid and that the enriched 3D environment supports the contextualized promotion of artifacts, products and services, which is an important growing demand from institutions and enterprises that want to valorize the resources of a territory.

INTRODUCTION

Local communities and institutions are becoming more aware of the need for promoting their region to a variety of audience, through techniques that would allow them to appreciate what it has to offer it in a pleasant and meaningful way. There are a number of attractions that characterize a territory and may be of interest to a diverse range of people. These attractions can include its cultural and natural heritage, buildings, history, speciality products, food, and accommodation, sport resorts, as well as the social values of its people. This promotion of a region can produce important commercial benefits as well as enhance interpersonal interaction of its people with the international community.

New Information and Communication Technologies (ICTs) are important for developing systems to support the promotion of a region (Arnold, 2008). In particular, the Web 2.0 technologies are providing tools (e.g. Social Networks, Forums, Interactive Maps, Travel Recommender and Booking Systems, Instant Communication Support, Conversational Digital Agents (Conrady, 2007)) that are greatly improving the services offered to tourists and general citizens. An important advancement for the future is likely to be the technology called Web 3.0, which is likely to embrace online 3D Virtual Worlds (VWs). Next generation websites will feature virtual environments that are able to provide the user a more compelling and involving experience (Brutzman & Daly, 2007). VWs are already popular among video gamers, and many large user communities have already established around famous Massive Multiplayer Online Games (MMOGs), such as World of Warcraft (Blizzard, 2008). Many technologies such as hardware video-chips and software tools developed for videogames can be used in other application fields such as 3D virtual worlds.

We are exploring these opportunities and challenges in the context of the "Travel in Europe" (TiE) project (Bellotti, Berta, De Gloria & Zappi, 2008), which is aimed at implementing an innovative means to promote and popularize European heritage. TiE is building a platform that will provide tools through which third party content developers will be able to build online 3D VWs, where users will live challenging and compelling experiences by interacting with virtual representations of the European heritage. From a business point of view -- which has been analyzed in an early survey phase of the project -- the TiE platform intends to meet the ever growing demand for advanced interactive systems to able to promote the European heritage on a wide scale (e.g. through the Internet) while being deeply root in the local regions. In particular, we predicated that the platform should be able to meet three major needs from cultural and tourism stakeholders' viewpoint:

- **Promotion of a region:** The proposed system can be thought of as an evolution of the current advertising systems used for promoting resorts and regions on TV/ magazines/journals.
- **Support for a geographic-context based knowledge acquisition:** The exploration of the various attractions should not be purely virtual, but also connected to the real world. The proposed approach intends to support knowledge acquisition/analysis

of the real systems, and connected with history-related experiences.

- **The resulting environments and users' virtual travels are not intended as a substitute for visits to real places:** Their aim should be to promote real visits, as in the current TV promotions, that stimulate the user's desire to visit the real places, by predesignating some important and attractive features of the region. The interaction should make users aware that the cultural trip presented through virtual reality is a reproduction of the real heritage that can be visited in European cities. It should encourage the user to develop and exploit an effective itinerary to make the most of her/his travels,e.g. by showing the important points necessary to adequately prepare for the travel. Furthermore, it should showcase the emotionally moving aspects of the destination, so as to turn a virtual visit into a real visit. This is particularly important for regions and destinations that, for various reasons, are not yet popular. Finally, TiE aims to meet the ever growing fascination with advanced interactive systems to promote European heritage on a wider scale by focusing on the following aspects:
- **Use the Internet as the communication media:** Maintain deep roots in the local regions, by geo-referencing cultural and historical aspects within the local urban or country environment.
- **Promote knowledge about the local resources**, e.g. handicrafts, food.

Based on these principles, the TiE platform aims at enabling new kinds of interaction, that link a region with its history and resources. This predicates the use of a 3D map for recreating a territory (e.g. a city, a region) as the reference system for a virtual visit to its historical sites. This is very similar to a real visit, where the tourist goes through a city, and learns about it and its history (e.g. by visiting museums, churches, and looking at palaces). In this new approach, any user is able to explore this 3D environment, through a simple web-browser plug-in. During the exploration, the user can get more in-depth information and live contextualized experiences (e.g. videos, games, quizzes) that are embedded in the environment.

As a work-in-progress demonstrator of the technology, we are building the Travel in Europe (TiE) online game, a cultural Serious Game (SG) aimed at promoting the European heritage. The game uses the engaging style of the SGs in order to improve the user's comprehension of the reality (high realism is a key-aspect of any SG). SG is a branch of the videogame industry which is acquiring ever more importance in the research community (Zyda, 2007). SGs typically provide highly realistic 3D simulation environments where users can face difficult tasks implemented as challenging adventures. SGs are now successfully employed in areas such as government (Raybourn, Deagle, Mendina & Heneghan, 2005), health (Sliney & Murphy, 2008), army (Losh, 2005), science (Mayo, 2007), and corporate training (Michael & Chen, 2006).

The TiE game exploits the concept of travel, which is engaging by itself and facilitates knowledge acquisition through geographic contextualization. A TiE player typically accomplishes a mission (as in a treasure-hunt game) by visiting some cities spread over the map of Europe. During the exploration, the player can learn about the local history/traditions/art by facing contextualized trial quizzes and games (e.g. a latin quiz or a history puzzle while exploring the remains of a roman market square). In each city, the player gains scores by facing some specific trials. Trial games are implemented as embedded 2D games, and are– concerned with the local artistic heritage in a given context. For instance, a game concerning Van Cleve's "Adoration of the Magi" triptych is played in the 3D reconstruction of the San Donato church in Genoa's historical center, where this picture is preserved.

The aim of this chapter is to present the design of the TiE framework, showing its suitability to meet the above mentioned requirements, and ianalye its potential impact and relevance for promoting tourism -- through an exposé of a region's culture and resources.

The rest of the chapter is organised as follows. The next section introduces the main features of the TiE project. The third section covers the related work of the paper. The fourth presents the peculiarities of the TiE virtual worlds, focusing in particular on the microGame concept, while the section following that shows the first TiE prototype. In the sixth section we briefly discuss possible perspectives for the future work. The final conclusions are drawn in the last section.

THE TiE PROJECT

The main objective of the TiE system is the design and development of an environment that supports users in performing adventures similar to the state-of-the-art videogames; moreover it is expected to include features, mechanisms, and patterns that provide a meaningful access to a region's resources, with aim of promoting its heritage. Having a complete operating environment is a significant added-value, since it will not mean developing a single case, but an extensible platform on the top of which a number of different applications may be built, each one of them being able to exploit the educational/cultural features, mechanisms, and functions provided by the TiE environment. Sample features include accurate 3D reconstructions and microGames (mGs, described in the next sub-section) that allow players to manipulate digital representations of the heritage entity.

In order to achieve the above mentioned goals, the TiE architecture is based on a state-of-the-art commercial game engine (Torque Game Engine (Maurina, 2006)), with Massive Multiplayer Online Games (MMOG) facilities that support access to multiple concurrent users, plus ad-hoc designed modules. These modules include:

- the algorithms for efficient collection of architectonic urban contents,
- efficient implementation of high-quality, realistic 3D models based on such contents;
- the algorithm to implement realistic 3D reconstructions of monuments;
- the TiE cultural game mechanisms and patterns; and
- the cultural mGs Templates.

TiE's target users are people who are interested in living compelling cultural experiences related to the cultural heritage. These people include high-school and university students and teachers, cultural tourists, and families. We aim to attract an even wider audience, because cultural heritage is of interest to all, and, if presented in the right ways, it can appeal to a larger audience.

Given the variety in the target audience, the TiE 3D environment has been designed to be highly configurable both by the author (i.e. the person who defines Points of Interest, possible paths, mGs, etc.) and by the system at runtime, in order to adapt events and games according to the user profiles. Thus, the TiE environment provides a number of features that are parametrizable in several terms (e.g. amount of information/detail provided, level of difficulty, number and type of objects) in order to provide suitable experiences for a variety of users.

The TiE concept, aims, on the one hand, at implementing a geo-referenced 3D environment reconstructed according to cultural validity principles, and, on the other hand, at providing tools for embedding these games and services that the system can control and adapt to the user's preferences

Exploiting this architecture, other objectives can be attained and further extensions easily implemented, for instance services and events that support promotion and commercialization of local products..

RELATED WORKS

The web 2.0 concept (O'Reilly, 2005) aims at overcoming the traditional barrier between content producers (e.g. newspaper, magazines, TV channels, portals) and passive audience (this was typical of web 1.0). Web 2.0 allows the end-users to publish their contents in a collaborative way, usually referred to as "social computing" (Schroth & Janner, 2007). The web 2.0 term thus includes all the services that users can exploit technologies for producing content and build communities of interest,e.g. blogs, wikis, forum, chats, social networking, geo-references, questionnaires, petitions, alerts, inter-personal communication support, etc. (Alexander, 2006).

Thanks to important enabling technologies, such as AJAX (Garrett, 2005), the Web 2.0 tools have moved the user interface rendering from the server side to the client side, reducing the temporal latency and promoting the development of sites with dynamic pages. In these sites, users can exploit within a web page the interaction modalities typical of stand-alone applications (e.g. drag & drop), and be able to do real-time editing. Moreover, users can access remote data (e.g. Google Maps, Amazon) by using suitable Application Programming Interfaces (APIs) and create new applications that are published and made available to all other users on the web. This concept is called mesh-up (Maximilien, Wilkinson, Desai & Tai, 2007). Mesh-ups have become popular due to the availability of off-the-shelf tool that make the programming task visual and easily accessible to users even without much computer programming skills.

Web 3.0 is the next step of this evolution and foresees the introduction of user interfaces based on 3D VWs for a variety of online services. VWs are computer simulated environments where users are represented as avatars (Hughes & Moshell, 1997). The concept of avatars was originally conceived for use in 2D graphics, however, it is readily being migrated to 3D environments.

Typical successful samples of VWs include MMOGs where millions of players interact in real-time (Blizzard, 2008). VWs are not limited to games, but can be used in other applications as well. such as chat, conferencing, entertainment and e-commerce (Kock, 2008). In the following, we mention VW projects and environments that are related to the system presented in this chapter.

Google has recently released an "Ancient Rome 3D" layer for their Google Earth geographic browser (Orndorff, 2008). This layer shows many of the buildings, structures and topography that made up the city in a specific moment in time - specifically June 21, 320 A.D., which was more or less the apex of the city's development as the capital of the Roman Empire. Some of the buildings even have interiors that can be visited.

VirtuyMall is a 3D mall now online in a beta version (Virtual Mall, 2008). The site allows visitors, represented as avatars, to walk through the halls and corridors, use lifts and escalators, chat with each other, look at the shop windows, and even try on shoes and clothes. This site involves 40 commercial activities and expects to decuplicate this figure within the next two years.

Second Life (SL) is a 3D virtual environment created by Linden Labs, which has gained wide popularity, in particular on the mass-media (Second Life, 2008). SL is organized as a set of VWs, structured as islands, where user avatars live a variety of experiences. Several islands have been built and used for various purposes, such as education, tourism, marketing, fantasy adventures, and pure entertainment.

The OpenSIM project is attempting to develop a similar VW environment that can be run on any server and would be free of any "for-profit" entity's control (OpenSim, 2008). The approach used for developing TiE is more specific, as it aims to give experience of real cultural heritage. Therefore, TiE provides specific mechanisms, procedures and tools aimed at supporting the building of culturally valid and realistic user experiences in an entertainment context. More generally, the founding concept of the TiE platform is strongly rooted on a realistic, geo-referenced representation of the physical reality. This approach is considered more appropriate for achieving a credible promotion of a territory represented within TiE.

TIE VIRTUAL WORLDS

TiE involves reconstructing a number of urban areas, such as culturally relevant cities and villages throughout Europe. This is a large, long-term effort that requires defining some fundamental principles in the design phase, so as to be time and cost efficient (Watson et al., 2008).

A 3D reconstruction of a city or a region for education/cultural purpose within an interactive environment is a process that requires a careful trade-off between the models' photorealism (in order to provide a highly impressive and culturally correct and meaningful experience) and the models' complexity and related computational weight (in order to allow interactive real-time online exploration).

The first term of the trade-off stresses the importance of having high-detail 3D reconstructions in order to realize a sound reconstruction of the heritage entity (in particular, making it believable is important to create a "sense of place" by the use of photorealistic models, weather effects, surround-sound audio, graspable virtual objects, natural lighting system, etc. (Fullerton, Swain, & Hoffman, 2004)). The second term highlights the performance problems that the TiE online environment has to overcome in order to provide users with a playable and enjoyable system. Moreover, complex systems are costly to implement, both for the 3D modeling aspect and for creating proper textures (which requires taking pictures, rectifying and equalizing them, and composing in the final textures that can be managed by the graphic engine at runtime).

In highly interactive system, such as a 3D exploration/games, the details of the reconstructed environment are not fundamental to building a believable display, as the players move rapidly within these environments. However, in the case of a cultural heritage game, the player is acting almost like an art detective, and has to carefully examine the details of particular entities.

In order to meet the above stated requirements, we have designed the reconstruction of each covered place (e.g. a city or several areas inside a city) as it follows:

- The 3D model is completely geo-referenced. The ground is elevated from a local 3D vectorial map. So, the placement of the buildings is precise. This allows compatibility/portability to various Geographic Information Systems (GISs) and expansibility of the system (e.g. possibility of upgrading the buildings' textures).
- In each covered area, a few Point-Of-Interests (POIs) are implemented. These buildings are rigorously reconstructed at a high level of detail. We use this approach for culturally meaningful buildings. For instance, for cathedrals, theaters, and Renaissance palaces.
- The textures for the rest of the palaces are built dynamically by the TiE system using a statistical template-based algorithm (Bellotti, Berta, Garnier-Rivers & Jacquet, 2008). Since several zones within a city are often characterized by relatively homogeneous buildings (one or more building having the same "style"), the idea is to exploit a statistical description of the architectonic parameters and build the buildings' virtual models accordingly, using a limited set of parametric building models, and of textures that are instances of the architectonic features representative of that area.

Plots and game rules are important aspects for creating a desirable user experience, with authentic feel for the reconstructed heritage. But, beside these aspects, that are external aspects dictated by the environment that define the logic of a particular game built on top of the TiE environment. We are interested tin identifying and analyzing mechanisms to be embedded in the 3D environment itself, so as to enrich it and further enhance its educational value (e.g. give more detail of particular sites, provide more in-depth information about them, present related local products and/or historical facts) and, where possible, the entertain the users, thereby combine education with entertainment, or provide edutainment.

The proposed MicroGames (mGs), present and discuss in the following, aim to fulfill the edutainment objective articulated in the preceding section.

MicroGames

MicroGames (mGs) are simple, short games that focus the player's attention on a particular item that is found during exploration of the 3D world. mGs are typically taken from well known game models, such as Puzzle, MemoryGame, and FindTheWrongDetails. The main concept that underpins mGs is that, they should be intuitive and easy to play, so that the player can focus on the contents rather than on learning how to play the game.

In order to re-use code and provide consistent and homogeneous interaction modalities (that can be quickly and easily learned by the player and then used several times), we have defined a library of mG Templates. Every mG is an instance of one of such templates. We broadly divide mG templates in to three categories, according to the cognitive skills t involved: observation games, reflection games, and action videogames.

- **Observation games**: These games focus the users' attention, encouraging them to investigate and explore the local environment. In general, these games tend to exploit the "knowledge in the world" in order to develop the cognition activity (Dickey, 2003), (Ducheneaut, Yee, Nickell & Moore, 2006), (Rovai, 2002). They aim to stimulate spatial processing skills. Such skills are important in cognitive development since they allow an individual to create meaning by manipulating visual images (Kahana, RSekuler, Caplan, Kirschen & Madsen, 1999), (Pillay, Brownlee & Wilss 1999).
- **Reflection games**: These games tend to favor reflection and discussion among team members, leading to analysis of questions and search for possible answers embedded in the clues available in the neighborhood being explored, and concepts learned previously in the same game.
- **Arcade videogames**: These games stimulate similar skills as observation games. Their specificity lies in the animated graphics and engaging interaction, which helps to create a convincing and pleasant experience. They stimulate fantasy and evoke images and atmospheres that can be used to convey educational messages which are easily memorized by the players.

Samples of mG Templates

Some samples of mG templates that have been developed in TiE include the following:

- **Puzzle (Observation)**: The Puzzle's 2D Graphic User Interface (GUI) displays a picture superimposed on the 3D environment. This picture is subdivided into a number of pieces, that have been randomly shuffled. The player has to reconstruct the original image by clicking on the pieces and dragging and dropping them to their expected correct place in the pcture. It is likely that user has already seen - during the exploration of the city - the element(s) featured in the picture, or the user's avatar in the VW may even be standing right in front of the 3D reconstruction of the building/place represented in the picture. The game aims at involving observation skills and memory, improving the ability to identify geometrical patterns, recognize colors and associate similar areas. The score is configurable by the author, who can create an instance from the template, and may reward either the speed of re-building the image, or accuracy (e.g. higher score for recreating the correct image by moving as few pieces as possible).

- **Quiz (Reflection)**: This is a simple multiple-choice question (or list of questions). The question is generally tied to the place where it is presented (e.g. a question at the Venice's Arsenal concerns the interpretation of a Dante's piece of the Divina Commedia in which Venice's Arsenal is described). Sample quizzes include: historical quizzes, guessing games, local dialect/language. Typical player skills include critical reasoning and evaluation of alternatives. We suggest that the quizzes be not related to the previous cultural knowledge of the player, but to the items that the player may learn/discover from current exploration of the reconstructed world, and of previously played mGs. In any case, the questions are prepared by the content author who is completely free to choose any set of questions. A version with images instead of written questions/answers is also available (VisualQuiz). Synthetic virtual characters (Virtual Humans enabled by Artificial Intelligence) that represent local people may be contacted by the player to ask for the meaning of a local word and other suggestions.
- **CatchIt (Arcade)**: In this a typical local character is placed in a higher position (e.g. a balcony, a bridge) and made to drop some objects: the player's avatar stands below and has to catch the right objects (i.e. those related to the local context) and avoid all the others. Objects can be representations of paintings, food items, and typical regional products. For example, in a game related to a church, the object in the game can be paintings and statues present there. The player is spurred on to quickly recognize every dropping objects and smartly move in order to save the right objects, while paying attention so as not to be hit by the other objects. The game's higher levels of difficulty typically involve higher speeds of fall, and fewer valid objects. The game is very dynamic and requires that the player be fully attentive, to be able to quickly recognize items and understand their meaning.

The proposed mG template samples are quite different from each other in terms of usability, target users and typology of information/service that can be provided. An author, who defines Point of Interests, paths and services inside a TiE VW, can choose to instantiate one mG template instead of another as per the expected preferences and educational needs of the target users. Finer degrees of adaptation can also be exploited, as explained in the following.

A fundamental feature of mG templates is the fact that they are parametric. Every mG instance consists of generic software module (one for each template) and an instance-specific XML configuration file that provides the values – defined by the content author – of the parametric features. The configuration file is easily editable by the content author, who is thus able to build simple games without detailed knowledge of the software. Configurability is important in order to support code-reuse and allow authors to easily instantiate services for their applications, according to their specific needs. Instantiation parameters involve both contents (i.e. text, images, difficulty levels, timings, etc.) and appearance (i.e. buttons, font colors, etc.).

Parameter values can also be subject to dynamic instantiation. This means that the author can specify more than one value for a given instance's parameter based on the actual value of parameterized rules. The Adaptation module of the TiE environment, which is responsible for storing the player's profile, does the matching at runtime in order to provide the user the most suitable content.

Beside the instantiation parameters of a mG, the content author must also specify the display rules. These define the conditions (e.g. elapsed time, player's score and position, player's profile features) under which that specific mG will become available to a player. For instance, a puzzle game could appear when the player is in front of a church, if the user has successfully passed the previous 3 games, she/he has collected a torch to light it, and the elapsed time is below a certain threshold.

mGs contents are usually correlated to the PoI (Point of Interest) in which these are embedded. For instance, contents and themes could touch upon the historical facts related to the site, or pieces of heritage preserved there. There are also other linking possibilities (in any case, a mG's contents are related with the visited area/city). For instance, an mG could be triggered as a bonus, or as a help to allow the user to collect useful information on an item, or could even be one or more questions asked by a virtual character met on the way. Also, a sequence of mGs may appear at the end of a user exploration of a city as a summative challenge to test the knowledge acquired in that place.

An important issue concerns the Human-Computer Interaction (HCI) modalities. We have investigated them in preliminary studies with early prototypes of mGs, getting useful information from young people and teachers involved in workshops. We highlight here the requirements for a third person point of view, with analogic-style indicators and a gamepad command console. From these studies we found that a map is very important to support virtual exploration.

Concerning the appearance of the mGs (that should somehow pop-up from the virtual world), the most appreciated interaction modality is through a mobile device reconstructed in the virtual world. It would be like a palm-top computer through which the player would manage all the aspects related to the mGs. An alternative would be represented by an external interaction window. We experimented this solution with a paper mock-up, but considered that it would be less engaging.

The Creative Toolkit

Rather than developing one single application, TiE has been designed an extensible technological framework that can be used to implement a number of edutainment applications with different types of contents and interaction modalities, such as event driven adventures and free walkthroughs. These applications are based on the TiE enriched 3D environment, and can be configured as required (e.g. by instantiating mG templates, adding new city models, defining game rules).

In order to make the authoring aspect accessible also to educational experts not familiar with programing, we are developing a visual Authoring Tool - namely the TiE Creative Toolkit - that supports the content author in configuring TiE games (rules that determine the plot, available worlds, etc.) and creating instances of mGs.

A content author can exploit her/his own multimedia contents to create games/quizzes for a given city/area by using the mG Designer, a dedicated part of the TiE Creative Toolkit . With this tool, a content creator is supported by a Wizard of Oz in instantiating a mG Template and specifying its configurable parameters. This is a significant advantage in implementing the modular design approach adopted in this project.

The possible range of applications from a User Generated Contents (UGC) perspective are many and varied: for instance, teachers could instantiate a set of mGs related to their lessons;

keen multimedia developers can use the online framework to create a complex, compelling and realistic adventure; generic end-users, by following some basic rules, can experience a simple online game construction; marketing experts can build appealing, interactive destinations in order to promote local products and services.

mGs allow the player to virtually interact with pieces of the heritage in their context and discover/investigate some details related to that area (e.g. we use some mGs as "portals" to have a short adventure in the past at the same place). In this way, mGs can be thought of as 1-level links in the "hypertext" represented by the 3D environment, where the player lives and partakes in cultural adventures. This approach is particularly useful for cultural tourism; furthermore, it can be exploited for general tourism and other applications, since it allows combining a compelling spatial exploration experience (similar to state-of-the-art 3D games) along with gaining in-depth information, by interacting with representations/products/services/tools/shops/natural resorts typical of that territory.

TIE GAME PROTOTYPE: GENOA CITY CENTER

As a first demonstration of the technological platform, we are implementing the TiE online game, a sort of cultural virtual treasure-hunting games through European cities. We are currently developing the environments for the cities involved in the TiE project consortium: Genoa, Strasbourg, Prague, Tomar, Plovdiv, Cuj-Napoca, Arousa-Norte and Maribor. As an example, we show here the case of Genoa as it has been implemented until now.

Genoa historical city center is one of the largest medieval urban centers in Europe (around 1x2 Km in area) with a high density of buildings. Buildings are thin and tall, separated by narrow pedestrian streets, namely "Carruggi". They show typically homogeneous features that we could efficiently model and process through the automatic generation statistical algorithm . Figure 1 shows an aerial view of the implemented model, while Figure 2 is a snapshot from a player's viewpoint during the exploration of the Genoa's historical center.

Inside the historical city, there is Strada Nuova, an area that contains outstanding palaces from the Renaissance and Baroque age, when Genoa

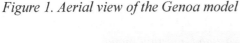

Figure 1. Aerial view of the Genoa model

Figure 2. Snapshot from a TiE game session in the Genoa historical city center

bankers had a key role in the financial arena. Strada Nuova was designed as the representative quarters for such families. Given their outstanding artistic and architectonic value, these palaces are implemented as PoIs. Figure 3 represents the reconstruction of "Palazzo Rosso" (an important museum in Strada Nuova) and "Palazzo Tursi" (now the prestigious seat of the municipality of Genoa).

In the reconstructed environment, the player's avatar can explore the main roads and the back alleys of the Genoa city centre. Some icons, linked to PoIs such as important palaces and churches, trigger mG sessions through which the user can virtually manipulate pieces of the artistic heritage and face quizzes concerning the history of Genoa. Sample mG Templates that have been instantiated include: TextQuiz, VisualQuiz, Puzzle, FindTheWrongDetails and FindTheMissingDetails (see Fig. 4).

In this work-in-progress environment we have made two types of preliminary tests. The first one

Figure 3. Strada Nuova area inside the Genoa city center: on the left there is the reconstruction of Palazzo Rosso, on the right the Palazzo Tursi, and in the foreground a virtual human.

Figure 4. Two snapshots of mGs (Puzzle and FindTheWrongDetails) about De Ferrari square in Genoa

involved high-school students and was aimed at investigating whether culturally-oriented Virtual Worlds enriched with mGs could provide an entertainment experience similar to that of state of the art commercial videogames. This is a key pre-requisite, in order to reach a broad audience who likes gaming but is not naturally keen on addressing cultural themes. Results – obtained in the context of a Serious Game concerning sea-side leisure-time activities are presented in (Bellotti, Berta, De Gloria & Primavera, 2009) - have been successful and show in particular that mGs can enhance the player experience in terms of ability demand, dynamism, engagement, emotional affect and realism.

The second type of tests involved also experts of art/history and education. The target was to get hints about usability and usefulness of the implemented environment in order to inform further design improvements in the implementation of the virtual environments of 15 cities/rural areas in other European countries. Based on this analysis, we have drawn indications on how to effectively integrate mGs in the 3D environment in order to enhance the visitor's experience of the reconstructed areas – we have reported them in (Bellotti, Berta, De Gloria & Zappi, 2008). Here, it is important to highlight that mGs are considered as very promising for showing and promoting the heritage preserved in the city, in museums, churches and other public or private areas. By having the possibility of virtually interacting with these artifacts and discovering more information about related personages, history and anecdotes/legends, the user gets familiarity with the environment and may draw a good motivation to have a real visit. Moreover, multimedia representations of the touched items (e.g. digital pictures and videos) may be granted as rewards to special winners and/or directly sold in a virtual book-shop, which would be an important show-case for promoting the digital heritage of a museum, in particular addressing also a customers' target, youngsters and videogamers, that may not be strongly self-motivated towards art and culture.

OPPORTUNITIES FOR FUTURE WORK

Extensive user testing is necessary in order to evaluate in depth the proposed approach and inform design of VWs aimed at supporting cultural tourism experiences. Investigating this research field opens a number of questions that will have to be addressed in the future by the research community. These involve in particular the development of a new generation of proactive agents that provide advanced services for personalized experiences, such as: effective presentation of the destination, scheduling and adaptation of mGs, combination of eCommerce and social networking, integration with Destination Management Systems.

CONCLUSIONS

Virtual Reality environments are ever more going online. This trend, opened by videogames, will spread to other kinds of applications and open new important opportunities to enhance tourism, and in particular cultural tourism given the possibility of creating compelling virtual adventures set in the context of artistic and natural beauties.

We are exploring these challenges in the context of the TiE project, and developing tools to build enriched virtual environments where the player could explore faithfully reconstructed places and live there information-rich, contextualized experiences. The whole should be perceived as a compelling, exciting and culturally meaningful story/adventure in which the player can get familiarity with items somehow available in the territory.

This concept can be thought of as the "digital analogy" of a visit of a city/region (which is typically enhanced by visits at museums, galleries, churches and other important buildings and/or memory places), which is the traditional way through which a number of people - from common tourists to specialized scholars - have elevated their spirit by appreciating foreign artifacts, habits and people, and developing knowledge about history, art, and geography. In other words, by discovering the world.

Extended user tests are necessary – and already planned in the context of the project – in order to achieve an appropriate assessment of the proposed approach. However, preliminary informal tests have suggested that the approach is valid and also allowed us to define guidelines about how to properly and smoothly integrate mGs in the environment, which is an important requirement in order not to startle/distract the player. Moreover, the enriched 3D environment supports the contextualized promotion of artifacts, products and services, which is an important growing demand from institutions and enterprises that want to valorize the resources of a territory.

REFERENCES

Active Worlds Inc. (2007). *Active worlds and education.* Retrieved January 7, 2009, from http://www.activeworlds.com/edu/index.asp

Alexander, B. (2006). Web 2.0: A new wave of innovation for teaching and learning? *EDUCAUSE Review, 41*(2), 32–44.

Arnold, D. (2008). Editorial for inaugural issue of JOCCH: Pasteur's quadrant: Cultural heritage as inspiration for basic research in computer science. *Journal of Computation in Cultural Heritage, 1*(1).

Bellotti, F., Berta, R., De Gloria, A., Pellegrino, M., & Primavera, L. (2007). Learning contents by videogame tricks. In *Proceedings of the Learning with game Conference.*

Bellotti, F., Berta, R., De Gloria, A., & Primavera, L. (in press). Enhancing the educational value of videogames. *ACM Computers in Entertainment.*

Bellotti, F., Berta, R., De Gloria, A., & Zappi, V. (2008). Exploring gaming mechanisms to enhance knowledge acquisition in virtual worlds. In *Proceedings of the International Conference on Digital Interactive Media in Entertainment and Arts.*

Bellotti, F., Berta, R., Garnier-Rivers, A., & Jacquet, E. (2008). *User requirements report* (TiE Project Tech. Rep.).

Brutzman, D., & Daly, L. (Eds.). (2007). *X3D: Extensible 3D graphics for Web authors*. San Francisco: Morgan Kaufmann.

Conrady, R. (2007). Travel technology in the era of Web 2.0. In *Trends and issues in global tourism* (pp. 165-184).

Corbit, M. (2002). Building virtual worlds for informal science learning. [AWEDU]. *Active Worlds Educational Universe, 11*(1), 55–67.

Dickey, M. D. (2003). Teaching in 3D: Pedagogical affordances and constraints of 3D virtual worlds for synchronous distance learning. *Distance Education, 24*, 105–121. doi:10.1080/01587910303047

Ducheneaut, N., Yee, N., Nickell, E., & Moore, R. J. (2006). Alone together?: Exploring the social dynamics of massively multiplayer online games. In *Proceedings of the SIGCHI Conference on Human Factors in Computing Systems*.

Explore Virtual Mall in 3D. (2008). *Virtual Mall*. Retrieved November 18, 2008, from http://www.virtuy.com

Fullerton, T., Swain, C., & Hoffman, S. (Eds.). (2004). *Proceedings of the Game design workshop. designing, prototyping and playtesting games*. San Francisco, CA: CMP Books.

Garrett, J. (2005). *Ajax: A new approach to Web applications*. Retrieved February 14, 2005, from http://www.adaptivepath.com/publications/essays/archives/000385.php

Google Earth. (2008). *Ancient Rome video*. Retrieved December 20, 2008, from http://earth.google.com/rome/

Grinter, R., Rodden, T., Aoki, P., Cutrell, E., Jeffries, R., & Olson, G. (Eds.). (2006). *Proceedings of the CHI Conference '06*. New York: ACM.

Hughes, C., & Moshell, E. J. (1997). Shared virtual worlds for experiment. *ACM Multimedia, 5*(2), 145–154. doi:10.1007/s005300050050

Kahana, M., Sekuler, R., Caplan, J., Kirschen, M., & Madsen, J. (1999). Human theta oscillations exhibit task dependence during virtual maze navigation. *Nature, 399*, 781–784. doi:10.1038/21645

Kock, N. (2008). E-collaboration and e-commerce in virtual worlds: The potential of Second Life and World of Warcraft. *International Journal of e-Collaboration, 4*(3), 1–13.

Livingstone, D., & Kemp, J. (2006). Massively multi-learner: Recent advances in 3D social environments. *Computing and Information Systms Journal, 10*(2).

Losh, E. (2005). In country with tactical Iraqi: Trust, identity, and language learning in a military video game. In *Proceedings of the Digital Arts and Culture Conference* (pp. 69-78).

Maurina, E. F., III, (Ed.). (2006). *The game programmer's guide to torque: Under the hood of the torque game engine*. Natick, MA: AK Peters, Ltd.

Maximilien, E. M., Wilkinson, H., Desai, N., & Tai, S. (2007). A domain specific-language for Web APIs and services mashups. In *Proceedings of the International Conference on Service Oriented Computing (ICSOC)*.

Mayo, M. J. (2007). Games for science and engineering education. *Communications of the ACM, 50*(7), 30–35. doi:10.1145/1272516.1272536

Michael, D., & Chen, S. (Eds.). (2006). *Serious games: Games that education, train, and inform*. Florence, KY: Thompson Course Technology PTR.

O'Reilly, T. (2007). *What is Web 2.0? Design patterns and business models for the next generation of software*. Retrieved September 20, 2007, from http://www.oreillynet.com/pub/a/oreilly/tim/news/2005/09/30/what-is-web-20.html

OpenSimulator Wiki. (2008). *Open simulator*. Retrieved November 18, 2008, from http://opensimulator.org/wiki/Main_Page

Orndorff, P. (2008). *Wired blog network*. Retrieved September 20, 2007, from http://blog.wired.com/geekdad/2008/11/explore-ancient.html

Pillay, H., Brownlee, J., & Wilss, L. (1999). Cognition and recreational computer games: Implications for educational technology. *Journal of Researeh on Computing in Education, 32*(1), 203–216.

Raybourn, E. M., Deagle, E., Mendina, K., & Heneghan, J. (2005). Adaptive thinking & leadership simulation game training for special forces officers. In *Proceedings of the Interservice/Industry Training, Simulation, and Education Conference*.

Rovai, A. P. (2002). Building sense of community at a distance. *International Review of Research in Open and Distance Learning*. Retrieved September 20, 2007, from http://www.irrodl.org/index.php/irrodl/article/ view/79/152

Schroth, C., & Janner, T. (2007). Web 2.0 and SOA: Converging concepts enabling the Internet of services. *IEEE IT Professional, 9*(3).

Second Life. (2008). *Linden Lab*. Retrieved December 2008, from http://www.secondlife.com

Sliney, A., & Murphy, D. (2008). JDoc: A serious game for medical learning. In *Proceedings of the First International Conference on Advances in Computer-Human Interaction* (pp. 131-136).

Watson, B., Muller, P., Wonka, P., Sexton, C., Veryovka, O., & Fuller, A. (2008). Procedural urban modeling in practice. *IEEE Computer Graphics and Applications, 28*(3), 18–26. doi:10.1109/MCG.2008.58

World of Warcraft. (2008). *Blizzard Entertainment*. Retrieved December 20, 2008, from http://www.blizzard.com/wow

Zyda, M. (2007). Special issue on serious games. *Communications of the ACM, 50*(7). doi:10.1145/1272516.1272535

Chapter 13
Itchy Feet:
A 3D E-Tourism Environment

Ingo Seidel
Matrixware Information Services GmbH, Austria

Markus Gärtner
Matrixware Information Services GmbH, Austria

Michael Pöttler
Vienna University of Technology, Austria

Helmut Berger
Matrixware Information Services GmbH, Austria

Michael Dittenbach
Matrixware Information Services GmbH, Austria

Dieter Merkl
Vienna University of Technology, Austria

ABSTRACT

In this chapter the authors describe an e-tourism environment that places emphasis on a community-driven approach to foster a lively society of travelers. It enables them to exchange travel experiences, recommend tourism destinations or just catch some interesting gossip. Moreover, business transactions such as booking a trip or getting assistance from professional travel agents are a constituent part of this environment. All these interactions happen in an integrated, game-like, 3D virtual world where each tourist is impersonated as an avatar. The authors draw a retrospective on the specification, design and implementation of this e-tourism environment and present the status quo. The authors describe how they applied electronic institutions, a framework developed and employed in the area of multi-agent systems, to the tourism domain. Furthermore, they present their approach to connect a 3D virtual world with electronic institutions. Our goal is to provide a test bed for assessing the acceptance of virtual environments, as a medium to overcome the non-tangible nature of tourism products.

DOI: 10.4018/978-1-60566-818-5.ch013

INTRODUCTION

In the last decades Information and Communication Technology (ICT) has revolutionized the global economy and almost every business including tourism. The rapid evolution of ICT enabled consumers to have access to a broader range of information services covering the whole tourism life cycle (Werthner & Klein, 1999).

A typical tour planning and execution cycle may be something like the following. Prior to booking, the customer is browsing the Internet to search for information and is using communication services such as forums or instant messaging to get the latest information directly from local people. Prices are compared and the cheapest offer is booked online. During the trip, the tourist uses her mobile device to get the latest news about local events. Activities and impressions are compiled in online diaries via the mobile device and made accessible to friends and family. After the trip, pictures are shared online and experiences are discussed. The majority of these activities take place in online tourism communities. An online community can be defined as the combination of commercial, technical, social and psychological aspects of groups of people (Eigner, Leitner, & Nausner, 2003). Following this trend many companies see the creation of "business-sponsored-communities" as an additional channel of distribution. In this context, companies analyze user profiles in order to provide personal advertisements and product-related information to community members. The tourism sector has been particularly active in this field, because customer loyalty not only depends on social interaction but also on the quality of the information provided, e.g., prices or opening times.

Furthermore, trip planning makes high demands on the information search (Pöttler, 2007). An online community is only successful when it attracts and retains a large number of members to reach critical mass (Wang, Yu, & Fesenmaier, 2002). The potential of online communities lies in the ability to be integrated in the value chain for product and service design. To tap its full potential, the creation of online communities has to be technically, operationally, strategically and economically planned to meet the users' requirements. Not only social interaction is of great importance during the process of community building, but community members want to communicate as well as using a technically sophisticated platform. This technological aspect has not been emphasized enough in the tourism domain. A study that compared different online tourism communities shows that technical innovations are introduced sparingly in these communities (Dippelreiter et al., 2009). Special focus should therefore be placed on the selection of the technological features and functionalities when creating a community in the tourism domain.

Another important aspect in tourism is the presentation of products. A tourism product is a virtual product that cannot be experienced in advance – it is a confidence product (Gratzer, Werthner, & Winiwarter, 2004). For a customer it is essential to get a good impression of the product before the trip, in order to know what to expect, so as not to be disappointed on site.

Traditionally the impression of a destination is conveyed by means of quality photos in travel catalogs and information from the travel agent. In addition, information gathering on the Internet and in online communities has become more important over the last few years. However, the presentation of the content is basically the same – textual descriptions and pictures are used to illustrate travel destinations. An approach that goes beyond these "classical" media types and provides more sophisticated visualization of tourism products are 3D product presentations.

The presentation of a product in a three dimensional space makes it easier to imagine the actual product and creates a completely new product experience. In a 3D Virtual World the user is impersonated as an avatar (a virtual, three dimensional representation of the user) and can explore the environment in a similar manner as the real world. This virtual world is composed of a landscape where the user can walk around; a virtual sky and sun resemble the natural atmosphere; furthermore, this environment is populated with buildings that can be entered through doors. For example, suppose a hotel has been visualized in the 3D Virtual World. The customer is then literally able to enter the hotel, experience its ambience, can see how the room will look like and how well the sea view can be enjoyed from the balcony in the virtual environment. Besides these advantages in product presentation, 3D Virtual Worlds also address social interaction implicitly. Just as in the real world, a user can see other users, is able to walk towards them and can start talking to them. It is fairly easy to get in touch with other people and new relationships can emerge quickly. Thus, we consider that a 3D Virtual World can be a good basis to build up an online community.

In light of these developments and new technologies, we are aiming at the creation of a novel 3D e-Tourism environment, henceforth referred to as Itchy Feet. With Itchy Feet we address the aspects of social interaction by providing instruments to interact and exchange experiences with other customers that go beyond the possibilities of conventional text-based chat rooms. It offers sophisticated visualization of tourism products, integrates travel agents and enables seamless access to the information richness of the Internet. The principal goal is to develop an instrument to support the complex interaction patterns of providers and consumers in an e-Tourism setting.

This principal goal subsumes three subgoals:

1. provide a 3D e-Tourism environment for both providers and consumers, to facilitate versatile interaction between participants including trading of tourism products;
2. provide a 3D e-Tourism environment that acts as a community facilitator to create and establish a lively and sustainable community involving both providers and consumers; and,
3. provide a 3D e-Tourism environment that is information-rich to provide transparent and unified access to disparate multimedia information sources.

The technological basis for this environment is formed by a 3D Virtual World that allows users to participate in Itchy Feet. The 3D Virtual World implements various community features such as profiles or forums, in order to become the cornerstone of a lively tourism community. Users have access to a wide range of information sources that are aggregated and presented in the 3D Virtual World. In order to provide these functionalities an agent-based approach is taken. According to Wooldridge (2001), agent-based solutions should be employed whenever the information is spread across several sources. This perfectly applies to the tourism domain where information is spread over the Internet and stored in databases on different organizational levels (regional, national, international).

In Itchy Feet, the software agents reside in a Multi-Agent System that is connected to a 3D Virtual World. To this end, we rely on a framework (Seidel & Berger, 2007) that combines a Multi-Agent System methodology, namely Electronic Institutions (Esteva, Rodriguez-Aguilar, Sierra, Garcia, & Arcos, 2001) with 3D Virtual Worlds. Our system is based on a three layered architecture. The 3D Virtual World is placed at the top layer, the Electronic Institution is at the bottom layer and both these two components are connected through the middleware layer.

An Electronic Institution is similar to a real world institution where processes and rules are predefined and involved parties have to act according to these processes and rules. In Itchy Feet, Electronic Institutions are used to define business processes and rules which are enforced in the 3D Virtual World. Every user in the 3D Virtual World is the principal of an agent in the

Electronic Institution that validates the actions of the user. Autonomous agents are visualized in the 3D Virtual World as avatars. Thus, the system enables active participation of humans in this agent-based society. The user is no longer restricted to controlling and observing the agent system, but is able to communicate with these agents just as with other human users.

The remainder of this chapter is structured as follows. The next section provides an overview of related work. The technological building blocks are presented in the third section. The general framework connecting Electronic Institutions with 3D Virtual Worlds is presented in the fourth section. In the section "Itchy Feet" the general framework is applied to the tourism domain and Itchy Feet is introduced. The different Electronic Institutions in this environment, the 3D Virtual World and the conceptual basis for data aggregation and presentation are presented. In the section, "Discussion" we discuss the environment and present opportunities for future research. The chapter is concluded in the last section.

RELATED WORK

e-Tourism has created new distribution channels for tourism resulting in the establishment of numerous online booking platforms. These services are increasingly used by customers to purchase tourism products. A survey comparing online booking with booking at traditional travel agents gives insights on the booking behavior of customers (Bogdanovych, Berger, Simoff, & Sierra, 2006). This survey showed that people are using online booking services primarily to book domestic trips, whereas international trips are more often booked with a travel agent. The main advantages of travel agents are their expertise and the face-to-face interaction when making difficult decisions. In contrast, online booking systems are more convenient, have lower response times and provide answers to inquiries in an environment familiar to most users. Note that these results were obtained in Australia and the booking behavior in other countries might be different, due to both sociological as well as geographical reasons.

Trust in e-Commerce systems is a domain of active research and different studies show that the social presence of a web site influences trust, enjoyment, perceived usefulness and loyalty. Social presence is the sense of awareness of other people in a communication medium. Hassanein & Head (2007) conducted a study where they investigated the influence of certain interface elements on perceived social presence. Three different online stores with low, medium and high levels of social presence were created. Test subjects had to complete a certain task – buying a piece of cloth – and reported their experiences in a questionnaire. The evaluation shows that the social presence of a web site can be influenced by certain user interface elements which in turn influences the trust, enjoyment and perceived usefulness of a web site.

In another work Cyr et al. (2007) argue that online shopping experiences lack human warmth as they are more impersonal, anonymous and do not provide face-to-face communication. They investigate how loyalty is influenced by social presence and if there are gender differences. Five e-Commerce web sites with different interactive elements were created and customers had to browse one of the websites and buy concert tickets. The results indicate that social presence influences loyalty as well as enjoyment, however, there are differences between males and females. For example, the direct impact of social presence on loyalty could only be shown for females but not for males.

Web sites in e-Tourism are rather dominated by conservative user interfaces. Especially on booking platforms users navigate through a plethora of drop down lists and selection boxes to search for tourism products. To overcome these disadvantages, new interface metaphors have been developed. One approach employs natural language interaction enabling users to formulate a query in natural language (Berger, Dittenbach, & Merkl, 2004). The advantages of this approach are the same as with online discussion forums, i.e. - users can express more complex queries when using their natural language and will get more appropriate results for their search. Furthermore, they do not have to learn a special query language and are not required to structure their request in a way the computer understands. A field trial showed that most of the participants considered the natural language interface to be more comfortable than standard interfaces and explicitly stated their preference for this kind of interface.

To get insights on the quality of information posted on forums, travel blogs, etc., Schwabe & Prestipino (2005) compared the information quality of online tourism communities with traditional guidebooks. They found that online communities provide more timely information, requests can be answered more completely, and personal requests can be accomplished better. The structure of the information is the only area where guide books are more sophisticated.

Another study compared different tourism online communities and investigated the use of Web 2.0 technologies (Dippelreiter et al., 2009). It is shown that online communities in e-Tourism mostly address the pre-trip and post-trip phase of the tourism life cycle, while support during the on-trip phase is mostly neglected. Communities are used to collect and aggregate information prior to the trip and to share experiences and pictures afterwards. Interestingly, Web 2.0 technologies such as interactive maps have only been introduced sparingly and many communities use conventional technologies. Discussion forums are also still the predominant way to elaborate on tourism topics and have not been replaced by other forms of collaborations.

Agent Technology

An interface determines how users are able to access and view the data in a system. The actual internal representation and structure of this data can be achieved by various means. Multi-Agent Systems are one possibility and have already been employed in the tourism domain for information gathering, representation and aggregation. For example, Chiu & Leung (2005) designed a virtual enterprise of independent tourism service providers as a Multi-Agent System. Agents make use of Semantic Web concepts to improve the planning stage and help customers in understanding and specifying their requirements and preferences. The authors' motivation was the lack of tourist portals that proactively assist tourists by adequately integrating disparate information sources and services. The Multi-Agent System developed by Chiu & Leung (2005) addresses these issues to create a ubiquitous tourist assistance system.

A similar approach, that also relies on agent technology to retrieve tourist information from distributed databases, has been presented by Yeung et al. (1998). A customer can use the system through a special interactive graphical user interface to enter search queries and to trace the information search and retrieval. In the background the information requests are processed by different types of software agents which communicate via the Knowledge Query and Manipulation Language (KQML) (Finin, Fritzson, McKay, & McEntire, 1994). Typically, a search request is passed to a specific information agent that has knowledge about the search topic. The information agent then queries a database and the result is sent back to the requesting agent. Special attention has been paid to platform independence – all system components are either implemented in Java or other platform independent technologies; and thus, KQML is used as a platform independent communication protocol.

The implementation of software agents usually follows a specific methodology aimed at defining the way agents need to be modeled. Several formal methodologies have been proposed in the literature. Dignum & Dignum (2001) introduced a formal methodology for the development of agent societies. They divide domain requirements into functional and interaction requirements. Functional requirements define what a system is supposed to do and interaction requirements define how the system is supposed to do it. In a subsequent work a methodology for the design of agent societies based on the type of coordination structure was presented (Dignum, Weigand, & Xu, 2001).

Gaia, a methodology for agent-oriented analysis and design was introduced by Zambonelli et al. (2003). It was the first formal methodology specifically developed for agent-based systems. The approach is based on designing a Multi-Agent System as a computational organization. Furthermore, the methodology has been extended for the analysis and design of Multi-Agent Systems. Clear guidelines for analysis and design are provided by Gaia. Juan et al. (2002) introduced a methodology based on Gaia to improve software engineering of agent-based open systems.

The Electronic Institution methodology was developed for modeling agent organizations effectively as institutionalized electronic organizations (Esteva, Rodriguez-Aguilar, Sierra, Garcia, & Arcos, 2001). The methodology is based on the notion of institutions. Institutions represent the framework within which human interaction takes place and define restrictions and permitted actions. Such definitions are mapped onto Electronic Institutions which are the electronic counterpart of institutions. Electronic Institutions are populated by heterogeneous software agents and humans that interact by means of speech acts.

3D Virtual Worlds

Research approaches taking advantage of 3D game engines have emerged over the last few years. One of the first examples is PSDoom by Dennis Chao (2001). In his work the Doom game engine is used as an interface for the management of Unix system processes where each process is represented as a monster. Killing the monster causes the corresponding process to "die". The intention of this work is to explore new interface metaphors that provide a more intuitive access to computers for computer illiterate people.

Moloney et al. (2003) developed an immersive design critique tool for architects. They use an open source game engine to create a collaborative virtual environment enabling students to create 3D architectural models. The environment allows students to iteratively alter the model and to directly view these changes. Moreover, reviewers are able to comment on the created models.

In the context of information visualization Kot et al. (2005) use a 3D game engine to improve data visualization for source code comprehension. This tool allows software developers to quickly perceive the structure of source code and the relationship between different source code files. Files are visualized as 3D objects in a 3D Virtual World. The user can explore the structure by walking through the virtual world. The content of a file is displayed when the user walks into a file object.

In another work Steve DiPaola & David Collins (2003) created a 3D Virtual World for the emulation of natural social paradigms. They believe that such environments convey tele-presence and help to achieve higher levels of socialization, learning and communication. The human voice is used as communication mechanism to represent the individuality of users and to create an immersion effect.

Multi-Agent Systems and 3D Virtual Worlds

Some works report on the combination of Multi-Agent Systems and 3D Virtual Worlds. Smith et al. (2003) present an approach where the agent logic is incorporated in a 3D environment. According to the authors most worlds are largely static and objects are used to trigger pre-programmed behavior. Agents are supposed to enrich the world and should make the environment more dynamic. The proposed framework consists of a society of agents in which each agent controls a 3D object. As an example, a conference room consisting of wall agents and a room agent is presented. Depending on the number of avatars in the room, the agents react and dynamically adapt the room size.

Adobbati et al. (2002) presented GameBots; a system that abstracts from the Multi-Agent System and provides a uniform interface to the 3D Virtual World. They have created a multi agent research test bed that is not limited to a specific task in a fixed environment and supports human testing and interaction. The GameBots environment supports humans-as-agents, is easily customizable (due to a scripting language), and supports multiple environments and tasks.

The Unreal Tournament Semi-Automated Force (UTSAF) project takes advantage of GameBots (Manojlovich, Prasithsangaree, Hughes, Chen, & Lewis, 2003). It is a framework that connects military simulations with a 3D visualization. The goal is to create a system that scales well on large and heterogeneous simulation environments. To this end, they developed a framework in which an agent system is used as the mediator between the military simulation and the 3D Virtual World. Agents monitor the status of the military simulation, filter relevant information and visualize entities of the simulation in a 3D Virtual World.

Nakanishi & Ishida (2004) developed a social interaction platform named FreeWalk/Q where software agents and human controlled avatars share the same environment, interaction model and scenario. They introduced different topologies and description levels to describe the behavior of an agent or a human's avatar for a more natural integration into their virtual environment.

Face-to-face communication in 3D worlds is addressed by Traum & Rickel (2002). They concentrate on issues such as proximity and attentional focus of others, the interplay between speech and nonverbal signals and the ability to maintain multipart conversations. They introduced an example scenario to demonstrate an initial implementation of their model.

A similar approach to seamlessly integrate agents and humans in a cohesive Multi-Agent System was introduced by Martin et al. (2003). In their work they describe a software prototype of a distributed collaboration and interaction system helping humans to act as an integrated part of a Multi-Agent System. They introduced so-called liaison agents which support human interaction with other non-human agents by arbitrating between them.

Payne et al. (2000) analyzed human-agent interaction and stated that agents can have different models of user interaction. In their work they describe a case study of a Multi-Agent System containing different agents, with some having functionally similar capabilities, but with different types of user interaction modalities. They argue that according to the type of user interaction a significant effect on the performance of the whole agent community can be ascertained.

Game Design

This paragraph describes the findings of the research conducted by Yee (2006 b), one of the leading researchers in the area of Massively Multi-User Online Role-Playing Games (MMORPGs). One of the aspects why people join a 3D environment is the motive of playing MMORPGs. They are a leisure activity practiced by millions of people worldwide, who are interacting with each other through graphical avatars to complete complex goals (Yee, 2006 b). However, little research has been conducted to explore the social interactions and relationships that develop between the users of MMORPGs.

Nick Yee was one of the first in this field, who focused on statistical analysis of motivation factors for playing MMORPGs (Yee, 2006 a). The stereotype that only teenagers are playing MMORPGs is a false premise. The average age of MMORPG users is 26.57 years, and on average they spend 22.72 hours each week playing their chosen MMORPG. Relating to social interaction, the majority of asked users had made more positive experiences in the 3D environment than in real life. While females emphasized the relationship, immersion and escapism within the 3D environment as the main motivation factors, the motivation for males lies in the manipulation and achievement of desired outcomes.

The reason why users are motivated to play MMORPGs has a lot to do with conceptualization and the design of the game. The difference between other entertainment products like books or music is that games are relatively unpredictable in their consumption (Hunicke, LeBlanc, & Zubek, 2004). In the field of game design there is a lot of literature related to the construction of specific games; however, there is less literature available about the best practices for designing games.

Rollings & Morris (2004) define a form of "Creative Road Map" for creating games, which comprises the following development stages: concept development, structure development and design; furthermore there are four phases of the creative process. It starts with inspiration, followed by synthesis, resonance and convergence. The inspiration phase is concerned with "where to get ideas"; synthesis means "combining the ideas", this is followed by the resonance which describes the "creation of synergy from ideas", and finally "finishing the concept" expressed by convergence.

They also describe the essentials of game design. Five useful questions can be asked by game designers who start to create a game: (i) Is it original? (ii) Is it coherent? (iii) Is it interactive? (iv) Is it interesting? (v) Is it fun? Another key aspect of game design is the concept of "meaningful play" (Salen & Zimmermann, 2004). The purpose of this concept is to create an exceptionally and meaningful game experience for the player.

Two diverse definitions are used for the concept of "meaningful play". The first, descriptive approach, specifies the interaction between the game system, the game-activity and the resulting outcome. It refers to the process in which the player undertakes activities, and the system responds. The second approach, called the evaluative approach specifies the game experience that needs to be created for the player.

TECHNOLOGICAL BUILDING BLOCKS

Multi-Agent Systems and 3D Virtual Worlds are the fundamental technologies used in our work. First, we will introduce Electronic Institutions and then present the employed 3D Virtual World. Electronic Institutions enable the specification of regulated and well structured environments. In particular, Electronic Institutions are taking control over security aspects to ensure participants adhere to the institutional rules and fulfill their obligations. They are computational realizations of real-world institutions enabling agents to interact with each other according to predefined conventions and rules (Esteva, Rodriguez-Aguilar, Sierra, Garcia, & Arcos, 2001). Literally speaking, an Electronic Institution is the guard to ensure that all actions performed by agents are in line with the rules and regulations that apply in the institution.

One of the first implementations of an Electronic Institution was an Auction House developed within the Multi-Agent System for Fish Trading (MASFIT) project (Cuni et al., 2004). The Electronic Institution methodology used in this project emerged from the FishMarket project. The FishMarket is an electronic realization of a real fish market created as test-bed for trading agents in electronic auction markets (Rodríguez-Aguilar, Martín, Noriega, Garcia, & Sierra, 1997).

The basic components of Electronic Institutions are i) the Dialogical Framework, ii) the Performative Structure, and iii) the Norms and behavioral rules.

The Dialogical Framework defines the language ontology and illocutionary particles that are used by the agents. It defines the organizational structure of the society of agents, comprising the agent roles as well as the relationships between them.

The Performative Structure determines the type of dialogues agents can engage in. These dialogues are named scenes. They are connected with each other to create sequences of activities or dependencies among them.

Norms and behavioral rules regulate the interaction and communication in a group of agents. They ensure the safety and stability of the system by prohibiting agents to behave in non-expected or non-accepted manners (Aldewereld et al., 2006). Norms are used to define the legality and illegality of actions, in a vague and abstract way to ensure they apply in different circumstances (Dignum, 2002).

The movement between scenes is realized via so-called transitions, which are responsible for routing agents. Agents leave scenes where they have been playing a given role and enter other scenes to play the same or a different role. A scene instance is generated by the owner of a scene. After a scene has been instantiated, agents may join this scene. For every scene a sub-language of the overall institutional language as well as its structure, by means of a Finite State Machine, are defined. Furthermore, certain states of the Finite State Machine have a list of agent roles, defining whether agents playing in these roles are eligible to join or leave. The arcs of the Finite State Machine are labeled with messages (illocutions). If a corresponding message is uttered, a state transition is performed by the Finite State Machine. The Norms and behavioral rules are expressed as pre- and post-conditions of the illocutions that are admissible in the Performative Structure of the Electronic Institution.

Figure 1 depicts an example of a Performative Structure and scene in auction setting. Every Performative Structure has an Entry and an Exit Point. Agents can move from one scene to another scene by using Xor, Or and And transitions. Consider two agents, one playing in the Seller role and the other one in the Buyer role. Both agents start from the Entry Point. The first transition, depicted as an arrow with an X inside, is a Xor transition. It restrains an agent from moving to more than one subsequent scene. In our example, the Seller has to move to Scene1 and the Buyer to Scene2. The second transition, depicted as a semicircle, is an And transition. An And transition defines a synchronization point which has to be passed by multiple agents simultaneously. An agent has to wait in such a transition until all required other agents have moved to that transition. Then they are able to move to the next scene simultaneously. In our case the Seller and Buyer agents have to synchronize after leaving Scene1 and Scene2. The And transition can only be passed if an agent playing in the Seller and an agent playing in the Buyer role are present in the transition. If only the Seller is present in the And transition it has to wait until the Buyer joins, before it can proceed. The third transition, depicted as an arrow without X, is an Or transition. An Or transition is less restrictive than the Xor transition and allows agents to join more than one subsequent scene. In our example only the Exit Point is reachable from the Or transition, therefore the Buyer and Seller can only move to the Exit Point.

Figure 1 also shows the scene protocol of the Trade Scene. Scene protocols are represented as Finite State Machines where state changes are triggered by uttering messages. All agents in a certain scene share the same scene protocol and state. A state defines the possible messages that

Figure 1. Performative structure and scene protocol of an electronic institution

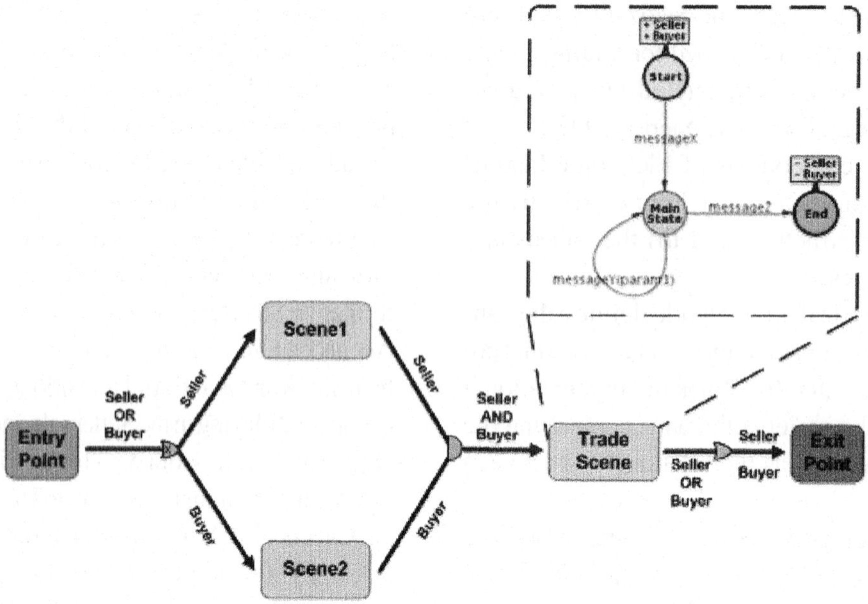

can be uttered and which roles are eligible to join or leave. In the Trade Scene Seller and Buyer agents are eligible to join the scene in the Start state and to leave it in the End state. In the Start state messageX can be uttered, while in the main state messageY or messageZ can be said.

3D Virtual Worlds

The second fundamental technology within the project are 3D Virtual Worlds. In order to identify a suitable 3D Virtual World, we evaluated four different 3D Virtual Worlds: two game engines - the Q Engine[1] and the Torque game engine[2]; one 3D virtual browser - Active Worlds[3]; and one 3D API - Java 3D[4]. Java 3D and Active Worlds did not provide enough functionality for our needs and could not be used. We then decided to choose the Torque game engine over the Q Engine as it has more features, is better proven and has a bigger developer community than the Q Engine.

The Torque game engine is an open source game engine developed by GarageGames. The feature list includes seamless indoor/outdoor rendering, animation support, a lighting engine, powerful editors, a scripting language and network functionality. Furthermore the royalty free licensing model allows developers to distribute and publish their games without further costs. The Torque game engine offers several editors and tools for the creation of games and 3D Virtual Worlds. These editors range from a world editor, used to arrange objects in the 3D Virtual World, over a terrain editor, used for the creation of the terrain, to a graphical user interface (GUI) editor, used for the design of the heads-up-display and the menu. The behavior of objects and the game logic is programmed via the scripting language. If the scripting language is not applicable (due to functional or speed limitations), it is possible to alter the game engine itself. The code is written in C++ and is directly compiled into the game engine executable.

Torque is an industry-proven game engine and has been used in numerous commercial and independent games. In the scientific world the Torque game engine has been utilized for research projects as well. The design critique tool from Moloney et al. (2003) is relying on the Torque game engine and IBM is using the engine for an internal research project on virtual worlds[5]. Moreover, the engine is widely used in education for teaching the principles of 3D game engines. The GarageGames web site[2] lists more than 200 schools and universities that use the Torque game engine in their class rooms.

A FRAMEWORK FOR 3D ELECTRONIC INSTITUTIONS

The role model for our environment is the concept of Massively Multi-User Online Role-Playing Games (MMORPGs). Millions of users interact, collaborate, socialize and form relationships with each other through avatars in such online environments (Castronova, 2005). For playing MMORPGs users must purchase a specific client and have to pay monthly subscription fees in the amount of 10 Euros to be able to access the central servers[6]. Users can view the virtual world in real time 3D graphics and use an avatar to interact with the environment. Commands are executed via user interfaces that are controlled by the mouse and keyboard.

The game World of Warcraft[7] is one of the most successful MMORPGs with more than 8 million users. In this virtual world, the collaboration becomes incredibly complex due to the interaction between beginner and advanced level types of users. In a common scenario users play in groups of 4 to 8 avatars where they fight against multiple computer controlled enemies. Other MMORPGs such as Star Wars Galaxies[8] have created collaboration scenarios of an entrepreneurial nature. Virtual goods are produced by the users themselves; supply, demand and prices are user driven. Many users say that they feel like they have a second job (Yee, 2006 b).

Conceptual Design

In our 3D e-Business environment two types of participants need to be considered: humans and agents. Agents are either autonomous or controlled by a human user. In the latter case, the couple human/agent is represented as an avatar in the 3D Virtual World. Humans and agents learn from each other and work together to collaboratively achieve certain goals. The user delegates tasks such as information gathering or product purchasing to the agent and learns from the agent which rules and restrictions apply in the environment. The user must act according to these rules. The movement and actions of the user in the 3D Virtual World are verified by the agent in the Electronic Institution.

Autonomous agents must be visualized in the 3D Virtual World such that users are able to interact and learn from them. An autonomous agent is a software agent that is capable of reacting to its environment and proactively makes its decisions based on the input from the environment and its internal decision model. The visualization of autonomous agents depends on their task. For example, an agent that actively participates in conversations may be visualized as an avatar, whereas a simple information agent may be visualized as an information monitor.

The dependence between the two systems requires that the 3D Virtual World is causally connected to the Electronic Institution. Causality refers to properties of the connection between a system and its representation (Maes & Nardi, 1988). In our case this means that whenever the 3D Virtual World changes, the Electronic Institution must change as well. Whenever the Electronic Institution evolves, the 3D Virtual World has to be modified in order to maintain a consistent relationship. Conceptually speaking, the system is composed of three layers whereof the 3D Virtual World is located at the top layer, the Electronic Institution is located at the bottom layer and both components are causally connected by the middleware layer.

Figure 2. An overview of the framework for connecting electronic institutions with 3D virtual worlds

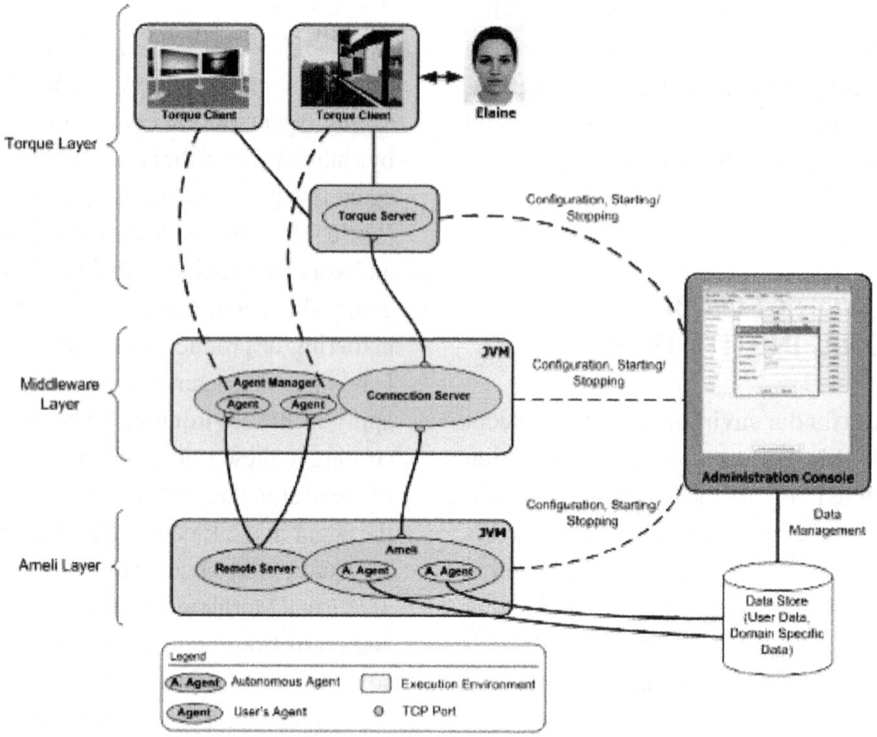

The Framework Architecture

An overview of the architecture is depicted in Figure 2. The rectangles define self-contained execution environments in which each application is running. These environments may run on the same computer or can be distributed across several machines. The communication between the layers is based on the TCP protocol. The components within each layer listen to network traffic and send messages on predefined ports.

The Administration Tool is connected to the data store and used for the administration of the components on every layer. The Electronic Institutions, the middleware as well as the Torque server can be started and stopped. The configuration is based on XML files that can be manipulated and managed via the Administration Tool. The connection to the data store enables administrators to create, manage and delete data that is used in the framework. There are generally two types of data: generic data that is used in every 3D e-Business environment and domain specific data which is only used in the context of the application domain. Examples of generic data are login data or user account data while examples of domain specific data could be flight or hotel data.

The bottom layer contains Ameli, the Electronic Institution runtime environment. The TCP port of the Ameli component is used to send all events that occur in the Electronic Institutions to the middleware. This also includes the actions of autonomous agents that run the Electronic Institutions. Depending on their roles, these agents have access to the data store and can access registration information, user profiles or domain specific data.

The Remote Server is responsible for the message exchange with external agents allowing them to participate in the Ameli system. A predefined communication protocol (which is specified in the Electronic Institutions Development Environment) enables the communication with external agents. Agents send action requests to the Remote Server which are then validated in the Ameli system according to the Electronic Institution specification. The Remote Server returns reply messages to the external agent.

Torque is running on the top layer following a client/server architecture. The server is running in dedicated mode controlling the state of the 3D Virtual World and observing the actions of the users. The server guarantees a consistent relationship with the Ameli system and changes the state of the 3D Virtual World if necessary. The connection between the Torque server and the middleware is used to exchange messages between these two layers.

The Torque client runs on the user's computer and is used to visualize the 3D Virtual World. When the client is started, a connection to the Torque server is established. The server and client run in different execution environments and may be distributed across several machines. In Figure 2, we can see that a user named Elaine has started the client and entered the 3D Virtual World with her avatar.

The middleware connects the upper layer with the lower layer. The connection to the Ameli system is used to listen to events that occur in this system and to enable the participation of user agents. The connection with the Torque layer is used to exchange messages with the Torque system. The user's agents are managed by the Agent Manager component. Every user in the 3D Virtual World is the principal of an agent in the Agent Manager. The connection between Elaine and her agent is depicted with a dotted line between the Torque client and the agent in Figure 2. Action requests from the user are sent to the middleware and forwarded to the user's agent in the Agent Manager component. These agents act as external agents and communicate with the Ameli system through the Remote Server.

Figure 3. The component interplay in the 3D e-business system

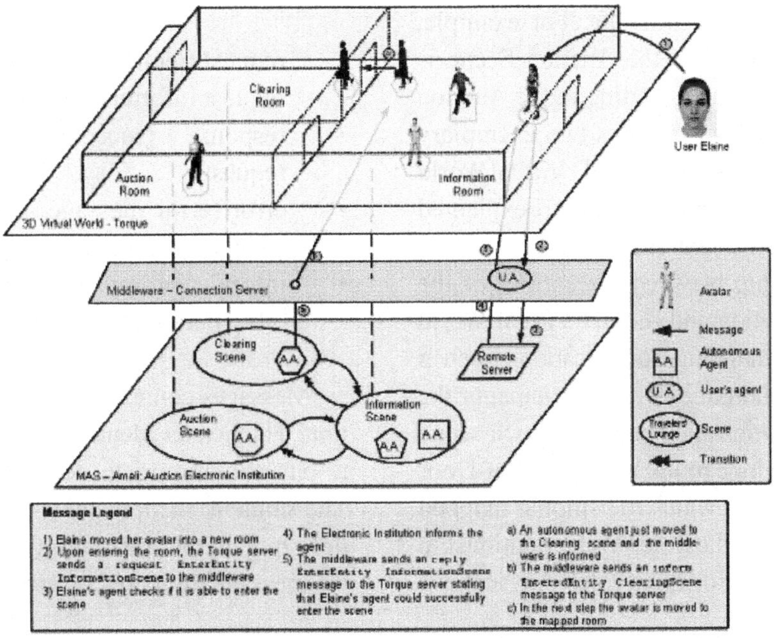

Connecting Electronic Institutions with 3D Virtual Worlds

To generate a mapping between entities of the 3D Virtual World and the Electronic Institution, two steps need to be carried out. First, a floor plan that specifies the layout of rooms and doors in the 3D Virtual World must be created. Second, the rooms and doors need to be linked to the entities of the Electronic Institution (scenes and transitions).

In a straightforward approach scenes are mapped onto rooms and transitions are mapped onto doors. This is illustrated in Figure 3, where the scenes of an Auction Electronic Institution are directly mapped onto rooms in the 3D Virtual World: the Information Scene is mapped onto the Information Room, the Auction Scene onto the Auction Room and the Clearing Scene onto the Clearing Room. If two scenes are connected in the Auction Electronic Institution, the corresponding rooms are connected by a door.

The 3D Virtual World in Figure 3 is populated by five avatars of which four are visual representations of autonomous agents and one avatar is controlled by Elaine. The relationship between agents in the Electronic Institution and the avatars in the 3D Virtual World is illustrated by the symbols underneath each avatar. For example, the autonomous agent in the Auction Scene is visualized by the avatar standing in the Auction Room. The figure also includes two exemplary message exchanges between the 3D Virtual World and the Electronic Institution. These are explained in more detail in the next Section.

The relationship between the entities of the Electronic Institution and the 3D Virtual World is defined in a mapping specification. Such a specification contains the following elements: the Scene-Room relationship specifies which scene is mapped onto which room, the Transition-Door relationship specifies which transition is mapped onto which door and the Role-Avatar relationship specifies visual cues for agent roles. A visual cue helps to visually identify the duties of a certain avatar. For example, the role of a sale agent might require the avatar to wear a specific work dress. The user is then able to easily identify a sales agent in the virtual world.

The mapping must be provided for each Electronic Institution individually and is defined in an XML document. This document is parsed by the Torque server in order to trigger the appropriate actions when a user moves between rooms. Furthermore, the Torque server uses the mapping information to appropriately visualize autonomous agents.

Message Protocol

Messages that are exchanged between the 3D Virtual World and the middleware layer are defined in a message protocol. These messages are organized in three different categories. Status messages are used to query Ameli about the current state of the system. Action messages are sent whenever an action takes place in the 3D Virtual World or in the Ameli system. Error messages are used to indicate a failure.

The message protocol is based on the following basic message types:

- request (request an action to be performed, request information)
- response (successful response to a request)
- error (error message, used as response to unsuccessful requests)
- inform (information message, inform the other part, no response is expected)

Messages contain a header and a content section. The header identifies the recipient in order to ensure appropriate delivery of the message. The content section holds the actual information. In general, the majority of the messages in the message protocol correspond to an event that

Listing 1. XML representation of an EnteredEntity message which is sent between the middleware and the 3D virtual world

```
<CS3DMessage id="32">
    <header>
        <particle>inform</particle>
        <platform>ItchyFeet</platform>
        <federation>ItchyFeet-Federation</federation>
        <ei>Auction</ei>
    </header>
    <content>
        <EnteredEntity direction="cs-3d">
                <entityType>scene</entityType>
                <name>InformationScene</name>
                <avatarid>Auctioneer</avatarid>
        </EnteredEntity>
    </content>
</CS3DMessage>
```

may occur in the Ameli system. The messages are used to abstract the events and to extract and forward only the relevant parts of each event. For example, if an autonomous agent enters a scene, the event EnteredSceneEvent occurs in Ameli. The middleware is notified that this event has happened and informs the 3D Virtual World with an inform EnteredEntity Scene message. The message protocol is implemented in XML and the XML representation of an EnteredEntity message is shown in Listing 1.

The communication between the middleware and the 3D Virtual World can be split into two different types of communication patterns.

First, the actions of autonomous agents must be visualized in the 3D Virtual World. To this end, the message protocol contains messages that are used to inform the 3D Virtual World about the movement or actions of agents. Examples of such messages are the different instances of EnteredEntity messages. They are used whenever an autonomous agent entered a certain entity in the Ameli system and the mapped avatar must perform a movement in the 3D Virtual World. In the case of an inform EnteredEntity Scene message, the autonomous agent entered a new scene and, as a consequence, the corresponding avatar must be moved to the mapped room in the 3D Virtual World. Whenever this message is received, the 3D Virtual World looks up in which room the scene is visualized and moves the avatar to the corresponding room.

An example of such a message exchange is shown in Figure 3 (messages a-c). In this example an autonomous agent has just entered the Clearing scene. The Ameli system sends out a message to the middleware layer (message a) which is forwarded to the corresponding avatar in the 3D Virtual World (message b). As a consequence, the avatar must be moved from the Information Room to the Clearing Room (message c).

Second, action requests by users must be validated in the Ameli system. Whenever a user performs an action in the 3D Virtual World, this action must be verified by her agent in the Ameli system. This communication consists of a request and a response message. Figure 3 exemplifies the use of these message types (messages 1-5). We can see that Elaine just entered the Information Room in the 3D Virtual World (message 1). Her corresponding agent also referred to as Controlled Agent must now move to the mapped scene in the Electronic Institution. For this reason a request EnterEntity InformationScene message is sent to the middleware (message 2). Elaine's Controlled Agent forwards the request to the Ameli layer where the agent tries to enter the Information Scene (message 3). The response is then sent to the agent (message 4) and forwarded to the 3D Virtual World by the agent (message 5).

If the agent could enter the scene the Ameli system reflects the same state as the 3D Virtual World. However, if the agent could not enter the scene, Elaine must leave the room in order to guarantee the consistent relationship between the system and its representation. This is resolved by teleporting the user out of the room.

Framework and User Administration

The management of users in the framework is accomplished by a dedicated Electronic Institution called Ether Electronic Institution. The Ether Electronic Institution is somewhat special, because it does not have a visual representation like the other Electronic Institutions in the framework. Services in the Ether Electronic Institution are accessible independent from a user's current location in the 3D Virtual World. The name is derived from the physical concept of Ether, a term used in ancient science to describe a medium that propagates light. The Ether was thought to be a substance above the clouds extending everywhere in space. In a similar manner, the Ether in our framework can be thought of as a medium that occupies every point in the 3D Virtual World.

In its general form, the Ether Electronic Institution provides services for user registration, user management and user login. Depending on the application domain of the 3D e-Business environment, additional functionalities can be added to the Ether Electronic Institution. For example, in a shopping related environment, the functionality of a shopping cart might be realized in the Ether Electronic Institution.

The administration of the framework can further be controlled by an Administration Tool. This tool enables administrators to start and stop the different components of the environment, to configure the system and to manipulate user accounts – i.e. user accounts can be created, modified and deleted. The administration interface of Itchy Feet is depicted in Figure 4. It contains a management for user accounts and has been extended by numerous other functions to be able to manipulate the domain specific data of Itchy Feet. The interplay of the interface with the other system components is shown in Figure 2.

Figure 4. The administration tool for the data model used in the framework

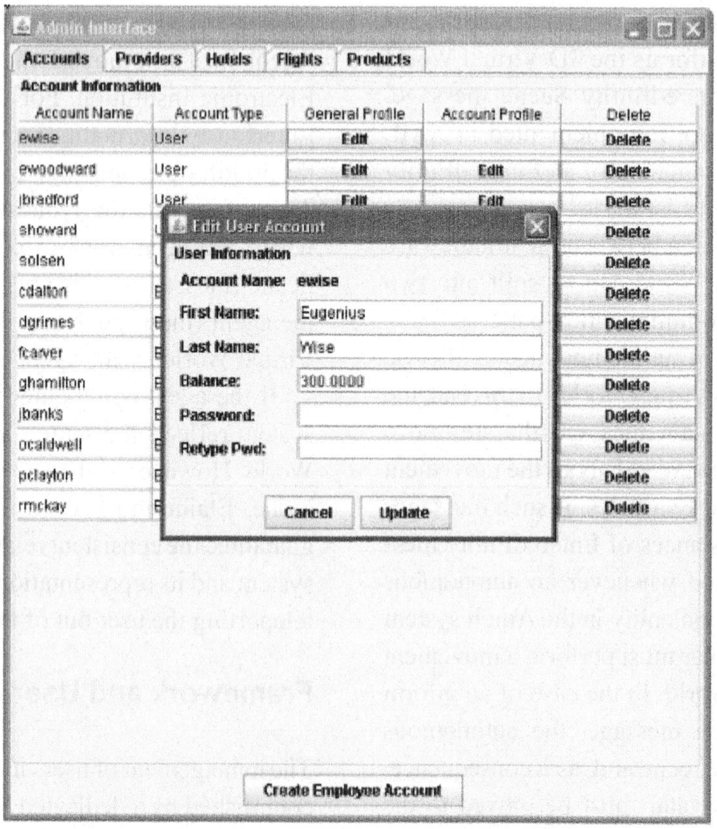

ITCHY FEET

The general e-Business framework is showcased by an application in the domain of tourism. This application is a trading environment where users can engage in the trade of tourism products through the interaction with software agents in the 3D Virtual World. The user is able to pass the whole process of purchasing a tourism good: from the search over the selection to the actual payment.

The landscape of Itchy Feet's 3D Virtual World is depicted in Figure 5. Itchy Feet is composed of three buildings connected by paths and the Ether. The Ether is a medium that surrounds users of Itchy Feet, providing location independent services to all users. Every building as well as the Ether is mapped onto an Electronic Institution in the Multi-Agent System layer. In the following we will give a description of the Electronic Institutions within Itchy Feet.

The Ether Electronic Institution

The Ether Electronic Institution is a validation and registration service. Every user who wants to participate within Itchy Feet has to register in the Ether Electronic Institution first. Every time a user logs into Itchy Feet her credentials are validated in the Ether Electronic Institution. The Ether Electronic Institution has three scenes: the Registration, the Validation and the Ether Scene.

The Registration and Validation Scenes implement the registration and validation service. The Ether Scene provides communication services and services for listing a user's inventory, shopping cart and profile. These services can be used inside and outside of any building in the 3D Virtual World. Figure 6 depicts the Performative Structure of the Ether Electronic Institution. The key symbols identify those agent roles that instantiate (open) new scenes. The different agent roles of the Ether Electronic Institution are shown in Table 1.

Figure 5. The landscape of Itchy Feet in the 3D virtual world

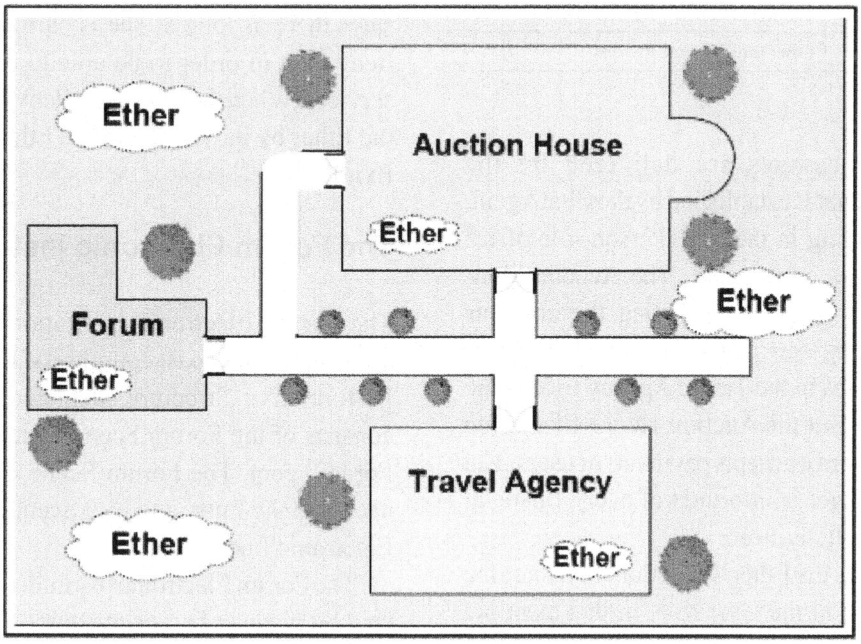

Figure 6. The performative structure of the ether electronic institution

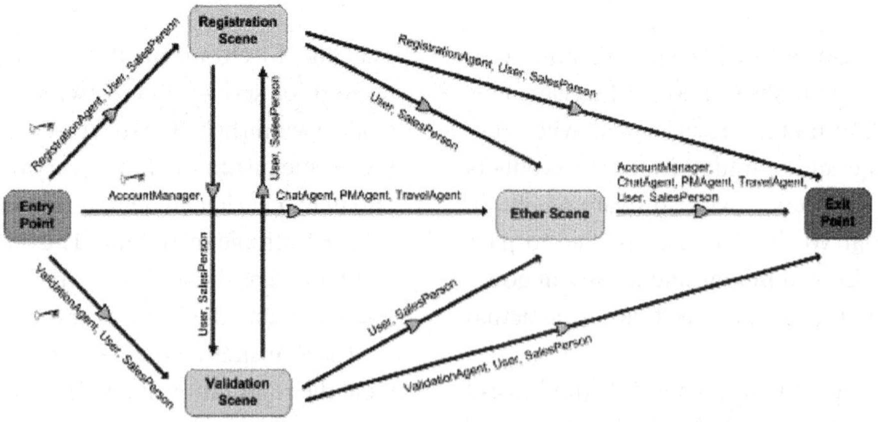

Table 1. The agent roles of the ether electronic institution

Agent role	Responsibilities
RegistrationAgent	Register new users
Validation Agent	Validate existing users
PMAgent	Deliver private messages between users
ChatAgent	Provide a chat facility to users
SalesPerson	Offer advice to users
User	Participant of Itchy Feet
AccountManager	Offer shopping cart and inventory administration services
TravelAgent	Offer travel advice to users

Private messages are delivered by the PMAgent. A chat is established by the ChatAgent. An agent playing in the SalesPerson role offers advice to users of the chat. The AccountManager provides services for listing the contents of the shopping cart and inventory. This agent also participates in the Travel Agency Electronic Institution and in the Auction House Electronic Institution where it accepts payments of users. The AccountManager is informed of every financial transaction in Itchy Feet.

To illustrate the Ether's functionality, imagine a user playing in the User role. In this example as well as in the upcoming examples we assume that all scenes of the Performative Structure have already been instantiated by their scene owners (marked with the key symbol). The User moves from the Entry Point to the Registration Scene and registers with the RegistrationAgent. The RegistrationAgent creates a new user account and profile. At every subsequent visit of Itchy Feet, the user will have to move to the Validation Scene instead of the Registration Scene to get her credentials validated and to gain access.

After the registration or validation procedure, the User moves directly to the Ether Scene. She stays there as long as she is participating within Itchy Feet in order to be able to use the Ether's services. When the User exits Itchy Feet she leaves the Ether by moving from the Ether Scene to the Exit Point.

The Forum Electronic Institution

The Forum Electronic Institution has only one scene and is the least complex of Itchy Feet. The Performative Structure, depicted in Figure 7, consists of the Forum Scene which is led by the ForumAgent. The Forum Scene is directly connected to the Entry and Exit Scenes of the Forum Electronic Institution.

The Forum Electronic Institution has been realized by means of an open source forum, namely jForum[9]. A Webservice has been implemented and

Figure 7. The performative structure of the forum electronic institution

exposes the main functions of the open source forum such as topic or thread creation to other software components. The ForumAgent uses a Webservice client to access these functions. Users solely interact with the ForumAgent, which forwards their requests to the actual forum. The different agent roles of the Forum Electronic Institution are shown in Table 2.

An agent playing in the DedicatedControlledAgent role provides information received from the ForumAgent to the public. Such an agent could be visualized as a panel in the 3D Virtual World where the most current or most interesting threads of the forum are displayed.

To illustrate the Forum's functionality, imagine an user playing in the User role. The user moves from the Entry Point straight to the Forum Scene. In the Forum Scene, the user queries the ForumAgent about the latest threads. She browses the threads and wants to comment on a certain discussion. A request to create a new forum posting is sent to the ForumAgent which creates the posting in the external web forum. The user then leaves the Forum Scene and moves to the Exit Point.

Table 2. The agent roles of the forum electronic institution

Agent role	Responsibilities
ForumAgent	Pass-through services of jForum
DedicatedControlledAgent	Provide information from the ForumAgent to the public
User	Participant of the Forum

The Travel Agency Electronic Institution

The Travel Agency Electronic Institution offers fixed price products. Customers may book flights, hotel rooms or all inclusive tours. The Travel Agency's Performative Structure is depicted in Figure 8.

In the Information Scene customers can inform themselves about products that are sold within the institution. Three Sale Scenes have been implemented for advising customers individually. Every Sale Scene is equipped with a SalesPerson, an external human travel agent, who shares its knowledge and expertise with customers helping them to establish a customized travel arrangement. Flights or hotel rooms can be booked in the Booking Scene and are paid in the Clearing Scene. Product information is conveyed to the Travel Agency by using a database and external data from travel agencies on the Internet. A customer performing a search in the Travel Agency will get product results from the Auction House as well. The payment is performed by credit card in the institution's Clearing Scene. The different agent roles of the Travel Agency Electronic Institution are shown in Table 3.

An agent playing either in the HotelDataFetcher or FlightDataFetcher role provides the Travel Agency with hotel and room data from external providers. When a user performs a search, the InformationAssistant agent will query one of these agents to get corresponding data from registered external providers. This data is aggregated and

Figure 8. Performative structure of the travel agency electronic institution

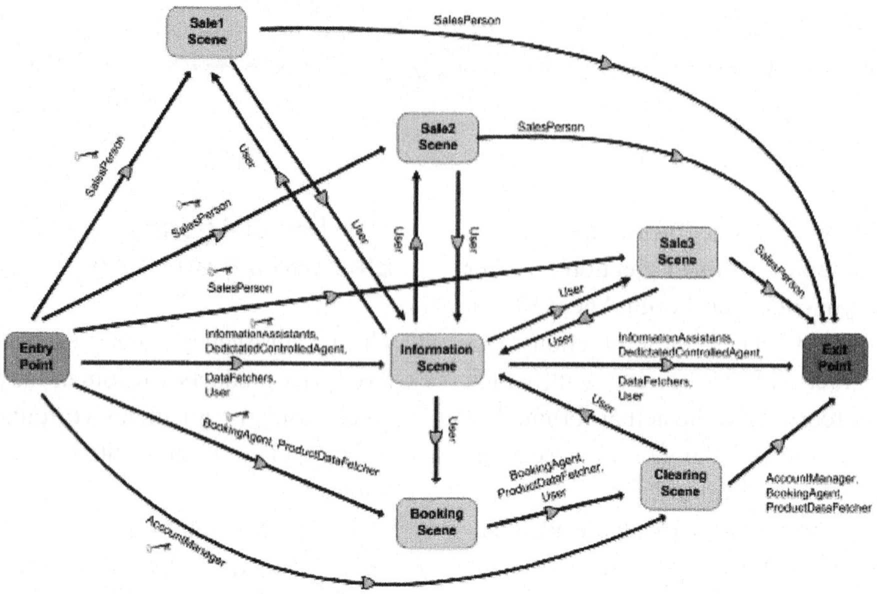

Table 3. The agent roles of the travel agency electronic institution

Agent role	Responsibilities
HotelDataFetcher	Fetch hotel and room data from external providers
FlightDataFetcher	Fetch flight data from external providers
ProductDataFetcher	Fetch detailed product information from external providers
HotelInformationAssistant	Provide hotel and room information to users
FlightInformationAssistant	Provide flight information to users
BookingAgent	Offer booking services to users
SalesPerson	Offer advice to users
AccountManager	Offer payment services to users
DedicatedControlledAgent	Offer hotel, room and flight data to the public
User	Participant of the Travel Agency

combined with existing hotel and flight data in the internal database and returned to the user.

A user who is undecided about her travel plans can move to one of the Sale Scenes and get advice from a SalesPerson. If a user spots a flight or hotel she is interested in, the product can be booked in the Booking Scene. To buy the flight or hotel arrangement a user moves to the Clearing Scene and settles the invoice with the AccountManager. An agent playing in the DedicatedControlledAgent role provides flight and hotel arrangements offered in the Travel Agency to the public, for example by means of a ticker.

To demonstrate the functionality of the Travel Agency, consider a user playing in the User role. Starting at the Entry Point the user moves to the Information Scene. In the Information Scene the user decides to move to the Sale2 Scene to get advice on traveling to Scotland. Well informed the user leaves the current scene and heads back to the Information Scene where she queries the FlightInformationAssistant about flights to Scotland. Having indentified a suitable flight, the user moves to the Booking Scene and books the flight. The flight is then paid in the Clearing Scene and the user leaves the Electronic Institution by moving to the Exit Point.

The Auction House Electronic Institution

In the Auction House Electronic Institution, flight and hotel room arrangements are auctioned. The Performative Structure, depicted in Figure 9, shares similarities with the Travel Agency.

The Auction House's Offering Scene is the central meeting place for the OfferManager, the DataScouts, the Auctioneers and the InformationTransferAssistent. DataScouts register products that have been fetched from the internal database with the OfferManager. The OfferManager then contacts the Auctioneers to sell them. Demand and supply is overseen by the OfferManager, which may instruct DataScout agents to bring in new products. The InformationTransferAssistant moves between the Information and the Offering Scene to provide the latest product information to the InformationAssistants.

The Information Scene is populated with Users and InformationAssistants. Users may query InformationAssistants about currently offered products. The products are auctioned in one of the three English Auction Scenes. Every auction scene is populated with an agent playing in the Auctioneer role and several users playing in the Customer role. A user changes its role from User to Customer as soon as she enters the Auction Scene. If a user has purchased a product, she has to move to the Clearing Scene to pay for it. The Clearing Scene is led by the AccountManager which accepts payment and assigns the ownership of a product to a customer. The different agent roles of the Auction House and their responsibilities are summed up in Table 4.

To illustrate the functionality of the Auction House, consider a user playing in the User role. Starting at the Entry Point, the user moves to the Information Scene and informs herself about ongoing auctions. An auction for a flight to Ibiza is held in the English Auction Scene 2. The user

Figure 9. The performative structure of the auction house electronic institution

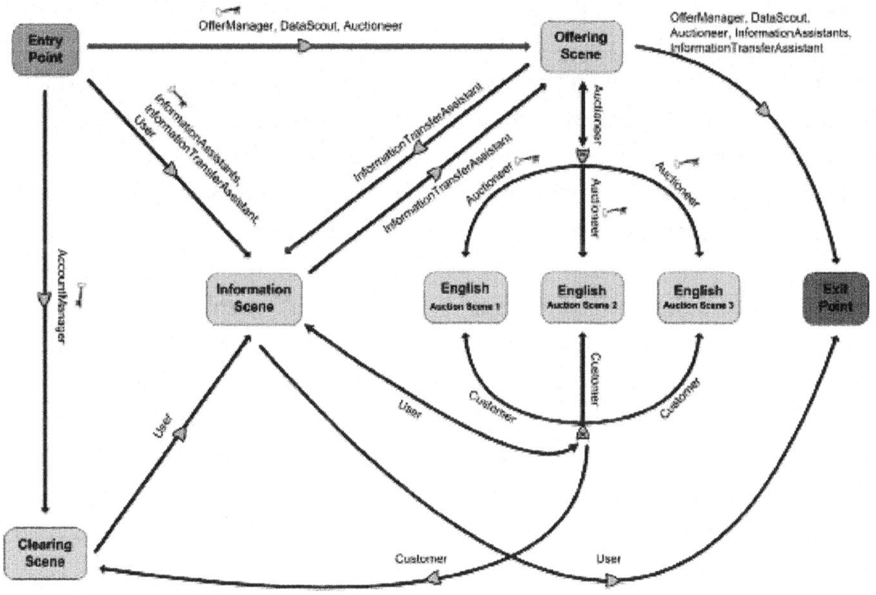

Table 4. The agent roles of the auction house electronic institution

Agent role	Responsibilities
OfferManager	Oversee demand and supply, instruct DataFetcher agents
Auctioneer	Lead auctions
DataScouts	Fetch detailed product information from external providers
HotelInformationAssistant	Provide hotel and room information to users
FlightInformationAssistant	Provide flight information to users
InformationTransferAssistant	Transfer information between Information and Offering Scene
AccountManager	Offer booking services to users
DedicatedControledAgent	Offer hotel, room and flight data to the public
User	Participant of the Auction House

is interested in travel arrangements for Ibiza and directly moves to this scene. In the English Auction Scene 2 the user engages in the auction, bids several times and is finally announced the winner. The user then moves to the Clearing Scene where she pays for the product and the ownership is transferred to the user.

The 3D Virtual World

The 3D Virtual World of Itchy Feet provides a visual representation of the presented Electronic Institutions. Except for the Ether Electronic Institution, the functionality of an Electronic Institution is within the scope of a building in the 3D Virtual World. Auctions can be performed in the Auction building, information gathering and product trade takes place in the Travel Agency building and participation in the forum is possible in the Forum building. The buildings have entry and exit doors and contain rooms that are connected via doors.

The Forum building contains one room, since all the functionality of the Forum Electronic Institution is provided in one scene. In this room, the user can launch a 2D forum interface and is able to browse the forum, create posts and start new threads. The forum interface is displayed in Figure 10. Elaine has started the forum interface and is currently showing the "Car rental in Romania" thread. She can engage in the conversation by entering a new message in a message box at the bottom of the list. Furthermore, the most interesting discussions will be projected onto walls where they can be read and followed by multiple users simultaneously.

The Auction building contains four rooms: an Information room, three Auction rooms and a Clearing room. In the Information room upcoming auctions are displayed, the three Auction rooms are used to conduct auctions and in the Clearing room products are paid. A user participates in an auction by entering the current bid into an input box and confirming the bid. The current state of the auction is broadcast to all participants and displayed on the user's interface. When a user wins an auction, the product is placed in her shopping cart and can be paid in the Clearing room. The payment information is entered via a 2D input mask. When the product has been paid, it is transferred to the user's inventory.

In the Travel Agency building information facilities are available and the trade of fixed price products takes place. The building consists of four rooms whereof three rooms are Sale rooms and one room is the main Information room. In the Sale rooms, users can get professional help from travel agents that are also logged in the 3D Virtual

Figure 10. The forum interface in the forum building

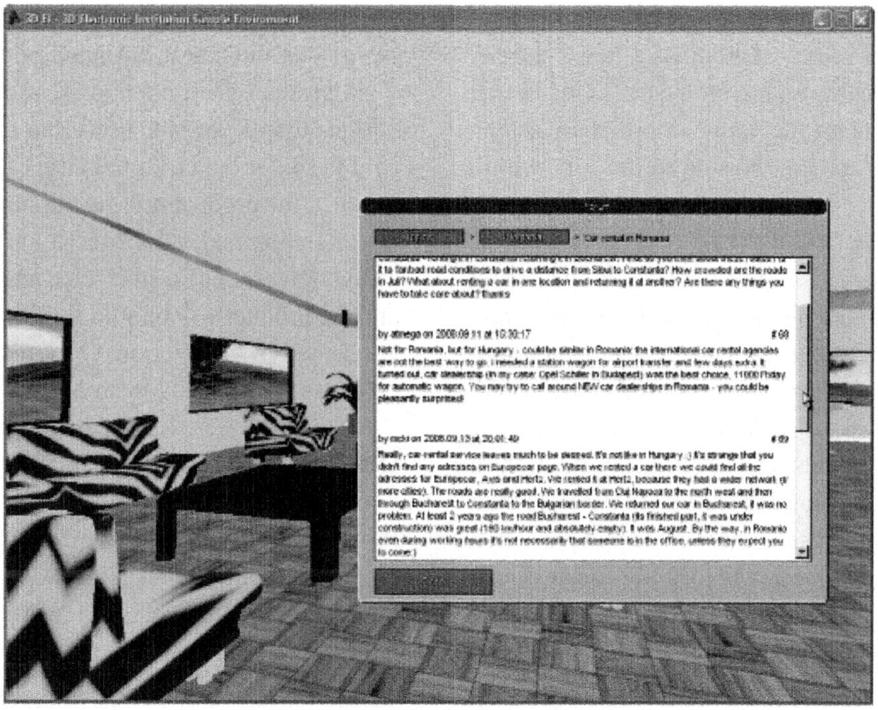

World and are represented as avatars. Similar to a travel agency, a user can directly interact with another human being, ask specific questions and let the travel agent take care of the booking. In the main Information room, the user is able to search for tourism products. The search facilities are 2D interfaces in which the query is entered and the aggregated results are presented in a list-style manner. Products that have been selected by the user are placed in the user's shopping cart. The payment of products is similar to the Auction building; the payment information is entered by the user via an input mask. As soon as the products have been paid, they are transferred from the cart to the user's inventory.

Trading

The current version of the prototype supports two different kinds of products: flights and hotels. A hotel product represents a reservation for a hotel room while a flight product represents a seat reservation for a certain flight. Furthermore, products can be distinguished by two additional attributes.

The first attribute defines how a product is sold. A product is either a fixed price product or an auction product. A fixed price product is sold for a fixed price in the Travel Agency building while an auction product is sold via an English auction in the Auction building.

The second attribute defines how products are added to the system. A product is either added manually to the system or via a third party product data provider. Products can be added manually with the Administration Tool - a wizard is used to define the attributes and content of the product. Alternatively, products are created automatically based on real world product information of third party tourism product providers.

When the user searches for a certain kind of product, e.g. a hotel room in Vienna, the software agents in the Ameli system query several hotel search interfaces on the Internet. The search results are merged and presented to the user in the 3D Virtual World. If the user decides to buy one of the externally retrieved products, a new "virtual" product is created within the system. This virtual product contains the same information as the external one and can be sold to the user within the system.

The product purchase process is the same as in known interfaces. The user enters the Travel Agency building in the 3D Virtual World and issues a search request. The request is then sent to the user's Controlled Agent which issues the request in the Ameli system. This triggers the autonomous agents to search for information in the internal database as well as in external data sources. All the results are merged and presented to the user in a coherent format. The user can browse the list and select certain offers that are placed in the user's shopping cart.

In a similar fashion to a real world store, the products are to be paid at a counter before the user leaves the building. The user is not allowed to leave the building if unpaid products remain in the shopping cart. The paying process is conducted with a credit card. The user enters the credit card information and the products move from the shopping cart to the user's inventory. If the user decided to buy a product that has been retrieved from an external data source, a new virtual product is created in the internal database. The creation process in the internal database is delayed until this moment in order to avoid a creation overhead and to only create products that are really needed internally.

The representation of products within the system closely resembles the way how tourism products are managed in the real world. We use the concept of room and flight contingents that can be purchased by so called providers.

A provider is a company that buys room contingents from hotels or seat contingents from air line companies and sells them to customers. The provider pays a fixed amount for a certain contingent and defines the prices for individual rooms and seats. In our model, a room or seat can only be sold if it is contained in the contingent of a provider and has an assigned price.

A product itself contains seat or room reservations identifying the seats and rooms that are sold in this product. In the case of a fixed price product, the product price is the sum of all rooms or seats contained in the reservation. In the case of an auction product, a start price has to be defined and the product will be sold for the end price that is reached in the auction. Only manually added products may be sold in an auction.

User Profiles

Profiles are one of the cornerstones of most successful and popular social networking sites like Facebook[10] or MySpace[11]. A profile is a concise representation of a user's personality and interests, allowing other users to easily get an impression of the person behind the nickname/avatar.

In Itchy Feet we also support profiles. They are filled out upon registration and can be modified later from within the 3D Virtual World. The profiles contain personal information like name, age or nationality and more touristic related information like traveler type, favorite countries or traveled countries. The Controlled Agent stores the profiles on the middleware layer and controls access to them. Hence, the Controlled Agent defines which other software agents/components are allowed to access which kind of information. A property that is especially important in the case of confidential information like credit card numbers.

Participation

This Section aims to give a general overview of the functionalities of the Itchy Feet platform by attending Elaine who visits the different places within the 3D Virtual World. Before she is able to visit the platform, Elaine must complete the registration process and is then able to use her personalized alter ego represented as a 3D character.

When Elaine walks around in the 3D Virtual World, her Controlled Agent performs the same movements in the Electronic Institution. We will illustrate how Elaine's agent moves around in the Electronic Institution and show which entities are entered and exited. Elaine will then post a question in the message forum and we will show how the message is sent to the ForumAgent in the Forum Electronic Institution.

In detail, users participate in the Itchy Feet system via the 3D front end, i.e. the 3D Virtual World. Currently we support two different types of user roles which are customer and employee. A customer is the common type of user that participates in the system to gather information, socialize with other users and purchase products. An employee works for a certain provider and can offer professional help to customers seeking for certain information or products. An employee is much like a travel agent in a travel agency.

The Login Procedure

The first time a user connects to the 3D Virtual World, she is guided through a series of screens where a user name has to be chosen and personal information about this user is gathered. A customer account can be created by anyone, while an employee account must already exist in the system before an employee connects for the first time. Upon finishing the registration, a new Controlled Agent is instantiated and associated with the new user. The entered data is stored by the Controlled Agent on the middleware layer, which also controls access to this data. Further, this Controlled Agent is used to represent the user within the Ameli system.

When the user has finished the registration phase or logs into the system, she is spawned as a new avatar in the 3D Virtual World. At the same time the Controlled Agent enters the Ameli system

Figure 11. The user Elaine has entered the 3D virtual world which triggered her controlled agent to enter the Ether Electronic Institution

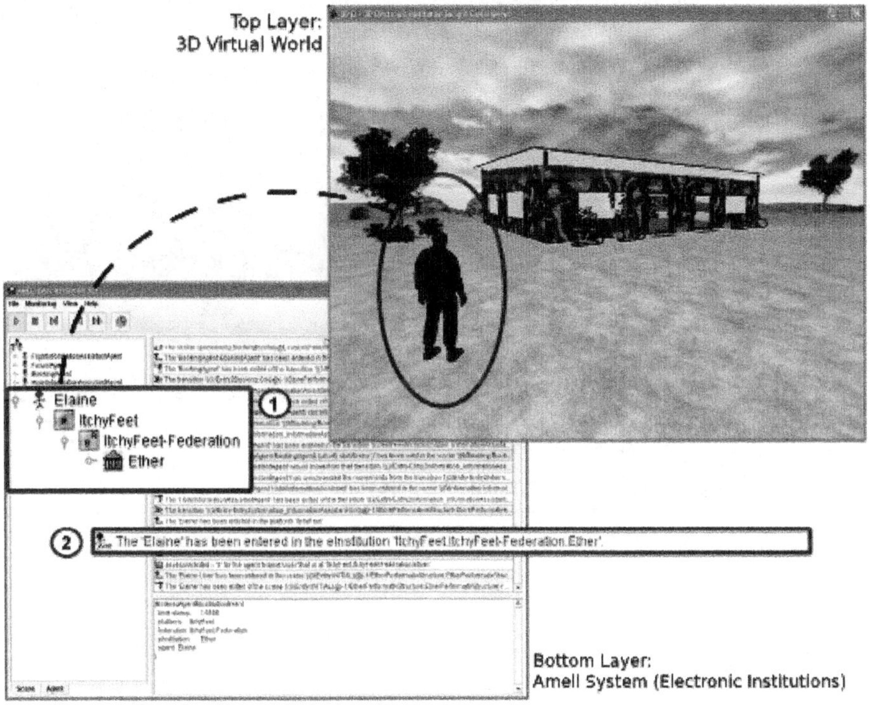

and also moves into the Ether Electronic Institution. This process is illustrated in Figure 11. The Figure shows the 3D Virtual World in the upper right corner and a monitoring tool of the Ameli system in the lower left corner.

The monitoring tool displays the current state of the Ameli system. In the left part all the agents that are currently present in the system are shown. In Ameli, Electronic Institutions are organized according to a three layered structure. An Electronic Institution is executed within a Federation, which is executed within a Platform. In the monitoring tool we can see that Elaine's agent has entered the Platform "ItchyFeet", the Federation "ItchyFeet-Federation" and the Electronic Institution "Ether". All the messages that have occurred in Ameli are shown in a list in the right part. In the area below the list, more detailed information for selected messages is displayed.

As can be seen in Figure 11, Elaine has been spawned in the 3D Virtual World as a new avatar. Note that Elaine is a gender bender and has selected a male avatar. The monitoring tool shows that her Controlled Agent has entered the system (1) and is now participating in the Ether Electronic Institution (1,2).

Moving Around in the 3D Virtual World

The avatar movement is controlled by the keyboard and the looking direction is controlled via the mouse. In the 3D Virtual World the user is able to either perform actions that are permitted in the Ether Electronic Institution or she can walk around in the world and enter one of the three buildings.

The user can enter a building by pressing a certain key when standing in front of a door. The

Figure 12. The user Elaine has moved into the forum building which triggered her controlled agent to enter the Forum Electronic Institution

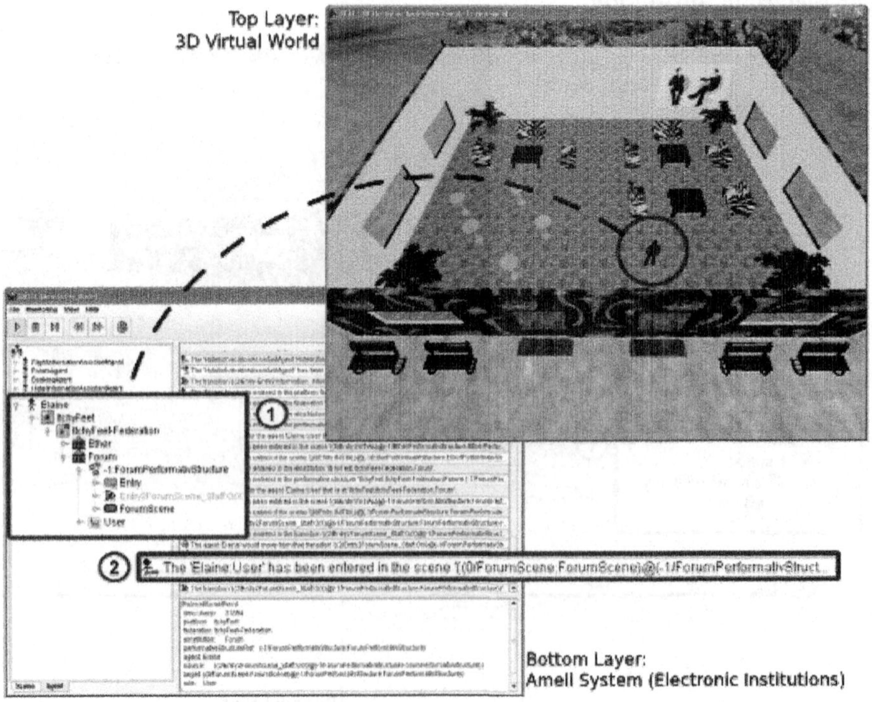

door will open and the user can enter the building. As soon as the building has been entered by the user, the Controlled Agent tries to enter the Electronic Institution that is mapped onto this building. Depending on the user's movement within the building, the Controlled Agent "follows the movement" in the Electronic Institution and tries to enter scenes and transitions.

This process is exemplified in Figure 12. Elaine has just entered the Forum building in the 3D Virtual World and is now standing inside the building. In order to maintain the consistent relationship with the Ameli system, Elaine's Controlled Agent must enter the Forum Electronic Institution. This action has been executed successfully and Elaine's agent is now also present in the Forum Electronic Institution (1) and has entered the Forum Scene (2) in this Electronic Institution.

Entering a Building

Inside a building, the user is able to execute the business processes that have been defined in the underlying Electronic Institution. In the case of the Forum building, the functionalities are defined in the Forum Electronic Institution. According to the Electronic Institution specification, a user is able to view threads and postings, can create new threads and is able to post messages.

These functions are realized in the 3D Virtual World via a 2D forum interface. Upon launching the interface, a request for the forum topics is sent to the user's Controlled Agent, which, in turn, sends a request to the ForumAgent for the currently available topics. The message is returned to the 3D Virtual World by the Controlled Agent and the topics are listed in the forum interface. The user is then able to browse the topics, show the threads of a topic and show the postings of a thread. The respective thread or post information is also retrieved via the user's Controlled Agent and the ForumAgent. The same applies to the creation of new threads and posts.

In Figure 13, Elaine has launched the forum interface and is currently viewing the topic "Romania" and the thread "Car rental in Romania". The posts of the thread are displayed in a scrollable list. A new post can be created via the text area at the bottom of the list. Elaine has just entered a new message and presses the button "Post Message" (1). A post creation request is sent to her Controlled Agent. The agent sends the message "post" to the ForumAgent in the Ameli system (2,3). The message is processed by the ForumAgent and a new post is created in the external web forum.

DISCUSSION

The presented framework utilizes ideas from different research approaches to create a new type of interactive social community platform. A 3D Virtual World is used to overcome the lack of human warmth and social presence which is often perceived in traditional online e-Commerce web sites. In a 3D Virtual World the awareness of other users is more explicit and the metaphors are more similar to the real world. These similarities might help users to engage in conversations and other familiar communication mechanisms, such as gestures, can be used as well.

The social presence that is established can help to increase the trust and loyalty of users into the e-Commerce system. A property that is especially crucial in e-Tourism systems where the quality of a product cannot easily be assessed and the customer needs to build up a trust relationship to the provider. In this context, the 3D Virtual World also enables new forms of product presentation through the visualization of a product in a 3D space. This can range from replications of hotel rooms over tourism destinations to material products such as backpacks or camping gear. The product can be experienced in more depth and the customer is able to get insights that might not have been possible with other presentation formats.

Figure 13. The user Elaine is posting a message in the forum building, her controlled agent is uttering the message in the Forum Electronic Institution

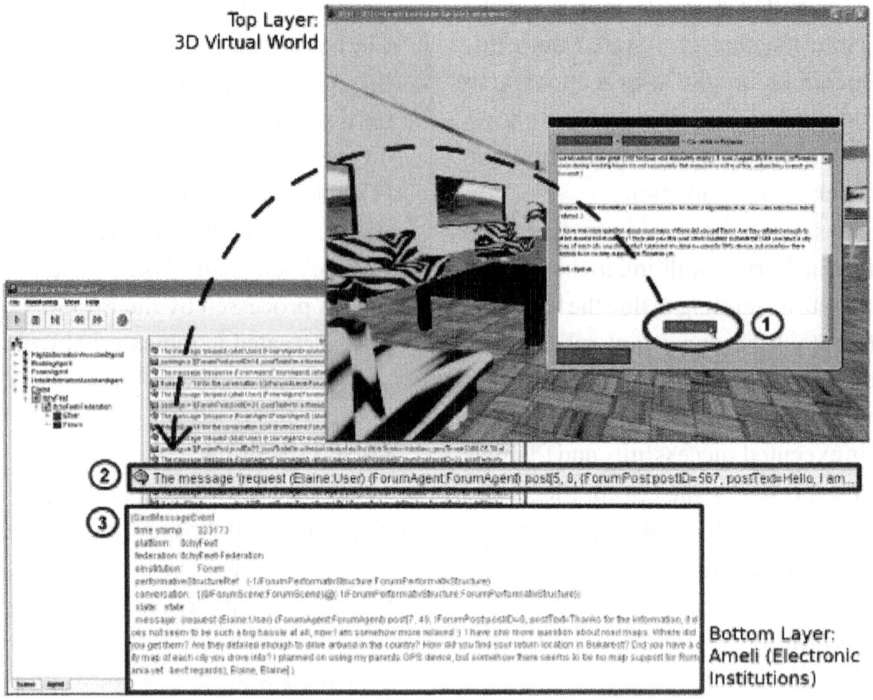

Electronic Institutions

The security of the system is warranted through Electronic Institutions. The business processes as well as the permitted actions of all participants are rigorously defined and verified by Electronic Institutions. Again, this is useful for building up a trust relationship between customer and provider and is advantageous for both parties. The customer can be sure that sensitive information and money transactions are handled correctly and the provider has the guarantee that only paid products are sold.

In the Electronic Institution software agents are responsible to carry out defined tasks within the limits of the formal specification. Besides being responsible for business transactions, software agents are used to fulfill additional functions. They carry out the tasks of information retrieval, aggregation and presentation as well. This further helps to satisfy the information demand of the customer and provides additional information for making a well-grounded buying decision.

Online Communities

The online community is a channel for the provision of up-to date touristic information and helps to create an active user base. One of the major future challenges within the project will be the development of strategies for fostering a lively society and establishing a successful online community. It is crucial to follow a certain strategy when developing an online community and to know which kind of community should be established.

In the area of community research three prevalent terms and conditions are defined: Community of Practice, Community of Interest and Community of Knowledge (Lindstaedt, 1998; Lave & Wenger, 1991). In the Community of

Interest social interaction and communication are the central aspects. In contrast, the Community of Knowledge is basically knowledge-oriented, is created within corporations and is not voluntary. The Community of Practice is defined as the concept of apprenticeship. It is a practice oriented consortium that focuses on the development of knowledge and methods to solve problems based on a communication process between apprentice, who asks a question and the supervisor who knows the answer.

When an online tourism community follows the Community of Interest approach it is usually created by individuals to share the collective interests of travelling, while in the Community of Practice approach the community is mostly business-initiated and focuses on the provision of knowledge. In this regard the business-initiated tourism community in Itchy Feet should be developed using the proven concept of Community of Practice to fulfill the aim of developing collective tourism knowledge. It consists of five phases of development as well as the promotion of a well-running community platform (Wenger, McDermott, & Snyder, 2002).

A Community of Practice comprises of three components: domain, community and practice. The domain is the common body of knowledge. The members of the community agree to the constraints of the domain, and decide which activities and content are relevant. The community is comprised of the social interaction between community members. The practice is defined by the concept of apprenticeship as described before.

A Community of Practice is developed in five phases. In the first phase one or more persons attend to a certain topic. In the second phase the basic structure, the tasks and communication channels are defined. The third phase is the main phase. It is characterized by the knowledge exchange and the evaluation of the aims, tasks and communication channels. In the fourth phase the knowledge exchange eventually results in community members no longer carrying out any activities within the community. Finally, in the fifth phase there is no further demand for information and the Community of Practice ceases to be an information exchange. In order to counteract the fourth and fifth phases a concept has been developed to make sustainable online communities: Design for evolution, open a dialogue between inside and outside perspectives, offer different levels of participation, develop both public and private places, focus on value, combine familiarity and excitement and create a rhythm for the community (Wenger, McDermott, & Snyder, 2002).

TECHNICAL DISCUSSION AND OPPORTUNITIES FOR FUTURE RESEARCH

The realization of the environment was started with the implementation of the general framework connecting arbitrary Electronic Institutions with 3D Virtual Worlds. A middleware layer had been developed for the message exchange between the two systems and for the control of the user's agent. The Torque game engine was extended to communicate with the middleware layer, to observe and control the user's movements and to control the visualization of autonomous agents. Originally it was planned that the framework is flexible enough to support an easy change of the 3D Virtual World. However, it turned out that the 3D Virtual World needed more additional functionality than we had initially thought. As we had already implemented these features in the Torque game engine, we decided to concentrate on this game engine and make it the primary 3D Virtual World for the framework.

After finishing a proof of concept implementation of the general framework, we focused on e-Tourism as specific application domain and started with the development of Itchy Feet. After a thorough requirements analysis and design, we implemented the domain specific data model and the Administration Tool to manage this data. At the same time, the Electronic Institutions were specified. By now the following features have been implemented:

- Tourism specific data model (e.g. including flights, hotels, contingents)
- Administration Tool for the management of the data model and configuration of the components
- Specification of all Electronic Institutions
- General Framework
- Forum Electronic Institution (agents, visualization, data binding to external open source forum)
- User participation in the 3D Virtual World and in the forum

Currently we are working on the implementation of the software agents and the visualization of the Electronic Institutions in the 3D Virtual World. The final application will include the following features:

- Implementation and visualization of all Electronic Institutions
- Users have access to all Electronic Institution functionalities in the 3D Virtual World
- Product search and purchase in the 3D Virtual World
- Community features – chat, profiles, instant messaging
- Support of multiple users
- Visualization of travel destinations and tourism products (e.g. hotel rooms)

In the process of development we encountered some restrictions and problems. The Ameli infrastructure and the Electronic Institutions Development Environment (EIDE) contain some bugs that occurred during development. The Agent Builder has problems with generating source code out of an agent specification and has difficulties with reading certain Electronic Institution specifications correctly. Sometimes the wrong scene or transition shows up when an agent's functionality is defined. The Islander, a tool to specify Electronic Institutions, has a saving issue and sometimes overwrites previously defined specifications with the current one.

The Torque game engine also turned out to be not as suitable as we had expected and contains some restrictions. The engine only provides very basic data structures and in order to use more sophisticated ones, the engine has to be manually patched and adapted. The editors are not a separate product but are mangled into the game engine and script code base. Thus, when custom changes are applied to the engine or the engine is updated, the editors can be affected of these changes and some functions may become inaccessible or the editors even stop functioning completely. Furthermore, it is difficult to add 3D content to the world as Torque requires models to have a certain structure that must be manually created in a 3D graphics application. Several other Torque internals have complicated the development even further.

CONCLUSION

In this chapter we have presented the concept of a 3D e-Business environment combining Electronic Institutions with 3D Virtual Worlds. Electronic Institutions are used to regulate the environment and to provide a framework for software agents. These software agents render the environment information rich with the ability to collect, aggregate and present data. Furthermore, they assist the user in the 3D Virtual World, help her to understand the environment and autonomously process tasks that the user has delegated to them. The 3D Virtual World provides familiar surroundings for users where the same metaphors apply as in the real world. Social interaction is implicitly addressed in such environments and the 3D Virtual World shall help to establish a lively community.

This general framework has been applied to the tourism domain in the Itchy Feet project. The proposed environment offers several advantages over traditional tourism information systems. The creation of a tourism community is in line with the current trend in ICT, where customers are using online communities to share knowledge and to get information on travel destinations. Furthermore, information needs are satisfied by software agents that collect and present information to the customer in the 3D Virtual World. The 3D presentation of products enables customers to get better insights on the final product; a feature that is especially important in the tourism domain where products usually cannot be tested in advance.

The acceptance of the developed system will be tested in a usability study. For this study we are going to create an evaluation framework for 3D Virtual Worlds. The basic framework will be general enough to also be used in other 3D Virtual World evaluations. A more specific version will be created that is tailored at the tourism domain and captures domain specific properties more accurately.

ACKNOWLEDGMENT

This work is funded by the FWF Austrian Science Fund (project reference: L363).

REFERENCES

Adobbati, R., Marshall, A. N., Scholer, A., Tejada, S., Kaminka, G., Schaffer, S., & Sollitto, C. (2002). Gamebots: A 3D virtual world test-bed for multi-agent research. *Communications of the ACM*, *45*(1), 43–45.

Aldewereld, H., Dignum, F., Garcia-Camino, A., Noriega, P., Rodriguez-Aguilar, J. A., & Sierra, C. (2006). Operationalisation of norms for usage in electronic institutions. In *Proceedings of the 5th international joint conference on Autonomous agents and multiagent systems (AAMAS '06)* (pp. 223-225). New York: ACM Press.

Berger, H., Dittenbach, M., & Merkl, D. (2004). User-oriented evaluation of a natural language tourism information system. *Information Technology and Tourism*, *6*(3), 167–180. doi:10.3727/1098305031436953

Bogdanovych, A., Berger, H., Simoff, S., & Sierra, C. (2006). Travel agents vs. online booking: Tackling the shortcomings of nowadays online tourism portals. In *Proceedings of the 13th International Conference on Information Technologies in Tourism (ENTER'06)* (pp. 418-428). Vienna, Austria: Springer-Verlag.

Castronova, E. (2005). *Synthetic worlds: The business and culture of online games*. Chicago: University of Chicago Press.

Chao, D. L. (2001). Doom as an interface for process management. In *Proceedings of the SIGCHI Conference on Human Factors in Computing Systems (CHI '01)* (pp. 152-157). New York: ACM Press.

Chiu, D. K., & Leung, H. (2005). Towards ubiquitous tourist service coordination and integration: A multi-agent and semantic web approach. In *Proceedings of the 7th International Conference on Electronic Commerce (ICEC '05)* (pp. 574-581). New York: ACM Press.

Cuni, G., Esteva, M., Garcia, P., Puertas, E., Sierra, C., & Solchaga, T. (2004). MASFIT: Multi-agent system for fish trading. In *Proceedings of the 16th European Conference on Artificial Intelligence (ECAI '04)* (pp. 710-714). Amsterdam, Netherlands: IOS Press.

Cyr, D., Hassanein, K., Head, M., & Ivanov, A. (2007). The role of social presence in establishing loyalty. *Interacting with Computers, 19*(1), 43–56. doi:10.1016/j.intcom.2006.07.010

Dignum, F. (2002). Abstract norms and electronic institutions. In *Proceedings of the International Workshop on Regulated Agent-Based Social Systems: Theories and Applications (RASTA '02)* (pp. 93-104).

Dignum, V., & Dignum, F. (2001). Modelling agent societies: Co-ordination frameworks and institutions. In *Proceedings of the 10th Portuguese Conference on Artificial Intelligence: Progress in Artificial Intelligence Knowledge Extraction, Multi-Agent Systems, Logic Programming, and Constraint Solving (EPIA '01)* (pp. 191-204). London: Springer-Verlag.

Dignum, V., Weigand, H., & Xu, L. (2001). Agent societies: Towards frameworks-based design. In M. Wooldridge, G. Weiß, & P. Ciancarini (Eds.), *Revised Papers and Invited Contributions from the Second International Workshop on Agent-Oriented Software Engineering II* (pp. 33-49). London: Springer-Verlag.

DiPaola, S., & Collins, D. (2003). A social metaphor-based 3D virtual environment. In *Proceedings of the International Conference on Computer Graphics and Interactive Techniques (SIGGRAPH '03)* (pp. 1-2). New York: ACM.

Dippelreiter, B., Grün, C., Pöttler, M., Seidel, I., Berger, H., Dittenbach, M., & Pesenhofer, A. (in press). Online tourism communities on the path to Web 2.0 - an evaluation. *Information Technology and Tourism.*

Eigner, C., Leitner, H., & Nausner, P. (2003). *Online-communities, Weblogs und die soziale rückeroberung des netzes.* Graz, Austria: Nausner & Nausner.

Esteva, M., Rodriguez-Aguilar, J. A., Sierra, C., Garcia, P., & Arcos, J. L. (2001). On the formal specifications of electronic institutions. In F. Dignum & C. Sierra (Eds.), *Agent mediated electronic commerce, the European AgentLink perspective* (pp. 126-147). London, UK: Springer-Verlag.

Finin, T., Fritzson, R., McKay, D., & McEntire, R. (1994). KQML as an agent communication language. In *Proceedings of the Third International Conference on Information and Knowledge Management (CIKM '94)* (pp. 456-463). New York: ACM.

Gratzer, M., Werthner, H., & Winiwarter, W. (2004). Electronic business in tourism. *International Journal of Electronic Business, 2*(5), 450–459. doi:10.1504/IJEB.2004.005878

Hassanein, K., & Head, M. (2007). Manipulating perceived social presence through the Web interface and its impact on attitude towards online shopping. *International Journal of Human-Computer Studies, 65*(8), 689–708. doi:10.1016/j.ijhcs.2006.11.018

Hunicke, R., LeBlanc, M., & Zubek, R. (2004). *MDA: A formal approach to game design and game research.* Paper presented at the AAAI Workshop on Challenges in Game AI, San Jose, CA.

Juan, T., Pearce, A., & Sterling, L. (2002). ROADMAP: Extending the gaia methodology for complex open systems. In *Proceedings of the First International joint Conference on Autonomous Agents and Multiagent Systems (AAMAS '02)* (pp. 3-10). New York: ACM Press.

Kot, B., Wuensche, B., Grundy, J., & Hosking, J. (2005). Information visualisation utilising 3D computer game engines case study: A source code comprehension tool. In *Proceedings of the 6th ACM SIGCHI New Zealand chapter's International Conference on Computer-Human Interaction (CHINZ '05)* (pp. 53-60). New York: ACM Press.

Lave, J., & Wenger, E. (1991). *Situated learning: Legitimate peripheral participation.* Cambridge, UK: Cambridge University Press.

Lindstaedt, S. (1998). *Group memories: A knowledge medium for communities of interest.* Boulder, CO: University of Colorado at Boulder.

Maes, P., & Nardi, D. (Eds.). (1988). *Meta-level architectures and reflection.* New York: Elsevier Science Inc.

Manojlovich, J., Prasithsangaree, P., Hughes, S., Chen, J., & Lewis, M. (2003). UTSAF: A multiagent-based framework for supporting military-based distributed interactive simulations in 3d virtual environments. In *Proceedings of the 35th Conference on Winter Simulation (WSC '03)* (pp. 960-968). Washington, DC: IEEE Computer Society.

Martin, C., Schreckenghost, D., Bonasso, P., Kortenkamp, D., Milam, T., & Thronesbery, C. (2003). An environment for distributed collaboration among humans and software agents. In *Proceedings of the Second International joint Conference on Autonomous Agents and Multiagent Systems (AAMAS '03)* (pp. 1062-1063). New York: ACM Press.

Moloney, J., Amor, R., Furness, J., & Moores, B. (2003). Design critique inside a multi-player game engine. In *Proceedings of the CIB W78 Conference on IT in Construction* (pp. 255-262). CIB Publication.

Nakanishi, H., & Ishida, T. (2004). FreeWalk/Q: Social interaction platform in virtual space. In *Proceedings of the ACM symposium on Virtual Reality Software and Technology (VRST '04)* (pp. 97-104). New York: ACM Press.

Payne, T. R., Sycara, K., & Lewis, M. (2000). Varying the user interaction within multi-agent systems. In *Proceedings of the Fourth International Conference on Autonomous Agents (AGENTS '00)* (pp. 412-418). New York: ACM Press.

Pöttler, M. (2007). *Die rolle von onlinecommunities in reise und tourismus.* Unpublished master's thesis, Vienna University of Technology, Vienna, Austria.

Rodríguez-aguilar, J. A., Martín, F. J., Noriega, P., Garcia, P., & Sierra, C. (1997). Towards a test-bed for trading agents in electronic auction markets. *AI Communications, 11*(1), 5–19.

Rollings, A., & Morris, D. (2004). *Game architecture and design.* Indianapolis, IN: New Riders Publishing.

Salen, K., & Zimmermann, E. (2004). *Rules of play: Game design fundamentals.* Cambridge, MA: MIT Press.

Schwabe, G., & Prestipino, M. (2005). *How tourism communities can change travel information quality.* Paper presented at the 13th European Conference on Information Systems, Information Systems in a Rapidly Changing Economy (ECIS '05), Regensburg, Germany.

Seidel, I., & Berger, H. (2007). Integrating electronic institutions with 3d virtual worlds. In *Proceedings of the 2007 IEEE/WIC/ACM International Conference on Intelligent Agent Technology (IAT'07)* (pp. 481-484). Washington, DC: IEEE Computer Society.

Smith, G., Maher, M. L., & Gero, J. S. (2003). Designing 3d virtual worlds as a society of agents. In *Proceedings of the 10th International Conference on Computer Aided Architectural Design Futures (CAADFutures '03)* (pp. 105-114). Dordrecht, The Netherlands: Kluwer Academic Publishers.

Traum, D., & Rickel, J. (2002). Embodied agents for multi-party dialogue in immersive virtual worlds. In *Proceedings of the First International joint Conference on Autonomous Agents and Multiagent Systems (AAMAS '02)* (pp. 766-773). New York: ACM Press.

Wang, Y., Yu, Q., & Fesenmaier, D. R. (2002). Defining the virtual tourist community: Implications for tourism marketing. *Tourism Management, 23*(4), 407–417. doi:10.1016/S0261-5177(01)00093-0

Wenger, E., McDermott, R., & Snyder, W. (2002). *Cultivating communities of practice.* Boston: Harvard Business School Press.

Werthner, H., & Klein, S. (1999). *Information technology and tourism, a challenging relationship.* Vienna, Austria: Springer-Verlag.

Wooldridge, M. J. (2001). *An introduction to multiagent systems.* New York: John Wiley & Sons, Inc.

Yee, N. (2006 a). The demographics, motivations, and derived experiences of users of massively multi-user online graphical environments. *Presence (Cambridge, Mass.), 15*(3), 309–329. doi:10.1162/pres.15.3.309

Yee, N. (2006 b). The psychology of massively multi-user online role-playing games: Emotional investment, motivations, relationship formation, and problematic usage. In R. Schroeder & A.S. Axelsson (Eds.), *Avatars at work and play: Collaboration and interaction in shared virtual environments* (pp. 187-207). New York: Springer-Verlag.

Yeung, C., Pang-Fei, T., & Yen, J. (1998). A multi-agent based tourism kiosk on Internet. In *Proceedings of the Thirty-First Annual Hawaii International Conference on System Sciences-Volume 4 (HICSS '98)* (p. 452). Washington, DC: IEEE Computer Society.

Zambonelli, F., Jennings, N. R., & Wooldridge, M. (2003). Developing multiagent systems: The gaia methodology. *ACM Transactions on Software Engineering and Methodology, 12*(3), 317–370. doi:10.1145/958961.958963

ENDNOTES

1 http://qdn.qubesoft.com/

2 http://www.garagegames.com/

3 http://www.activeworlds.com/

4 http://java3d.dev.java.net/

5 http://eightbar.co.uk/2007/05/08/the-ibm-innovate-quick-internal-metaverse-project/

6 http://www.legendmud.org/raph/gaming/mudtimeline.html

7 http://www.worldofwarcraft.com/raf-splash.htm

8 http://starwarsgalaxies.station.sony.com/players/index.vm

9 http://www.jforum.net/

10 http://www.facebook.com/

11 http://www.myspace.com/

Chapter 14
The Use of Photographs on Consumer Generated Content Websites:
Practical Implications for Destination Image Analysis

Doris Schmallegger
James Cook University, Australia

Dean Carson
Charles Darwin University, Australia

Damien Jacobsen
Charles Darwin University, Australia

ABSTRACT

Word-of-mouth is an important source of information for tourists making decisions about what destinations to visit. Word-of-mouth has a strong influence on shaping the image of a destination, particularly for remote destinations which are in part characterised by limited market penetration in terms of more formal marketing communications. There has been some research situating consumer generated content in Web 2.0 applications as word-of-mouth that has the potential to influence destination images for some destinations and among some markets. Less attention has been paid to consumer generated photographs although photographs and other non-text media are becoming increasingly pervasive on Web 2.0 websites. This chapter argues that photographs make a substantial contribution to word-of-mouth exchange online, and that there is a need for tools to help destinations interpret photographic content. Mapping photographs to Echtner and Ritchie's (1993) destination image framework is one approach that shows some promise as it allows for comparison between the images projected by marketing bodies and consumers.

DOI: 10.4018/978-1-60566-818-5.ch014

INTRODUCTION

The increasing popularity of the Internet, and particularly the emergence of Web 2.0 applications, has dramatically changed the way in which 'word-of-mouth' exchange occurs among tourism consumers. Most significantly, consumer generated content (CGC) such as blogs, wikis and consumer forums allows word-of-mouth to extend beyond limited networks of friends, family and fellow travellers met along the way. The sharing of opinions and the telling of experiences can now occur more readily between strangers, with limited mediation and few barriers beyond language and access to technology.

A growing body of literature has recognised the importance of tourism CGC for tourism businesses and destination marketing organisations (DMOs) (Puehringer & Taylor, 2008; Schegg et al., 2008; Pan, MacLaurin & Crotts, 2007). The existing literature has focused exclusively on the texts posted by consumers on blogs, in travel review sites and virtual communities, and in wikis. This chapter argues that photographs (and other media) are at least as important as texts in communication between travel consumers. The efforts underway to develop tools to analyse CGC texts for marketing research purposes, as for example proposed by Waldhoer and Rind (2008), need to be extended to include CGC photographs.

There have been two broad approaches proposed for the analysis of CGC texts, including structured and unstructured content analysis techniques. Several researchers in the past (Wenger, 2008; Carson, 2008; Pan et al., 2007) attempted to analyse the themes that emerged from texts without imposing any framework or model over their content analysis. Other researchers (Douglas & Mills, 2006; Schmallegger & Carson, 2009) analysed texts within particular frameworks, such as a brand personality framework or a destination image framework. Carson (2008) commented that the free form and diversity of information (not all of it related directly to the travel experience) in blog texts made it difficult to apply unstructured content analysis techniques. Structured techniques, while necessarily limiting what the analysis can be about (Tapachai & Waryszak, 2000), reduce 'noise' and provide outputs more directly related to the intent of the analysis. The issues addressed by this chapter include whether structured techniques are also of value when analysing CGC photographs.

The chapter progresses as follows. The following section looks at the ways in which consumer generated photographs are used in Web 2.0 applications. It then reviews the importance of CGC for tourism marketers, with a particular focus on how CGC can influence destination image. We then discuss the technologies and methodologies available for analysing photographic content, and propose that formal destination image frameworks may be of value for structured analysis. Finally, the chapter looks at what might happen in the future as non-text media becomes more pervasive and technologies for automatically analysing image content begin to emerge. An example of CGC photograph analysis, based around a destination in outback Australia, is used to illustrate the theory presented in the chapter.

CONSUMER GENERATED TRAVEL PHOTOGRAPHS

Despite being mostly taken by 'amateurs', tourist photographs contain a wealth of meaning beyond the obvious appearances (la Grange 2005). Tourists take photographs out of a variety of motivations including reproducing existing place discourses (Jenkins, 2003), portraying personal accomplishments (Lemelin, 2006), actualising social roles (Larsen, 2006) and attempting to capture the un-photographable meaning and aura of special places (Garlick, 2002).

Researchers have found that tourists often tailor the nature of their photographs according to their desired future audience (Crang, 1999), and how they would like to be seen by their peers (Wells, 2004). Tourist photographs tend to capture experiences that tourists want to take back home with them and share with a chosen audience. Slideshows and photographs are a common way to communicate personal trip experiences and perceived destination images to peers and hence constitute a significant form of word-of-mouth in tourism (Milne, Grekin & Woodley 1998; Brown & Chalmers, 2003; Van Dijck, 2008). More recently, new online applications facilitating consumer generated content and peer-to-peer communication have emerged that enable users to share their travel experiences with other like minded people. This new generation of online technologies, also commonly referred to as 'Web 2.0' (O'Reilly, 2005), has made it possible to make travel related virtual word-of-mouth information available to a much wider audience than traditional face-to-face word-of-mouth.

The recording of travel experiences through Web 2.0 applications on the Internet is becoming increasingly popular (Schmallegger & Carson, 2008; Gretzel, Yoo & Purifoy, 2007). More frequently visited CGC websites in the Web 2.0 genre include MySpace.com, YouTube.com, TripAdvisor.com and Flickr.com. These websites enable users to participate in web forums and message boards, perform product ratings and trip evaluations, participate in virtual community games, and publish their own travel stories in the form of blogs, photos, podcasts, or online videos (Laboy & Torchio, 2007). Recent developments in Web 2.0 also include trends such as 'mobile blogging', where users can post their latest travel experiences online as they go from mobile devices, such as mobile phones or personal digital assistants (PDAs) (Repo, Hyvonen & Saastamoinen, 2006).

With Internet up- and download capacities increasing, CGC websites often encourage the use of non-text media, such as photos, videos, or audio, as a form of communication. The tremendous growth in popularity of digital photography over the last decade, fuelled by rapid developments in the digital camera and photo equipment sector, has led to an explosion of digital images on the Internet (Snavely, Seitz & Szeliski, 2006). Today, cameras for private use are available for relatively moderate prices and are increasingly being integrated into other mobile devices, making it easy for travellers to take large numbers of digital photographs during a trip. As travel related CGC keeps increasing and technological capacities keep improving, we can expect more non-textual information, and in particular digital photographs, to become more important in online word-of-mouth communications.

CONSUMER GENERATED PHOTOGRAPHS OF THE FLINDERS RANGES

Our research on consumer generated photographs of the Flinders Ranges region in South Australia analysed photographs on private blog sites, public travel blog sites and online travel communities (www.travelblog.org and www.travelpod.com) as well as in photograph sharing websites such as www.flickr.com. Photographs were located through a manual sampling process using in-site search functions on public travel websites (www.travelblog.org, www.travelpod.com and www.flickr.com) and a generic blog search engine (www.blogsearch.google.com).

While most private blogs contained just one or two entries about the Flinders Ranges, and the text in these entries was typically no more than one or two hundred words, there was an average of fifteen photographs of the Flinders Ranges posted by each user. Travel specific websites, such as public travel blog sites, on the other hand, contained more text and fewer photographs per user. There were 53 users who reported on trips to the Flinders Ranges on public travel blog sites, and they collectively posted 452 photographs (8.5 photographs per user). Not surprisingly, the 40 Flinders Ranges tourists located on the online photo sharing website Flickr.com posted more photographs each on average (19 photographs per user) than those posting through private or travel specific blog sites.

Even though there appear to be some differences in the amount and structure of photographs on different types of CGC websites, the research highlights the importance of photographs and visual images in CGC about travel and tourism, at least in the case of the Flinders Ranges destination. The Flinders Ranges is fairly typical of remote destinations in Australia, with the images being based largely on landscape and scenery. These images are very visually appealing, and therefore, may be more suited to photographic recording than many other destinations. There has been no published research yet on the extent to which different types of destinations inspire different amounts of photography, but it will become an important issue as market research using CGC increases in popularity.

CONSUMER GENERATED CONTENT AND DESTINATION IMAGE

'Word-of-mouth' is commonly used in marketing literature as a label for the consumer-to-consumer exchange of information about products or services (Carl, 2006). In tourism, it is usually assumed to involve past or current visitors passing on descriptions and recommendations to current or potential visitors (Morgan et al., 2003). As an informal information source, word-of-mouth content is difficult to capture and analyse in the way that might be done for more formal sources such as guide books and popular media (Murphy et al., 2007).

Until recently, research into word-of-mouth communication in tourism made assumptions about the relationships between the sender and receiver of information (Anderson, 1998). It was assumed, for example, that the two key factors in determining transmission of information were physical proximity and strength of relationship. The less well known senders were, the more that word-of-mouth communication relied on physical interaction (meeting someone in person) (Anderson, 1998). Communication at a distance, through telephone or mail, could best occur between people who were well known to each other (Sheth & Parvatylar, 1995). Face-to-face interaction was seen as necessary in helping the receiver assess the credibility of the source of information where credibility had not previously been established through a personal relationship. It is the concept of credibility established through a personal trust relationship that is seen as contributing to the power of word-of-mouth communication (Beerli & Marton, 2004).

Litvin, Goldsmith and Pan (2008) described how online forms of communication, including CGC, were changing the accepted view of word-of-mouth communication in tourism. Physical proximity has become less important in forming relationships, and other techniques have emerged through which people establish trust relationships. Relatively easy access to lots of different sources of information allows cross checking of specific messages (recommendations for places to visit, for example). The ways in which blog sites are often organised as components of virtual communities also lends credibility to individual messages (Berger, Dittenbach & Merkl, 2006). 'Incorrect' information is likely to be quickly identified by other members of the community (Eigner et al., 2003). As more people both create and sustain personal relationships through Web 2.0 applications, the transition from physical proximity to virtual attachment in determining the reach of word-of-mouth will continue.

Literature about electronic or online word-of-mouth in tourism has focused on the nature of blog content (Wenger, 2008; Carson, 2008) and the attributes of messages delivered through travel specific review sites (Gretzel et al., 2007). There are other settings in which word-of-mouth exchange can occur, including online travel forums on special interest web sites and virtual travel communities (Lueg, 2006).

Analysing online word-of-mouth on CGC sites as a new form of market research is becoming increasingly popular in tourism research. Given the very casual flow of information and the wide range of experiences described, it has recently been argued that CGC sites might reflect the opinions and attitudes of travellers in a more genuine and representative way than other, more traditional methods of consumer research (Pan et al., 2007; Bulkeley, 2005). Several researchers have therefore argued that CGC analysis can be a powerful tool to assess the image of a destination among a certain target market, especially for traveller groups which are otherwise hard to reach (Schmallegger & Carson, 2008; Wenger, 2008; Choi et al., 2007; Pan et al., 2007).

Destination images are usually formed by the sum of a consumer's beliefs and impressions, which are generated by information received and processed from a variety of sources over time (Baloglu & McCleary, 1999; Gartner, 1993; MacKay & Couldwell, 2004). Images emerge as a result of cognitive evaluations and emotional interpretations of a destination's perceived attributes. Inputs in the form of external information sources can contribute immensely to the formation of overall impressions of a destination. These have been referred to in the literature as induced inputs (for example purposeful and targeted marketing information by the destination) and organic inputs (communications not developed by the destination) (Baloglu & McCleary, 1999; MacKay & Couldwell, 2004; Gallarza, Gil & Calderón, 2002). Of these organic inputs, word-of-mouth has often been described as the most critical (Baloglu & McCleary, 1999; Andreu et al., 2000; Hanlan & Kelly, 2005).

Many destination image studies in the past have focused on examining specific attributes, while neglecting more holistic and integrated impressions and images of the destination (MacKay & Couldwell, 2004). Echtner and Ritchie (1993) addressed these issues by proposing a destination image framework which included a multidimensional continuum approach for destination image analysis. They suggest that destination image is composed of attribute-based and holistic components, both of which contain functional (tangible) and psychological (intangible, symbolic) characteristics (see Figure 1).

Functional attributes for tourism destinations might include climate, prices, physical scenery, hard infrastructure or entertainment venues. Psychological attributes describe the personal interpretation and evaluation of these attributes, such as the friendliness of locals or the quality of products and services. Holistic elements, then, reflect the imagery produced by functional and psychological attributes. They might include holistic mental pictures of physical characteristics on the one side, and the general mood or atmosphere created by these elements on the other.

CONSUMER GENERATED DESTINATION IMAGES OF THE FLINDERS RANGES

Our research in the Flinders Ranges looked at the destination images as revealed by photographs in the DMO touring guide and compared these with photographs posted by international visitors (1401 photographs from 92 users) and domestic visitors (461 photographs from 44 users) on a range of Web 2.0 websites, including public and private blog sites, online travel communities and photo sharing websites. A combination of content analysis and semiotic analysis was used to identify functional, psychological, attribute-based and holistic image components of the Flinders Ranges.

Both content and semiotic analysis are common methodologies used in the analysis and interpretation of photographic imagery. Content analysis is attribute-based and primarily concerned with describing quantitatively the appearance of certain themes and attributes, allowing the main focal

Figure 1. The components of destination image (Source: Echtner & Ritchie, 1993)

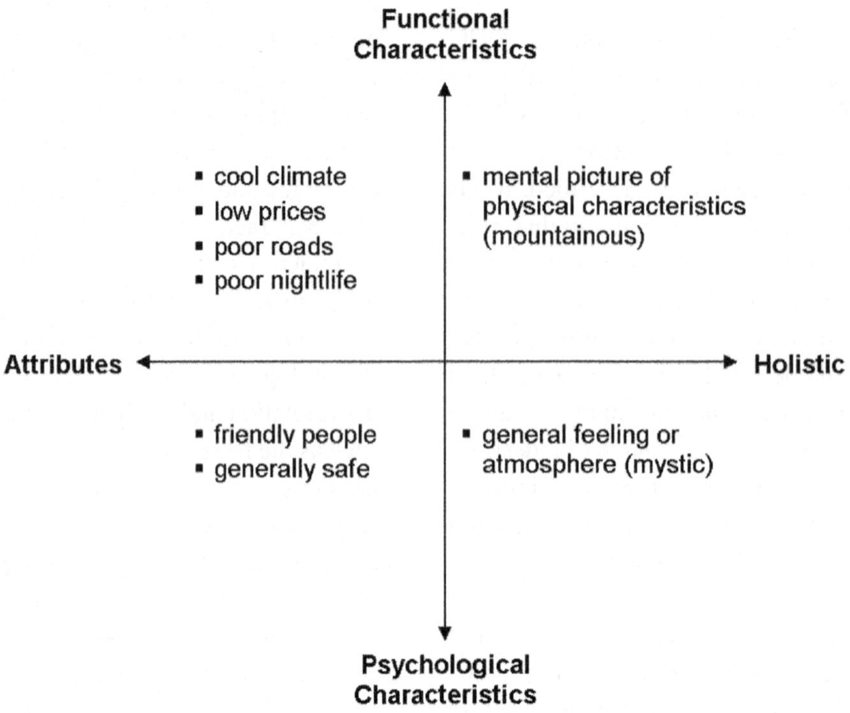

themes of pictures to be identified (Cooper, 1994; Jenkins, 2003). While content analysis normally breaks the picture down into a number of categories, semiotic analysis considers the picture as a whole, and is concerned with investigating how the content and composition of a picture communicate certain messages through signs and symbols about the place or the object they depict.

During the content analysis process the researchers developed a range of descriptive categories that they thought would best describe the content of the photos. Table 2 provides a short outline of the most common themes identified. The most common objects photographed by Flinders Ranges visitors included: 1) natural characteristics of the destination (e.g. mountains, gorges, or wildlife); 2) cultural attractions (e.g. historic ruins, heritage trains, or Aboriginal rock art); 3) activities (e.g. four-wheel-driving, bushwalking, or camping); and 4) people (e.g. members of the family or travel group).

In addition, a more subjective semiotic interpretation of the photos was used to establish what particular photo objects could signify about the destination and to identify the main psychological attributes and holistic feelings captured in the pictures. All identified codes were then grouped around Echtner and Ritchie's destination image framework to describe the destination's functional, psychological, attribute-based and holistic image components.

Figure 2 shows a brief summary of the destination image map created from photographs posted by domestic travellers. Functional attributes included a range of attractions and activities that were commonly depicted on photos, such as mountains, gorges, wildlife, or four wheel driving. The functional holistic image quadrant included holistic images associated with the physical characteristics of the destinations, such as the wide open space, the dry landscape, or breathtaking views. The psychological quadrant sections

Table 1. Most common themes in consumer generated photographs

	Domestic		International	
Themes	**nr. of users**	**% of users**	**nr. of users**	**% of users**
Natural characteristics				
mountain ranges	34	77.3%	60	65.2%
gorges	21	47.7%	35	38.0%
vegetation	17	38.6%	32	34.8%
dry landscape	15	34.1%	32	34.8%
breathtaking views	14	31.8%	28	30.4%
wide open space	13	29.5%	22	23.9%
wildlife	13	29.5%	57	62.0%
colourful sunsets	9	20.5%	27	29.3%
Wilpena Pound	4	9.1%	24	26.1%
Cultural attractions				
historic ruins	9	20.5%	19	20.7%
Outback towns	8	18.2%	16	17.4%
heritage trains	5	11.4%	13	14.1%
waterfront jetties	4	9.1%	4	4.3%
Aboriginal rock art	3	6.8%	14	15.2%
Activities				
bushwalking	16	36.4%	31	33.7%
4WDing	12	27.3%	12	13.0%
camping	9	20.5%	23	25.0%
scenic drives (non 4WD)	3	6.8%	16	17.4%
People				
family members	6	13.6%	8	8.7%
group activities	5	11.4%	18	19.6%
individuals posing with sights	5	11.4%	28	30.4%
Total number of users	*44*	*100.0%*	*92*	*100.0%*

contained personal experiences and evaluations that travellers tried to communicate through their photographs. Identified psychological attributes included, for example, a sense of adventure or that the Flinders Ranges were a place for a family holiday or to 'get away from it all'. Psychological holistic interpretations of the place were identified as 'lonely and isolated', 'peaceful', 'inspiring', or 'majestic'.

COMPARING CONSUMER GENERATED IMAGES WITH OFFICIAL DMO IMAGES

It is always difficult to assess what 'the most appropriate' destination image is for a specific place as the images can be different for different markets (Russell et al., 2005; Fakeye & Crompton, 1991; Leisen, 2001). Images captured by tourists can depend on a variety of factors, including

Figure 2. A destination image map created from consumer generated photographs

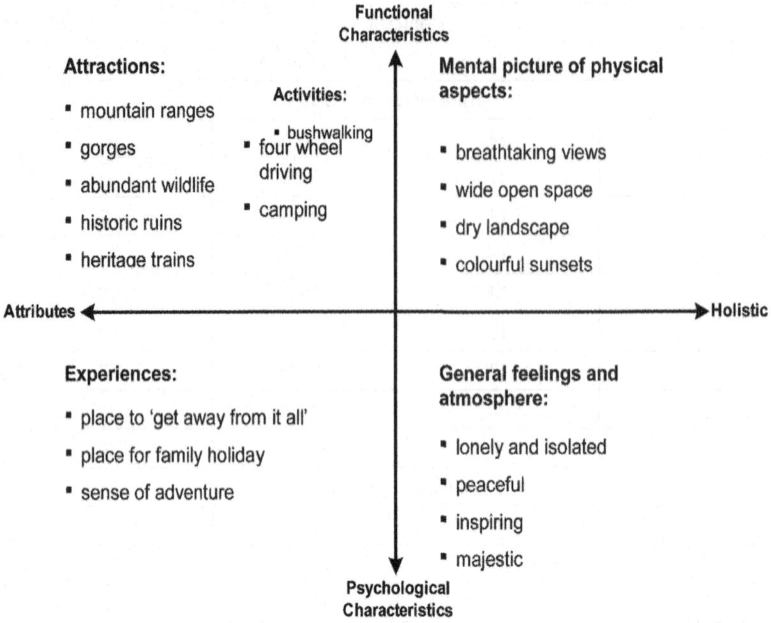

demographic factors or the level of familiarity with the destination (MacKay, 2004; Fakeye & Crompton, 1991). Our research in the Flinders Ranges, for example, has identified substantial differences between domestic and international travellers in terms of demographic characteristics and trip patterns.

Domestic travellers were generally older than international travellers and were mainly travelling as families with children or as older retired couples. Domestic visitors typically stayed in the Flinders Ranges between three days and one week. The international sample was dominated by a much younger age group and included mainly single backpackers or young couples who were often travelling as part of an organised tour group. They were mainly from the UK, continental Europe (Germany, France, and the Netherlands) or North America (United States and Canada). In general, international travellers were on longer trips around Australia and included a visit to the Flinders Ranges as a short two or three-day stop on the way from Adelaide up to central Australia.

Considering these fundamental market differences, it is very likely that domestic visitors view and experience the same destination in different ways than international visitors. Different approaches to destination marketing will therefore be required for these two markets. Holiday brochures and other marketing collateral are only successful if they manage to establish a link between the target destination and a market's motivations, goals or preferences (Jenkins, 2003; Dann, 1996). Understanding how various markets perceive the destination and to what extent official projected images are contested or reinforced can help to develop better targeted destination promotion strategies. A framework, such as that provided by Echtner and Ritchie (1993), allows for the comparison of destination images between destinations, as well as within destinations, between different markets and official destination marketing agencies.

Schmallegger and Carson (2009) argued that CGC could influence destination image in at least three ways: Firstly, images provided by consumers could contest the images promoted by destination marketing organisations or tourism businesses. This would happen if consumers disagreed with a formally promoted component of the destination image. Secondly, CGC images reinforce formal images when they are in agreement. Finally, CGC images may add to the formal image by revealing and introducing new aspects not promoted by DMOs or local businesses.

Figure 3 highlights some of the aspects of the formal Flinders Ranges destination image projected by the DMO and provides a short overview of how consumer generated photographs of international and domestic visitors compare to the formal DMO images. This simple analysis indicates how two different markets perceive the destination in different ways. Understanding this might help the DMO (and individual businesses) more effectively target each market.

A comparative analysis of destination image revealed that consumer images generally tended to reinforce DMO images, especially in relation to the functional images. Images of scenic mountain ranges, the ruggedness of the country, or the wide open space were reinforced by both domestic and international markets. Also psychological impressions, such as a sense of adventure or the peaceful atmosphere, were reinforced by both markets.

Our research could not identify consumer images that were contesting any of the images projected by the DMO. However, there were some important differences in the ways in which the three groups perceived and portrayed the destination. Some images that were extensively promoted by the DMO were not replicated by the consumers. A particularly interesting component of the DMO image was the attention paid to regional cuisine. Food and wine images feature prominently in the touring guide, promoting regional cuisine as one of the key attractions in the Flinders Ranges. These images were completely absent in both international and domestic visitor photo sets. Similarly, the DMO promoted a wide range of activities as part of the destination image (mountain biking, camel riding, scenic flights and so on), but again these were not present in consumer images either. Positive images of friendly locals or quaint little Outback towns were also missing in the consumer photo sets.

On the other hand, consumers included a range of new experiences in their photos which had not been promoted by the DMO. Such newly introduced images were relating to new activities, such as mountain climbing and camping under the stars, or images portraying the destination as a place to 'get away from it all'. Both traveller markets introduced new images of ruins and abandoned homesteads and promoted images which highlighted the isolation, desolation and loneliness of the destination, and how difficult it would be to live there permanently (see Figure 4).

There were some other substantial differences in the ways photos were taken. While consumer photos of landscape did not include people in order to highlight impressions such as isolation, loneliness or 'being in the middle of nowhere', DMO photographs mostly included people in landscape photos, showing that it is not a hostile and isolated place to be. International tourists did include people in photographs of activities, capturing the social atmosphere experienced within the travel group. Domestic travellers' photographs, on the other hand, focused more on landscape and wildlife and tended not to have people in any of their images.

MARKET RESEARCH TECHNIQUES FOR CONSUMER GENERATED PHOTOGRAPHS

Analysing photographs taken by tourists is considered a useful method to elicit destination image, as photographs not only include individual attributes of a place but tend to capture holistic and psychological impressions as well, which reflect the 'lived experience' of tourists (MacKay & Couldwell, 2004). Markwell (1997) noted that the content and images produced in tourists' photographs

Figure 3. Comparative analysis of destination image maps

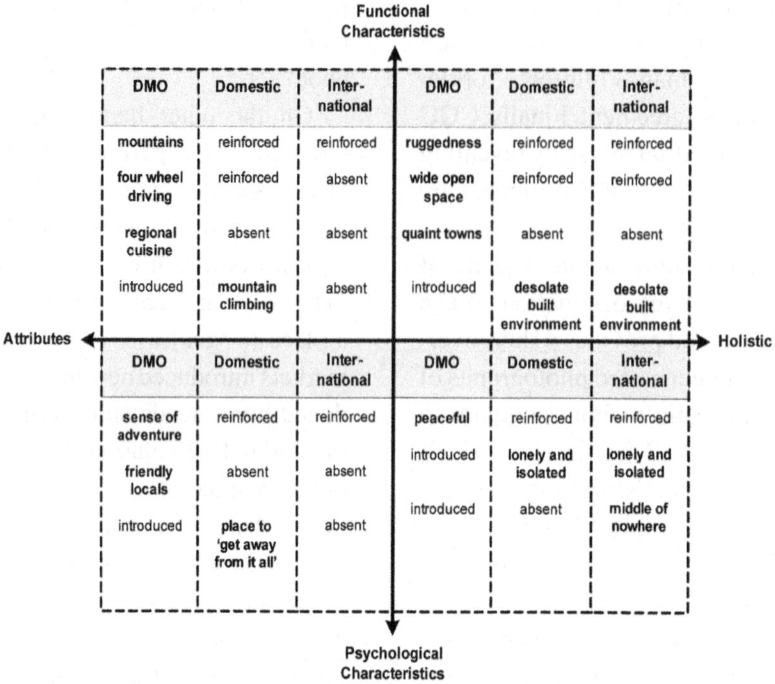

often reflect the way in which tourists want to see the destination, hence their personal perceptions and interpretations that they have accumulated about the place. The use of consumer generated photographs – in the literature also referred to as 'visitor-employed photography' (Cherem & Driver, 1983) – in tourism and leisure research is becoming increasingly recognised by researchers, principally due to the potential of yielding rich marketing data (Markwell, 1997). However, despite the wide spread use of photos and visual stimuli in tourism promotion, destination image research has mostly been based on text analysis and there have only been few studies analysing the role of visual images in destination image formation (Jenkins, 2003; MacKay & Fesenmaier, 1997; MacKay & Couldwell, 2004).

Visitor-employed photography research has traditionally involved distributing cameras to research participants (or allowing them to use their own cameras) who were then instructed to photograph specific scenes or items depending on the stated research objectives (MacKay & Couldwell, 2004). While this approach was a very time consuming and cost intensive process in the past (participants had to be recruited, cameras and photo film had to be purchased, photos had to be printed etc.) the Internet now provides easy access to a wealth of data, albeit less structured than in previous studies. The rapid development of new technologies, particularly in the digital photography and camera sector, in combination with increasing bandwidth and Internet up- and download capacities, have lead to an increasing number of photographs being posted on travel blogs or online photo sharing websites.

The continuing lack of research into consumer generated photographs in tourism may be partially because of the lack of well established automatic ways of classifying CGC on the Internet. Research into developing automatic systems for image retrieval and interpretation is still in its early stages (Spaniol, Klamma & Lux, 2007) and to date, there is no software application readily available which

Figure 4. Example of qualitative interpretation of photographs (© 2008 Simon Waterhouse. Used with permission) Title of photo: "Desolation"

allows researchers, DMOs or tourism businesses to automatically analyse what consumer generated photographs have to say about a particular business or destination.

CHALLENGES FOR CONSUMER GENERATED PHOTOGRAPH ANALYSIS

Our research has identified a number of challenges associated with image analysis using manual approaches and techniques. Particularly, the manual sampling and data collection process makes it difficult to filter out irrelevant photographs from the enormous amount of consumer generated data that most of the search engines and in-site search functions return. More than half of all returned results were irrelevant because they were either not about travel to the destination, did not contain any photos of the destination, or were posted by commercial interests rather than private consumers. Similar issues were identified by Carson (2008), who collected and analysed CGC texts in blogs about the Northern Territory.

One of the main challenges in locating online photographs is that search engines are largely incapable of understanding and interpreting the semantic content of photographs (Kennedy et al., 2007). Content classification of photographs on the Internet relies mainly on textual metadata, including 'tags' and keywords, that are manually assigned to the photos by the content creator to describe and classify the content of the picture. However, 'tagging' on CGC websites is not a consistent or standardised process and can be very different from consumer to consumer. Tags might be inaccurate, ambiguous or used in ways that do not necessarily reflect the real content of the picture (Spaniol et al., 2007).

In our case, identifying and locating photos from different market segments or specific niche markets turned out to be a substantial challenge. Similar to what previous studies about travel related CGC found (Douglas & Mills, 2006; Wenger, 2008; Carson, 2008), the results of the Flinders

Ranges research suggest again that the majority of CGC about a tourism destination is created by younger and mostly international travellers who are on longer, multiple destination trips. Searching and collecting photographs from other markets, particularly from domestic travellers, was far more time consuming. Unless researchers know or have access to special interest websites or travel communities that are frequently used by the market segments they wish to analyse, the use of general search engines or in-site search functions can be a very tedious process.

Another significant challenge lies in the analysis and interpretation of photographs. While common techniques such as content analysis or semiotic analysis are widespread in photographic analysis and used to identify common themes and messages in photographs, the real art is in the interpretation of these results. In our research based on the Flinders Ranges, for example, we identified the lack of consumer generated photographs featuring food and wine, a strong theme in DMO provided photographs. It requires some thought to assess whether this absence of an image element represents contesting the image, or simply reflects that food and wine are uncommon subjects of photographs. Similarly, it can be challenging to interpret the meaning behind content – whether a photographer is trying to communicate the fascinating beauty of a scene (of an abandoned farm-house, for example as in Figure 4), or the undesirability of the location as a residence.

A photograph is always ambiguous and open to the interpretation by the viewer (Wells, 2004). Personal experiences and familiarity with the destination as well as personal characteristics and demographic factors can have a tremendous impact on how a spectator perceives a picture (MacKay, 2004). Hence, manual qualitative interpretation of photographs is a subjective process. In our research we found that this subjectivity can sometimes be significantly reduced if photographs are analysed and evaluated in combination with the text that accompanies them. Apart from designated online photo albums, most pictures posted in blogs, forums or photo sharing websites included some sort of textual explanation, either in the form of titles, short captions or even entire paragraphs describing the situation in which the photo was taken (Figure 4).

Caption: "Somewhere West of Wilpena Pound, just off the road to Parachilna in the Flinders Ranges. (...) Its hard to beleive [sic] anyone would bother building here in the first place."

The real meaning of a photograph is difficult to derive in the absence of any explanatory text. The same has been found in other contexts, such as contemporary art, where words and captions are used to reveal the ambiguous meanings of photographs (Hapkemeyer & Weiermair, 1996). Even though the photograph analysis proved to be a useful tool for establishing which official DMO images were reinforced, omitted or introduced, it could not be used to identify whether consumers are actually contesting existing images, or agreeing with them. This is only possible in conjunction with some text analysis, for example when users clearly stated that they disagreed with the way the destination was officially projected.

The difference between text analysis and photographic analysis was the apparent lack of language as an issue in analysis. Given the prominence of international consumer generated entries, text analysis has often been limited according to the language skills of the researcher or the analysis program (Carson, 2008; Choi et al., 2007; Pan et al., 2007). Analysing visual images has got some potential in developing cross cultural market insights. However, images in photographs can themselves be culturally determined (Sontag, 1977; Crang, 1997; MacKay & Fesenmaier, 2000), i.e. the travellers' cultural background is likely to have some impact on the photographs they take.

Notwithstanding the challenges identified in the preceding section, DMOs will find it very useful to monitor and maintain a collection of consumer generated photographs about their destination, which they can compare to the images they are trying to promote. Analysis of the collection can reveal where promoted images are not being taken up, and may also reveal opportunities to adjust the image used for destination promotion, to better deal with specific markets. As with all tourism market research, the value of consumer generated photograph analysis will really lie in developing an understanding of the target markets and the messages most useful in promoting the destination. Consequently, different collections could be used for different markets. Photograph sets (i.e. the photographs provided by a single user) can be tagged with different market profiles (sociographic, demographic, seasonal, activity-based etc), so that multiple analyses can take place. In our research, we have tagged international and domestic visitors, but also visitors who engage in different activities (such as four wheel drive touring) and belong to different travel party types (such as families and older couples). The destination image maps described in this chapter are one way to present the results of analyses.

FUTURE TRENDS AND OPPORTUNITIES FOR RESEARCH

Digital photographic equipment continues to be incorporated into mobile telephones, personal digital assistants (PDAs) and other devices that are compact and require few specialist skills to use. Photographs taken with such equipment can be easily loaded to Web 2.0 websites and personal home pages. Photographs are easier to take and manage than text in many cases – photographs can reach across language and cultural barriers, and their production does not require high levels of literacy. The continuing growth in use of Web 2.0 applications -- not just among younger consumers -- and the desirable status of travel and tourism as popular topics among web users will have important implications for tourism businesses and destinations. Word-of-mouth communication in the online environment theoretically has greater reach than even the most carefully constructed formal marketing campaigns using the more traditional media. The literature suggests that it has a substantial impact on people's travel decisions. The future will see market analysts increase the attention paid to how best to identify, analyse, and respond to CGC.

The attention currently being paid to automated analysis of CGC text for tourism market research (Waldhoer & Rind, 2008) will surely have to extend to consumer generated photographs. Image interpretation software development is a high priority for the major search engines (Lew at al., 2006; Spaniol et al., 2007), and the technologies developed for searching images will surely be useful for the types of analysis described in this chapter.

As with many new developments, however, the capacity to access information is just one challenge. The information must also be judicially processed (Malhotra, 2001) so that it is appropriately organised, analysed, and converted into knowledge and ultimately leads to innovation. As technicians work on ways of collating photographs with similar themes or subjects, more work needs to be done on how destinations and businesses can interpret the content of the photographs and relate such analysis to their business evaluation and marketing. Some of the areas where future research can focus include:

- **Structured Content Analysis:** It may be more valuable to take a structured approach to content analysis, such that the applications of the research are understood before the analysis takes place.
- **Comparative Analysis:** This analysis can include initially comparing the messages in word-of-mouth communication with the desired messages of the business or destination, and then comparing messages between market segments.

- **Contextual Analysis:** Photographs are rarely posted in isolation. There is usually some contextual information about the user, and some text that accompanies the photos (even if it is simply a tag or caption for the photograph). Research using CGC needs to consider both text and graphic elements of entries along with their context.
- **Semantic Analysis:** Most entries contain multiple photographs, and analysis should consider the meaning of the sets of photographs as well as each photograph individually.

There is still much to be learned about the sorts of destinations, markets, and trip types that are likely to attract coverage (text or photographs) on Web 2.0 websites, and how these might change over time. Our research in the Flinders Ranges involved a relatively remote, nature based destination with high scenic values. The photographs we located came primarily from young travellers, and there was a much higher representation of international compared with domestic tourist photographs. International visitors are certainly less familiar with travel to remote Australia than domestic tourists. The Flinders Ranges DMO has a relatively small marketing budget, and its formal marketing exposure is very limited. Limited reach of official marketing messages in combination with a high degree of unfamiliarity with a destination might contribute significantly to a stronger exposure of the destination in consumer generated online environments. It may also be that novel experiences and experiences that are perceived as more exotic are more likely to be talked about on CGC websites (Wenger, 2008). Future research will have to look at whether other types of destinations (less remote and with different market characteristics) will be treated differently on CGC websites.

There is clearly a need for more research into how photographs are used by tourists to communicate with each other, and how this has transferred to the online environment. This chapter reveals a field of investigation in its infancy, with questions remaining about how much impact consumer generated photographs (in conjunction with, or in addition to text) have on destination selection decisions. What can be concluded, however, is that DMOs and tourism businesses have greater access than ever before to what consumers have to say about them. Market research needs to develop better tools and methods for interpreting this form of virtual word-of-mouth.

CONCLUSION

Our research on CGC about the Flinders Ranges shows that photographs are a substantial part of online word-of-mouth exchange. They can tell us a great deal about the perceived destination images of different visitor markets. Using structured techniques for image analysis, such as mapping photographs to Echtner and Ritchie's (1993) destination image framework, is recommended to identify the various components of complex and multilayered destination images. This approach was found to be very useful as it allows for comparison between official images promoted by the DMO and consumer generated images. It can reveal which official DMO images are reinforced or omitted in consumer generated images, or whether consumers introduce new destination images. It can help identify to what extent image projections by destination marketing bodies are in line with consumer perceptions, or where there are potential gaps in a destination's promotional efforts. However, the proposed technique is not free of limitations. The main difficulties were associated with the manual sampling and data collection process, as well as with the subjective interpretation of photographic content. This chapter concludes that the meaningfulness of photographic content analysis can be greatly enhanced by using multiple angles of analysis, including structured, comparative, contextual and semantic analysis techniques.

REFERENCES

Anderson, E. W. (1998). Customer satisfaction and word-of-mouth. *Journal of Service Research, 1*(1), 5–17. doi:10.1177/109467059800100102

Andreu, L., Bigné, E. J., & Cooper, C. (2000). Projected and perceived image of Spain as a tourist destination for British travellers. *Journal of Travel & Tourism Marketing, 9*(4), 47–67. doi:10.1300/J073v09n04_03

Baloglu, S., & McCleary, K. W. (1999). A model of destination image formation. *Annals of Tourism Research, 25*(4), 868–897. doi:10.1016/S0160-7383(99)00030-4

Beerli, A., & Martin, J. D. (2004). Factors influencing destination image. *Annals of Tourism Research, 31*(3), 657–681. doi:10.1016/j.annals.2004.01.010

Berger, H., Dittenbach, M., & Merkl, D. (2006). Let's get social in e-tourism: The "itchy feet" way. In *Proceedings of the 7th Asia-Pacific Conference on Computer Human Interaction (APCHI 2006)*, Taipei, Taiwan.

Brown, B., & Chalmers, M. (2003). Tourism and mobile technology. In K. Kuutti, E.H. Karsten, G. Fitzpatrick, P. Dourish, & K. Schmidt (Eds.), *Proceedings of the 8th European Conference on Computer-Supported Cooperative Work,* Helsinki, Finland (pp. 335-354).

Bulkeley, W. (2005). Marketers scan blogs for brand insights. *Wall Street Journal, 23*(June). Retrieved August 18, 2007, from http://online.wsj.com/public/article/SB111948406207267049-qs710svEyTDy6Sj732kvSsSdl_A_20060623.html?mod=blogs

Carl, W. J. (2006). What's all the buzz about? Everyday communication and the relational basis of word-of-mouth and buzz marketing practices. *Management Communication Quarterly, 19*(4), 601–634. doi:10.1177/0893318905284763

Carson, D. (2008). The 'blogosphere' as a market research tool for tourism destinations: A case study of Australia's Northern Territory. *Journal of Vacation Marketing, 14*(2), 111–119. doi:10.1177/1356766707087518

Cherem, G., & Driver, B. (1983). Visitor employed photography: A technique to measure common perceptions of natural environments. *Journal of Leisure Research, 15*, 65–83.

Choi, S., Lehto, X. Y., & Morrison, A. M. (2007). Destination image representation on the Web: Content analysis of Macau travel related Web sites. *Tourism Management, 28*, 118–129. doi:10.1016/j.tourman.2006.03.002

Cooper, D. (1994). Portraits of Paradise: Themes and images of the tourist industry. *Southeast Asian Journal of Social Science, 22*, 144–160. doi:10.1163/030382494X00142

Crang, M. (1997). Picturing practices: Research through the tourist gaze. *Progress in Human Geography, 21*(3), 359–373. doi:10.1191/030913297669603510

Crang, M. (1999). Knowing, tourism and the practices of vision. In D. Crouch (Ed.), *Leisure/tourism geographies: Practices and geographical knowledge* (pp. 238-256). London: Routledge.

Dann, G. (1996). tourists' images of a destination – an alternative analysis. *Journal of Travel & Tourism Marketing, 5*(1/2), 41–55. doi:10.1300/J073v05n01_04

Douglas, A. C., & Mills, J. E. (2006). Logging brand personality online: Website content analysis of Middle Eastern and North African destinations. In M. Hitz, M. Sigala, & J. Murphy (Eds.), *Information and communication technologies in tourism 2006* (pp. 345-346). New York: Springer.

Echtner, C. M., & Ritchie, J. R. B. (1993). The measurement of destination image: An empirical assessment. *Journal of Travel Research, 31*(4), 3–14. doi:10.1177/004728759303100402

Eigner, C., Leitner, H., Nausner, P., & Schneider, U. (2003). *Online-communities, weblogs und die soziale rückeroberung des netzes*. Graz, Austria: Nausner & Nausner.

Fakeye, P., & Crompton, J. (1991). Image differences between prospective, first-time and repeat visitors to the lower Rio Grande Valley. *Journal of Travel Research, 30*(2), 10–16. doi:10.1177/004728759103000202

Gallarza, M. G., Saura, I. G., & Garcia, H. C. (2002). Destination image: Towards a conceptual framework. *Annals of Tourism Research, 29*(1), 56–78. doi:10.1016/S0160-7383(01)00031-7

Garlick, S. (2002). Revealing the unseen: Tourism, art and photography. *Cultural Studies, 16*(2), 289–305. doi:10.1080/09502380110107599

Gartner, W. C. (1993). Image formation process. *Journal of Travel & Tourism Marketing, 2*(2/3), 191–215.

Gretzel, U., Yoo, K. H., & Purifoy, M. (2007). *Online travel review study: Role and impact of online travel reviews.* Texas A&M University: Laboratory for Intelligent Systems in Tourism. Retrieved September 14, 2007, from http://www.tripadvisor.com/pdfs/OnlineTravelReviewReport.pdf

Hanlan, J., & Kelly, S. (2005). Image formation, information sources and an iconic Australian tourist destination. *Journal of Vacation Marketing, 11*(2), 163–177. doi:10.1177/1356766705052573

Hapkemeyer, A., & Weiermair, P. (1996). *Photo text text photo: The synthesis of photography and text in contemporary art.* Kilchberg, Switzerland: Edition Stemmle.

Jenkins, O. H. (2003). Photography and travel brochures: The circle of representation. *Tourism Geographies, 5*(3), 305–328. doi:10.1080/14616680309715

Kennedy, L., Naaman, M., Ahern, S., Nair, R., & Rattenbury, T. (2007). How Flickr helps us make sense of the world: Context and content in community-contributed media collections. In *Proceedings of the 15th International Conference on Multimedia* (pp. 631-640). Augsburg, Germany: ACM. Retrieved November 12, 2008, from http://portal.acm.org/citation.cfm?id=1291384

La Grange, A. (2005). *Basic critical theory for photographers*. London: Focal Press.

Laboy, F., & Torchio, P. (2007). *Web 2.0 for the travel marketer and consumer: A white paper.* E-site Marketing and the International Association of Online Communicators. Retrieved August 12, 2007, from http://www.wesitemarketing.com/web2-travel-marketing.php

Larsen, J. (2006). Picturing Bornholm: Producing and consuming a tourist place through picturing practices. *Scandinavian Journal of Hospitality and Tourism, 6*(2), 75–94. doi:10.1080/15022250600658853

Leisen, B. (2001). Image segmentation: The case of a tourism destination. *Journal of Services Marketing, 15*(1), 49–66. doi:10.1108/08876040110381517

Lemelin, R. H. (2006). The gawk, the glance, and the gaze: Ocular consumption and polar bear tourism in Churchill, Manitoba, Canada. *Current Issues in Tourism, 9*(6), 516–534. doi:10.2167/cit294.0

Lew, M. S., Sebe, N., Lifl, C. D., & Jain, R. (2006). Content-based multimedia information retrieval: State of the art and challenges. *ACM Transactions on Multimedia Computing . Communications and Applications, 2*(1), 1–19.

Litvin, S. W., Goldsmith, R. E., & Pan, B. (2008). Electronic word-of-mouth in hospitality and tourism management. *Tourism Management, 29*, 458–468. doi:10.1016/j.tourman.2007.05.011

Lueg, C. (2006). Mediation, expansion and immediacy: How online communities revolutionize information access in the tourism sector. In *Proceedings of the 14th European Conference on Information Systems*, Goteborg, Sweden.

MacKay, K. J. (2004). Is a picture worth a thousand words? Snapshots from tourism destination image research. In J. Aramberri & R. Butler (Eds.), *Tourism development: Issues for a vulnerable industry* (pp. 44-65). Clevedon, UK: Channel View Publications.

MacKay, K. J., & Couldwell, C. M. (2004). Using visitor employed photography to investigate destination image. *Journal of Travel Research, 42*, 390–396. doi:10.1177/0047287504263035

MacKay, K. J., & Fesenmaier, D. R. (1997). Pictorial element of destination promotions in image formation. *Annals of Tourism Research, 24*, 537–565. doi:10.1016/S0160-7383(97)00011-X

Mackay, K. J., & Fesenmaier, D. R. (2000). An exploration of crosscultural destination image assessment. *Journal of Travel Research, 38*(4), 417–423. doi:10.1177/004728750003800411

Malhotra, Y. (2001). Knowledge management for e-business performance: Advancing information strategy to 'Internet time'. In Y. Malhotra (Ed.), *Knowledge management and business model innovation* (pp. 2-16). Hershey, PA: Idea Group Publishing.

Markwell, K. W. (1997). Dimensions of photography in a nature-based tour. *Annals of Tourism Research, 24*(1), 131–155. doi:10.1016/S0160-7383(96)00053-9

Milne, S., Grekin, J., & Woodley, S. (1998). Tourism and the construction of place in Canada's eastern Arctic. In G. Ringer & C.L. Cartier (Eds.), *Destinations: Cultural landscapes of tourism* (pp. 101-121). London: Routledge.

Morgan, N. J., Pritchard, A., & Piggott, R. (2003). Destination branding and the role of stakeholders: The case of New Zealand. *Journal of Vacation Marketing, 9*(3), 285–299. doi:10.1177/135676670300900307

Murphy, L., Moscardo, G., & Benckendorff, P. (2007). Exploring word-of-mouth influences on travel decisions: Friends and relatives versus other travellers. *International Journal of Consumer Studies, 31*(5), 517–527. doi:10.1111/j.1470-6431.2007.00608.x

O'Reilly, T. (2005). *What is Web 2.0: Design patterns and business models for the next generation of software*. Retrieved September 14, 2007, from http://www.oreillynet.com/pub/a/oreilly/tim/news/2005/09/30/what-is-web-20.html

Pan, B., MacLaurin, T., & Crotts, J. (2007). Travel blogs and their implications for destination marketing. *Journal of Travel Research, 46*(1), 35–45. doi:10.1177/0047287507302378

Puehringer, S., & Taylor, A. (2008). A practitioner's report on blogs as a potential source of destination marketing intelligence. *Journal of Vacation Marketing, 14*(2), 177–187. doi:10.1177/1356766707087524

Repo, P., Hyvonen, K., & Saastamoinen, M. (2006). Traveling from B2B to B2C: Piloting a moblog service for tourists. In *Proceedings of the International Conference on Mobile Business*. Retrieved November 12, 2008, from http://www2.computer.org/portal/web/csdl/doi/10.1109/ICMB.2006.46

Russell, R., Thomas, P., & Fredline, E. (2005). Mountain resorts in summer: Defining the image. In C.M. Hall & S. Boyd (Eds.), *Nature-based tourism in peripheral areas: Development or disaster?* (pp. 75-90). Clevedon, UK: Channel View Publications.

Schegg, R., Liebrich, A., Scaglione, M., & Ahmad, S. F. S. (2008). An exploratory field study of Web 2.0 in tourism. In P. O'Connor, W. Hoepken, & U. Gretzel (Eds.), *Proceedings of the International Conference on Information and Communication Technologies in Tourism 2008,* Innsbruck, Austria (pp. 152-161). New York: Springer.

Schmallegger, D., & Carson, D. (2008). Blogs in tourism: Changing approaches to information exchange. *Journal of Vacation Marketing, 14*(2), 99–110. doi:10.1177/1356766707087519

Schmallegger, D., & Carson, D. (2009). Destination image projection on consumer generated content websites: A case study of the Flinders Ranges. *Journal of Information Technology and Tourism.*

Sheth, J. N., & Parvatylar, A. (1995). Relationship marketing in consumer markets: Antecedents and consequences. *Journal of the Academy of Marketing Science, 23*(4), 255–271. doi:10.1177/009207039502300405

Snavely, N., Seitz, S. M., & Szeliski, R. (2006). Photo tourism: Exploring photo collections in 3D. *ACM Transactions on Graphics, 25*(3), 835-846. Retrieved August 22, 2008, from http://portal.acm.org/citation.cfm?id=1141911.1141964&coll=GUIDE&dl=GUIDE&CFID=172983&CFTOKEN=91862526

Sontag, S. (1977). *On photography.* London: Penguin Books.

Spaniol, M., Klamma, R., & Lux, M. (2007). Imagesemantics: User-generated metadata, content based retrieval & beyond. In *Proceedings of the 1st International Conference on New Media Technology*, Graz, Austria. Retrieved November 12, 2008, from http://mathias.lux.googlepages.com/imagesemantics-imedia-2007-preprint.pdf

Tapachai, N., & Waryszak, R. (2000). An examination of the role of beneficial image in tourist destination selection. *Journal of Travel Research, 39*(August), 37–44. doi:10.1177/004728750003900105

Van Dijck, J. (2008). Digital photography: Communication, identity, memory. *Visual Communication, 7*(1), 57–76. doi:10.1177/1470357207084865

Waldhoer, K., & Rind, A. (2008). etBlogAnalysis – mining virtual communities using statistical and linguistic methods for quality control in tourism. In P. O'Connor, W. Hoepken, & U. Gretzel (Eds.), *Proceedings of the International Conference on Information and Communication Technologies in Tourism 2008,* Innsbruck, Austria (pp. 453-462). New York: Springer.

Wells, L. (2004). *Photography: A critical introduction* (3rd ed.). London: Routledge.

Wenger, A. (2008). Analysis of travel bloggers' characteristics and their communication about Austria as a tourism destination. *Journal of Vacation Marketing, 14*(2), 169–176. doi:10.1177/1356766707087525

Section 4

Selected Further Readings

Chapter 15
Developing Visual Tourism Recommender Systems

Mohan Ponnada
Victoria University, Australia

Roopa Jakkilinki
Victoria University, Australia

Nalin Sharda
Victoria University, Australia

ABSTRACT

Tourism recommender systems (TRS) have become popular in recent years; however, most lack visual means of presenting the recommendations. This paper presents ways of developing visual travel recommender systems (V-TRS). The two popular travel recommender systems being used today are the TripMatcher™ and Me-Print™. Tour recommendation using image-based planning using SCORM (TRIPS) is a system that aims to make the presentation more visual. It uses SCORM and CORDRA standards. Sharable content object reference model (SCORM) is a standard that collates content from various Web sites, and content object repository discovery and registration/resolution architecture (CORDRA) aims to locate and reference SCORM repositories throughout the Internet. The information collected is stored in the form of an XML file. This XML file can be visualised by either converting it into a Flash movie or into a synchronized multimedia integration language (SMIL) presentation. A case study demonstrating the operation of current travel recommender systems also is presented. Further research in this area should aim to improve user interaction and provide more control functions within a V-TRS to make tour-planning simple, fun and more interactive.

INTRODUCTION

Recommender systems have become popular with the advent of e-commerce. The development of this technology is being strengthened as more people start using the Internet for making purchases. Recommender systems are used by Amazon.com (Linden, Smith, & York, 2003) to recommend books, and movies are recommended on MovieLens (Miller, Albert, Lam, Konstan, & Riedl, 2003). In recent years there has been much work done to improve recommender systems. With increasing Internet adoption, business transactions on the Internet are likely to grow substantially; this encourages vendors to add recommendation capabilities to their Web sites (Peddy & Armentrout, 2003). Tourism is one of the most successful and dynamic industries in the world, and is constantly evolving with continuous technological advancements that include Internet based systems. One such advancement is visual travel recommender systems (V-TRS).

Travel recommender systems (TRSs) are increasingly being adopted to support the tourism industry, some examples of this include Triplehop's TripMatcher™ (Delgado, 2001; Starkov, 2001), and VacationCoach's expert advice platform Me-Print™ (VacationCoach, 2002). A TRS allows tourists to access an informed recommendation for travel planning via an artificial intelligence-based engine. However, current TRSs do not provide tourists with the facility to visualise their complete holiday itinerary, integrating location, transportation, accommodation, attractions, and entertainment. The tourist has to browse through individual Web pages to build a mental picture of the planned tour. In this chapter we introduce the concept of a visual TRS, which can overcome this limitation.

The main objectives of this chapter are:

- To understand recommender systems
- To provide an insight into current application of recommender systems in the tourism industry
- To gain an understanding of services provided by TRS systems, their benefits and limitations
- To present the framework of a visual travel recommender system
- To present a case study demonstrating the operation of current travel recommender systems
- To discuss the future trends in travel recommender systems

BACKGROUND INFORMATION

Recommender Systems

"Recommender Systems are an attempt to mathematically model and technically reproduce the process of recommendations in the real world" (Berka & Plößnig, 2004). Recommender systems are being used by e-commerce Web sites to make suggestions to their customers (Schafer, Konstan, & Riedl, 1999). These recommendations can be made on various factors such as demographics, past buying behaviour of the customers, and prediction of the future buying behaviour.

Recommender systems enhance sales in three different ways (Schafer et al., 1999):

- **Browsers to buyers:** A good Web site can turn visitors of the site into buyers by helping them find the products they wish to purchase.
- **Cross-selling:** Well linked Web pages can improve cross-selling by suggesting additional products for the customer to purchase.
- **Loyalty:** Recommender Systems can improve loyalty by creating a relationship of trust between the Web site and the customer.

Classification of Recommender Systems

The process of recommendation varies depending on the application and the system in question. However, the general concepts underpinning recommender systems are the same. Recommender systems can be classified into four recommendation paradigms (Stabb et al., 2002), namely:

- **Content-based recommender systems**
- **Collaborative-filtering recommendation systems**
- **Knowledge-based recommendation systems**
- **Hybrid recommender systems**

Content-Based Recommender Systems

In content-based recommender systems, the users express their needs, desires and constraints. The recommender system makes a recommendation by matching the user profile with the product information, using information retrieval techniques. The system understands the user's desires and preferences based on the characteristics and ratings provided, and by looking at past user preferences.

However, this system has a number of limitations (Balabanovi, 1997; Shardanand, 1995):

- Firstly, the "new user problem" comes into play since the user has to rate a sufficient number of items before a content-based recommender system understands the user's preferences.
- Secondly, the number of features associated with an item influences this type of system. To extract sufficient features, the content must be in a text form, or features should be assigned to items manually. Such feature extraction is difficult for graphics, audio and video streams.
- A third disadvantage is that a content-based recommender system recommends items that match against the user profile, this provides little opportunity to the users to experience the item being recommended (Shardanand, 1995).

Collaborative-Filtering Recommender Systems

Collaborative-filtering recommender systems are the most widely used recommender system, where user feedback, reviews and rating given by other users are relied upon to recommend an item (Hill, Stead, Rosenstein, & Furnas, 1995). For example, suppose if a user is looking for a book on the Java language in an online book store, the system recommends books which have high ratings based on the feedback from readers who have read various Java books. These systems work well if there is a large volume of ratings for each item.

Reliance on these types of systems is problematic for the recommendation of new items or where the number of reviews is low. Also, it does not account for divergence in preferences between new and previous users. Pazzani (1999) suggests one way of overcoming this limitation via the use of a hybrid recommender system, that combine collaborative, content-based, and demographic filtering approaches.

Knowledge-Based Recommendation Systems

Knowledge-based recommender systems combine the knowledge about the user and the products and services on offer to make a recommendation. If a user visits an online book store, the system recommends other books in related topics. The system knows what the user is looking for, and based on this the system recommends additional products (Burke, 2000). These systems do not need extensive knowledge about an item to make a decision, but like the content-based recommender systems, they require knowledge about the user and his/her buying patterns, which can be acquired by a series of queries.

Hybrid Recommender Systems

Hybrid recommender systems combine two or more recommendation methodologies. These systems were developed in order to overcome the limitations of each of the individual systems. Most often, collaborative-filtering is combined with some other methodology. Decisions are made by combining two or more techniques, including artificial neural networks (Pazzani & Billsus, 1997), information retrieval techniques (Hull, 1998), and Bayesian classifiers (Mooney, Bennett, & Roy, 1998).

In the modern Internet world, recommender systems have the ability to act as key tools that influence the success of a business. "Recommender systems are changing from novelties used by a few e-Commerce sites, to serious business tools that are re-shaping the world of e-Commerce" (Schafer et al., 1999), these systems are supporting many Web sites that help customers find the right product.

Current Travel Recommendation Systems

Since the mid 1990s, tourism Web sites have flourished, allowing users to plan and view their holiday locations online. As tourists began using online tourism information, TRSs were developed to recommend holiday locations and activities. The two most popular recommender systems for tourism and travel presently in use are TripMatcher™ (Delgado, 2001; Starkov, 2001) used by Ski-Europe, and Me-Print™ (VacationCoach, 2002) used by Travelocity.

TripleHop's Trip Matcher™

Traditionally, when a person wanted to go on a holiday, they visited a travel agent and had a counselling session. After having analysed the requirements and specifications of the customer, the travel agent made recommendations as to what would be an ideal place for them to visit. TripleHop's Trip Matcher™ tries to mimic the counselling scenario by allowing the users to search for advice on available destinations. The technical process behind the system is designed so that when the user specifies his/her requirements and constraints, the system matches the specified preferences with the services and items on the catalogue, or the database. This system is being used by Ski-Europe.com.

Ricci (2000) explains, "TripleHop's matching engine uses a more sophisticated approach to reduce user input. It guesses importance of attributes that the user does not explicitly mention. It then combines statistics on past user queries with a prediction computed as a weighted average of importance assigned by similar users."

The system then advises users about potential destinations they may book, based on their interest and browsing pattern. The software learns about user preferences by remembering navigation patterns each time he/she browses through the Web site, enabling it to provide useful recommendations. From an algorithm perspective, it uses contextual filtering and attribute-based collaborative filtering.

VacationCoach Me-Print™

Me-Print™ relies on three important components to give personalised travel advice, namely, intelligent profiling, expert knowledge base, and robust advice engineering. Me-Print™ uses profiling of users to categorize them. It exploits user profile such as their unique lifestyle and leisure preferences in relative terms. For example, if a user likes golf, the algorithm considers user's preference for golf in comparison to other sports such as tennis, or swimming. These multiple preferences are used to provide advice based on priorities and interests.

Services Offered by Current TRS

A travel recommender system allows users to choose their holiday while sitting in front of a computer. A simple user interface provided by the recommender system offers an interactive and simple means of communicating with the system. These systems aim at making the interaction time brief, by reducing the time needed for visiting various Web sites to gather information. At times the system has to deal with issues relating to under, or, over specification of user requirements. The system suggests appropriate repair actions such as "constraint relaxation" if the user has over-specified the requirements, and "tightening," if details have been under specified. The framework for this system is based on case-based reasoning (Ricci, 2002).

The system has the ability to formulate queries and offer various examples to users if they are not experienced enough to come up with a proper query. Ricci (2002) states that an effective TRS should not only support active preference construction, but also should allow users to explore the different options available.

Benefits of Integrating TRS in Today's Business

A TRS system can be very helpful in tourism business, as it displays a list of products retrieved by a query to the system, and allows the user to make an informed selection. After the choice has been made, the initial query is saved along with the selected destination, this enables the system to identify and suggest a better set of products in the future. An information feedback technique such as Rocchio's method (the relevance feedback technique) is used to add new terms and constraints into the original query based on the selections made (Ricci, 2002). Research shows that an accurate recommendation, even if not taken up by the customer, can increase the user's trust in the system, which is necessary for future recommendation acceptance.

Some TRSs interact with the users in multiple stages and pose a sequence of questions, each question raised as a result of previous interaction. If these systems are designed to manage the human-machine interaction effectively they help to grow the business, as the users are not expected to be familiar with the system to begin with. This draws in more potential buyers who need help in making decisions.

Limitations of Current Travel Recommender System

Recommendations from a TRS aim to help the tourist in making informed decisions about their travel plans. However, current TRSs deal only with the first stage of planning a trip, that is, destination selection. Present TRSs are unable to generate a complete travel itinerary which includes information such as accommodation and tourist attractions. Furthermore, a tourist is unable to visualise the planned holiday by using the current TRS technology. New information presentation models are required to increase user's confidence in the selected destination, such as providing the user a view of his/her trip, and allowing comparison between different options on a given trip.

Visual Travel Recommender Systems (V-TRS)

Visual travel recommender system (V-TRS) is a TRS that uses visual information, along with audio, to enhance the presentation of the recommendations made to the user. Two models aiming to develop the V-TRS are presented in the following.

Tourism Recommendation Using Image-Based Planning (TRIP)

Most of the TRSs available today don't provide a complete itinerary, but rather focus solely on the destination selection. This forces travellers to spend a lot of time browsing the Internet, looking for different attractions at their chosen destination. In addition to the suggestions provided by the recommender system, there can be a number of factors that effect the tourist's decision. Generally, tourists seek a second opinion from their acquaintances (relatives and friends). Often, many changes, and some backtracking is required before a travel itinerary is finalised. All of these factors make travel planning a complex undertaking.

As more people rely on the Internet to book their travel plans, it is important for travel Web sites to not only provide textual information, but also visual information. This will further help travellers in their decision-making process. A recommender system with more visual presentation and reasoning enables tourists to get a feel of the destination. The tourism recommendation using image-based planning (TRIP) proposed by Kimber, Georgievski, and Sharda (2006) aims to achieve this.

TRIP Overview

Before booking a holiday package, the traveller would want to have an idea of what he/she is going to experience on the trip. "How am I going to organize my trip?" and "How can I get the maximum value for my time and money?" are the major questions that occur at that point in time. Most of the time, it is difficult to find the right details about the trip, and one has to go though the time consuming process of visiting Web sites, gathering chunks of information and then sorting the details. The TRIP system aims to overcome this drawback by presenting the details visually. The presentation can be customised based on the user's requirements. This will enable the user to have a clear idea as to what he/she is going to experience on the trip. The presentation provided by the visual travel recommender system will include details about the user's selection such as hotels, the services offered by the hotels, the places that he/she is going to visit, and other major activities.

Tour planning is influenced by experiences, thus, the recommender system should provide the tourist with visual clues to assist them in decision making. Planning a complete tour involves various components and decisions, which can be categorised into travel, accommodation, interesting places to visit and hospitality considerations. Some hindrances to decision making can be the time required to gather and analyse information about the destination, balancing schedules with other activities, and ensuring that the travel experience is satisfying.

Keen and Rawlings (2004) have proposed a system which facilitates the decision making process by using a visual language. Their prototype demonstrates tourism products available in Northern Tasmania, Australia. Users are provided information on a wide range of tourism products in the form of images and videos. As the user explores the information, the system keeps track of their browsing pattern, and a logic-based statistical profile is constructed. The profile building is a continuous process—the more the user uses the system, the better the profile becomes. This profile influences the system's interaction with the user in the future and any information of interest to the user is stored in an electronic scrapbook (e-scrapbook).

The e-scrapbook is a personalised area in which the user can place information about items of interest. Typical information could be travel schedule, accommodation booking, and recreational activities. The user can place different products in the e-scrapbook, for example, cost of accommodation at various hotels. The user can easily delete items from the e-scrapbook, and also save items in it for future use. This gives flexibility to the user, and helps in gathering information over a period of time.

The system also allows past users to post their e-scrapbooks on a Web site, thereby allowing new searchers to import partial or entire e-scrapbooks from experienced users. This facility gives new users a demonstration of how to plan a trip, and gives valuable feedback. Once the user is happy with all the information in the e-scrapbook they can purchase the products. This method of travel recommendation using image-based planning helps user to narrow their choices until they are satisfied, and, at the same time, provide a graphical overview.

Tour Recommendation Using Image-Based Planning with SCORM (TRIPS)

In the present Internet environment, tourists have to visit a number of Web sites in an attempt to visualise their tour. The proposed tour recommendation using image-based planning with SCORM (TRIPS) system, will allow tourists to visualise their entire vacation by collating content from various Web sites. TRIPS uses the sharable content object reference model (SCORM) to store tourism information on various Web servers. If tourism Web sites post their information based on the SCORM standard, the proposed system could assemble relevant multimedia content from different sites and present it to the user to create a virtual experience. The SCORM standard has originally been developed as a reference model for Web-based e-learning technology. It is possible for us to adapt this standard for creating a visual experience generator for tourists.

The SCORM standard was proposed by The Department of Defence (DoD) and Advanced Distributed Learning (ADL) laboratories in 1997 to standardise the format of e-learning contents on the Web. The SCORM model aims to improve performance and reduce costs of e-learning systems. It was created by collating various e-learning specifications used by the Institute of Electrical and Electronics Engineers (IEEE). The main objectives of SCORM standards are to define reusable learning objects and to develop content and assessment models. SCORM, as an e-learning standard, enables portability of learning contents, thereby allowing content to be used across different courses. In addition to SCORM, an extension is being developed to enable content registration and resolution of all relevant information throughout the Internet, this is called the content object repository discovery and registration/resolution architecture (CORDRA).

CORDRA

The CORDRA model also is an undertaking of the Department of Defense (DoD) and Advanced Distributed Learning (ADL), and aims to extend the current SCORM standard. This model is being developed so that one can locate and reference SCORM repositories throughout the Internet. Figure 1 presents a conceptual model of how CORDRA will achieve this. CORDRA searches the World Wide Web, much the same way current search engines do. Once the required resources are discovered, their location is resolved; making the resources accessible to SCORM based systems as the sharable content objects (SCOs). Even though SCORM and CORDRA standards have been developed for e-learning systems, these can be used to create visual TRSs. If the tourism Web sites store information using SCORM, then based on a user query, the CORDRA system can collate all related information from the Web. However, the collated information needs to be combined into presentations that the user can view in a controlled manner.

Visual Tour Planning Using TRIPS

The TRIPS system uses sharable content objects (SCOs); these are Web information objects such as pictures, videos, and descriptions of places. Once a traveller's destination is finalised, further options need to be explored. For example, if a traveller is travelling to Melbourne (Australia) in January, options could include watching the Australian Open (tennis), visiting beaches, cruising over the Yarra River, or visiting historic sites. Depending on the number of days available, the tourist can visit all the places mentioned, or visit a selection of places based on priorities. The TRIPS system contains information about the tourist's destination and their interests, and gathers SCOs related to the tourist's interests. Once the tourist finalises his/her selection, TRIPS can create an

Figure 1. Finding and delivering content as SCOs

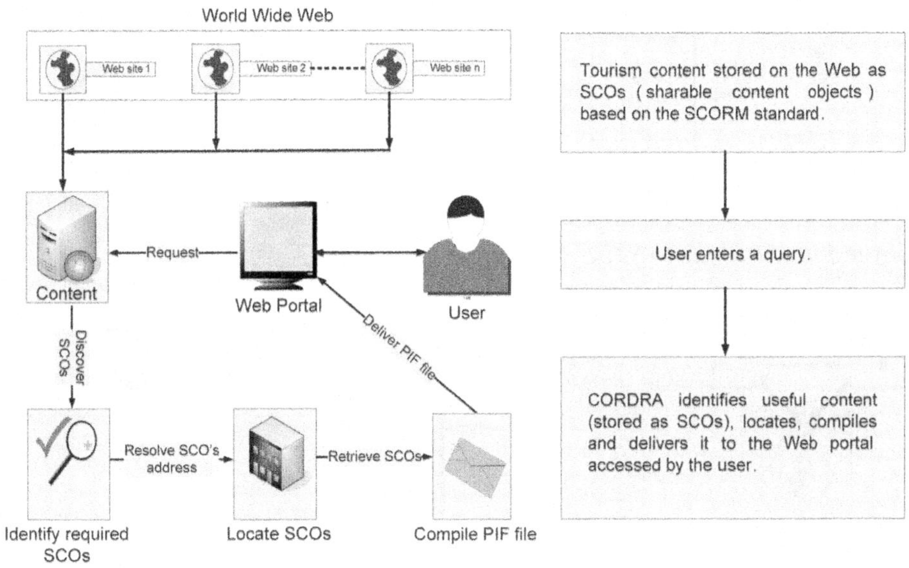

activity tree of the itinerary, and deliver the useful content (SCOs) as a package interchange file (PIF). The PIF contains an XML file (imsmanifest.xml) with all control files and resources referenced in the contents pages. The PIF, therefore contains information about the activities available to the tourist, structured in a hierarchy.

Conversion to Flash Movie

Next, the TRIPS system needs to provide options for delivering content in a user-defined sequence. This enables the user to control the sequence of on-screen displays. The Melbourne tourist may want to consider visiting the Australian Open on the first day and then take a half-day wine tour of the Yarra valley, and relax on a beach in the afternoon, followed by a dinner cruise on the Yarra River. SCOs with information relating to these activities will be collated in the PIF file. The aim is to present to the tourist a short presentation of the travel itinerary being considered. One way to do this is to convert the imsmanifest.xml file to a format compatible with ActiveSWF (Activeswf, 2005) tool which can convert an XML file to a Flash movie. The duration of the movie can be selected by the user bearing in mind the number of options to be viewed. Figure 2 shows the conversion of imsmanifest.xml file to swfmanifest.xml (ActiveSWF readable xml file), and then to a Flash movie.

Conversion to SMIL Movie

The conversion of PIF file into a presentation also can be achieved by using the SMIL standard, as shown in Figure 3. The synchronized multimedia integration language (SMIL) is a W3C recommendation that makes use of XML for creating descriptive multimedia presentations. It defines different mark-ups such as timing mark-up, layout mark-up, animations, and visual transitions. The translated SMIL file can be sent to any user device, such as a Web browser on a computer, or on a portable device. The program checks for parameters such as screen resolution, bandwidth, and customises the SMIL presentation to match the system parameters. This process can optimise the presentation suitable for display on the specific user device.

Figure 2. Conversion of PIF file to Flash movie file using ActiveSWF software

Figure 3. Conversion of PIF file to SMIL file using a translator

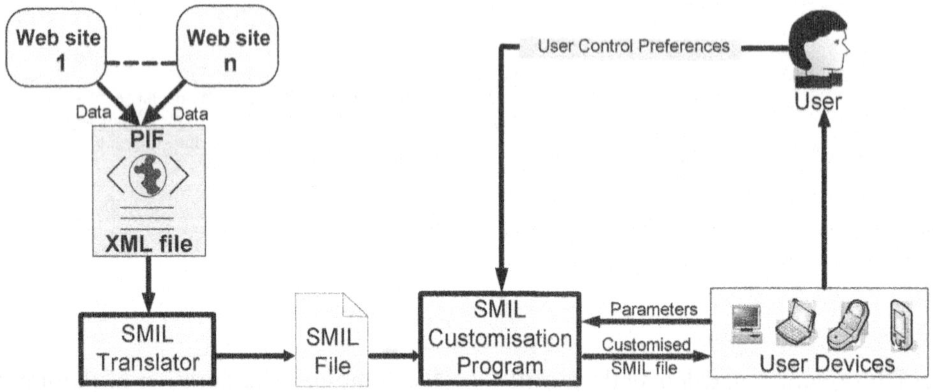

As shown in Figure 3, SCOs from various Web sites are collected and stored into the PIF file, this file is sent to a translator which translates the file into a SMIL file, and the SMIL file is then sent to a customisation program which checks the parameters on the user device. The SMIL file is modified according to these parameters and then sent to the user device for viewing.

TRIPS Architecture

Based on the characteristics of SCORM, a new model has been developed for creating the TRIPS system. This new model allows tourism information to be converted into reusable content packages. These packages will be searchable and accessible through the local SCORM repositories, as well as through the CORDRA enhancement. The advantage of this is that all information stored using the SCORM standard will be more interoperable, accessible, reusable, maintainable and adaptable. The overall architecture of the TRIPS system is shown in Figure 4.

The process of converting imsmanifest.xml to a presentation file (swfmanifest.xml or .smil) takes place on the server-side. On the client-side, a graphical user-interface is used to browse potential destinations and their components.

The TRIPS architecture can be broken down into five main components: visual-TRS Web portal, learning management system (LMS) using SCORM, dynamic tourism information repository, repository access, and CORDRA. This system has three types of users: tourist, system administrator, and content producers.

V-TRS Web Portal

The tourist interacts with the system via the V-TRS portal. This portal works with a SCORM-based learning management system (LMS).

Figure 4. Tour recommendation using image-based planning with SCORM (TRIPS) model

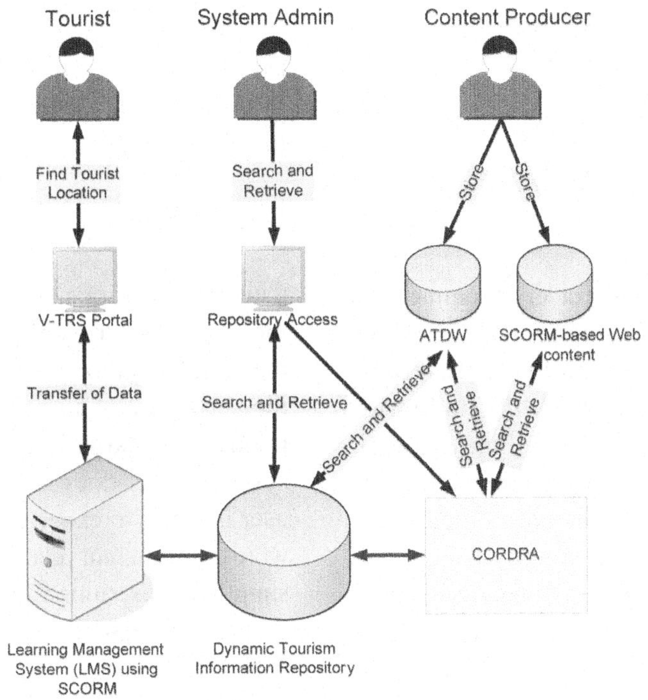

Learning Management System (LMS)

As SCORM is a standard designed for e-Learning, the system designed to use it are called learning management system (LMS). The TRIPS system can use any of the standard LMSs available, and adapt it to work as a V-TRS.

Dynamic Tourism Information Repository

Dynamic tourism information repository is a central storage system. This repository can be set up as a single server or a network of shared resources. The primary function of this repository is to store all the sharable content objects (SCOs) that will be used for tour visualisation.

Repository Access

Repository access is a console or a portal used by the system administrator to access the information within the repository. Unlike the tourist, who gains admittance through the LMS, the system administrator accesses the SCOs in their raw format and can even modify these, if required.

Role of CORDRA

CORDRA, though currently under development, already shows great promise when considering the possibility of incorporating it into the TRIPS model. CORDRA will pave the way for a far superior search facility due to its access to the World Wide Web, which is an ever expanding resource of tourism information. Currently, the Australian Tourism Data Warehouse (ATDW) stores tourism product and destination information that relates to Australian tourism (ATDW, 2005). In order to implement the functionality promised by CORDRA, the ATDW's expanding database could be included. The data from various databases, when combined with information on the Web, creates a huge data source that can be accessed by TRIPS. This provides TRIPS the opportunity to become a universally accessible V-TRS.

FUTURE TRENDS

How Visual TRS Can Enhance the Current TRS

Even though the current travel recommender systems make quality recommendations to the user, these recommendations are not presented in a way that lets the user visualise the entire trip. Future recommender systems will make use of audio-visual media to provide an in-depth view of the user's trip, where, the human-computer interaction is made more interesting by using audio and video in innovative ways. Dynamic text will be displayed along with the images to provide a description of each destination. Narration of this text in different languages also will be possible. TRIPS can be used in a distributed environment using CORDRA. If all tourism related Web sites are SCORM and CORDRA compliant, then information from any Web site can be retrieved and used to recommend a complete holiday plan, including travel, accommodation, and other activities. Tourists will then have an easy and effective way of planning their personal or business travel. This also will improve the credibility of the World Wide Web as an effective vehicle for travel planning.

Case Study

Current recommender systems are not very interactive in terms of presenting the details of the tour. Even though the recommendations that they make are of a good quality, their presentation is more textual and rather unappealing. The system output does not give a feel of what the user is going to experience on the trip. In other words, the current recommender systems give a simplistic description of the different available destinations and offers.

For the purpose of this case study, we have developed a Web site that emulates how current TRSs work and make suggestions based upon user's choices and other criterion. We discuss this system and present screen shots of its user interface.

Figure 5 shows the input screen for the recommender system. First, one must answer some

Figure 5. Input screen of the travel recommender system

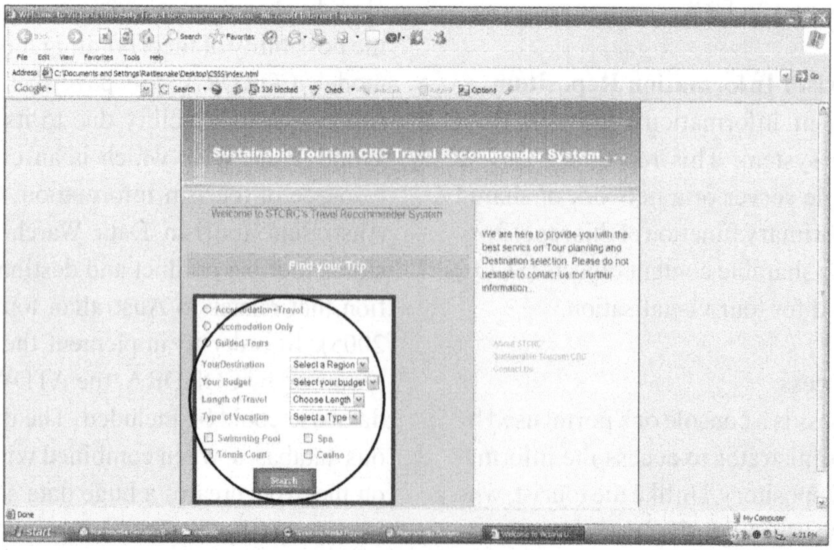

Figure 6. Screen showing the recommendations made by the system

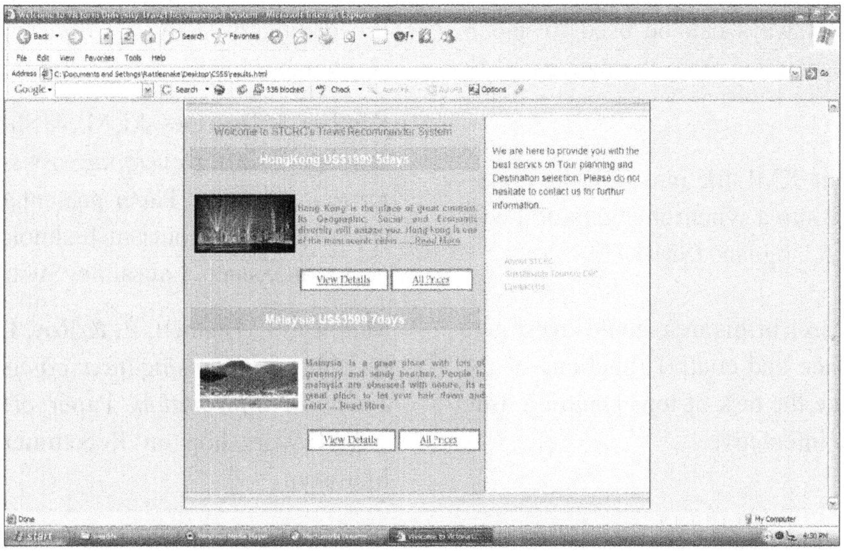

questions, such as the region, budget, desired length of vacation, type of vacation and other such preferences.

The user input is analysed and the system makes recommendations with brief details of different packages which match the user's preferences. In this case, if the user wants to know what is included in each package, he/she needs to visit different Web links. Figure 6 shows a screen capture of how recommendations are often displayed.

To some extent, recommendations made by such systems are useful; however, they fail to hold the user's attention. Our aim is to present these recommendations in a more appealing and attractive manner. We want to make the process of making recommendations more fun and interactive, by changing the way information is presented to the user. Rather than displaying the recommendations in the form of text, we are introducing audio, video and text narration, thereby taking the concept of travel recommender systems to the next level.

CONCLUSION

The technology of recommender systems is improving constantly as more people use the Internet for making purchases. Vendors all over the world are encouraged to add recommender capabilities to their Web sites to attract more online business. This chapter discussed how the limitations of current travel recommender systems (TRS) can be eliminated by using visual travel recommender systems (V-TRS). Recommender systems are classified as content-based, collaborative, knowledge-based and hybrid. The most widely used travel recommender systems today are the TripMatcher™ and MePrint™. Current TRSs only deal with the first stage of tour planning, that is, destination selection, and are unable to provide a visual presentation of the entire tour. The proposed V-TRS aims to save time, while making the systems more interactive, and providing a visual presentation to give the tourist a feel of the entire trip. In this chapter we have proposed a sharable content object reference model (SCORM) based architecture to visualise the tour, and suggested ways to use the content object repository discovery and registration/resolution architecture (CORDRA) enhancement.

Two different ways can be used to generate a video presentation from the data in XML format:

- Convert the XML file into a Flash movie
- Convert it into a synchronized multimedia integration language (SMIL) file

Further research in this area should investigate the user interface and control functions of the V-TRSs to make the task of tour planning, fun, easy, and more interactive.

REFERENCES

Activeswf. (2005). *Software ActiveSWF Prof 1.9.3.* Retrieved December, 2005 from http://www.activeswf.com

ATDW. (2005). *Australian Tourism Data Warehouse.* Retrieved December, 2005 from http://www.atdw.com.au

Balabanovi, M., & Shoham, Y. (1997). Fab: Content-based, collaborative recommendation. *ACM Communication, 40*(3), 66-72.

Berka, T., & Plößnig, M. (2004). Designing recommender systems for tourism. In *Enter 2004*, Kairo.

Burke, R. (2000). Knowledge-based recommender systems. *Encyclopedia of Library and Information Systems, 69*(32).

Delgado, J. (2001). *Who's who in recommender systems.* Paper presented at the ACM SIGIR Workshop on Recommender Systems, New Orleans.

Hill, W., Stead, L., Rosenstein, M., & Furnas, G. (1995). *Recommending and evaluating choices in a virtual community of use.* Paper presented at the CHI-95 Conference, Denver, CO.

Hull, A. D. (1998). *The TREC-7 filtering track: description and analysis.* Paper presented at the Proceedings of TREC-7, 7th Retrieval Conference, Gaithersburg, US.

Kimber, J., Georgievski, M., & Sharda, N. (2006, January 18-20). *Developing a visualisation tool for tour planning.* Paper presented at the IFITT Global Travel & Tourism Technology and eBusiness Conference, Lausanne, Switzerland.

Mooney, R., Bennett, P., & Roy, L. (1998). *Book recommending using text categorzation with extracted information.* Paper presented at the AAAI Workshop on Recommender Systems, Madison.

Pazzani, J. M. (1999). A framework for collaborative, content-based and demographic filtering. *Artificial Intelligence Review, 13*, 393-408.

Pazzani, J. M., & Billsus, D. (1997). Learning and revising user profiles: The identification of interesting Web sites. *Machine learning, 27*(3), 313-331.

Ricci, F. (2002). Travel recommender systems. *IEEE Intelligent Systems*, 55-57.

Schafer, J. B., Konstan, J. A., & Riedl, J. (1999). *Recommender systems in electronic commerce.* Paper presented at the ACM Conference on Electronic Commerce.

Shardanand, U., & Maes, P. (1995). *Social information filtering: Algorithms for automating "word of mouth."* Paper presented at the Proceedings of ACM conference on Human Factors in Computing Systems.

Stabb, S., Werther, H., Ricci, F., Zipf, A., Gretzel, U., Fesenmaier, D. R., et al. (2002). Intelligent systems for tourism. *Intelligent Systems, IEEE [see also IEEE Intelligent Systems and Their Applications], 17*(6), 53-66.

Starkov, M. (2001). *How to turn lookers into bookers—Recommendation engines in travel and hospitality*, Retrieved May 10, 2006, from http://www.hotel-online.com/News/PR2001_3rd/Aug01_EnginesinTravel.html

VacationCoach. (2002). *Using knowledge personalization to sell complex products*. Retrieved January 20, 2006, from http://crm.ittoolbox.com/pub/LK032002.pdf

This work was previously published in Information and Communication Technologies in Support of the Tourism Industry, edited by W. Pease, M. Rowe, and M. Cooper, pp. 162-179, copyright 2007 by IGI Publishing (an imprint of IGI Global).

Chapter 16
A Framework for Ontology-Based Tourism Application Generator

Roopa Jakkilinki
Victoria University, Australia

Nalin Sharda
Victoria University, Australia

ABSTRACT

This chapter provides an overview of tourism ontology and how it can be used for developing e-tourism applications. The Semantic Web is the next generation Web; it uses background knowledge captured as an ontology and stored in machine-processable and interpretable form. Ontologies form the core of the Semantic Web and can be used to develop intelligent applications. However, generating applications based on ontology still remains a challenging task. This chapter presents a framework that provides a systematic process for developing intelligent e-tourism applications by using a tourism ontology.

INTRODUCTION

Tourism is one of the most successful and dynamic industries in the world, and it is constantly evolving because of technological advancements. Information technology is being used to enhance tourism services such as travel bookings, itinerary planning, destination marketing, and information sharing. These services use dynamic Web applications.

The current tourism applications rely on static information sources such as Web sites to create tourism products and services. These applications lack intelligence; for example, an itinerary planner in the current scenario will allow the tourist to make bookings, but it cannot suggest an itinerary based on the travellers preferences. A Semantic Web application using an ontology, generic profiling, and semi-structured query tools can overcome the technical limitations of the current systems, and help build intelligent e-tourism tools, or applications.

This chapter discusses the purpose of developing a tourism ontology and proposes a model to develop intelligent tourism applications based on the same. The second section presents the background knowledge, followed by a proposed model for developing e-tourism applications, the following section demonstrates the working of an itinerary planner, and we finish with the conclusions.

The main objective of this chapter is to present a framework for developing ontology based e-tourism applications. The specific foci of the chapter are:

- To provide an understanding of the Semantic Web and ontologies
- To introduce various existing travel ontologies and applications based on the same
- To describe a process model for developing e-tourism applications
- To present a case study using an intelligent itinerary planner

BACKGROUND

Semantic Web

The Semantic Web was thought up by Tim Berners-Lee as a mesh of information linked up in such a way so as to be easily processable by machines. It is not intended to be read by people, as it describes relationships between data that software will interpret (Palmer, 2001). Figure 1 represents the Semantic Web stack which has a layered architecture, it is based on a hierarchy of languages, each language both exploiting the features, and extending the capabilities of the layers below (Butler, 2003). A brief introduction to the Semantic Web layers is presented in the following:

- **Uniform resource identifier (URI):** The Web naming and addressing convention, like the strings starting with "http" or "ftp"; they are short strings used to identify resources on the Web. Anyone can create new URIs. Example: http://melba.vu.edu.au/roopa.txt.
- **Unicode:** A replacement for the older ASCII code and can cope with multiple languages. It is a 16-bit code that can be used to represent the characters in most of the world's scripts.
- **Extensible Markup Language (XML):** A standard format for serializing data using tags; XML file can contain data like a database, it is derived from Standard Generalized Markup Language (SGML) and is somewhat similar to Hypertext Markup Language (HTML). XML schema is a schema language used for describing XML data as well-defined schemas or data models. XML namespaces (NS) is an extension to XML for managing a collection of names identified by URIs.
- **Resource description framework (RDF):** This allows users to add metadata to describe the core data; RDF Schema is a language for describing RDF vocabularies (Bray, n.d.); in other words, RDF schema provides a way of organizing a large set of RDF vocabulary.
- **Ontology vocabulary:** A data model that represents the terminology used in a domain; it also is used to reason about the objects in that domain and the relations between them. Web Ontology Language (OWL) and Darpa Agent Markup Language + Ontology Interchange Language (DAML+OIL) are some of the languages used to describe ontologies.
- **Logic:** The Logic layer allows carrying out reasoning on a set of data, based on predefined rules, in order to draw conclusions. Inference engines or reasoners (Inference Engine, n.d.), such as, Racer, Fact, and Pellet work at this layer.
- **Proof and trust:** The proof and trust layers are still nascent. In most applications construction of proof is done by using some

rules, the other party can use these rules to see whether or not a statement is true. Trust layer allows the creation of digital signatures for authentication and encryption.

What are Ontologies?

An ontology is a data model that represents a domain; it can be used to reason about the objects in that domain and the relations between them. Ontologies represent knowledge about the world or some part of it, they consist of: classes, collection of objects; attributes, properties an object can have and share; relations, represent the way the objects are related; and individuals, which are instances of the class (Chandrasekaran, Josephson, & Benjamins, 1999).

An ontology can be a domain ontology and theory ontology (Swartout, Patil, Knight, & Russ, 1997). A domain ontology models a specific domain; it represents the particular meanings of terms as they apply to that domain, for example, tourism. A theory ontology provides a set of concepts for representing some aspect of the world, such as time and space.

Need for Tourism Ontology

Ontologies are especially useful where multiple entities such as researchers and organisations are active in the same domain, but each entity uses their own data model for that domain. For example, in the tourism domain, different entities such as travel agents, hotel chains, national, and regional tourism organisations have their own way of representing their services to the consumer (accommodation, events, attractions, services, etc.) using different data models. Furthermore, these data models maybe represented using different software technologies. This leads to interoperability problems, that is, software developed for one system cannot access data on another.

If tourism entities need to communicate with one another, a common data representation is needed. This common representation needs to represent both the concepts in the domain, and the relationships between these concepts. In addition, it should be possible for each tourism entity to map its data models to that used in a common ontology.

Having an ontology is very useful in this situation; as it models the domain in a structured

Figure 1. The Semantic Web stack, and its layers covered in this chapter

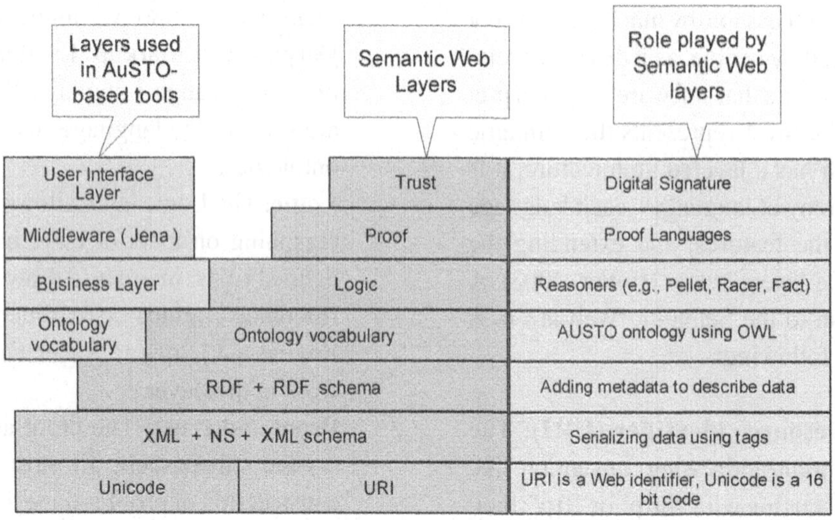

manner, all entities will be able to use the ontology to communicate with all other entities, by mapping their source data model to the common ontology and then using the existing mappings between the ontology and the other destination data models (Clissmann & Höpken, n.d.).

Another benefit of ontologies is that they make it possible to carry out reasoning on the domain, they also act as back ends for intelligent applications, that is, they provide the ability to derive domain knowledge for developing intelligent applications. These applications, with the help of a reasoner, can infer facts from the domain ontology. Creating an ontology for tourism will allow knowledge sharing between different tourism organizations, and also will allow for the creation of intelligent e-tourism tools such as search engines and tour planners.

Travel Ontologies

A variety of tourism ontologies have been developed to date. In this section we give an overview of a number of tourism related ontologies. The Harmonise ontology is not only a minimun standard ontology, but also a means of reconciling various ontologies.

OTA Specification

The Open Travel Alliance specifications have been designed to serve two purposes, namely to act as a common language for travel related services, and to provide a mechanism for information exchange between travel industry members (The Open Travel Alliance, n.d.). It is possible to view the OTA specifications as a comprehensive ontology, defining concepts such as AirSchedule, GolfCourseReservation, HotelContentDescription, HotelPreferences, and so on. The OTA specification has already been utilised in a travel related project called Agentcities (Gordon, Kowalski, Paprzycki, Pelech, Szymczak, & Wasowicz, 2005).

MONDECA

MONDECA's tourism ontology defines tourism concepts based on the World Tourism Organization (WTO) thesaurus (MONDECA, n.d.). These include among others, terms for tourism object profiling, tourism and cultural objects, tourism packages, and tourism multimedia content. MONDECA has created a proprietary system called the Intelligent Topic Manager (ITM) that is used to manage its travel ontology.

TAGA Ontology

The Travel Agent Game in Agentcities (TAGA) is an agent framework for simulating the global travel market on the Web. Its purpose is to demonstrate the capabilities of Agentcities (Agentcities, n.d.) and Semantic Web technologies. TAGA works on the Foundation for Intelligent Physical Agents (FIPA) compliant platforms within the Agentcities environment (The Foundation for Intelligent physical agents, n.d.). In addition to the FIPA content language ontology, TAGA defines two domain ontologies to be used in simulations. The first ontology covers basic travel concepts such as itineraries, customers, travel services, and service reservations. The second ontology is devoted to auctions and defines different type of auctions, roles the participants play in them, and the protocols used. TAGA ontologies are limited in their usability, and are rather unrealistic due to the nature of the TAGA simulations.

Harmonize Ontology

Harmonize is an attempt at ontology-mediated integration of tourism systems following different standards (E-Tourism, n.d.). Its goal is to allow organizations to exchange information without changing their data models. The Harmonize project also involves sub-domains that are partially related to the world of travel: geographical and geo-spatial concepts, means of transportation, political, temporal, and gastronomy, and so forth. These sub-domain concepts can be used within the travel system.

Numerous ontologies have been developed for the domain of tourism. Defining and agreeing on the right ontology is a difficult task. One could argue that the choice of the right ontology is purely subjective, because the meaning of various terms differs across domains, users, and situations. Each of these ontologies have been developed with a specific task in mind and specialises in a particular aspect of the tourism domain; for example, a tourism ontology that specialises in tourism events can be used to develop an event planner. Most of the ontologies have been developed with a tool in mind, and their scope is limited to that tool. We have developed an abstract ontology called the Australian sustainable tourism ontology (AuSTO) which covers all the general concepts used in tourism, both from the customer perspective and from the enterprise perspective; subsequently several intelligent tools such a tour planner, search engines and travel recommender systems are planned for development based on the AuSTO ontology.

Applications Based on Travel Ontologies

A number of intelligent applications such as search engines, tour planners, and location-based tour guides have been developed using ontologies. These applications help the traveller as well as tour operator to plan trips and find information about destinations. In this section we describe two such applications and their usage.

On Tour

On Tour can be considered as an intelligent search engine. The main objective of the On Tour system is to connect isolated pieces of information, that is, to assist the user in finding information from a variety of sources, and to allow individualized use of the same (Daniel, 2005). As a search engine, On Tour allows for the querying of distributed data as well as considering the semantics of discovered concepts and instances. It allows the user to specify preferences like maximum budget and minimum comfort, and define further constraints such as personal schedule. This system helps the user to plan a vacation from the beginning to the end. In later phases of development On Tour will act as a recommender system by giving advice on best restaurants, venue for musicals, and so on. It also will provide support for mobile devices. On Tour approach is to extract pieces of information from structured Web pages and conduct constraint based reasoning for the integration of multiple information sources.

Talea

Talea is a platform aimed at supporting the development of Web-based tourism applications (Levi, Vagliengo, & Goy, 2005). This software was designed and developed within the Diadi 2000 (Dissemination of Innovation in Industrial Decline areas) project. The Diadi 2000 project aims at applying ICT technologies to small and medium enterprises (SMEs) to increase the value of their businesses. Talea provides for multi device access, where customers and suppliers can use PDAs or smart phones to buy and offer tourism services. This software acts as a matchmaker by matching service provision with request; tourism suppliers can advertise their services such as room availability, car rentals, and so on, and customers can perform a search for a particular service.

Dynamic Packaging System

An important type of e-tourism application that has evolved in recent years is a dynamic packaging system (Cardaso, 2005). It is used by airlines, hotels, tour operators, and travel agencies to create customised packages for individual consumers. Dynamic packaging can be defined as the combining of different travel components, bundled and priced in real-time, in response to the request from a consumer or a booking agent. They have created an e-tourism ontology that allows interoperability through the use of shared vocabulary and meanings for terms. Semantic mediators are used to support a virtual view that integrates semantically annotated e-tourism information sources. Final dynamic package processes are created using conditional planning ranking and selection. Once the dynamic package processes are evaluated they are presented to the tourist and the tourist can select the package that he finds most appealing or suitable according to his preferences.

TOURISM APPLICATION GENERATOR ARCHITECTURE

Figure 2 presents the underlying model for generating ontology based e-tourism applications; called the e-tourism application generator architecture (e-TAGA). The e-TAGA model consists of three layers: the ontology layer (OL), the business logic layer (BLL) and the graphical user interface layer (GUIL). The OL provides persistence for the tourism ontology; the business logic layer includes two common components and parts of the tourism applications themselves. The two common components in the BL are the inference engine (IE) and the custom logic (CL). The GUI layer includes the graphical user interface (GUI) components of individual tourism applications and some common GUI elements.

Ontology Layer (OL)

The ontology layer consists of the ontology which embodies knowledge about the domain and some additional specifications. This layer is the core of all Semantic Web systems. We will use the AuSTO ontology to exemplify the operation of the various layers.

Tools for Ontology Development

In any ontology development project one needs to begin by selecting an ontology development tool. In the AuSTO project three different tools were compared in order to decide which one of these would be most suitable for our tourism ontology development. The three tools considered were Protégé 2000, Ontolingua, and OntoEdit free. This comparison was based on ontological aspects and usability aspects. Our study indicated that Protégé 2000 is far superior in usability and ontology as-

Figure 2. A tourism application generator architecture (e-TAGA)

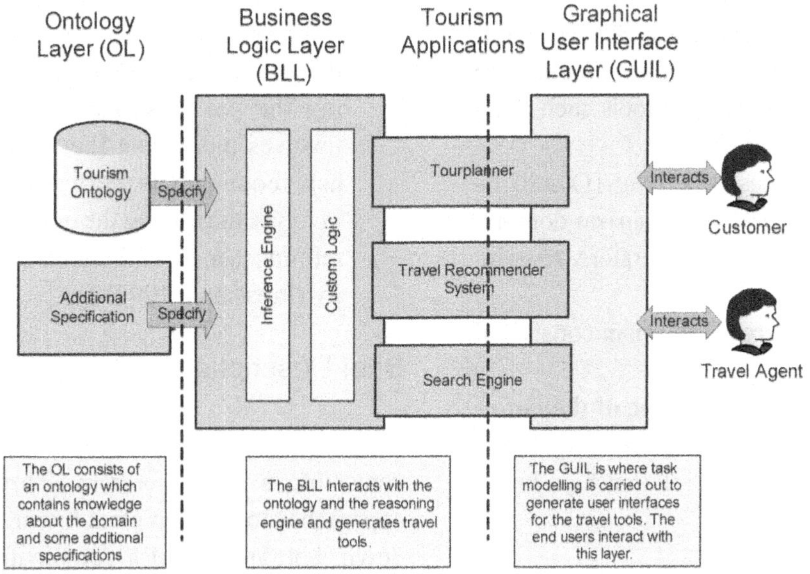

pects as compared to Ontolingua and OntoEdit free (Jakkilinki, Sharda, & Georgievski, 2005), hence Protégé2000 was selected. Protégé2000 (Protégé, n.d.) comprises an open architecture that allows programmers to insert arbitrary components into the tool. This feature can be exploited during the development of Semantic Web applications based on the ontology. An additional benefit of Protégé 2000 toolkit is developers can package the implementation of the application as a Protégé plug-in and test how the system behaves in response to any changes in the ontology.

Methodology Followed to Develop AuSTO Ontology

Ontology development methodology includes tools, techniques and process followed in order to develop the ontology. The methodology followed to develop the AuSTO ontology is as follows (Jakkilinki et al., 2005).

1. **Identify the purpose behind ontology development:** The pertinent questions are listed here, along with their answer for AuSTO development.
    - Why is the ontology being built? In the case of AuSTO, the ontology is being built to describe the tourism domain.
    - What is its intended use? AuSTO ontology will be used as a knowledge base to develop intelligent tools such as an itinerary planner.
    - Who are the users? AuSTO will be used by operators in tourism domain, such as the tourist operators, tourism vendors.
2. **Ontology capture mechanism** consists of three different stages:
    - **Determining the scope of the ontology:** This involves identifying all the key concepts and relationships in the domain.
    - **Selecting a method to develop the ontology:** The method we followed to develop AuSTO is the top-down approach.
    - **Defining the concepts in the ontology:** This involves taking closely related terms and grouping them as classes.
3. **Coding the ontology:** Coding refers to representing the ontology in some formal language. A suitable ontology editor has to be selected, in the case of AuSTO the ontology editor used is Protégé. Once the ontology editor is selected the classes have to be entered as concepts and their attributes are entered as slots.
4. **Refinement:** This consists of two phases, namely intra-coding refinement and extra-coding refinement. Intra-coding refinement refers to the refinement done during the coding phase, whereas extra-coding refinement refers to the changes made to overcome the errors uncovered during the testing and maintenance stages.
5. **Testing:** The testing process uncovers any defects in functional logic and implementation. Testing should be carried out during all stages of development.
6. **Maintenance:** This can be corrective, adaptive or perfective. Corrective maintenance involves correcting the ontology to overcome the errors discovered by users while querying the ontology. Adaptive maintenance involves modifying the ontology to fulfil new requirements. Perfective maintenance involves improving the ontology by further refining it, in order to enhance its functionality (Pressman, 1997).

Brief Description of Classes in AuSTO

Creating an ontology involves delineating concepts into a class hierarchy. Three important approaches to develop class hierarchies are top-down, bottom-up and a combination approach

(Uschold & Gruninger, 1996). In the top-down approach the development process starts with the definition of the most general concepts in the domain, followed by specialised concepts. In the bottom-up approach the development process starts with the definition of the most specific classes, which form the leaves of the class hierarchy tree, with subsequent grouping of these classes into more general concepts. The combined approach uses a combination of top-down and bottom-up processes. The approach followed for AuSTO is the bottom-up approach. This approach is usually driven by the need for having a workable vocabulary quickly and then enhancing it as the project progresses. AuSTO is written in OWL (Web Ontology Language), Figure 3 is a screen shot of AuSTO ontology in Protégé. The AuSTO ontology consists of a class hierarchy shown on the left, each class has properties and one can create individuals, or instances of a class, using the instance tab in the Protégé interface.

AuSTO being tourism ontology it contains classes from the tourism domain. Following list gives some of the important classes in AuSTO:

- **Involved party** can be traveller, vendor, operator, and so forth.
- **Requirement** refers to travel requirements
- **Offering** includes travel products and services.
- **Solution** refers to systems outputs such as itineraries.
- **Resource** can be reserved or rented items.
- **Specification** allows for both offering specifications and requirement specifications
- **Preference** includes traveller's preferences such as date, time, location, or price range.

Each of these classes can represent a plethora of tourism information. For example, requirement represents diverse travel requirements such as accommodation, entertainment, transport, and offering represents the wide range of travel products and services that vendors make available to the traveller, often as part of a packaged solution.

Business Layer

The business logic layer (BLL) uses an inference engine and custom logic, and is responsible for generating outcomes; that is, it returns results based on user interactions. Figure 4 describes the BLL for the applications based on AuSTO.

Figure 3. A screen shot of the AuSTO ontology

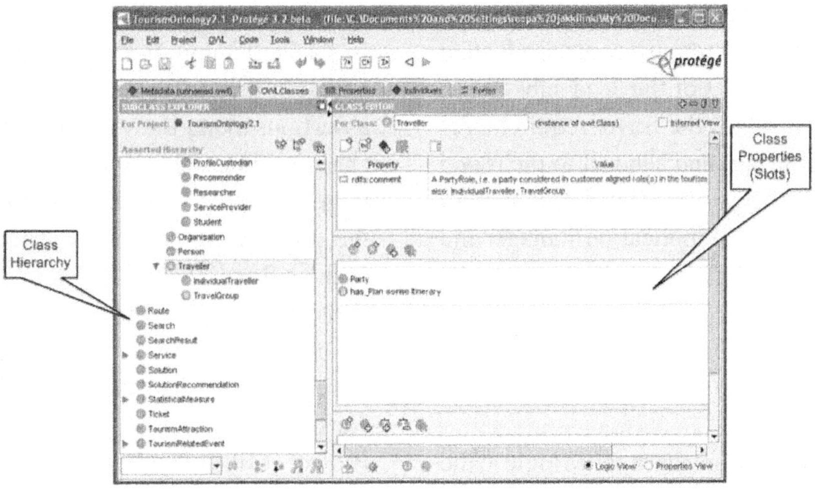

Figure 4. Architecture for the business layer

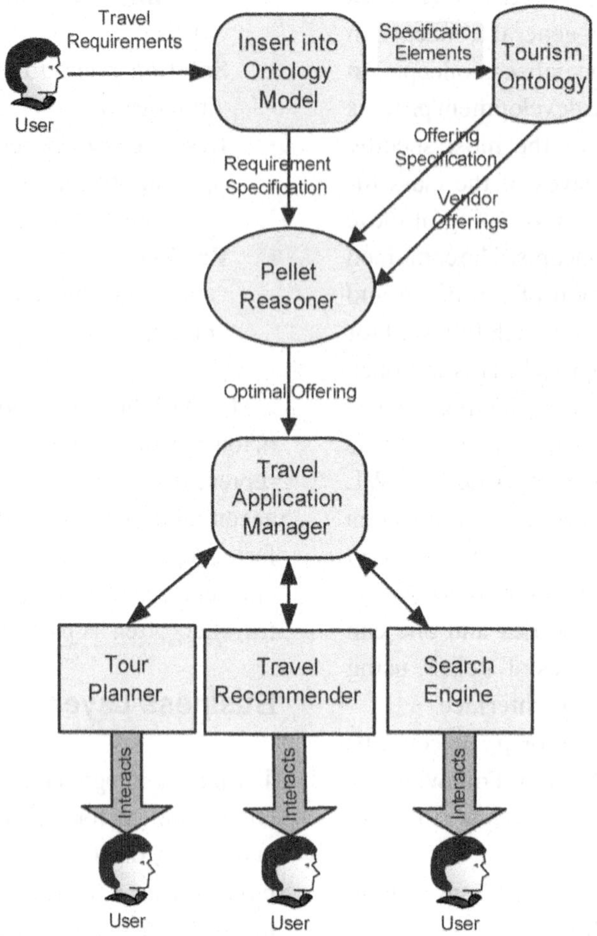

A user specifies his travel requirements in the ontology and the tourism vendor advertises his offerings which are tourism services in the ontology. The offerings and requirements are loaded into the ontology model of the Jena subsystem. Pellet reasoner matches the travel requirements to the vendor offerings and sends it to the travel application manger. Travel tools such as tour planners can query the travel application manager and produce the travel solution, which in this case is an itinerary.

What are Reasoners?

The reasoner is a software that applies logic to the knowledge embodied in the ontology for arriving at some conclusions (*Inference Engine*, n.d.). We generally recognize two types of inferencing, namely forward chaining, and backward chaining. In forward chaining one proceeds from a given situation towards a desired goal by adding new assertions along the way; whereas, in backward chaining one starts with the desired goal and then attempts to find the method for arriving at the goal. A number of reasoners are available, such as Racer, FaCT, Pellet, and F-OWL. Pellet is the reasoner used in the AuSTO project, it is an open-source Java-based OWL DL reasoner developed by the Maryland Information and Network Dynamics Lab Semantic Web Agents Project (Mindswap, n.d.).

Role Played by Jena

Jena is a Java framework for building Semantic Web applications, it is open source and has been developed by HP (Hewlett Packard) Labs. Jena acts as a middleware which connects the ontology, reasoner and the user interface. In Jena all operations are done by manipulating the Jena model. Therefore, to manipulate an ontology it needs to be loaded into the Jena model first. Jena has four subsystems: query engine, database interface, reasoning engine, and ontology management. Jena's architecture allows external reasoners to be plugged into the Jena models.

User Interface Layer

One of the most difficult aspects of building an application is designing the user interface. User Interface design is the design of the graphical elements on the computer screen with which a user interacts to conduct application tasks. The user interface is as important as the functionality of the application, and plays an important role in the success of any product. User interfaces accomplish two fundamental tasks: communicating information from the computer to the user and communicating information from the user to the computer.

The benefits of a good user interface design include: lower training costs, less user stress, consistency in application usage, increased ability to recover from errors, better user control, less clicks to find information, ability to store more information per screen, easier to use the software, selection amongst many choices using limited space, see all selections at all times, better understanding of the software, save screen space, and higher data entry speed (Miller, n.d.).

Task analysis and modelling techniques are increasingly being used in designing user interfaces, they form an important part of user interface design process and help design more intuitive interfaces.

What are Task Analysis and Task Modelling?

Task analysis involves the study of a system functionality as a collection of tasks. Generally the systems function is divided into a set of top-level tasks, and each one of these is further divided into sub-tasks, and so forth to develop a task-tree. This process can be used to guide the design of new systems beginning with user requirement capture. One of the most important applications of task analysis is designing user interfaces, in which menus are based on the task trees. The top level menus can be labelled after the top level tasks and the sub menus after the next level tasks (Dix, Finlay, Abowd, & Beale, 1998).

After an informal task analysis where the main tasks and their attributes have been identified, task modelling is used to understand the relationships among the various tasks in order to better address the design of interactive applications.

As task modelling is used to model the behaviour of a system from user's perspective, it captures the system requirements and actions defined as a set of tasks, and models the behaviour of the system as a scenario of tasks. This allows the designers to improve the human computer interaction aspects when designing a system's operation (Georgievski & Sharda, 2003). Although task models have long been considered in human-computer interaction, only recently have user interface developers and designers realized their importance to obtain more effective and consistent solutions (Giulio, Paterno, & Santaro, 2002). Task models play an important role because they represent the logical activities that should support users in reaching their goals, and knowing the tasks necessary to attain a goal is fundamental to any good design (Paterno, 2002).

There are two types of task models: user task model and system task model. A user task model states the problems to be solved by the system, and thus consists of overlapping user scenarios (Georgievski & Sharda, 2003). Actors involved in a user task model are generally human; however, it may include external systems and the environment. A system task model forms the basis for specifying a solution in the form of system requirements. Actors involved in a system task model are generally subsystems, interfaces, and, at times humans.

Tools for Task Modelling

One of the main problems in task modelling is that it is a time-consuming and sometimes tedious process. To overcome this problem interest has been increasing in tools that support task analysis and modelling. However, current tools are outcomes of research projects, and are used mainly by groups that have developed them.

The concur task tree environment (CTTE) is a Java Applet based tool developed by Human Computer Interaction Group – ISTI (Pisa). CTTE provides the ability to build task models from a visual perspective where the user can define and structure the tasks in a logical fashion using the graphical editor provided in the tool. CTTE enables the user to focus on the activities of their model and thus allowing the user to identify the requirements of the model and organize them into a logical hierarchy of task and subtasks (Georgievski & Sharda, 2003).

The main features of the CTTE tool are (Giulio et al., 2002):

- **Focuses on activities:** Allows designers to concentrate on the activities that a user has to perform, rather than programming details.
- **Hierarchical structure:** Provides a wide range of granularity allowing large and small task tree structures to be developed and reused.
- **Graphical syntax:** Facilitates easy interpretation of the logical task structure using graphical representation.
- **Concurrent notation:** Provides rich set of possible temporal relationships that can be used to specify the relationship between the tasks.
- **Distinct task representations:** Uses distinct icons to represent user task, application task, interaction task, and abstract task

CTTE provides the ability to build two types of task models: single user task models and cooperative task models. Single user task models are used to represent systems that a single user controls. A cooperative task model is similar to a single user task model; however it includes tasks executed by two or more users.

Other useful features of CTTE tool are model comparison, reachability analysis, and interactive task model simulator (Giulio et al., 2002).

ITINERARY PLANNER CASE STUDY

In this section we describe the task model created to represent the user interface for the itinerary planner. This task model guide the development of the user interface by focusing on the various functions the user interface needs to perform.

CTTE allows the following types of tasks to build the entire task model:

- **Abstract tasks** define a set of subtasks to be performed at a conceptual level
- **User tasks** denoted the operation/tasks executed by the user
- **Interaction tasks** represent tasks that carry out communication between entities within the task model.
- **Application tasks** are of tasks executed by the system or application entities in the process model

CTTE uses transition notations to describe the temporal relationships between tasks and the execution sequence for the task model. The

Table 1. Temporal operators used in CTTE

Syntax	Notation	Description
T1 [] T2	Choice	A choice between two or more tasks
T1>>T2	Enabling	T1 enables T2 when T1 is terminated
T1[]>>T2	Enabling with Information Exchange	T1 provides some information to T2 besides enabling it
T1|> T2	Suspend/Resume	T2 can interrupt T1, and when T2 is terminated T1 can be reactivated from the state reached before the interruption
T*	Iteration	Tasks performed repetitively

temporal operators used in CTTE are described in Table 1.

We have implemented the task model for itinerary planner as a single user task model that represents the overall function of the user interface from a user perspective. We represent these tasks as tree diagrams in Figures 5 to 11. In the task tree diagram we define the execution sequence for each task using the temporal operators described in Table 1.

Figure 5: This shows the itinerary planner abstract task model. It illustrates the tasks the

Figure 5. Itinerary planner abstract model

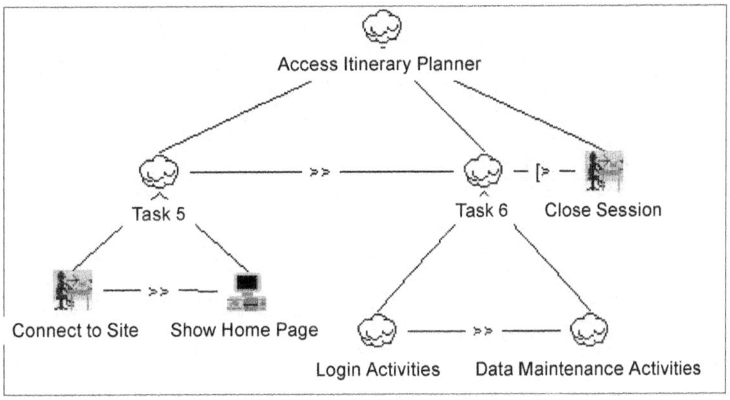

Figure 6. Login activities

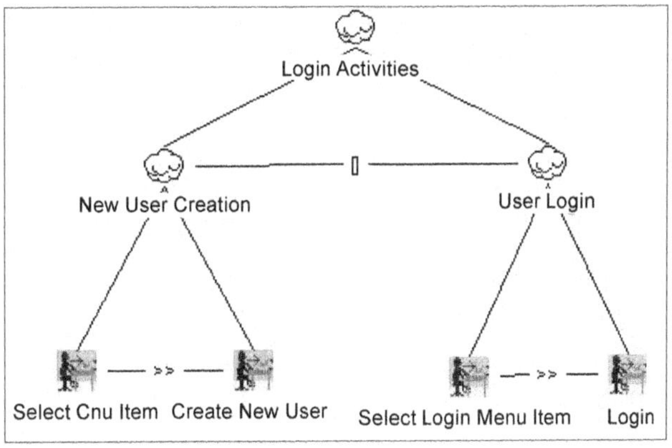

Figure 7. Data maintenance activities

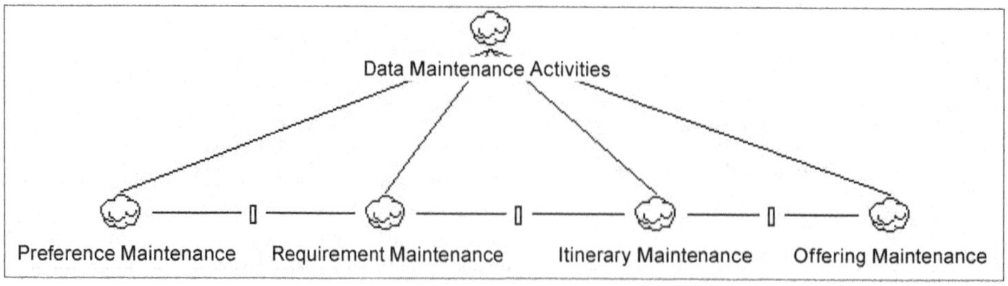

Figure 8. Preference maintenance activities

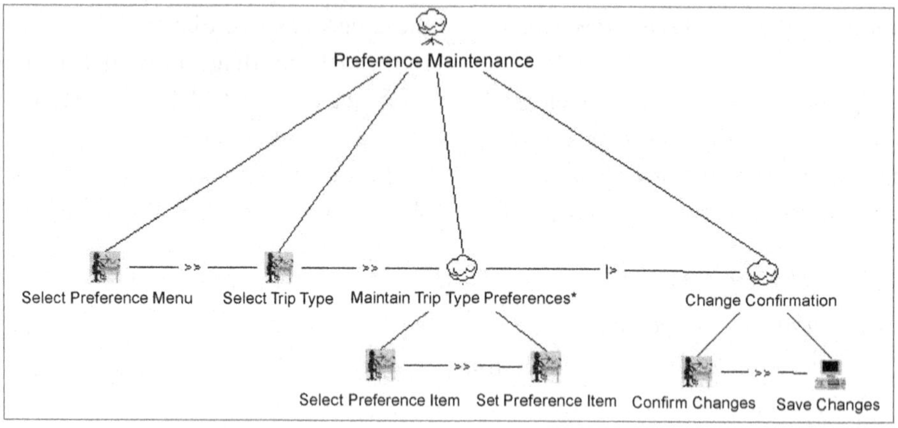

Figure 9. Requirement maintenance activities

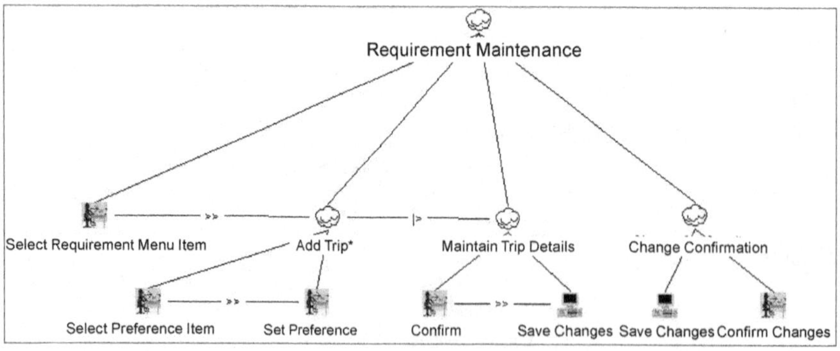

user can perform on connecting to the itinerary planner Web site. Task 5 consists of connecting to the Web site and viewing the home page. Task 6 involves logging into the Web site and then carrying out the data maintenance activities. Figures 8 to 13 expand on these activities.

Figure 6: This shows the task model that expands the Login Activity task. Login Activities describe the tasks to be performed for the user to login, it allows for an existing user, as well as new user.

Figure 7: Data Maintenance Activities task tree, which provides a choice between four ab-

Figure 10. Itinerary maintenance activities

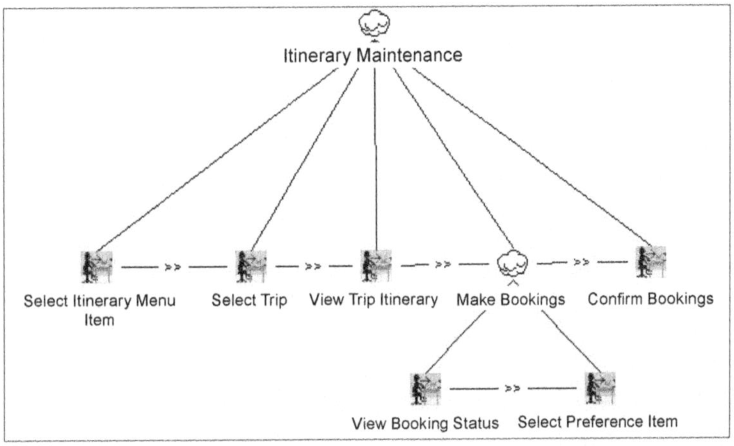

Figure 11. Offering maintenance activities

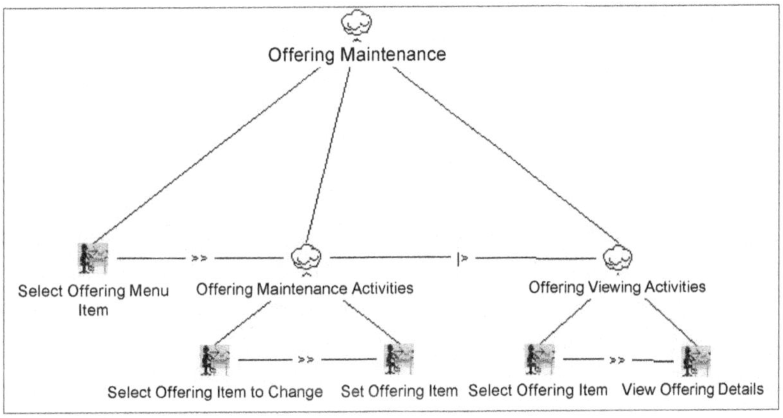

stract tasks: Preference Maintenance, Requirement Maintenance, Itinerary Maintenance, and Offering Maintenance.

Figure 8: Preference Maintenance Activities task tree, which consists of the tasks involved in maintaining the preferences of the traveler. Here preferences refer to what of the traveler likes, with regard to various facilities such as accommodation, transport, and so forth.

Figure 9: Requirement Maintenance Activities task tree, which describes the tasks involved in maintaining the traveler requirements. Requirements refer to the travelers demands for the tour, for example the traveler may want 5-star accommodation and a business class flight.

Figure 10: Itinerary Maintenance Activities task tree, which describes the tasks involved in creating an itinerary for the traveler. An itinerary is generated by matching the traveler's requirements with the offerings available.

Figure 11: Offering Maintenance Activities task tree, which describes the tasks involved in maintaining the offerings being provided by various travel vendors. Tourism vendors can advertise their services such as room availability, tickets availability through this option.

Working of an Itinerary Planner

In this section we describe the operation of a travel itinerary planner; this itinerary planner has

Figure 12. New user screen

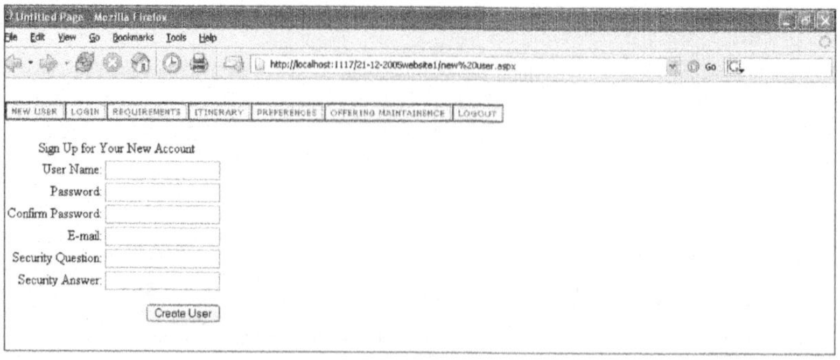

Figure 13. Login screen

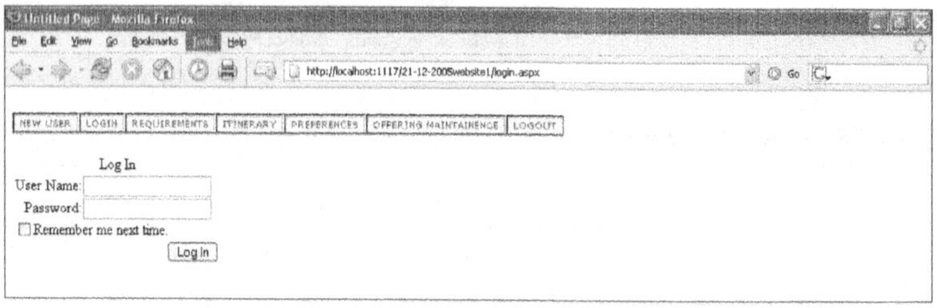

been developed based on the application generator framework. It consists of AuSTO ontology, a user interface created using ASP.net, and a business logic layer, which acts as a connector between the ontology and the user interface. The AuSTO ontology is populated by a tourism domain expert, the application allows tourism operators to advertise their offerings in the offerings page, and the offerings are stored in the ontology. The end user or the tourist can specify his requirements in the requirements page, these requirements are stored in the ontology, and the tourist also can specify his preferences which also are be stored in the ontology. The itinerary planner matches the requirements with the offerings, and produces an itinerary; the end user can either reject the itinerary offerings or accept these and confirm bookings in the itinerary page. The user interface for the itinerary planner has been developed based on the task model described in the previous section. This application is explained in some more detail with the help of screen shots in the following.

Figure 12: This shows the new user screen, which allows the creation of a new user. It is necessary to have an account in order to use the application.

Figure 13: This shows the user login screen where an existing user can login into the application. Once the user logs in, he has access to facilities such as storing preferences or specifying requirements.

Figure 14: This shows the requirements screen where a tourist can enter his requirements for a trip. Once the requirements are entered the tourist clicks the Add Trip button and a new leg can be added.

Figure 15: This shows the itinerary screen, the tourists' requirements are matched with the vendor offerings and an itinerary is produced. The tourist can accept offerings in the itinerary with the help of the checkboxes, and make booking by clicking on the Make Bookings button and then confirm bookings.

Figure 16: This shows the preferences screen, which allows the user to store his preferences for

Figure 14. Requirements screen

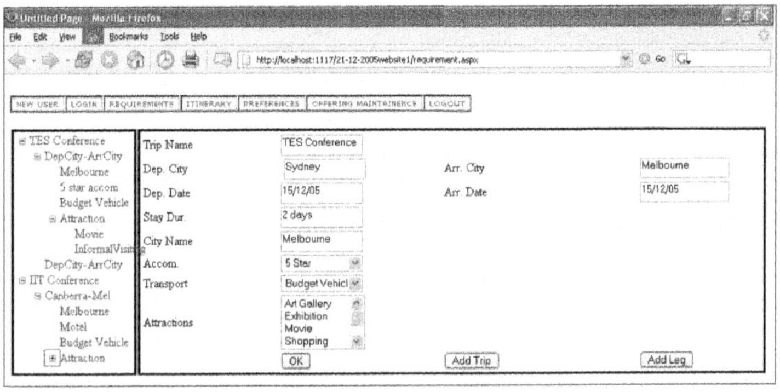

Figure 15. Itinerary screen

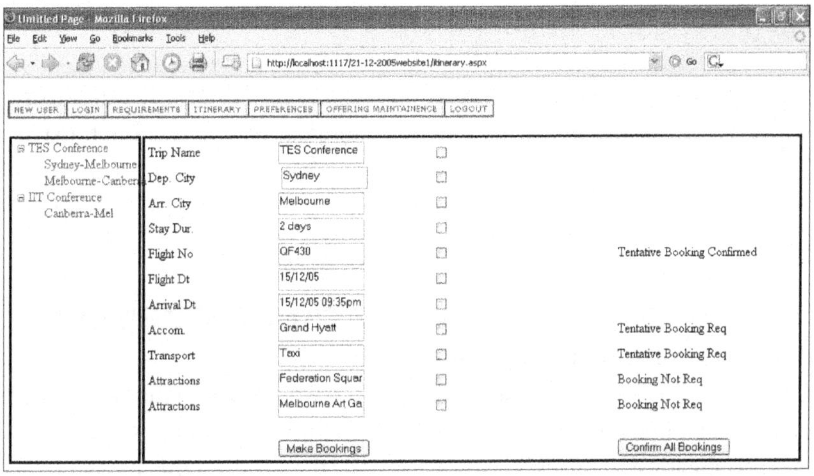

Figure 16. Preferences screen

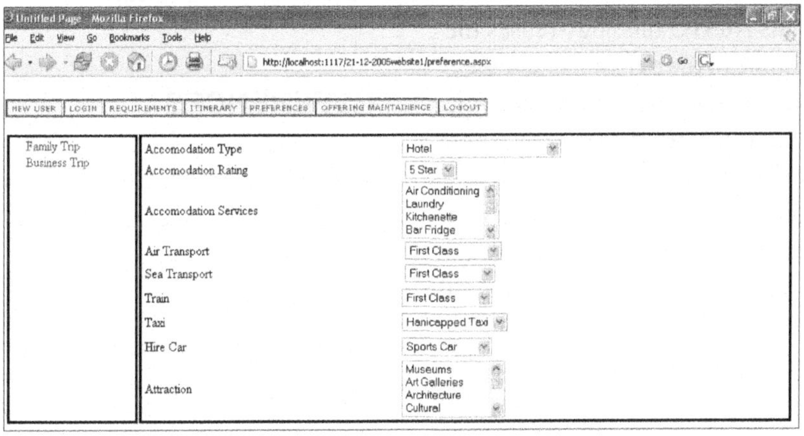

accommodation, transport facilities and other such services. Different preferences for different kind of trips can be stored, such as family trip and business trip.

Figure 17: This shows the offerings maintenance screen, tourism vendors such as hotels or transport providers can advertise their offerings on this page. For example, hotels can advertise

Figure 17. Offerings maintenance screen

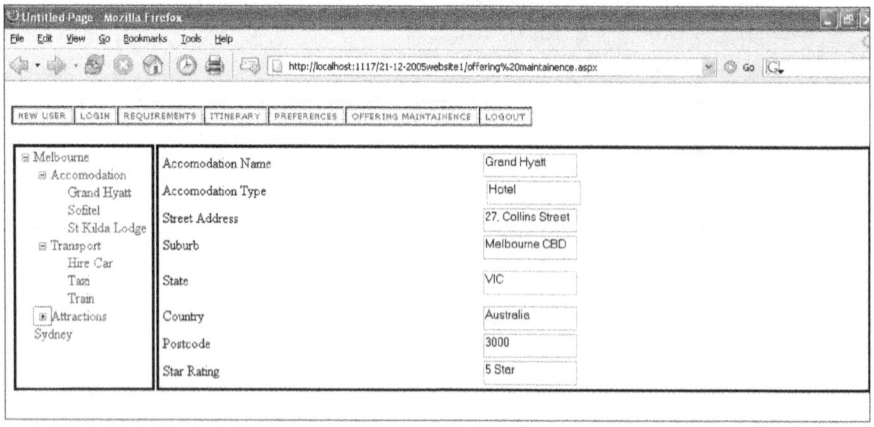

their room availability, and transport providers can advertise their vehicle availability.

CONCLUSION

There is a need for standardisation of definitions and concepts in the field of tourism; the solution is to develop travel ontologies. Number of travel ontologies have been developed in recent times, each with an application in mind; we have developed an Australian sustainable tourism ontology (AuSTO), specifically for the Australian tourism sector. This AuSTO ontology reuses the knowledge from some of the existing ontologies. Ontologies enable the development of Semantic Web applications, but ontology driven application development is still a nascent field. We are developing an intelligent travel application generator based on the AuSTO ontology. The application generator framework enables the production of different intelligent travel tools such as Itinerary planners, and recommender systems. We are building an itinerary planner by using this framework, and this intelligent itinerary planner can match the user requirements specified in the ontology with vendor offerings specified in the ontology and produce an itinerary as a solution. This chapter presented an overview of the Semantic Web, introduced different tourism ontologies and some applications based on tourism ontologies, and describes in detail a framework for developing e-tourism applications based on ontologies.

ACKNOWLEDGMENTS

We would like to thank Sustainable Tourism Cooperative Research Center (STCRC), Australia, for the funding this research. We also would like to thank Henk Meijerink and Paul Mohinyan for their help in this research.

REFERENCES

Agentcities. (n.d.). Retrieved August 15, 2005, from http://www.agentcities.org

Bray, T. (n.d.). *What is RDF.* Retrieved May 31, 2006, from http://www.xml.com/pub/a/2001/01/24/rdf.html?page=2

Butler, M. H. (2003). *Is the Semantic Web hype?* Retrieved May 31, 2006, from http://www.hpl.hp.com/personal/marbut/isTheSemanticWebHype.pdf

Cardaso, J. (2005). *E-tourism: Creating dynamic packages using Semantic Web processes.* Paper presented at the W3C Workshop on Frameworks for Semantics in Web Services.

Chandrasekaran, B., Josephson, J. R, & Benjamins, V. R. (1999). What are ontologies, and why do we need them? *IEEE, 14*(1), 20-26.

Clissmann, C., & Höpken, W. (n.d.). *Harmonise ontology user manual.* Retrieved from www.harmo-ten.info/harmoten_docs/D2_2_Ontology_User_Manual_V3.2.0.3.doc

Daniel, B. (2005). *On tour, the Semantic Web and its benefits to the tourism industry.* Retrieved May 25, 2006, from http://etourism.deri.at/ont/docu2004/OnTour%20%20Semantic%20Web%20and%20its%20benefits%20to%20the%20tourism%20industry.pdf

Dix, A., Finlay, J., Abowd, G., & Beale, G. R. (1998). *Human-computer interaction.* Prentice Hall.

E-tourism. (n.d.). Retrieved August 16, 2005, from http://deri.at/research/projects/e-tourism

Foundation for Intelligent Physical Agents, The. (n.d.). Retrieved August 15, 2005, from http://www.fipa.org

Georgievski, M., & Sharda, N. (2003). *Task modelling for a holistic quality of service model—TRAQS.* Paper presented at the IEEE India Council Annual Convention and Exhibition, India.

Giulio, M., Paterno, F., & Santaro, C. (2002). CTTE: Support for developing and analyzing task models for interactive system design. *IEEE Transaction on Software Engineering, 28*(9), 1-17.

Gordon, M., Kowalski, A., Paprzycki, M., Pelech, T., Szymczak, M., & Wasowicz, T. (2005). Ontologies in a travel support system. *Internet 2005*, 285-300.

Inference engine. (n.d.). Retrieved May 15, 2006, from http://www.emclab.umr.edu/consortium/Whatis/node17.html

Jakkilinki, R., Sharda, N., & Georgievski, M. (2005). *Developing an ontology for multimedia design and planning pyramid.* Paper presented at the International Symposium on Information and Communications Technologies, Petaling Jaya Malaysia.

Levi, G., Vagliengo, A., & Goy, A. (2005). *Talea: An ontology-based framework for e-business applications development.* Paper presented at the 2nd Italian Semantic Web Workshop on Semantic Web Applications and Perspectives, Trento, Italy.

Miller, R. H. (n.d.). *Web interface design: Learning form our past.* Retrieved May 25, 2006, from http://www.cs.rutgers.edu/~shklar/www4/rmiller/rhmpapr.html#background

Mindswap. (n.d.). Retrieved May 15, 2006, from http://www.mindswap.org/2003/pellet/index.shtm

Mondeca. (n.d.). Retrieved August 15, 2005, from http://www.mondeca.com

Open Travel Alliance, The. (n.d.). Retrieved August 15, 2005, from http://www.opentravel.org

Palmer, S. B. (2001). *The Semantic Web: An introduction.* Retrieved May 25, 2006, from http://infomesh.net/2001/swintro/

Paterno, F. (2002). *Task modelling: Where we are, where we are headed.* Paper presented at the First International Workshop on Task Models and Diagrams for User Interface Design, Tamodia, Bucharest, Romania.

Pressman, R. S. (1997). *Software engineering, a practitioner's approach* (4th ed.). McGraw-Hill.

Protégé. (n.d.). Retrieved May 25, 2006, from http://protege.stanford.edu/

Swartout, B., Patil, R., Knight, K., & Russ, T. (1997). *Towards distributed use of large scale ontologies.* Paper presented at the Symposium on Ontological Engineering of AAAI, Stanford, CA.

Uschold, M., & Gruninger, M. (1996). Ontologies: Principles, methods and applications. *Knowledge Engineering Review, 11*(2).

This work was previously published in Information and Communication Technologies in Support of the Tourism Industry, edited by W. Pease, M. Rowe, and M. Cooper, pp. 26-49, copyright 2007 by IGI Publishing (an imprint of IGI Global).

Compilation of References

Aaron, M. (2003). Universal, ubiquitous, user-interface design for the disabled and elderly. *Interaction, 10*(2), 23–27. doi:10.1145/637848.637858

Active Worlds Inc. (2007). *Active worlds and education.* Retrieved January 7, 2009, from http://www.activeworlds.com/edu/index.asp

Activeswf. (2005). S*oftware ActiveSWF Prof 1.9.3.* Retrieved December, 2005 from http://www.activeswf.com

Adobbati, R., Marshall, A. N., Scholer, A., Tejada, S., Kaminka, G., Schaffer, S., & Sollitto, C. (2002). Gamebots: A 3D virtual world test-bed for multi-agent research. *Communications of the ACM, 45*(1), 43–45.

Adomavicius, G., & Tuzhilin, A. (2005). Toward the next generation of recommender systems: A survey of the state-of-the-art and possible extensions. *IEEE Transactions on Knowledge and Data Engineering, 17*, 734–749. doi:10.1109/TKDE.2005.99

Agentcities. (n.d.). Retrieved August 15, 2005, from http://www.agentcities.org

Aldewereld, H., Dignum, F., Garcia-Camino, A., Noriega, P., Rodriguez-Aguilar, J. A., & Sierra, C. (2006). Operationalisation of norms for usage in electronic institutions. In *Proceedings of the 5th international joint conference on Autonomous agents and multiagent systems (AAMAS '06)* (pp. 223-225). New York: ACM Press.

Alexander, B. (2006). Web 2.0: A new wave of innovation for teaching and learning? *EDUCAUSE Review, 41*(2), 32–44.

Alfaro, I., Nardon, M., Pianesi, F., Stock, O., & Zancanaro, M. (2004). Using cinematic techniques on mobile devices for cultural tourism. *Journal of Information Technology & Tourism, 7*(2), 61–71. doi:10.3727/1098305054517309

Allison, A., Currall, J., Moss, M., & Stuart, S. (2005). Digital identity matters. *Journal of the American Society for Information Science and Technology, 56*(4), 364–372. doi:10.1002/asi.20112

Al-Nazer, A., & Helmy, T. (2007). A Web searching guide: Internet search engines and autonomous interface agents collaboration. In *Proceedings of the wi-iatw*, Los Alamitos, CA, USA (pp. 424-428).

Alva, M. E. O., Martínez, A. B., Cueva, J. M., Sagástegui, H. T. C., & López, B. P. (2003). Comparison of methods and existing tools for the measurement of usability in the Web. In *Web engineering* (LNCS 2722, pp. 386-389). Berlin, Germany: Springer.

Ambite, J. L., Knoblock, C. A., Muslea, M., & Minton, S. (2005). conditional constraint networks for interleaved planning and information gathering. *IEEE Intelligent Systems, 20*(2), 25–33. doi:10.1109/MIS.2005.24

amodt, A., & Plaza, E. (1994). Case-based reasoning: Foundational issues, methodological variations, and system approaches. *AI Communications, 7*(1), 39–59.

Anderson, E. W. (1998). Customer satisfaction and word-of-mouth. *Journal of Service Research, 1*(1), 5–17. doi:10.1177/109467059800100102

Andreu, L., Bigné, E. J., & Cooper, C. (2000). Projected and perceived image of Spain as a tourist destination for British travellers. *Journal of Travel & Tourism Marketing, 9*(4), 47–67. doi:10.1300/J073v09n04_03

Anil, S., Juan, Q., Sergiu, M. D., Sushil, J. L., & Monica, N. N. (2007). Sycophant: An API for research in context-aware user interfaces. (pp. 83-83). In *Proceedings of the 2nd International Conference on Software Engineering Advances (ICSEA). Cap Esterel.*

Ardissono, L., Goy, A., Petrone, G., Segnan, M., & Torasso, P. (2001). Tailoring the recommendation of tourist information to heterogeneous user groups. In *Proceedings of the Hypermedia: Openness, Structural Awareness, and Adaptivity, Int. Workshops OHS-7, SC-3 and AH-3* (LNCS 2266, pp. 280-295). Berlin, Germany: Springer Verlag.

Armstrong, A., & Hagel, J. (1996). The real value of on-line communities. Harvard Business Review, (May-June). boyd, d. m., & Ellison, N. B. (2007). Social network sites: Definition, history, and scholarship. *Journal of Computer-Mediated Communication, 13*(1).

Arnold, D. (2008). Editorial for inaugural issue of JOCCH: Pasteur's quadrant: Cultural heritage as inspiration for basic research in computer science. *Journal of Computation in Cultural Heritage, 1*(1).

ATDW. (2005). *Australian Tourism Data Warehouse.* Retrieved December, 2005 from http://www.atdw.com.au

Averjanova, O., Ricci, F., & Nguyen, Q. N. (2008). Map-based interaction with a conversational mobile recommender system. In *Proceedings of the 2nd International Conference on Mobile Ubiquitous Computing, Systems, Services and Technologies.*

Axhausen, K., & Gärling, T. (1992). Activity-based approaches to travel analysis - conceptual frameworks, models, and research problems. *Transport Reviews, 12*(4), 323–341. doi:10.1080/01441649208716826

Baader, F., & Sattler, U. (2001). An overview of tableau algorithms for description logics. *Studia Logica, 69,* 5–40. doi:10.1023/A:1013882326814

Baader, F., Calvanese, D., McGuinness, D., Nardi, D., & Patel-Schneider, P. (2003). *The description logic handbook: Theory, implementation and applications.* Cambridge, UK: Cambridge University Press.

Backhaus, K., Erichson, B., Plinke, W., & Weiber, W. (2003). *Multivariate analysemethoden* (10th ed.). Berlin, Germany: Springer.

Balabanovi, M., & Shoham, Y. (1997). Fab: Content-based, collaborative recommendation. *ACM Communication, 40*(3), 66-72.

Baloglu, S., & McCleary, K. W. (1999). A model of destination image formation. *Annals of Tourism Research, 25*(4), 868–897. doi:10.1016/S0160-7383(99)00030-4

Banavar, G., Bergman, L., Cardone, R., Chevalier, V., Gaeremynck, Y., & Giraud, F. (2004). An authoring technology for multi-device Web applications. *IEEE Pervasive Computing / IEEE Computer Society [and] IEEE Communications Society, 3*(3), 83–93. doi:10.1109/MPRV.2004.1321033

Bandelloni, R., & Paterno, F. (2004). Flexible user interface migration. In *Proceedings of the 9th international conference on Intelligent user interfaces* (pp. 148-155).

Baus, J., Cheverst, K., & Kray, C. (2005). A survey of map-based mobile guides. In L. Meng, A. Zipf, & T. Reichenbacher (Eds.), *Map-based mobile services: Theories, methods and implementations* (pp. 193-209). Berlin, Germany: Springer.

Beerli, A., & Martin, J. D. (2004). Factors influencing destination image. *Annals of Tourism Research, 31*(3), 657–681. doi:10.1016/j.annals.2004.01.010

Bellotti, F., Berta, R., De Gloria, A., & Primavera, L. (in press). Enhancing the educational value of videogames. *ACM Computers in Entertainment.*

Bellotti, F., Berta, R., De Gloria, A., & Zappi, V. (2008). Exploring gaming mechanisms to enhance knowledge acquisition in virtual worlds. In *Proceedings of the International Conference on Digital Interactive Media in Entertainment and Arts.*

Bellotti, F., Berta, R., De Gloria, A., Pellegrino, M., & Primavera, L. (2007). Learning contents by videogame tricks. In *Proceedings of the Learning with game Conference*.

Bellotti, F., Berta, R., Garnier-Rivers, A., & Jacquet, E. (2008). *User requirements report* (TiE Project Tech. Rep.).

Ben-Bassat, T., Meyer, J., & Tractinsky, N. (2006). Economic and subjective measures of the perceived value of aesthetics and usability. *ACM Transactions on Computer-Human Interaction, 13*(2), 210–234. doi:10.1145/1165734.1165737

Berelson, B. (1952). *Content analysis in communication research*. New York: Free Press.

Berger, H., Dittenbach, M., & Merkl, D. (2004). User-oriented evaluation of a natural language tourism information system. *Information Technology and Tourism, 6*(3), 167–180. doi:10.3727/1098305031436953

Berger, H., Dittenbach, M., & Merkl, D. (2006). Let's get social in e-tourism: The "itchy feet" way. In *Proceedings of the 7th Asia-Pacific Conference on Computer Human Interaction (APCHI 2006)*, Taipei, Taiwan.

Berka, T., & Plößnig, M. (2004). Designing recommender systems for tourism. In *Proceedings of The Eleventh International Conference on Information Technology in Travel & Tourism, ENTER 2004*, Cairo, Egypt.

Bisignano, M., Di-Modica, G., & Tomarchio, O. (2006). An intent-oriented approach for multi-device user interface design. In *Proceedings of the 20th International Conference on Advanced Information Networking and Application* (Vol. 2, pp. 186-194).

Bogdanovych, A., Berger, H., Simoff, S., & Sierra, C. (2006). Travel agents vs. online booking: Tackling the shortcomings of nowadays online tourism portals. In *Proceedings of the 13th International Conference on Information Technologies in Tourism (ENTER'06)* (pp. 418-428). Vienna, Austria: Springer-Verlag.

Bolan, K., Canada, M., & Cullin, R. (2007). Web, library, and teen services 2.0. *Young Adult Library Services, 5*(2), 40–43.

Bouguila, L., & Sato, M. (2002). Virtual locomotion system for large scale virtual environments. In *Proceedings of Virtual Reality* (pp. 291–292). Washington, DC: IEEE.

Braun, E., Hart, A., & Muhlhauser, M. (2004). Authoring for multi-device interfaces. In *Adjunct Proceedings of the 8th ERCIM Workshop* (pp. 186-194.).

Bray, T. (n.d.). *What is RDF.* Retrieved May 31, 2006, from http://www.xml.com/pub/a/2001/01/24/rdf.html?page=2

Breslow-Sardone, S. (2006). *Travel 2.0.* Retrieved May 12, 2008, from http://web.archive.org/web/20060811192611/http://honeymoons.about.com/od/smarttravel/qt/travel-2pointoh.htm

Brewster, S., Leplatre, G., & Crease, M. (1998). Using non-speech sounds in mobile computing devices. In *Proceedings of the First Workshop on Human Computer Interaction of Mobile Devices*, Glasgow, Scotland (pp. 224-259).

Bridge, D. (2002). Towards conversational recommender systems: A dialogue grammar approach. In *Proceedings of the Workshop in Mixed-Initiative Case-Based Reasoning, at the 6th European Conference in Case-Based Reasoning*, Aberdeen, Scotland (pp. 9-22).

Bridge, D., Göker, M., McGinty, L., & Smyth, B. (2005). Case-based recommender systems. *The Knowledge Engineering Review, 20*(3), 315–320. doi:10.1017/S0269888906000567

Brown, B., & Chalmers, M. (2003). Tourism and mobile technology. In K. Kuutti, E.H. Karsten, G. Fitzpatrick, P. Dourish, & K. Schmidt (Eds.), *Proceedings of the 8th European Conference on Computer-Supported Cooperative Work*, Helsinki, Finland (pp. 335-354).

Brown, B., Chalmers, M., Bell, M., Hall, M., MacColl, I., & Rudman, P. (2005). Sharing the square: Collaborative leisure in the city streets. In *Proceedings of the 9th European Conference on Computer Supported Cooperative Work* (pp. 427-447).

Brutzman, D., & Daly, L. (Eds.). (2007). *X3D: Extensible 3D graphics for Web authors*. San Francisco: Morgan Kaufmann.

Buffett, S., Keping, J., Liu, S., Spencer, B., & Wang, F. (2004). Negotiating exchanges of P3P-labeled information for compensation. *Computational Intelligence*, *20*(4), 663–677. doi:10.1111/j.0824-7935.2004.00259.x

Buhalis, D. (1999). Information technology for small and medium sized tourism enterprises: Adaptation and benefits. *Information Technology & Tourism*, *2*(2), 79–95.

Buhalis, D. (2002). The future e-tourism intermediaries. *Tourism Management*, *23*, 207–220. doi:10.1016/S0261-5177(01)00085-1

Buhalis, D. (2003). E-tourism: Information technologies for strategic tourism management. New York: Financial Times Prentice Hall.

Buhalis, D., & Law, R. (2008). Progress in information technology and tourism management: 20 years on and 10 years after the Internet - the state of e-tourism research. *Tourism Management*, *29*, 609–623. doi:10.1016/j.tourman.2008.01.005

Bulkeley, W. (2005). Marketers scan blogs for brand insights. *Wall Street Journal*, *23*(June). Retrieved August 18, 2007, from http://online.wsj.com/public/article/SB111948406207267049-qs710svEyTDy6Sj732kvSsSdl_A_20060623.html?mod=blogs

Burgess, S., Sellitto, C., & Karanasios, S. (2009). *Effective Web Presence Solutions for Small Businesses: Strategies for Successful Implementation*, Hershey, PA: IGI Global

Burigat, S., Chittaro, L., & De Marco, L. (2005). Bringing dynamic queries to mobile devices: A visual preference-based search tool for tourist decision support. In *Proceedings of the 10th IFIP TC13 International Conference on Human-Computer Interaction (INTERACT 2005)* (pp. 213-226).

Burke, R. (2000). Knowledge-based recommender systems. In J. E. Daily, A. Kent, & H. Lancour (Eds.), *Encyclopedia of library and information science*. New York: Marcel Dekker.

Burke, R. (2002). Interactive critiquing for catalog navigation in e-commerce. *Artificial Intelligence Review*, *18*(3-4), 245–267. doi:10.1023/A:1020701617138

Burke, R. (2007). Hybrid Web recommender systems. In P. Brusilovsky, A. Kobsa, & W. Nejdl (Eds.), *The adaptive Web: Methods and strategies of Web personalization* (pp. 377-408). Heidelberg, Germany: Springer.

Burns, J., & Gregory, R. M. (2001). A framework for effective user interface design for Web-based electronic commerce applications. *International Journal of an Emerging Transdiscipline*, *4*, 67–75.

Butler, M. H. (2003). *Is the Semantic Web hype?* Retrieved May 31, 2006, from http://www.hpl.hp.com/personal/marbut/isTheSemanticWebHype.pdf

Calì, A., Calvanese, D., Colucci, S., Di Noia, T., & Donini, F. M. (2004). A logic-based approach for matching user profiles. In M. Gh. Negoita, R. J. Howlett, & L. C. Jain (Eds.), *Proceedings of the Knowledge-Based Intelligent Information and Engineering Systems, 8th International Conference, KES 2004*, Wellington, New Zealand (pp. 187-195).

Calvanese, D., De Giacomo, G., & Lenzerini, M. (1998). On the decidability of query containment under constraints. In *Proceedings of the 17th ACM SIGACT SIGMOD SIGART Symposium on Principles of Database Systems (PODS'98)* (pp. 149-158).

Camacho, D., Molina, J. M., Borrajo, D., & Aler, R. (2002). MAPWEB: Cooperation between planning agents and Web agents. *Information & Security*, *8*(2), 209–238.

Canter, L., & Siegel, M. (1994). *How to make a fortune on the information superhighway*. New York: Harper Collins.

Cantoni, L., & Tardini, S. (2006). *Internet*. New York: Routledge.

Cantoni, L., Tardini, S., Inversini, A., & Marchiori, E. (2009). From paradigmatic to syntagmatic communities: a socio-semiotic approach to the evolution pattern of online travel communities. In W. Hopken, U. Gretzel, & R. Law (Eds.), *Information and Communication Technologies in Tourism 2009 - Proceedings of the International Conference*, Amsterdam, The Netherlands (pp. 13-24). Wien, Austria: Springer.

Cardaso, J. (2005). *E-tourism: Creating dynamic packages using Semantic Web processes.* Paper presented at the W3C Workshop on Frameworks for Semantics in Web Services.

Carenini, G., Smith, J., & Poole, D. (2003). Towards more conversational and collaborative recommender systems. In *Proceedings of the 8th International Conference on Intelligent User Interfaces,* Miami, FL (pp. 12-18). New York: ACM Press.

Carl, W. J. (2006). What's all the buzz about? Everyday communication and the relational basis of word-of-mouth and buzz marketing practices. *Management Communication Quarterly*, *19*(4), 601–634. doi:10.1177/0893318905284763

Carmagnola, F., Cena, F., Gena, C., & Torre, I. (2005). A multidimensional approach for the semantic representation of taxonomies and rules in adaptive hypermedia systems. In *Proceedings of the PerSWeb'05 workshop (UM 2005).*

Carrasco, J., Miller, E., & Wellman, B. (2006). *Spatial and social networks: The case of travel for social activities.* Paper presented at the 11th International Conference on Travel Behaviour Research.

Carson, D. (2008). The 'blogosphere' as a market research tool for tourism destinations: A case study of Australia's Northern Territory. *Journal of Vacation Marketing*, *14*(2), 111–119. doi:10.1177/1356766707087518

Castronova, E. (2005). *Synthetic worlds: The business and culture of online games.* Chicago: University of Chicago Press.

Chandrasekaran, B., Josephson, J. R, & Benjamins, V. R. (1999). What are ontologies, and why do we need them? *IEEE, 14*(1), 20-26.

Chao, D. L. (2001). Doom as an interface for process management. In *Proceedings of the SIGCHI Conference on Human Factors in Computing Systems (CHI '01)* (pp. 152-157). New York: ACM Press.

Cherem, G., & Driver, B. (1983). Visitor employed photography: A technique to measure common perceptions of natural environments. *Journal of Leisure Research*, *15*, 65–83.

Chiclana, F., Herrera, F., & Herrera-Viedma, E. (1998). Integrating three representation models in multipurpose decision making based on preference relations. *Fuzzy Sets and Systems*, *97*, 33–48. doi:10.1016/S0165-0114(96)00339-9

Chiu, D. K., & Leung, H. (2005). Towards ubiquitous tourist service coordination and integration: A multi-agent and semantic web approach. In *Proceedings of the 7th International Conference on Electronic Commerce (ICEC '05)* (pp. 574-581). New York: ACM Press.

Choi, S., Lehto, X. Y., & Morrison, A. M. (2007). Destination image representation on the Web: Content analysis of Macau travel related Web sites. *Tourism Management*, *28*, 118–129. doi:10.1016/j.tourman.2006.03.002

Chung, J. Y., & Buhalis, D. (2008). Web 2.0: A study of online travel community. In *Proceedings of ENTER 2008: International Conference on Information and Communication Technologies in Tourism*, Innsbruck, Austria (pp. 70-81).

Chung, J. Y., & Buhalis, D. (in press). Information needs in online social networks. *Journal of Information Technology and Tourism.*

Clissmann, C., & Höpken, W. (n.d.). *Harmonise ontology user manual.* Retrieved from www.harmo-ten.info/harmoten_docs/D2_2_Ontology_User_Manual_V3.2.0.3.doc

Collins, C., Buhalis, D., & Peters, M. (2003). Enhancing SMTEs' business performance through the Internet and e-learning platforms. *Education and Training, 45*(8/9), 483–494. doi:10.1108/00400910310508874

Comscore. (2008). *Social networking explodes worldwide as sites increase their focus on cultural relevance.* Retrieved August 12, 2008, from http://www.comscore.com/press/release.asp?press=2396

Conrady, R. (2007). Travel technology in the era of Web 2.0. In *Trends and issues in global tourism* (pp. 165-184).

Constantine, S. (2000). *User interfaces for all: Concepts, methods and tools.* Mahwah, NJ: Lawrence Erlbaum Associates, Inc.

Cook, K. S., & Whitmeyer, J. M. (1992). Two approaches to social structure: Exchange theory and network analysis. *Annual Review of Sociology, 18*, 109–127. doi:10.1146/annurev.so.18.080192.000545

Cooper, C., & Buhalis, D. (1998). The future of tourism. In C. R. Cooper (Ed.), Tourism: Principles and practices. London: Addison Wesley Longman.

Cooper, D. (1994). Portraits of Paradise: Themes and images of the tourist industry. *Southeast Asian Journal of Social Science, 22*, 144–160. doi:10.1163/030382494X00142

Corbit, M. (2002). Building virtual worlds for informal science learning. [AWEDU]. *Active Worlds Educational Universe, 11*(1), 55–67.

Costa, G., Dobbin, M., & Klisanin, R. (2008). *Facebook hunt for missing Melbourne woman.* Retrieved September 25, 2008, from http://www.theage.com.au/national/facebook-hunt-for-missing-melbourne-woman-20080925-4nux.html

CouchSurfing. (2008). CouchSurfing statistics. Retrieved August 8, 2008, from http://www.couchsurfing.com/

Couclelis, H. (1992). Location, place, region, and space. In R. Abler, M. Marcus, & J. Olson (Eds.), *Geography's inner worlds* (pp. 215-233). New Brunswick, NJ: Rutgers University Press.

Cox, C., Burgess, S., Sellitto, C., & Buultjens, J. (2008). *The influence of user-generated content on tourist travel behaviour.* Lismore, NSW: Australian Regional Tourism Research Centre.

Crang, M. (1997). Picturing practices: Research through the tourist gaze. *Progress in Human Geography, 21*(3), 359–373. doi:10.1191/030913297669603510

Crang, M. (1999). Knowing, tourism and the practices of vision. In D. Crouch (Ed.), *Leisure/tourism geographies: Practices and geographical knowledge* (pp. 238-256). London: Routledge.

Cresswell, T. (1996). *In place/out of place.* Minneapolis, MN: University of Minnesota Press.

Culler, J. (1981). Semiotics of tourism. *American Journal of Semiotics, 1*, 127–140.

Cuni, G., Esteva, M., Garcia, P., Puertas, E., Sierra, C., & Solchaga, T. (2004). MASFIT: Multi-agent system for fish trading. In *Proceedings of the 16th European Conference on Artificial Intelligence (ECAI '04)* (pp. 710-714). Amsterdam, Netherlands: IOS Press.

Cyr, D., Hassanein, K., Head, M., & Ivanov, A. (2007). The role of social presence in establishing loyalty. *Interacting with Computers, 19*(1), 43–56. doi:10.1016/j.intcom.2006.07.010

Daniel, B. (2005). *On tour, the Semantic Web and its benefits to the tourism industry.* Retrieved May 25, 2006, from http://etourism.deri.at/ont/docu2004/OnTour%20%20Semantic%20Web%20and%20its%20benefits%20to%20the%20tourism%20industry.pdf

Dann, G. (1996). tourists' images of a destination – an alternative analysis. *Journal of Travel & Tourism Marketing, 5*(1/2), 41–55. doi:10.1300/J073v05n01_04

Daramola, J. O., Adigun, M. O., & Olugbara, O. O. (2008). A product line architecture for evolving intelligent component services in tourism information systems. In P. O. Connor, W. Hopkin, & U. Gretze (Eds.), *Information and communication technologies in tourism* (pp. 118-145). Berlin, Germany: Springer.

David, T., Joelle, C., & Gaelle, C. (2001). A unifying reference framework for the development of plastic user interfaces. In *Proceedings of the 2001 Engineering of Human—Computer Interaction Conference (EHCI'2001)* (pp. 173-192).

deKleer, J. (1986). An assumption-based tms, extending the ATMS, and problem solving with the ATMS. *Artificial Intelligence, 28*(2), 127–224. doi:10.1016/0004-3702(86)90080-9

Delgado, J. (2001). Who's who in recommender systems. In *Proceedings of the ACM SIGIR Workshop on Recommender Systems*, New Orleans, LA.

Dickey, M. D. (2003). Teaching in 3D: Pedagogical affordances and constraints of 3D virtual worlds for synchronous distance learning. *Distance Education, 24*, 105–121. doi:10.1080/01587910303047

Dignum, F. (2002). Abstract norms and electronic institutions. In *Proceedings of the International Workshop on Regulated Agent-Based Social Systems: Theories and Applications (RASTA '02)* (pp. 93-104).

Dignum, V., & Dignum, F. (2001). Modelling agent societies: Co-ordination frameworks and institutions. In *Proceedings of the 10th Portuguese Conference on Artificial Intelligence: Progress in Artificial Intelligence Knowledge Extraction, Multi-Agent Systems, Logic Programming, and Constraint Solving (EPIA '01)* (pp. 191-204). London: Springer-Verlag.

Dignum, V., Weigand, H., & Xu, L. (2001). Agent societies: Towards frameworks-based design. In M. Wooldridge, G. Weiß, & P. Ciancarini (Eds.), *Revised Papers and Invited Contributions from the Second International Workshop on Agent-Oriented Software Engineering II* (pp. 33-49). London: Springer-Verlag.

DiPaola, S., & Collins, D. (2003). A social metaphor-based 3D virtual environment. In *Proceedings of the International Conference on Computer Graphics and Interactive Techniques (SIGGRAPH '03)* (pp. 1-2). New York: ACM.

Dippelreiter, B., Grün, C., Pöttler, M., Seidel, I., Berger, H., Dittenbach, M., & Pesenhofer, A. (in press). Online tourism communities on the path to Web 2.0 - an evaluation. *Information Technology and Tourism.*

Dix, A., Finlay, J., Abowd, G., & Beale, G. R. (1998). *Human-computer interaction.* Prentice Hall.

Douglas, A. C., & Mills, J. E. (2006). Logging brand personality online: Website content analysis of Middle Eastern and North African destinations. In M. Hitz, M. Sigala, & J. Murphy (Eds.), *Information and communication technologies in tourism 2006* (pp. 345-346). New York: Springer.

Doyle, J. (1979). A truth maintenance system. *Artificial Intelligence, 12*(3), 231–272. doi:10.1016/0004-3702(79)90008-0

Ducheneaut, N., Yee, N., Nickell, E., & Moore, R. J. (2006). Alone together?: Exploring the social dynamics of massively multiplayer online games. In *Proceedings of the SIGCHI Conference on Human Factors in Computing Systems.*

Dugundji, E., Paez, A., & Arentze, T. (2008). Social networks, choices, mobility and travel. *Environment and Planning. B, Planning & Design, 35*(6), 956–980. doi:10.1068/b3506ged

Dulworth, M. (2008). *The connect effect: Building strong personal, professional, and virtual networks.* San Francisco: Berrett-Koehler Publishers.

Dunlop, M. D., Elsey, B., & Montgomery Masters, M. (2007). Dynamic visualisation of ski data: A context aware mobile piste map. In *Proceedings of the 9th International Conference on Human Computer Interaction with Mobile Devices and Services (Mobile HCI 2007)* (pp. 211-214).

Dunlop, M. D., Morrison, A., McCallum, S., Ptaskinski, P., Risbey, C., & Stewart, F. (2004). Focussed Palmtop information access combining Starfield displays with profile-based recommendations. In *Proceedings of Workshop on Mobile and Ubiquitous Information Access* (pp. 79-89).

Echtner, C. M., & Ritchie, J. R. B. (1993). The measurement of destination image: An empirical assessment. *Journal of Travel Research, 31*(4), 3–14. doi:10.1177/004728759303100402

Egger, R., & Buhalis, D. (2008). E-tourism case studies: Management & marketing issues in eTourism. Oxford, UK: Butterworth Heinemann Oxford.

Eigner, C., Leitner, H., Nausner, P., & Schneider, U. (2003). *Online-communities, weblogs und die soziale rückeroberung des netzes.* Graz, Austria: Nausner & Nausner.

Elliott, C. (2008). Next up: Travel 2.0. *National Geographic Traveler, 25*(2), 14–18.

Emerson, D. (2008). *Facebook friends not real friends: Judge.* Retrieved March 27, 2008, from http://www.smh.com.au/news/technology/facebook-friends-not-real-judge/2008/03/27/1206207279597.html

Engdahl, S. (Ed.). (2007). *Online social networking.* Farmington Hills, MI: Greenhaven Press.

Esteva, M., Rodriguez-Aguilar, J. A., Sierra, C., Garcia, P., & Arcos, J. L. (2001). On the formal specifications of electronic institutions. In F. Dignum & C. Sierra (Eds.), *Agent mediated electronic commerce, the European AgentLink perspective* (pp. 126-147). London, UK: Springer-Verlag.

E-tourism. (n.d.). Retrieved August 16, 2005, from http://deri.at/research/projects/e-tourism

Explore Virtual Mall in 3D. (2008). *Virtual Mall.* Retrieved November 18, 2008, from http://www.virtuy.com

Fakeye, P., & Crompton, J. (1991). Image differences between prospective, first-time and repeat visitors to the lower Rio Grande Valley. *Journal of Travel Research, 30*(2), 10–16. doi:10.1177/004728759103000202

Felfernig, A., Friedrich, G., Jannach, D., & Zanker, M. (2007). An integrated environment for the development of knowledge-based recommender applications. *International Journal of Electronic Commerce, 11*, 11–34. doi:10.2753/JEC1086-4415110201

Fesenmaier, D. R., Werthner, H., & Wöber, K. (Eds.). (2006). *Destination recommendation systems: Behavioral foundations and applications.* London: CAB International.

Finin, T., Fritzson, R., McKay, D., & McEntire, R. (1994). KQML as an agent communication language. In *Proceedings of the Third International Conference on Information and Knowledge Management (CIKM '94)* (pp. 456-463). New York: ACM.

Fink, J., & Kobsa, A. (2000). A review and analysis of commercial user modeling servers for personalization on the World Wide Web. *User Modeling and User-Adapted Interaction, 10*(3-4), 209–249. doi:10.1023/A:1026597308943

Fisher, R. J., & Price, L. L. (1991). International pleasure travel motivation and post vacation cultural attitude change. *Journal of Leisure Research, 23*, 193–208.

Fiske, J. (1990). *Introduction to communication studies* (2nd ed.). London: Routledge.

Fodor, O., & Werthner, H. (2005). Harmonise: A step toward an interoperable e-tourism marketplace. *International Journal of Electronic Commerce, 9*(2), 11–39.

Forsyth, T. (1997). Environmental responsibility and business regulation: The case of sustainable tourism. *The Geographical Journal*, 163.

Foundation for Intelligent Physical Agents, The. (n.d.). Retrieved August 15, 2005, from http://www.fipa.org

Frank, A., Bittner, S., & Raubal, M. (2001). Spatial and cognitive simulation with multi-agent systems. In D. Montello (Ed.), *Spatial Information Theory - Foundations of Geographic Information Science, Proceedings of COSIT 2001,* Morro Bay, CA, USA (Vol. 2205, pp. 124-139). Berlin, Germany: Springer.

Friedman-Hill, E. (1995). *Jess: The rule engine for the Javaplatform*. Retrieved from http://herzberg.ca.sandia.gov/jess/

Fullerton, T., Swain, C., & Hoffman, S. (Eds.). (2004). *Proceedings of the Game design workshop. designing, prototyping and playtesting games*. San Francisco, CA: CMP Books.

Gallarza, M. G., Saura, I. G., & Garcia, H. C. (2002). Destination image: Towards a conceptual framework. *Annals of Tourism Research, 29*(1), 56–78. doi:10.1016/S0160-7383(01)00031-7

Garlick, S. (2002). Revealing the unseen: Tourism, art and photography. *Cultural Studies, 16*(2), 289–305. doi:10.1080/09502380110107599

Gärling, T., Säisä, J., Book, A., & Lindberg, E. (1986). The spatiotemporal sequencing of everyday activities in the large-scale environment. *Journal of Environmental Psychology, 6*, 261–280. doi:10.1016/S0272-4944(86)80001-9

Garrett, J. (2005). *Ajax: A new approach to Web applications.* Retrieved February 14, 2005, from http://www.adaptivepath.com/publications/essays/archives/000385.php

Gartner, W. C. (1993). Image formation process. *Journal of Travel & Tourism Marketing, 2*(2/3), 191–215.

Gelter, H. (2006). Towards an understanding of experience production. In M. Kylänen (Ed.), *Digital media & games* (pp. 28-51). Rovaniemi, Finland: University of Lapland Press.

Georgievski, M., & Sharda, N. (2003). *Task modelling for a holistic quality of service model—TRAQS.* Paper presented at the IEEE India Council Annual Convention and Exhibition, India.

Georgievski, M., & Sharda, N. (2006). Re-engineering the usability testing process for live multimedia systems. [EIMJ]. *Journal of Enterprise Information Management, 19*(2), 223–233. doi:10.1108/17410390610645094

Gillmor, D. (2008). Bloggers and mash. *New Scientist, 197*(2649), 44–47. doi:10.1016/S0262-4079(08)60675-2

Giulio, M., Paterno, F., & Santaro, C. (2002). CTTE: Support for developing and analyzing task models for interactive system design. *IEEE Transaction on Software Engineering, 28*(9), 1-17.

Golledge, R., & Stimson, R. (1997). *Spatial behavior: A geographic perspective*. New York: Guilford Press.

Gomez-Jacinto, L., & Martin-Garcia, J., & Bertiche-Haud'Huyze, C. (1999). A model of tourism experience and attitude change. *Annals of Tourism Research, 26*(4), 1024–1027. doi:10.1016/S0160-7383(99)00063-8

Goodchild, M. (2007). Citizens as sensors: The world of volunteered geography. *GeoJournal, 69*, 211–221. doi:10.1007/s10708-007-9111-y

Google Earth. (2008). *Ancient Rome video*. Retrieved December 20, 2008, from http://earth.google.com/rome/

Gordon, M., Kowalski, A., Paprzycki, M., Pelech, T., Szymczak, M., & Wasowicz, T. (2005). Ontologies in a travel support system. *Internet 2005*, 285-300.

Graef, G., & Gaedke, M. (2000). Construction of adaptive Web-applications from reusable components. In *Proceedings of the 1st International Conference on Electronic Commerce and Web Technologies*(EC-Web) (pp. 1-12).

Granovetter, M. (1985). Economic action and social structure: The Problem of embeddedness. *American Journal of Sociology, 91*, 481–493. doi:10.1086/228311

Gratzer, M., Werthner, H., & Winiwarter, W. (2004). Electronic business in tourism. *International Journal of Electronic Business, 2*(5), 450–459. doi:10.1504/IJEB.2004.005878

Gravetter, F. J., & Wallnau, L. B. (2003). Statistics for the behavioral sciences (6th ed.). Belmont, CA: Wadsworth/ Thomson Learning.

Greaves, M. (2007). Semantic Web 2.0. *IEEE Intelligent Systems, 22*(2), 94–96. doi:10.1109/MIS.2007.40

Gretzel, U., & Fesenmaier, D. (2005). Persuasiveness of preference elicitation processes in destination recommendation systems. In *Proceedings of the 12th International Conference on Information and Communication Technologies in Travel and Tourism* (*ENTER 2005*) (pp. 194-204).

Gretzel, U., & Fesenmaier, D. (2007). Persuasion in recommender systems. *International Journal of Electronic Commerce, 11*, 81–100. doi:10.2753/JEC1086-4415110204

Gretzel, U., Yoo, K. H., & Purifoy, M. (2007). *Online travel review study: Role and impact of online travel reviews.* Texas A&M University: Laboratory for Intelligent Systems in Tourism. Retrieved September 14, 2007, from http://www.tripadvisor.com/pdfs/OnlineTravelReviewReport.pdf

Grinter, R., Rodden, T., Aoki, P., Cutrell, E., Jeffries, R., & Olson, G. (Eds.). (2006). *Proceedings of the CHI Conference '06*. New York: ACM.

Grundy, J. C., & Jin, W. (2002). Experiences developing a thin-client, multi-device travel planning application. In *Proceedings of 2002 New Zealand Conference on Computer-Human Interaction*, Hamilton, New Zealand.

Gupta, A., & Srivastava, M. (2001). *Integrated java technology for end-to-end m-commerce*. Retrieved June 4, 2008, from http://developers.sun.com/mobility/midp/articles/mcommerce/

Haddawy, P., Ha, V., Restificar, A., Geisler, B., & Miyamoto, J. (2003). Preference elicitation via theory refinement. *Journal of Machine Learning Research, 4*, 317–337. doi:10.1162/153244304773633843

Hägerstrand, T. (1970). What about people in regional science? *Papers / Regional Science Association. Regional Science Association. Meeting, 24*, 7–21.

Hammond, K. (1989). *Case-based planning: Viewing planning as a memory task.* San Diego, CA: Academic Press.

Hanlan, J., & Kelly, S. (2005). Image formation, information sources and an iconic Australian tourist destination. *Journal of Vacation Marketing, 11*(2), 163–177. doi:10.1177/1356766705052573

Hapkemeyer, A., & Weiermair, P. (1996). *Photo text text photo: The synthesis of photography and text in contemporary art.* Kilchberg, Switzerland: Edition Stemmle.

Hariharan, R., & Hornsby, K. (2000). *Modeling intersections of geospatial lifelines.* Paper presented at the First International Conference on Geographic Information Science, GIScience 2000, Savannah, Georgia, USA.

Harvey, D. (1989). *The condition of postmodernity.* Oxford, UK: Basil Blackwell.

Hassanein, K., & Head, M. (2007). Manipulating perceived social presence through the Web interface and its impact on attitude towards online shopping. *International Journal of Human-Computer Studies, 65*(8), 689–708. doi:10.1016/j.ijhcs.2006.11.018

Hassenzahl, M., & Tractinsky, N. (2006). User experience - a research agenda. *Behaviour & Information Technology, 25*, 91–97. doi:10.1080/01449290500330331

Hecht, B., & Raubal, M. (2008). GeoSR: Geographically explore semantic relations in world knowledge. In L. Bernard, C. Friis-Christensen, & H. Pundt (Eds.), *The European Information Society - Taking Geoinformation Science One Step Further (Proceedings of the 11th AGILE International Conference on GIScience 2008, Girona, Spain)* (pp. 95-113). Berlin, Germany: Springer.

Hendricks, M., Egenhofer, M., & Hornsby, K. (2003). Structuring a wayfinder's dynamic space-time environment. In W. Kuhn, M. Worboys, & S. Timpf (Eds.), *Proceedings of the Spatial Information Theory - Foundations of Geographic Information Science, International Conference, COSIT 2003, Kartause Ittingen, Switzerland, September 2003* (Vol. 2825, pp. 75-92). Berlin, Germany: Springer.

Hill, W., Stead, L., Rosenstein, M., & Furnas, G. (1995). Recommending and evaluating choices in a virtual community of use. In *Proceedings of the CHI-95 Conference*, Denver, USA.

Hodgkinson, T. (2008). *With friends like these...* Retrieved January 14, 2008, from http://www.guardian.co.uk/technology/2008/jan/14/facebook

Höpken, W., Fuchs, M., Zanker, M., Beer, T., Eybl, A., & Flores, S. (2006). etPlanner: An IT framework for comprehensive and integrative travel guidance. In [Berlin, Germany: Springer.]. *Proceedings of the Information and Communication Technologies in Tourism, ENTER, 2006*, 125–133. doi:10.1007/3-211-32710-X_20

Horrocks, I., Patel-Schneider, P. F., & van Harmelen, F. (2003). From SHIQ and RDF to OWL: The making of a Web ontology language. *Journal of Web Semantics*, *1*(1), 7–26. doi:10.1016/j.websem.2003.07.001

Horrocks, I., Patel-Schneider, P. F., Boley, H., Tabet, S., Grosof, B., & Dean, M. (2004). *SWRL: A Semantic Web rule language combining OWL and RuleML* (W3C Member Submission, 21 May 2004). Retrieved from http://www.w3.org/Submission/2004/SUBM-SWRL-20040521/

Houghton, J. W. (2007). Online delivery of tourism services: Development, issues, and challenges. In W. Pease, M. Rowe, & M. Cooper (Eds.), *Information and communication technologies in support of the tourism industry* (pp. 1-25). Hershey, PA: IGI Publishing.

Huang, C. M., & Chao, Y. C. (2001). Universal WWW access for heterogeneous client devices. In *Proceedings of the 27th Euromicro Conference* (pp. 315-322).

Hughes, C., & Moshell, E. J. (1997). Shared virtual worlds for experiment. *ACM Multimedia*, *5*(2), 145–154. doi:10.1007/s005300050050

Huhns, M. N., & Bridgeland, D. M. (1991). Multiagent truth maintenance. *IEEE Transactions on Systems, Man, and Cybernetics*, *21*(6), 1437–1445. doi:10.1109/21.135687

Hull, A. D. (1998). *The TREC-7 filtering track: description and analysis.* Paper presented at the Proceedings of TREC-7, 7th Retrieval Conference, Gaithersburg, US.

Hunicke, R., LeBlanc, M., & Zubek, R. (2004). *MDA: A formal approach to game design and game research.* Paper presented at the AAAI Workshop on Challenges in Game AI, San Jose, CA.

Inference engine. (n.d.). Retrieved May 15, 2006, from http://www.emclab.umr.edu/consortium/Whatis/node17.html

Interrante, E. V., Ries, B., & Anderson, L. (2007). Seven league boots: A new metaphor for augmented locomotion through moderately large scale immersive virtual environments. In *Proceedings of the Symposium on 3D User Interfaces* (pp. 167–170). Washington, DC: IEEE.

Interrante, V., Anderson, L., & Ries, B. (2006). Distance perception in immersive virtual environments, revisited. In *Proceedings of Virtual Reality* (pp. 3–10). Washington, DC: IEEE.

Ipadeola, A. O., Olugbara, O. O., Adigun, M. O., & Xulu, S. S. (2008). A system for dynamically generating user centric interfaces for mobile applications and services. In I. Y. Song, et al. (Eds.), *Proceedings of the ER Workshops 2008* (LNCS 5232, pp. 175-184). Berlin, Germany: Springer-Verlag.

Ipadeola, A. O., Olugbara, O. O., Xulu, S. S., & Adigun, M. O. (2008). Polymorphic logical description for automatic generation of user centric, multi-device interfaces. In *Proceedings of the third International Conference on Pervasive Computing*, Alexandria, Egypt.

Iwata, H., Yano, H., Fukushima, H., & Noma, H. (2005). CirculaFloor. *IEEE Computer Graphics and Applications*, *25*(1), 64–67. doi:10.1109/MCG.2005.5

Jakkilinki, R., & Sharda, N. (2007). A framework for ontology-based tourism applications. In W. Pease, M. Rowe, & M. Cooper (Eds.), *Information and communication technologies in support of the tourism industry* (pp. 26-49). Hershey, PA: IGI Publishing.

Jakkilinki, R., Sharda, N., & Georgievski, M. (2005). *Developing an ontology for multimedia design and planning pyramid.* Paper presented at the International Symposium on Information and Communications Technologies, Petaling Jaya Malaysia.

James, L. (2002). Damask a tool for early-stage design and prototyping of cross-device user interfaces. In *Proceedings of the Conference Supplement of UIST 2003: ACM Symposium on User Interface Software and Technology* (pp. 13-16).

Jameson, A., Baldes, S., & Kleinbauer, T. (2004). Two methods for enhancing mutual awareness in a group recommender system. In *Proceedings of the Working Conference on Advanced Visual interfaces*, Gallipoli, Italy (pp. 447-449). New York: ACM.

Janelle, D. (2004). Impact of information technologies. In S. Hanson & G. Giuliano (Eds.), *The Geography of Urban Transportation* (3rd ed., pp. 86-112). New York: Guilford Press.

Jank, M., & Pospischil, G. (2005). Device independent mobile multimodal user interfaces with the MONA multimodal presentation server. In *Proceedings of the Eurescom Summit* (pp. 89-93).

Jannach, D. (2006). Finding preferred query relaxations in content-based recommenders. In *Proceedings of the IEEE Intelligent Systems Conference IS'2006*, Westminster, UK (pp. 355-360).

Jannach, D., & Kreutler, G. (2005). Personalized user preference elicitation for e-services. In *Proceedings of the IEEE International conference on e-Technology, e-Commerce and e-Service*, Hong Kong (pp. 304-611).

Jannach, D., & Kreutler, G. (2007). Rapid development of knowledge-based conversational recommender applications with advisor suite. *Journal of Web Engineering, 6*(2), 165–192.

Jannach, D., Zanker, M., Jessenitschnig, M., & Seidler, O. (2007). Developing a conversational travel advisor with ADVISOR SUITE. In A. J. Frew (Ed.), *Information and communication technologies in tourism* (pp. 43-52). Berlin, Germany: Springer.

Jenkins, O. H. (2003). Photography and travel brochures: The circle of representation. *Tourism Geographies, 5*(3), 305–328. doi:10.1080/14616680309715

Jerald, J., Peck, T., Steinicke, F., & Whitton, M. (2008). Sensitivity to scene motion for phases of head yaws. In *Proceedings of the Applied Perception in Graphics and Visualization* (pp. 155–162). New York: ACM.

Joachims, T. (2002). Optimizing search engines using clickthrough data. In *Proceedings of the 8th ACM SIGKDD International Conference on Knowledge Discovery and Data Mining (KDD-02)* (pp. 133-142). New York: ACM Press.

Juan, T., Pearce, A., & Sterling, L. (2002). ROADMAP: Extending the gaia methodology for complex open systems. In *Proceedings of the First International joint Conference on Autonomous Agents and Multiagent Systems (AAMAS '02)* (pp. 3-10). New York: ACM Press.

Kacprzyk, J. (1986). Group decision making with a fuzzy linguistic majority. *Fuzzy Sets and Systems, 18*, 105–118. doi:10.1016/0165-0114(86)90014-X

Kahana, M., Sekuler, R., Caplan, J., Kirschen, M., & Madsen, J. (1999). Human theta oscillations exhibit task dependence during virtual maze navigation. *Nature, 399*, 781–784. doi:10.1038/21645

Kai, R. (2005). A transformational approach to multi-device interface. In *Proceedings of the human Factor in computer System*, Portand OR, USA (pp. 1126-1127).

Keates, S., Laddon, P., Clarkson, P. J., & Robinson, P. (2002). User models and user physical capability. [UMUAI]. *Journal of User Modeling and User-Adapted Interaction, 12*, 139–169. doi:10.1023/A:1015047002796

Kelly, M. (2007). *Heard about user generated content? It's the new word of mouth (Travel trends: Incorporating travel trends and novacancy).* Retrieved April 18, 2008, from http://web.archive.org/web/20070313203812/http://www.traveltrends.biz/ttn17-user-generated-content

Kennedy, L., Naaman, M., Ahern, S., Nair, R., & Rattenbury, T. (2007). How Flickr helps us make sense of the world: Context and content in community-contributed media collections. In *Proceedings of the 15th International Conference on Multimedia* (pp. 631-640). Augsburg, Germany: ACM. Retrieved November 12, 2008, from http://portal.acm.org/citation.cfm?id=1291384

Keßler, C., Rinner, C., & Raubal, M. (2005). An argumentation map prototype to support decision-making in spatial planning. In F. Toppen & M. Painho (Eds.), *Proceedings of the AGILE 2005 - 8th Conference on Geographic Information Science* (pp. 135-142). Lisboa, Portugal: Instituto Geografico Portugues (IGP).

Kim, W. G., Lee, C., & Hiemstra, S. J. (2004). Effects of an online virtual community on customer loyalty and travel product purchases. *Tourism Management, 25*, 343–355. doi:10.1016/S0261-5177(03)00142-0

Kimber, J., Georgievski, M., & Sharda, N. (2006, January 18-20). *Developing a visualisation tool for tour planning.* Paper presented at the IFITT Global Travel & Tourism Technology and eBusiness Conference, Lausanne, Switzerland.

Knight, M. (2007). Web 2.0. *Communications Engineer, 5*(1), 30–35. doi:10.1049/ce:20070104

Kobsa, A. (2000). *User modeling as a key factor in system personalization.* Retrieved September 16, 2005, from http://www.zurich.ibm.com/~mrs/chi2000/contributions/kobsa.html

Kock, N. (2008). E-collaboration and e-commerce in virtual worlds: The potential of Second Life and World of Warcraft. *International Journal of e-Collaboration, 4*(3), 1–13.

Kohli, L., Burns, E., Miller, D., & Fuchs, H. (2005). Combining passive haptics with redirected walking. In [). New York: ACM.]. *Proceedings of the Conference on Augmented Tele-Existence, 157*, 253–254. doi:10.1145/1152399.1152451

Kolbitsch, J., & Maurer, H. (2006). The transformation of the Web: How emerging communities shape the information we consume. *Journal of Universal Computer Science, 12*(2), 187–213.

Kolodner, J. (1993). *Case-based reasoning.* San Mateo, CA: Morgan Kaufmann.

Kot, B., Wuensche, B., Grundy, J., & Hosking, J. (2005). Information visualisation utilising 3D computer game engines case study: A source code comprehension tool. In *Proceedings of the 6th ACM SIGCHI New Zealand chapter's International Conference on Computer-Human Interaction (CHINZ '05)* (pp. 53-60). New York: ACM Press.

Kozinets, R. V. (2002). The field behind the screen: Using netnography for marketing research in online communities. *JMR, Journal of Marketing Research, 39*, 61–72. doi:10.1509/jmkr.39.1.61.18935

Kwan, M.-P. (2000). Analysis of human spatial behavior in a GIS environment: Recent developments and future prospects. *Journal of Geographical Systems, 2*(1), 85–90. doi:10.1007/s101090050034

Kwan, M.-P. (2004). GIS methods in time-geographic research: Geocomputation and geovisualization of human activity patterns. *Geografiska Annaler B, 86*(4), 267–280. doi:10.1111/j.0435-3684.2004.00167.x

La Grange, A. (2005). *Basic critical theory for photographers.* London: Focal Press.

Laboy, F., & Torchio, P. (2007). *Web 2.0 for the travel marketer and consumer: A white paper.* E-site Marketing and the International Association of Online Communicators. Retrieved August 12, 2007, from http://www.wesitemarketing.com/web2-travel-marketing.php

Lappe, M., Bemmer, F., & van den Berg, A. V. (1999). Perception of self-motion from visual flow. *Trends in Cognitive Sciences, 3*(9), 329–336. doi:10.1016/S1364-6613(99)01364-9

Larsen, J. (2006). Picturing Bornholm: Producing and consuming a tourist place through picturing practices. *Scandinavian Journal of Hospitality and Tourism*, *6*(2), 75–94. doi:10.1080/15022250600658853

Larsen, J., Urry, J., & Axhausen, K. (2006). *Mobilities, networks, geographies*. Aldershot, England: Ashgate.

Lave, J., & Wenger, E. (1991). *Situated learning: Legitimate peripheral participation*. Cambridge, UK: Cambridge University Press.

Lee, J. K., & Mills, J. E. (2007). Exploring tourist satisfaction with mobile technology. In *Proceedings of ENTER 2007: 14th annual conference of IFITT, the International Federation for IT & Travel and Tourism*, Ljubljana, Slovenia (pp. 141-152).

Leiper, N. (1990). Tourism systems: An interdisciplinary perspective. New Zealand: Massey University.

Leisen, B. (2001). Image segmentation: The case of a tourism destination. *Journal of Services Marketing*, *15*(1), 49–66. doi:10.1108/08876040110381517

Leiss, W., Kline, S., & Jhally, S. (1990). *Social communication in advertising: Persons, products and images of well-being* (2nd ed.). Ontario, Canada: Nelson Canada.

Lemelin, R. H. (2006). The gawk, the glance, and the gaze: Ocular consumption and polar bear tourism in Churchill, Manitoba, Canada. *Current Issues in Tourism*, *9*(6), 516–534. doi:10.2167/cit294.0

Lenntorp, B. (1976). Paths in space-time environments: A time-geographic study of the movement possibilities of individuals. *Lund Studies in Geography, Series B*(44).

Levi, G., Vagliengo, A., & Goy, A. (2005). *Talea: An ontology-based framework for e-business applications development*. Paper presented at the 2nd Italian Semantic Web Workshop on Semantic Web Applications and Perspectives, Trento, Italy.

Lew, M. S., Sebe, N., Lifl, C. D., & Jain, R. (2006). Content-based multimedia information retrieval: State of the art and challenges. *ACM Transactions on Multimedia Computing . Communications and Applications*, *2*(1), 1–19.

Lexhagen, M. (2005). The importance of value-added services to support the customer search and purchase process on travel websites. *Journal of Information Technology and Tourism*, *7*(2), 119–135. doi:10.3727/1098305054517336

Lin, K.-J. (2007). Building Web 2.0. *Computer*, *40*(5), 101–102. doi:10.1109/MC.2007.159

Linden, G., Hanks, S., & Lesh, N. (1997). Interactive assessment of user preference models: The automated travel assistant. In *Proceedings of User Modeling*.

Lindstaedt, S. (1998). *Group memories: A knowledge medium for communities of interest*. Boulder, CO: University of Colorado at Boulder.

Lituchy, T. R., & Rail, A. (2000). Bed and breakfast, small inns, and the Internet: The impact of technology on the globalization of small businesses. *Journal of International Marketing*, *8*(2), 86–97. doi:10.1509/jimk.8.2.86.19625

Litvin, S. W., Goldsmith, R. E., & Pan, B. (2008). Electronic word-of-mouth in hospitality and tourism management. *Tourism Management*, *29*, 458–468. doi:10.1016/j.tourman.2007.05.011

Livingstone, D., & Kemp, J. (2006). Massively multi-learner: Recent advances in 3D social environments. *Computing and Information Systms Journal*, *10*(2).

Lorenzi, F., & Ricci, F. (2005). Case-based recommender systems: A unifying view. In *Intelligent techniques for Web personalization* (pp. 89-113). Berlin, Germany: Springer.

Losh, E. (2005). In country with tactical Iraqi: Trust, identity, and language learning in a military video game. In *Proceedings of the Digital Arts and Culture Conference* (pp. 69-78).

Lueg, C. (2006). Mediation, expansion and immediacy: How online communities revolutionize information access in the tourism sector. In *Proceedings of the 14th European Conference on Information Systems*, Goteborg, Sweden.

Lutz, C. (2003). Description logics with concrete domains - a survey. In P.Balbiani, N.-Y. Suzuki, F. Wolter, and M. Zakharyaschev (Eds.), *Advances in modal logics* (Vol. 4). London: King's College Publications.

Macho, S., Torrens, M., & Faltings, B. (2000). A multi-agent recommender system for planning meetings. In *Proceedings of the Workshop On Agent-Based Recommender Systems (WARS'2000).*

MacKay, K. J. (2004). Is a picture worth a thousand words? Snapshots from tourism destination image research. In J. Aramberri & R. Butler (Eds.), *Tourism development: Issues for a vulnerable industry* (pp. 44-65). Clevedon, UK: Channel View Publications.

MacKay, K. J., & Couldwell, C. M. (2004). Using visitor employed photography to investigate destination image. *Journal of Travel Research, 42*, 390–396. doi:10.1177/0047287504263035

MacKay, K. J., & Fesenmaier, D. R. (1997). Pictorial element of destination promotions in image formation. *Annals of Tourism Research, 24*, 537–565. doi:10.1016/S0160-7383(97)00011-X

Mackay, K. J., & Fesenmaier, D. R. (2000). An exploration of crosscultural destination image assessment. *Journal of Travel Research, 38*(4), 417–423. doi:10.1177/004728750003800411

Maechling, P., Chalupsky, H., Dougherty, M., Deelman, E., Gil, Y., & Gullapalli, S. (2005). Simplifying construction of complex workflows for non-expert users of the Southern California Earthquake Center community modeling environment. *SIGMOD Record, 34*(3), 24–30. doi:10.1145/1084805.1084811

Maes, P. (1994). Agents that reduce work and information overload. *Communications of the ACM, 37*(7), 30–40. doi:10.1145/176789.176792

Maes, P., & Nardi, D. (Eds.). (1988). *Meta-level architectures and reflection.* New York: Elsevier Science Inc.

Mahmood, T., Ricci, F., Venturini, A., & Höpken, W. (2008). Adaptive recommender systems for travel planning. In *Proceedings of ENTER 2008: International Conference on Information and Communication Technologies in Tourism*, Innsbruck, Austria (pp. 1-11).

Mailharro, D. (1998). A classification and constraint-based framework for configuration. *AI in Engineering . Design and Manucturing, 12*, 383–397.

Malhotra, Y. (2001). Knowledge management for e-business performance: Advancing information strategy to 'Internet time'. In Y. Malhotra (Ed.), *Knowledge management and business model innovation* (pp. 2-16). Hershey, PA: Idea Group Publishing.

Manojlovich, J., Prasithsangaree, P., Hughes, S., Chen, J., & Lewis, M. (2003). UTSAF: A multiagent-based framework for supporting military-based distributed interactive simulations in 3d virtual environments. In *Proceedings of the 35th Conference on Winter Simulation (WSC '03)* (pp. 960-968). Washington, DC: IEEE Computer Society.

Markwell, K. W. (1997). Dimensions of photography in a nature-based tour. *Annals of Tourism Research, 24*(1), 131–155. doi:10.1016/S0160-7383(96)00053-9

Marten, P. S. (2007). The transformation of the distribution process in the airlines industry empowered by information and communication technologies. In W. Pease, M. Rowe, & M. Cooper (Eds.), *Information and communication technologies in support of the tourism industry* (pp. 76-113). Hershey, PA: IGI Publishing.

Martin, C., Schreckenghost, D., Bonasso, P., Kortenkamp, D., Milam, T., & Thronesbery, C. (2003). An environment for distributed collaboration among humans and software agents. In *Proceedings of the Second International joint Conference on Autonomous Agents and Multiagent Systems (AAMAS '03)* (pp. 1062-1063). New York: ACM Press.

Mason, C., & Johnson, R. R. (1989). DATMS: A framework for distributed assumption based reasoning. *Distributed Artificial Intelligence, 2*, 293–317.

Maurina, E. F., III, (Ed.). (2006). *The game programmer's guide to torque: Under the hood of the torque game engine*. Natick, MA: AK Peters, Ltd.

Maximilien, E. M., Wilkinson, H., Desai, N., & Tai, S. (2007). A domain specific-language for Web APIs and services mashups. In *Proceedings of the International Conference on Service Oriented Computing (ICSOC).*

Mayo, M. J. (2007). Games for science and engineering education. *Communications of the ACM, 50*(7), 30–35. doi:10.1145/1272516.1272536

McCarthy, K., Salamó, M., Coyle, L., McGinty, L., Smyth, B., & Nixon, P. (2006). Group recommender systems: A critiquing based approach. In *Proceedings of the 11th international Conference on intelligent User interfaces*, Sydney, Australia (pp. 267-269). New York: ACM.

McGinty, L., & Smyth, B. (2006). Adaptive selection: An analysis of critiquing and preference-based feedback in conversational recommender systems. *International Journal of Electronic Commerce, 11*(2), 35–57. doi:10.2753/JEC1086-4415110202

McIntyre, P. (2008). *Using social media for commercial gain.* Retrieved December 4, 2008, from http://www.theage.com.au/news/technology/biztech/using-social-media-for-commercial-gain/2008/12/04/1228257189521.html

McMillan, S. J. (2000). The microscope and the moving target: The challenge of applying content analysis to the World Wide Web. *Journalism & Mass Communication Quarterly, 77*(1), 80–98.

McSherry, D. (2005). Retrieval failure and recovery in recommender systems. *Artificial Intelligence Review, 24*, 319–338. doi:10.1007/s10462-005-9000-z

Meng, L., Zipf, A., & Winter, S. (2008). *Map-based mobile services: Design, interaction and usability.* Berlin, Germany: Springer.

Mernik, M., Heering, J., & Sloane, A. M. (2005). When and how to develop domain-specific languages. *ACM Computing Surveys, 37*(4), 316–344. doi:10.1145/1118890.1118892

Merritt, J. (2006). Web 2.0 becomes travel standard. *Business Travel News, 23*(20), 28–30.

Michael, D., & Chen, S. (Eds.). (2006). *Serious games: Games that education, train, and inform.* Florence, KY: Thompson Course Technology PTR.

Milic-Frayling, N., Jones, R., Rodden, K., Smyth, G., Blackwell, A., & Sommerer, R. (2004). Smartback: Supporting users in back navigation. In *Proceedings of the 13th conference on World Wide Web*, New York, USA.

Miller, H. (1991). Modeling accessibility using space-time prism concepts within geographical information systems. *International Journal of Geographical Information Systems, 5*(3), 287–301. doi:10.1080/02693799108927856

Miller, H. (1999). Measuring space-time accessibility benefits within transportation networks: Basic theory and computational methods. *Geographical Analysis, 31*(2), 187–212.

Miller, H. (2005). A measurement theory for time geography. *Geographical Analysis, 37*(1), 17–45. doi:10.1111/j.1538-4632.2005.00575.x

Miller, H. (2005). What about people in geographic information science? In P. Fisher & D. Unwin (Eds.), *Re-presenting geographical information systems* (pp. 215-242). New York: John Wiley.

Miller, R. H. (n.d.). *Web interface design: Learning form our past.* Retrieved May 25, 2006, from http://www.cs.rutgers.edu/~shklar/www4/rmiller/rhmpapr.html#background

Milne, S., Grekin, J., & Woodley, S. (1998). Tourism and the construction of place in Canada's eastern Arctic. In G. Ringer & C.L. Cartier (Eds.), *Destinations: Cultural landscapes of tourism* (pp. 101-121). London: Routledge.

Mindswap. (n.d.). Retrieved May 15, 2006, from http://www.mindswap.org/2003/pellet/index.shtm

Mirzadeh, N., & Ricci, F. (2007). Cooperative query rewriting for decision making support and recommender systems. *Applied Artificial Intelligence, 21*, 1–38. doi:10.1080/08839510701527515

MIT. (2008). *Usability guidelines (Massachusetts Institute of Technology)*. Retrieved April 17, 2008, from http://web.mit.edu/is/usability/usability-guidelines.html

Mohapatra, D., & Suma, S. B. (2005). Survey of location based wireless services. In *Proceedings of the 2005 IEEE International Conference on Personal Wireless Communications* (pp. 358-362).

Moloney, J., Amor, R., Furness, J., & Moores, B. (2003). Design critique inside a multi-player game engine. In *Proceedings of the CIB W78 Conference on IT in Construction* (pp. 255-262). CIB Publication.

Mondeca. (n.d.). Retrieved August 15, 2005, from http://www.mondeca.com

Monge, P. R., & Contractor, N. S. (2003). Theories of communication networks. New York: Oxford University Press.

Montaner, M., Lopez, B., & de la Rosa, J. L. (2003). A taxonomy of recommender agents on the Internet. *Artificial Intelligence Review, 19*(4), 285–330. doi:10.1023/A:1022850703159

Montello, D. (2001). Scale, in geography. In N. Smelser & P. Baltes (Eds.), *International encyclopedia of the social & behavioral sciences* (pp. 13501-13504). Oxford, UK: Pergamon Press.

Mooney, R., Bennett, P., & Roy, L. (1998). *Book recommending using text categorization with extracted information.* Paper presented at the AAAI Workshop on Recommender Systems, Madison, WI.

Morgan, N. J., Pritchard, A., & Piggott, R. (2003). Destination branding and the role of stakeholders: The case of New Zealand. *Journal of Vacation Marketing, 9*(3), 285–299. doi:10.1177/135676670300900307

Morgan, N., Pritchard, A., & Pride, R. (2004). *Destination branding: Creating the unique destination proposition.* Oxford, UK: Elsevier.

Mori, G., Paterno, F., & Santoro, C. (2004). Design and development of multi-device user interface through multiple logical descriptions. In *Proceedings on Software Engineering* (pp. 507-520).

Morrison, A. M., Taylor, S., Morrison, A. J., & Morrison, A. D. (1999). Marketing small hotels on the World Wide Web. *Information Technology & Tourism, 2*(1-4), 97–113.

Moses, A. (2008). *Coming soon... Facebook: The movie.* Retrieved September 1, 2008, from http://www.theage.com.au/news/web/coming-soon--facebook-the-movie/2008/09/01/1220121111266.html

Murphy, J. (1988). *The power of your subconscious mind.* London: Simon & Schuster.

Murphy, L., Moscardo, G., & Benckendorff, P. (2007). Exploring word-of-mouth influences on travel decisions: Friends and relatives versus other travellers. *International Journal of Consumer Studies, 31*(5), 517–527. doi:10.1111/j.1470-6431.2007.00608.x

Mutlu, B. D. (2004). *The chaotic nature of human experience: Insights on the subject matter of design towards establishing a science of design.* Unpublished master's thesis, Carnegie Mellon University, USA.

Nakanishi, H., & Ishida, T. (2004). FreeWalk/Q: Social interaction platform in virtual space. In *Proceedings of the ACM symposium on Virtual Reality Software and Technology (VRST '04)* (pp. 97-104). New York: ACM Press.

Nash, K. (2008). *A peek inside Facebook.* Retrieved August 31, 2008, from http://www.pcworld.com/businesscenter/article/150489/a_peek_inside_facebook.html

Nasseam, E. (2003). *A Web services strategy for mobile phones.* Retrieved June 4, 2008, from http://webservices.xml.com/pub/a/ws/2003/08/19/mobile.html

Neuman, W. L. (2006). *Social research methods: Qualitative and quantitative approaches* (6th ed.). Boston: Allyn and Bacon.

Newitz, A. (2008). Web 3.0: What will the next era of Web culture bring? *New Scientist, 197*(2649), 42–43. doi:10.1016/S0262-4079(08)60674-0

Nguyen, Q. N., & Ricci, F. (2004). User preferences initialization and integration in critique-based mobile recommender systems. *Proceedings of the 5th International Workshop on Artificial Intelligence in Mobile Systems*, 71-78.

Nguyen, Q. N., & Ricci, F. (2007). Replaying live-user interactions in the off-line evaluation of critique-based mobile recommendations. In *Proceedings of the 2007 ACM Conference on Recommender Systems* (pp. 81-88).

Nguyen, Q. N., & Ricci, F. (2008). Long-term and session-specific user preferences in a mobile recommender system. In *Proceedings of the 2008 International Conference on Intelligent User Interfaces* (pp. 381-384).

Nguyen, Q. N., & Ricci, F. (2008). Conversational case-based recommendations exploiting a structured case model. In *Proceedings of the 9th European Conference on Case-Based Reasoning.*

Nickols, F. (2003). *Communities of practice: An overview*, Retrieved January 2009, from http://home.att.net/~discon/KM/CoPOverview.pdf

Niedzviecki, H. (2008, November 1). With 700 friends like these, who needs…? [Insight section]. *Age*, 3.

Nielsen, J. (1993). *Usability engineering.* Boston, MA: Academic Press.

Nielsen, J. (2000). *Designing Web usability: The practice of simplicity.* New York: New Riders Publishing.

Nielsen, J. (2007). *Web 2.0 can be dangerous.* Retrieved April 21, 2008, from http://www.useit.com/alertbox/web-2.html

Nielsen, J., & Loranger, H. (2006). *Prioritorizing Web usability.* Berkeley, CA: New Riders Publishing.

Nielsen, J., & Tahir, M. (2002). *Homepage usability.* Salem, VA: New Riders Publishing.

Niininen, O., Buhalis, D., & March, R. (2007). Customer empowerment in tourism through consumer centric marketing (CCM). *Qualitative Market Research, 10*(3), 265–282. doi:10.1108/13522750710754308

Niininen, O., March, R., & Buhalis, D. (2006). Consumer centric tourism marketing. In D. Buhalis & C. Costa (Eds.), Tourism management dynamics: Trends, management and tools (pp. xxiii, 279). London: Butterworth Heinemann.

Niklfeld, G., Anegg, H., Gassner, A., Jank, M., Pospischil, G., Pucher, M., et al. (2005). Device independent mobile multimodal user interfaces with the MONA multimodal presentation server. In *Proceedings of the Eurescom Summit. W3C Workshop on Multi-Modal Interaction.*

Nisbet, R. A. (1970). *The sociological tradition.* London: Heinemann Educational.

Noy, N. F., Fergerson, R. W., & Musen, M. A. (2000). The knowledge model of Protege-2000: Combining interoperability and flexibility. In *Proceedings of the 2nd International Conference on Knowledge Engineering and Knowledge Management (EKAW'2000),* Juan-les-Pins, France.

Nusair, K. K., Yoon, H.-J., & Parsa, H. G. (2008). Effect of Utilitarian and hedonic motivations on consumer satisfaction with travel websites. *Information Technology & Tourism, 10*(1), 75–89. doi:10.3727/109830508785058977

Nyaupane, G. P., Teye, V., & Paris, C. (2008). Innocents abroad: Attitude change toward hosts. *Annals of Tourism Research, 35*(3), 650–667. doi:10.1016/j.annals.2008.03.002

O'Connor, M. J., Knublauch, H., Tu, S. W., & Musen, M. A. (2005). Writing rules for the Semantic Web using SWRL and Jess. In *Proceedings of the 8th International Protege Conference, Protege with Rules Workshop,* Madrid, Spain.

O'Connor, M., Cosley, D., Konstan, J. A., & Riedl, J. (2001). PolyLens: A recommender system for groups of users. In W. Prinz, M. Jarke, Y. Rogers, K. Schmidt, and V. Wulf (Eds.), *Proceedings of the Seventh Conference on European Conference on Computer Supported Cooperative Work* (pp. 199-218). Norwell, MA: Kluwer Academic Publishers.

O'Reilly, T. (2005). *What Is Web 2.0: Design patterns and business models for the next generation of software*. Retrieved March 2009, from http://www.oreillynet.com/pub/a/oreilly/tim/news/2005/09/30/what-is-web-20.html

O'Sullivan, T., Hartley, J., Saunders, D., Montgomery, M., & Fiske, J. (1994). *Key concepts in communication and cultural studies* (2nd ed.). London: Routledge.

Olsen, D., Jefferies, S., Nielsen, T., Moyes, W., & Fredrickson, P. (2000). Cross-modal interaction using XWeb. In *Proceedings of the 13th Annual Symposium on User Interface Software and Technology*, CA, USA (pp. 191-2000).

Open Travel Alliance, The. (n.d.). Retrieved August 15, 2005, from http://www.opentravel.org

OpenSimulator Wiki. (2008). *Opensimulator*. Retrieved November 18, 2008, from http://opensimulator.org/wiki/Main_Page

Orndorff, P. (2008). *Wired blog network*. Retrieved September 20, 2007, from http://blog.wired.com/geekdad/2008/11/explore-ancient.html

Palmer, S. B. (2001). *The Semantic Web: An introduction*. Retrieved May 25, 2006, from http://infomesh.net/2001/swintro/

Pan, B., MacLaurin, T., & Crotts, J. (2007). Travel blogs and their implications for destination marketing. *Journal of Travel Research*, *46*(1), 35–45. doi:10.1177/0047287507302378

Park, M. H., Hong, J. H., & Cho, S. B. (2007). Location-based recommendation system using Bayesian user's preference model in mobile devices. In *Proceedings of the 4th International Conference on Ubiquitous Intelligence and Computing* (pp. 1130-1139).

Paterno, F. (2002). *Task modelling: Where we are, where we are headed*. Paper presented at the First International Workshop on Task Models and Diagrams for User Interface Design, Tamodia, Bucharest, Romania.

Paterno, F. (2005). Model-based tools for pervasive usability. *Interacting with Computers*, *17*(3), 219–315. doi:10.1016/j.intcom.2004.06.017

Paterno, F. (2005). Multimodality and multi-device interfaces. In *Proceedings of the W3C Workshop on Multimodal Interaction*.

Payne, T. R., Sycara, K., & Lewis, M. (2000). Varying the user interaction within multi-agent systems. In *Proceedings of the Fourth International Conference on Autonomous Agents (AGENTS '00)* (pp. 412-418). New York: ACM Press.

Pazzani, J. M. (1999). A framework for collaborative, content-based and demographic filtering. *Artificial Intelligence Review*, *13*, 393-408.

Pazzani, J. M., & Billsus, D. (1997). Learning and revising user profiles: The identification of interesting Web sites. *Machine Learning*, *27*(3), 313–331. doi:10.1023/A:1007369909943

Peck, T., Whitton, M., & Fuchs, H. (2008). Evaluation of reorientation techniques for walking in large virtual environments. In *Proceedings of Virtual Reality* (pp. 121–128). Washington, DC: IEEE.

Piaget, J., & Inhelder, B. (1969). *The psychology of the child*. New York: Basic Books.

Pillay, H., Brownlee, J., & Wilss, L. (1999). Cognition and recreational computer games: Implications for educational technology. *Journal of Researeh on Computing in Education*, *32*(1), 203–216.

Pitchford, S. (2008). *Identity tourism: Imaging and imagining the nation*. Bingley, UK: Emerald Group Publishing.

Ponnada, M., & Sharda, N. (2007). A high level model for developing intelligent visual travel recommender systems. In *Proceedings of ENTER 2007: 14th annual conference of IFITT, the International Federation for IT & Travel and Tourism*, Ljubljana, Slovenia (pp. 33-42).

Ponnada, M., Jakkilinki, R., & Sharda, N. (2007). Developing Visual Tourism Recommender Systems, in *Information and Communication Technologies in Support of the Tourism Industry, Pease, W., Rowe, M. & Cooper, M. (Eds.), IGI Global, 162-179.*

Pospischil, G., Umlauft, M., & Michlmayr, E. (2002). Designing LoL@, a mobile tourist guide for UMTS. In *Proceedings of the 4th International Conference on Human Computer Interaction with Mobile Devices and Services* (*Mobile HCI 2002*) (pp. 140-154).

Pöttler, M. (2007). *Die rolle von onlinecommunities in reise und tourismus.* Unpublished master's thesis, Vienna University of Technology, Vienna, Austria.

Pourret, O., Naïm, P., & Marcot, B. (2008). *Bayesian networks: A practical guide to applications.* New York: Wiley.

Preece, J. (2000). Online communities: Designing usability, supporting sociability. New York: John Wiley.

Pressman, R. S. (1997). *Software engineering, a practitioner's approach* (4th ed.). McGraw-Hill.

Pretes, M. (2003). Tourism and nationalism. *Annals of Tourism Research, 30*(1), 125–142. doi:10.1016/S0160-7383(02)00035-X

Procaccino, D. J., & Miller, R. F. (2000). Tourism on the World Wide Web: A comparison of Web sites of United States- and French-based businesses. *Information Technology & Tourism, 1-4*(1), 173–183.

Protégé. (n.d.). Retrieved May 25, 2006, from http://protege.stanford.edu/

Puehringer, S., & Taylor, A. (2008). A practitioner's report on blogs as a potential source of destination marketing intelligence. *Journal of Vacation Marketing, 14*(2), 177–187. doi:10.1177/1356766707087524

Pultar, E., Cova, T. J., Yuan, M., & Goodchild, M. (2009a). EDGIS: A dynamic GIS based on space time points. *International Journal of Geographical Information Science.*

Pultar, E., Raubal, M., & Goodchild, M. (2008) GED-MWA: Geospatial exploratory data mining Web agent. In H Samet, C. Shahabi, & O. Wolfson (Eds.), *Proceedings of the 16th ACM International Symposium on Geographic Information Systems, SIGSPATIAL ACM GIS 2008,* Irvine, CA (pp. 499-502).

Pultar, E., Raubal, M., Cova, T. J., & Goodchild, M. (2009b). Dynamic GIS case studies: Wildfire evacuation and volunteered geographic information. *Transactions in GIS, 13*(s1), 85–104. doi:10.1111/j.1467-9671.2009.01157.x

Raubal, M., Miller, H., & Bridwell, S. (2004). User-centred time geography for location-based services. *Geografiska Annaler B, 86*(4), 245–265. doi:10.1111/j.0435-3684.2004.00166.x

Raubal, M., Winter, S., Teßmann, S., & Gaisbauer, C. (2007). Time geography for *ad-hoc* shared-ride trip planning in mobile geosensor networks. *ISPRS Journal of Photogrammetry and Remote Sensing, 62*(5), 366–381. doi:10.1016/j.isprsjprs.2007.03.005

Raybourn, E. M., Deagle, E., Mendina, K., & Heneghan, J. (2005). Adaptive thinking & leadership simulation game training for special forces officers. In *Proceedings of the Interservice/Industry Training, Simulation, and Education Conference.*

Razzaque, S. (2005). *Redirected walking.* Unpublished doctoral dissertation, University of North Carolina, Chapel Hill.

RDF Core Working Group W3C Semantic Web Activity, W3C. (2004). *Resource description framework (RDF)* (W3C Recommendation, 10 February 2004). Retrieved from http://www.w3.org/TR/rdf-primer/

Reactive. (2007). *Web 2.0 for the tourism & travel industry.* Melbourne, Australia: Reactive.

Reilly, J., McCarthy, K., McGinty, L., & Smyth, B. (2005). Incremental critiquing. *Knowledge-Based Systems, 18,* 143–151. doi:10.1016/j.knosys.2004.10.005

Reilly, J., Zhang, J., McGinty, L., Pu, P., & Smyth, B. (2007). Evaluating compound critiquing recommenders: A real-user study. In *Proceedings of the 2007 ACM Conference on Electronic Commerce* (pp. 114-123).

Ren, F., & Kwan, M.-P. (2007). Geovisualization of Human hybrid activity-travel patterns. *Transactions in GIS*, *11*(5), 721–744. doi:10.1111/j.1467-9671.2007.01069.x

Repo, P., Hyvonen, K., & Saastamoinen, M. (2006). Traveling from B2B to B2C: Piloting a moblog service for tourists. In *Proceedings of the International Conference on Mobile Business*. Retrieved November 12, 2008, from http://www2.computer.org/portal/web/csdl/doi/10.1109/ICMB.2006.46

Resnick, P., & Varian, H. R. (1997). Recommender systems. *Communications of the ACM*, *40*(3), 56–58. doi:10.1145/245108.245121

Resnick, P., Iacovou, N., Suchak, M., Bergstrom, P., & Riedl, J. (1994). GroupLens: An open architecture for collaborative filtering of netnews. In *Proceedings of the ACM Conference On Computer-Supported Cooperative Work* (pp. 175-186).

Rheingold, H. (1991). Virtual reality. New York: Summit Books.

Ricci, F. (2002). Travel recommender systems. *IEEE Intelligent Systems*, *17*(6), 55–57.

Ricci, F., & DelMissier, F. (2004). Supporting travel decision making through personalized recommendation. In B. C.-M. Karat & J. Karat (Eds.), *Designing personalized user experiences for ecommerce* (pp. 231-251). Amsterdam: Kluwer Academic Publisher.

Ricci, F., & Nguyen, Q. N. (2007). Acquiring and revising preferences in a critique-based mobile recommender system. *IEEE Intelligent Systems*, *22*(3), 22–29. doi:10.1109/MIS.2007.43

Ricci, F., & Werthner, H. (2002). Case-based querying for travel planning recommendation. *Information Technology and Tourism*, *4*, 215–226.

Ricci, F., Arslan, B., Mirzadeh, N., & Venturini, A. (2002). ITR: A case-based travel advisory system. In S. Craw & A. D. Preece (Eds.), *Proceedings of the 6th European Conference on Advances in Case-Based Reasoning* (LNCS 2416, pp. 613-627). London: Springer.

Richter, K. (2005). A transformation strategy for multi-device menus and toolbars. In *Proceedings of the CHI '05 Extended Abstracts on Human Factors in Computing Systems* (pp.1741-17).

Riecken, D. (2000). Introduction: Personalized views of personalization. *Communications of the ACM*, *43*(8), 27–28.

Riesbeck, C. K., & Schank, R. C. (1989). *Inside case-based reasoning*. Hillsdale, NJ: Lawrence Erlbaum.

Rodrigo, O. (2006). Mobile access to Web systems using a multi-device interface design. In *Proceedings of 2006 World congress in Computer Science, Computer Engineering and Applied Computing* (pp. 332-334).

Rodríguez-aguilar, J. A., Martín, F. J., Noriega, P., Garcia, P., & Sierra, C. (1997). Towards a test-bed for trading agents in electronic auction markets. *AI Communications*, *11*(1), 5–19.

Rojek, C. (1997). Indexing, dragging, and social construction. In C. Rojek & J. Urry (Eds.), *Touring cultures: Transformations of travel and theory* (pp. 52-74). London: Routledge.

Rollings, A., & Morris, D. (2004). *Game architecture and design*. Indianapolis, IN: New Riders Publishing.

Root, G., & Recker, W. (1983). Towards a dynamic model of individual activity pattern formulation. In S. Carpenter & P. Jones (Eds.), *Recent advances in travel demand analysis* (pp. 371-382). Aldershot, England: Gower.

Rovai, A. P. (2002). Building sense of community at a distance. *International Review of Research in Open and Distance Learning*. Retrieved September 20, 2007, from http://www.irrodl.org/index.php/irrodl/article/view/79/152

Russell, R., Thomas, P., & Fredline, E. (2005). Mountain resorts in summer: Defining the image. In C.M. Hall & S. Boyd (Eds.), *Nature-based tourism in peripheral areas: Development or disaster?* (pp. 75-90). Clevedon, UK: Channel View Publications.

Saaty, T. L. (1980). *The analytic hierarchy process*. New York: McGraw-Hill.

Salen, K., & Zimmermann, E. (2004). *Rules of play: Game design fundamentals*. Cambridge, MA: MIT Press.

Sarwar, B., Karypis, G., Konstan, J., & Riedl, J. (2001). Item-based collaborative filtering recommendation algorithms. In *Proceedings of the 10th International WWW Conference*, Hong Kong.

Savidis, A., Alex, P., Demosthenes, A., & Constantine, S. (1997). Designing user-adapted interfaces: The unified design method for transformable interactions. In *Proceedings of the Symposium on Designing Interactive Systems* (pp. 323-334).

Schafer, J. B., Konstan, J., & Riedl, J. (1999). Recommender systems in e-commerce. In *Proceedings of the ACM Conference on Electronic Commerce* (pp. 158-166).

Schegg, R., Liebrich, A., Scaglione, M., & Ahmad, S. F. S. (2008). An exploratory field study of Web 2.0 in tourism. In P. O'Connor, W. Hoepken, & U. Gretzel (Eds.), *Proceedings of the International Conference on Information and Communication Technologies in Tourism 2008,* Innsbruck, Austria (pp. 152-161). New York: Springer.

Schild, K. (1991). A correspondence theory for terminological logics: Preliminary report. In *Proceedings of IJ-CAI-91, 12th International Joint Conference on Artificial Intelligence,* Sydney, Australia (pp. 466-471).

Schlungbaum, E. (1997). Individual user interfaces and model based user interface software tools. In *Proceedings of International Conference on Intelligent User Interfaces*.

Schmallegger, D., & Carson, D. (2008). Blogs in tourism: Changing approaches to information exchange. *Journal of Vacation Marketing, 14*(2), 99–110. doi:10.1177/1356766707087519

Schmallegger, D., & Carson, D. (2009). Destination image projection on consumer generated content websites: A case study of the Flinders Ranges. *Journal of Information Technology and Tourism.*

Schroth, C., & Janner, T. (2007). Web 2.0 and SOA: Converging concepts enabling the Internet of services. *IEEE IT Professional, 9*(3).

Schwabe, G., & Prestipino, M. (2005). *How tourism communities can change travel information quality.* Paper presented at the 13th European Conference on Information Systems, Information Systems in a Rapidly Changing Economy (ECIS '05), Regensburg, Germany.

Scott, J. (2000). Social network analysis: A handbook (2nd ed.). Thousands Oaks, CA: Sage Publications.

Second Life. (2008). *Linden Lab*. Retrieved December 2008, from http://www.secondlife.com

Seidel, I., & Berger, H. (2007). Integrating electronic institutions with 3d virtual worlds. In *Proceedings of the 2007 IEEE/WIC/ACM International Conference on Intelligent Agent Technology (IAT'07)* (pp. 481-484). Washington, DC: IEEE Computer Society.

Selic, B. (2003). The pragmatics of model-driven development. *IEEE Software*, *20*(5), 19–25. doi:10.1109/MS.2003.1231146

Sellitto, C. (2005). A study of emerging tourism features associated with Australian winery websites. *Journal of Information Technology and Tourism*, *7*(3/4), 157–170. doi:10.3727/109830505774297283

Sellitto, C., & Burgess, S. (2007). Planning and implementing the websites of Australian SMTEs. *Journal of Information Technology and Tourism*, *9*(2), 115–131. doi:10.3727/109830507781367366

Shahabi, C., & Chen, Y. (2003). Web information personalization: Challenges and approaches. In *Proceedings of the 3nd International Workshop on Databases in Networked Information Systems (DNIS 2003),* Aizu-Wakamatsu, Japan (pp. 5-15).

Sharda, N. (1999). *Multimedia information networking.* Upper Saddle River, NJ: Prentice Hall.

Sharda, N. (2008). *Creating ambient multimedia experience on-demand.* In *Proceedings of the Semantic Ambient Media Experience Workshop (SAME 2008) in conjunction with ACM Multimedia 2008,* Vancouver, BC, Canada (pp. 41-48).

Sharda, N., Jakkilinki, R., Georgievski, M., & Ponnada, M. (2008). *Intelligent visual travel recommender systems model for e-tourism websites.* Queensland, Australia: CRC.

Shardanand, U., & Maes, P. (1995). *Social information filtering: Algorithms for automating "word of mouth."* Paper presented at the Proceedings of ACM conference on Human Factors in Computing Systems.

Shavlik, J., & Towell, G. (1989). An approach to combining explanation-based and neural learning algorithms. *Connection Science, 1*(3), 233–255. doi:10.1080/09540098908915640

Shearin, S., & Lieberman, H. (2001). Intelligent profiling by example. In *Proceedings of the International Conference on Intelligent User Interfaces (IUI 2001),* Santa Fe, NM (pp. 145-152).

Sheldon, P. (1997). *Tourism information technology.* Wallingford, CT: CAB International.

Sheth, J. N., & Parvatylar, A. (1995). Relationship marketing in consumer markets: Antecedents and consequences. *Journal of the Academy of Marketing Science, 23*(4), 255–271. doi:10.1177/009207039502300405

Sinner, A., Kleemann, T., & von Hessling, A. (2004). Semantic user profiles and their applications in a mobile environment. In *Proceedings of the Artificial Intelligence in Mobile Systems 2004 (AIMS 2004).*

Sliney, A., & Murphy, D. (2008). JDoc: A serious game for medical learning. In *Proceedings of the First International Conference on Advances in Computer-Human Interaction* (pp. 131-136).

Smith, G., Maher, M. L., & Gero, J. S. (2003). Designing 3d virtual worlds as a society of agents. In *Proceedings of the 10th International Conference on Computer Aided Architectural Design Futures (CAADFutures '03)* (pp. 105-114). Dordrecht, The Netherlands: Kluwer Academic Publishers.

Smyth, B. (2007). Case-based recommendation. In *The adaptive Web* (pp. 342-376). Berlin, Germany: Springer.

Snavely, N., Seitz, S. M., & Szeliski, R. (2006). Photo tourism: Exploring photo collections in 3D. *ACM Transactions on Graphics, 25*(3), 835-846. Retrieved August 22, 2008, from http://portal.acm.org/citation.cfm?id=1141911.1141964&coll=GUIDE&dl=GUIDE&CFID=172983&CFTOKEN=91862526

Sontag, S. (1977). *On photography.* London: Penguin Books.

Spaniol, M., Klamma, R., & Lux, M. (2007). Imagesemantics: User-generated metadata, content based retrieval & beyond. In *Proceedings of the 1st International Conference on New Media Technology,* Graz, Austria. Retrieved November 12, 2008, from http://mathias.lux.googlepages.com/imagesemantics-imedia-2007-preprint.pdf

Stabb, S., Werther, H., Ricci, F., Zipf, A., Gretzel, U., & Fesenmaier, D. R. (2002). Intelligent systems for tourism. *IEEE Intelligent Systems, 17*(6), 53–66. doi:10.1109/MIS.2002.1134362

Starkov, M. (2001). *How to turn lookers into bookers—Recommendation engines in travel and hospitality,* Retrieved May 10, 2006, from http://www.hotel-online.com/News/PR2001_3rd/Aug01_EnginesinTravel.html

Steel, N., Huppert, F. A., McWilliams, B., & Melzer, D. (2004). *Physical and cognitive function.* Retrieved from http://www.ifs.org.uk/elsa/report03/ch7.pdf

Steinfield, C. (2004). The development of location based services in mobile commerce. In B. Preissl, H. Bouwman, & C. Steinfield (Eds.), *E-Life after the dot com bust* (pp. 177-197). New York: Springer.

Steinicke, F., Bruder, G., Jerald, J., Frenz, H., & Lappe, M. (2008). Analyses of human sensitivity to redirected walking. In *ACM Proceedings on Virtual Reality and Software Technology* (pp. 149-156). New York: ACM.

Steinicke, F., Bruder, G., Kohli, L., Jerald, J., & Hinrichs, K. (2008). Taxonomy and implementation of redirection techniques for ubiquitous passive haptic feedback. In *Cyberworlds*. Washington, DC: IEEE Press.

Steinicke, F., Bruder, G., Ropinski, T., & Hinrichs, K. (2008). Moving towards generally applicable redirected walking. In *Proceedings of the Virtual Reality International Conference (VRIC)* (pp. 15-24). Washington, DC: IEEE Press.

Stepchenkova, S., Mills, J. E., & Jiang, H. (2007). Virtual travel communities: Self-reported experiences and satisfaction. In M. Sigala, L. Mich, & J. Murphy (Eds.), Information and communication technologies in tourism 2007 (pp. 163-174). New York: Springer-Verlag Wien.

Stock, O., Werthner, H., & Zancanaro, M. (2006). Futuring travel destination recommendation systems. In D. R. Fesenmaier, H. Werthner, & K. W. Wober (Eds.), *Destination recommendation systems: Behavioural foundations and applications* (pp. 297-314). Oxfordshire, UK: CAB International.

Sugiyama, K., Hatano, K., & Yoshikawa, M. (2004). Adaptive Web search based on user profile constructed without any effort from users. In *Proceedings of the WWW 2004*, New York, USA (pp. 675-684).

Swartout, B., Patil, R., Knight, K., & Russ, T. (1997). *Towards distributed use of large scale ontologies.* Paper presented at the Symposium on Ontological Engineering of AAAI, Stanford, CA.

Szekely, P. (1996). Retrospective and challenges for model-based interface development. In *Proceedings of the 2nd International Workshop on Computer-Aided Design of User Interfaces*, A Presses Universitaires de Namur, Namur (pp. 21-44).

Taboada, M., & Mann, W. C. (2006). Applications of rhetorical structure theory. *Discourse Studies*, *8*(4), 567–588. doi:10.1177/1461445606064836

Tapachai, N., & Waryszak, R. (2000). An examination of the role of beneficial image in tourist destination selection. *Journal of Travel Research*, *39*(August), 37–44. doi:10.1177/004728750003900105

ten Hagen, K., Kramer, R., Hermkes, M., Schumann, B., & Mueller, P. (2005). Semantic matching and heuristic search for a dynamic tour guide. In *Proceedings of the 12th International Conference on Information and Communication Technologies in Travel and Tourism* (*ENTER 2005*) (pp. 149-159).

Thompson, C. A., Göker, M. H., & Langley, P. (2004). A personalized system for conversational recommendations. *Journal of Artificial Intelligence Research*, *21*, 393–428.

Thyne, M. A., Lawson, R., & Todd, S. (2006). The use of conjoint analysis to assess the impact of the cross-cultural exchange between hosts and guests. *Tourism Management*, *27*, 201–213. doi:10.1016/j.tourman.2004.09.003

Torrens, M., Faltings, B., & Pu, P. (2002). SmartClient: Constraint satisfaction as a paradigm for scaleable intelligent information systems. *Constraints: An International Journal*, *7*(1), 49–69. doi:10.1023/A:1017940426216

Towle, B., & Quinn, C. (2000). *Knowledge-based recommender systems using explicit user models* (Tech. Rep. WS-00-04, 74-77). Paper presented at the AAAI workshop.

Traum, D., & Rickel, J. (2002). Embodied agents for multi-party dialogue in immersive virtual worlds. In *Proceedings of the First International joint Conference on Autonomous Agents and Multiagent Systems (AAMAS '02)* (pp. 766-773). New York: ACM Press.

Urry, J. (1990). *The tourist gaze: Leisure and travel in contemporary societies.* London: Sage Publications.

Urry, J. (1995). *Consuming places.* London: Routledge.

Usability Net. (2003). *International standards for HCI and usability.* Retrieved July 2004, from http://www.usabilitynet.org/tools/r_international.htm

Uschold, M., & Gruninger, M. (1996). Ontologies: Principles, methods and applications. *Knowledge Engineering Review, 11*(2).

US-GSA. (2006). *Research-based Web design & usability guidelines.* Washington, DC: U.S. Department of Health and Human Services (HHS) and the U.S. General Services Administration (GSA).

VacationCoach. (2002). *Using knowledge personalization to sell complex products.* Retrieved January 20, 2006, from http://crm.ittoolbox.com/pub/LK032002.pdf

Van Dijck, J. (2008). Digital photography: Communication, identity, memory. *Visual Communication, 7*(1), 57–76. doi:10.1177/1470357207084865

Venkataiah, S., Sharda, N., & Ponnada, M. (2008). A comparative study of continuous and discrete visualisation of tourism information. In *Proceedings of ENTER 2008: International Conference on Information and Communication Technologies in Tourism,* Innsbruck, Austria (pp. 12-23).

Vogt, C. A., & Fesenmaier, D. R. (1998). Expanding the functional information search model. *Annals of Tourism Research, 25*(3), 551–578. doi:10.1016/S0160-7383(98)00010-3

Waldhoer, K., & Rind, A. (2008). etBlogAnalysis – mining virtual communities using statistical and linguistic methods for quality control in tourism. In P. O'Connor, W. Hoepken, & U. Gretzel (Eds.), *Proceedings of the International Conference on Information and Communication Technologies in Tourism 2008,* Innsbruck, Austria (pp. 453-462). New York: Springer.

Wallace, M., Maglogiannis, I., Karpouzis, K., Kormentzas, G., & Kollias, S. (2004). Intelligent one-stop-shop travel recommendations: Using an adaptive neural network and clustering of history. *Information Technology & Tourism, 6*(3), 181–193. doi:10.3727/1098305031436971

Wang, Y., & Fesenmaier, D. R. (2004). Towards understanding members' general participation in and active contribution to an online travel community. *Tourism Management, 25*(6), 709–722. doi:10.1016/j.tourman.2003.09.011

Wang, Y., Yu, Q., & Fesenmaier, D. R. (2002). Defining the virtual tourist community: Implications for tourism marketing. *Tourism Management, 23*(4), 407–417. doi:10.1016/S0261-5177(01)00093-0

Wasserman, S., & Faust, K. (1994). Social network analysis: Methods and applications. New York: Cambridge University Press.

Watson, B., Muller, P., Wonka, P., Sexton, C., Veryovka, O., & Fuller, A. (2008). Procedural urban modeling in practice. *IEEE Computer Graphics and Applications, 28*(3), 18–26. doi:10.1109/MCG.2008.58

Watson, I. (1997). *Applying case-based reasoning: Techniques for enterprise systems.* San Francisco: Morgan Kaufmann.

Web Ontology Working Group W3C Semantic Web Activity, W3C. (2004). *OWL Web ontology language* (W3C Recommendation, 10 February 2004). Retrieved from http://www.w3.org/2001/sw/WebOnt/

Wellman, B. (1983). Network analysis: Some basic principles. *Sociological Theory, 1,* 155–200. doi:10.2307/202050

Wells, L. (2004). *Photography: A critical introduction* (3rd ed.). London: Routledge.

Wenger, A. (2008). Analysis of travel bloggers' characteristics and their communication about Austria as a tourism destination. *Journal of Vacation Marketing, 14*(2), 169–176. doi:10.1177/1356766707087525

Wenger, E., McDermott, R., & Snyder, W. (2002). *Cultivating communities of practice.* Boston: Harvard Business School Press.

Werry, C., & Mowbray, M. (2001). *Online communities: Commerce, community action and the virtual university.* Upper Saddle River, NJ: Prentice Hall.

Werthner, H., & Klein, S. (1999). *Information technology and tourism, a challenging relationship.* Vienna, Austria: Springer-Verlag.

Werthner, H., & Ricci, F. (2004). Tourism and development II: E-commerce and tourism. *Communications of the ACM, 47*(12), 101–105. doi:10.1145/1035134.1035141

Whittaker, S., Issacs, E., & O'Day, V. (1997). Widening the Net. Workshop report on the theory and practice of physical and network communities. [ff]. *SIGCHI Bulletin, 29*(3), 27–30. doi:10.1145/264853.264867

Whitton, M., Cohn, J., Feasel, P., Zommons, S., Razzaque, S., Poulton, B., & Brooks, F. (2005). Comparing VE locomotion interfaces. In *Proceedings of Virtual Reality* (pp. 123–130). Washington, DC: IEEE.

Wilkinson, S. (2004). Focus group research. In D. Silverman (Ed.), *Qualitative research: Theory, method and practice* (2nd ed.) (pp. 177-199). London: Sage Publications.

Williamson, J. (1978). *Decoding advertisements: Ideology and meaning in advertising.* London: Marion Boyars.

Wooldridge, M. J. (2001). *An introduction to multiagent systems.* New York: John Wiley & Sons, Inc.

Worboys, M. F. (2001). Nearness relations in environmental space. *International Journal of Geographical Information Science, 15*(7), 633–651. doi:10.1080/13658810110061162

World of Warcraft. (2008). *Blizzard Entertainment.* Retrieved December 20, 2008, from http://www.blizzard.com/wow

Wu, S., Ghenniwa, H., Zhang, Y., & Shen, W. (2006). Personal assistant agents for collaborative design environments. [f]. *Computers in Industry, 57*(8), 732–739. doi:10.1016/j.compind.2006.04.010

Wu, Y.-H., & Miller, H. (2001). Computational tools for measuring space-time accessibility within dynamic flow transportation networks. *Journal of Transportation and Statistics, 4*(2/3), 1–14.

Yamakami, T. (2007). MobileWeb 2.0: Lessons from Web 2.0 and past mobile Internet development. In *Proceedings of the International Conference on Multimedia and Ubiquitous Engineering (MUE'07)*, Korean Bible University, Seoul, Korea. Washington, DC: IEEE Computer Society.

Yang, J., Yang, W., Denecke, M., & Waibel, A. (1999). Smart sight: A tourist assistant system. In *Proceedings of the. 3rd Int. Symposium. Wearabale computers*, San Francisco, CA (pp. 73-78).

Yang, Y. (2006). *Towards spatial Web personalization.* Unpublished doctoral dissertation, Naval Academy Research Institute, France.

Yang, Y., & Claramunt, C. (2004). A flexible competitive neural network for eliciting user's preferences in Web urban spaces. In P. Fisher (Ed.), *Developments in spatial data handling* (pp. 41-57). Berlin, Germany: Springer-Verlag.

Yao, Y. (1995). Measuring retrieval effectiveness based on user preference of documents. *Journal of the American Society for Information Science American Society for Information Science, 46*(2), 133–145. doi:10.1002/(SICI)1097-4571(199503)46:2<133::AID-ASI6>3.0.CO;2-Z

Yee, N. (2006). The demographics, motivations, and derived experiences of users of massively multi-user online graphical environments. *Presence (Cambridge, Mass.), 15*(3), 309–329. doi:10.1162/pres.15.3.309

Yee, N. (2006). The psychology of massively multi-user online role-playing games: Emotional investment, motivations, relationship formation, and problematic usage. In R. Schroeder & A.S. Axelsson (Eds.), *Avatars at work and play: Collaboration and interaction in shared virtual environments* (pp. 187-207). New York: Springer-Verlag.

Yeung, C., Pang-Fei, T., & Yen, J. (1998). A multi-agent based tourism kiosk on Internet. In *Proceedings of the Thirty-First Annual Hawaii International Conference on System Sciences-Volume 4 (HICSS '98)* (p. 452). Washington, DC: IEEE Computer Society.

Yu, H., & Shaw, S.-L. (2008). Exploring potential human activities in physical and virtual spaces: A spatio-temporal GIS approach. [ff]. *International Journal of Geographical Information Science*, *22*(4), 409–430. doi:10.1080/13658810701427569

Zambonelli, F., Jennings, N. R., & Wooldridge, M. (2003). Developing multiagent systems: The gaia methodology. *ACM Transactions on Software Engineering and Methodology*, *12*(3), 317–370. doi:10.1145/958961.958963

Zanker, M., Aschinger, M., & Jessenitschnig, M. (2007). Development of a collaborative and constraint-based Web configuration system for personalized bundling of products and services. In B. Benatallah et al. (Eds.), *Proceedings of the 8th International Conference on Web Information Systems Engineering*, Nancy, France (pp. 273-284). Berlin, Germany: Springer.

Zanker, M., Bricman, M., Gordea, S., Jannach, D., & Jessenitschnig, M. (2006). Persuasive online-selling in quality & taste domains. In Proceedings of the*International Conference on Electronic Commerce and Web technologies - EC-WEB*, Krakow, Poland (pp. 51-60). Berlin, Germany: Springer.

Zanker, M., Fuchs, M., Höpken, W., Tuta, M., & Müller, N. (2008). Evaluating recommender systems in tourism - a case study from Austria. In P. O'Connor et al. (Eds.), *Proceedings of the Information and Communication Technologies in Tourism (ENTER 2008)* (pp. 24-34). Berlin, Germany: Springer.

Zappen, J. P., Harrison, T. M., & Watson, D. (2008). A new paradigm for designing e-government: Web 2.0 and experience design. In *Proceedings of the 2008 international conference on Digital government research, Digital Government Society of North America* (pp. 17-26).

Zyda, M. (2007). Special issue on serious games. *Communications of the ACM*, *50*(7). doi:10.1145/1272516.1272535

About the Contributors

Nalin Sharda gained B.Tech. and Ph.D. degrees from the Indian Institute of Technology, Delhi. He teaches and leads research in innovative applications of multimedia and internet systems at the School of Engineering and Science at Victoria University, Australia. He has published the Multimedia Information Networking text book, and over 100 papers and handbook chapters. He has led research projects for the Australian Sustainable Tourism CRC to develop e-Tourism systems using Semantic Web technologies, and innovative visualization methodologies. Dr. Sharda has been invited to present lectures and seminars in the Distinguished Lecturer series for the Prolearn program of the European Union, and as Erasmus Mundus Visiting Research Professor at RWTH Aachen University, Germany.

***

Mara Abel is graduated in Geology and doctor in Computer Science, Artificial Intelligence. She is professor in Knowledge Engineering at the Institute of Informatics of Universidad Federal do Rio Grande do Sul (UFRGS), Brazil; and the Director of the Informatics Enterprise Center of Brazil. She is also the co-founder of the company ENDEEPER Rock Knowledge System, an spin-off of her research group that provides knowledge management solutions for petroleum companies.

Prof. **Matthew O Adigun** received his PhD in Computer Science from Obafemi Awolowo University, Nigeria in 1989. He is currently with University of Zululand, South Africa where he heads both the Department and Research Centre for Mobile E-Services. In his capacity as a Professor of Computer science since 1989, he has been leading a number of research initiatives sponsored by the South African National Research Foundation from 1999 to date. The latest initiative which started in 2007 is titled *ICT Infrastructure for Electronic Commerce and Services*. His research interest are in Software Engineering, application of grid services to recommender and other e-Commerce systems, and wireless mesh network as a viable connectivity for SMME-enabling technologies.

Olga Averjanova was born on 1983.01.12 in Vilnius, Lithuania. She received her Bachelor degree in Computer Science from Vilnius University in 2005. She was Erasmus student for one year at Aalborg University, Denmark, Computer Science faculty. Her bachelor thesis was devoted to experimenting data mining algorithms in the prediction of bank loans client's reliability. Averianova completed her Master studies at Free University of Bozen-Bolzano in 2008 where she specialized in intelligent location-based mobile recommender systems. Averianova conducted also research and development activities in software engineering related to some techniques for administrating PROM plug-ins and applications.

Currently Averianova is working as a software engineer in a London, UK, based company, designing image processing applications.

Ana Bazzan received her PhD in 1997 from the University of Karlsruhe, Germany, and an MSc in computer science from the Institute of Informatics at the University of Rio Grande do Sul (UFRGS) in Porto Alegre, Brazil. From 1997 to 1998, she had a postdoc research associate position in the Multi-Agent Systems Laboratory at the University of Massachusetts in Amherst, under the supervision of prof. Victor Lesser. In 1999 she joined the Institute for Informatics at UFRGS as a professor and got tenure three years later. During 2006 and 2007 she had a fellowship from the Alexander von Humboldt Foundation at the University of Würzburg in Germany. She is affiliated with the research groups on Artificial Intelligence and Multi-Agent Systems at UFRGS. Her research interests include: game-theoretic paradigms for coordination of agents, multiagent learning, coordination and cooperation in MAS, agent-based simulation, RoboCup Rescue, and traffic simulation and control. Other professional activities: associate editor of the journal Advances in Complex Systems, chair of program committee for the 17th Braz. Symp. on Artificial Intelligence (2004), and member of the advisory committee of IJCAI 2009.

Francesco Bellotti is a researcher at the ELIOS laboratory of the University of Genoa. He is involved in research projects concerning Serious Games. mobile computing, Human-Computer Interaction and multimedia systems in the automotive environment. He received a Ph.D. in Electrical Engineering from the University of Genoa. Prof. Bellotti has authored over 80 papers in international journals and conferences. Contact him at: franz@elios.unige.it

Helmut Berger is Head of the Information Retrieval Group at Matrixware Information Services GmbH, Vienna, Austria. His research concentrates on information retrieval, human-computer interaction, adaptive information systems, e-Tourism, and multi-agent systems. In these areas, Helmut has published about 55 papers in books, conference proceedings and journals. He has studied Computer Science at the Vienna University of Technology. Helmut received his master's degree in Computer Science in 2001 and his PhD in 2003 from the Vienna University of Technology.

Riccardo Berta is a research consultant at the Department of Biophysical and Electronic Engineering of the University of Genoa. He received his degree in Electronic Engineering (Master Degree) from the University of Genova, in 1999, with a thesis on project and development of an optimizing environment for Java bytecode. His current research interests include design, implementation and evaluation of Serious Games and innovative modalities of Human-Computer Interaction for mobile devices. Dr. Berta has authored about 50 papers in international journals and conferences.

Gerd Bruder is a PhD student at the University of Münster, Germany, where he received a Diploma in Computer Science in 2009. In his diploma thesis he developed virtual locomotion interfaces, which allows user to explore any virtual environment by real walking. His research interests include locomotion techniques in virtual reality, perception in immersive virtual environments and computer graphics at the Department of Computer Science at the University of Münster.

Prof. **Dimitrios Buhalis** is currently Established Chair in Tourism, Deputy Director of the International Centre for Tourism and Hospitality Research at Bournemouth University and Professorial

Observer at the Bournemouth University Senate. Professor Buhalis is leading eTourism research and is working with the Bournemouth team for introducing technology in all aspects of tourism research and teaching. He was previously Programme Leader MSc in Tourism Marketing and MSc in eTourism, Reader in Business Information Management, Leader of eTourism Research and member of the Senate at the University of Surrey. He has been Adjunct Professor at ESSEC in Paris, Visiting Professor at Hong Kong Polytechnic University, China, Professor Associado at the University of Aveiro, Portugal, and Visiting Professor and Member of the University Assembly at Modul University in Vienna, Austria. He has written or co-edited a total of 12 books, including Tourism Business Frontiers and Tourism Management Dynamics published by Elsevier, eTourism: Strategic Information Technology for Tourism published by Pearson (Prentice Hall/Financial Times) and Tourism Distribution Channels (Thomson), Managing alliances in the global hospitality and tourism industry as well as a series of three books on IT and Tourism. Dimitrios has also served as Chairman of the Scientific Committee of the ENTER'98, '99, and 2000 conferences on Tourism and Information Technology, as well as ENTER Destinations Chair for 2002 and ENTER Overall Chair in 2003 and 2009. He has served as Vice President of the International Federation of Information Technology for Travel and Tourism (IFITT) of which he is a founding member whilst he often Chairs conferences for EyeForTravel.

Stephen Burgess completed his PhD in the School of Information Management and Systems at Monash University. His thesis was in the area of small business interactions with customers via the internet. His research and teaching interests include the use of ICTs in small businesses (particularly in the tourism field), the strategic use of ICTs, and B2C electronic commerce. He has received a number of competitive research grants in these areas. He has completed several studies related to website features in small businesses and how well websites function over time. He has authored or edited three books and special editions of journals in topics related to the use of ICTs in small business and been track chair at the international ISOneWorld, IRMA, Conf-IRM and ACIS conferences in these areas.

Jeremy Buultjens is the Director of the Australian Regional Tourism Research. Jeremy teaches Tourism Planning and the Environment, Indigenous Tourism and Economics. Jeremy's research interests include Indigenous tourism, tourism in protected areas, regional tourism and employment relations in the hospitality industry. He has conducted consultancies for the NSW National Parks and Wildlife Service, the NSW Crown Solicitor's Office, W.A. Department of Conservation and Land Management, and the Northern Rivers Area Consultative Committee. Jeremy has published in employment relations, tourism and hospitality journals. He is joint editor of the Journal of Economic and Social Policy.

Dean Carson is the Head of Population Studies at the School for Social and Policy Research, Charles Darwin University. His expertise is in the examination of human mobility, and its consequences for regional development and technological innovation. He has published extensively on the challenges presented by tourist mobility in regional Australia. The focus of that research has been on the potential for regional destinations to act as systems of innovation. He has also published on mobility patterns of residents of outback Australia (including the Northern Territory). He is currently finalising an academic edited book on the demographic characteristics of remote areas in Australia, Canada, the United States and Scandinavia.

Jin Young Chung holds an MSc in tourism marketing from the University of Surrey, U.K., and is currently a Ph.D. researcher in the Department of Recreation, Park, and Tourism Sciences at the Texas A&M University, U.S.A. He has extensive working experience in Information Technology industry. His research interests include online social network and tourist behavior from a social psychological perspective. In particular, his overall research agenda is geared towards exploring social networks in tourism virtual communities and also better understanding price fairness perception in tourism context.

Carmen Cox is a Senior Lecturer in Marketing in the Graduate College of Management at Southern Cross University's Tweed Gold Coast Campus. Her industry experience is in the hospitality sector where she has worked as Marketing & Research Manager for a 5-star integrated resort. Carmen's research interests focus on marketing and consumer behavior issues primarily in the fields of tourism and hospitality. She has published articles in the areas of consumer loyalty; tourist travel behavior and other hospitality topics in journals including the Journal of Travel Research; Journal of Hospitality and Tourism Research; Tourism, Culture & Communication; Journal of Vacation Marketing and Tourism Analysis.

Prof. **Alessandro De Gloria** is full professor of electronics at the University of Genoa. He is the leader of the ELIOS (Electronics for the Information Society) laboratory of the Department of Electronics and Biophysical Engineering at the University of Genoa. His research interests include Serious Games, virtual reality, mobile computing, Human-Computer Interaction and embedded system design. He has participated and directed several European research projects on these items. Prof. De Gloria has authored over 120 papers in international journals and conferences.

Michael Dittenbach is Senior Research Scientist at Matrixware and member of the Information Retrieval Group. He also lectures at the Vienna University of Technology. From 2000 until 2007 he was Senior Researcher at the E-Commerce Competence Center - EC3, Vienna, an institute for applied research in the area of e-Commerce. He received his MSc in computer science in 2000 and his doctoral degree in 2003 from the Vienna University of Technology, Vienna, Austria. His main research interests include, but are not limited to, information retrieval, text mining, natural language processing, digital libraries, user interfaces and neurocomputing.

Dr. **Harald Frenz** studied biology at the Ruhr-University in Bochum, Germany. In 2003 he received the PhD in the Department of Biology of the Ruhr-University Bochum, Germany. His research focus is the perception of visually simulated self-motion. Currently he is working in the lab of Markus Lappe at the University of Münster, Germany.

Markus Gärtner received his bachelor's degree in Information Systems from the Vienna University of Technology in 2005 and his master degree in 2007. In his master thesis he developed a prototype of an e-Commerce Trading Environment based on the Multi Agent System paradigm. He is currently working as a PhD student in the itchy feet project, incorporating part of his previous work, and responsible for the development of the framework architecture. Furthermore he studies Media Informatics, which he will finish in 2009. His research interests include Multi Agent- / Distributed Systems, agent technology, embedded systems, security, project management, software engineering as well as Virtual and Augmented Reality.

Abayomi. O. Ipadiola is with the University of Zululand where he acts as a research assistant in the department of computer science. He is currently pursuing a Master of Science degree in Computer Science. Mr Ipadeola obtained his first Bachelor of Science (Honors) degree in computer science at University of Ilorin in Nigeria. His research interests include: pervasive grid computing and artificial intelligence.

Damien Jacobsen is currently a PhD candidate at Charles Darwin University. He has a Master of Business (research) which focused on domestic tourists and social myths about Aboriginal people. Other past work has included innovation in regional communities, while his current research interests include Aboriginal people in tourism, domestic tourist experiences and the effects of colonialism on (post)colonial states. In his recent research, Damien examined the photographic behaviour of domestic tourists in desert Australia. He is particularly interested in how photographs reflect the unique ways in which domestic visitors view remote places like the desert.

Dietmar Jannach is a full professor at the University of Technology in Dortmund, Germany and the head of the e-Services Research Group. His research interests include interactive recommender systems and conversational preference elicitation, engineering of knowledge-based systems and web applications as well as the application of Artificial Intelligence in industry. Dietmar Jannach has authored and co-authored more than 100 scientific papers in these areas and published papers in journals such as Artificial Intelligence, AI Magazine, IEEE Intelligent Systems and on conferences such as IJCAI and ECAI.

Jason Jerald received a Bachelor in Computer Science with specialization in Computer Graphics and minors in Electrical Engineering and Mathematics from Washington State University in 1998. Jason has worked at several research institutions in the United States including Battelle Pacific Northwest National Laboratories, Argonne National Laboratories, HRL Laboratories, the Navy Research Laboratories, and NASA Ames Research Center. Jason's current research investigates motion perception in virtual environments. He plans to graduate with a PhD in Computer Science from The University of North Carolina at Chapel Hill by the summer of 2009.

Markus Jessenitschnig is a research assistant and lecturer at the University Klagenfurt since 2008. From 2006 to 2008 he was a member of the eTourism Competence Center Austria. He received his MS in Computer Science and he is a Ph.D. candidate in Computer Science at the University Klagenfurt. His research interests include user modeling, recommender systems and system architectures.

Prof. Dr. **Markus Lappe** holds a PhD in physics from the University of Tübingen, Germany. He did research work on computational and cognitive neuroscience of vision at the Max-Planck Institute of Biological Cybernetics in Tübingen, the National Institutes of Health, Bethesda, USA, and the Department of Biology of the Ruhr-University Bochum, Germany. In 1999 he was awarded the BioFuture prize of the Federal Ministry of Education and Research. Since 2001 he is a full professor of experimental psychology at the University of Münster. He is also a member of the Otto Creutzfeldt Center for Cognitive and Behavioral Neuroscience at the University of Münster.

Fabiana Lorenzi is master in Computer Science and PhD student at the Federal University of Rio Grande do Sul (UFRGS) under the supervision of Prof Dr Ana Bazzan and Prof Dr Mara Abel, where she is working with multiagent recommender systems. She teaches Artificial Intelligence at the Lutheran University of Brazil (ULBRA). Her current research interests include: multiagent recommender systems, case-based reasoning and swarm intelligence.

Dieter Merkl is Associate Professor at the Department of Software Technology and Interactive Systems, Vienna University of Technology. He received his diploma and doctoral degrees in social and economic science from University of Vienna in 1989 and 1995, respectively. From 2004 to 2005 he held the position of an Associate Professor at the School of Computing and Information Technology, University of Western Sydney. Dieter Merkl was leading the Adaptive Multilingual Interfaces project at the Electronic Commerce Competence Center-EC3 from 2000 to 2003. His current research interests focus on Collaborative Virtual Environments, Data Mining, and Neurocomputing. He has published widely in these areas, with more than 140 publications at conferences and in journals.

Quang Nhat Nguyen is a lecturer and research staff in the faculty of Information Technology, Hanoi University of Technology, Vietnam. He received his bachelor and master degrees in computer science from Hanoi University of Technology, Vietnam in 1997 and 2000 respectively, and his PhD in computer science from the International Doctorate School, University of Trento, Italy in 2006. He was a research assistant in the Electronic Commerce and Tourism Research Laboratory, ITC-irst institute, Italy. He was a research staff and lecturer in the faculty of Computer Science, Free University of Bozen-Bolzano, Italy. He was leading software development teams in several Vietnam and U.S. software companies in Vietnam. His current research interests include recommender systems, machine learning, and decision-making support for mobile users.

Oludayo, O. Olugbara received the B.Sc. degree (first class honors) in Mathematics, M.Sc. degree in Mathematics (Computer Science Specialization) and PhD degree in Computer Science. He is currently a senior lecturer in the Department of Computer and Information Sciences, Covenant University, Nigeria. His research interests include database compression and data mining, artificial intelligent techniques, mobile computing, image processing, software engineering methodologies and object/service-oriented software development. He has published more than forty articles.

Michael Pöttler has received his bachelor's degree in business informatics from the Vienna University of Technology in 2006 and completed his master studies in 2007. He is currently working as a PhD student in the itchy feet project where he is responsible for the development of the community area as well as the evaluation of the usability aspects. His research interests include virtual communities, 3D-architectures and game design.

Ludovica Primavera is a PhD student in computer science in the Department of Biophysical and Electronic Engineering, University of Genoa. Her research interests include experience evaluation of video games and Serious Games design. She received an MS in psychology from the University of Padua, with a thesis on semantic memory deficits in Lewy Body Dementia, Alzheimer's disease and Herpes Simplex Encephalitis.

Edward Pultar is a Ph.D. Student in the Department of Geography at the University of California, Santa Barbara (UCSB). He received B.S. degrees in computer science and geography in 2005 and an

M.S. degree in geography in 2007 from the University of Utah. Edward's research interests include Geographic Information Science and Systems (GIS) and travel behavior with spatiotemporal data representation, visualization, querying, and decision-making of particular interest. He won first place for a paper and presentation in the GIS Specialty Group Student Paper Competition at the 2007 Association of American Geographers (AAG) Annual Meeting.

Francesco Ricci is associate professor at the faculty of Computer Science, Free University of Bozen-Bolzano, Italy. His current research interests include recommender systems, intelligent interfaces, constraint satisfaction problems, machine learning, case-based reasoning and mobile services. F. Ricci is interested in the design, development and evaluation of concrete and fully operational recommender systems. Trip@dvice, the recommendation technology, which he designed in the last years, has been reengineered by a spin-off company (ectrsolutions.com), and it is currently exploited by many operational web sites. He is the author of more than one hundred scientific publications appeared on international journals (User Modeling and User Adapted Interaction, Applied AI, Communication of ACM, IEEE PAMI, IEEE Expert, Applied Intelligence, Int. J. of Int. Systems, Journal of Information Technology and Tourism etc.) and conferences proceedings (ICML, ICCBR, ICTAI, ITS, etc.). He has co-chaired national and international conferences (RecSys08, ICCBR2005, Enter 2005, ARS'05, RPEC'02, IWCBR98,) and acts as a referee of several scientific Journals. He is in the editorial board of Information Technology and Tourism Journal.

Martin Raubal is Associate Professor at the Department of Geography at the University of California, Santa Barbara (UCSB). He is also an affiliated faculty member at the Department of Computer Science and a faculty member of the Cognitive Science Program at UCSB. Martin received his Ph.D. in Geoinformation from Vienna University of Technology in 2001 with honors. He also holds a M.S. degree in Spatial Information Science and Engineering from the University of Maine and a Dipl.-Ing. in Surveying Engineering from Vienna University of Technology. Martin's research interests lie in the area of cognitive engineering for geospatial services, more specifically he focuses on representing and modeling people's cognition and spatio-temporal behavior, and the integration of such models into geospatial applications for the enhancement of people's decision-making support. Martin is currently a board member of the University Consortium for Geographic Information Science (UCGIS) and serves on the editorial boards of Transactions in GIS, Journal of Location Based Services, and Geography Compass. He has authored and co-authored more than 50 books and research papers published in refereed journals and conference proceedings.

Doris Schmallegger completed a Masters degree in Tourism and Leisure Management in 2007 at the IMC University of Applied Sciences in Krems, Austria. She is currently a PhD candidate at James Cook University in Cairns, and conducts research into remote systems of innovation in the Flinders Ranges in South Australia. Doris also works as research associate at the School for Social Policy and Research at Charles Darwin University. Her research interests include tourism development and innovation in remote areas, self-drive tourism, and new information and communication technologies. She has recently published in the field of consumer generated content and its potential role in tourism research.

Ingo Seidel has received his bachelor's degree in Software Engineering from the Vienna University of Technology in 2005 and completed his master studies in the field of Computational Intelligence in

2007. He is currently working as a PhD student in the itchy feet project where he is responsible for the development of the framework architecture, the system evaluation and usability testing. His research interests include software engineering, usability design and virtual communities.

Carmine Sellitto has investigated innovation, e-commerce/marketing adoption across a variety of business domains including tourism providers and Australian-based wineries. He gained his PhD from RMIT University where he was awarded the prize for PhD innovation. Dr Sellitto has published widely on topics associated with e-business, information management and technology, website analysis, tourism and IT, Internet-marketing, information quality and the adoption of technology by small business. His articles have appeared in the International Journal of Retail & Distribution Management, Journal of Information Science, Journal of the American Society for Information Science and Technology and Market Management.

Dr. **Frank Steinicke** holds an Assistant Professor position in Computer Science at the University of Münster, Germany. He received his PhD (2006) in computer science from the University of Münster. His research interests include human-computer interaction with special consideration on VR, perception and cognition in computer generated environments and visualizations. In many interdisciplinary projects his research efforts aim on the challenge to provide natural and effective user interfaces for VR-based environments.

Leanne White is a lecturer in Marketing and a research associate with the Centre for Tourism and Services Research at Victoria University in Melbourne, Australia. She has taught Marketing, Public Relations, Communications, Politics and Australian Studies at universities since 1988. Leanne has also worked in the areas of public relations, research and policy in government and higher education. Her research interests include: advertising, national identity, commercial nationalism, tourism, sports marketing, and the Olympic movement. Leanne's doctoral thesis examined the manifestations of official nationalism and commercial nationalism at the Sydney 2000 Olympic Games.

Yanwu Yang received Ph.D degree in Computer Science from the doctoral school of the Ecole Nationale Superieure d'Arts et Metiers (ENSAM), France in 2006. He joined the Complex Systems and Intelligence Sciences Laboratory at Institute of Automation, Chinese Academy of Sciences, in 2007. His current interests include user model, Human-Computer Interaction and text mining.

Markus Zanker is an assistant professor in the Department for Applied Informatics at University Klagenfurt and cofounder and director of ConfigWorks GmbH, a provider of interactive selling solutions. He received his MS and Ph.D. degree in Computer Science and MBA in business administration from University Klagenfurt. His research interests focus on knowledge-based systems, in particular in the fields of interactive sales applications such as product configuration and recommendation. Furthermore, he is emphasizing on knowledge acquisition and user modeling for personalization.

Index

O

P

R

S

T

U

Lightning Source UK Ltd.
Milton Keynes UK
UKOW07n0634111117
312426UK00014B/126/P

9 781605 668185